# STRATEGIC
# MANAGEMENT
# AND BUSINESS POLICY

# McGraw-Hill Series in Management

**Fred Luthans and Keith Davis,** *Consulting Editors*

**Allen:** The Management Profession

**Arnold and Feldman:** Organizational Behavior

**Benton:** Supervision and Management

**Buchele:** The Management of Business and Public Organizations

**Cascio:** Managing Human Resources: Productivity, Quality of Work, Life, Profits

**Cleland and King:** Management: A Systems Approach

**Cleland and King:** Systems Analysis and Project Management

**Dale:** Management: Theory and Practice

**Davis and Frederick:** Business and Society: Management, Public Policy, Ethics

**Davis and Newstrom:** Human Behavior at Work: Organizational Behavior

**Davis and Newstrom:** Organizational Behavior: Readings and Exercises

**Del Mar:** Operations and Industrial Management: Designing and Managing for Productivity

**Dobler, Lee and Burt:** Purchasing and Materials Management: Text and Cases

**Dunn and Rachel:** Wage and Salary Administration: Total Compensation Systems

**Feldman and Arnold:** Managing Individual and Group Behavior in Organizations

**Finch, Jones, and Litterer:** Managing for Organizational Effectiveness: An Experiential Approach

**Flippo:** Personnel Management

**Gerloff:** Organizational Theory and Design: A Strategic Approach for Management

**Glueck and Jauch:** Business Policy and Strategic Management

**Glueck and Jauch:** Strategic Management and Business Policy

**Glueck and Snyder:** Readings in Business Policy and Strategy from *Business Week*

**Hampton:** Contemporary Management

**Hicks and Gullett:** Management

**Hicks and Gullett:** Modern Business Management: A Systems and Environmental Approach

**Hicks and Gullett:** Modern Business Management: A Systems and Environmental Approach

**Hicks and Gullett:** Organizations: Theory and Behavior

**Jauch and Townsend:** Cases in Strategic Management and Business Policy

**Johnson, Kast, and Rosenzweig:** The Theory and Management of Systems

**Karlins:** The Human Use of Human Resources

**Kast and Rosenzweig:** Experiential Exercises and Cases in Management

# CASES IN STRATEGIC MANAGEMENT AND BUSINESS POLICY

**LAWRENCE R. JAUCH**
*Southern Illinois University—Carbondale*

**JAMES B. TOWNSEND**
*Kansas State University*

McGraw-Hill Book Company

*New York   St. Louis   San Francisco   Auckland   Bogotá   Hamburg
Johannesburg   London   Madrid   Mexico   Montreal   New Delhi
Panama   Paris   São Paulo   Singapore   Sydney   Tokyo   Toronto*

**CASES IN STRATEGIC MANAGEMENT AND BUSINESS POLICY**

2 3 4 5 6 7 8 9 0 D O C D O C 8 9 8 7 6

ISBN 0-07-032299-6

This book was set in Century Schoolbook by J. M. Post Graphics, Corp.
The editor was John R. Meyer;
the cover was designed by Laura Stover;
the production supervisor was Marietta Breitwieser.
Project supervision was done by Publishing Synthesis, Ltd.
R. R. Donnelley & Sons Company was printer and binder.

Library of Congress Cataloging in Publication Data
Main entry under title:

Cases in strategic management and business policy.

(McGraw-Hill series in management)
1. Strategic planning—Case studies. 2. Corporate planning—Case studies. 3. International business enterprises—Case studies. I. Jauch, Lawrence R. II. Townsend, James B., date . III. Series.
HD30.28.C39 1986     658.4'012     85-16572
ISBN 0-07-032299-6

# ABOUT THE AUTHORS

**Lawrence R. Jauch** is Professor of Management at Southern Illinois University—Carbondale. His Ph.D. in Management was completed in 1973 at the University of Missouri-Columbia. Professor Jauch is the coauthor of 12 texts and supplements, and has published over 60 papers, cases, and monographs. He has consulted with planning executives in several countries. Dr. Jauch is in his second third-year term on the editorial review board of the *Academy of Management Review*. He chaired the Business Policy and Planning Division of the Academy in 1983–84.

**James B. Townsend** is Associate Professor of Management at Kansas State University. He earned his D.B.A. in 1976 from George Washington University. Among his other activities he serves as worldwide construction programmer for USAF and executor of international study programs at the Industrial College of the Armed Forces. Professor Townsend's *Extraterritorial Antitrust: The Sherman Act versus American Business Abroad* was nominated for a national award, and his pioneering studies in licensing are being widely used by the Licensing Executives Society. He has been a member of the Business Policy and Planning Division (BPP), of the Academy of Management since 1977 and the Academy's Placement Chairman since 1984.

# CONTENTS

# PREFACE

The business policy and strategic management course is now well entrenched in professional business schools and colleges. The primary pedagogical vehicle used in this course continues to be case studies of enterprises facing challenges of the future. The collection of cases included here was designed to encourage students to apply strategic management concepts by examining the firm as a whole from the perspective of top management. Many of the 24 cases are either completely new or are updates of "tried and true" predecessors. A range of organizational type, size, and complexity is available to suit the different needs of instruction and issue development. To stimulate student interest and involvement, a number of cases concern well-known companies or deal with products or services with which students can readily identify.

Most of the cases are of relatively recent origin in terms of the time periods in which the organizations operate. Many contain sufficient data for application of decision-making techniques and managerial interpretation from which to draw meaningful conclusions.

The beginning section of the book introduces the student to the overall strategic case analysis approach. A special feature is the inclusion of two sections outlining recommendations for better written and oral reports. Our students have found these helpful as they begin the demanding task of integrating a comprehensive set of analyses and proposals within a strategic framework.

The remaining four sections of the book organize the cases by "segment of economic activity." That is, Section II presents cases of entrepreneurial and start-up organizations. Section III deals with firms involved in international activities, or which are multinational in their operations. Section IV encompasses businesses with manufacturing as their basis. Finally, Section V contains cases involving nonprofit and service-oriented firms. Since the careers of students with diverse interests will likely lead them into many different segments of activity, exposure to these various examples should prove valuable. In all these cases, however, we believe that the concepts of strategy formation and/or implementation apply to the enterprise as a whole. Hence these cases are not chosen to "represent" selected types of functional issues per se.

With the foregoing in mind, we believe the book as a whole can be used in several ways. First, selected cases can be assigned in conjunction with other text material (such as Glueck/Jauch *Strategic Management and Business Policy,* 2nd ed.). On the other hand, if another approach is preferred by the instructor, it can be used as a stand-alone casebook to support other text material or the instructor's own lectures or to complement a strategy-simulation game. Of course, a concepts-readings-case package could also successfully incorporate this material.

We would be remiss if we failed to acknowledge the contributions of the various casewriters who have permitted us to use their work. Too often, the hard work of capturing the essence of organizational activities and relating it in a few pages goes unrecognized. The authors represented here, from various regions of the country, have contributed more than they know to the education of the next generation of managers. We are grateful for their efforts and contribution to this volume through sharing their instructional materials with our colleagues.

We also wish to acknowledge several reviewers of earlier drafts of this book—William E. Burr, II, University of Oregon; Phillip Jones, Xavier University; Robert Kempt, Drake University; Fred Luthans, University of Nebraska, Lincoln; John Mahon, Boston University; and Jack Sullivan, Oklahoma State University. These individuals advised us on the selection of appropriate case materials and their organization, as well as ways in which to introduce the overall case analysis process.

Finally, John Meyer was most helpful in the development of the concept of this volume and in promoting a successful conclusion in timely fashion.

Comments about your experiences in using these materials will be most welcome. Hopefully, the errors have been minimized, but your willingness to call our attention to any you find will be appreciated.

**Lawrence R. Jauch**
**James B. Townsend**

# PART ONE

# CASE ANALYSIS: APPLYING THE STRATEGIC MANAGEMENT PROCESS

This casebook has been prepared to help you apply knowledge about strategic management practices. Case analysis is the most widely used method to help you understand the complexity of integrating strategic decisions from a top-management perspective. This part of the book introduces you to the case method and the strategic management process. Parts Two through Five present the cases that you can use to "practice" the ideas you are learning about, in order to become a more accomplished professional.

This chapter briefly describes the case method. Then an approach to strategic management that can be used for case analysis is outlined. Finally, some ideas are offered about how you might prepare reports and present analyses. Since you will eventually prepare analyses and make presentations to your peers and supervisors in organizations, it is useful to obtain some practical experience in doing so.

## THE CASE METHOD [1]

A case is a written description of an enterprise (like a business, industry, hospital, or arts organization). A case usually contains information about numerous facets of the enterprise: its history, environment, and internal operations. And cases usually provide some information about key managers in the organization. The cases used in *Cases in Strategic Management and Business Policy* are multifaceted, containing material on many aspects of the organizations. Thus your analysis is expected to be comprehensive.

Cases are based on material gathered about real organizations. Many of the cases in this book are undisguised; that is, real names are used. There are also some disguised cases of companies that wished to remain anonymous; their names and locations have been changed. This does not change the reality of challenges and problems facing these firms, and it serves no useful purpose for you to try to guess their identity.

**ARE CASES COMPLETE?** There is no such thing as a *complete* case study. The amount of detail required would make the case too long to read and too detailed to analyze. One reaction that frequently is heard is, "I don't have enough information." In reality, the manager *never* has enough information because it is not available, it is not available at this time, or it is too costly to acquire.

What does the manager do then? The manager makes the necessary decisions on the basis of the information at hand after making reasonable assumptions about the unknowns. So, with cases, you must work with the information you have and make reasonable assumptions. The case contains enough information for the analyst to examine and then determine the crucial factors that confront management at the time.

**IS ALL THE CASE INFORMATION IMPORTANT?**

When you get your mail, some of it is important, some useless, some of minor interest. At work, managers are bombarded with information. It too consists of a mix of the relevant, the partially relevant, and the useless. So it is with cases. When case writers gather information, some will become crucial to analysis. Other pieces of information are not especially useful. Since you are training to be a manager, it is your job to do the manager's job: separate the wheat from the chaff. You also have to sort through sometimes conflicting evidence or opinions, and so learn to deal with uncertainty.

**WHY ARE CASES USED IN MANAGEMENT EDUCATION?**

Case studies allow a different kind of learning to take place—close to a learn-by-doing approach. Cases are intended to simulate the reality of the manager's job. The material in the case provides the data for analysis and decision making. Cases become the laboratory materials for applying what we have learned about how to be effective business executives or administrators.

Cases require you to make decisions about the situations presented and to defend those decisions with your peers. In real decision making, you will need to persuade your peers and superiors that your analysis and solution are the best. So these communication and interpersonal skills are vital to success in management. Cases provide you with the opportunity to improve these skills too.

**WHAT ROLES DO STUDENTS AND INSTRUCTORS PLAY IN THE CASE METHOD?**

Typically, the instructor serves a different role from that of lecturer. Instructors encourage students to analyze problems and recommend solutions. Instructors question and criticize and encourage their students' peers to do the same. At the end of class the instructor may summarize or simply walk away, refusing to answer questions like, "what would you do?" or "what did the managers do?" The relevant answer is the one proposed and logically defended by the analysts in class.

The student can play several roles. Standard roles include those of the board chairperson, the president, and consultant. We prefer the consultant's role. Thus the student can analyze and recommend what should be done, given the nature of the problem and the nature of the top executives. If students feel that the suggestion they would like to make is likely to be unacceptable to the president, they should discuss both solutions or present a particularly convincing argument to make the recommendation acceptable and overcome objectives.

# GUIDELINES FOR ANALYZING CASES [2]

So far we have discussed the rationale of the case method. Now let's look at the content of a good case analysis.

**THE STRATEGIC PROBLEM AND THE STRATEGIC MANAGEMENT PROCESS**

The strategic problem in general is to determine how the organization can accomplish objectives or develop plans to meet new objectives. The strategic management process helps you to determine the nature of this problem. That is, top managers may be changing, or goals are not being met. Or the environment (e.g., competitors, economic conditions, etc.) may be changing. Changes can create problems (threats or opportunities). Or the firm may have internal problems (e.g., insufficient capital, weak marketing, etc.) or strengths (e.g., good production processes). Various phases of analysis will help you sort through causes of problems or new opportunities to which managers can apply strengths. Other phases of analysis help you systematically explore ways to solve problems and recommend plans for action. That is, you will develop a strategy for the firm to follow. A strategy is an integrated and comprehensive plan for the firm to use to solve problems and accomplish objectives. Hence, the strategic management process involves analysis of potential goal and management change, strategy formulation, and implementation of an action plan to solve problems.

At all times in your analysis you need to keep in the back of your mind the ideas you are ultimately trying to integrate. What is the current mission and what are the objectives? What is the enterprise's business definition? What are the firm's products and markets, and what functions does this enterprise perform? What is its environmental situation? What is its distinctive competence? Will the current strategy allow the firm to reach its objectives and the goals of its managers, or will it encounter problems in accomplishing its mission in the future? Can the firm invent a creative solution to these problems? How can the firm organize and manage itself to the full advantage of its resources and implement an innovative solution? The whole thrust of your analysis should generally focus on those issues.

Exhibit 1.1 summarizes these ideas in a simple model of the strategic management process. The following sections elaborate on this model to help you focus on key questions and makes suggestions you will want to address as you do your case analysis. For some cases, all these questions may not be directly applicable. For others, you may have to make some assumptions or do library research. However, the more questions you address, the more likely you will do a good analysis.

**Exhibit 1.1** A Model of Strategic Management

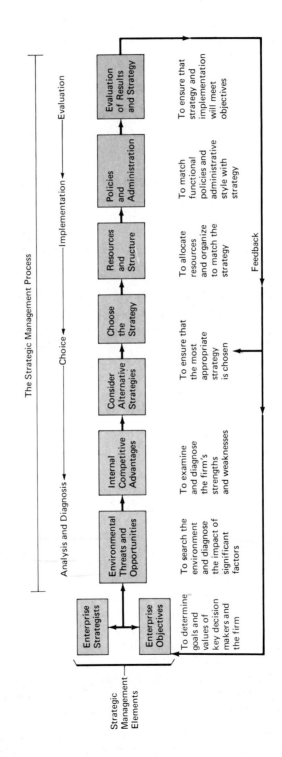

The Strategic Management Process

Analysis and Diagnosis —— Choice —— Implementation —— Evaluation

Strategic Management Elements

| Enterprise Strategists / Enterprise Objectives | Environmental Threats and Opportunities | Internal Competitive Advantages | Consider Alternative Strategies | Choose the Strategy | Resources and Structure | Policies and Administration | Evaluation of Results and Strategy |
|---|---|---|---|---|---|---|---|
| To determine goals and values of key decision makers and the firm | To search the environment and diagnose the impact of significant factors | To examine and diagnose the firm's strengths and weaknesses | To ensure that the most appropriate strategy is chosen | | To allocate resources and organize to match the strategy | To match functional policies and administrative style with strategy | To ensure that strategy and implementation will meet objectives |

Feedback

**THE STRATEGIC ELEMENTS**

You need to assess the mission and objectives of the organization and the strategists involved. These elements are important first steps in determining the nature of the strategic problem.

What is the mission of the business? What is its business definition and past strategy? Prepare a statement that summarizes these elements. The case may not state these clearly, but you need to attempt to determine the mission and past strategy. In particular, look for synergies in the business definition. Also try to itemize a list of objectives. Then ask if these objectives help to define the organization, provide standards, and coordinate decisions, or if there is conflict. Since organizations usually have multiple objectives, how are they currently ranked? Are they long- or short-term? Are goals specific or broad? Do they need to be more specific? Are existing goals being achieved? Are there pressures to change goals? Refer to Exhibit 1.2 and identify any forces that may be leading to changes in objectives. At this point, you may be able to identify whether objectives are being met or whether a new set of desired goals is emerging.

Of course, one of the forces for change deals with the values and goals of top management. Who are the key people with decision power in this case? What do they want? How do they make decisions? How much risk are managers willing to assume? Does the board support the chief executive officer (CEO)? If you are going to ultimately make realistic recommendations that have some probability of acceptance, you must understand who has the power (in the case) to implement your proposals. If you are playing the consultant role, you must convince the manager(s) with power that your recommendation will fit his or her goals and values and be best for the organization.

**ANALYSIS AND DIAGNOSIS**

The strategic problems may be caused by either external or internal changes. Thus the next phase of case analysis focuses on change factors.

**EXHIBIT 1.2**
Forces
Affecting
Objectives

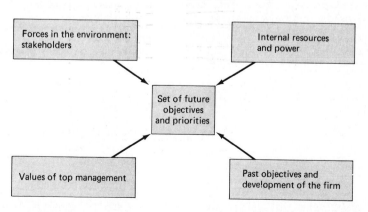

*Note:* Each of those factors represents a set of constraints on the establishment of the priorities among future objectives. The set of objectives considered at any one time will be affected by these forces.

### The Environment

It's important to examine threats and opportunities from the environment. You need to analyze and diagnose the socioeconomic, technological, supplier, competitor, and governmental sectors of importance to the firm. Exhibit 1.3 provides the key overall questions. What are the assumptions about the environment on which current strategy is based? What predictions do you make for the future? Are there any gaps in those assumptions and predictions? If so, will the gaps lead to changes in objectives or strategy? What is the level of uncertainty about the environment? In other words, will the environment change and cause a strategic problem or opportunity?

For the case you are analyzing, which of your key predictions are creating threats and opportunities? You should focus your diagnosis on the critical areas—the sectors on which the firm is most dependent and that allow greater development, complexity, and volatility. In these areas, much greater in-depth analysis should be done to try to reduce some of the uncertainty. Exhibit 1.4 sketches various factors that could provide threats or opportunities to a given firm. Each area should be assessed in more or less detail depending on the importance of expected changes to the firm in question. If the case data are insufficient, you may want to search for information in the library or establish key assumptions about the expected scenario of the firm's environment in each key category.

If you want to do a more sophisticated analysis, you could prepare several scenarios that may ultimately lead to preparation of contingency proposals. In any case, you should prepare a commentary based on your summary of the key environmental issues. That is, you should elaborate on data and estimates of revenue or cost implications and estimates of the likelihood of events and their timing. In the end, go back to the key questions: Where are the opportunities? Where are the threats? What strategic impact do these changes have?

---

**EXHIBIT 1.3**    The Environmental Analysis and Diagnosis Process

| Environment of the Firm | Strategists analyze and diagnose gaps |
|---|---|
| Socioeconomic<br>Technological<br>Supplier<br>Competitor<br>Government | Analysis<br>1. Identify the current strategy the firm uses to relate to the environment. What are the assumptions or predictions about the environment on which current strategy is based?<br>2. Predict the future environment. Are the assumptions or predictions the same as in step 1? Is there a gap?<br>Diagnosis<br>3. Assess the significance of the gap between the current and future environments for the firm. Are changes in objectives needed? Do changes in strategy appear useful to consider? Will they reduce the gap? |

| **EXHIBIT 1.4** | Examples of Environmental Factors to be Analyzed and Diagnosed* |
|---|---|

Socio-economic Sector
    Economic conditions and trends
    Demographic factors and changes
    Geographic factors and conditions
    Social factors and changes
Technological Sector
    Product/service life cycle changes
    Operations or distribution tools and techniques
    Raw materials factors
Supplier Sector
    Power of suppliers, number of suppliers, entry and exit of suppliers
    Availability and cost of: raw materials, energy, money, labor
Competitor Sector
    Entry and exit of competitors
    Availability of substitute products or services
    Major strategic changes of competitors
Government Sector
    Federal, State and Local segments
    Executive, Legislative and Judicial branches
    Tax, fiscal and monetary policies
    Regulatory agencies
    Import/export policies and trade regulations

*Note:* Some of these factors are more or less important for a given firm. If the factor is more volatile and uncertain (rapid unpredictable change), or if the firm's performance is influenced by or more dependent on a given factor, (e.g. suppliers of labor may be more important than money suppliers, or vice versa), then that issue needs more detailed analysis and diagnosis as to its potential impact on the firm in the future. Further, recognize that these factors often overlap and influence one another (e.g. fiscal policies influence economic conditions, or social changes may influence competitor strategy).

Reconsider the strategic problem. Will the changes you anticipate in the environment prevent you from reaching existing goals, or allow you to reach desired goals?

**Internal Conditions**

Like environmental factors, the internal factors may create problems or help the organization attain its goals. Thus you need to analyze a firm's internal strengths and weaknesses.

Examine Exhibit 1.5, which identifies areas of a business where strengths and weaknesses can exist. Which are the most important areas for the firm in the case? Those should receive your greatest attention. Identify distinctive competencies in critical areas by asking key questions: What does the firm do

**EXHIBIT 1.5**   Analysis of Internal Strengths and Weaknesses

### Corporate Resources and Personnel

1. Corporate image and prestige
2. Effective organization structure and climate
3. Company size in relation to the industry (barrier to entry)
4. Strategic management system
5. Enterprise's record for reaching objectives: How consistent has it been? How well does it do compared with similar enterprises?
6. Influence with regulatory and governmental bodies
7. Effective corporate-staff support systems
8. Effective management information and computer systems
9. High-quality employees
10. Balanced functional experience and track record of top management: Are replacements trained and ready to take over? Do the top managers work well together as a team?
11. Effective relations with trade unions
12. Efficient and effective personnel relations policies: staffing, appraisal and promotion, training and development, and compensation and benefits
13. Lower costs of labor (as measured by compensation, turnover, and absenteeism)

### Finance and Accounting

1. Total financial resources and strength
2. Low cost of capital in relation to the industry and competitors because of stock price and dividend policy
3. Effective capital structure, allowing flexibility in raising additional capital as needed; financial leverage and cash flow forecasting and control
4. Amicable relations with owners and stockholders
5. Advantageous tax conditions
6. Efficient and effective financial planning, working capital, and capital budgeting procedures
7. Efficient and effective accounting systems for cost, budget and profit planning, and auditing procedures
8. Inventory valuation policies

### Marketing and Distribution

1. Competitive structure and market share: To what extent has the firm established a strong market share in the total market or its key submarkets?
2. Efficient and effective market research system
3. The product-service mix: quality of products and services
4. Product-service line; completeness of product-service line and product-service mix; phase of life cycle and main products and services are in
5. Strong new-product and new-service leadership

6. Patent protection (or equivalent legal protection for services)
7. Positive feelings about the firm and its products and services on the part of the ultimate consumer
8. Efficient and effective packaging of products (or the equivalent for services)
9. Effective pricing strategy for products and services
10. Efficient and effective sales force: close ties with key customers. How vulnerable are we in terms of concentrating on sales to a few customers?
11. Effective advertising: Has it established the company's product or brand image to develop loyal customers?
12. Efficient and effective marketing promotion activities other than advertising
13. Efficient and effective service after purchase
14. Efficient and effective channels of distribution and geographic coverage, including internal efforts

### Production and Operations Management

1. Lower total cost of operations compared with competitors' total costs
2. Capacity to meet market demands
3. Efficient and effective facilities
4. Raw materials and subassemblies costs
5. Adequate availability of raw materials and subassemblies
6. Efficient and effective equipment and machinery
7. Efficient and effective offices
8. Strategic location of facilities and offices
9. Efficient and effective inventory control systems
10. Efficient and effective procedures: design, scheduling, quality control
11. Efficient and effective maintenance policies
12. Effective vertical integration

### R&D and Engineering

1. Basic research capabilities within the firm
2. Development capability for product engineering
3. Excellence in product design
4. Excellence in process design and improvements
5. Superior packaging developments being created
6. Improvements in the use of old or new materials
7. Ability to meet design goals and customer requirements
8. Well-equipped laboratories and testing facilities
9. Trained and experienced technicians and scientists
10. Work environment suited to creativity and innovation
11. Managers who can explain goals to researchers and research results to higher managers
12. Ability of unit to perform effective technological forecasting

**EXHIBIT 1.6**  A Summary of the Financial Position of a Firm

| Ratios and Working Capital | 1979 | 1980 | 1981 | 1982 | 1983 | Trend | Standard | Interpretation |
|---|---|---|---|---|---|---|---|---|
| Liquidity: Current | | | | | | | | |
| Quick | | | | | | | | |
| Leverage: | | | | | | | | |
| (etc.) | | | | | | | | |
| Working-capital position | | | | | | | | |

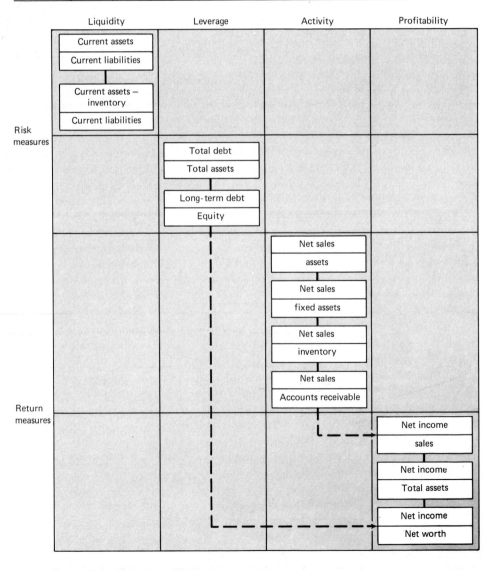

well? Do these count? What does the firm do poorly? Does it matter? Your analysis should focus on the data and indicators based on relative comparisons: How do current conditions relate to past and future needs? How do the areas relate to one another? How do the areas relate to relevant competitors?

Also prepare any supporting documents and commentary about distinctive competencies. Very often you will want to prepare a summary of the firm's financial position (see Exhibit 1.6) if data are available. The basic financial data need interpretation and point to other areas of the firm that may need to be examined. You could also prepare a break-even analysis or analyze sales data and so on if they are available. In a few cases, where the data are sufficient, you might prepare a resource deployment matrix like that shown in Exhibit 1.7. Such information gives the manager an overall view of the internal past strategy of the firm as it has been implemented through budgetary allocations.

As you did for the environment, you should prepare a summary statement indicating the results of your assessment of enterprise strengths and weaknesses. Your commentary should attempt to determine how the strengths and

**EXHIBIT 1.7**  A Resource Deployment Matrix

| Functional Areas | Resource-Deployment Emphasis | 5 years ago | 2 years ago | This year | Next year | 3 years from now |
|---|---|---|---|---|---|---|
| R&D/ Engineering | % of dollars invested focus of efforts | | | | | |
| Manufacturing | % of dollars invested focus of efforts | | | | | |

*Note*: Complete similar information for Marketing, Finance, and Management to fill out the *Functional Area* Matrix.

| Strategic Business Units | Resource-Deployment Emphasis | 5 years ago | 2 years ago | This year | Next year | 3 years from now |
|---|---|---|---|---|---|---|
| Division A | % of dollars invested Returns focus of efforts | | | | | |

*Note:* Complete similar information for Divisions B, C, etc. to fill out the *Strategic Business Unit* Matrix.

weaknesses have been used for competitive advantage and how they might be used later. In doing this, don't forget your environmental analysis. Begin to ask yourself whether the competitive advantages (the ones that exist or that could be developed) relate to new opportunities you identified earlier. Also determine whether increased resources might be needed to offset any threats, where those resources are now and where they need to be. In other words, how can the firm most effectively exploit the opportunities and meet the threats the environment is presenting?

**STRATEGY ALTERNATIVES AND CHOICE**

Before proceeding, reexamine your analyses and diagnoses in relation to the strategic problem. Do your environmental and internal analyses point to a need to change strategy because existing objectives won't be met or new objectives can be achieved?

The next issue to consider is the various alternatives a firm might pursue. The central factor examined at the beginning of the consideration of strategic alternatives is the business of the firm. This was partly answered by your earlier analysis of the past mission and strategy. Products, markets, and functions need to be identified. Once the firm's business has been defined, various questions (such as Should we get out of this business entirely? or Should we try to expand?) will help the strategist focus on the type of strategic alternative the firm should pursue.

The grand strategy alternatives are to expand, stabilize, or retrench. This can be done in ongoing activities or by changing the business definition of products, markets, or functions. Combinations of simultaneous activities or sequential options are included. All strategy alternatives can be designed to improve performance, but different propositions are offered whenever one is more likely to be successful than another.

**Proposition 1:**
Stability is more likely if the firm is doing well, the environment is not excessively volatile, and the product or service has reached the stability or maturity stage of the life cycle.

**Proposition 2:**
Expansion is more likely in highly competitive, volatile industries, particularly early in the product-service life cycle.

**Proposition 3:**
Retrenchment is more likely if the firm is not doing well, greater returns can be gained elsewhere, or the product or service is at a later stage of the life cycle.

**Proposition 4:**
Combinations are more likely for multiple-SBU firms, in periods of economic transition, and during changes in the product-service life cycle.

Now examine Exhibit 1.8. Focus on the strategic problem and your analyses of internal and external conditions overall. Focus on the grand strategy most relevant for the situation in the case. Also compare this analysis with our four propositions. Note that if your environmental analysis shows stability and your internal analysis shows strength, a stability strategy is more likely, but expansion may occur where the firm is strong. Conversely, if the environment shows threats and the firm is weak, retrenchment is a more likely alternative. Prepare a list of advantages and disadvantages of following the grand strategy you are analyzing. Does the grand strategy solve the strategic problem? Will it do a better job than other alternatives?

Various approaches to the grand strategies can also be identified. That is, the way in which the grand strategy is carried out depends upon the specifics of your analyses of internal and external conditions and the nature of the goals and strategic problem. First, think in terms of products (or services), markets, and functions. For example, if the firm has an environmental opportunity and internal strength in *product development,* you could recommend new products, new product features, quality variations, or additional models and sizes. On the other hand, competitor threats or proliferation in the product line might call for retrenchment by eliminating unprofitable products or pruning the line. *Market development* is another category for consideration. Additional (or fewer) geographic territories could be considered as well as getting into (or out of) various market segments (customer niches). Adding new markets or retrenching out of old ones is, of course, dependent on the particular combination of distinctive competencies and environmental conditions facing the firm. Similarly, a firm could decide to penetrate existing markets with current products to gain market share. *Developing functions* is yet a third category for potential strategic activity. A given firm could expand functions by backward or forward vertical integration (moving closer to sources of supply or to end users is one way in which a firm provides added value). Conversely, the firm might dis-

**EXHIBIT 1.8**    Focusing Strategic Alternatives

| PREDOMINANT ENVIRONMENTAL CONDITIONS | PREDOMINANT INTERNAL CONDITIONS | |
|---|---|---|
| | Weakness | Strength |
| More Stable | Stability with possible retrenchment in some areas | Stability in some areas, expansion in others |
| Mainly Opportunities | Improve weak areas with an operating turnaround | Expand in new products, markets or functions |
| Mainly Threats | Retrench in areas of weakness | Expand in some areas, retrench in others |

continue some functions if it is weak in a given area (for example, by focusing on distribution only instead of production and distribution).

Of course, the firm could remain *stable* in some or all of its products, markets, and functions if it is satisfied with its goal attainment, perceives no threats or opportunities, and is relatively strong internally. Or, without changing products, markets, or functions, it might improve its operations by cost cutting to improve margins. Quite frequently, firms will maintain stability in one important area to provide a comfortable operating position, combined with expansion into new areas where managers see opportunity and believe they have or can develop the internal capabilities to achieve growth goals. Hence combinations of approaches should be considered, either simultaneously or over time.

Aside from thinking about products, markets, and functions, strategies can be pursued in other ways. Depending on the strengths or weaknesses, a firm could attempt any of the grand strategies alone or with the involvement of others. The most common example is expansion through a merger or acquisition. The retrenchment corollary would be to sell to another firm or liquidate a division or the whole business. In some cases, retrenchment could be a recommended strategy to avoid a threat, eliminate a weakness, or take an advantage of an opportunity to use resources better in other lines of business. Another approach firms are more frequently considering is the use of joint ventures. If two or more companies lack a necessary component for success in a given environment, they might join forces to create a new enterprise or engage in a given project for a period of time.

Another possible strategic option concerns the extent to which proposed changes in products, markets, or functions are similar or different from the past strategy. If the changes considered are similar or somehow related to past activities, then synergy is more likely. If the changes are more unrelated, this is known as diversification. Once again, there are pros and cons to either approach. For example, diversification might reduce some kinds of risk associated with being tied to economic cycles; but this type of move requires different kinds of strategic capabilities.

It is beyond the purpose of this overview to discuss the numerous reasons and conditions supporting a given strategy and how it can be carried out. The preceding discussion has only pointed you in several key directions for consideration. However, using Exhibit 1.8 as a guide, focus on one or two grand strategies first, then consider the various possible approaches for carrying those out.

Again, the basis for your recommendations should be the particular combination of internal and external conditions in relation to solving the strategic problem for the enterprise in question. You should also realize that there are potential advantages and disadvantages to pursuing any given alternative. You should elaborate the pros and cons of alternatives.

At this point you will want to consider which of these strategic alternatives you would recommend. For instance, will a particular option help the firm reach its goals better than other alternatives? Does the strategy use competitive advantages? Will it build new ones and allow the firm to develop a sustained distinctive competence? Does the strategy meet the challenges and opportunities in the environment? Does it change the nature of the business? Will such a change be acceptable to the power holders?

For a multidivisional firm, you will need to consider the portfolio of strategies of the firm as a whole. Some divisions may be stable, others may expand, or others retrench. Next, settle on a tentative choice for which you will develop a plan of implementation. Following that, the evaluation stage will be applied to confirm a final choice.

If you are doing a sophisticated analysis, you would compare several contingency strategies to go along with the scenarios that we suggested you prepare earlier. Hence you might have a worst case – best case – most likely set of strategies.

**IMPLEMEN-TATION**   Exhibit 1.9 outlines several major areas managers need to consider for a plan to implement the strategy. For any given case, it is unlikely you will be able to obtain some of the needed detail. However, one or two major elements of a plan might be included to "flesh out" your strategy recommendation.

**EXHIBIT 1.9**
A Strategic
Implementation
Process

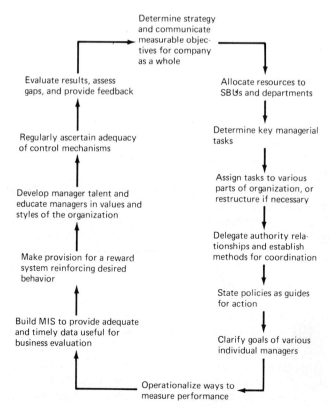

Determine strategy and communicate measurable objectives for company as a whole

Allocate resources to SBUs and departments

Determine key managerial tasks

Assign tasks to various parts of organization, or restructure if necessary

Delegate authority relationships and establish methods for coordination

State policies as guides for action

Clarify goals of various individual managers

Operationalize ways to measure performance

Build MIS to provide adequate and timely data useful for business evaluation

Make provision for a reward system reinforcing desired behavior

Develop manager talent and educate managers in values and styles of the organization

Regularly ascertain adequacy of control mechanisms

Evaluate results, assess gaps, and provide feedback

In some cases, a major implementation focus could deal with resource allocation. What major changes in resource allocations are implied by your strategy? If a multi-SBU firm is involved, will the firm need to shift resources from one SBU to another? Will some functional areas need more resources? Where will resources come from? If your strategy is to sell some assets, how much do you expect to get from the sale? If your strategy is expansion, will the firm use internal funds, debt, or equity, and what will be the impact on the balance sheet? If your strategy is a joint venture, what kind of equity agreement do you recommend? A sophisticated analysis would present pro

**EXHIBIT 1.10**    Alternative Business Strategies and Plans*

| Strategy | Marketing- Product Line Plans | Manufacturing Plans | Human Resources Plans | Financial Plans | Timing |
|---|---|---|---|---|---|
| Retrenchment | Identify product lines for divestment— those with low sales or margins. | Identify plants to close on the basis of capacity utilization. | Reduce personnel on the basis of skills needed in the future and seniority. | Eliminate or reduce dividends, and manage cash flows. | Sell plants and reduce personnel in 1 year; cut dividends now. |
| Stability | Push the high-margin products in the line. | Defer plant and equipment investments over $200,000. | Invest in training programs to improve management skills. | Develop good bank relations, maintain steady dividends, and strengthen the balance sheet. | Continue for three years unless trends show high opportunity. |
| Expansion | Extend and improve product lines; volume is more critical than margins. | Expand plant capacity to support new products as necessary. | Hire additional sales, R&D, and production workers and managers. | Increase the debt-equity ratio by one-third. Consider the impact of dividend policy on cash-flow needs. | Evaluate market share position and financial condition after 2 years. |

*Note: The foregoing presents brief examples of a few policy issues for each type of grand strategy. More generally, policies for each functional area need to be established as follows:
1. Financial mix: (a) capital, (b) leasing versus buying, (c) investment risk, (d) use of assets, (e) accounting and tax treatment
2. Marketing mix: (a) products and markets, (b) distribution and promotion, (c) price, (d) quality
3. Production-operations mix: (a) capacity and utilization, (b) location of facilities, (c) maintenance and replacement, (d) sourcing
4. R&D mix: (a) products and processes, (b) basic and applied research, (c) offensive and defensive research
5. Personnel: (a) recruiting, (b) allocating, (c) developing, (d) maintaining
6. Legal issues
7. Public relations

forma balance sheet and income statement exhibits based on realistic assumptions of the plan based on the strategy.

In other cases, a plan for implementation might address key major changes needed in the organization structure. Usually in a case analysis, structural change would occur only if major redefinitions of the business result from your proposed strategy. However, some cases may focus on organizational issues. Here, you would probably be provided with data on which to base more detailed recommendations. Still, you should consider the strategic reason why any changes you propose would be necessary. For example, is the firm moving from related to unrelated product or market areas? If so, a change to divisional forms could probably be useful. Other characteristics of the firm and its environment related to the strategy should be considered as well. In a few cases you may want to address the role of a planning staff as it relates to the future of the organization.

For most cases, plans and policies for the functional areas would be considered. Exhibit 1.10 suggests an example of the kinds of issues you might consider. Greater detail and more specifics for the case in question could be needed, but these are illustrations. The list in the note to Exhibit 1.10 suggests key functional decisions you might make. For a case analysis, you should *focus on* the *major policy* issues in the critical functional areas that managers will need to address as a consequence of pursuing the strategy you recommend. In other words, deal primarily with the areas that have greatest significance for your strategic proposal and that require changes. Before drawing up your final proposal, look back over any functional policies you might propose and ask yourself, Are they consistent with one another? Are they consistent with the strategic choice? Are they related to the major strategic issue?

Your plan might also consider leadership, if that is important to the case. Are changes needed in current leadership? If yes, in what positions? What kinds of leader changes are to be made? Is it feasible to recommend firing the president if he or she holds the power? Would a career development plan make sense? Can reward systems be set up to motivate managers to enact the strategic choice? How much effort will be needed to carry out your plan?

**EVALUATION**  After you have finished your analysis and prepared a plan to implement the tentative strategy, reevaluate the entire process, looking at it as a whole. Is your plan comprehensive, unified, and integrated? Are the strategy and plans you developed consistent, appropriate, and workable? Will the plan solve the strategic problem? If not, but your plan is the best available given your analyses and diagnoses, then you will have to convince management that their expectations about goal attainment will have to be modified. In other words, after your set of recommendations is put together, be sure you are solving the major problems.

In preparing your final set of recommendations, it might be useful to think in terms of a PERT network. That is, what are the *critical activities* that must be accomplished *over a period of time* to accomplish goals or solve the strategic problem? For example, *what* new products need to be developed? *When* should managers abandon unprofitable markets? What are the events on a "critical path" to accomplish the strategy you have chosen, and how can those events be managed? Remember that there are probably several key activities that need to be related to one another in a unified way. When the activities are aligned, working together, and pointed in the same direction, then the plan has a greater chance of being a success.

You should realize that managers have to control and evaluate performance of a plan over time. Managers often set up benchmarks for evaluation (see Exhibit 1.11) and indicate when and how information should be delivered

**EXHIBIT 1.11**  Benchmarks for Evaluation: An Example*

| Key Success Factors | Overall Objectives or Assumptions | Expected Performance at This Time | Current Performance | Existing Deviations | Projected Deviations |
|---|---|---|---|---|---|
| Financial: | | | | | |
| Reduce overhead cost | 5% | 2% | 3% | +1% | +1% |
| Profit on sales | 12% | 5% | 9% | +4% | +2% |
| Marketing: | | | | | |
| Analyze new-product proposals | 10 | 4 | 2 | −2 | −3 |
| Sales per employee | $7000 | $6800 | $6900 | +$100 | +$100 |
| Personnel: | | | | | |
| Number of key managers needed | 6 | 2 | 3 | +1 | +1 |
| Ratio of indirect cost to direct cost | 12% | 14% | 13% | −1% | 0% |
| R&D: | | | | | |
| Recruitment of senior engineers | 20 | 16 | 10 | −6 | −6 |
| Increase R&D-sales ratio | 5% | 4% | 3% | −1% | −1% |
| Operations: | | | | | |
| Increase production capacity | 50% | 40% | 40% | 0% | 0% |
| Competitor reactions: | | | | | |
| Increased R&D | 4% | 3% | 4% | +1% | +1% |
| Product changes | 4 | 2 | 3 | +1 | +1 |

*Note: Managers will want to compare *progress to date* with *expectations to date*. Of primary interest are those factors where an existing deviation might lead to a *projected deviation* of some importance requiring corrective action. The idea is to establish specific performance indicators for measurement at a given time period. Indicate the overall key success factors, benchmarks for attainment at specific times, how they should be measured, and possible contingency plans to put into effect if given benchmarks are not attained at a given time.

Many cases might not require this detail. However, you should be aware that managers need tools like this to evaluate strategic performance.

to the right managers at the right time. Most cases may not require this degree of detail. But thinking about these issues might help you pinpoint critical activities that you may have overlooked as you try to solve the major problems.

Finally, if you are doing more sophisticated planning, show how your plan is flexible enough to provide for contingencies. Indicate the conditions for and the time when a contingency strategy should be put into effect.

**PROBLEMS IN ANALYSIS**

We have taken you through our suggestions for a comprehensive basic case analysis. We should point out that most cases will not directly address all the questions we just raised for you to analyze. In some cases financial data are not available, or competitor or other environmental data are lacking. In other cases, the focus may be on a more limited set of issues or problems. The key is to focus on critical issues. In a few cases you have several other options:

- Do some library work to get additional data.
- Make assumptions and proceed.
- Recognize that the case focus is limited and apply the most directly relevant material you have learned.

Like managers, you will often need to be creative, put together your own data, and "read between the lines" to answer some questions and deal with significant strategic issues. We hope you will invest the time it takes to do that.

Finally, you may be using other text material that organizes strategic management concepts a bit differently, or that uses another classification scheme for various approaches to types of strategy a firm might pursue. Authors present material in their own style. If you face this situation, it is up to you to choose the approach you wish to follow. Regardless of your choice, the use of the cases should help illustrate the factors top management needs to consider as it positions its firms for better performance in the future.

# THE CASE PREPARATION PROCESS [3]

There are a large number of possible approaches to case preparation. The approach below has worked for some of our students.

1. Read the case. Underline and comment on parts that you think are important. Then you might try to determine what the major and minor problems are, jotting down how you might analyze them. Do some preliminary analysis to see if your impressions are correct. Identify the mission and strategy and list the objectives of the firm. Put the case aside for a while.
2. Read the case again. This time prepare analyses of goals, values, and internal and external factors. This requires an analysis, as we described earlier. At about this point, if you find it comfortable (and if your instructor

allows it), you might sit down and discuss the case with several friends who have different interests or majors. You and your friends can help each other with the problem, and you can learn to understand your friends' point of view, too. (We hope the instructor allows it, for in real life if managers have a problem that has ramifications for other areas, they probably visit friends in those areas to get their points of view.)

You are then ready for real analysis. Examine your statements for implicit assumptions. Fill in areas where no "hard" data were presented with reasonable assumptions, and state them carefully.

3. Prepare a list of the major opportunities and problems. Rank-order these factors in terms of importance. Prepare a list of alternative strategies. Consider the advantages and disadvantages of the viable alternatives for this enterprise, using your previous analyses. Make recommendations that you have carefully thought through by asking such questions as: If I recommend they do $X$ in marketing, how will it affect finance, or $Z$ company, or the sales manager?

4. Analyze the alternatives in terms of the problems and opportunities and make a choice that seems to meet the objectives of the enterprise and considers the values of strategists and internal and external factors.

5. Clarify how the organization can implement your suggested strategy. Prepare a plan that specifies the major implementation issue(s) (e.g., resource needs, functional policies, organization design, or administrative systems supporting the strategy).

6. Reevaluate your proposal. Point out any possible problem areas and how and when key activities should be evaluated as the plan is put into effect.

7. Prepare notes for an oral presentation (and practice it), or prepare a final written report. Our last section discusses these topics at more length.

It is equally easy to spend too much or too little time on case analysis. Plan to spend anywhere from 10 to 15 hours over a four- or five-day period in the analysis phases. Another 5 to 10 hours may be needed to prepare a report. You may spend more time if the case represents a real challenge to you. However, there is a danger that you may begin to lose perspective if you get unnecessarily bogged down in detail.

**STAGES OF ANALYSIS**  Our students seem to go through stages in handling cases. The amount of time spent in each stage varies with the student, but most seem to go through these stages:

*Stage 1: Factual Level.* The first stage is characterized by the development of the ability to choose the pertinent facts from all the data in the case. In real life, managers are bombarded by cues, facts, and information. On the factual level, the student learns to separate the important from the unimportant and to see where the problems(s) is (are).

*Stage 2: Preanalytical Level.* This stage is characterized by rudimentary use of the "tools of the trade." Thus if from Stage 1 students perceive a problem in the financial area, they now say so and present a page of ratios, various financial statements, cash budgets, and the like.

*Stage 3: Analytical Stage.* Realizing that "facts do not speak for themselves," students enter a new stage. They now interpret the facts. They not only compute the ratios but also explain them meaningfully. They say, "The current ratio is 1 : 1. This is less desirable than the normal 2 : 1 ratio found in this industry [or risk class, etc.] and means that this firm. . . ."

Students are now on the threshold of asking the right questions and establishing relationships (perhaps even cause-and-effect relationships) and can begin to apply their knowledge, experience, and judgment.

*Stage 4: Problem-Solving Stage.* Students have now reached the stage of "knowing" what the problem(s) is (are). What is to be done about the problem? Usually, students attempt to dream up potential ways of accomplishing what they want to do. They develop several potential solutions. They tell us about the solutions, attempt to show the implications for each alternative, and weigh them as better or worse.

*Stage 5: Decision-Making Stage.* Students now must choose a solution to the problem. To do this, they need a weighing device. Normally, students attempt to consider maximum goal achievement with least effort. But there are many objectives for a firm, and sometimes, in fact often, goals conflict with one another.

This final stage in the process is in many ways the least "rational." In many of the earlier stages, the analysis can be fairly objective. "Facts" have been weighed as rationally as possible by using as sophisticated tools as are appropriate. But at this stage, it is difficult to determine which alternative is the best. Many of the alternatives have been based on estimates. Even with the use of decision trees and the like, there is still the problem of setting probabilities of occurrence. The final stage then involves "judgment." More emotional, more intuitive factors are used than in other stages. One value we have in our business society is rationality; we like to "stick to the facts." But these decisions have fewer "hard facts" on which to rely, so the choice is based upon values and judgment and the experience of the executive. We may as well face this openly. Students also show that their solution, strategy, or plan will "solve" the problem seen in the case.

*Stage 6: Implementation Stage.* After making a choice, students now realize that the decisions must be implemented by adjusting the organization or setting up policies or a control and evaluation system.

We hope you will progress through all six stages, for they represent the kinds of strategic management decision processes that executives go through.

# REPORTING YOUR RECOMMENDATIONS [4]

Each of us has our own style for presenting the results of our analysis. Now and in the future you will be asked to present, discuss, justify, and defend your recommendations, both in oral form and in writing. So we conclude by offering some suggestions for how you might make more effective presentations, assuming those are backed up by the type of analysis we just outlined.

**WRITTEN
PRESEN-
TATIONS**

Written reports are the end product of a comprehensive managerial process. The intent is to communicate concisely and effectively the results and conclusions of your analysis so that your recommendations are justified and ultimately accepted.

Most written reports of case analyses tend to be relatively short (6 to 10 pages plus exhibits), though each instructor has different expectations. Occasionally even shorter "management summaries" might be called for. In either case, a key guideline is to attempt to apply one principle—keep it simple. Unfortunately, after hours of analysis and note taking, you will want to share all your analysis to show what you have done. If you try that, it is likely that you won't keep your presentation simple. Keeping it simple and straightforward does not necessarily imply you have done a sloppy job or that it lacks comprehensiveness. If the report is put together well, it will be apparent that the conclusions are grounded in good analysis.

If, as we suggested, you prepare and include supporting exhibits (such as commentary and predictions of internal and external factors, ratio summaries, breakeven analyses, pro forma financial statements, benchmarks for evaluation, and so on), you will provide powerful evidence to justify your major arguments and recommendations, and you will show that you have thought through the issues involved.

Do not be a "slave" to the particular format used in your analysis, such as writing a page on past strategy, another on the environment, and so on. Rather, when you begin to write, start writing from the *end* of your analysis. Sum up your major recommendations in one or two sentences or a paragraph. Then build a topical outline for the paper around these conclusions. What are the key messages from your analysis that support and build to this recommendation? The commentary should be tightly integrated and logically flow from beginning to end so that the reader is led to agree with you. Remember, you are trying to convince your reader that your proposal should be adopted and that the recommendations will accomplish objectives of interest. Proper presentation of those exhibits will help. (Give the exhibit a clear title, and the source should be clear without having to refer to the text.)

Aside from these general comments, we have some other suggestions for preparing a written report that is likely to be complete, accurate, and convincing, assuming it is grounded on substantive analysis.

### Guides for Written Reports
Here are some suggestions for preparing more effective written presentations:

1. *Provide a cover letter/memo or executive summary.* Consider the needs of the individual for whom the report is intended (e.g., board chairperson, president, etc.), and convey how reading the report and following its recommendations will serve your reader's interests. An executive summary or cover letter allows readers to quickly judge the relevance of the material and their need for the information. The summary/letter/memo should high-

light major recommendations and basic rationale in terms of goal attainment (organizational or personal). It forces the author to reach definite recommendations and select essential supporting arguments that convince the reader of their validity or usefulness. Such a summary also allows the reader to more easily follow the logic of the report to its ultimate convincing conclusions.

2. *Provide a table of contents.* A one- or two-page outline can be a useful introduction. It permits faster reading with clearer comprehension since the reader can follow the logical structure of the report. Such an outline can aid you in making sure you have a logical sequence and flow of concepts in the final report. Section and subsection titles and short descriptive sentences help the reader see how you are integrating your ideas.

3. *Structure the report logically.* The reader should sense a natural flow of ideas from one topic to the next in a logical sequence that leads to support for the final recommendation. Headings, subheadings, and supportive detail assist immensely. Titles of primary sections should be underlined and set off from the double-spaced typed body of the report. Subsections might be numbered or the text indented or single-spaced for contrast. Supporting details are often best placed in the form of charts, graphs, tables, and so on.

   a. Section structure. Each section should deal with primarily one topic. The coverage of the topic should be complete.

   b. Subsection content. This should be limited to one concept and should generally be supported by some type of exhibit.

   c. Paragraph structure. Paragraphs should start with a topic sentence. They should vary in length, depending on the need for explaining the topic. Successive paragraphs should have an obvious sequence (ordered by time, activity, or importance) that leads to natural transitions from point to point and ultimately builds to a logical conclusion.

   d. Sentence structure. Rules of syntax and grammar are important. Your meaning should be clear. Jargon and informal tone may be used depending on the assumed relationship to the reader. That is, you may address the reader in the first person—"We recommend that your firm . . ." is preferable to "It is recommended that the firm . . ." And sentence length should be variable, but usually the shorter the better.

   e. Exhibits. Matrices, graphs, figures, tables, diagrams, charts, and the like can convey information quickly or provide evidence to support conclusions and analysis. The text should refer the reader to well-labeled, numbered, and titled exhibits.

4. *Provide definite recommendations.* Take a position and support it. The reader should clearly understand your proposal and the reasons for it. It is difficult to hedge without appearing obvious. Where possible, refrain from conditional conclusions. However, you may want to indicate under what circumstances another recommendation might be put into action (e.g., recommend contingency strategies if certain assumptions about the future take place).

5. *Provide a conclusion.* Don't leave the end of the report hanging. Summarize your key recommendations and reasons for your proposal, and explain how

its acceptance and implementation will contribute to the interests of the reader to whom the report is written.

6. *Prepare concise, precise reports.* With regard to style, we prefer concise cases written in specifics. Generalities without clear precise meaning are not particularly helpful. For example, do not say that the firm's past performance has been poor and leave it at that. Indicate that specific objectives (rate of sales growth, profits as percent of sales, or whatever) have not been reached or have missed the mark by a certain amount. Don't say "this firm needs more formal planning." If it does, indicate the nature and types of planning the firm needs.

7. *Write several drafts.* Good writers do not turn in their first draft. Ask someone else to read it, or read it out loud to yourself. When you hear what you say and how you say it, you are likely to find rough areas to clean up; or you may find out you have not said what you mean or failed to say something you needed to.

**ORAL PRESENTATIONS AND DISCUSSIONS**

You may have a chance to present your recommendations to a group who will question and challenge you. We hope you do since it is good experience to justify a position. Oral reports and meetings in business organizations require you to be prepared and to be able to "think on your feet." As with written reports, you are trying to communicate information or gain acceptance of proposals.

Obviously, oral presentations are different from written. You should not just read your report. You will have to be even more precise, more specific, and more convincing. In written form, if clearly presented, many of the facts "speak for themselves." In an oral presentation, that can't happen; there is not time for listeners to digest exhibits that a reader might have. You should still use exhibits (handouts or overheads), but they will have to be less detailed and more to the point of summarizing key aspects of your presentation. As with the written presentation, you need to organize well in advance and prepare notes to yourself of the high points.

### Guides for Oral Presentations and Discussion

Some suggestions for making more effective oral presentations are included below:

1. *Define your audience.* You need to gain audience attention and interest; consider the level of sophistication and preparation of your audience as you prepare your report. For example, if you assume the audience will follow a detailed technical explanation of a financial analysis, you would proceed differently than if you assume the audience could not understand such an analysis. By the way, the attention span of most audiences is little more than 20 minutes or so; so plan accordingly.

2. *Prepare a complete outline.* Members of an audience may not understand the sequence or relationship of topics being discussed. The outline should

help give an overview of the presentation so the audience does not get lost. Generally, oral presentations start with "telling the audience what you are going to tell them"; then you tell them the message; you conclude by "telling them what you told them." The outline helps your audience understand where you are going and how various topics are interrelated. In essence, the content of main sections and subheadings should say to the audience, "This is why this material is important, so keep listening; these are the topics we are going to discuss, in this order."

3. *Provide supportive detail.* To provide justification for a position, the audience must sense you know what you are talking about. Exhibits of supportive analysis help, but you cannot provide orally the detail contained in a written presentation. Thus describe supportive detail selectively. The two or three most important analytical conclusions should be presented with a brief description of the data and the assumptions and approach used to make calculations. Don't bore or irritate the audience with long, drawn-out descriptions of endless tables of numbers.

4. *Prepare clear visual aids.* Blackboards, flip charts, scale models, or overheads and slides should be prepared in advance. Wording should be brief; letters and figures should be legible when projected; numbers should be rounded; graphics and charts should be clear. The discussion about an exhibit should discuss the concepts; do not just read the statements, but explain their significance.

5. *Introduce your topic.* Explain the purpose of the presentation, present the agenda or outline, briefly describe the methodology (how you went about your analysis), and briefly summarize the major recommendations.

6. *Present material clearly and confidently.* Stand for the presentation; maintain eye contact with the audience; start without delay; maintain a steady pace; rehearse your presentation with note cards.

7. *Come to a natural conclusion.* Don't just end your presentation with, "Well, that's it." Restate the outline of the report, briefly. And restate the recommendations of the report and major rationale for the position.

8. *Respond to questions positively.* Expect aggressive or hostile attacks and be prepared for them. Don't hurry your response, but carefully consider the intent of the question. Don't ramble in your response; address the question directly without diverting to side issues. Don't try to bluff; if you don't know the answer, admit it. On the other hand, don't avoid direct confrontation—you may be able to answer the question with another question, asking the audience to respond or the questioners to present their point of view.

9. *Listen.* As a presenter, listen carefully to the question before answering. Furthermore, many times you will be asked to listen to someone else's presentation or participate in a group discussion of a case. Once again, full and complete analyses need to be done. But here, instead of a formal presentation, you are being asked to challenge the position of others and defend your own. Do this with facts, figures, assumptions, and logic. Do not attack a position unless you have a counterposition with reasons to back it up. But do not be afraid to express your viewpoint if it differs. On

the other hand, don't waste group time by repeating the same points and reasoning over and over.

10. *Avoid repetition.* In a case presentation or discussion, refrain from reviewing or rehashing the entire case background. Everyone (presumably) is familiar with that. What is of interest is your analysis of the material and your interpretations. Also, clearly distinguish between facts and assumptions.

11. *Go for it.* Take a defensible position and support it. Obviously there is some risk that you will be attacked, but don't be afraid to be criticized. You may as well learn what such criticism is like, and learn to deal with it. Different positions can always be taken based on the same facts. Since there is no one "right" answer to a case, discussion and criticism will help you hone your skills in justifying a position.

# SUMMARY

Some of our suggestions may vary from your style or approach, or the requirement others (your instructor or your boss) may expect of you. Each of us has our own style and format preferences. But the suggestions may help you as you go about the task of trying to effectively analyze and communicate the results of your case study.

The approach we have suggested is really a general approach to problem solving. Some might argue that it is little more than common sense. That is not quite true. Hard analysis as we have suggested here may end up appearing to be "common sense" when it is all done. But the method is a specialized application of the scientific approach. Sometimes that method leads us to conclusions that are contrary to common sense but later appear quite "natural." For example, common sense tells us that the sun revolves around the earth. Our earth-bound perspective and senses tell us the sun "rises" in the east and "sets" in the west. Until science proved otherwise, people believed that the earth was stationary. So it is with an elegant recommendation for strategy. The creative proposal *appears* simple in the end and *seems* to be nothing more than common sense. Yet this "simple common-sense" solution is likely to be the unique approach that no one else ever dreamed of.

# REFERENCES

[1]    McNair, M. P. (ed.): *The Case Method at the Harvard Business School* (New York: McGraw-Hill, 1954).
       Postman, N., and C. Weingarten: *Teaching as a Subversive Activity* (New York: Delacorte Press, 1969).
[2]    Glueck, W. F., and L. R. Jauch: *Strategic Management and Business Policy* (New York: McGraw-Hill, 1984).

[3]    Edge, A. G., and D. R. Coleman: *The Guide to Case Analysis and Reporting* (Honolulu: System Logistics, 1978).

Kepner, C. H., and B. B. Tregoe: *The Rational Manager* (New York: McGraw-Hill, 1976).

Raymond, R.: *Problems in Business Administration* (New York: McGraw-Hill, 1964).

Schnelle, K. E.: *Case Analysis and Business Problem Solving* (New York: McGraw-Hill, 1967).

[4]    Hodgetts, R. M., and M. S. Wortman, Jr.: *Administrative Policy: Text and Cases in Strategic Management* (New York: Wiley, 1980).

Hosmer, L. T.: *Strategic Management* (Englewood Cliffs, N.J.: Prentice-Hall, 1982), esp. Chap. 14.

Ronstadt, R.: *The Art of Case Analysis: A Student Guide* (Needham, Mass.: Lord Publishing, 1977).

# PART TWO

## CASES ON ENTREPRENEURIAL ORGANIZATIONS

# 1

# COLONIAL AMERICAN KITCHENS, INC.

## James E. Weir

It was a beautiful cool autumn day in the New England town of Big Town in October 1979. Sixty-eight-year-old Bill Bradley, the president of Colonial American Kitchens (CAK), and inventor of a newly shaped hot dog bun and hamburger bun, sat in his small one-room office reviewing the events of the past two years. His company was experiencing financial and technical difficulties which no one could have forseen, he concluded. Mr. Bradley remarked: "If we could just solve the automation problem, our troubles would be over. At this time we are only able to produce our Good Buns in a semiautomated manner using a scrapless moline table cutter running at a rate of 100 dozen buns per hour. We must find a way to get that rate up to 1,000 dozen buns per hour before they will become acceptable to the big wholesale producers." At the present time he concluded that he had only two alternatives. He could market the buns more slowly on a local basis, using bread routemen who would sell them to a few key bakeries on a commission basis. At the same time he and his associate, Bob Towers, would continue to search for an automated production machine which would produce the buns at the required 1,000 dozen rate. The second alternative was to sell his bread pan and baking process patents to a large baking company for approximately one million dollars and pay off his debts. That might be the end of his dream to revolutionize the traditional hot dog and

hamburger buns. The Good Buns produced by Colonial American Kitchens are illustrated in Exhibit 1.

Bill Bradley was born in south Big Town in 1911. He entered the baking trade early in his career, working in a number of small and large-size bakeries. Over time, Bill began to develop an idea for a new hot dog bun shaped like an ice cream cone. The goal of his efforts was to try to design a bun shaped in a way that would prevent condiment spillage. He began to experiment with different mixtures of dough and cone-shaped buns in his home kitchen. None proved successful because they were hard to form and would not cook uniformly in the usual flat horizontal baking pans. One day he experimented with a banquet dinner tin by forming a hump in the center of the tin and placing dough around it. He baked it. Much to his surprise it worked. The discovery of the upside-down raised-indentation baking form was now experimentally proven. From 1972 to 1974 he began to experiment with handmade wooden molds and tin foil materials in his basement workshop. He was successful. He showed his invention to his baker friends at work. They continued to encourage him to form a company since he had acquired a patent. One of the bakers went so far as to circulate a list of persons who would like to buy stock in Bill's new invention. Twenty-five thousand dollars in savings were initially pledged to Bill's new invention. In 1975, Bill began to get publicity in local newspaper articles. The pressures continued to build to form a company and seek additional process patents. In 1975, Bill retired from his bakery job and began to pursue his life's dream:

**Exhibit 1**
Colonial
American
Kitchens, Inc.
Hamburger and
Hot Dog Buns

## THE BAKERY FOODS INDUSTRY

he wanted to be known as the man who revo-lutionized the traditional hot dog and ham-burger buns.

The major segments of bakery foods industry are shown in Exhibit 2. Preliminary data from the 1977 census show some remarkable trends in the bakery foods industry. Whereas from 1967 to 1972 there was a 3% drop in the volume of wholesale bakery shipments, this trend has been reversed by a 3% increase over the 1972–77 period. Consumption of white bread has de-clined from a high in 1967 of 8.7 billion pounds of white pan bread to 6.8 billion pounds in 1977. *Bakery* magazine predicts a further decline to 5.7 billion pounds by 1982, with an overall hike in bakery food products of 5.1% in the 1977–82 period.

Bakers have responded to the trend toward nutritional concerns by producing white hearth breads, variety breads, buns, and rolls. The new product market strategy is an attempt on the part of bakers to reposition bakery products as "natural" and "nutritional" as quickly as pos-sible. The figures presented in Exhibit 2 dem-onstrate that this strategy is working well. For example, in 1978 the Metz Baking Company of Sioux City, Iowa, introduced seven variety breads, including two enriched white breads under the label "Nature's Harvest." The Jewell Corporation of Chicago introduced 20 variety breads using the "Natural Harvest" label. The Rhodes Bake-N-Serve Company of Portland, Oregon, has recently emphasized the promotion of dark bread in its Minneapolis market using the advertising theme "Nutrition Never Tasted Better."

In a recent survey conducted by the Inde-pendent Bakers Association, 39% of the health and diet conscious respondents said that they were deciding bakery food purchases on the ba-sis of nutrients; 31% were more concerned in balancing their food budgets; 24% were con-cerned with watching their weight; 7% were not

**EXHIBIT 2**  American Colonial Kitchens, Inc. The Bakery Product Mix Changes, 1979

| | Volume (millions of pounds) | | | % of Wholesale Bakery Foods | | |
|---|---|---|---|---|---|---|
| | 1972 | 1977 | 1982* | 1972 | 1977 | 1982* |
| TOTAL BAKERY FOODS | 22,807 | 23,581 | 24,799 | 100% | 100% | 100% |
| TOTAL BREADS/ROLLS | 14,879 | 14,954 | 15,401 | 65% | 63% | 62% |
| White Bread | 8,657 | 6,793 | 5,717 | 38 | 29 | 23 |
| Variety Breads | 1,543 | 2,020 | 2,600 | 7 | 9 | 10 |
| Hots and Hams | 2,356 | 2,652 | 3,092 | 10 | 11 | 12 |
| Hearth Breads, Rolls | 1,136 | 2,096 | 2,660 | 5 | 9 | 11 |
|    White Hearth Bread | 550 | 1,377 | 1,700 | 2 | 6 | 7 |
|    Hearth Rolls | 586 | 388[1] | 560 | 3 | 2[1] | 2 |
|    English Muffins | NA | 331[1] | 400 | NA | 1[1] | 2 |
| Brown & Serve Rolls | 376 | 264 | 185 | 2 | 1 | 1 |
| Bread Crumbs, etc. | 114 | 222 | 233 | .4 | 1 | 1 |
| Break, nsk | 669 | 687 | NA | NA | NA | NA |
| Rolls, nsk | 28 | 220 | NA | NA | NA | NA |
| TOTAL SWEET GOODS | 2,996 | 3,015 | 2,975 | 13% | 13% | 12% |
| Donuts | 618 | 577 | 550 | 3 | 2 | 1 |
|    Yeast | 229 | 223 | 211 | 1 | 2 | 2 |
|    Cake | 389 | 354 | 340 | 2 | 2 | 1 |
| Coffee Cakes, etc. | 682 | 715 | 750 | 3 | 3 | 3 |
| Soft Cakes | 1,121 | 1,225 | 1,247 | 5 | 5 | 5 |
|    Snack Cakes | NA | 804[1] | 868 | NA | 3 | 4 |
|    Other | NA | 421 | 379 | NA | 2 | 1 |
| Pies | 575 | 498 | 428 | 3 | 2 | 2 |
| COOKIES, CRACKERS | 4,006 | 4,213 | 4,423 | 18% | 18% | 18% |
| FROZEN | 926** | 1,400* | 2,000 | 4% | 6% | 8% |

[1]Listed separately for first time in 1977.
*Source:* 1977 Census of Manufacturers, preliminary data; Bakery Production and Marketing.
*BPM estimate.
**Frozen Food Census.

sure how they made up their minds. Bakers are much more concerned about other trends in the market place besides price increases. One of the most important trends is the reduction in size of the average U.S. family. In 1975 for the first time in history, the average household dropped below three persons. Experts expect this trend to continue at such a rate as to produce an average of 2.4 persons per household by 1990. The response from bakers has been to reduce the size of all types of bakery food products. For example, Pepperidge Farms, Sara Lee, and

Morton's have all introduced small-size cakes and pies for shoppers with small families. A second very important trend is the increase in number of women working outside the home. In 1960, 31% of U.S. women were in the labor force; by 1977 that number had increased to 47% of all U.S. women. The implications of this trend have been quickly grasped by innovative bakers. Women will have less time to cook for their families. They will be attracted to convenience foods, like bakery products, requiring little food preparation. Associated with the working women trend is the tendency for families to eat an increasing number of meals out each week. According to *Advertising Age,* in 1969, 11% of all meals were eaten away from home; in 1979 that figure increased to 17%, currently accounting for 37% of the consumer's food budget. This trend presents bakers with increased opportunities to sell bakery products, since restaurants tend to promote a variety of bakery foods. For example, these foods include toast at breakfast, crackers in soup, bread baskets containing hearth breads, and desserts of all kinds.

The 25% decline in per capita consumption of white pan bread has been offset by a 31% increase in variety breads, and a 13% increase in hot dog and hamburger buns. The boom in hot dog and hamburger buns continues to be propelled by consumers' appetite for fast foods, at home or in restaurants. *Bakery* estimated that 60 new bun plants were opened in 1977 and 1978. Since 1975 there has been a virtual explosion in all types of capital expenditures in the bakery products field; 1975, 280 million; 1976, 340 million; 1977, 360 million; 1978; 391 million; 1979, 259 million estimated expenditures. These expenditures include new plants, new equipment, and the modernization of existing plants.

The consumption of soft buns—the "hots and hams"—has increased to a robust $1.5 billion business at wholesale in 1978. This boom is rooted in the growing preference for eating more meals away from home. Fast food firms, such as McDonald's, demand the largest share of this market. For example, McDonald's buys 270 million dozen hamburger buns per year at an estimated $100 million wholesale value. Soft buns, in addition to variety buns, are the fast-growing segments of the wholesale bakery industry. The food service industry has been growing at a 10% annual rate and is a $40 billion industry. Fast food operations account for $12 to $15 billion of this amount. Fast food chains which emphasize hamburgers contribute $6 billion annually to this total. Market Research Corporation of America uses a consumer panel to keep diaries of their food consumption. Their "revenue census" shows the following results of annual eatings of bread-type products per 1,000 capita, 1972–1978 (Table 1):

Supermarkets are aggressively going after bakery food business. The number of in-store bakeries have increased from 4,000 in 1974 to 10,000 in 1979. Correspondingly, sales have in-

## TABLE 1

| | In Home | Net* Change | Away from Home | Net* Change | Total | Net* Change |
|---|---|---|---|---|---|---|
| Hamburger Buns | 13,259 | +21% | 22,066 | +20 | 35,355 | +47 |
| Hot Dog Buns | 8,777 | +35% | 4,885 | +31 | 13,662 | +32 |

*Adjusted for population increases.

creased from $500 million to $3 billion over this same time period. This trend is firmly established as evidenced by the fact that 75% to 85% of new supermarkets plan to include in-bakery facilities. Gross profits for such facilities run from 65–70%. Many supermarkets are experimenting with combining their bakery shop with a coffee shop or deli. As a result these combined operations tend to chalk up 7–8% of total grocery sales. ITT Continental Baking Corporation advises its customers that bakery department provides an opportunity for one of the biggest dollar producers per square foot in the supermarket. One supermarket in Effingham, Illinois, averages $8.75 in sales per square foot of bakery department space.

## INITIAL MARKET TEST OF GOOD BUNS

Colonial American Kitchens' management believed that the market gains Good Buns might make during 1978, its first full year of test marketing, would be at the expense of conventional bun sales. They believed consumers would be eager to try the new hamburger or hot dog bun even at the cost of a slight price premium of five cents over conventional buns. An agreement was made with a regional bakery, United States Bakery, to test market approximately fifty thousand packages in 20 Big Town supermarket chains in a six-week period, May through June. Various radio and television advertising spots were used to tempt consumers to buy Good Buns. It was hoped that homemakers and teenagers would be eager to purchase the product for its uniqueness and convenience. Both the boat-shaped hot dog bun and the round hamburger bun were market tested during the market test period. It was believed that six weeks would be a long enough period to see if consumers would switch from either conventional buns to the unique bun. The test buns would be baked by the semi-automated molding table technique requiring manual intervention. This was the first time a large number of buns were baked.

The initial market introduction was not successful from two points of view. United States Bakery, using the molding table method, said that it cost too much to produce the fifty thousand buns. They had trouble producing the buns using the semi-automated method. They said it cost too much to place the proofed dough on the special crown-type molds by hand. Even more discouraging, the consumers seemed unwilling to purchase the eight-pack buns for a five-cent premium over conventional buns priced at 79 cents per package. Only two-thirds of the buns were sold in supermarkets. Most unsold buns were returned or found their way into day-old bread stores. Mr. Bradley concluded that consumer buying habits were too difficult to change in four months. A more sustained advertising program was necessary. The firm didn't have the money for that in the summer of 1978. He began to rethink the pricing policy adopted for the new buns. Apparently, Good Buns were priced too high to get consumers to try them for the first time. Even with the coupons offered in daily newspapers, the five-cent premium was still too high. The bun market proved to be much tougher to penetrate than anyone suspected, even the United States Bakery executives. Mr. Bradley was convinced more than ever that the key to success lay in getting the automated production perfected. During 1978 and 1979 he devoted his entire energies to achieving this goal.

## PRODUCTION PROBLEMS

Exhibit 3 illustrates the production process which was designed to produce 100 dozen Good Buns per hour. Ingredients are mixed using the special Colonial American flour selected for Good Buns. It is rolled into sheets of dough, cut into exact dough shapes by a special cookie-cutter roller assembly, placed on crown-type molds in baking pans, put in the proofing boxes to cure,

**Exhibit 3**
Colonial
American
Kitchens, Inc.
Semi-Automated
Production
Process

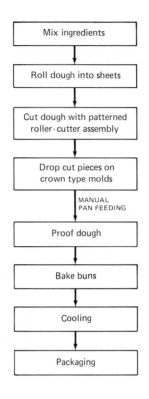

Mix ingredients

↓

Roll dough into sheets

↓

Cut dough with patterned
roller-cutter assembly

↓

Drop cut pieces on
crown type molds

MANUAL
PAN FEEDING

Proof dough

↓

Bake buns

↓

Cooling

↓

Packaging

a bottom pan is used to form the dough on the indentation molds, baked, cooled, wrapped, and packed into cartons.

During the latter part of 1978 the Baking Division of the Johnson Food Service Group, a large supermarket chain, began to work with CAK to perfect a cookie-cutter roller assembly and ingredient mixture which would allow molding table production of the new buns. The initial tests demonstrated the feasibility of this manual production technique which produces correctly cut dough ready to be baked in CAK baking pans. However, Johnson has discontinued experimentation to perfect the ingredient mixture and to conduct test production runs. Various problems developed in finding a proper ingredient mixture, to reduce dough sticking on the roller assembly. They felt that CAK should bear the expenses for these experiments. A favorable test report would be necessary before Johnson will allow CAK to approach their

chain store owners selling Good Buns distributorship rights. After headquarters approval, CAK expects to approach the Johnson chain store owners for the purpose of selling contracts for frozen Good Buns dough to be baked in their stores. When the technology is perfected, Johnson representatives have stated that they will send a product approval letter to their chain stores in exchange for exclusive production rights and other considerations. CAK has yet to negotiate this total package of rights, responsibilities, and duties.

Since 1977 Mr. Bradley has worked to perfect a roller cutter assembly attachment and the associated production process which will be used to cut the round and long dough shapes, roll them, and finally drop them precisely in the center of a special mold producing the exact indentations necessary for the hollow buns. Various production problems were encountered and solved in the development of this process. The roller cutter assembly was not satisfactorily perfected by the first engineering consultant hired. A new design tested by Johnson Food Services seemed to work well even if it continued to cause sticking dough. A Teflon coating is expected to solve this problem. There were continuing problems in establishing a suitable ingredient mixture which would produce a nonsticking dough necessary to yield a precise dough-drop on to the identation mold. However, the most important technological problem facing the firm was to develop a high-speed production system which would automatically drop the dough precisely on to the center of the molds. This critical production problem must be solved before CAK can go into fully automated mass production necessary to serve large numbers of consumers. Mr. Bradley has faith that this problem can be solved. He has arranged to have the Donut Corporation of America (DCA) advise him on the feasibility of using the fully automated baking technique employing one of their modified donut baking units. Their initial report is due to be sent to Mr. Bradley in early 1980.

## THE FIRM'S CHIEF MARKET ASSUMPTION

Mr. Bradley believes that homemakers of middle-class income families and above will wish to purchase Good Buns on a regular once-a-week basis after full acceptance has been obtained. He believes that market research data would assist the firm in establishing a profile of the typical consumer who would tend to purchase both hot dog and round bun styles. It remains to be seen if the shape of the bun itself is satisfactory in order to win new buyers away from the conventional buns. Mr. Bradley believes that some middle-class consumers may be taste-conscious as well as convenience-oriented. He restated the firm's chief market assumption: Good Buns will be accepted by consumers primarily based upon the convenience of having an enclosed and fillable bun structure. However, taste is thought to be of utmost importance. The firm may later engage in product development activities in order to observe the effects of a variety of grains on consumer

product acceptance. These developmental activities were to be postponed until well into the next phase of product development, the regional test market period. Mr. Bradley admitted that the firm has not engaged in extensive market research to test this critical assumption. The most important problem he sees now is to perfect the mass production process to produce 1,000 dozen buns per hour.

## POTENTIAL DISTRIBUTION CHANNELS

Ultimately, Mr. Bradley believes that there are two major multiregional channels of distribution feasible for Good Buns. The first is the regional mass market units, the supermarkets, in which Mr. Bradley expects to capture 80% of the firm's total sales after full consumer acceptance of the product concept. After the introductory phase, full product acceptance will include the use of those supermarkets which have their own baking facilities. Bradley believes it will be easier for him to monitor su-

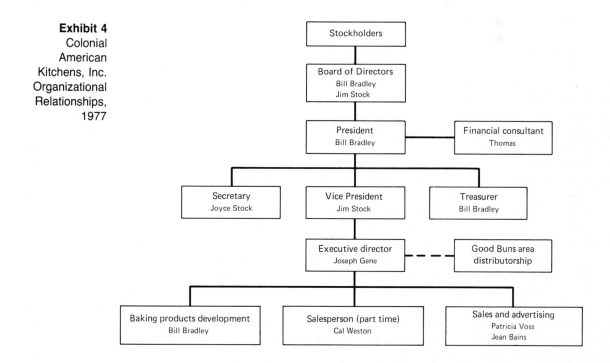

**Exhibit 4**
Colonial American Kitchens, Inc. Organizational Relationships, 1977

permarket bakeries and control any baking production problems which might arise during this period. At a later stage of acceptance the products will be produced for all types of supermarkets and quick shop stores. The other 20% of fillable buns sales will come from fast food restaurants as either an addition to the usual product line, or as a product base around which a potential franchise could be oriented. When asked if these plans have been formalized in writing, Mr. Bradley pointed out that the plans were still in the "talking stage" at this time, since he does not have the staff to conduct formalized planning.

**EXHIBIT 5**   Colonial American Kitchens, Inc.

A-Balance Sheet
October 31, 1977
(Unaudited)
(Cents Omitted)

### ASSETS

| | | |
|---|---:|---:|
| Cash* | | $ 4,046 |
| Deposit—Royalty | | 1,000 |
| Prepaid expenses: | | |
| Insurance | $ 601 | |
| Advertising/sales promotion | 25,909 | 26,510 |
| Research/development (Unamortized portion) | | |
| Consulting fees | 103,782 | |
| Travel | 6,215 | |
| Product development | 18,510 | 128,507 |
| Equipment (Net book value) | | 3,300 |
| | | $163,363 |

### SHAREHOLDERS' EQUITY

| | | |
|---|---:|---:|
| Capital stock: | | |
| Common stock | | |
| "A" $1 par—400,000 authorized | | |
| issued and outstanding—156,500 | $156,500 | |
| "B" 5¢ par—600,000 authorized | | |
| issued and outstanding—590,000 | 26,375 | |
| | 182,875 | |
| Paid in surplus | 37,500 | $220,375 |
| Deficit | | |
| Balance—January 1, 1977 | ( 8,874) | |
| Current operations** | (48,138) | (57,012) |
| | | $163,363 |

*$27,500 additional cash due to distributorship contributions and $18,000 increase in paid-in surplus for a total cash balance of $49,546.
**November expenses $6,750.

## THE FIRM'S MANAGEMENT

At the height of CAK's growth the firm consisted of the personnel shown in Exhibit 4. Joyce and Jim Stork were silent partners who played no active part in the firm's daily management. Very early in this venture Bill Bradley realized his knowledge of marketing was limited. In 1976 he decided he needed someone to help him put his product on the market. A few of his friends suggested he should be attempting to franchise the buns. One day he went to the library and found the name of a local listee in a franchising periodical. That person was Joseph Gene, who agreed to become Bill's executive director. Mr. Gene was an impulsive, fast-moving, self-educated salesman who had little formal education and a habit of keeping his cryptic sales expense records on his checkbook stub. He had been successful in forming and selling for a profit a number of franchises. He had no formal or practical knowledge of marketing, management, or finance. He immediately began to aid Mr. Bradley in setting up and operating the Colonial American Kitchens Corporation. Next, he formulated a plan for licensing bun production with the right of establishing regional distributorships by states and aggressively began selling activities across the country. Within the next two years more than four licensing contracts had been signed. Cash began to flow into the company. In October 1977 a shareholder and investors' meeting was held. The officers of the firm distributed the financial information contained in Exhibits 5 and 6. More than fifty people attended the informal meeting. A dinner was held later that night at a local restaurant. The firm appeared to be doing well since Mr. Gene appeared on the scene. His salesmanship seemed to more than adequately make up for any lack of formal knowledge or experience concerning marketing research, finance, planning, or record-keeping.

The technical problems persisted, however. One avenue after another was pursued. Consultants were hired to help find a way to produce dough on a fully automated production scale using Pan-O-Matic attachments. Other

**EXHIBIT 6** B-Statement of Operations for the Period January 1, 1977, to October 31, 1977
(Unaudited)
(Cents Omitted)

| | | $— |
|---|---:|---:|
| INCOME | | |
| OPERATING EXPENSES | | |
| Selling costs | $ 1,663 | |
| Rent/Storage | 2,320 | |
| Telephone | 3,662 | |
| Office supplies | 734 | |
| Donation | 314 | |
| Equipment depreciation | 825 | |
| Sales promotion/advertising | 1,888 | |
| Travel | 2,870 | |
| Insurance | 500 | |
| Amortization—Reserve and development | 33,362 | 48,138 |
| NET (LOSS) | | ($48,138) |

**EXHIBIT 7**    Colonial American Kitchens, Inc. October 31, 1979

Dear Stockholders:

I would like to provide you with a summary of what we have been doing to turn the company's situation around. Enclosed is a financial summary for the year 1978. As you can see, we are currently in a loss situation. Let me advise you of the steps the company has been taking to turn our venture around.

The biggest technological problem is to achieve automated bun production quantities of 1,000 dozen per hour. At the present time our semi-automatic technology will produce 100 dozen per hour and it requires manual intervention. We are investigating two pieces of equipment which we believe can be satisfactorily modified to produce the desired production rate while maintaining the desired product quality. One is produced by the Donut Corporation of America, a division of DCA Food Industries, Incorporated, with headquarters in New York City. We have visited one of their production facilities located here in Big Town. Their production processes have certain apparent advantages which we are now evaluating. A second system which may be suitable for modification to produce our buns is manufactured by Autoprod, Incorporated, of Hyde Park, New York. Feasibility studies are now under way. We will keep you advised of our progress as we continue to evaluate these and other systems.

United States Bakery has tested our existing semi-automated processes and have not achieved desirable results. Basically, we concluded that the consumers wanted the product, as evidenced by the June 1978 market introductory program. During a three-month period we sold 46,000 packages of Good Buns. However, American Bakeries could not foresee the possibility of producing the buns at the 1,000 dozen bun rate with their existing technology.

Our company has loaned pans to twelve companies or individuals for further baking tests. For example, Inglish Rolls Bakers is now producing our Good Buns for the Coca Cola vendor carts.

Our creditors are trying to help us by being patient in collecting what we owe. We are making every effort to meet our obligations to them. I have worked with no salary since October 1978. I will continue to work without salary because I believe that consumers want our buns and, most importantly, I want to strive to protect your intersts. I have loaned the company funds to meet our current operating expenses.

What is your company doing to try to find a solution to these problems? We are moving very vigorously to solve our major technological problem. We expect to have some results on this soon. Second, we have moved to establish independent sales and delivery merchandisers using our semi-automated production techniques in local bakeries. We feel we can ultimately be successful using this slower marketing approach. However, our major priority continues to be to seek an automated process.

I want to make a personal request of you. I need your continued patience while implementing the plans I have sketched above. Time is needed to work out these problems. I feel we are near to discovering how to achieve the desired production rate. Once that is accomplished, we will have the means to make our futures secure.

My pledge to you is to work as hard as I can to solve the problems I have outlined. I will keep you advised on the moves that are being made. If you have any questions, please call me.

Sincerely,

Bill Bradley, President

**EXHIBIT 8**   Colonial American Kitchens, Inc

| BALANCE SHEETS | Beginning of Taxable Year 1977 | | End of Taxable Year 1978 | |
|---|---|---|---|---|
| ASSETS | (A) Amount | (B) Total | (C) Amount | (D) Total |
| 1.   Cash | | 7625- | | 288- |
| 2.   Buildings and other fixed depreciable assets | 10254- | | 61364 | |
|    (a) Less accumulated depreciation | 1185- | 9067- | 4889- | 56475- |
| 3.   Total assets | | 16694- | | 56703- |
| **LIABILITIES AND STOCKHOLDERS' EQUITY** | | | | |
| 4.   Accounts payable | | | | 144609- |
| 5.   Capital stock: | | | | |
|    (a) Preferred stock | | | | |
|    (b) Common stock | 228965- | 228965- | 412985- | 412985- |
| 6.   Paid-in or capital surplus | | 111981- | | 209021- |
| 7.   Retained earnings— Unappropriated | | (324252-) | | (709912 ) |
| 8.   Total liabilities and stockholders' equity | 16694- | | | 56703- |
| **ANALYSIS OF UNAPPROPRIATED EARNING PER BOOKS** | | | | |
| 9.   Balance at beginning of year | (324252-) | | | |
| 10.  Net income per books | (385660-) | | | |
| 11.  Total | (709912-) | | Balance at end of year (709912-) | |

technical problems were under consideration. Roller assemblies, one for the long and round buns, had to be designed so that the dough would not stick to the rollers. The designs for two different styles of baking pans had yet to be firmly established for high-speed production processes. The ingredient mixture required coordinated development as well. The firm operated on the assumption that these problems would eventually be solved. During this period no budgets of any type were formulated or used control expenditures. In November 1977, Richard Thomas, one of the firm's investors began advising Mr. Bradley on financial matters.

## THE CURRENT SITUATION

With the test market failure in the summer of 1978, events began to run against the firm. The sale of licensing agreements was halted for legal reasons. Cash flow problems arose immediately. The staff was advised that the firm had no available funds. Mr. Bradley sought legal assistance but continued to work on the technical problems of meeting the 1,000 dozen per hour production requirement. In October 1979 the letter illustrated in Exhibit 7 and financial statement of Exhibit 8 were prepared for mailing to each stockholder.

# 2

# THE MINI-STORAGE BUSINESS

## Marjorie G. Prentice

*Georgia College*

Dick and Judy LaVergne early in 1979 acknowledged that they have long wanted to expand their opportunities beyond full-time employment to include part-time management of a small business venture. The thrill of private entrepreneurship and the opportunity to make a substantial return on investment are key elements in their long term goals.

After much preliminary investigation into a variety of possible business ventures such as racquetball courts, fast food franchises, and self-serve car washes, Dick and Judy have narrowed their consideration to an investment in the rapidly growing mini-storage industry. The decision to consider investing in this industry was made in response to their desire to find a business which (1) did not require a high level of technical expertise, (2) would have a high year-round customer demand, and (3) would be relatively easy to enter and operate.

At last they have reached the point of decision. Should they build in a mini-storage business? If they decide to build a mini-storage facility, where should it be located and what should be the mix of unit sizes? Can they handle the operations of a mini-storage business on a part-

time basis? All of these questions, and many more, pass through Dick's mind as he and his wife review the information they have gathered over the past year.

## GENERAL BACKGROUND

The LaVergnes live in Sacramento, the capital of California. Sacramento is surrounded by a number of "bedroom" communities, some relatively stable, and others growing rapidly. As the center of the state, county, and city government, Sacramento has a large percentage of its labor force in service occupations. Within the extended metropolitan area there are two major Air Force Bases, Mather and McClellan, each with a relatively transient military population.

Beyond the immediate metropolitan area, there are still large expanses of undeveloped land which are of increasing interest to major industries wishing to expand or relocate in California. Such industries need space, not only for plant, facilities, but for a major influx of production workers if a local labor supply is not already available. Hewlett Packard is one such firm considering expansion in the Roseville area northeast of Sacramento. Should Hewlett Packard exercise their land option, it is estimated that they will need 4,500 employees by 1985.

The mild climate of the Sacramento area is particularly appealing to the American public in the face of increasing energy costs for home heating. This asset to home owners, coupled with the property tax relief resulting from California's 1979 "Proposition 13," is encouraging increased migration to the area. Outdoor recreational opportunities are an important feature of California living. Within two hours, Sacramentoans can have their R. V.s in the campgrounds of the Sierra Nevada mountains. Within less than one hour, most Sacramento sailers, boaters, and water skiers can be at the highly developed facilities of Lake Folsom, just northeast of the city. These combined factors make Sacramento a very desirable place for a family to locate.

## INDUSTRY BACKGROUND

The mini-storage business, often referred to as private storage rooms, or by such terms as "rent-a-space" facilities or "U-lock-it" units, provides private and secure individual storage units for such varied items as household goods, business records, retail-wholesale inventory, sports and out-of-season equipment, and recreational vehicles. Most present firms operating mini-sized self storage units tend to use a similar design known as modified warehouse units. Typically, each location has eight or more cinderblock buildings subdivided by wooden partitions into 350 to 800 units. These individual storage units vary in size from 4' × 6' closets to 10' × 30' indoor rooms. Many facilities also include outdoor parking areas for cars, campers, and boats. Each facility is surrounded by a chain link fence and has high-intensity lighting and other extensive security precautions.

### Customer Consideration

Customer access to most individual units is from the outside of the building through individually keyed steel roll-up doors; however, some of the smaller units have only interior hallway access. The facilities are usually open daily, with entrance controlled through a key card or with a sign-in-out sheet in the manager's office. Units are rented on a monthly basis, with charges in relation to both unit square footage and demand.

*Demand* As both residential and business construction costs have risen, architects and owners have tended to decrease the internal storage space of living and working accommodations. With storage space at a premium, mini-storage units have become increasingly popular. In addition to business storage needs for records and inventories, and apartment and residential dweller's needs for household and recreational storage, a currently expanding demand for storage exists for mobile home owners. The early 1980's recession appears not to have hurt the mobile home industry in California as it has conventional home construction.

According to managers of several operating mini-storage facilities, the demand for mini-storage units has resulted in a 90–92% average occupancy rate for all sizes of units during the late 1970's. They say the greatest demand is for the smaller units of 5' × 10' and under. Presently, mini-storage firms have larger numbers of these smaller units available, but there are still waiting lists for these small-sized units. This is not to imply that the larger units are not needed, but only that the 10' × 10' and larger sizes are less popular than the smaller units.

*Competition* At the present time there is such a high demand for self-storage units from conventional and mobile home owners, small business managers, and sports enthusiasts that competition does not seem to present a problem. Two examples support this view. Three mini-storage facilities operate adjacent to the Folsom Boulevard and Sunrise Boulevard freeway interchange in Rancho Cordova, just east of Sacramento. The two older original facilities have 95–100% occupancy and the newest firm is reported to be filling quickly without causing any decrease in demand for the others. The second example is a storage facility currently being constructed in Roseville adjacent to an older established firm. The manager of the operating firm expects no decrease in her demand, and predicts sufficient demand for the new company to operate profitably. This apparently favorable climate may continue for the immediate future.

However, in the long run, conditions may vary, depending upon the location selected.

## Management Consideration

There are several major advantages for the owner of a mini-storage business. Three of these are (1) low maintenance, requiring little in addition to trash removal; (2) relative low original land costs, as facilities can be built close to freeways, on odd-shaped parcels of commercially zoned land, or other less desirable locations; and (3) below average construction costs, due to limited requirements for plumbing, interior finishing work, and other items requiring high-cost skilled labor.

Two of the primary problems in the mini-storage business are day-by-day management and security. Most owners hire one or more resident managers to maintain a residence at the mini-storage facility on a 24-hour basis. However the storage facilities are usually open to the customer only from 7:00A.M. to 11:00P.M., seven days a week. The restrictive life-style coupled with the heavy paperwork flow required by high-turnover customers, especially those with seasonal or inventory-related needs, are undoubtedly reasons for the high turnover rate of resident managers within the industry.

An effective security system requires a perimeter chain link fence and high-intensity lighting. Of the dozens of variations of security systems available, there seem to be three main types which are appropriate for this industry:

1 An alarm, deactivated by a key, installed in each door of each unit. The security key is issued to the customer at the time the unit key is issued.
2 Zoning surveillance and electronic monitoring, which relies on a centralized system. Each door is monitored to signal the central office whenever that door is entered.

**EXHIBIT 1**   Estimated "Start Up" Costs

1979 cost estimates for a "typical" self-storage facility in the Sacramento area:

| | |
|---|---:|
| Land acquisition | 75,000 |
| Architect fees | 16,400 |
| Construction costs for storage units | 660,000[1] |
| Additional construction costs for live-in management | 20,000 |
| Asphalting costs | 70,000 |
| Fencing costs | 6,300 |
| Security system | 20,000 |
| Legal fees (incorporation) | 2,300 |
| Working capital (1st year) | 30,000 |
| | $900,000 |

The greater number of smaller units, the higher will be the total costs. For example, within a space of 10' × 20' you can build one storage unit at a cost of $2200, four 5' × 10' units at a cost of $2,400 or six 5' × 6' units at a cost of $2520. (Based on construction costs as follows:)

10 × 30 units at $11.50/sq. ft.
10 × 20 units at $11.00/sq. ft.
10 × 10 units at $10.75/sq. ft.
 5 × 10 units at $12.00/sq. ft.
 5 ×  6 units at $14.00/sq. ft.

3 Guard dogs, usually German Shepherds or Doberman Pinschers, can be either owned or rented. The dogs are usually used in pairs, and are in addition to the resident manager. The rental, per dog, per month, in the Sacramento area is $195, including transportation and required care. Dogs are used by most of the companies in the Sacramento area, often in combination with one or more other security devices.

## FINANCIAL INFORMATION

From banks, credit unions, building contractors, real estate firms, and government agencies, the LaVergnes have carefully gathered a great deal of financial information. They feel they now are in a position to make a decision on entering the mini-storage business. They have learned that a typical facility would need about 2.5 acres of land (a lot approximately 210 × 520 feet). The entire area must be enclosed by a high-quality chain link fence and the entire surface within the fence must be asphalt covered, with the exception of the actual building footage.

Investigation has disclosed that, in the industry, the IRS expects the building to depreciate over a 30-year period, and fencing and asphalt to be depreciated over a 20-year period; accelerated depreciation is not permitted. A 65 percent occupancy rate is common for the first year, with a "conservative" 90 percent occupancy rate each year thereafter. Expenses and

---

**EXHIBIT 2**    Estimated Annual Operating Costs

Expenses for a "typical" medium-sized facility (575 units), include, but are not limited to, the following annual costs:

| | |
|---|---:|
| Insurance | $ 4,000 |
| Security[1] | $ 5,000 |
| Payroll—wages and fringes | $ 12,000 |
| Advertising expenses | $ 5,000 |
| Office supplies | $ 500 |
| Property taxes | $ 14,000 |
| Repairs and maintenance | $ 2,000 |
| Depreciation[2] | $ 26,500 |
| Utilities | $ 4,000 |
| Loan repayment[3] | $102,800 |
| Legal fees | $ 1,000 |
| Accounting and auditing fees | $ 1,000 |
| Corporate tax rate[4] | + |

[1]Rental of two guard dogs for periods when the facility is not open.
[2]Actual Depreciation based on initial construction costs.
[3]Actual Loan payment based on size of loan; payment includes principal and interest (14%, 30-year loan on $720,000).
[4]Corporate form of structure is deemed advisable to minimize liability.
Corporate tax rates:

| | |
|---|---|
| 0–$ 25,000 | 17% |
| $25,001–$ 50,000 | 20% |
| $50,001–$ 75,000 | 30% |
| $75,001–$100,000 | 40% |
| over $100,000 | 46% |

revenues should increase at the same rate over the foreseeable future.

Architectural considerations will influence the initial investment cost. For example, commercial building codes, maximizing fire and theft prevention while minimizing construction costs, and special code requirements for a live-in management unit must be considered in estimated cost projections.

Estimates of construction costs and actual operating expenses are shown in Exhibits 1 and 2, respectively. Through the liquidation of several prior investments, Dick presently has the ability to raise $180,000 for the required 20 percent down payment on the $900,000 he will need for this new business. Thirty-year loans are available at 14% interest through commercial outlets which will cover the remaining 80 percent needed for initial construction costs and first-year working capital requirements.

## SITE LOCATION INFORMATION

There seems to be a great deal of pricing consistency within the industry, at least in the Sacramento area. A comparison of unit sizes, numbers of units, and rental fees for three established firms is shown in Exhibit 4.

In order to maintain a high-unit occupancy rate, location is a primary consideration. Land availability, land costs, zoning laws, freeway/thoroughfare access, high-density population, and ease of travel from LaVergne's home are all important. His preferences for location are in the area north-northeast of the metropolitan area, in either Sacramento or Placer counties.

## EXHIBIT 3

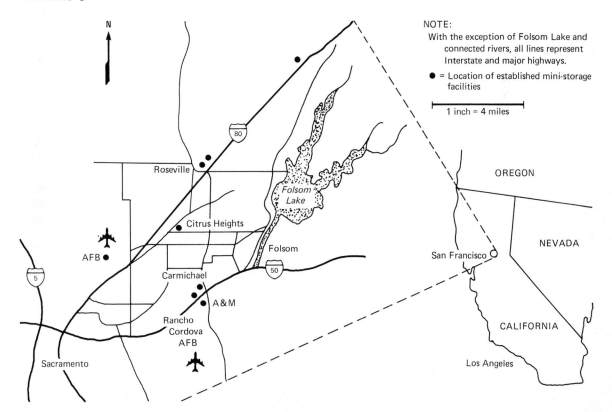

NOTE:
With the exception of Folsom Lake and connected rivers, all lines represent Interstate and major highways.

● = Location of established mini-storage facilities

1 inch = 4 miles

From this general area, he chose four sites to investigate; Folsom, Citrus Heights, Carmichael, and Roseville. (See Exhibit 3 for a map of the area and Exhibit 5 for population figures of the area.)

*Folsom* would be a high-demand area because of the excellent recreational developments around Folsom Lake and the resulting need for storage of boats and other recreational equipment. Folsom has many parcels of available commercial land for building. The drawbacks, however, are in the strict zoning limitations to protect the natural environment, and the absence of good freeway access to the available land within the city.

*Citrus Heights* also seems to be a good site due to the fact that many new homes are being built in the area, most of which are smaller than in the past decade, and therefore, with limited built-in storage. There is also a present lack of competition from other storage firms in this area. The primary problems for a Citrus Heights lo-

cation are (1) the limited availability of any easily accessible commercial land of sufficient size to handle this proposed development and (2) strict zoning regulations which would limit site and design options.

*Carmichael* is the nearest of the four cities to downtown Sacramento. It already has a high, relatively stable population. Many parts of the city are comprised primarily of older homes with an average larger amount of internal storage as well as basements and garages. Commercial land availability is limited due to the high residential population already established in the community.

*Roseville's* Chamber of Commerce reports that this city has a good growth potential, a wide variety of available commercial land near freeway access, and more new home construction under way than in the other three areas. In addition, a major firm has a land option for a proposed plant which will employ 4,500 persons within the next few years.

**EXHIBIT 4**    Pricing and Size of Typical Competition in Sacramento Area

| Unit Size | A & M Storage | | Mini-Warehouse | | Capital City Storage | |
|---|---|---|---|---|---|---|
| | No. of Units | Monthly Rental per unit | No. of Units | Rental per unit | No. of Units | Rental per unit |
| 4 × 6 | — | — | 67 | $15 | — | — |
| 5 × 6 | 15 | $15 | — | — | 12 | $15 |
| 5 × 10 (attic) | — | — | 11 | $21 | — | — |
| 5 × 10 (ground) | 290 | $22 | 299 | $21 | 150 | $21 |
| 6 × 10 | 76 | $23 | — | — | — | — |
| 10 × 10 | 89 | $36 | 69 | $34 | 60 | $34 |
| 10 × 12 | — | — | 28 | $38 | — | — |
| 10 × 15 | — | — | 42 | $42 | 50 | $42 |
| 10 × 20 | 80 | $54 | 85 | $52 | 55 | $52 |
| 10 × 25 | — | — | 34 | $54 | 30 | $64 |
| 10 × 30 | 36 | $70 | 47 | $74 | 25 | $74 |
| Parking Space for R.V. Units | | | | | | |
| 10 × 20 | 36 | $15 | 60 | $13 | — | — |
| 10 × 28 | — | — | 38 | $18 | — | — |
| 10 × 30 | 24 | $17 | — | — | — | — |

**EXHIBIT 5**   Population Figures for Target Area Locations

|      | Folsom | Citrus Heights | Carmichael | Roseville |
|------|--------|----------------|------------|-----------|
| 1970 | 6,618  | 45,324         | 37,608     | 18,139    |
| 1971 | 6,312  | 45,328         | 38,391     | 18,600    |
| 1972 | 7,102  | 47,052         | 39,914     | 19,100    |
| 1973 | 7,073  | 51,459         | 40,199     | 19,800    |
| 1974 | 7,037  | 54,459         | 40,773     | 20,500    |
| 1975 | 6,858  | 55,520         | 41,489     | 20,850    |
| 1976 | 7,837  | 57,301         | 41,780     | 20,500    |
| 1977 | 7,900  | 62,492         | 42,125     | 21,050    |

Recognition of site location is an important element in the mini-storage industry. Presently, the primary sources of advertising are (1) multi-column space in the *Yellow Pages* of the telephone directory and (2) on-building signs painted or mounted on the freeway-adjacent storage units. As other companies enter the market, there will undoubtedly be the need for other forms of advertising. A location away from major freeway visibility would make additional promotional strategies necessary.

## OPERATIONAL INFORMATION

Once a facility is in operation, maintenance is usually at a minimum, with trash control often being the most complicated task. If customer turnover is high, office records can be a problem.

Operating considerations are directly related to the number of buildings containing the individual units to be managed. In addition, excessive turnover rates for live-in managers pose a critical problem which must be solved if the operation is to function effectively and profitably.

Based on a series of interviews with present managers, the LaVergnes have decided that if they build, the facility should have no more than five sizes of units: 5 × 6, 5 × 10, 10 × 10, 10 × 20, and 10 × 30. The expected annual occupancy rate, after the first year is 95% for the two smaller-size units, 90% for the 10 × 10 size, and 85% for the two larger-size units. Dick wants to spend no more than $660,000 for construction costs and expects a payback of his total investment within seven years.

# 3 THE PHELPS QUALITY DRUG COMPANY[1]

## Lawrence R. Jauch

*Southern Illinois University–Carbondale*

## BACKGROUND OF FIRM

The Phelps Quality Drug Company operates three drugstores in Springfield, IL. Springfield is a central Illinois city having a population of about 95,000. The stores are owned by a partnership of two brothers (Paul and Jerry Phelps), Mark Horne, and Tom Buske. All partners except Mr. Buske are registered pharmacists.

The company is an old and well-established firm, having started as the Quality Drug Company in 1940. Paul Phelps began working for the company's store as an assistant pharmacist in 1949. Later, Jerry Phelps attended pharmacy school and joined the firm in 1952.

In the mid-1950's, the store experienced difficulties because of declining profits. The two Phelps brothers were convinced that they could improve the store's performance and made an offer to buy the store and go into business for themselves. The owners said that they would sell the business, but the price they set was too high for the brothers to afford. They therefore convinced two other men, Dave Snyder and Dan Smith, to join the partnership. The sale was completed in late 1958 and the Quality Drug Company became known as the Phelps Quality Drug Company. Mr. Snyder died in 1967 and his share of the business was sold to Mr. Buske.

[1]This is a disguised case. That is, the facts in it are based on a real organization. But the names of the persons involved, the location, and the quantitative data have been changed because the organization requested it. It serves no useful purpose to try to determine which organization is the "real" organization. Based on a case originally prepared by William F. Glueck.

Mr. Rhodes retired in 1979 and sold his share to Mr. Horne, another registered pharmacist. All partners share equally in the ownership of the firm.

As a result of the increase in life expectancies of many Americans during the fifties and sixties the demand for drugs and pharmacies grew rapidly during the sixties. In response to this growth, Phelps bought out another drug company in 1972 and took over its store, which was only two years old at the time. An opportunity for further expansion occurred in 1975 when the owner of a small drugstore in the southern part of the town died. The Phelps Company acquired this store. Currently Phelps owns three stores. No further expansion has been considered. The existing stores have been remodeled from time to time; the number one downtown store and the number three "southside" store are rather old-fashioned in design and appearance. All three facilities are leased.

In 1978 the Phelps Quality Drug Company entered into an agreement with Rexall, the national drug manufacturer, to sell Rexall products. The agreement gives Phelps exclusive rights to sell Rexall products within a 25-mile area. In exchange for this privilege, the partners were obligated to buy a small amount of Rexall stock.

For a while after the Rexall agreement, business grew and profits rose. The high point was reached in 1981, when sales exceeded $4 million. Since that time, however, sales have dropped somewhat. In a conversation with the case writer, Paul Phelps explained why he thought the business was not growing as it should: "It's those new 'supers'—the large discount stores—that have cut into our business," he stated. "Why, I don't even consider them as drugstores. They sell everything—even groceries. Drugs are only a sideline. I can't really understand why people would want to fill their prescriptions at these stores; service is so impersonal. But they're growing and we're not. That's a fact that we have to face."

To illustrate the trend in sales, Mr. Phelps showed the case writer some of his firm's fi-

nancial statements for the past few years (see Tables 1, 2, and 3).

## ORGANIZATION AND MANAGEMENT

Paul Phelps, Jerry Phelps, and Mark Horne work as pharmacist-managers at the three stores. Jerry Phelps is manager of store 1, the original store; his brother has the responsibil-

**TABLE 1** Phelps Quality Drug Company Comparative Balance Sheets for the Years Ended June 30

|  | 1983 | 1984 | 1985 |
|---|---|---|---|
| **Assets** | | | |
| Current assets | | | |
| Cash on hand | $502,168 | $414,040 | $471,735 |
| Accounts receivable | 195,781 | 141,965 | 147,560 |
| Prepaid expenses | 8,751 | 6,735 | 8,490 |
| Inventory | 487,416 | 548,340 | 530,720 |
| Total current assets | $1,191,116 | $1,111,080 | $1,158,505 |
| Fixed assets | | | |
| Furniture, equipment | $348,203 | $406,135 | $413,765 |
| Leasehold improvements | 2,510 | 6,620 | 9,195 |
|  | $350,713 | $412,755 | $422,960 |
| Less accumulated depreciation | 303,039 | 319,665 | 333,285 |
| Net fixed assets | $47,674 | $93,090 | $89,675 |
| Other Assets: stock | 6,500 | 6,500 | 5,250 |
| Total Assets | $1,248,290 | $1,210,670 | $1,253,430 |
| **Liabilities and net worth** | | | |
| Current liabilities | | | |
| Accounts payable | $177,183 | $159,180 | $159,100 |
| Notes payable | 2,500 | 2,500 | 2,500 |
| Accrued taxes | 35,264 | 27,025 | 28,710 |
| Other | 17,416 | 5,955 | 6,535 |
| Total current liabilities | $232,363 | $194,660 | $196,845 |
| Partner's accounts | | | |
| Balance at June 1 | $953,823 | $1,015,928 | $1,016,010 |
| Add net profit for period | 192,596 | 132,582 | 178,670 |
| Deduct withdrawals | 130,491 | 132,500 | 138,095 |
| Balance at end of period | $1,015,928 | $1,016,010 | $1,056,585 |
| Total liabilities and net worth | $1,248,291 | $1,210,670 | $1,253,430 |

**TABLE 2**　Phelps Quality Drug Company Comparative Income Statements for the Years Ended June 30

|  | 1983 | 1984 | 1985 |
|---|---|---|---|
| Net sales | $3,641,553 | $3,323,620 | $3,498,905 |
| Cost of sales | 2,125,273 | 2,068,615 | 2,085,370 |
| Gross profit | $1,516,280 | 1,255,005 | 1,413,535 |
| Operating expenses | 1,075,831 | 1,004,510 | 1,066,055 |
| Operating income | $ 440,449 | $ 250,495 | $ 347,480 |
| Federal taxes | 247,853 | 117,913 | 168,935 |
| Net income | $ 192,596 | $ 132,582 | $ 178,545 |

ity for store 3; and Mr. Horne manages store 2. Mr. Buske is a local factory owner. As a "not-so-silent" financial partner, he frequently offers his advice and helps make major policy or planning decisions.

Paul Phelps explained that each store is managed almost independently of the others. For example, each store orders its own stock and sets its own prices. Nearly all major decisions, including decisions to buy major equipment or redecorate the stores, are made by each store manager. Decisions involving a large cap-

**TABLE 3**　Phelps Quality Drug Company Income Statements by Stores for the Years Ended June 30

|  | Store 1 | Store 2 | Store 3 |
|---|---|---|---|
| Revenue |  |  |  |
| Net sales | $808,240 | $2,007,920 | $682,745 |
| Cost of sales | 461,835 | 1,216,375 | 407,160 |
| Gross profit on sales | $346,405 | $791,545 | $275,585 |
| Operating expenses |  |  |  |
| Salaries | 168,620 | 336,025 | 184,435 |
| Payroll taxes | 6,160 | 10,290 | 4,205 |
| Advertising | 5,865 | 12,463 | 4,870 |
| Trading stamps | 10,500 | 32,000 | 9,500 |
| Depreciation | 7,745 | 11,120 | 3,425 |
| Utilities | 9,275 | 20,240 | 8,645 |
| Repairs | 3,460 | 5,020 | 1,260 |
| Rent | 3,400 | 44,150 | 20,700 |
| Store supplies | 6,690 | 15,845 | 4,855 |
| Bookkeeping services | 7,965 | 11,707 | 8,605 |
| Taxes and insurance | 12,790 | 15,835 | 7,425 |
| Office expenses | 3,515 | 7,985 | 3,275 |
| Other and miscellaneous | 8,400 | 18,360 | 9,430 |
| Total operating expenses | $245,385 | $541,040 | $270,630 |
| Operating income | $ 92,020 | $250,505 | $ 4,955 |

ital outlay, such as store expansion, require the joint approval of all three working partners. Also, the stores do join together in some of their promotional efforts. Bookkeeping procedures are standardized, with one accounting firm serving all three stores. "Really, just about the only reason we even have a formal partnership is so we can trade under the Phelps name," Mr. Phelps said. "People know and trust that name."

In 1982, Mr. Buske and Mr. Horne presented a plan to incorporate the business. Convinced of the possibility of tax savings and of the advantages of limited liability, Mr. Buske tried to persuade his partners to follow the plan. The two Phelps brothers strongly opposed such a move, saying that they believed that the four men would lose all control of the company if outside shareholders were brought in. The matter was dropped from any further discussion. Jerry Phelps told the case writer that "our present arrangement keeps us out of each other's hair. I'm not sure that we could maintain our present excellent relationship if we incorporated."

## THE MARKET AND COMPETITION

The three stores serve separate market areas within the city. Store 1, located in the downtown area, caters mainly to persons working downtown and to downtown shoppers from other parts of town. Business in the downtown area has tapered off in recent years, partly because of a parking problem and also because of the growth of shopping centers in the outlying districts. Store 2 is in a shopping center at the fringe of a well-to-do residential area. The largest of the three stores, it accounts for 60 percent of total sales. The third store is located directly across the street from one of the city's hospitals. It is in a predominantly low-income area.

All three stores offer basically the same types of products and services. The three main categories are prescription service, fountain service, and sundries. Rexall products are promoted the most vigorously. This is because, ac-

cording to one of the partners, they have a lower unit cost and higher markup. Other pharmaceutical products are used to supplement the Rexall line, however. Drinks, dairy products, sandwiches, and other snack items are served at the fountain bars. Sundry products include tobacco products, magazines, some cosmetic products, small household items, etc.

Phelps' competition comes from both the small neighborhood-type pharmacies and the large "super" drug discount stores. The services and products offered by the neighborhood pharmacies are usually limited to prescriptions and drugs; few sundry items are carried. There is little price competition from the smaller stores, since they buy in smaller volume and have high overhead costs.

Phelps' competition mainly comes from four large stores. Two such stores, owned by the Baldwin Drug Company, are located very close to the Phelps stores 1 and 2. Both Baldwin stores, which are operated as franchises for a major retail drug firm, are larger than the Phelps stores. Recently, the Baldwin stores broadened their product lines to include such things as small appliances, school supplies, toys, etc., and began offering discount prices on some proprietary drugs and other items.

Within the past three years, two large discount drugstores have been built at suburban shopping center locations in Springfield. One is located three blocks from Phelps store 2. These stores carry a full line of merchandise, including appliances, clothing, a full assortment of household goods, hardware items, and other goods. They do a high-volume discount drug business, with drugs and cosmetics sold at substantially lower prices than those of Phelps' or most of the other drug firms.

The two new discount stores are typical of the giant discount stores. These stores carry a broad line of merchandise, including many high-margin items (electric hair dryers, etc.), as well as household goods, paper goods, soft goods, toys, photographic equipment, small appliances, records, hardware, and some automotive supplies.

The growth of such stores may be explained in several ways. They are usually able to get better sites in the large shopping centers. Also they can price more competitively with supermarkets and other competitors. They generally have more merchandising experience, and enjoy economies in buying.

Another type of competitor is the smaller discount drugstore, averaging 2,000 to 3,000 square feet in size and featuring fast-moving health and beauty aid products. Markups for such stores are modest, with turnover rapid. At present, there is one such store in Springfield.

In a brief conversation with the case writer, Mr. Horne stated that he was very much concerned about the impact of the new discount stores. He explained that before the new stores were even opened, he told his partners that Phelps would lose sales. At that time, he suggested that they examine their profit margin item by item to see if some prices could be cut to meet the competition. This idea was immediately rejected by the two brothers, who did not want to lose their profit margins. When Phelps sales actually did begin to decline the Phelpses still resisted any move to lower prices. At that time Paul Phelps remarked, "Our main selling point is the personal service we offer. We can't continue to offer this service if margins are cut."

## PROMOTION

For the most part, advertising is done independently by the three stores. Newspaper ads are run on the average of once a month for each store. Because the stores rarely offer special prices on goods, most of the advertisements mainly promote the store name. A typical ad is headlined: "Thirty Years of Service: You Can Depend on Us."

The Rexall Company furnishes the materials for newspaper insertions and in addition, pays one-half of the advertising costs. Rexall also runs nationwide ads in many leading magazines, at no cost to the Phelps stores. These advertisements are meant to promote the Rexall name and do not name individual franchises.

Generally speaking, Rexall offers no discounts on its products to druggists. One exception to this policy is the annual summer "one-cent sale." During this sale of Rexall products, the stores offer "two for the price of one plus a penny." The Rexall wholesaler offers sale goods to the individual stores at a reduced price for this sale. Mr. Horne said that this sale is usually successful, but it has not produced the results in recent years that it did in the past.

Although not as low as the prices in discount stores, the prices on Rexall products are, by and large, lower than those for the more famous name brands. Rexall aspirin, for example, may sell for 15 to 20 cents cheaper per 100 than a better-known brand. Prescription drugs vary less from brand to brand.

The partners proudly point to one aspect of the traditional neighborhood store which remains in their stores: the fountain bar. "This is almost an institution in this country," said Jerry Phelps, "but I'm afraid it's dying out. Although we don't realize much in the way of a profit from these bars, we still feel they give our stores a warmer atmosphere. Besides, when the kids come in to get a sundae, their parents often have them buy something else while they're here."

Another aspect of the firm's "personal touch" is the credit given to customers. Most customers, in fact, do business at Phelps stores on credit. Paul Phelps said that the stores did not profit directly from carrying customers on credit (no interest or service fee is charged), but the availability of credit was popular among the "old-timers." Credit applications are rarely checked, since most persons applying for credit are known by the employees. Delivery service is also offered by all three stores.

## OPERATIONS

Each store manager is responsible for the purchase and control of all inventory. The department heads assist the managers in buying the goods needed for their own departments. Most purchases are made through salesmen who visit the stores up to twice a week.

Inventories are not kept at fixed levels. Instead, a "short list" is kept in all departments. Thus, when a clerk or department head notices that an item is low or depleted, an entry is made on the list. Whenever a salesman appears, any items that he carries and that are on the short list are ordered. The person doing the ordering decides the quantity. Conceivably, anyone working in the store can order when a salesman visits. Buying trips are made by the three partners about three times per year. At these times, merchandise is selected for the Christmas, summer, and back-to-school seasons.

A physical count of inventory is made for all stores once each year. This occurs between Christmas and the first of the year, before preparation of the financial statements. The permanent records kept on inventory consist of order slips, shipping invoices, and ending inventory listings.

Pricing is done on a cost-plus basis. Three classes of items are marked up by different percentages of costs. All tobacco products are marked up by 25 percent above invoice price. Magazines, books, and periodicals carry a 20 percent markup, and most other items are marked up by one-third of the invoice price. This does not apply to Rexall brand items, which carry a markup of 50 percent above cost. The partners follow "fair trade" practices and do not use price cutting as a tool to increase sales volume. The partners believe that this policy allows them adequate profits and at the same time makes marketing easier.

An accounting firm keeps track of credit sales records. A bookkeeper comes to each of the three stores to record credit slips three times per week. It is possible for an individual to have a separate credit account at all three stores and at the end of the month receive a statement from each. Credit at one store guarantees a person that he may receive credit at the other two.

## DECIDING THE FUTURE

The Phelps brothers, who are both in their mid-sixties, have been thinking about retirement for some time. They were therefore quite receptive to a recent offer by a national food store chain to buy the Phelps Company drugstores. Presently, the food chain operates a chain of discount drugstores, and is anxious to become established in the Springfield area. If it buys the Phelps stores, it plans to remodel them completely and convert them to high-volume discount stores.

According to the terms of the merger proposal, the grocery firm would offer common stock having a book value equivalent to twice the partners' capital accounts in exchange for the Phelps Company's assets. The market value of the stock is presently close to book value. There is no offer for the three Phelps partners to continue in their present capacities, although it was mentioned that "they could probably work as pharmacists at other stores in the chain, if they so desire."

The offer has drawn mixed reactions from the partners. Paul and Jerry Phelps both think that it "looks like a good deal," but neither one says that he is quite ready to retire. Mr. Horne, who at 35 is much younger, is bitterly opposed to the sale. Mr. Buske has not expressed his feelings, but it is felt that he would go along with the sale.

In a private conversation, Mr. Horne told the case writer why he opposed the sale of the business: "To begin with, I think I have a lot of potential," he said. "We've already got some of the best locations in town. It's just a matter of tapping into a market that is already there. Oh sure, the new discount stores have hurt us a little, but only because we've let them. We've got to change our image—perhaps do some remodeling. But above all, we must become more competitive price-wise. I'm hoping that you can convince my partners to stick with it a while longer, and perhaps help us lay down some guidelines for the future."

# 4     PLAYPARTS

## Christine Hale and Richard Levin

*School of Business Administration University of North Carolina at Chapel Hill*

"Leigh, I finished those drawings during lunch today. When we get Andy settled for the night, I want to have a serious talk about our business plans." Rick Cooke shifted the bag of groceries to the other arm and opened the apartment door. Leigh, carrying a briefcase in one arm and their four-year-old son in the other, followed him in.

"I've done some serious thinking about it already, Rick. In fact, I've worked out some sound numbers for us to work with."

"I don't doubt that," smiled Rick. Her comment reminded him once again of their sharply differing personalities. "You're an accountant through and through," he always teased her. "You're the only person I know who has to have her pencils all pointed the same direction in the drawer and begins every explanation with the words, 'Now think of it as a T-account . . .' "

In contrast to Leigh's neatly organized desk, Rick's workspace in the home consisted chiefly of a cluttered drafting board and a desk and bookcase overflowing with engineering journals. "Rick is interested in everything and good at most of them," friends often said. Rick, though he had an engineering background and was employed as a quality assurance engineer in a furniture manufacturing plant, was an outdoor sportsman, a skilled draftsman, and an avid reader on many subjects. Leigh was a fast-rising member of a prestigious public accounting firm. Friends saw her as the perfect foil to Rick; her cool purposefulness contrasting with his easygoing manner.

Recently, Rick had developed an idea for a business of his own, involving the creation, manufacture, and sale of modular playground equipment. He had built a play area for Andy and other neighborhood children on the apartment complex grounds from wooden beams and old truck tires. It had been a tremendous success with the children, and other parents had praised the creativity. The operators of the day care center where Andy had spent his days had then approached Rick about building a similar play area. As he drafted his plans for that project, Rick had become fascinated with the idea of creating a line of standardized modular playground equipment, using durable materials such as truck tires and weather-proofed hardwood coated with a durable, low-gloss sealer.

The equipment Rick envisioned, called PlayParts, was designed to be mixed and matched in any number of positions. The play area would be built around the Basic Unit (see Drawing 1). The Basic Unit would act as support for almost all of the other PlayParts (see Drawings 2 and 3). The pieces would be constructed using precut tongue-and-groove planks,

This case was prepared by Christine Hale and Richard Levin of the University of North Carolina at Chapel Hill as a basis for class discussion rather than to illustrate either effective or ineffective handling of an administrative situation.

Support for this work was provided by the Business Foundation of North Carolina.

**DRAWING 1**

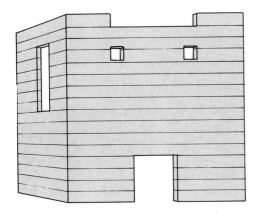

hardwood pegs, and glue at major joints, strengthened by steel bolts in assembly. The Basic Unit would be secured to the ground with two-foot-long anchor posts sunk in cement.

"We've already had some indication of the reception this type of play equipment will get from children and parents. Parents at the center have told me many times that they feel my designs are safer than most existing equipment, and everyone seems to feel they are much more stimulating to a child's imagination than are conventional swing sets and slides," Rick said as he and Leigh settled down for the discussion.

"And it will be of excellent quality," added Leigh. "It is sturdy, more attractive than conventional equipment, and can be guaranteed against normal wear and tear and weather damage for, say, three years. That should be another selling point for value-conscious parents."

"Actually, I think we will have to direct our product at the institutional market because that quality equipment is going to have to command a quality price. To justify paying the price, the purchasers are going to have to be serving a number of children. That's why I'm thinking

**DRAWING 2**

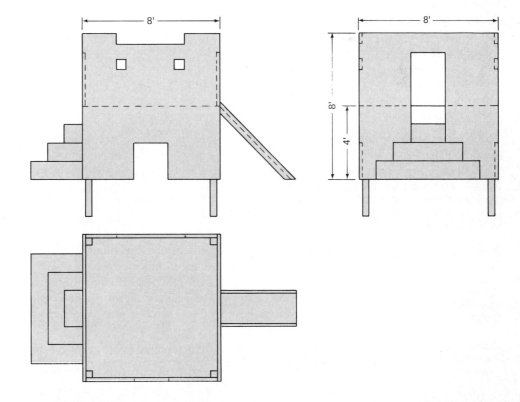

**DRAWING 3**

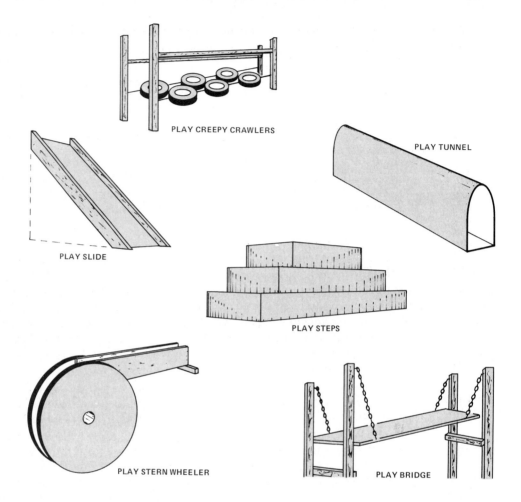

PLAY CREEPY CRAWLERS

PLAY TUNNEL

PLAY SLIDE

PLAY STEPS

PLAY STERN WHEELER

PLAY BRIDGE

of targeting mainly large day care centers and municipal parks."

"Rick, your designs do fit right in with the trend toward more creative play areas and equipment. But all the play areas of this type that I've seen have been homemade."

"Yes, but my designs will offer the same originality and durability and be just as economical because of the big price difference between wholesale and retail lumber. The big advantage of mine is its standardization, which will allow people to begin with the Basic Unit and put together a play area in a variety of ways, adding pieces as they can afford them."

"Let's see, we should be dealing with an expanding market due to the increase in the number of working mothers," said Leigh.

"I happen to have been doing a little reading to determine market potential. I haven't found the most recent figures, but according to the 1976 *Statistical Abstract,* the number of women in the labor force with children under six increased about 18% from 1972 to 1975.[1] The number of day care centers doubled from 1967 to 1972. Look, I jotted some figures down on that one. (See Exhibit 1.) And the number

---

[1]*Statistical Abstract of the U.S. 1976,* U.S. Department of Commerce, Bureau of the Census, July 1976, p. 359.

**EXHIBIT 1**  Number and Capacity of Licensed or Approved Day Care Centers

| | March 1967 | 1968 | 1969 | 1970 | 1971 | 1972 |
|---|---|---|---|---|---|---|
| Day Care Centers | 10,400 | 11,700 | 13,600 | 16,700 | 18,400 | 20,319 |
| Family Day Care Centers | 24,300 | 27,400 | 32,700 | 40,700 | 55,400 | 60,967 |
| Total | 34,700 | 39,100 | 46,300 | 57,400 | 73,800 | 81,286 |
| Capacity | 475,000 | 535,000 | 638,300 | 774,000 | 911,700 | 1,021,202 |

Source: Child Care Data and Materials, Committee on Finance, U.S. Senate, October 1974, p. 58.

of county and municipal parks increased nearly 26% in the ten years from 1960 to 1970."[2]

"Sounds like you went wild with the *Statistical Abstract.* All those figures tell us is that there probably are more potential buyers than there used to be. What about some absolute numbers?"

"Look at this information. There were over 81,000 day nurseries in the U.S. even in 1972.[3] There were nearly 20,000 municipal and county parks and recreation areas in 1970.[4] So that gives us roughly 100,000 facilities as a conservative figure for potential market size. Besides, the current trend toward more neighborhood parks expands the potential market . . ."

"But there is competition in that market, Rick."

"Right. There is the conventional backyard equipment found in larger department catalog stores. And there are kits marketed through trade catalogs for $400 to $1,000. The conventional is low priced and generally lower quality than what I propose to offer. The kits offer good quality equipment, but they don't offer the pos-

sibilities of varied playground configurations and gradual add-ons that my equipment will offer. PlayParts will have a longer guarantee, sturdiness, a flexible configuration, and an attractive natural appearance. And neither of those forms of competition for PlayParts utilizes personal selling to any great degree."

"So you mean to go with personal selling? Won't that be very expensive?"

"Well, I realize that at first we won't be able to because of the wide dispersion of facilities we mean to target. We'll advertise through institutional catalogs, trade literature, and direct mailings. Our sales will initially be mail order in response to those ads, but personal selling will follow up requests for information. Our salespeople can offer an additional service by helping institutions plan their equipment needs and by suggesting equipment configurations."

"What sort of initial sales force are you thinking about?"

"I think two full-time salespeople can call on 500 to 600 customers each per year initially," answered Rick. "Later, when the product is better known, calls should become more geographically convenient. Then the salespeople can increase the number of calls from that two or three per day figure. The sales effort will be directed from the home office."

"Wait a minute. Let's try to put some hard numbers on some of these ideas," interrupted

[2]Ibid., p. 216.

[3]*Child Care Data and Materials,* Committee on Finance, U.S. Senate, October 1974, p. 58.

[4]Op. cit., p. 217.

| Year | Ave. Price/Unit | New Units | Repl'mt. Volume | Exp'n. Volume | Total Dollars |
|------|-----------------|-----------|------------------|----------------|----------------|
| 1 | $500 | 500 | — | — | $250,000 |
| 2 | 500 | 800 | — | $12,500 | 412,500 |
| 3 | 500 | 1,000 | — | 45,000 | 545,000 |
| 4 | 550 | 1,200 | $27,500 | 63,250 | 750,750 |
| 5 | 605 | 1,400 | 78,650 | 105,000 | 1,030,650 |

Leigh. "You mentioned 100,000 facilities as potential buyers. Let's aim very conservatively for a .5% market penetration. That gives us a first-year sales target of five hundred units. Give me a price for the average configuration."

"$500. I've got some preliminary cost figures for the various pieces . . ."

"Hold it. We'll get to that. Let me push out a little sales forecast with that average price." (See table above.)

"Those would appear to be reasonable numbers to work with in the beginning, Rick. The increase in units sold incorporates market growth, consumer acceptance of the product, and expansion and replacement of existing equipment. Constant prices for the first three years should help establish client relations."

"Later those price increases may be absolutely necessary due to increased supply prices. Some years, lumber shortages have caused the price of lumber to skyrocket."

"Now, how about those cost projections, Rick?"

"Here's what I've worked up. You'll notice the margin is slightly lower on the Basic Unit. That piece should attract the purchase of the higher-margin accessory pieces." (See table below.)

"How about distribution costs? That'll be pretty stiff given the weight and bulk of the pieces."

"Leigh, we'll probably have to subsidize the freight costs initially. By Year 3, with volume at 1,000 units per year, shipping costs per average set of equipment should be about $100. I'm basing this on the assumption that with low volume we will ship by independent motor carriers. Later, we'll have multiple production facilities near the markets and perhaps a company truck system. That will really help get those distribution costs down."

"So those prices you just showed me do not include any freight charges?"

"No . . ."

"And of course the equipment will have to be shipped disassembled."

| | Basic Unit | Steps | Slide | Tunnel |
|---|-----------|-------|-------|--------|
| Wood (finished) | $150 | $12 | $13 | $20 |
| Wood (support) | 10 | 10 | — | — |
| Hardware and attachment assembly | 10 | 10 | 10 | 15 |
| Glue | 5 | 3 | 2 | 5 |
| Sealer | 25 | 10 | 10 | 10 |
| Labor | 20 | 10 | 10 | 15 |
| Total costs | $220 | $55 | $45 | $65 |
| Prices | $300 | $80 | $65 | $95 |

"It can be shipped in no more than five disassembled parts, no larger than eight feet by eight feet and one to two feet at the widest point. The purchaser can assemble the equipment without any special tools. Simple assembly was a major consideration in my designs."

"Speaking of assembly, what sort of manufacturing process and facilities will this product require?"

"Again, it is relatively simple. All materials can be purchased in partially finished condition. We can contract for blemished truck tires from major manufacturers. Cable rolls can be easily purchased from utility companies, giving us a predictable, inexpensive, and high-quality supply."

"Won't the wood be the major cost?" asked Leigh.

"Yes, wood supply would be a good thing to look at for future vertical integration. But for the first year, hardwood can be purchased with precut tongue-and-groove features and planed surfaces. Later on, those finishing operations can be performed at the assembly facilities."

"So assembly in the plant will basically entail fitting and gluing things together?"

"Yes," replied Rick, "specifically, assembly means cutting wood to the appropriate lengths, drilling holes, placing pegs, marking the pieces for further assembly, gluing the tongue-and-groove planks, coating with the sealer, and inspection."

"OK, Rick, I know practically nothing about woodworking and assembly. I'll just take your word for what equipment and floor space this plant would need."

"We'll need an average of two units per day produced to meet our first-year sales target. That production level will require one bench saw, one drill press, and several large wood presses for gluing. Cost on that sort of equipment

**EXHIBIT 2**  Incremental Financing Needs

| Year | 1 | 2 | 3 | 4 | 5 |
|---|---|---|---|---|---|
| Machinery and Equipment | 1,500 | 1,500 | — | 1,500 | — |
| Working Capital | | | | | |
|    Inventory | 3,000 | 2,000 | 2,000 | 2,000 | 3,000 |
|    Receivables | 20,000 | 15,000 | 10,000 | 15,000 | 25,000 |
|    Cash and Other WC | 5,000 | 3,000 | 2,500 | 3,500 | 5,000 |
| Loan repayment | — | — | — | 10,000 | 10,000 |
| Loss financing | 26,000 | — | — | — | — |
| Incorporation costs | 5,000 | — | — | — | — |
|    Totals | 60,500 | 21,500 | 14,500 | 32,000 | 43,000 |
| Incremental financing will be provided by: | | | | | |
| Creditor financing | 12,500 | 8,300 | 4,700 | 8,300 | 12,500 |
| Earnings after taxes | — | 20,500 | 22,100 | 52,600 | 81,000 |
| Depreciation | 150 | 300 | 300 | 450 | 450 |
|    Subtotal | 12,650 | 29,100 | 27,100 | 61,350 | 93,950 |
| Required capital financing | 47,850 | — | — | — | — |
| Available for reinvestment | | | | | |
|    or distribution to owners | — | (8,100) | (12,600) | (29,350) | (50,950) |
|    Totals | 60,500 | 21,000 | 14,500 | 32,000 | 43,000 |

runs . . . let me see . . . $500, $380, and $600, respectively. Maybe less if I can get good used equipment."

"And what are the floor space requirements?"

"I'd say about 4,000 square feet of space on one floor. Most of that is for raw materials and finished goods storage. The facilities will need no special features except a 220 volt electrical source and adequate ventilation for gluing and sealing operations."

"Then we should be able to rent space of that type for about $500 a month, including utilities. Renting will keep the capital needs lower and give us more flexibility until we see if the product takes off."

"The other capital outlays will occur step-wise as sales increase," added Rick. "Using our sales forecast, the second year the machinery requirements will double to two table saws, two drill presses, and more wood presses."

"Assuming we continue to rent for five years, let's figure the incremental financing." (See Exhibit 2.) "Rick, these figures show a need for about $50,000 for the initial financing."

"We ought to be able to put in $5,000."

"Oh, Rick, not the house down-payment-fund . . ."

"Then if we offer $20,000 in private debt placement at about 10% . . . and another $25,000 could be raised by offering maybe 30% of the common stock of PlayParts, Inc., to the holders of this private debt."

"Just a minute. If you're talking about a

**EXHIBIT 3**   Abbreviated Income Statement

| | Years | | | | |
|---|---|---|---|---|---|
| | 1 | 2 | 3 | 4 | 5 |
| Revenues | $250,000 | 412,500 | 545,000 | 750,750 | 1,030,650 |
| Cost of Sales | 180,000 | 300,000 | 400,000 | 540,000 | 740,000 |
| Gross Margin | 70,000 | 112,500 | 145,000 | 210,750 | 290,650 |
| Operating Expenses: | | | | | |
|   Rent | 6,000 | 6,000 | 8,000 | 8,000 | 10,000 |
|   Depreciation | 150 | 300 | 300 | 450 | 450 |
|   Sales—direct efforts | 40,000 | 40,000 | 60,000 | 60,000 | 80,000 |
|     —catalog sales | 5,000 | 6,000 | 8,000 | 9,000 | 10,000 |
|   Promotion and adver. | 25,000 | 20,000 | 20,000 | 22,000 | 22,000 |
|   General and Admin. | | | | | |
|   (Incl. interest | | | | | |
|   on debt) | 20,000 | 20,000 | 22,000 | 23,000 | 25,000 |
| Net income (Loss) | (26,150) | 20,200 | 26,700 | 89,300 | 143,200 |
| before taxes | | | | | |
| Income Taxes | — | — | 4,600 | 35,700 | 62,200 |
| (net of ITC) | | | | | |
| Net Income after taxes | (26,150) | 20,200 | 22,100 | 52,600 | 81,000 |
| Return on Original Investment | | | | | |
|   Total = $50,000 | — | 40% | 44% | 105% | 162% |
|   Minority interest (30%) | — | 24% | 26% | 63% | 97% |
|   = $25,000 | | | | | |

debt burden, we'd better check the cash flow. Using our projected revenue figures, what sort of *pro forma* p & l do we come up with?" (See Exhibit 3 for a projected income statement.)

"See, Leigh, the debt could be repaid over the fourth and fifth years. And the return on the minority investment will be between 24% in the second year and 97.2% in the fifth year."

"I think that's probably a little optimistic . . ."

"Of course you do. Now that return can't include any dividends, at least for the first five years. The return to me, as founder, is in salary. $8,000 in Year 1 and increased thereafter."

"$8,000 is a bit of a salary cut from your present position, Rick."

"Yes, Leigh, but that is only in the beginning."

"Still, the money you take out won't be entirely under your control. Who else will be on the board of directors besides you and presumably me?"

"I was casting myself as president and chairman of the board, with you and about three members chosen by the minority shareholders comprising the board. It won't be a big operation. The first year, I'll have authority over the two salespeople, the three production employees, and an administrative secretary. You'll be responsible for installing a comprehensive accounting and management information system."

# 5

# TEXAS, INC.

## Clayton G. Smith and Arnold Cooper

*Purdue University*

In December 1976, Texas, Inc. appeared to be on the verge of bankruptcy. The small restaurant business had a negative net worth, and a number of its food bills were two months past due. The co-owners of the business, Jim Christensen and Mike O'Farrell, were blaming each other for the firm's difficulties. During the fall, their arguments had become more and more severe as the financial situation of the company worsened. By December, the disagreement was so strong that the co-owners were only talking through their lawyers.

Jim Christensen and Mike O'Farrell also jointly owned two other businesses—Dusty's, Inc. and an Athens Cove franchise outlet. While these two businesses continued to be profitable, the co-owners felt that they could be financially ruined if Texas, Inc. went under.

## BACKGROUND

Jim Christensen was 24 years old when he obtained his MBA in accounting from Indiana University. After graduating in 1971, he joined Coopers and Lybrand, one of the country's largest accounting firms. At the urging of a friend of his, Bill Bishop, Jim left his job in early 1973 and together they opened an outlet of the new Athens Cove chain of pizza restaurants in

Bloomington, Indiana. Due to a substantial earnings loss and a business disagreement, Jim subsequently sold his share of the business.

Despite their experience, Jim had come to enjoy the idea of being in business for himself, and he felt that he could be successful at it. In January of 1974, he decided to team up with an old friend of his from high school, Ken Matthews, and begin a new business. Neither Jim nor Ken had strong feelings as to the type of business they should go into.

Jim did feel, however, that they needed more capital than they collectively had. Jim and his wife, Ellen, had a combined net worth of just under $50,000. She worked as a radiologist for several hospitals near Indiana University, which provided an income of $17,000 a year. Matthews had served in the Army for four years in Vietnam. "With the pay that the Army gives you, I wasn't able to save much while I was in," said Matthews, "and when I was on leave I spent most of what I saved." With Jim's consent, Matthews therefore called George Crowley, an old "boozing buddy" of his, and invited him to join the venture. Crowley, a stockbroker who worked in New York City, agreed to make a modest investment in whatever type of business was decided upon (assuming the idea was sound).

## AN OUTSIDE INVESTOR

In March of 1974, Jim began to look for another investor, one who would be a silent partner. His lawyer, John Heagney, happened to know a couple who were interested in investing in a business venture. Heagney introduced Jim to Mike and Donna O'Farrell.

Mike, 27 years of age, had recently left his job with a consulting firm in Chicago. He had worked as a staff member for the company, earning $15,600 a year (plus expenses). "Given the fact that I was putting in 70–80 hours a week," said Mike, "I felt that I should have been making a lot more. The job was also creating a lot of family pressure. When our daughter was born in '73, I was so tied up on business in New York, that it was three days before I was able to get home to see my wife and child. If I had hopped a plane when I first got the news that Michele had been born, I probably would have been fired. Anyway, I finally came to the conclusion that the only way to make what you are really worth, and to have any control over your life is to be in business for yourself. After talking it over with Donna, I decided to leave my job. It was my intention to get into a business, and take an active part in its operation."

Together, Mike and Donna had a net worth of almost $275,000, about $200,000 of which came from an inheritance that Donna had received some years earlier. Most of the inheritance had been in the form of stocks and bonds. Mike and Donna were favorably impressed with Jim Christensen, and agreeable to a role for Mike as a silent partner in spite of their original intention to take an active role in any business they went into. "I felt that Mike would make a good business partner," said Jim, "and so without much formality he came on board."

## IDEAS EXPLORED

Jim, Ken, Mike and Donna explored a number of ideas, and kept Crowley posted (who was back in New York). Together, they looked at a welding job shop, a small fountain syrup company in Chicago, a tennis club, and a taco franchise outlet.

Jim and Mike came up with one idea that came very close to being carried out—a drive-through liquor store. Designs for the building were drawn up whereby the customer would drive through a long breezeway with glass window displays on both sides of the car. The customer would then place his order via an intercom system, drive down a little further and pick up the order. To comply with Indiana state law, which said that a person could not be served liquor in his car, the customer would get out of his car and stand in a booth to receive his package.

By the time all the details had been squared away, however, the 1975 money crunch had hit. Interest rates soared to a level that the lending banks felt that Jim and his partners could not handle; the bank decided not to loan them the money.

With money virtually unavailable at this point, they began to look for investments that they could finance entirely with their own money.

## TUMBLEDOWN TAVERN

Ken got the idea of leasing a warehouse, which was located very close to Indiana University in Bloomington, and turning it into a bar and sandwich place. The Bloomington area had a population of approximately 100,000; the student population of the school was over 50,000. Jim and Ken negotiated the lease with help from Jim's lawyer, John Heagney. They arranged for a one-year lease with an option for four two-year extensions, reasoning that if the business failed, the liability for lease payments would not be too great.

Jim figured the initial capitalization requirements to be $20,000, and it was agreed that Mike and Donna would contribute $10,000 for a 1/3 equity share of the business. As the partnership agreement was being drawn up, however, Jim realized that the initial capitalization level would be inadequate. He asked Mike and Donna to raise their contribution to $20,000 and offered them a 40% share of the business; but Mike refused.

After a fair amount of haggling among the partners, the final capitalization structure was agreed upon:

| | Contribution | Equity Share (%) |
|---|---|---|
| Mike O'Farrell | $17,500 | 40 |
| George Crowley | 10,000 | 20 |
| Jim Christensen | 2,500 | 20 |
| Ken Matthews | 2,500[1] | 20 |
| | $32,500 | 100 |

The business, which they named Tumbledown Tavern, was set up as a Subchapter S Corporation (see Appendix A on Subchapter S Corporations). It was the closest bar to Indiana University. It quickly came to be known for its rowdy clientele. "Fights were very common," said Donna, "toilets were ripped off the walls, and bathroom doors were ripped from the hinges. Between the fighters, the thieves, and the drug pushers, we wound up having bouncers in every room."

## MIKE AND DONNA'S EMERGING ROLE

While Mike was supposed to be a silent partner, he (and Donna) gradually became more involved in the affairs of the business (See Exhibit 8). According to Mike, this was partly due to their concern over the way things were being run, but it was also because they were enthusiastic about the idea of being in business.

Jim quickly came to appreciate Mike's help in the business. Jim's MBA in Accounting had given him a strong background in financial management, tax preparation, and administrative detail. Mike, on the other hand, had a Masters of Science in Marketing (Purdue University, 1972), and he had also worked part-time as a bartender in college. He proved to be very adept at developing effective promotion schemes, merchandising the liquor display behind the bar, dealing with personnel, and day-to-day business operations. And because Mike was 6'2" and 200 lbs., he was fairly good at breaking up

[1]Ken borrowed the money from Jim.

fights among the patrons. At 5'8" and 140 lbs., Jim usually called for assistance when fights broke out.

The two partners came to feel that they were perfect complements for each other—Jim with his accounting degree as the "detail man," Mike with his marketing degree as the "concept man." "We were both somewhat skilled in the other fellow's area," said Jim, "but we felt that expertise in both areas was vital to success." It was also apparent that Ken was not much help at all in running the business. Because of his years in the service, he had never acquired much in the way of business experience, and he did not seem to be interested in learning how. Matthews did help to break up a lot of the fights that occurred, but he spent his time drinking with the customers. "For the most part, Ken was never in on any of the important decisions," said Mike.

By the end of the first year, in June of 1975, the business had earned a $12,000 profit on the $32,500 investment. But, as Mike put it, "Both Jim and I came from structured environments, and we were tired of the fights and hassles." They decided to buy out Ken Matthews and George Crowley for $10,000 each.

## DUSTY'S

The business was reorganized, again as a Subchapter S Corporation, and renamed "Dusty's"; Mike now held a 60% equity position in the business, and Jim held 40%. Profits and losses were to be shared 60/40 according to the equity positions of the parties. However, a stockholder agreement allocated voting rights equally. Mike and Donna felt that it was only fair that Jim and Ellen have an equal say in the running of the business.

Jim and Mike cleaned the place up over the summer of 1975, investing another $15,000 in the business for improvements; they intended to attract a more law-abiding clientele by changing the image of the business. The im-

---

**EXHIBIT 1**   Initial Number of Employees at Each Business Owned.*

|            | Full-Time | Part-Time |
|------------|-----------|-----------|
| Dusty's    | 5         | 5         |
| Athens Cove | 7[1]      | 14        |
| Texas, Inc. | 7         | 19[2]     |

*For all the businesses, most employees were paid the minimum wage.
[1]Includes one Manager and one Assistant Manager
[2]Includes one day manager, and one night manager; Jim, Mike, and Donna took turns for the day and night shifts in filling these positions.

---

provements included a new bar which replaced a long formica table, bench seat booths which replaced plastic chairs and tables, and carpeting for the eating area. Jim and Mike also decided to raise prices by roughly 25%, figuring that it would encourage some of the "rowdy" clientele to go elsewhere. (For instance, the price of a mixed drink was raised from $1.10 to $1.40.)

It was also in the summer of 1975 that Jim and Ellen bought a house that was just two houses away from Mike and Donna's. Ellen's job as a radiologist kept her from becoming involved in running the business, but Jim, Mike, and Donna were together constantly after the Christensens moved next door—at home, and at Dusty's. According to Donna, "It was like we were living with each other." Jim and Mike came to be close friends during the period. Mike enjoyed Jim's sense of humor very much, and Jim admired Mike's open nature. Both appeared to have very similar interests in going into business:

- the idea of wheeling and dealing
- making lots of money
- entrepreneurial freedom
- exciting investments (stocks and bonds were too mundane)

According to Mike, "Dusty's was just the entree. We were figuring on opening a number of businesses, so that we could really make it big."

## JIM'S PREVIOUS BUSINESS PARTNER

One evening Jim told Mike and Donna about his experience with his previous business partner. Bill Bishop, a friend of his from college, held franchise rights for an outlet of Athens Cove, a new chain of pizza restaurants that was just getting started in the Midwest. Bishop suggested to Jim that they go into business together to exploit what appeared to be an exciting business opportunity. Together, they formed a Subchapter S Corporation. Because Bishop had the franchise rights, Jim agreed to invest 60% of the capital for a 25% equity position. (Profits and losses were to be shared according to each person's equity position. Voting rights were similarly weighted.) Jim also agreed that, while he would be an officer in the corporation, he would function as a silent partner in the beginning and become a working partner later on.

They also drew up what both men thought was an excellent buy/sell agreement, whereby if one party made an offer to buy the other out, the second party could accept, or come back with a higher offer which the first party would *have to* take. This seemed to assure that the party who sold his shares would receive a fair offer from the other party.

A substantial earnings loss was incurred before they had been in business for long.

Through his greater voting power, Bishop was able to pressure Jim not to draw any salary and to drop his title as a corporate officer until earnings recovered. This was done even though Bishop continued to draw his full salary. Feeling that he was being used, Jim decided to get out of the business. Bishop then arranged to have a third party make Jim an offer for his share of the business—a contingency not dealt with in the buy/sell agreement. Jim thought that the offer was substantially below market value, but, because he could not find a third party to whom he could sell his shares at a better price, he decided to accept the offer. Said Jim of the experience, "I really got burnt, but I learned a lot and got off fairly light."

Mike and Donna didn't see Jim's previous partnership experience as being a source of difficulties. "We weren't like Bishop," said Donna, "and we all had a big dream and a common goal." They all came to feel that they were "perfect partners," and that with their combined business experience they could run anything.

## SHORTCOMINGS RECOGNIZED

Jim and Mike did recognize shortcomings in each other, however, and did have their share of disagreements.

Mike sometimes questioned Jim's judgment in operational decisions. For example, Jim purchased $6,000 worth of furnishings for Dusty's at an auction, without telling Mike; Mike thought that $6,000 for the merchandise was "way out of line." Jim also purchased a cash register for $1,800 for better accounting and control procedures—again without telling Mike. Mike did not feel they needed "such an elaborate machine." And according to Mike, Jim did not deal with subordinates well. Mike felt that Jim was too willing to overlook mistakes by subordinates, and unable to fire employees who weren't working out. Said Mike, "Jim could never separate personalities from the needs of the business." Mike also felt that Jim was unable to assign unpleasant tasks. "A lot of times," said Mike, "when a customer threw up in the bathroom, Jim cleaned it up himself."

For Jim's part, he felt that Mike was much too impatient and demanding of the employees. "Most of the help that we have are minimum wage workers—mainly students from the University. I think Mike expects too much from these kids when they haven't had all that much work experience." Jim thought that Mike was slightly impulsive. "We had a little disagreement over how we should price the drinks. Mike wanted to pass the 4% sales tax, on to the customers, and I felt that it should be absorbed by the business. He didn't give any thought at all to how people might be turned off by the higher price." Jim also felt that Mike was too willing to spend money on intangibles, such as advertising and promotion. "You do need some 'hype' when you start a business," said Jim, "but equipment and furnishings are much more important in the early stages."

However, they both liked each other well enough to overlook each other's weaknesses, and they both felt that they could make up for the other fellow's weak spots as well.

## ATHENS COVE

By early 1976, Dusty's seemed sufficiently established (see Exhibit 2) so that Jim and Mike decided they could open another business. As part of Jim's buy/sell agreement at Athens Cove, he had obtained the right to purchase a new Athens Cove franchise in the area.

Because Jim owned the franchise rights, he conducted the negotiations. The Athens Cove people had the final say as to the location. "Because the prices of Athens Cove pizzas were at the top of the line, people with higher incomes were more attracted to Athens Cove outlets than people with lower incomes," said Jim. Inexplicably, the franchisor wanted to locate the business on a lot in the lower-middle-class section of Elliotsville (which is about 16 miles outside of Bloomington.) Jim and Mike surmised that Athens Cove had a financial relationship with

**EXHIBIT 2** Dusty's, Inc. Statements of Income

| | | | Twelve Months Ending May 31, 1976 | | Seven Months Ending December 31, 1976 | |
|---|---|---|---|---|---|---|
| Net Sales | | | $221,453 | | $114,966 | |
| Cost of Goods Sold | | | 88,581 (40.0%) | | 43,687[2] | |
| Gross Margin | | | 132,872 (60.0%) | | 71,279 (62.0%) | |
| Operating Expenses | | | | | | |
| Wages | 53,148 (24.0%) | | | | 32,180[3] (28.0%) | |
| Supplies | 5,760 (2.6%) | | | | 3,478 (3.0%) | |
| Utilities | 8,640 (3.9%) | | | | 5,267 (4.6%) | |
| Taxes, state | 350 (0.2%) | | | | 223 (0.2%) | |
| Taxes, payroll | 4,746 (2.1%) | | | | 2,874 (2.5%) | |
| Insurance | 3,600 (1.6%) | | | | 2,194 (1.9%) | |
| Repair and Maintenance | 9,745[1] (4.4%) | | | | 2,998 (2.6%) | |
| Advertising | 4,763 (2.2%) | | | | 2,959 (2.6%) | |
| Laundry | 2,193 (1.0%) | | | | 1,311 (1.1%) | |
| Depreciation, Equipment | 6,750 (3.0%) | | | | 3,938 (3.4%) | |
| Interest Expense, Equipment | 2,160 (1.0%) | | | | 1,260 (1.1%) | |
| Rent | 9,600 (4.3%) | | | | 6,300[4] (5.5%) | |
| | | | 111,455 (50.3%) | | 64,982 (56.5%) | |
| | | | $ 21,417 (9.7%) | | $ 6,297 (5.5%) | |

[1]Includes $4,000 for bathroom doors.
[2]Cost of goods sold reduction reflects fact that sales tax was passed through to customers through increased prices; it had been absorbed by the firm in the previous year.
[3]Increase reflects additional help hired when Texas, Inc. was started.
[4]Rent was raised by $100/month in June 1976.

the owner of the prospective property. Jim pressed for a more favorable location, but was unable to get Athens Cove to change its position. Mike thought that Jim could have been more insistent. In spite of their reservations, however, Jim and Mike and their wives all decided to go ahead with the deal.

Jim and Mike gave a note for $7,500 to Athens Cove for the amount of the franchise cost. Jim contributed $1,500 to the business, while Mike invested $2,500. To get an SBA guaranteed loan for $70,000, the amount needed for equipment and working capital, Donna put $100,000 of her stocks and bonds up as collateral.[2] Mike and Jim had the building built to their specifications. They made an agreement

[2]The loan was obtained from a local bank, with 90% of the amount guaranteed by the Small Business Administration. Jim filled out the SBA application, which was very complex. The application was 45 pages long. Jim's thoroughness led the loan officer at the bank to comment that it was the best SBA application he had ever seen.

**EXHIBIT 3**  Balance Sheet of Dusty's Inc. as of December 31, 1976

**Assets**

| | |
|---|---|
| Cash | $ 1,542 |
| Inventory | 2,079 |
| Misc. Prepayments | 1,150 |
| Current Assets | 4,771 |
| Equipment and Fixtures | 30,000 |
| Less: Accumulated Depreciation | 6,000 |
| Net Fixed Assets | 24,000 |
| Leasehold Improvements, Net | 12,138 |
| Total Assets | 40,909 |

**Liabilities and Owners' Equity**

| | |
|---|---|
| Accounts Payable | $ 2,147 |
| Stockholders' Equity | |
| Capital Stock | 32,500 |
| Retained Earnings | 6,262 |
| Total Stockholders' Equity | 38,762 |
| Total Liabilities and Owners' Equity | 40,909 |

**EXHIBIT 4**  Athens Cove Restaurant Statement of Income for Ten Months Ending December 31, 1976

| | | |
|---|---|---|
| Sales | | $276,511 |
| Cost of Goods Sold | | 96,778 (35%) |
| Gross Margin | | 179,733 (65%) |
| Operating Expenses | | |
| Wages and Salaries | 73,275 (26.5%) | |
| Employee Meals | 4,373 (1.6%) | |
| Supplies | 8,148 (2.9%) | |
| Utilities | 9,329 (3.4%) | |
| Taxes, state | 770 (0.3%) | |
| Taxes, payroll | 6,543 (2.4%) | |
| Insurance | 5,331 (1.9%) | |
| Repair and Maintenance | 1,493 (0.5%) | |
| Advertising | 12,443 (4.5%) | |
| Laundry | 7,396 (2.7%) | |
| Depreciation, Equipment | 20,187 (7.3%) | |
| Interest Expense, Equipment | 4,665 (1.7%) | |
| Interest Expense, Building Mortgage | 16,250 (5.9%) | |
| Land Lease | 4,000 (1.4%) | |
| Total Operation Expenses | | 174,203 (63.0%) |
| Earnings Before Taxes | | $ 5,530 (2.0%) |

with the owner of the land which allowed them to use the land for 15 years without cost. In return, the building would become the property of the land owner at the end of the 15 years. To help secure a $175,000 loan for the building, they obtained a subordination from the land owner in favor of the bank. This meant that, in the event of liquidation, the land owner would receive any settlement only after the bank received the full amount owed to it.

Jim, Ellen, Mike, and Donna each had to sign personal guarantees for all loans extended to the business. Hence, all four were jointly liable for the debts of the business, and potentially any of them could be sued separately for the full amount of any of the loans.

The new business was set up as a Subchapter S Corporation, separate from Dusty's. As at Dusty's the equity shares in the business were divided 60/40, with Mike holding the 60% position. Profits and losses were again divided according to the party's equity positions, and

voting power was to be shared equally in this business as well.

At this point, Jim did make up a list of rules and responsibilities for the parties. It turned out, however, that they were never followed in practice. Said Mike, "If one person spent 60 hours at the businesses during a given week, the other would feel obliged to put in an equivalent amount of time." They had also talked about a formal buy/sell agreement for the two businesses, but never got around to it. Jim and Mike reasoned that, if either of them ever wanted out, they would work it out on friendly and equitable terms. "I think that we all feared having things in writing," said Mike. "I think we feared that it would ruin the aura of our dream."

John Heagney, who knew both couples very well by this time, didn't pressure them to formalize the relation more—he knew how good their friendship was. Said Heagney, "At the time, I felt that it would only make the relationship unnecessarily rigid."

**EXHIBIT 5**  Balance Sheet of Athens Cove Restaurant as of December 31, 1976

| Assets | | Liabilities and Owners' Equity | |
|---|---|---|---|
| Cash | $4,054 | Accounts Payable | $5,745 |
| Inventory | 4,145 | Franchise Fee Payable | 2,500 |
| Misc. Prepayments | 1,673 | LT Notes Payable-Current Portion | 11,333 |
| Current Assets | 9,872 | Current Liabilities | 19,578 |
| Equipment and Fixtures | 74,521 | | |
| Less: Accumulated Depreciation | 8,872 | | |
| | 65,649 | | |
| Delivery Vehicles | 7,600 | Loan for Building (15 years) | 163,278 |
| Less: Accumulated Depreciation | 904 | Notes Payable (7 years) | 60,667 |
| | 6,696 | Notes Payable (3 years) | 5,055 |
| | | Long-Term Liabilities | 229,000 |
| Building | 175,000 | | |
| Less: Accumulated Depreciation | 9,722 | Stockholders' Equity | |
| | 165,278 | Capital Stock | 4,000 |
| | | Retained Earnings | 2,000 |
| Net Fixed Assets | | Total Stockholders' Equity | 6,000 |
| Franchise Rights (15-yr. term) | 7,083 | | |
| Total Assets | 254,578 | Total Liabilities and Owners' Equity | 254,578 |

**EXHIBIT 6** Texas, Inc. Statement of Income for Seven-Months Ending December 31, 1976*

| | | |
|---|---|---|
| Net Sales | | $178,000 |
| Cost of Goods Sold | | 97,900 (55%) |
| Gross Margin | | 80,100 (45%) |
| Operating Expenses | | |
| Wages | 56,960 (32.0%) | |
| Supplies | 4,216 (2.4%) | |
| Utilities | 6,897 (3.9%) | |
| Taxes, state | 687 (0.3%) | |
| Taxes, payroll | 5,087 (2.9%) | |
| Insurance | 3,193 (1.8%) | |
| Repair and Maintenance | 1,166 (0.7%) | |
| Advertising | 1,500 (0.8%) | |
| Laundry | 1,699 (0.9%) | |
| Depreciation, Equipment | 7,583 (4.2%) | |
| Rent, Building and Land | 14,000 (7.9%) | |
| Rent, Equipment | 2,100 (1.2%) | |
| Interest Expense | 2,333 (1.3%) | |
| Total Operating Expenses | | 107,421 (60.3%) |
| Earnings Before Taxes | | ($ 27,321) |

*Note—the annual charge for the liquor license would be reflected on next year's Income Statement.

The Athens Cove restaurant opened on March 1, 1976, and sales took off immediately. (See Exhibit 4.) Jim and Mike felt that there was no stopping them now.

## TEXAS, INC.

Mike got the idea of starting a Bar-B-Que restaurant just outside of Bloomington that would serve relatively inexpensive ($4–$7) Bar-B-Que foods. Jim liked the idea, and so they went ahead. Although there were more than 40 restaurants in Bloomington, this would be the first Bar-B-Que restaurant in the area. Mike defined the market, drew up a menu, and decided on pricing and promotion. He also designed the building.

Jim and Mike were able to obtain an SBA guaranteed loan for $50,000 for equipment and working capital.[3] The partners made the fol-

lowing contributions to the new business: Donna pledged another $50,000 of her stocks and bonds, so that the business could obtain a five-year lease of the land and building; Jim put $15,000 into the business from his and Ellen's savings account. Jim and Ellen had most of their money in the three businesses now. In addition, they also had personal car payments to make, and a third mortgage on their house.

As at Athens Cove, Jim, Ellen, Mike, and Donna all had to sign personal guarantees for each of the loans, which made each person jointly and separately liable for the debts of Texas, Inc.

Here too, the business was set up as a Subchapter S Corporation. Mike gained a 60% equity position, with Jim receiving 40%. According to the Shareholders Agreement (see Exhibit 9) profits and losses were to be shared according to equity positions and voting power was equally divided.

[3]Again, Jim prepared the SBA application.

**EXHIBIT 7**   Balance Sheet of Texas, Inc. as of December 31, 1976

**Assets**

| | |
|---|---:|
| Cash | $ 3,073 |
| Inventory | 3,996 |
| Misc. Prepayments | 1,037 |
| Current Assets | 8,106 |
| Equipment and Fixtures | $60,000 |
| Less: Accumulated Depreciation | 7,583 |
| Net Fixed Assets | 52,417 |
| Leasehold Improvements, Net | 4,927 |
| Total Assets | 65,450 |

**Liabilities and Owners' Equity**

| | |
|---|---:|
| Accounts Payable | $17,771 |
| Notes Payable—Current | 10,000 |
| Current Liabilities | 27,771 |
| Notes Payable—Long-Term | |
| (7 years) | 40,000 |
| Stockholder Loans | 10,000 |
| Long-Term Liabilities | 50,000 |
| Stockholders' Equity | |
| Capital Stock | 15,000 |
| Retained Earnings | (27,321) |
| Total Stockholders' Equity | (12,321) |
| Total Liabilities Equity | 65,450 |

## TWO PROBLEMS

Jim and Mike knew that they would have to deal with two problems at Texas, Inc.

The greatest problem was that neither had had any experience in running a full-line restaurant. Mike and Donna wanted to hire an experienced restaurant manager who would train them to set up and run the business, and also manage some of the day-to-day operations himself. The salary of a professional manager would be approximately $16,000 a year. Jim did not feel that they could afford to spend the money at this time. "The more Mike tried to persuade him," said Donna, "the more upset he got." The argument continued, virtually non-stop, for two days.

Finally, a compromise was reached. Jim and Mike agreed to make John Moss, one of the full-time employees at Dusty's, the manager at Athens Cove (at a salary of $10,000 a year), so that they would have more time to devote to Texas, Inc. Jim and Mike had each been putting in an average of 50 hours a week at Dusty's and Athens Cove, while Donna had been devoting six hours a week to the two businesses.[4] The compromise seemed acceptable to all.

[4]It was around this time that Donna found out that she was pregnant with her second child. However, Mike and Donna figured that she could put in about 20 hours a week until the baby came, and then come back to work after she was on her feet again. The babysitter who took care of Michele, their first child, could also take care of the new baby.

**EXHIBIT 8**    Hours Worked by Jim, Mike, and Donna

|  | Jim | Mike | Donna |
|---|---|---|---|
| Hours worked when owned Dusty's alone. | 40 | 20 | 6 |
| Hours worked when owned Dusty's and Athens Cove. | 50 | 50 | 6 |
| Hours worked when owned Dusty's, Athens Cove, Texas, Inc. | 80 | 80 | 40 |

*Note:* Jim, Mike, and Donna drew $3.00 an hour when they were doing work that the help would otherwise do. Two-thirds of the time that they spent at the businesses involved such work. They did not draw fixed salaries at the businesses; their compensation *as owners and managers* of the firms came through dividends only.

The other problem had to do with the laws of the county where the business was to be located. According to county law, Indiana corporations formed for the purpose of establishing a restaurant business within the county limits had to be in business for six months and realize $100,000 in sales before they could apply for a liquor license. This meant that it would be late 1976 or early 1977 before they would be able to serve alcoholic beverages at the restaurant.

The cost of such a liquor license was approximately $1,400 a year.

Since the business was to be located just outside of Bloomington, the city law which governed within the city limits and provided for the immediate purchase of a liquor license upon incorporation did not apply. It was under the city law that Mike and Jim had obtained the liquor license for Dusty's.

Both Jim and Mike realized that their rel-

**EXHIBIT 9**    Shareholders Agreement for Texas, Inc.

This agreement, entered into on the 1st day of May, 1976, by and between Michael T. O'Farrell, and James A. Christensen, hereinafter sometimes referred to as the "shareholders," WITNESSETH:

WHEREAS the shareholders have caused a Subchapter S Corporation to be formed under the laws of the State of Indiana, of the name Texas, Inc. (hereafter sometimes referred to as "the corporation"); and

WHEREAS the corporation is authorized, and has, issued 1,000 shares of common stock of zero par value, to the shareholders, for valid consideration in the following proportions

| | |
|---|---|
| Michael T. O'Farrell | 600 shares |
| James A. Christensen | 400 shares |

Now, THEREFORE in consideration of the forgoing it is agreed:

1. Profits and losses of the corporation shall be shared, according to the equity positions of the shareholders.

*Continued*

**EXHIBIT 9** *Continued*

2. Irrespective of the shareholders' equity positions in the corporation, the voting power of each of the shareholders shall be equally divided.

3. Each shareholder shall, so long as he remains a shareholder, vote his shares for the election of the other shareholder as a director of the corporation. Further, each shareholder shall use his voting power, either as a shareholder or director, to uphold the letter and the spirit of this agreement.

4. If a shareholder becomes incapacitated for a period longer than one year, or dies, the remaining shareholder shall have the option, for a period of 60 days after the expiration of one year, or after notice of death, to purchase his shares at a price to be determined by an appraisal. The appraiser shall be appointed by the remaining shareholder, and the incapacitated or deceased shareholder's legal representative. The appraiser shall have full discretion in the determination of the value of the shares and the remaining shareholder and the incapacitated or deceased shareholder's representative shall be bound by the appraiser's determination.

5. The life of each shareholder shall be insured for the pro rata benefit of the other shareholder in proportion to the shares they hold, for $250,000. Each shareholder agrees that to the extent that the proceeds of the policy are paid to him, he will exercise his option to purchase shares from the estate of the deceased shareholder.

6. The shareholders expressly agree that they will each retain sole interest in the shares that they respectively own.

7. The duration of this agreement shall be from the date of its execution until December 31, 1980, and thereafter it shall be renewed every two years unless one of the shareholders shall, at least 90 days in advance of such renewal date, give notice in writing to the other shareholder of his desire to terminate the agreement on such date.

8. No modification or waiver of any provision of this agreement shall be valid unless it is made in writing and signed by both shareholders, or a shareholder's legal representative.

IN WITNESS WHEREOF the parties hereto have executed this agreement the day and year above mentioned.

_____

_____

                                      _____

                                        _____

Confirmed and Agreed to:
    Texas, Inc.
      By _____

Attest:

_____, Secretary of Texas, Inc.

ative lack of experience and the absence of a liquor license would pose problems for the first few months. However, neither thought that the problems would be insurmountable.

## THE OPENING

Texas, Inc. opened its doors in June of 1976, and "it seemed as though we had nailed the market," said Mike. Customers were lined up four abreast into the parking lot on the first night. They rang up $1,800 in sales and gave away another $600 worth of food and beverages. But it was also a very chaotic night. A number of dinners went to the wrong patrons; and some meals were poorly cooked and sent back to the kitchen by customers. Around 9:00 P.M. one of the two new grills that they had purchased for the business caught fire.

On the second night the other grill caught fire, and they found out that they had purchased the wrong kind of equipment. The salesman who had sold them the grills had recommended that they purchase two units of a *surface* heating model. In making inquiries after the second fire, however, Mike found out that, for the amount of cooking they were doing on the grills, a *penetrating* heat model was required. Surface heating grills were meant for lower volumes and cooked food more slowly. Mike said, "We thought the salesman knew what he was talking about, and we followed his advice—he obviously didn't know what he was talking about." The cost of the grills was $5,000 each. Jim and Mike decided to keep the grills and cook the food more slowly, rather than disrupting operations while the grills were replaced.

John Moss, the new manager at Athens Cove, didn't seem to be handling his tasks very well either. According to Mike, "He didn't make any really bad decisions, but there were no good decisions. When something broke, he made the quickest and cheapest repair possible. He didn't keep the place very clean, which is always im-

portant in a franchise outlet. Basically, he didn't seem to care about how things were run." And according to Donna, he was not very good at handling people. "His attitude rubbed off on the employees—they weren't going to work hard if it didn't matter to him—and he also made a poor impression on customers."

The Athens Cove people were upset that John Moss wasn't keeping the place as clean as they expected. They also didn't like the fact that he was overweight, and wore a beard. They felt he conveyed a poor image of an Athens Cove manager. "He almost looked like a rumpled Sabastian Cabot with acne," said Donna. Mike wanted to let him go, but Jim felt that they should give him "a little more time to come around."

## "BUSINESS JUST DIED"

During the three months, from June through August, things did improve at Texas, although slowly. A lot of food was wasted during the first few months of operation, due to poorly cooked meals and spoilage. "The head chef was not very skilled," said Mike, "and as it turned out, he was an alcoholic." "None of the people in the kitchen were really qualified," said Donna "and what made it worse was that we didn't have a head in the kitchen who cared."

Gradually, Jim and Mike began to get the problems under control as they learned more about food preparation. The quality of the meals and service gradually improved. "During the first few weeks, when you asked people if they had enjoyed their meals, they said yes, but you could tell they hadn't," said Donna. "By the end of August, their answers seemed to be a little more genuine."

"Business was never as good as it had been in the first week," said Mike, "but it was fairly good right through Labor Day. But after Labor Day, business just died." As they tried to figure out what had happened, Mike said, "I think we got a reputation for bad service, and it caught up with us, just as we were getting things under control."

The situation worsened during the fall, and by early November, Jim's $15,000 contribution had been spent. Jim and Mike wondered how they could keep the business going until they could get things turned around. A large portion of Donna's stocks and bonds were used as collateral already, and she did not want to pledge any more of her assets. However, Jim felt that this was the only way out. He and Ellen were in heavy debt, while Mike and Donna still had some stocks that she could pledge on a new loan. He reasoned that Mike and Donna would be saving her investment (and the stocks and bonds Donna had pledged), and that the only alternative was bankruptcy for everyone.

Donna was adamant about "not throwing good money after bad," and resented the fact that Jim was pressing the issue so hard. She was especially resentful because she felt that Jim was the cause of all their problems. "He wouldn't agree to hire a professional manager," said Donna, "this whole mess is his fault. We knew everything except food, the physical product we were selling."

Jim became very bitter because he felt, in his words, that he was being put "through the ringer" again. At first Mike attempted to mediate between Jim and Donna. Said Mike, "I tried to keep everyone calm, so that we could find a way out. We finally received the liquor license during the second week of December, and I figured that this would be a cause for hope for everyone."

However, Donna remained convinced that she was about to lose all that she had pledged, which caused Mike and Donna's marriage to become very strained. "My marriage seemed like it was about to break up," said Mike, "and Donna was six months pregnant at this point. There was no way that I could take an unbiased position."

## "URGES TO KILL"

By the end of December, the firm had lost over $27,000 (see Exhibit 6). Texas Inc.'s accounts payable were more than $17,000 (see Exhibit 7), and many of its food bills were two months past due. By this time Jim was sure that Mike and Donna were waiting until he sold out before pledging her stocks on a new loan. During one angry meeting Jim told Mike and Donna, "You want me out of here, don't you!" The fight was carried to such extremes that the two couples would only talk through their lawyers. "We were honest behind each other's backs when it came to managing the affairs of the businesses," said Mike, "but face to face anything went. On several occasions, I actually had urges to kill Jim." At one meeting involving Jim and Ellen, Mike and Donna, and their lawyers, John Heagney apologized for not having urged them to make their relationship more formal.

Mike and Donna decided that they had three basic alternatives:

1. Drive everyone into bankruptcy by ruining Texas, Inc. "We contemplated this one," said Donna, "just for the sheer satisfaction it would give us."
2. Find a buyer for Texas, Inc. (but who would buy the firm in such shape?).
3. Buy Jim and Ellen out of Texas and try to turn things around (but what would they do about Dusty's and Athens Cove?).

# APPENDIX A: SUBCHAPTER S CORPORATIONS

One of the disadvantages of the corporate form is that the earnings of such a business are subject to double taxation—earnings are taxed once via the corporate income tax, and then again to the extent that net income is distributed as dividends to the stockholders of the company.

There is a way of preserving most of the benefits of corporateness while avoiding the burden of double taxation. Elimination of the corporate tax is possible by "Subchapter S election," if the corporation is eligible as a "small business corporation" under Subchapter S of the Internal Revenue Code. Under Subchapter S, no tax is paid at the corporate level, but all corporate income is taxable to the shareholders individually (based on each shareholder's proportionate share of net income), whether or not the income is distributed.

A corporation must meet the following requirements to be considered as a "small business corporation," and thus eligible for Subchapter S election.

1. It must have no more than 10 shareholders.
2. It may not have a shareholder as a person (other than an estate), who is not an individual.
3. It may not have a non-resident alien as a shareholder.
4. There may be no more than one class of shares.

*Source: Case and Materials on the Laws of Corporations,* by Harry G. Henn (St. Paul, Minn.: West Publishing Co., 1974). Pages 101, and 610–617.

As of 1974, 268,000 American Corporations had elected treatment as a Subchapter S Corporation.

# APPENDIX B Retail Trade: Eating and Drinking Places

| Item Description For Accounting Period 7/74 Through 6/75 | A Total | Size of Assets in Thousands of Dollars (000 omitted) | | | | | | | | | | |
|---|---|---|---|---|---|---|---|---|---|---|---|---|
| | | B Under 100 | C 100 to 250 | D 250 to 500 | E 500 to 1,000 | F 1000 to 5,000 | G 5,000 to 10,000 | H 10,000 to 25,000 | I 25,000 to 50,000 | J 50,000 to 100,000 | K 100,000 to 250,000 | L 250,000 and over |
| 1. Number of Establishments | 76601 | 56340 | 12923 | 5031 | 1554 | 618 | 58 | 40 | 14 | 11 | 12 | — |
| 2. Total receipts (in millions of dollars) | 28828.2 | 8874.4 | 5516.4 | 3737.2 | 1896.0 | 2389.8 | 729.3 | 1151.7 | 860.0 | 1037.5 | 2635.9 | — |
| **Selected Operating Factors in Percent of Net Sales** | | | | | | | | | | | | |
| 3. Cost of operations | 46.1 | 48.4 | 44.0 | 43.1 | 42.4 | 44.7 | 46.3 | 44.5 | 45.8 | 51.7 | 49.7 | — |
| 4. Compensation of officers | 3.5 | 5.4 | 4.1 | 4.1 | 3.2 | 2.3 | 1.2 | .9 | .5 | .4 | .3 | — |
| 5. Repairs | 1.2 | 1.2 | 1.3 | 1.4 | 1.3 | 1.2 | 1.2 | 1.2 | 1.1 | 1.1 | 1.1 | — |
| 6. Bad debts | .1 | .1 | — | .1 | .1 | .2 | .6 | .2 | .2 | .2 | .3 | — |
| 7. Rent on business property | 4.9 | 5.1 | 5.0 | 4.5 | 4.8 | 4.3 | 5.5 | 4.6 | 4.8 | 3.9 | 6.1 | — |
| 8. Taxes (and Federal tax) | 3.8 | 3.9 | 4.0 | 3.7 | 3.9 | 3.6 | 3.7 | 3.8 | 3.7 | 3.7 | 3.6 | — |
| 9. Interest | 1.3 | .6 | 1.2 | 1.7 | 2.1 | 1.8 | 2.2 | 1.2 | 1.7 | 2.0 | 2.2 | — |
| 10. Deprec/Deplet/Amortiz† | 2.8 | 2.1 | 2.9 | 3.0 | 3.4 | 3.1 | 3.6 | 3.2 | 3.8 | 3.2 | 3.2 | — |
| 11. Advertising | 1.7 | 1.3 | 2.1 | 1.8 | 2.1 | 1.8 | 1.9 | 2.5 | 1.6 | 1.9 | 1.6 | — |
| 12. Pensions & other benef plans | .4 | .2 | .4 | .5 | .5 | .6 | .6 | .8 | 1.1 | .5 | .6 | — |
| 13. Other expenses | 34.3 | 33.1 | 33.3 | 35.1 | 35.7 | 37.4 | 38.7 | 38.3 | 36.9 | 29.5 | 34.1 | — |
| 14. Net profit before tax | * | * | 1.6 | 1.0 | .5 | * | * | * | * | 1.8 | * | — |
| **Selected Financial Ratios (number of times ratio is to one)** | | | | | | | | | | | | |
| 15. Current ratio | 1.0 | .9 | .9 | .8 | .7 | .8 | 1.0 | .8 | 1.0 | .7 | 1.8 | — |
| 16. Quick ratio | .6 | .6 | .6 | .6 | .4 | .6 | .6 | .5 | .7 | .4 | 1.2 | — |
| 17. Net sls to net wkg capital | — | — | — | — | — | — | — | — | 193.9 | — | 8.1 | — |
| 18. Net sales to net worth | 7.5 | 24.4 | 9.7 | 8.3 | 6.7 | 7.0 | 4.9 | 4.1 | 3.6 | 3.6 | 2.9 | — |
| 19. Inventory turnover | 19.3 | 28.8 | 21.3 | 19.6 | 19.3 | 16.9 | 10.3 | 14.5 | 12.2 | 12.6 | 13.1 | — |
| 20. Total liab to net worth | 2.2 | 4.1 | 2.6 | 2.8 | 2.7 | 2.6 | 2.0 | 1.2 | 1.2 | 1.6 | 1.5 | — |
| **Selected Financial Factors in Percentages** | | | | | | | | | | | | |
| 21. Current liab to net worth | 90.9 | 171.8 | 103.1 | 122.0 | 113.0 | 114.8 | 72.4 | 63.9 | 57.0 | 65.9 | 44.9 | — |
| 22. Inventory to curr assets | 21.6 | 26.4 | 19.9 | 20.9 | 20.0 | 20.5 | 25.4 | 29.6 | 23.2 | 33.9 | 16.0 | — |
| 23. Net income to net worth | 9.2 | — | 22.1 | 16.5 | 9.7 | 9.4 | 1.9 | 4.6 | 3.5 | 6.7 | 7.6 | — |
| 24. Retained earn to net inc | 51.2 | — | 72.1 | 78.3 | 74.7 | 72.7 | 66.8 | 74.5 | -1.4 | 89.6 | 54.6 | — |

†Depreciation largest factor.
Source: Almanac of Business and Industrial Financial Ratios.

# 6

# VIDEOSHOP— MARK-TELE, INC.

## Michael P. Mokwa
## Karl Gustafson

*Arizona State University*

Cable television began to spread rapidly across the United States during the late 1970s. It was promoted to subscribers predominantly as an entertainment media that would provide an expanded choice of high-quality television programming.

Some advertising and marketing experts perceived cable television differently. They saw it as opening a revolutionary new dimension in commercial communications. In the short run, cable television would generate new advertising and direct marketing opportunities. As telecommunication technology improved in the long run, cable television could become a direct threat to conventional shopping systems. Most experts, however, forecasted that significant changes in consumer shopping patterns were at least a decade or two away. Mr. Richard Johnson disagreed. He was the managing director of Mark-Tele, Inc., one of the most innovative and aggressive cable television companies.

During the fall of 1981, Mr. Johnson began to prepare a proposal for presentation to his board of directors at their forthcoming winter meeting. The proposal would suggest that Mark-Tele develop several new television channels. These channels would be unconventional. Most cable channels involved either an entertainment, educational, or public information format.

mat. The proposed new channels would involve innovative commercial formats using telecommunications technology that would allow organizations to market and sell directly to consumers in their own homes. A new marketplace would be created. Mr. Johnson named this concept "VideoShop."

## THE NEW VENTURE

Several months earlier, Mr. Johnson had created a new ventures task force. The mission of this task force was to generate and study novel programming formats that could be developed into new cable channels in the near term, and possibly into new networks in the long run. These new channels would be used by Mark-Tele to generate additional revenues, to increase its subscription base, and to allocate operating costs more effectively.

The current capacity of the Mark-Tele cable system was fifty-two different channels, but only thirty-one were in use. When Mark-Tele began operations, they had only twelve channels but had grown steadily. Costs had been relatively constant regardless of the number of channels that Mark-Tele operated. Thus, Mr. Johnson perceived Mark-Tele's cost structure as highly fixed, and he foresaw the development of new channels as a means of distributing these costs. Mr. Johnson expected that new channels would draw new subscribers, that subscription rates could be raised as more channels were added, and that subscription revenue could grow faster than corresponding operating costs.

The new ventures task force was carefully selected. It included the operations and sales managers from Mark-Tele, two product development specialists form Mark-Tele's parent company, and a consultant from the communications industry. An excerpt of their report to Mr. Johnson is presented in the Appendix.

The task force recommended that Mark-Tele should develop several new cable channels using the television as the medium for shopping. Each Mark-Tele subscriber could "tune into" these shopping channels. The subscriber could control and execute an entire shopping experience in the home. Products and services could be purchased directly, or the subscriber could gather specific information about a particular product or service and competitive offerings before making an important buying decision. The task force report indicated that eleven different product or service lines appeared viable for the new shopping concept.

Mr. Johnson was thrilled with the new venture idea and the task force report. He wanted to develop and implement the concept quickly. First, he selected a distinctive name for the venture, identifying it as VideoShop. Next, he met informally with some prospective salespeople, distributors, and retailers from different product and service fields. Most of these meetings were casual lunches or dinners. Mr. Johnson sensed some strong, but very cautious interest and support from some prospective suppliers. Then, he carefully reviewed and screened the list of product and service lines that had been proposed in the task force report.

Mr. Johnson felt that each of the proposed lines was feasible, but he wanted to focus his efforts on those products and services (a) that appeared to be easiest and most profitable to implement in the near term, and (b) that appeared to have the strongest interest among the prospective suppliers with whom he had met. Five lines were selected for development:

1. Catalog sales by regional and national retailers.
2. Ticket reservations for concerts, plays, and sporting events, as well as reservations at local restaurants.

3. Airline ticket reservations and vacation planning.
4. A multiple-listing service for real estate companies to display homes and commercial property that were for sale in the area or possibly from areas across the country.
5. Grocery products.

Mr. Johnson expected that he could find outstanding firms from each product or service field to participate in the VideoShop venture under terms that Mark-Tele would set forth. He thought the costs to each firm would be small when compared with the benefits of newly accessible markets.

## MARK-TELE'S BACKGROUND

Mark-Tele was founded in 1977, as a wholly owned subsidiary of Intertronics, Inc., a large corporation based in New York City. Intertronics was founded in 1973 as a joint venture among three well-respected, multinational firms. One firm was primarily in the information processing industry. Another was a publishing and broadcasting conglomerate, and the third was a high-technology producer in electronics. The mission of Intertronics was to design, develop, and implement innovative, applied telecommunications systems for domestic consumer markets. Intertronics received financial support and full technological cooperation from its parent companies, but was operated as an autonomous venture. Intertronics managed each of its subsidiaries using the same orientation.

During 1978, Mark-Tele bid to install cable television systems in several large metropolitan areas in the United States. Late that year, Mark-Tele was granted the right to install a cable television system in a large growing southwestern metropolitan area. Mark-Tele's management was excited to begin operations and to enter this particular area.

The area had more than a sufficient number of households to profitably support a cable television company according to industry standards. More importantly, the population was growing rapidly. National and international companies were locating headquarters or building large manufacturing facilities in the area. The growth of industry meant a tremendous increase in the number of families relocating into the area. This growth was projected to continue for at least the next fifteen years, thus representing a very attractive cable market for Mark-Tele. Intertronics would use Mark-Tele's location as the test site for a new type of cable television technology. The traditional type of cable used in cable television systems was a "one-way" cable because a "signal" could be directed only from the cable television company *to* the individual households attached to the service.

Recently, Intertronics had developed a "two-way" cable that was capable of transmitting and receiving signals both from the cable television company and from individual households connected to the system. As such, a home could send signals *back* to the cable television company. Two-way cable communication processes were used in a few other areas of the country, but these cable systems required the use of a telephone line along with the one-way cable. The cost of the new two-way cable was nearly four times the cost of the one-way cable. Because Mark-Tele was a test site, they and their subscribers received the cable system at a substantially reduced cost.

To implement the two-way cable, Mark-Tele installed an interactive device to the television set of each of its subscribers. These devices facilitated communication between the Mark-Tele building and individual homes. The interactive devices resembled a small desk-top electronic calculator. These devices were expensive to install, but Intertronics absorbed most

**EXHIBIT 1**　VideoShop—Mark-Tele, Inc.
Income Statement Mark-Tele, Inc. Fiscal Years Ending December 31, 1979 and 1980

| | 1979* | 1980** |
|---|---|---|
| **Revenues** | | |
| Subscription revenue | $4,560,000 | $6,600,000 |
| Pay service revenue | 4,104,000 | 5,400,000 |
| Total Revenue | $8,664,000 | $12,000,000 |
| **Expenses** | | |
| Operation expense (includes salaries) | $3,852,000 | $5,248,000 |
| Sales expensed | 1,913,400 | 2,610,300 |
| Interest expense | 136,200 | 136,200 |
| Depreciation expense | 74,800 | 74,800 |
| Rent expense | 46,000 | 46,000 |
| Equipment maintenance expense | 32,500 | 34,700 |
| Total Expense | $6,054,900 | $8,150,000 |
| Gross Profit | $2,609,100 | $3,850,000 |
| Taxes @ 47% | $1,226,277 | $1,848,000 |
| Net profit | $1,382,823 | $2,002,000 |

*Based upon subscriptions of 38,000 homes with a subscription rate of $10.00 per month per home, and average home "pay service" of $9.00 per month per home.
**Based upon total subscriptions of 50,000 homes with a subscription rate of $11.00 per month per home, and average home "pay service" of $9.00 per month per home.

of the installation cost. The remaining cost was reflected in slightly higher-than-average monthly subscription charges paid by subscribers. The subscription charge for basic cable services from Mark-Tele was $11 per month. The comparable rate that Mark-Tele would charge for one-way cable would be $8.50 per month.

Mark-Tele's first year of operations concluded with 5,000 subscribers and a small negative net operating profit. In the following year, Mark-Tele subscriptions increased to 38,000, generating a net profit of almost 1.4 million dollars. In 1980, Mark-Tele continued to aggressively attract more subscribers, reaching 50,000 total. Net profit increased to exceed 2 million dollars. Financial statements for 1979 and 1980 are presented in Exhibit 1.

Research by Mark-Tele suggested that the potential number of homes for the cable network in their market area exceeded 400,000 over the next five years. In ten years, the market potential was forecasted to be nearly 750,000 homes. A demographic profile of current subscribers is presented in Exhibit 2.

Mark-Tele offered many different channel formats. These channels provided a wide variety of programming for virtually any type of viewer. Several of the channels were "pay tele-

---

**EXHIBIT 2**     VideoShop—Mark-Tele, Inc.
1980 Demographic Analysis of Mark-Tele Subscribers*

| Family Size | Age of Paying Subscriber |
|---|---|
| 1—17.6% | 18–25—22.4% |
| 2—22.8 | 26–35—19.2 |
| 3—10.8 | 36–45—19.6 |
| 4—19.3 | 46–55—17.7 |
| 5—15.1 | 56–65— 7.1 |
| 6— 5.8 | 66–75— 8.3 |
| 7+—8.6 | 76+ — 5.7 |
| **Family Income** | **Residency** |
| $0K– $8K— 1.3% | Home owners—71.6% |
| $ 9K–$18K—15.7 | Renters—28.4% |
| $19K–$28K—18.3 | |
| $29K–$35K—17.5 | |
| $36K–$45K—19.6 | |
| $46K–$59K—12.7 | |
| $60,000+ —14.9 | |
| **Number of Hours Home Television Active per Week** | **Number of Years of Education of Paying Subscribers** |
| 0 – 7— 2.5% | 0 – 8— 1.4% |
| 8 –14—15.1 | 9 –11—22.5 |
| 15–21—17.2 | 12– —21.8 |
| 22–28—40.7 | 13–15—26.3 |
| 29–35—20.8 | 16+ years—28.0 |
| 36+ hours—3.7 | |

*Based upon 50,000 subscribers.

**EXHIBIT 3**  VideoShop—Mark-Tele, Inc. Channel Allocation Schedule

| Cable Channel Number | Designated Programming/Service |
|:---:|:---|
| 1 | Mark-Tele Channel Listing* |
| 2 | Program Guide* |
| 3 | Local Transit Schedule* |
| 4 | Classified Ads and Yard Sales* |
| 5 | Weather Radar and Time* |
| 6 | Dow Jones Cable News* |
| 7 | Reserved for Future Use |
| 8** | Home Box Office* |
| 9** | Showtime* |
| 10** | The Movie Channel* |
| 11** | Golden Oldies Channel* |
| 12 | Reserved for Future Use |
| 13 | Reserved for Future Use |
| 14 | Cable News Network* |
| 15 | Reserved for Future Use |
| 16 | UPI News Scan* |
| 17 | Government Access* |
| 18 | Music Television* |
| 19** | Stereo Rock Concert* |
| 20 | Educational Access* |
| 21 | Educational Access: New York University* |
| 22 | Proposed Educational Access |
| 23 | Proposed Interactive Channel for Lease |
| 24 | Proposed Interactive Channel for Lease |
| 25 | Proposed Interactive Channel for Lease |
| 26 | VideoShop: *Retail Sales Channel* |
| 27 | VideoShop: *Entertainment Tickets and Restaurants* |
| 28 | VideoShop: *Grocery Products* |
| 29 | VideoShop: Reserved |
| 30 | VideoShop: Reserved |
| 31 | USA Network* |
| 32 | WTBS, Atlanta, Channel 17* |
| 33 | WOR, New York, Channel 9* |
| 34 | K///, Local ABC Affiliate |
| 35 | Christian Broadcasting Network* |
| 36 | ESPN (Sports) Network* |
| 37 | K///, Local Station, Channel 15* |
| 38 | K///, Local NBC Affiliate, Channel 8* |
| 39 | K///, Local CBS Affiliate, Channel 11* |
| 40 | Proposed Channel for Lease |

*(continued)*

**EXHIBIT 3** VideoShop—Mark-Tele, Inc. Channel Allocation Schedule (*continued*)

| Cable Channel Number | Designated Programming/Service |
|---|---|
| 41 | Concert Connection* |
| 42 | WGN, Chicago, Channel 9* |
| 43 | Public Access: Cultural Bulletin Board* |
| 44** | Proposed Games Channel |
| 45 | Public Access: Library Information* |
| 46 | Proposed Public Access |
| 47 | Public Broadcasting System |
| 48 | Reserved for Future Banking Transactions |
| 49 | VideoShop: *Airline Tickets and Travel* |
| 50 | VideoShop: *Real Estate Showcase* |
| 51 | Reserved for Future Use |
| 52 | Reserved for Future Use |

*Active channel.

**Optional pay service.

vision." For these, a household would pay an additional charge beyond the basic monthly rate. Pay television services were very successful. The revenue from pay services nearly matched basic subscription revenue for Mark-Tele in 1980. A schedule for the allocation of Mark-Tele's fifty-two channel capacity is presented in Exhibit 3. Both current and prospective channels are listed.

## CABLE TELEVISION TECHNOLOGY

Cable television became increasingly popular during the 1970s. This can be attributed largely to significant advances in computer and communications technologies, as well as regulatory and legal changes, in the telecommunications industry.

The Mark-Tele cable television system was controlled by a sophisticated configuration of minicomputers with high-speed communications between each processor. Three computers, each used for a different task, insured that viewers would have access to the cable network at all times.

The main computer transmitted cable signals to each individual home using the two-way cable lines. The second computer's function was to back up the main computer in the event that a system failure might occur. The second computer would be a vital element of the VideoShop system because it could be used as an update system for suppliers to amend information regarding their products or services. This computer also could be used to transmit the orders or reservations placed by "shopping" subscribers directly to prospective suppliers. The third computer functioned as another back up, if system failures would occur simultaneously to the main computers. A very sophisticated software application integrating the communication network and operating system had been developed to assure ninety-nine percent uptime for the cable system. A diagram sketching the Mark-Tele cable system is presented in Exhibit 4.

The cable system incorporated two different types of storage devices. The first type of storage disk (a magnetic disk) was used to store data, such as billing information about a par-

**EXHIBIT 4**

VIDEOSHOP-MARK-TELE, INC.
Mark-Tele Two way Cable System

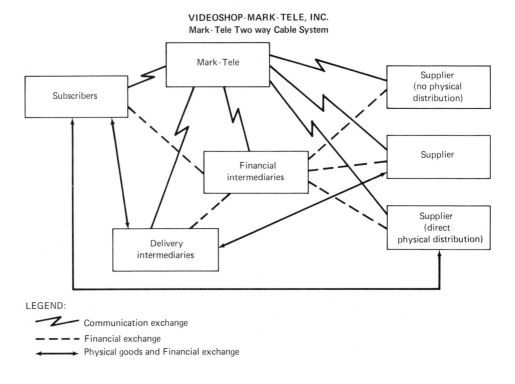

LEGEND:

⟋⟋ Communication exchange

– – – – Financial exchange

◄——————► Physical goods and Financial exchange

ticular subscriber. The second type of disk involved an innovative technology that could be used extensively by the VideoShop system. The disk, called a "video disk unit," was capable of storing images or pictures like a movie camera. VideoShop suppliers could store images of their products and services on these disks so that subscribers to the cable system could access the images at any time. Only through the use of the new two-way cable developed by Intertronics would it be possible to incorporate the video disk units (VDU) into the cable network. The two-way cable allowed signals to travel from the main computer to an individual television, and from the television back to the main computer.

Two-way communication was possible through the use of the interactive indexing device attached to each subscriber's television. This indexing device was a small box, about the size of a cigar box. It contained special electronics allowing the device to transmit data back to

the main computer. On top of the indexing device, there were twelve keys simply called the keypad. An individual subscriber could use the keypad to call up "menus," sort through a menu, and send data back to the main computer. A menu is a computer term used to describe listings of general categories from which additional information can be drawn.

Using a prospective VideoShop example, a menu for a channel containing airline information could first indicate to a viewer the different airlines from which to choose. The viewer could then push the key on the keypad that corresponds to the airline that he or she was interested in using. The next menu could show all the different cities to which the chosen airline flies. The viewer then could push the key on the keypad that corresponds to the city to which he or she wishes to travel. The following screen could provide the flight numbers and times during which flights are available. From the information on that screen, the user could make a reservation which would be transmitted to the airline's computer through the Mark-Tele computer. Finally, the reservation would be logged, confirmed, and ticket(s) mailed to the viewer. The entire transaction would take only a few minutes to execute. The shopper would control the entire experience in the home environment. It would be simple and efficient.

## VIDEOSHOP CHANNELS

Mr. Johnson believed that the most significant factors that would affect the successful acceptance of VideoShop by consumers were (a) the quality of the picture viewed by the subscribers; (b) the accuracy of the information provided by suppliers to shoppers; (c) the convenience and ease of using the system to shop; (d) the technical reliability of the system; and (e) the delivery, billing, and return policies of suppliers. Mr. Johnson felt strongly that control over suppliers would be vital to assure the success of VideoShop. He thought that Mark-Tele should

form a small consumer satisfaction department to conduct VideoShop consumer studies, to review the VideoShop policies and operations of all involved suppliers, and to resolve all consumer problems and complaints.

Mr. Johnson felt that the five shopping channels that he had selected from the list generated by the task force would work well given the nature of the success factors that he perceived to be important. He prepared a brief description for each of the prospective shopping channels and a pro forma income statement. He would use these to build his presentation for the forthcoming board meeting and to develop a prospectus to sell the VideoShop concept to suppliers. The pro forma statement is presented in Exhibit 5.

### The Catalog Sales Channel(s)

National and regional retailers could use the VideoShop system to sell and promote their entire merchandise lines including their most current items and prices. Shoppers would have

---

**EXHIBIT 5** VideoShop—Mark-Tele, Inc. Pro Forma Income Statement VideoShop Operation*

| | |
|---|---:|
| **Revenue** | |
| Catalog Purchase Channel | $300,000 |
| Airline Reservation Channel | 400,000 |
| Ticket Sales and Restaurant Channel | 150,000 |
| Multiple-Listing Service Channel | 36,000 |
| Total Revenue | $886,000 |
| **Expenses** | |
| Salaries | $240,000 |
| Administrative Expense | 52,000 |
| Communication Expense (Telephone Lines) | 19,200 |
| Depreciation Expense | 15,700 |
| Interest Expense | 13,820 |
| Equipment Maintenance | 4,200 |
| Total Expenses | $344,920 |
| Contribution | $541,080 |

*Based upon 50,000 subscription base and task force projections.

the opportunity to view merchandise on the television screen in their own home, avoiding the inconvenience of a shopping trip or the boredom of thumbing through a catalog book. Information about products and prices could be presented in a format similar to catalog books, or innovative action formats could be developed to simulate a store environment or create some novel context.

Retailers would be responsible for developing appropriate video disk units and keeping information current. Mark-Tele could provide a consulting service to help suppliers produce effective video disks. Mark-Tele could also reserve the right to reject any material that was felt to be inappropriate. However, Mark-Tele would attempt to be open-minded. For example, products that consumers find embarrassing to purchase at a store could be considered a prime prospect for Video-Shop, if presentations were tasteful.

A shopper could use the interactive indexing device to direct and control an entire shopping experience. This could involve viewing information about product features and prices from one retailer, and then quickly switching to another retailer's presentation for comparative information. In addition, a shopper desiring more extensive information could access a brief demonstration or informative advertisement about a product. After selecting a product, the interactive device could transmit the order through Mark-Tele's computing system directly to the retailer's processing system. The retailer could present alternative payment programs and specific delivery schedules or instructions. The shopper could charge purchases using national or store credit cards, and could pick up the merchandise directly (but conveniently) or could have it delivered.

Mark-Tele could charge each retailer a service fee based upon a fixed percentage of shoppers' invoice values (before taxes). Individual retailers could be billed monthly and various payment programs could be formulated. The new ventures task force estimated that an av-

erage home would purchase a minimum of $300 worth of retail merchandise annually through VideoShop. They proposed a service charge rate of 2%. Mark-Tele could also generate revenue selling video consulting services to the suppliers.

This shopping and marketing scenario could be the prototype for all the VideoShop channels. Adaptations for different product or service lines and shopping patterns would be relatively easy to implement.

**Ticket Sales and Restaurant Reservation Channel**

VideoShop could provide detailed information concerning local entertainment alternatives to subscribers. Entertainment organizations could present exciting promotional spots using the video disk technology and sell tickets directly to VideoShop subscribers.

Entertainment shoppers could use video menus to select a particular entertainment form such as movies, theater, or sporting events. On another menu, they could view all the relevant alternative events, and then access specific promotional spots about events which interested them. These spots could blend information about performance schedules and locations with features about or highlights of the event. The shopper could select an event and a specific performance, then purchase tickets. Tickets could be sold using conventional diagrams of seating arrangements, innovative graphic formats, or the shopper could actually be presented with the view from a specific seat or area of seating using the video disk technology. When tickets were purchased, these could be paid for using credit cards at the time of purchase, or payment could be mailed or made at the time of the event. Likewise, tickets could be mailed or picked up.

Another dimension of this channel could be a restaurant promotion and reservation feature. Restaurant menus and promotional spots could be made accessible for diners. Once diners have chosen a particular restaurant using the memo and spots, they could make a reservation and even select a specific table (if the restaurant developed, as part of its VideoShop system, a seating arrangement routine similar to that of the entertainment organizations).

All VideoShop ticket purchases and reservations could be transmitted directly from the shopper's home through Mark-Tele computers to the restaurant or ticket outlet. Most restaurants and small entertainment organizations would have to purchase or lease a small "intelligence" computing terminal to receive reservations or ticket orders and to keep information updated. Intertronics could supply these.

The task force felt that this channel could generate at least $150,000 revenue per year given the current subscriber base. They recommended a $25 per month minimum charge to restaurants and a 50¢ service fee per ticket reservation. They were unsure of a fee schedule for entertainment organizations that would only promote events and would not be selling tickets directly through VideoShop. However, they thought that rates similar to commercial advertising rates would be appropriate.

### Airline Ticket Sales and Travel Accommodations Channel

Discussions with the task force concluded that an airline ticket sales channel could be the easiest for Mark-Tele to implement and operate in the short run, and also could be most lucrative financially. Projected revenue for the first year of operating this channel was $400,000 based upon a very conservative usage rate and an extremely competitive pricing policy.

This channel could allow subscribers to make airline reservations, purchase their tickets, and select travel accommodations using the same fundamental interactive shopping procedures as other VideoShop channels. Shoppers could avoid the aggravating inconveniences of current airline reservation systems, and could quickly do comparative shopping which current systems have inhibited. Research has shown that comparative shopping for airline fares often can save hundreds of dollars. Once a flight has

been selected, the subscriber also could make hotel or motel reservations. VideoShop could allow hotels and motels to visually present rooms and surroundings and to promote themselves to *all* travelers.

Perhaps the most important characteristic of this channel could be the potential ease of implementation, once cooperation was secured from the airlines. The format and basic system used within the airlines industry to transmit, display and process schedules, fares, and ticket information appeared to be compatible with the Mark-Tele system. Mark-Tele computers and cable lines could be used to link shoppers directly with airline ticket reservation systems, bypassing reservationists and travel agents. Subscribers could select itineraries, then secure reservations and pay using major credit cards. Tickets could be mailed or picked up at airport ticket counters or other service locations.

Mark-Tele could record each ticket purchase and charge the appropriate airline a fixed fee of $4.00 per ticket. This rate was half of the $8.00 rate charged by most travel agents. The task force believed that a minimum average of two tickets would be purchased by each subscribing household per year. Revenue estimates were not made for the travel accommodations feature of this channel.

### Multiple Listing Service Channel

A few large local realtors expressed strong interest in the VideoShop concept. Traditional promotional tools used to stimulate buyers' interest and assist them make decisions about what properties to see in person included classified newspaper ads, newspaper supplements, brochures, "for sale" signs, the multiple-listing catalog, and photographs of properties posted on an agency's wall. Most realtors and buyers found these boring. More importantly, these simply did not present most properties effectively. A frequent complaint among realtors and buyers was the high cost in time and dollars wasted traveling to and viewing personally properties that were not represented well in a promotion or informational item. VideoShop could provide an exciting and effective method for presenting realty.

While this VideoShop channel could be accessed by any subscriber, the channel would open a new commercial consumer market for Mark-Tele cable subscriptions—the realty agencies. Many agencies had a television on premise to entertain clients and their children or to provide a means "to catch the news" when business was slow. Some agencies already had purchased cable service from Mark-Tele.

A general issue was raised by the task force whether to charge a commercial subscriber different fees than a residential subscriber. A more specific issue regarding this channel was whether to limit access to realty agencies and others willing to pay an additional fee for it, or to open it for public access. The task force recommended open access and suggested that a minimum of thirty realty agencies would need to participate. Each could be charged a monthly fee of $100 or an annual fee of $1,000. The realtor would be responsible for producing and maintaining high-quality video disks with accurate and updated information. Mark-Tele could provide technical assistance and would monitor this channel carefully.

### Grocery Products Channel

One of the most exciting prospects for VideoShop could be a grocery products channel. It was the most interesting but difficult channel for which to design a format.

Grocery products are purchased very frequently, and everyone must buy. Consumers have tended to develop relatively consistent grocery shopping patterns. Expenditures on grocery items have been swelling. Many consumers find going shopping to be tedious, laborious, and inconvenient. Others such as people with handicaps or shut-in simply cannot get to stores or cannot shop freely and comfortably in modern superstores. Likewise, groceries producers, wholesalers, and retailers have been threatened by escalating cost structures that reduce their margins substantially.

A VideoShop grocery channel, thus, could provide consumers with convenience, comfort, low shopping risks, and potential savings. For suppliers, it could generate increased control over operations and costs and higher profits. However, this VideoShop channel directly would attack an expensive, firmly established distribution network and basic, traditional patterns of shopping. Strong resistance from many consumers could be anticipated, and suppliers not involved in the venture could be expected to retaliate competitively. Also, there could be critical barriers to providing shoppers a total assortment of grocery products including frozen and "fresh" items and to implementing a cost/effective delivery service or pickup procedure. Undoubtedly, these "bugs" could be worked out. The recommendation for this channel was to maintain its high priority as a channel to develop in the near term, but initially and quickly to invest funds in more design and research before contacting any specific prospective suppliers.

### CONCLUSION—A TIME FOR REFLECTION AND . . . OR ACTION

One more time, Mr. Johnson critically reviewed the task force report and his brief descriptions of prospective VideoShop channels. He felt simultaneously excitement, enthusiasm, and some frustration. He and the task force had worked hard and creatively to formulate the idea of VideoShop. They thought that most technological barriers could be overcome, and they projected a very favorable cost structure. Definitely, VideoShop was a concept whose time had arrived! Mark-Tele's board, composed largely of Intertronics personnel, would have to be convinced.

Mark-Tele was a small company with only a few people and tight resources. It already was a high-investment and high-risk experimental venture receiving considerable financial support and subsidy from Intertronics. Would Intertronics feel that VideoShop was an extension of the Mark-Tele experiment or a contamination of it? Could the board be convinced to provide more resources and assistance, and what would they expect in return?

If VideoShop received approval and support from the board, Mr. Johnson was not exactly sure in which direction to proceed. While he had identified the primary prospective channels, which specific channel or channels should be developed first? What would be the operational design for a channel, and what type of marketing program would be needed to maximize market awareness and shopper adoption?

Mr. Johnson was also concerned that some of his assumptions and some of those of the task force might be too optimistic, particularly those concerning the costs to suppliers. The task force had recommended that prospective suppliers should incur most of the start-up and maintenance expenses, and the risks. Yet, it appeared that Mark-Tele would skim the VideoShop revenues without much direct cost or risk. Would suppliers accept Mark-Tele's conditions for operations? The entire supply issue would require significant attention. Which specific suppliers would contribute most to VideoShop? Which suppliers would work best with Mark-Tele, and what type of relationships would evolve? How would a marketing program be formulated to reach prospective suppliers?

Suddenly, Mr. Johnson realized that he was vascillating. If Mark-Tele didn't implement VideoShop soon, someone would. VideoShop was a great idea. Mr. Johnson simply lacked the strategic plan that he could use to convince the board and to market VideoShop to suppliers and shoppers.

# APPENDIX: NEW VENTURE TASK FORCE REPORT PROPOSING A TELECOMMUNICATIONS SHOPPING SYSTEM*

We recommend that Mark-Tele design and implement a telecommunication shopping (TCS) system immediately. This proposed new venture appears to be a natural extension of Mark-Tele's experimental mission and an excellent application of Mark-Tele's distinctive technological capabilities in the telecommunications field.

A TCS system would allow a Mark-Tele subscriber to become an active shopper and buyer in the privacy of the home using only the television. Facilitated by Mark-Tele's sophisticated communications and computing technologies, a TCS system subscriber would be able to view and buy a large variety of products and services that conventionally would have required the shopper to leave the home and travel to view and purchase. A TCS system would also serve the suppliers of many different products and services with an opportunity to break away from costly traditional market channels and to inexpensively expand their market coverage and increase sales substantially.

For Mark-Tele, a TCS system would increase revenues, diversify its revenue base, and distribute its high fixed costs efficiently. A TCS system could be used as a promotional tool to build and maintain Mark-Tele's local subscription base. Current subscription rates could be

*This is an abridged version of the committee's report. The authors thank Ms. Sherri Katz for her contribution to this report.

raised with the addition of the TCS system, or an additional fee could be charged to subscribers who desire to participate in the TCS system. Suppliers and shopping subscribers would also be charged for services that Mark-Tele would provide in the development and operation of the TCS system. In the longer run, Mark-Tele could potentially develop TCS networks that could be sold to other cable systems. Clearly, early entry into the TCS field would be lucrative financially for Mark-Tele.

In the remainder of this report, we will discuss (1) significant environmental factors that influence the TCS market; (2) a general strategy for targeting the TCS system; (3) prospective product and service offerings; and (4) developmental issues for promoting the TCS system.

## THE ENVIRONMENT OF TCS

Economic, technological, legal and regulatory, and social trends are emerging in support of a TCS system.

Increased consumer spending is predicted to continue, but gains for retailers will be restricted by inflationary pressures. There will be a slower pace of store expansion during the 1980s. Many of the major metropolitan areas are overbuilt with retail space, and developers often are experiencing difficulty obtaining sites and financing. Retailers similarly are experiencing rising rents. Sales growth at many shopping centers has fallen due to slow growth of suburban communities and shrinking distances that consumers are willing to travel to shop as gasoline prices continue to advance.

Retailers are attempting to boost productivity, consolidate store space, and cut costs to improve returns. Inflation has increased operating costs more rapidly than sales during the last ten years. Many retailers have been attracted to discount pricing policies. The catalog showroom has become one of the fastest-growing segments of discount merchandising featuring national-brand products at discount prices while operating on lower overhead than department stores.

Considering sociocultural trends, women are continuing to enter the work force, thus having less time to engage in shopping for staples, as well as for discretionary purchases. Greater emphasis on recreational activities continues, and individuals are reluctant to sacrifice leisure time to shop in stores. Convenience is emerging as a high priority.

Consumers are emphasizing their self-identity. As such, consumers are demanding more individuality in goods and services, often desiring distinctive products that individual stores may not be able to afford to inventory and display. Definitely, there has been more intense consumer preferences for specialty items and services difficult to find in the Mark-Tele market area.

An increase in the number of single-parent and single-person households has led to increased in-home shopping. Nonstore innovations such as pay-by-phone, specialty mail-order catalogs, and toll-free phone ordering have become increasingly popular. Catalog shopping currently offers a full line of merchandise together with prices and features that permit a consumer to comparison shop at home without having to spend time inefficiently searching for products in crowded stores, waiting for sales help, or at times being annoyed by overzealous clerks.

In addition, the increasing age of the population, proliferation of retirement communities, and declining mobility of individuals in their later years make catalog shopping very attractive.

There are significant technological advances that will influence the TCS system. In the past, alphanumerics and graphics but not still or moving "pictures" could be retrieved from a data bank and displayed on a television screen; however, Intertronics' innovative technologies have advanced moving picture capabilities. This new technology has permitted the consumer to control the timing, sequence, and content of information through the use of the keypad. As such, the convenience of purchasing on impulse without need for either a telephone or advance credit arrangements is viable. Purchases can be charged automatically to a bank or credit card account.

Development of videodiscs and video cassettes, which to date have been used by viewers to record television programs, have significant promise for advertising and catalog media. Potential exists for suppliers to mail lower-cost video catalogs on a complimentary basis or in lieu of printed direct-mail offerings.

Consumers are being exposed to and are accepting complex technical items such as videotape recorders, home computers, and debit cards for use with automatic teller machines. Home computers and the development of "videotex," the generic term for home information-retrieval systems, will provide functions compatible with those of the TCS system. Many consumers will easily develop the technical skills and sophistication needed to actively participate in the TCS system.

The political-legal context is confusing. The Federal Communications Commission has decided that cable franchising is mainly the province of local jurisdictions. All cable companies must interact with local governments to obtain and maintain authority to operate. While Mark-Tele has secured exclusive rights in their metropolitan area, changes in federal and local policy must be monitored, and good rapport with local leaders should be cultivated continuously.

The TCS venture raises questions concerning supplier and financial contractual arrangements. The antitrust implications of arrangements with some large institutions should be studied in more detail on a case-by-case basis. Moreover, movement into the retail sector by Mark-Tele through the TCS system will mean closer scrutiny by federal and local consumer protection agencies such as the Federal Trade Commission and Consumer Product Safety Commission. Finally, Mark-Tele will need to carefully consider protection of the privacy of personal, financial, and transactional data about subscribers of the TCS system. Controls must be established to prevent unauthorized access to information in the system data banks and to guard against unauthorized purchasing.

## THE GENERAL COMPETITIVE CONTEXT

Industry observers clearly are divided when projecting the evolution of electronic shopping and its acceptance by both consumers and the industry. Consumers appear interested in the potential convenience, extended selections, fuel economies, discount prices, and time savings offered by the concept of shopping at home. Furthermore, at least ten thousand firms have expressed interest in the concept of electronic shopping. Currently, all forms of nonstore retailing are growing rapidly, and continued growth is forecasted. Major developments in nonstore retailing will be reviewed.

### Mail-order Catalogs

General department store merchandisers, catalog showrooms, and specialty houses periodically mail catalogs to targeted groups of consumers. An average mail-order house distributes from six to twenty catalog issues yearly at a cost often approaching two dollars each. Circulations range from about one hundred thousand to over a million for each mailing. The results have been outstanding. Over $26 billion was spent by consumers on mail-order items in 1978—an increase of $12 billion in three years. By comparison, in-store retailing sales grew at a rate less than half of the mail-order rate. Mail-order firms' after-tax profits averaged seven percent during this period.

Specialty firms such as L. L. Bean, Dallas' Horchow Collection, Talbot's of Massachusetts, and Hammacher-Schlemmer of New York have become more prominent in the field. Specialty-oriented catalogs are accounting for seventy-five percent of total mail-order sales, and mail-order catalogs currently contribute fifteen percent of the total volume of Christmas season sales.

Telephone and mail generated orders received by traditional store retailers such as Bloomingdales, Penneys, and Sears are increasing three to five times faster than in-store sales. Sears found that 9.1 percent of its sales came from outside catalogs in 1977 and an additional 11.4 percent from catalog counters in the stores. Montgomery Ward derived 13 percent of its sales from catalogs.

In-flight shopping catalogs used by major airlines are additional evidence of the increasing popularity of nonstore shopping. Master Card, American Express, and Visa have increased their direct mail offerings to their credit card holders and are expanding their assortments of merchandise.

### The Catalog Showrooms

The catalog showroom is one of the fastest growing fields of retailing. Catalogs are used to promote and feature jewelry, housewares, appliances, sporting goods, and toys at discount prices. Customers visit the showroom to inspect merchandise and to make purchases. Analysts suggest that eighty-five percent of sales are generated by the catalogs and the remainder by test selling products promoted on the showroom floor. Sales for 1980 are estimated to be $7.8 billion, an increase of eleven percent from 1979. Forecasts for 1981 suggest a twenty percent gain in sales revenue. The number of showrooms across the country is nearly 2,000.

### Non-interactive Shopping Using the Cable

Comp-U-Card of Stamford, Connecticut, is a seven-year-old telephone merchandising firm. For an annual fee of $18, it offers members a discount on a broad line of durable goods. Members shop around familiarizing themselves with products and prices. Then, they call Comp-U-Card toll-free for specific information about an item's availability and price. If a purchase decision is made, the consumer provides membership and credit card numbers to an operator, and the merchandise is prepared for delivery. An experimental project has been proposed in which Comp-U-Card would use cable systems and satellite transmission to present product and price information to its subscribers. A transmitted schedule would alert subscribers to the time when particular product information would be presented. Subscribers would continue to use the telephone when ordering. In October 1980, Federated Department Stores acquired a substantial interest in Comp-U-Card.

Telephone purchasing systems using cable presentations are currently operating in Europe. In March 1979, the British Post Office, which runs Britain's telephone system, opened a "viewdata" service called "Prestel." Viewers are presented listings of games, restaurants, and consumer product evaluations. Products and services can be purchased on credit by phone. France launched a similar service called "Antiope" in 1979.

A few U.S. companies are testing similar systems. Viewdata Corp., a subsidiary of the Knight-Ridder Newspaper chain, proposes to install a permanent system in southern Florida by 1983. First Bank System of Minneapolis will be testing a "videotex" system in North Dakota similar to the Antiope System of France.

### Interactive Cable Systems and Videotex

Since December 1977, Warner Communications and American Express have been involved with a $70 million joint venture testing the QUBE two-way system of Warner Amex Cable in Columbus, Ohio. Currently, the system serves 30,000 of the 105,000 homes in its service area. American Express and Warner Communications propose to build other QUBE systems in such metropolitan areas as Houston, Pittsburgh, and Cincinnati. Both Sears and Penneys currently are testing the QUBE system.

In May 1981, American Telephone & Telegraph (AT&T) endorsed a videotex concept in which a home computer terminal must be purchased. AT&T has set out to develop its own system. AT&T would be a formidable opponent to anyone in the market, considering the firm's capabilities and financial strength. Thus, there are a number of legal actions being undertaken to prevent AT&T's direct entry into the videotex market, fearing it could become a monopoly power. However, strong deregulation sentiments may overcome the opposition and facilitate AT&T's entry into the market.

In summary, the TCS market is embryonic. Growth in nonstore retailing is providing a solid foundation upon which TCS systems can build. Over $100 million already has been invested by U.S. firms to design and test various TCS systems, and at least eighty-three experimental projects are being conducted around the world. As a result, Mark-Tele must be prepared to match formidable competition, and we feel confident that Mark-Tele can.

## TARGET MARKET CONSIDERATIONS

The TCS system must be carefully tailored and targeted to meet market demands and expectations. There are two different markets that must be considered when developing this venture: (1) the suppliers, and (2) the shoppers.

We propose that the TCS system be targeted to the ultimate *user*—the subscribing shopper. A TCS system that is designed well will sell itself to suppliers. Suppliers, therefore, should be considered as a dimension of the "total product" that will be offered to target shoppers. This approach will allow Mark-Tele to retain maximum control and autonomy in the design and implementation of this venture.

### The Target Market—Shoppers

A careful review of the size and characteristics of the current and potential Mark-Tele subscription base indicates substantial market potential and buying power. However, critical analysis of shopping and buying behavior is necessary to isolate the most lucrative prospective customer segments and to understand their prospective TCS behavior. Three buying factors appear to be very important: (1) risk perceptions, (2) convenience orientations, and (3) buyer satisfaction.

*Risk* Buying is a complex experience filled with uncertainty and related risks of unfavorable consequences. Fundamentally, consumers confront the uncertainty of achieving their buying goals and risks such as embarrassment or wasting time, money, or effort in a disappointing buying or shopping experience. Consumers usually are not highly conscious of these until they face new, different, or very important buying decisions or situations. In general, shopping is used to reduce uncertainty, risk, and potential disappointment. More specifically, consumers shop to help refine their buying goals, to search for and evaluate specific products and terms, to execute transactions, and to favorably reinforce past purchase behaviors.

When consumers consider TCS experiences, they must feel comfortable and in control. All shopping and buying uncertainties, risks, and potential negative consequences must be minimized throughout the total TCS experience. Initially, the consumer must learn how to operate/interface with the TCS system. One positive experience should build into others.

During the TCS experience, some traditional risk-reduction tactics such as personal inspection of merchandise or interaction with salespeople will not be available to the shopper. However, there are significant risk-reduction tactics that will be accessible. These include

- Visual and audio comparison of a wide assortment and range of products and services;
- Information access and collection controlled by the shopper;
- Information availability regarding many product features and all terms of sale and delivery;

- Promotional messages that present products and services in attractive, exciting, and believable formats;
- Past experiences with the product, service, brand, or supplier;
- Personal experiences shared by significant friends, relatives, or peers;
- Testimonials from respected celebrities, peers, or experts;
- Continuous building of positive shopping experiences with the TCS system.

These risk-reduction tactics should be incorporated into the TCS system design and promoted during operations.

In short, we suggest (a) that uncertainty and risk can be significantly reduced by presenting TCS, and its products and services, as personal and uncomplicated; and (b) that shopping confidence can be built by involving shoppers in positive TCS experiences. For example, some exploratory studies have been indicated that shoppers feel confident ordering merchandise by television when (1) the product or service is easily recognizable and clearly identified by brand, retailer, size, color, and/or other relevant properties; (2) consumers could access the information when they felt ready to actually make the purchase; and (3) consumers had purchased the product or service previously.

*Convenience*  Shopping is a problem-solving activity. The TCS system offers solutions to many nagging problems encountered when shopping conventionally. Consider the following common aggravations: having to carry merchandise; adapting to limited store hours; poor and confusing displays of merchandise; difficulty finding desired items; dealing directly with salespeople; spending time and money traveling to the store; crowds of shoppers; boredom and fatigue of going from department to department and store to store. These are some of the inconveniences of conventional shopping systems that TCS can overcome.

A strong need or orientation for conven-

ience is an appropriate base for identifying and understanding the primary target market for the TCS system. The following customer characteristics should be used to identify target market boundaries and to isolate specific segments within the primary target market. In the future, these could be cross-tabulated with other demographic, behavioral, and media characteristics to further refine target segment definitions and to tailor market programs.

Primary target customers for the TCS system are those Mark-Tele subscribers:

- With greater than average need or desire for convenience;
- With restricted mobility because children are at home;
- With appropriate buying power and media (credit cards);
- Who compile shopping lists regularly;
- Who are frequent catalog shoppers;
- Who rely extensively on newspaper, magazine, or television advertising;
- Who are loyal to specific brands or suppliers;
- Who do not like to travel or find it very difficult to travel;
- Who do not like to deal with crowds;
- Who are handicapped physically;
- Who are actively engaged in time consuming leisure activities;
- Who are senior citizens.

*Satisfaction.*  A consumer must have a satisfying experience each time that the TCS system is used. Otherwise, it is very likely that the consumer will not use TCS again and may discuss the bad experience with other shoppers and discourage their future use of the system. Thus, Mark-Tele must maintain tight control over suppliers. A consumer satisfaction department should be formed within Mark Tele. This group should monitor all TCS activities, conduct market research, investigate all consumer complaints, and make certain that all consumers are fully informed and satisfied with TCS.

## Supplier Market Implications

After selecting general product and service categories and designing a general format for each TCS channel, Mark-Tele should direct attention to the supplier market. At that time, Mark-Tele should evaluate prospective suppliers regarding the relevance of their product or service assortment, their delivery and financial capabilities, the quality of their promotional strategies, and their desire to enter into this unconventional market. We feel that Mark-Tele's technical competence and captive subscription base will provide substantial leverage in all negotiations with suppliers. The actual marketing effort should involve personal selling programs custom designed for each prospective target supplier.

## Prospective Products and Services

Preliminary research on TCS systems have uncovered a number of product and service lines that are appropriate for our target market and appear to be financially and technically feasible. As this innovative approach to shopping evolves and consumer acceptance and involvement grows, many other products and services could be incorporated. However, the most feasible products and services currently are:

- Standard catalog items;
- Staple grocery items;
- Gifts and specialty items;
- Appliances and home entertainment equipment;
- Toys, electronic games and equipment, basic sporting goods;
- Banking and financial services;
- Classified ads;
- Multiple-listing service of local properties;
- Ticket, restaurant, and accommodations reservations;
- Educational classes;
- Automobiles.

We cannot stress too strongly that TCS will involve a high degree of risk perceived by consumers. This must be reduced by offering products and services with which consumers are familiar and comfortable and that involve a minimum number of simple shopping decisions for consumers.

The consumer must *learn* to use the TCS system. Mark-Tele must guide this learning experience and make sure that consumers have consistent, positive shopping experiences that become reinforcing. The following services/features should be incorporated into the TCS system to reduce shopping risks and facilitate consumer satisfaction:

- Easy to use indexing devices;
- Top-quality visual and audio representation;
- Professional promotions;
- Up-to-date information on specials;
- Competitive pricing policies and convenient payment methods;
- TCS availability 24 hours per day, seven days per week;
- Maintenance service availability 24 hours per day, seven days per week;
- Accurate order-taking and -filling;
- Prompt delivery or pickup services;
- Quick and equitable handling and resolution of customer complaints;
- Exceptional reliability.

Eventually, the TCS product and service assortment could be broadened and channel features changed. However, the products and service lines outlined in this report appear to involve minimal consumer risks, high potential for competitive advantage and target consumer satisfaction, and substantial returns for Mark-Tele.

## THE COMPETITIVE ADVANTAGE AND TCS PROMOTION

A competitive advantage over conventional suppliers can be achieved by Mark-Tele if the TCS system is designed to serve the needs and expectations of the identified target market by actively considering their prepurchase deliberations, by guiding their purchase activities, and by reinforcing their postpurchase satisfaction. This must be complemented with accurate and reliable order processing and with prompt, efficient logistical support. Above all, Mark-Tele must communicate and promote its distinctive capabilities. We believe that the following distinctive features of the TCS system should be emphasized:

- The extensive variety and depth of product and service assortments;
- The vast amount of relevant information that is easily accessible and allows consumers to make better choices;
- The excitement, involvement, convenience, and satisfaction of shopping in the privacy of one's home using space-age technology and the simplicity of the television;
- The insignificant, negligible, and indirect costs to consumers particularly when compared with the opportunities and benefits.

We feel that the best medium for promotion of the TCS system will be the television itself. Promotional information should be presented on all television channels other than pay channels. The TCS system initially should be portrayed as a new, exciting service available to all Mark-Tele subscribers. After this campaign, the theme should be changed to focus on *how* the TCS system works *for* and *with* the subscriber/consumer. A final campaign should be developed to reinforce and to encourage extended usage of the TCS system.

Enclosures and brochures in billing statements should be used extensively in support of the television campaigns to alert subscribers to the availability of the TCS system, to detail operational dimensions, and to discuss changes and additions to the system before these occur. Demonstration projects probably can be executed using the television rather than personal contact.

Mailing, print media, and personal selling appear to be appropriate means for reaching prospective subscribers as the cable system expands, as well as a means to retrack and increase penetration of cable services in areas in which these already are available. However, the TCS system should be promoted as only one dimension of the total Mark-Tele cable package to prospective subscribers.

Finally, "word of mouth" will be a vital factor underlying acceptance and use of TCS. Active stimulation and encouragement of this free, highly effective form of promotion should be implemented and maintained using both creative advertising strategies and other promotional tactics such as special cable rates to subscribers who get friends or relatives to sign up and use the system.

## CONCLUSION

The recommendation of our committee is that Mark-Tele design and implement the proposed new venture concept—a tele-communication shopping system. We have identified the target customer and viable products and services to satisfy their needs and Mark-Tele's objectives. Development of the supplier market and control over suppliers also has been discussed.

Overall, the distinct advantages of the TCS concept would include (a) the wide variety of products and services that would be available to consumers; (b) the unique and novel process of shopping; (c) the ease, convenience, and privacy of shopping and buying; and (d) the special buying incentives such as comparative sales prices and controlled access to extensive amounts of information regarding products and services.

We recommend immediate action on this proposal to ensure and enact a competitive advantage in this revolutionary marketplace.

# PART THREE

# CASES ON INTERNATIONAL/ MULTINATIONAL ORGANIZATIONS

# 7

# EADCOR, A.G. (A)

**John H. Grant**

*University of Pittsburgh*

"Our firm seems to be facing two crucial questions as we approach the mid-1980s, and the answers to both will be instrumental in guiding our future posture in Africa. First, how can we as a private development bank (PDB) most effectively position ourselves to participate in the long-term economic changes in the equatorial region of Africa? Second, we're concerned about how we can best monitor and guide our lending, investment, and service activities from our headquarters here in Basle.

"If your analyses reveal other equally important issues which I should pursue with our Board of Directors, I will naturally appreciate your assessments and suggestions!" With these general remarks, Rudolph Garner, President of EADCOR (Equatorial African Development Corporation) opened his first meeting with a consultant whom he hoped would be able to assist with any needed revisions to EADCOR's evolving strategy.

The private development banking industry was comprised of various institutions which could develop and promote, finance, and provide supportive services to bankable projects in various parts of the world. Funding syndication, project management, market research, and employee training were among the services provided by the PDBs.

## CORPORATE BACKGROUND

EADCOR was founded in the early 1970s by the Richland family, and other equity investments soon followed from major multinational corporations (MNCs) headquartered in Europe and the United States. The Richlands' wealth had been accumulated from international trading, manufacturing, and natural resource development, including mining in South Africa. Each of the several investors felt a substantial responsibility to aid in the economic development of equatorial Africa, but they all also recognized that significant profits might eventually be earned by firms which knew the most effective ways to participate in such economic changes.

The investments of a few hundred thousand Swiss francs (one SF at the time = $.50 U.S.) from each MNC were relatively small in relation to their corporate size, but the combined resources thus available to EADCOR gave it the base for potentially significant participation in dozens of projects simultaneously. As a matter of practice, EADCOR sought to maintain less than a controlling equity interest in its projects in order both to stimulate local entrepreneurial initiatives and to simplify compliance with various countries' regulatory requirements.

The goals of EADCOR were known to be viewed somewhat differently by various constituents, but the executives felt that job creation, export enhancement, profitability, and public image were the prime criteria. Each project, however, could be seen as offering a potentially different mix of such payoffs.

During its initial years of operation, EAD-COR's portfolio reflected a conservative investment philosophy and earned a steady stream of interest income, mostly from the U.S. and Europe. More recently, however, investments and loans to more than thirty projects across several countries in the equatorial region of Africa had resulted in some encouraging growth situations, but losses had been incurred on six projects. With total assets of SF 76,000,000 and revenue of SF 8,000,000, the firm earned after-tax profit of SF 800,000 in 1981.

EADCOR's initial image as being a "South African operation" because of close association with the Richland family had slowly faded, so the credibility of its involvement with Black African nations was beginning to improve.

The appropriate management processes and investment mix remained unclear, however, in part because of the differing perspectives between the branch offices in Zimbabwe and Swaziland and the headquarters in Switzerland.

## CONTRASTING BUSINESS CONTEXTS

The senior executives of EADCOR had been recruited from earlier careers in international business, with particular emphasis in banking. While they were familiar with the dynamic operating environments in equatorial Africa, they were also comfortable with the sophisticated banking environments in Zurich, London, and New York. The corporate offices were located in a modern, though not elegant building in Basle's central business district, and the firm leased an apartment in a nearby hotel for use by visiting executives from out of town.

Various small businesses in Malawi, Kenya, and Swaziland faced numerous operating difficulties arising from erratic sources of material, changing government regulations, frequently untrained labor forces, and limited sources of equity capital. Attempts to coordinate the operating goals and results were often hampered by poor communications systems between the individual businesses, the regional office, and corporate headquarters.

Because some of the local managers had more political savvy than they had economic skills or concerns, they often misinterpreted the financial risks they were taking and the informational needs expected by the executives in Basle. Similar difficulties, of course, faced the managers of many competing intermediary institutions as they sought to provide similar services in developing countries.

## "INTERMEDIARY" INSTITUTIONS

The PDBs were but one of several types of organizations which provided competing and complementary services between the suppliers and users of financial capital. Intergovernmental organizations like the World Bank Group and the Arab Development Funds were instrumental in major projects. Various countries' banks and parastatal development finance institutions were focused toward specific geopolitical areas. On the other hand, foreign-based MNCs and private consulting firms tended to specialize by tasks or industries. The PDBs thus were often seen as hybrid organizations which could provide both financial and managerial services to either established or newly developing firms.

Several PDBs operated in developing regions of the world, e.g., Latin America, Asia, and Africa. Operating with names like SIFIDA, FRIDA, ADELA, and PICA, such PDBs ranged in size from that of EADCOR to others seven times as large. The economic performance of these firms was very difficult to judge, however, because of the varying project relationships, timing of profit recognition, and methods of accounting.

Different intermediary institutions developed reputations and skills at various levels and degrees of efficiency. Performance could vary along dimensions such as responsiveness to local needs, capacity to attract foreign investment, management development, and skill in project identification and implementation. The various intermediaries could thus develop differential comparative advantages in various project settings.

One rather aggregate dimension along which the intermediaries differed was the extent of project participant interaction. For example, the World Bank Group and consultants tended to pursue a high degree of interaction with other supporting agencies, but most local banks and PDBs pursued little collaboration with related organizations.

The extent of assistance needed from development banking institutions tended to vary by a country's level of economic devleopment. In the least developed countries, the investment opportunities (or "absorptive capacity") tended to be quite limited, but as development progressed the need for supportive financial institutions increased. However, beyond a certain stage of sophistication, countries' markets for capital and services were so efficient that development banks became much less important. As different economic and political trends moved through sub-Saharan Africa, the demand for PDBs' services varied substantially.

## TRENDS AFFECTING EQUATORIAL AFRICA

While loans to businesses in sub-Saharan African countries had increased sixfold to a level of almost SF 14 billion during the decade ending in 1980, the total private investment remained at slightly less than SF 2 billion. At the same time, 75 percent of the latter funds were concentrated in Nigeria and Ivory Coast. Such increases in funding could not realistically be expected to continue, however, because declining oil prices would cause some of the OPEC countries to become net users rather than investors or lenders of funds. In addition, slow economic growth in most OECD countries was leading those governments to reduce their overseas developmental assistance (ODA).

Within many of the equatorial African countries themselves, the general economic conditions were deteriorating, so equity investments often appeared less attractive. GNP per capita growth had declined, export volume fell in absolute terms, and agricultural productivity was weak except for crops like rice. In some countries, loans had to be "rescheduled," so the banks developed even more conservative attitudes toward the region. The net effect of these trends was an increasing need for the types of intermediary services which PDBs could provide at a time when the potential suppliers had fewer resources or less economic incentive to participate in the development of such economies.

## EADCOR'S OPERATIONS

The diverse activities of the corporation remained highly centralized in the office of Rudolph Garner. Although some efforts had been made to delegate certain decisions, the Vice President, Henry Reed, the various employees, consultants, and project managers continued to seek "Rudy's" input or agreement to many decisions. (Figure 1 presents the firm's organization chart.)

Between 1976 and 1982, EADCOR's project investments had become spread across more countries (see Figure 2), and commitments had increased in agricultural and industrial sectors at the expense of handicrafts (see Figure 3 for more detail). The processes for selecting projects varied substantially, with some being proposed by EADCOR's stockholders, others being recommended by the Field Offices, and still others arising from direct contacts with the corporate office by institutions and entrepreneurs in various countries.

The system for planning and control in use at EADCOR placed rather heavy reliance on financial forecasts and subsequent comparisons. Data for budgeting projections typically came from the field office, the existing or proposed project manager, and the corporate headquarters. The bases for differing projections from

**FIGURE 1**

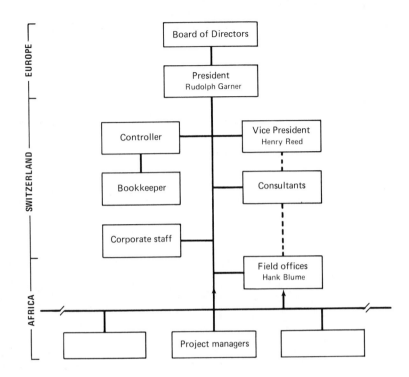

**FIGURE 2**

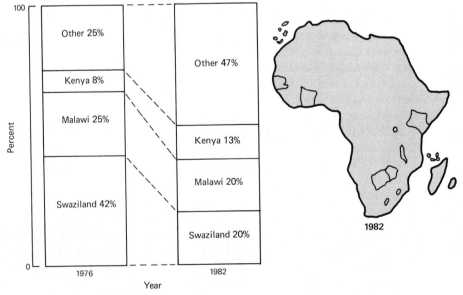

Source: EADCOR's Project Files

**FIGURE 3**

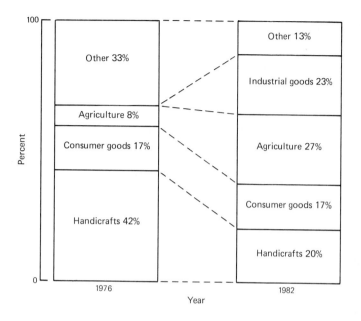

various sources were often not well documented, so the headquarters staff often made the final decisions regarding the project estimates, participation levels, etc.

Recent experiences with the procedures revealed that the budgets sometimes were not fully consistent with the strategic plans for the projects. Further, budgetary changes for on-going projects were often changed without there having been a thorough review of the related assumptions and controllable factors causing the changes. As Hank Blume explained, "these rather loose procedures reflect the fact that project managers' competencies are sometimes overestimated, government policies often change with virtually no notice, and expected materials are occasionally in very short supply." Coordination difficulties across the thirty existing projects was also seen as being particularly difficult because managers at different levels viewed the risks and potential payoffs much differently. For example, some project managers were willing to assume a "quick gamble with other people's money" while others were seeking to "save the economy of their village."

In Basle, the senior executives wanted to be able to demonstrate some genuine short-term progress toward their various goals so the stockholders would consider larger investments, but they simultaneously realized that the long-term employment and developmental objectives would be difficult to achieve.

While there were persistent problems with certain aspects of EADCOR's operations, Garner and Reed felt that substantial progress had been made in recent years, and they were anxious that future changes build on past accomplishments rather than destroy them.

## FUTURE DIRECTIONS

"Given the situation in which we find ourselves," commented Henry Reed, "it seems that we must incorporate several elements into our strategy, but the number of possible alternatives appears to be unlimited. This chart [see Figure 4] summarizes some of our thinking, but the weighting and timing of our efforts clearly must be added. Perhaps an entirely different approach would be even better."

EADCOR's executives realized that changes in their range of services could affect both their

**FIGURE 4**

ALTERNATIVE STRATEGIES

| | "Interaction" strategy | "Wide-service" strategy |
|---|---|---|
| Credibility (or reputation) | | |
| Interaction with related organizations | | |
| Technical competence in project management | | |
| Size of bank | | |
| Specialized services capability | | |
| Acceptability in Africa | | |

ELEMENTS

relative competency level as well as the risks they would be assuming. In addition, efforts to establish effective interaction with other agencies required substantial administrative effort, and such relationships often became specialized with regard to particular countries or types of business opportunities.

As various strategic alternatives and implementation systems were being considered, the possible economic consequences also had to be assessed. While the vast majority of EADCOR's income had always been in the form of interest, other PDBs had substantial portions of their revenues from service fees, operating income, and capital gains. Implicit in such re-

sults were differences in the depth, scope, and duration of involvement by the PDBs in particular projects.

"EADCOR must do more than just provide money," Garner observed as his meeting with the consultants drew to a close. "The countries need more than money if they are to develop. On the other hand, we've had more experience with complex financing than with the general management of projects. We have no advantage as consultants or teachers! Whatever you recommend, I'll want your advice about how to make it work, because we can all see that our present approach will be even less adequate in the future if we hope to grow."

# 8

# INCO, LIMITED

## Lawrence R. Jauch and Nancy Owens

*Southern Illinois University–Carbondale*

## HISTORY, OWNERSHIP, AND MANAGEMENT

Directly and through its subsidiaries, INCO is the world's largest producer of nickel. It is a major producer of copper and other metals and formed metal products. INCO's 30,000 employees operate plants and mines in more than 20 countries. Total combined assets of this fully integrated company and its two major divisions approach $3.15 billion with net sales of $1,173.421 million for the year ended December 31, 1983.

Nickel was discovered in Ontario in 1848, but not until 1883 was a large nickel–copper deposit found in the Sudbury district. In 1886, S. T. Ritchie organized the Canadian Copper Company and the first smelter in the Sudbury district was blown in 1888.

In 1902, Canadian Copper merged with six other metals manufacturers in the U.S., Britain, and France, creating INCO (New Jersey). In 1916, the International Nickel Company Canada, Limited, was formed to consolidate some of the subsidiaries of INCO (New Jersey) in Canada.

By 1928, INCO (New Jersey) stock was exchanged for INCO (Canada) stock and the former became inoperative. Also in 1928, INCO merged with the Mond Nickel Company. One of the reasons for this merger was the ownership by each of a portion of property known as the Frood Mine, the largest and richest copper–nickel deposit known in the world. By the later 1960s, however, INCO's control of the world nickel market declined appreciably, some estimating their market share as less than one-half.

In 1974, ESB Ray-O-VAC was acquired, and in 1976, the corporate name INCO, Limited was adopted, to replace the previous one, The International Nickel Company of Canada, Limited. In 1977, Inco Metals Company was established as a unit of INCO, Limited to operate the company's primary metals business. Inco Metals is responsible for marketing and production of primary metal products on an international basis, and also is responsible for certain technical and administrative service. In 1978 INCO, Limited organized around three principal product groups: primary metal products (INCO Metals, currently referred to as Primary Metals), formed metal products (Formed Metal Products Group, now called INCO Alloy Products Company), and batteries and related products (ESB Ray-O-Vac). The latter group subsequently became INCO Electro Energy Corporation.

In 1980, the market outlook for primary batteries was considered promising by Inco management. Management's expectations included an increased demand for primary batteries during the 1980s as a result of the need for packaged energy in micro-miniaturized items such as calculators, watches, and electronic games.

A once promising future for primary batteries turned bleak with the recessionary conditions, and the concomitant drop in the demand for nickel pervaded the early 1980s (1981 demand fell to a low equal to 1979 levels). The dampened outlook continued with decreased demand for all the primary metals, putting INCO in a position of financial weakness. Inco Electro Energy operated at a loss during 1981 as well as 1980. By February 1983, INCO had divested itself of all the Electro Energy units and the company's structure stood as shown in Exhibit 1.

## Management

An extensive restructuring of the corporation was effected during 1982, reflecting the regrouping of Inco Metals Company, the forma-tion of Inco Alloy Products Limited in the United Kingdom, and the divestiture of Inco Electro Energy Corporation.

The streamlining of the company's man-agement structure reduced the number of cor-porate officers worldwide to 22 compared with 33 at January 1982.

As a part of the restructuring, the board promoted Charles F. Baird, formerly President, to Chairman and Chief Executive Officer. Charles F. Baird has been President since 1976. He was previously Vice Chairman of the Com-pany and since 1979 has served as a director.

---

**EXHIBIT 1**    INCO and Subsidiaries, 1983

Inco Metals Company:
   Canada—mining & processing of metals
   Indonesia—metal, mining & processing
   U.K.—refining
   Japan—nickel processing (minority interests)
Inco Alloy Products Company:
   Huntington Alloys Inc.—Rolling mills in Virginia and Kentucky
   Wiggins Alloys Ltd.—production of high nickel alloys in Birmingham, England
   Daniel Doncaster & Sons Ltd.—Forging and machining of high-performance metal components
     at six locations in the United Kingdom
   Turbo Products, Inc.—Machines, gas turbine blades. Acquired September, 1980
   Canadian Alloys Division—Production of nickel strip to the Canadian mint. Carries out
     experimental work on current and new alloys
   Daido Inco Alloys Ltd.—Daido Inco Alloys Ltd. owned equally between Daido Steel Co. and Inco
     Ltd. Located in Japan, Daido Ltd. markets specialty and high-nickel alloys in Japan
Other business concerns of Inco includes the following:
   Inmetro
   Pittsburgh Pacific Processing Co.
     Inmetro and Pittsburg Pacific are both involved in metals and reclamation and recycling
   Inco Energy Resources Ltd.—Hydrocarbon explorations and development
   MPD Technology—Promotes sale of new products based on Inco research
   Venture Capital Programs
Exmibal—In its continued effort to curb operating losses, Inco elected to write off the investment
  associated with its 80% owned Guatemalan subsidiary, a nickel plant which was already shut
  down

Mr. Baird joined Inco in 1969 as a Vice President of Finance and was a Senior Vice President from 1972 to 1976. He obtained a degree from the Graduate School of Business at New York University. He is currently a Director of the Bank of Montreal, ICI Americas Inc., as well as Aetna Life & Casualty Company.

Donald J. Phillips, in addition to his responsibilities as President of Inco Limited, was elected to Chief Operating Officer.

Walter Curlook, formerly president, Inco Metals Company, was elected Executive Vice President of Inco Limited. Mr. Curlook also serves as Vice President for the Mining Association of Canada, Director of Great-West Life Assurance Company, and is a member of both the American Institute of Mining, Metallurgy & Petroleum Engineers as well as the Canadian Institute of Mining & Metallurgy. Curlook received his degree from the University of Toronto.

Ian McDougall, formerly Senior Vice President, Inco Limited, now presides as Executive Vice President with increased responsibilities. Mr. McDougall received a degree from Columbia University in 1958. He also serves as a Director of The Bank of Nova Scotia.

John H. Page serves as President of Inco Alloy Products Company and is also President of Inco United States, New York.

Phillip C. Jessup, Jr., Vice President, General Counsel & Secretary, received degrees from Yale University and Harvard Law School. Mr. Jessup is a member of the American Bar Association, American Society of International Law, and American Society of Corporate Secretaries. He also serves as Chairman of Inco Gulf E. C. as well as trustee for Olior Inc.

## THE NICKEL INDUSTRY AND COMPETITION

The following describes demand and supply conditions facing the original and principal business of Inco-nickel.

### The Markets for Nickel

More than 90% of the nickel is used in the form of metal, principally in alloys. Nickel's ability to impart corrosion resistance, strength, and specific physical properties in alloys leads to its wide use in many producer and consumer goods. The chemical properties of nickel lead to its use in batteries, dyes, and pigments as a catalyst, and in insecticides. Of the total nickel consumed in 1979, 22% was consumed in chemicals and allied products and in petroleum refining and allied products; 13% in electrical equipment machinery and supplies; 10% in aircraft and parts; 10% in motor vehicles; 9% in machinery; 9% in construction; 9% in fabricated metal products; 7% in household appliances; 4% in ship and boat building and repairing; and 7% in other uses.

### Demand Forecasts

Total U.S. domestic demand for nickel in the year 2000 is forecast to be between 430,000 and 650,000 tons. Within this range, the expected level of demand is 600,000 tons, representing an annual growth rate of 4% between 1978 and 2000.

The demand for primary nickel in the United States is expected to be 300,000 to 480,000 tons in the year 2000. Primary nickel demand in the rest of the world is expected to increase at a somewhat higher rate than in the United States. Annual world growth rates of between 2.8% and 4.6% during 1978 through 2000 accordingly will require from 1.10 million to 1.6 million tons in the year 2000. The developed countries use nickel for essentially the same purposes as does the United States. These uses are likely to grow at rates equal to U.S. rates, and by the year 2000 will account for most of the rest-of-the-world consumption. (See Appendix 1 for details of demand forecasts.)

Despite large reserves and other sources of nickel, large complex mines, processing and refining plants make it difficult to quickly adjust the supply of nickel to meet demand. Inversely, if ore production continues even with low demand, as it did during 1975 to 1978, costs remain high.

Prices of nickel, of course, vary by grade and product. One of the basic guides on these prices is the cost of basic electrolytic nickel, the history of which is traced in Exhibit 2. Prior to 1977, INCO's posted prices were the guide to the industry. But in 1977 INCO refrained from publishing prices and treated this as confidential business information. Also in 1975, most nickel was sold on a contract basis, a new occurrence in the industry.

## Nickel Availability and Production

In 1980, world reserves were estimated at 60 million tons. Lateritic ores, or nickel oxides, are principally found in tropical climates or areas with unusually heavy rainfall. This type of ore is increasingly important in current production. Primary sources include Cuba, Guatemala, Dominican Republic, Puerto Rico, Philippines, Indonesia, and New Caledonia. The other type of nickel deposits, sulfide ores, are said to have been segregated from the rock mass at depth, and are concentrated into veins, stringers, and fissure fillings in the host rock. INCO's older facilities are concentrated on mining of sulfides. Lateritic mining has become economical and feasible within the past few years, and INCO's new facilities mine this ore in Indonesia.

A new source of nickel has been explored by INCO along with the United States, West Germany, and Japan. Exploration of mineral resources of the deep seabeds, principally manganese nodules containing substantial quantities of nickel, copper, and cobalt, may be of considerable economic significance. (Some sources estimate there are 1.5 trillion tons of nodules at depths ranging from 100 to 10,000 feet, and are continually formed at a rate of 10 million tons per year.) But legal and economic questions as to their recovery remain unanswered.

---

**EXHIBIT 2**    Selected Nickel Prices, Cents per Pound

Realized Price, F.O.B. Port Colborne, Canada

| | | | |
|---|---|---|---|
| November | 1966 | 85 | |
| December | 1968 | 103 | |
| October | 1970 | 133 | |
| September | 1972 | 153 | |
| June | 1974 | 285 | |

Realized Price, F.O.B. New York

| | | | | | | |
|---|---|---|---|---|---|---|
| June | 1974 | 162.0 | April | 1979 | 242.5 |
| July | 1974 | 185.0 | May | 1979 | 305.0 |
| January | 1975 | 201.0 | June | 1979 | 305.0 |
| August | 1975 | 201.0 | December | 1979 | 315.0 |
| September | 1975 | 220.0 | January | 1980 | 325.0 |
| September | 1976 | 220.0 | March | 1980 | 350.0 |
| October | 1976 | 241.0 | September | 1980 | 305.0 |
| August | 1977 | 241.0 | January | 1981 | 350.0 |
| September | 1977 | 215.5 | January | 1982 | 329.0 |
| January | 1978 | 207.0 | January | 1983 | 329.0 |
| December | 1978 | 196.5 | | | |

*Source:* 1983 Commodity Yearbook, p. 231.

**EXHIBIT 3**  World Mine Production of Nickel (In Thousands of Short Tons of Contained Nickel)

| Year | Australia[3] | Philippines | Canada | Cuba | Finland | Indonesia | Brazil | Dom. Republic | Zimbabwe | N. Caledonia | Greece | Botswana | South Africa | USSR | United States | World Trade |
|---|---|---|---|---|---|---|---|---|---|---|---|---|---|---|---|---|
| 1974 | 22.0 | | 296.0 | 37.4 | 6.6 | 23.3 | 3.9 | 33.6 | 12.7 | 148.3 | 31.4 | | 24.4 | 138.0 | 16.6 | 849.3 |
| 1975 | 40.0 | 10.3 | 367.0 | 40.3 | 6.1 | 21.2 | 3.5 | 29.7 | 11.0 | 146.9 | 31.0 | | 22.9 | 168.0 | 17.0 | 890.5 |
| 1976 | 91.0 | 16.8 | 265.5 | 40.7 | 7.2 | 31.7 | 5.8 | 26.9 | 16.1 | 121.2 | 18.8 | | 24.7 | 155.0 | 16.5 | 873.4 |
| 1977 | 94.7 | 40.5 | 256.3 | 40.5 | 6.7 | 36.5 | 4.7 | 27.4 | 18.4 | 124.9 | 24.9 | 13.3 | 25.1 | 162.0 | 14.3 | 412.9 |
| 1978 | 90.8 | 32.5 | 141.4 | 38.3 | 5.1 | 34.6 | 4.0 | 15.8 | 17.3 | 71.8 | 20.4 | 17.7 | 31.6 | 164.0 | 13.5 | 722.8 |
| 1979 | 76.8 | 36.7 | 139.4 | 35.6 | 6.4 | 34.2 | 3.3 | 27.7 | 16.1 | 88.7 | 22.2 | 17.8 | 33.3 | 166.0 | 15.1 | 748.8 |
| 1980[1] | 81.9 | 42.2 | 203.7 | 42.1 | 7.2 | 33.6 | 2.8 | 18.0 | 16.6 | 95.5 | 16.8 | 17.0 | 28.3 | 170.0 | 14.7 | 820.9 |
| 1981[2] | 81.6 | 40.8 | 176.0 | 44.6 | 7.6 | 28.7 | 2.6 | 21.5 | 12.7 | 82.1 | 17.2 | 18.2 | 29.1 | 174.0 | 12.1 | 772.0 |
| 1982[2] | 70.0 | 35.0 | 90.0 | 35.0 | | 14.0 | | | | 35.0 | 17.0 | 18.0 | 29.0 | 170.0 | 3.2 | 576.0 |

[1]Preliminary.
[2]Estimate.
[3]Content of nickel sulfate and concentrates.
*Source:* Bureau of Mines.

Extraction methods vary by the type of deposit to be mined. Sulfide deposits are mined underground. The principal method of extraction is cut and fill stopping. These sulfide ores are ground and then carried through various separation processes. In the operations at INCO, three concentrates are separated for processing. Nickel-bearing iron sulfide is treated chemically to remove nickel, then residue is sintered (formed into solid mass without melting), and sold as iron ore pellets to the steel industry. The copper-bearing nickel goes through multiple processes and is separated into copper sulfide and precious metals. Also nickel powder can be recovered with the addition of other processes.

Oxide or lateritic ores can be converted to nickel oxide to be sold directly, or can be further processed. Processes vary and have been greatly improved.

Exhibit 3 presents world mine production by country. As can be noticed, many countries are entering the market, due in part to the feasibility of lateritic ore recovery. Although there are many sources of lateritic ores, the processing costs depend critically on energy costs. It is estimated that each dollar increase per million BTUs used in production could increase costs of Canadian nickel to 6 percent, and lateritic by 21 percent. (Access to water power in Canada accounts for much of the difference.)

**Competition**

Aside from the relative worldwide demand pattern, the nickel industry has witnessed some changes recently. In 1974, AMAX Nickel, a division of AMAX Incorporated, entered the market, opening a mine in Africa with a rated annual nickel capacity of 80 million pounds (along with other minerals). AMAX previously was involved in sales of other metals and alloying agents, and planned to use their leverage in the alloying industry to enter this market. Other competitors in the industry include Falconbridge and Sherritt Gordon. These companies are all international and vertically integrated in that they mine nickel ores and process them to a product acceptable to the industrial consumer. Selected data on Falconbridge and AMAX are included in Exhibit 4.

**EXHIBIT 4**    Two Competitors in the Industry

| Company | Pertinent Trends ($ in Millions except share data) | | | | |
|---|---|---|---|---|---|
| | 1982 | 1981 | 1980 | 1979 | 1978 |
| Falconbridge Nickel | | | | | |
| Sales | 483 | 713 | 758 | 650 | 508.0 |
| Net Profit | 85 | 9 | 109 | 35 | 5.5 |
| Long-Term Debt | 467 | 465 | 423 | 275 | 295.0 |
| Earnings per Share | 17.12 | 1.81 | 20.61 | 6.00 | 0.15 |
| AMAX | | | | | |
| Sales | 2415 | 2799 | 2949 | 2650 | 1751.1 |
| Net Profit | 390 | 231 | 470 | 375 | 160.0 |
| Long-Term Debt | 1308 | 1235 | 1125e | 900 | 791.8 |
| Earnings per Share | 6.53 | 3.31 | 7.48 | 6.50 | 2.76 |

e = estimated.

**EXHIBIT 5** Principal Properties, Plants, Laboratories, and Products Owned and Operated by INCO Nickel Operations, 1982

Operating Mines
  Sudbury, Ontario—Copper Cliff South, Creighton, Frood, Garson, Levack, Little Stobie, McCreedy West, Stobie.
  Shebandowan, Ontario—Shebandowan.
  Thompson, Manitoba—Thompson, Pipe Open Pit.
  Soroako, Indonesia.
Mines on Standby
  Sudbury, Ontario—Clarabelle, Coleman, Copper Cliff North, Crean Hill, Murray, Totten.
  Thompson, Manitoba—Birchtree, Soab, Pipe #1.
Concentrators
  Sudbury, Ontario—Clarabelle, Copper Cliff, Frood-Stobie.
  Shebandowan, Ontario.
  Thompson, Manitoba.
Smelters
  Sudbury, Ontario.
  Thompson, Manitoba.
  Soroako, Indonesia.
Iron Ore Recovery Plant
  Sudbury, Ontario—Nickel oxide, sulphuric acid.
Matte Refining
  Sudbury, Ontario—Nickel oxide sinter, INCOMET* nickel.
Refineries
  Sudbury, Ontario—Nickel pellets and powders, electrolytic copper and copper wire bar, gold, silver, selenium, tellurium, semi-refined plantinum-group metals, nickel sulphide.
  Port Colborne, Ontario—S and R-ROUNDS*, electrolytic nickel, utility nickel shot and pig, foundry additives, semi-refined platinum group metals, cobalt oxide.
  Thompson, Manitoba—Electrolytic nickel, cobalt oxide.
  Clydach, Wales—Nickel pellets and powders, nickel salts, cobalt oxides.
  Acton (London), England—Gold, platinum, palladium, rhodium, ruthenium, iridium.
Research Laboratories and Pilot Plants
  Sheridan Park (Mississauga), Sudbury and Port Colborne, Ontario.
  Clydach, Wales.

*Trademark of the Inco family of companies.

## INCO'S OPERATIONS

This section describes the operations of INCO'S two basic diversions.

### Primary Metals

Exhibit 5 outlines the principal productive assets owned by INCO. The primary operations are at Copper Cliff (1 mile west of Sudbury). These facilities are served by the Canadian National and Canadian Pacific railways. The Copper Cliff concentrator and the two smelters were renovated and added to in 1961, at a total cost of $55 million. This added a new process to produce nickel oxide sinter, and tripled capacity of iron ore recovery. Also in 1972, new plants were added to refine copper and precious metals. In 1971, a new Sudbury concentrator became operational, with a 35,000-ton daily capacity. In 1967, a 22,500-ton daily capacity concentrator was in operation, transmitting concentrate via pipeline for four miles to Copper Cliff.

In 1977 a $140 million refinery came into production at Copper Cliff, with a capacity of 100 million pounds of nickel pellets and 25,000,000 pounds of nickel powder per year. In 1972 pollution control equipment and a system to recycle 85 percent of the 150 million gallons of water used each day at Sudbury operations were installed with costs of $26 million and $10 million, respectively.

The Thompson complex became operational in 1961. In 1969 additions and improvements were made, raising the capacity to 170 million pounds of nickel annually. The original facility at Port Colborne was built in 1918, updated between 1929 and 1936, allowing production of electrolyte nickel. In 1937, a new process was added to increase capacity, and in 1972 Port Colborne had a capacity of 3.7 million pounds per month of nickel used for electroplating. In 1972, an additional plant was added to Port Colborne to produce 25 million pounds of nickel magnesium per year. The latest research station was opened in 1967.

The Port Colborne nickel refinery which has been on standby for several years was reopened February 7, 1983.

To control inventories and conserve cash, INCO reduced production at all locations in 1982. For example:

Capital expenditures were cut back at all operating locations.

Closed leaching section of Sudbury non-ore recovery plant.

Discontinued production of cobalt salts.

Converted the Acton, England refinery to a more cost-efficient process for separation of gold, platinum, and palladium.

Manitoba Divison operations were shut down November 1, 1982; production was resumed in January 1983 with four-day work weeks.

Production at P.T. Inco Indonesia was maintained at a reduced level in 1982.

The nickel refinery section in Wales was shut down in May 1982 and reopened in January 1983.

Mothballing of the Guatemalan project was completed in 1982.

Exhibit 6 summarizes sales and operating data for the Primary Metals Group.

### INCO Alloy Products

The reorganization of INCO in 1977 created this group, composed of various companies: Huntington Alloys Inc., Henry Wiggins and Company, Daniel Doncaster & Sons Limited, Canadian Alloys Division, Daido Special Alloys, Ltd., and Turbo Products International. Wiggins and Doncaster were later grouped together for greater efficiency. Manufacturing and marketing worldwide, basic products include numerous types of forgings, high nickel alloys in the form of sheet, strip, tubing and bar, and wielded products. These products are used in many industries (see Appendix 1). This unit has

**EXHIBIT 6**    Sales and Operating Data for Primary Metals Group

|  | 1982 | 1981 | 1980 |
|---|---|---|---|
| Sales by product |  |  |  |
| Primary nickel | $552 | $891 | $917 |
| Refined copper | 117 | 194 | 286 |
| Precious metals | 68 | 103 | 157 |
| Cobalt | 24 | 58 | 39 |
| Other products | 24 | 24 | 12 |
| Net sales to customers | 785 | 1270 | 1411 |
| Operating earnings (loss) | $130 | $281 | $569 |
| Deliveries (pounds in millions) |  |  |  |
| Primary nickel and intermediates | 216 | 298 | 292 |
| Nickel contained in alloy products | 35 | 44 | 53 |
| Total nickel | 251 | 342 | 345 |
| Copper | 167 | 240 | 288 |
| Other operating data |  |  |  |
| Manshifts worked (thousands) | 2642 | 4555 | 4855 |
| Capital expenditures ($millions) | 67 | 110 | 93 |
| Employees | 19,057 | 23,180 | 24,623 |

a dual role: to purchase INCO nickel at market prices (largest single consumer of INCO's primary nickel products), and to operate profitably within itself.

Through INCO Alloy Products Company (IAPC), INCO is a leading producer of high nickel rolling mill alloys as well as forged and machined components made for these other alloys.

At IAPC's principal U.S. division, Huntington Alloys, Inc., 1982 revenues were $226 million, some 20 percent below 1981. Huntington produces alloys for various users. The rolling mill at Huntington, West Virginia was built in 1922.

A modernization program was begun in 1972 at Acton, England to provide capabilities to treat metal concentrates yielding precious and other metals. A facility was also built in 1977 to reclaim chromium in Burnaugh, Kentucky. IAPC's U.K. operating unit, Inco Alloy Products Limited, incurred an operating loss in pounds sterling which, because of the accounting treatment of changes in currency exchange rates, was disproportionately larger when results were translated into U.S. dollars. Revenues were $195 million, about 32 percent below 1981. The revenue decrease was due almost equally to lower prices and lower volume. Results were affected in particular by severely depressed conditions in the European aerospace industry.

Rolling mill facilities near Birmingham were successfully commissioned, adding new production capabilities in 1982.

Turbo Products International, Inc. in the U.S., Canadian Alloys Division, and Daido Inco Alloys Ltd. of Japan all had sales declines. Nevertheless, Turbo and Daido remained profitable. Canadian Alloys Division received a contract from the Royal Canadian Mint to supply coinage material, assuring high production at this facility well into 1983.

During 1982 IAPC continued to develop and market new alloys, including mechanically al-

**EXHIBIT 7**   Sales and Operating Data for Inco Alloy Products Company

| | 1982 | 1981 | 1980 |
|---|---|---|---|
| Net sales to customers | $437 | $600 | $731 |
| Operating earnings (loss) | $(17) | $ 22 | $ 87 |
| Other operating data | | | |
|   Capital expenditures ($millions) | 17 | 23 | 28 |
|   Working capital ($millions) | 256 | 348 | 472 |
|   Employees | 6054 | 7201 | 8292 |

loyed materials produced by powder metallurgy. Sales volume increased for these products, but Exhibit 7 indicates the operating results for this unit as a whole.

Exhibit 8 summarizes the effect of the worldwide economic situation and depressed demand for nickel on the combined operations of INCO.

**Industrial Relations**

The final aspect of INCO's operations explored here is its managerial relationships with employees. INCO negotiates with several different unions at various operating divisions. A series of strikes and shutdowns by mines and other employees seems to be a problem which INCO managers must periodically deal with in Canada, England, America, and elsewhere. For example, the litany includes:

1969—125-day strike, Sudbury-United Steelworkers
1970—120-day strike, Clybach, South Wales
1973—42-day strike, Huntington
1973—150-day strike, Henry Wiggins
1978—work stoppage, Burnaugh, Kentucky
1978—work stoppage, ESB Ray-O-Vac
1978—140-day strike, Huntington Alloys
1978—150-day strike, Sudbury
1980—140-day strike, Clybach, South Wales
1981—88-day strike at Manitoba Division

In 1977, INCO placed full-time industrial relations representatives at all principal mines and plants to resolve complaints and grievances more quickly. Also, a training course in labor relations was conducted for 3,000 management and supervisory personnel.

**EXHIBIT 8**   Supplementary Operating Data for Combined Operations at INCO

| | 1982 | 1981 | 1980 |
|---|---|---|---|
| Capital expenditures ($millions) | 95 | 152 | 143 |
| Nickel production (pounds in millions) | 201 | 330 | 394 |
| Nickel inventories (pounds in millions) | 106 | 144 | 155 |
| Employees* | 25,798 | 31,678 | 33,975 |

*From continuing operations only.

Personnel policies vary by division at INCO. For example, the Ontario division practices a mass shutdown in July for three weeks' vacation by all employees. Other divisions use different approaches, but INCO does review its programs of retirement, insurance, and savings plans periodically so "they compare favorably" with current industrial practice. Exhibit 8 presents data on numbers of employees at INCO worldwide.

## THE INFLUENCE OF GOVERNMENTS

As a large multinational, INCO must deal with a number of governments and different policies. For example, in August of 1982, the FTC began a probe of INCO, U.S. Falconbridge, U.S. Societe Metallurgique LeNickel, and Western Mining Co. When the probe was later dropped it was revealed to have been a price-fixing probe. These companies account for approximately 55% of the non-communist world's nickel production. Some governments are also involved with financing projects and provide various tax regulations. Nickel is a strategic metal whose use in wartime increases much faster than the overall economy. This strong, tough, durable metal is used for military armaments and hardware. Therefore, governments tend to stockpile the metal. The value of nickel has meant favorable tax structures for producers. For example, U.S. producers are granted an income depletion allowance on domestic and foreign mine production. And the United States pays 50 percent of approved costs of exploring for nickel deposits.

The Canadian government provides assistance in discovery and development of mineral resources. New laws may be in the offing, but new mining operations and cost of exploration and development in Canada have been allowed exemptions on taxes. Although Canada dropped some tax exemptions for mining in 1974, this was almost offset in 1976 when Canada dropped taxes on exports.

Aside from taxation, governments regulate and legislate. In Canada the possible nationalization of Quebec, supported by French separatists, suggests possible legal problems for the future. (INCO has some exploration, but no current production in Quebec.) And speculation about possible nationalization of certain parts of the mining industry is not unheard of in Canada. Laws regarding mining of seabeds have yet to be finalized by various international agreements. Of course, governments play a role in industrial relations, too. For example, in 1976, a three-year contract was signed with the production and maintenance employees at the Thompson complex. This agreement was submitted jointly by the union and INCO to Canada's anti-Inflation Board; but the board rolled back the wage increase, and two work stopages totaling 14 days ensued. Finally, all international companies must be concerned with worldwide financial markets and exchange rates of various currencies.

Operationally, another major area of governmental influence in industrialized countries is protection of the environment and the work force.

### Environmental Health and Safety

The various mining and production operations INCO is involved with are subject to regulations promulgated by governments to protect health and safety of workers and the public. This is of particular importance in Canada and the United States.

In 1975, the U.S. National Academy of Sciences published an exhaustive study of the medical and biological effects of nickel as a potential environmental pollutant. The report suggests harmful effects of nickel, but suggests that modern smelting and refining processes have diminished the risks somewhat. The Academy did recommend that companies should maintain exhaustive health records of employees, and investigations should continue.

As of 1977, INCO was in compliance with many of the regulations that the Ontario Ministry of Labour had developed for occupational safety and health. Also in 1977, INCO was developing computerized systems for recording individual work histories and in-plant environmental data.

In the United States, the Occupational Safety and Health Administration (OSHA) announced its intention to develop revised standards for occupational exposure to nickel and its compounds. INCO, along with other producers, was conducting extensive research on their own, and are assessing the technical and economic feasibility of complying with more stringent controls. In Ontario, the Joint Occupational Health Committee of INCO and United States Steel Company is studying the dermatological and epidemiological effects of nickel on workers. This study is based on the previously implemented employee health data bank, and will be sent to OSHA along with studies by other producers and users of nickel.

Other environmental issues INCO must be concerned with include questions of land use (particularly reclaiming mined land and conservation of natural resources), and metal recycling. While the latter is of environmental concern, it may also have significant impact on demand/supply conditions. The specialized recycling industry for high-temperature and purity alloys and supper alloys is correlated with stainless steel production and can supply firms with sufficient raw material for production during varying economic conditions. Finally, the issue of acid rain has become increasingly important in Canada and the United States.

## RECENT ACTIVITIES AND PERFORMANCE OF INCO

During its history, INCO has witnessed many changes within the industry. In the late 1920s and 1930s, INCO controlled above 85 percent

**EXHIBIT 9**    Five-Year Supplementary Operating Statistics

| Year ended December 31 | 1982 | 1981 | 1980 | 1979 | 1978 |
|---|---|---|---|---|---|
| CANADIAN OPERATIONS: | | | | | |
| Proven and probable ore reserves at year end (tons in millions) | 491 | 502 | 543 | 514 | 462 |
| Nickel content (tons in millions) | 7.3 | 7.7 | 8.1 | 7.6 | 7.5 |
| Copper content (tons in millions) | 4.5 | 4.6 | 4.9 | 4.8 | 4.7 |
| Ore mined (tons in millions) | 6.3 | 12.2 | 14.5 | 8.4 | 10.1 |
| Average grade of ore mined | | | | | |
| Nickel | 1.52% | 1.42% | 1.48% | 1.53% | 1.56% |
| Copper | .96% | 1.09% | 1.07% | 1.02% | 1.07% |
| INDONESION OPERATIONS: | | | | | |
| Proven and probable ore reserves at year end (tons in millions) | 66 | 42 | | | |
| Nickel content (tons in millions) | 1.2 | 0.8 | | | |

*continued*

**EXHIBIT 9**  (*Continued*)

| Year ended December 31 | 1982 | 1981 | 1980 | 1979 | 1978 |
|---|---|---|---|---|---|
| Ore mined (tons in millions) | 0.7 | 1.2 | 1.5 | 0.7 | Pre-operating Year |
| Average grade of nickel in ore mined | 2.16% | 2.09% | 1.00% | 2.03% | |
| COMBINED CANADIAN, INDONESIAN, AND GUATEMALAN OPERATIONS*: | | | | | |
| Production (pounds in millions) | | | | | |
| Nickel | 201.0 | 330.1 | 393.8 | 255.0 | 267.3 |
| Copper | 135.0 | 244.0 | 290.8 | 146.1 | 197.5 |
| Average prices realized | | | | | |
| Nickel per pound | | | | | |
| -Historical/nominal dollars | $2.55 | $2.99 | $3.14 | $2.43 | $1.98 |
| -Constant/average 1982 dollars | $2.55 | $3.17 | $3.68 | $3.23 | $2.93 |
| Copper per pound | | | | | |
| -Historical/nominal dollars | $0.71 | $0.82 | $1.00 | $0.91 | $0.61 |
| -Constant/average 1982 dollars | $0.71 | $0.87 | $1.17 | $1.21 | $0.90 |
| INTERNAL CASH FLOWS ($millions) | | | | | |
| Positive (negative) | (55) | (197) | (110) | 19 | 46 |

*Note:* Canadian ore mined, and nickel and copper production were affected by strikes in 1978, 1979, 1981, and 1982 and by shutdowns in 1982.

*Ore mined at the Guatemalan facilities in 1979 and 1980 totaled 0.9 million tons; such facilities did not operate in 1981 and were mothballed in 1982.

*Shareholders*

At year-end 1982, 69 percent of the shareholders having general voting rights (the Common and the Series B Preferred shareholders) had addresses in Canada, 29 percent in the United States, and 2 percent elsewhere. Of these voting shares, Canadian residents of record held 50 percent, United States residents of record held 38 percent, and residents of record in other countries 12 percent.

*Dividends*

On February 7, 1983, the Board of Directors declared a regular quarterly dividend of 5 cents a common share, payable March 15 to shareholders of record on February 17. The Company paid total dividends per common share of 20 cents in 1982 and 59 cents in 1981.

*Optional Stock Dividend Program*

Under the Company's Optional Stock Dividend Program, common shareholders have the right to elect to receive a stock dividend, valued at a 5 percent discount from the market price of the Company's Common Shares, in lieu of a cash dividend. Holders of 33 percent of the Company's outstanding Common Shares are now participating in the Program. The Program permits many shareholders to receive certain tax benefits, including the deferral of income taxes and the elimination of Canadian withholding taxes, and also provides Common shareholders with a simple and convenient method of obtaining additional Common Shares at a 5 percent discount and without payment of brokerage commissions or service charges.

**EXHIBIT 10**  Ten-Year Review, Inco Limited and Subsidiaries

| | 1982 | 1981 | 1980 | 1979 |
|---|---|---|---|---|
| **Summary of operations** (in thousands) | | | | |
| Net sales* | $1,236,000 | 1,885,900 | 2,150,000 | 1,611,300 |
| Cost of sales and operating expenses* | $1,264,600 | 1,454,400 | 1,352,300 | 1,116,400 |
| Selling, general, and administrative expenses* | $ 123,200 | 144,400 | 144,500 | 109,400 |
| Interest, net of amounts capitalized* | $ 148,300 | 147,100 | 124,800 | 109,900 |
| Income and mining taxes* | $ (106,600) | 81,200 | 250,400 | 121,200 |
| Earnings (loss) from continuing operations before extraordinary charges* | $ (204,200) | 20,400 | 249,600 | 135,800 |
| Net earnings (loss) applicable to common shares | $ (232,300) | (497,500) | 193,200 | 118,500 |
| Per common share | $ (2.82) | (6.51) | 2.56 | 1.58 |
| Common dividends | $ 16,100 | 45,000 | 52,100 | 37,400 |
| Per common share | $ 0.20 | 0.59 | 0.69 | 0.50 |
| Common shares outstanding (weighted average) | 82,247 | 76,395 | 75,464 | 74,762 |
| **Other financial data** (in thousands) | | | | |
| Capital expenditures* | $ 95,300 | 152,200 | 143,300 | 85,400 |
| Depreciation and depletion* | $ 110,300 | 139,900 | 142,500 | 111,000 |
| Pension expense* | $ 34,300 | 59,800 | 61,600 | 54,700 |
| Research and development expense* | $ 35,800 | 37,000 | 34,100 | 26,600 |
| Exploration expense* | $ 19,200 | 32,700 | 26,900 | 13,900 |
| Working capital | $ 746,800 | 981,500 | 1,039,500 | 943,100 |
| Net property, plant and equipment | $2,109,000 | 2,136,100 | 2,542,400 | 2,523,400 |
| Total assets | $3,406,000 | 3,777,400 | 4,642,800 | 4,335,400 |
| Total debt | $1,203,400 | 1,331,400 | 1,351,700 | 1,274,100 |
| Preferred shares | $ 338,600 | 341,800 | 345,000 | 348,300 |
| Common shareholders' equity | $1,173,000 | 1,291,100 | 1,817,300 | 1,657,900 |
| Return on total assets | — | — | 4.7% | 3.3% |
| Return on common shareholders' equity | — | — | 10.6% | 7.1% |
| **Operating data** (in thousands) | | | | |
| Ore mined—short tons | 7,500 | 13,400 | 16,400 | 9,600 |
| Nickel produciton—pounds | 201,300 | 330,100 | 393,800 | 255,000 |
| Nickel deliveries—pounds | 250,800 | 341,800 | 345,400 | 393,600 |
| Copper deliveries—pounds | 167,400 | 239,800 | 288,300 | 129,100 |
| Platinum-group metals and gold deliveries—troy ounces | 310 | 317 | 349 | 326 |
| **Other statistics** | | | | |
| Employees at year end* | 25,798 | 31,678 | 33,975 | 33,864 |
| Common shareholders at year end | 55,759 | 62,054 | 67,609 | 74,541 |

*Amounts reported are for continuing operations only.

| 1978 | 1977 | 1976 | 1975 | 1974 | 1973 |
|---|---|---|---|---|---|
| 1,298,000 | 1,247,800 | 1,442,600 | 1,198,000 | 1,450,600 | 1,172,800 |
| 992,900 | 917,800 | 946,600 | 756,400 | 768,400 | 693,300 |
| 102,500 | 97,200 | 91,000 | 79,500 | 78,900 | 66,300 |
| 59,000 | 52,600 | 56,500 | 38,500 | 38,900 | 42,300 |
| 72,600 | 65,500 | 130,200 | 125,400 | 244,000 | 120,500 |
| 61,700 | 87,700 | 178,500 | 179,800 | 296,700 | 225,600 |
| 57,300 | 92,300 | 196,800 | 186,900 | 298,600 | 225,600 |
| 0.77 | 1.24 | 2.64 | 2.51 | 4.01 | 3.02 |
| 52,200 | 93,200 | 119,300 | 119,300 | 119,300 | 89,400 |
| 0.70 | 1.25 | 1.60 | 1.60 | 1.60 | 1.20 |
| 74,595 | 74,593 | 74,576 | 74,552 | 74,541 | 74,535 |
| 193,400 | 402,500 | 434,900 | 315,800 | 141,400 | 88,800 |
| 89,700 | 96,900 | 98,100 | 96,600 | 92,100 | 76,800 |
| 47,900 | 46,500 | 47,400 | 33,700 | 32,000 | 21,300 |
| 31,400 | 39,400 | 34,100 | 32,200 | 31,200 | 26,700 |
| 14,200 | 22,400 | 34,200 | 26,500 | 18,200 | 15,200 |
| 961,900 | 826,200 | 595,300 | 589,500 | 648,000 | 537,800 |
| 2,540,500 | 2,436,700 | 2,119,400 | 1,785,000 | 1,560,200 | 1,395,400 |
| 4,145,600 | 4,075,800 | 3,628,300 | 3,025,700 | 2,799,700 | 2,248,800 |
| 1,307,000 | 1,315,600 | 1,251,600 | 803,300 | 621,900 | 466,500 |
| 351,600 | 353,300 | — | — | — | — |
| 1,566,700 | 1,561,600 | 1,562,400 | 1,484,400 | 1,416,400 | 1,236,900 |
| 1.9% | 2.5% | 5.4% | 6.2% | 10.7% | 10.0% |
| 3.7% | 5.9% | 12.6% | 12.6% | 21.1% | 18.2% |
| 10,900 | 19,600 | 19,800 | 21,200 | 22,000 | 19,700 |
| 267,300 | 416,700 | 461,600 | 458,900 | 509,600 | 469,200 |
| 377,400 | 312,300 | 409,800 | 351,100 | 549,100 | 517,000 |
| 224,600 | 341,200 | 356,000 | 334,600 | 367,200 | 327,100 |
| 468 | 438 | 554 | 301 | 317 | 413 |
| 33,326 | 38,216 | 38,696 | 37,755 | 32,459 | 31,311 |
| 75,067 | 77,875 | 78,014 | 84,369 | 86,795 | 90,660 |

**EXHIBIT 11**    Consolidated Balance Sheet, INCO Limited and Subsidiaries, December 31

| | 1982 | 1981 | 1980 |
|---|---|---|---|
| | (in thousands) | | |
| CURRENT ASSETS | | | |
| Cash and marketable securities | $18,651 | 34,669 | 53,283 |
| Receivables | 241,503 | 314,387 | 585,019 |
| Inventories | 784,713 | 1,005,510 | 1,305,613 |
| Prepaid expenses | 8,254 | 11,561 | 17,977 |
| Investment in discontinued business | 70,000 | 205,000 | — |
| TOTAL CURRENT ASSETS | 1,123,121 | 1,571,127 | 1,961,892 |
| Property, plant and equipment | 3,571,856 | 3,523,833 | 3,951,238 |
| Less—Accumulated depreciation and depletion | 1,462,872 | 1,387,691 | 1,408,882 |
| | 2,108,984 | 2,136,142 | 2,542,356 |
| OTHER ASSETS | 173,922 | 70,139 | 137,551 |
| TOTAL ASSETS | $3,406,027 | $3,777,408 | $4,651,799 |
| CURRENT LIABILITIES | | | |
| Notes payable | $74,146 | $229,380 | $306,906 |
| Accrued payroll, vacation and trade accounts payable | 94,745 | 126,674 | 204,865 |
| Other payables and accrued liabilities | 203,754 | 211,635 | 249,205 |
| Income and mininmg taxes payable | 3,688 | 21,903 | 161,458 |
| TOTAL CURRENT LIABILITIES | 376,333 | 589,592 | 922,434 |
| Other liabilities | | | |
| Long-term debt | 1,129,293 | 1,101,981 | 1,044,780 |
| Deferred income and mining taxes | 346,800 | 412,100 | 445,000 |
| Pension benefits and minority interest | 41,966 | 40,790 | 67,244 |
| TOTAL LIABILITIES | 1,518,059 | 1,554,871 | 1,557,024 |
| STOCKHOLDERS' EQUITY | | | |
| Preferred stock | 338,594 | 341,798 | 345,040 |
| Common stock | 272,053 | 141,794 | 125,413 |
| Paid-in capital in excess of par value | 61,036 | 61,036 | 61,036 |
| Retained earnings | 839,952 | 1,088,317 | 1,630,852 |
| TOTAL STOCKHOLDERS' EQUITY | 1,511,635 | 1,632,945 | 2,162,341 |
| TOTAL LIABILITIES AND STOCKHOLDERS' EQUITY | $3,406,027 | $3,777,408 | $4,641,799 |

**EXHIBIT 11A**   INCO, Limited and Subsidiaries, Long-Term Debt

| December 31 | 1982 | 1981 | 1980 |
|---|---|---|---|
| | (in thousands) | | |
| Inco Limited | $797,429 | $765,953 | $464,176 |
| P.T. International Nickel Indonesia | 267,666 | 299,781 | 431,383 |
| Exmibal | 42,594 | 52,957 | 62,799 |
| Inco Europe Limited and Subsidiaries | 27,469 | 20,776 | 33,731 |
| Other Indebtedness | 62,106 | 38,667 | 28,036 |
| Total continuing operations | 1,197,264 | 1,178,134 | 1,020,125 |
| Discontinued business segments | — | — | 164,915 |
| | 1,197,264 | 1,178,134 | 1,185,040 |
| Long-term debt due within one year | | | |
|   Continuing operations | 67,971 | 76,153 | 89,139 |
|   Discontinued business segments | — | — | 51,121 |
| | 67,971 | 76,153 | 140,260 |
| Long-term debt | $1,129,293 | $1,101,981 | $1,044,780 |

The average interest rate on long-term debt at December 31, 1982, was 9.6%. Approximately 37% of such debt carries interest rates that are subject to periodic adjustments based on market interest rates. Long-term debt is payable in the following currencies: 76% U.S. dollars, 15% Canadian dollars, 5% pounds sterling, and 4% other currencies.

Interest expense on long-term debt for the years 1982, 1981, and 1980 was $129,091,000, $119,830,000, and $106,276,000, respectively. Total interest expense is net of interest income earned from formal intercompany loans to discontinued business segments, at market interest rates, which totaled $3,645,000 in 1982, $19,438,000 in 1981, and $9,573, 000 in 1980.

At the end of 1982, the Company has unutilized committed credit facilities of $460 million. Certain of these facilities contain covenants which require that the ratio of the Company's consolidated debt to its net worth not exceed 55:45 through 1984 and thereafter not exceed 50:50; at December 31, 1982, this ratio was 45:55. Under these facilities, net worth is essentially defined as the sum of preferred shares and common shareholders' equity, and consolidated debt is defined to include borrowings, guarantees, and certain minimal obligations.

of the world's nickel consumption. INCO has lost its overwhelming dominance. Yet, even in the 1970s, an industry trade association still did not exist because, as one of INCO's competitors states, "INCO was it."

Financial data for INCO are presented in Exhibits 9 to 13. This suggests that INCO is still a dominant force in this industry, but that it has experienced substantial changes recently.

The recessions in 1975 and 1980 revealed a general weakening of demand and reduced shipments of nickel significantly. Despite weak demand, INCO held strong to its steady pro-

duction policy in 1976, and did not order any cutbacks, avoiding costs of closing and reopening facilities. In late 1976, INCO announced a 9.6 percent price increase for basic electrolytic nickel and the industry was startled. In 1977 INCO rescinded this price increase since others in the industry had refused to follow. Also in 1977 INCO stopped publishing prices for nickel. INCO's listed prices were previously used as an industry yardstick, and competitors and customers were shocked by this move. Price wars were forecasted to occur, and implications regarding the Robinson Patman Act were voiced.

**EXHIBIT 12**   INCO Limited and Subsidiaries, Consolidated Statement of Earnings, Year Ended December 31

|  | 1982 | 1981 | 1980 |
|---|---|---|---|
|  | (in thousands) | | |
| Revenues | $1,276,993 | $1,911,600 | $2,187,009 |
| Costs and expenses | | | |
| Cost of sales and operating expenses | 1,264,564 | 1,454,430 | 1,352,255 |
| Selling, general, and administrative expenses | 123,180 | 144,378 | 144,536 |
| Research, development and exploration | 54,953 | 69,649 | 61,006 |
| Interest expense | 148,298 | 147,130 | 124,783 |
| Currency translation adjustments | (3,161) | (5,616) | 4,391 |
| Income and mining taxes | (106,628) | 81,162 | 250,413 |
|  | 1,481,206 | 1,891,133 | 1,937,384 |
| Earnings before extraordinary charges | (204,213) | 20,467 | 249,625 |
| Extraordinary charges | — | 489,985 | 30,218 |
| Net earnings (loss) | $(204,213) | $(469,518) | $219,407 |
| Net earnings (loss) per common share | $(2.82) | $(6.51) | $2.56 |

Consolidated Statement of Retained Earnings

| Year ended December 31 | 1982 | 1981 | 1980 |
|---|---|---|---|
|  | (in thousands) | | |
| Retained earnings at beginning of year | $1,088,317 | $1,630,852 | $1,489,678 |
| Net earnings (loss) | (204,213) | (469,518) | 219,407 |
| Preferred dividends | (28,053) | (28,017) | (26,179) |
| Common dividends—$.20 per share (1981—$.59, 1980—$.69) | (16,099) | (45,000) | (52,054) |
| Retained earnings at end of year | $839,952 | $1,088,317 | $1,630,852 |

(This act outlaws preferential treatment to customers.)

However, by 1982, nickel's slide had continued to thrash INCO. In 1982 even Mr. Baird conceded that since 1974 the nickel market has been absolutely flat. Adding further to the decline of INCO's financial health was the fact that the company had borrowed heavily in order to expand to meet a 1980 forecast of 1 million tons of nickel worldwide. The actual demand turned out to be closer to 565,000 tons.

INCO's acquisition of the Electro Energy division was viewed by many analysts as being inappropriate with respect to the expertise of INCO's management. Indeed, by the end of 1982, INCO had completely divested itself of that product group taking a write-off of $290 million in an effort to reduce debt and escape from a

**EXHIBIT 13** INCO Limited and Subsidiaries, Consolidated Statement of Changes in Financial Position for the Year Ended December 31

|  | 1982 | 1981 | 1980 |
|---|---|---|---|
|  | (in thousands) | | |
| Working Capital Provided (used) by operations | $(169,304) | $ 4,691 | $382,177 |
| Reclassification of Discont. Bus. Segment | (100,300) | — | — |
| Capital Expenditures | (95,290) | (185,639) | (191,561) |
| Long-Term Borrowing | 41,177 | 127,537 | (30,651) |
| Common Stock Transactions | 133,122 | 26,285 | 14,505 |
| Dividends Paid | (44,152) | (73,017) | (78,233) |
| Increase (Decrease in Working Capital | $(234,747) | $ (57,923) | $ 96,337 |
| ANALYSIS OF CHANGES IN WORKING CAPITAL | | | |
| Increase (decrease) in current assets | | | |
| Cash and marketable securities | $(16,018) | $(18,614) | $(20,691) |
| Accounts and tax refunds receivable | (72,884) | (170,632) | 66,759 |
| Inventories | (220,797) | (300,103) | 223,969 |
| Prepaid expenses | (3,307) | (6,416) | 6,429 |
| Investment in discontinued business segments | (135,000) | 205,000 | — |
| Total | $(448,006) | $(390,765) | $276,466 |
| Increase (decrease) in current liabilities | | | |
| Note payable and other debt | $(155,234) | $(77,526) | $105,102 |
| Payable and accrued liabilities | (39,810) | (115,761) | 38,163 |
| Income and mining taxes payable | (18,215) | (139,842) | 180,129 |
| Total | $(213,259) | $(332,842) | $180,129 |
| Increase (decrease) in working capital | $(234,747) | $(57,923) | $96,337 |

business in which the company was being battered. Investment bankers thought that INCO had paid too much for ESO Ray-O-Vac in the first place. In what has sometimes been termed an unfriendly acquisition, the battery maker was finally acquired for $41 a share.

Further evidence of the financial effect of the depressed nickel industry is related to INCO's Guatemalan nickel plant (Exmibal). The Guatemalan plant had been on standby since 1980. During 1981 the company elected to mothball the entire operation. This resulted in a write-down of $220 million (the company's total investment) when it was concluded by management that it was very unlikely that the facility could operate profitably in the foreseeable future. It is management's intention that subsequent operations will benefit in that losses and cash outflows associated with the Guatemalan operations will be sharply reduced.

All of these problems came at a time when capital improvements were needed at existing facilities. The company has been unable to finance itself through operations as can be seen from the results of operations. Following this period of retrenchment, top management was wondering what strategic moves would be in the best interests of the company.

# APPENDIX 1
# FORECAST FOR NICKEL DEMAND

The statistical projections for the demand for nickel in the year 2000 was derived from the classical regression analysis based upon the historical end-use data from 1960 through 1978.

Once the statistical projection for 2000 was obtained, contingency assumptions that would cause significant increases or decreases were considered. The following are analyses of the contingency assumptions made for nickel demand in each of the major end uses during 1978–2000 and the forecast range of demand in the year 2000.

*Transportation* (Aircraft and Parts)—Substitution of cobalt, columbium, or other elements for nickel in super alloys or substantial use of ceramic components could place nickel demand at the low range. But if the use of nickel in super alloys is unchanged and maraging steels are used in airframes the demand could reach the high range as indicated by Table 1. The most probable demand for nickel in aircraft and parts by 2000 is the middle range because nickel will continue its important role in aerospace application to achieve higher operating temperatures and thus greater efficiencies in aircraft power plants.

*Ship- and Boat-Building and Repairs*—Assuming that the growth rate of shipbuilding will exceed the growth in population and reflect continued prosperity, the demand for nickel in

this industry could reach the high end of the projected forecast. The most probable forecast is slightly less because U.S. ship- and boat-building is expected to remain rather stable, and the high-speed navy will be dependent primarily on gas turbines for propulsion.

*Chemical Manufacturing*—Moderate growth could effect a reduced demand for nickel by 2000 due to the use of substitute metals for plasters. However, expanded use of nickel in corrosive environments, construction of large-scale desalinization plants, and exploitation of the ocean as a source of food and raw material could also increase the demand. The most probable demand favors the high end of the range because of the growing need for materials that will withstand corrosive environments and the probability that aquaculture will become important prior to 2000.

*Petroleum*—Projections for demand in the petroleum industry range from 53,000 to 73,000 in 2000. The most probable demand favors the high end of the range because of the growing need for corrosion-resistant pollution control equipment and the increasing need for equipment in the petroleum and newly developing synfuels industry.

*Fabricated Metals Products*—Projections for nickel use in fabricated metal products exhibit a moderately narrow range in 2000. The low

**TABLE 1** Projections and Forecasts for U.S. Nickel Demand by End Use (thousand tons)

| | | | 2000 | | |
| | | | Contingency forecasts for United States | | |
| | | Statistical projections | Forecast range | | Probable |
| | 1978 | | Low | High | |
|---|---|---|---|---|---|
| Transportation: | | | | | |
|   Aircraft and parts | 23.3 | 50* | 45 | 65 | 55 |
|   Motor vehicles and equipment | 24.2 | 9* | 28 | 47 | 40 |
|   Ship- and boat-building and | | | | | |
|     repairs | 9.6 | 20* | 8 | 15 | 14 |
|   Total | 57.1 | — | 81 | 127 | 109 |
| Chemicals | 33.6 | 110* | 87 | 130 | 125 |
| Petroleum | 18.5 | 68* | 53 | 73 | 71 |
| Fabricated metal products | 22.5 | 38* | 35 | 50 | 48 |
| Electrical | 31.2 | 73* | 70 | 110 | 105 |
| Household appliances | 16.7 | 4* | 20 | 25 | 22 |
| Machinery | 20.3 | 0* | 33 | 40 | 37 |
| Construction | 22.5 | 75* | 25 | 60 | 55 |
| Other | 17.2 | 0* | 26 | 35 | 30 |
|   Total | 182.5 | — | 349 | 523 | 491 |
|   Grand Total | 239.6 | — | 430 | 650 | 600 |

[1]Statistical projections, provided by the Branch of Economic Analysis, are derived from regression analyses based on 20-year historical time series data and from forecasts of economic indications such as GNP and FRB index. A statistical projection of zero indicates that demand will vanish at or before the year 2000, based on the historical relationship. Projection equations with a coefficient of determination (R-squared) less than 0.70 are indicated by an asterisk(*).

end of the range assumes past substitution trends will continue. However, higher living standards may require more metal products of superior quality and thus raise the demand. The probable estimate favors the high end of the range.

*Electrical*—Increasing sophistication of power-generating and distribution equipment would effect a substantial increase in nickel demand by 2000. However, the relatively high price of nickel may result in large-scale substitution for nickel in resistance alloys, whereby usage would be much lower. The forecast of most probable demand in 2000 is set above the middle of the range, because it is anticipated that cogeneration systems for large coal-fueled power stations will become important by 2000.

*Household Appliances*—Projection for nickel use in household appliances is expected to decrease in 2000 because of peaks in the historical curve in 1966 and 1974, associated to some extent with a throwaway economy that will not likely be repeated. Assuming population increase will be minimal in the next 20 years, and the trend away from stainless and plated decorative items will continue, the usage of

**TABLE 2**   Summary of Forecasts of U.S. and Rest-of-World Nickel Demand (thousand tons)

| | 1978 | 2000 Forecast range[1] | | Probable | | Probable average annual growth rate 1978–2000 (percent) |
| | | Low | High | 1990 | 2000 | |
|---|---|---|---|---|---|---|
| **United States** | | | | | | |
| Primary | 180.5 | 300 | 480 | 300 | 440 | 3.7 |
| Secondary | 59.1 | 130 | 170 | 100 | 160 | 4.6 |
| Total | 239.6 | 430 | 650 | 400 | 600 | 4.0 |
| Cumulative (primary) | | 5,500 | 7,200 | 3,000 | 6,700 | = |
| **Rest of world** | | | | | | |
| Primary | 602 | 1,100 | 1,600 | 950 | 1,400 | 3.9 |
| Secondary | 130 | 320 | 630 | 270 | 500 | 6.3 |
| Total | 732 | 1,420 | 2,230 | 1,220 | 1,900 | 4.4 |
| Cumulative (primary) | | 18,400 | 23,100 | 9,300 | 21,100 | = |
| **World** | | | | | | |
| Primary[2] | 783 | 1,400 | 2,080 | 1,250 | 1,840 | 3.9 |
| Secondary[2] | 189 | 450 | 800 | 370 | 660 | 5.8 |
| Total | 972 | 1,850 | 2,880 | 1,620 | 2,500 | 4.3 |
| Cumulative[2] (primary) | | 23,900 | 30,300 | 12,300 | 27,800 | — |

[1]Calculated from 1978 trend value: U.S. primary 196; U.S. secondary 59; rest-of-world primary 500; rest-of-world secondary 130.
[2]Rounded.

nickel in appliances will remain relatively static. Therefore, a small increase is reflected in the projection.

*Machinery*—Larger, more sophisticated machines of wide variety will be required in the future and will incorporate nickel-containing alloy steels, especially in the massive parts for large mining and earth-moving machines. Projecting recent trends, the forecast lies approximately in the mid-range of the expected high and low demand.

*Construction*—A limited use of stainless steel for decorative siding and of nickel-bearing alloys for construction is the basis for low range here. However, the likelihood of widespread use of nickel-bearing high-strength steels projects a much higher value. The probable forecast most closely approximates the high range.

*Other*—The probable demand for nickels use in the other category is 30,000 tons. The high level of nickel activity in applied research laboratories will probably result in development of new uses.

# 9 MOBIL CORPORATION

## M. Edgar Barrett

*Southern Methodist University*

It was early March 1984. Richard Collier, Exploration Manager of Mobil Oil Corporation's Rocky Mountain Division, had just heard the news of Mobil Corporation's $5.7 billion offer for Superior Oil Company. This piece of information came as no great surprise to Collier, since it had been well known that Superior had been looking for a merger partner and that its owners had approached Mobil's board of directors several months ago. Also, this type of move was not uncommon for Mobil. This was, in fact, the company's eighth acquisition attempt since 1979 (three were successful). Perhaps understandably in his position, however, Collier wished Mobil would begin placing more emphasis on replacing reserves from its own exploration activities.

## COMPANY OVERVIEW

Mobil Corporation was the third largest industrial company in the United States (behind Exxon and General Motors), with revenue from operations in 1983 of nearly $55 billion. Mobil consisted of one of the world's largest petroleum

This case was written by Robert R. Gardner, Associate Director of the Maguire Oil and Gas Institute, under the direction of M. Edgar Barrett, Director of the same institute. It was based, in part, on earlier versions written by Bill Clark and Mary Pat Cormack. The character and situation described in the first and last paragraphs of the case are fictional. Data provided elsewhere are drawn entirely from public sources. This case was prepared as the basis for class discussion rather than to illustrate either effective or ineffective handling of an administrative situation.
Copyright © 1985 by M. Edgar Barrett

operations, a growing chemical business, a paperboard packaging business, and a nationwide retailing operation. Mobil companies conducted business in more than 100 countries and employed more than 178,000 people.

The company had total assets in 1983 of $35 billion. Net income was $1.5 billion. Total return to investors in 1983 was 22.39%. Over the previous ten years, Mobil averaged a 15.17% return to investors—highest among the major oil companies.[1] With a 5.69% share of the domestic market, Mobil ranked as the fifth largest gasoline retailer in 1983.

## HISTORICAL BACKGROUND

Mobil's corporate roots could be traced in one direction back to the formation of Vacuum Oil in 1866, and in another, to John D. Rockefeller's Standard Oil Trust, which later absorbed the smaller company. Vacuum Oil was founded by Hiram Bond Everest and Mathew Ewing, who had invented in 1865 a new process of distilling crude oil under a vacuum. At that time, a gallon of kerosene sold for twice as much as a barrel of crude oil, and Ewing believed that his vacuum process could produce more kerosene from a barrel of crude than was possible with other known refining methods. Everest, on the other hand, recognized the possibilities of using the oily residue from the distilling process as a petroleum lubricant for machinery and leather. Everest decided to finance the new venture, and Vacuum Oil was founded in 1866.

[1] "The 500 Largest U.S. Industrial Corporations," *Fortune,* April 30, 1984, pp. 276–277.

**EXHIBIT 1**    Mobil Corporation Income Statement

| (Millions) | 1983 | 1982 | 1981 | 1980 | 1979 |
|---|---|---|---|---|---|
| Revenues | | | | | |
| Sales and services | | | | | |
| Petroleum operations ................. | $43,433 | $49,182 | $53,298 | $49,189 | $35,403 |
| Chemical .......................... | 2,230 | 2,034 | 2,235 | 1,812 | 1,562 |
| Paperboard packaging .............. | 1,685 | 1,869 | 1,998 | 1,880 | 1,600 |
| Retail merchandising ................. | 6,003 | 5,584 | 5,742 | 5,497 | 5,251 |
| Services and other ................... | 1,256 | 1,277 | 1,215 | 1,132 | 905 |
| Total sales and services ............ | 54,607 | 59,946 | 64,488 | 59,510 | 44,721 |
| Excise and state gasoline taxes .......... | 3,389 | 3,168 | 3,129 | 3,313 | 2,764 |
| Interest ................................ | 513 | 460 | 335 | 414 | 339 |
| Dividends and other income ............. | 92 | 142 | 19 | 22 | 80 |
| Equity in earnings of certain affiliated companies ............................ | 397 | 392 | 616 | 467 | 388 |
| Total Revenues .................... | 58,998 | 64,108 | 68,587 | 63,726 | 48,292 |
| Costs and Expenses | | | | | |
| Crude oil, products, merchandise, and operating supplies and expenses ........ | 38,404 | 43,997 | 46,178 | 41,301 | 30,477 |
| Exploration expenses ................... | 618 | 847 | 803 | 524 | 359 |
| Selling and general expenses ........... | 4,967 | 5,312 | 5,181 | 4,957 | 4,265 |
| Depreciation, depletion, and amortization .. | 1,892 | 1,736 | 1,586 | 1,399 | 1,086 |
| Interest and debt discount expense ....... | 814 | 663 | 608 | 479 | 459 |
| Taxes other than income taxes | | | | | |
| Excise and state gasoline taxes ........ | 3,389 | 3,168 | 3,129 | 3,313 | 2,764 |
| Windfall profit tax .................... | 447 | 630 | 936 | 267 | — |
| Import duties ........................ | 3,395 | 3,500 | 3,825 | 4,155 | 3,756 |
| Property, production, payroll, and other taxes ............................. | 858 | 959 | 942 | 655 | 564 |
| Total taxes other than income taxes .. | 8,089 | 8,247 | 8,832 | 8,390 | 7,084 |
| Income taxes ......................... | 2,711 | 2,093 | 2,966 | 3,863 | 2,555 |
| Total costs and expenses ........... | 57,495 | 62,895 | 66,154 | 60,913 | 46,285 |
| Income Before Extraordinary Item .......... | 1,503 | 1,213 | 2,433 | 2,813 | 2,007 |
| Extraordinary Item—Gain on sale of interest in Belridge Oil Company (less income taxes of $189) .................................. | — | — | — | 459 | — |
| Net Income ........................... | $ 1,503 | $ 1,213 | $ 2,433 | $ 3,272 | $ 2,007 |
| Memo: | | | | | |
| Income less foreign inventory profits ........ | $ 1,503 | $ 1,213 | $ 2,332 | $ 2,169 | $ 1,707 |

*Source:* Mobil Corporation Financial and Operating Statistics 1983.

**EXHIBIT 2**  Mobil Corporation Balance Sheet

| (Millions) | December 31, | | | | |
| --- | --- | --- | --- | --- | --- |
| | **1983** | **1982**[a] | **1981** | **1980** | **1979** |
| **Assets** | | | | | |
| Current assets | | | | | |
| Cash | $ 507 | $ 542 | $ 782 | $ 698 | $ 621 |
| Marketable securities, at cost | 1,046 | 1,133 | 1,262 | 1,220 | 1,257 |
| Accounts and notes receivable | 4,832 | 5,135 | 5,440 | 5,718 | 5,060 |
| Inventories | | | | | |
| Crude oil and petroleum products | 3,070 | 3,678 | 4,320 | 4,518 | 3,114 |
| Chemical products | 317 | 338 | 333 | 315 | 237 |
| Paperboard packaging | 128 | 137 | 172 | 181 | 158 |
| Retail merchandising | 937 | 893 | 937 | 975 | 1,080 |
| Other, including materials and supplies | 626 | 737 | 718 | 474 | 362 |
| Total Inventories | 5,078 | 5,783 | 6,480 | 6,463 | 4,951 |
| Prepaid expenses | 427 | 367 | 256 | 203 | 174 |
| Total current assets | 11,890 | 12,960 | 14,220 | 14,302 | 12,063 |
| Investments and long-term receivables | 2,854 | 2,563 | 2,423 | 2,213 | 2,030 |
| Properties, plants, and equipment, at cost | 31,673 | 30,029 | 27,612 | 24,581 | 20,676 |
| Less accumulated depreciation, depletion, and amortization | 11,795 | 10,714 | 9,902 | 8,741 | 7,573 |
| Net properties, plants, and equipment | 19,878 | 19,315 | 17,710 | 15,840 | 13,103 |
| Deferred charges and other assets | 450 | 378 | 423 | 350 | 310 |
| Total Assets | $35,072 | $35,216 | $34,216 | $32,705 | $27,506 |
| **Liabilities and Shareholders' Equity** | | | | | |
| Current liabilities | | | | | |
| Notes and loans payable | $ 1,185 | $ 2,187 | $ 1,692 | $ 949 | $ 1,064 |
| Accounts payable and accrued liabilities | 6,847 | 7,332 | 7,604 | 7,880 | 7,113 |
| Income, excise, state gasoline, and other taxes payable | 2,246 | 2,393 | 2,486 | 3,218 | 2,377 |
| Deferred income taxes | 163 | 316 | 704 | 546 | 467 |
| Long-term debt and capital lease obligations maturing within one year | 372 | 198 | 219 | 126 | 170 |
| Total current liabilities | 10,813 | 12,426 | 12,705 | 12,719 | 11,191 |
| Long-term debt | 5,162 | 4,404 | 3,284 | 3,256 | 2,962 |
| Capital lease obligations | 328 | 313 | 320 | 315 | 342 |
| Reserves for employee benefits | 336 | 385 | 410 | 412 | 398 |
| Deferred credits and other noncurrent obligations | 1,074 | 845 | 653 | 605 | 294 |
| Accrued restoration and removal costs | 315 | 265 | 208 | 148 | 114 |
| Deferred income taxes | 3,000 | 2,665 | 2,442 | 2,087 | 1,605 |
| Minority interest in subsidiary companies | 92 | 106 | 97 | 94 | 87 |
| Shareholders' equity | 13,952 | 13,807 | 14,657 | 13,069 | 10,513 |
| Total Liabilities and Shareholders' Equity | $35,072 | $35,216 | $34,776 | $32,705 | $27,506 |

[a] Restated.

*Source:* Mobil Corporation Financial and Operating Statistics 1983.

**EXHIBIT 3**    Mobil Corporation Changes in Financial Position

| (Millions) | 1983 | 1982[a] | 1981 | 1980 | 1979 |
|---|---|---|---|---|---|
| Sources of Funds | | | | | |
| Operations | | | | | |
| Income before extraordinary item ........ | $1,503 | $1,213 | $2,433 | $2,813 | $2,007 |
| Depreciation, depletion, and amortization | 1,892 | 1,736 | 1,586 | 1,399 | 1,086 |
| Deferred income tax charges ........... | 487 | 166 | 425 | 482 | 585 |
| Dividends in excess of (less than) equity in income of unconsolidated companies | (158) | 44 | (41) | 129 | (50) |
| Funds available from operations ...... | 3,724 | 3,159 | 4,403 | 4,823 | 3,628 |
| Extraordinary item ....................... | — | — | — | 459 | — |
| Book value of properties, plants, and equipment sold ...................... | 140 | 209 | 116 | 99 | 78 |
| Other, net ............................. | (30) | 195 | 123 | 410 | 84 |
| Funds available before financing ...... | 3,834 | 3,563 | 4,642 | 5,791 | 3,790 |
| Application of Funds | | | | | |
| Cash dividends to shareholders ........... | 813 | 836 | 851 | 733 | 541 |
| Capital expenditures .................... | 3,073 | 3,821 | 3,571 | 3,525 | 2,641 |
| Major acquisitions[b] .................... | — | 500 | — | 715 | 792 |
| Increase (decrease) in: | | | | | |
| Accounts and notes receivable .......... | (303) | (302) | (278) | 658 | 870 |
| Inventories .......................... | (705) | (545) | 17 | 1,512 | 823 |
| Prepaid Expenses .................... | 60 | 111 | 53 | 29 | 32 |
| Investments and long-term receivables ... | 133 | 77 | 169 | 312 | 136 |
| (Increase) decrease in: | | | | | |
| Accounts payable and accrued liabilities | 485 | 266 | 276 | (767) | (1,437) |
| Income, excise, state gasoline, and other taxes payable ...................... | 147 | 93 | 732 | (841) | (637) |
| Foreign exchange translation effects on working capital, debt, and other items, net ................................. | 206 | 203 | — | — | — |
| Application of funds before financing ... | 3,909 | 5,060 | 5,391 | 5,876 | 3,761 |
| Increase (decrease) in funds before financing .......................... | (75) | (1,497) | (749) | (85) | 29 |
| Total Financing* | | | | | |
| Increases in long-term debt .............. | 1,208 | 1,424 | 375 | 525 | 202 |
| Decreases in long-term debt ............. | (450) | (305) | (347) | (231) | (287) |
| Increase (decrease) in capital lease obligations .......................... | 15 | (7) | 5 | (27) | (20) |
| Increase (decrease) in notes and loans payable .......................... | (1,002) | 495 | 743 | (115) | 461 |

*continued*

**EXHIBIT 3**   (*Continued*)

| (Millions) | 1983 | 1982ª | 1981 | 1980 | 1979 |
|---|---|---|---|---|---|
| Increase (decrease) in long-term debt and capital lease obligations maturing within one year | 174 | (21) | 93 | (44) | 1 |
| Purchase of common stock for treasury | (11) | (471) | — | — | — |
| Issuance or sale of common stock | 19 | 12 | 6 | 17 | 10 |
| Total financing increase (decrease) | (47) | 1,128 | 875 | 125 | 367 |
| Increase (Decrease) in Cash and Marketable Securities | $ (122) | $ (369) | $ 126 | $ 40 | $ 396 |

*Excludes the increase (decrease) in financing of two major unconsolidated subsidiaries:

| | | | | | |
|---|---|---|---|---|---|
| Mobil Oil Credit Corporation | $ (16) | $ (101) | $ — | $ 193 | $ 187 |
| Montgomery Ward Credit Corporation | 36 | (315) | (281) | (99) | 498 |
| Total | $ 20 | $ (416) | $ (281) | $ 94 | $ 685 |

ª Restated.

ᵇ Includes acquisition of a working interest in certain holdings of The Anschutz Corp., 1982, and acquisition of operations of TransOcean Oil , Inc., 1980, and General Crude Oil Co., 1979.

*Source:* Mobil Corporation Financial and Operating Statistics 1983.

After some initial consumer resistance, the quality and utility of Everest's lubricants were proven in the marketplace, and Vacuum Oil began growing rapidly. The favorable reputation of Vacuum Oil finally attracted the attention of Rockefeller's Standard Oil Company, and in 1879, Rockefeller bought a controlling interest in the smaller company. Under Standard's aegis, Vacuum Oil evolved into a company whose primary functions were refining, domestic and foreign marketing, domestic manufacturing, and distribution of speciality products. By 1912, Vacuum had become an international lubricating oil company, two-thirds of whose business volume was outside the United States.

Standard Oil Company of New York (Socony) was the other of Mobil's immediate ancestors. When the huge Standard Oil Trust was broken up in the historical antitrust action of 1911, Socony was one of 33 fragments of the original company. In 1912, Socony had both an extensive export business and a wide marketing outlet system. However, the company had no crude oil resources, nor was it involved in the lubricating products business. In fact, after leaving the Standard Oil Trust, neither Socony nor Vacuum Oil had any significant strength in exploration or production. Consequently, both companies began trying to integrate operations in the United States and abroad in order to shore up their respective weaknesses. In 1918, Socony acquired 70% of the stock of a Texas oil producing company called Magnolia Petroleum Company, which had crude oil production, reserves, refineries, and pipeline in the Southwest. Later, in 1925, Socony, which had assets of $90 million, acquired all of the properties of Magnolia Petroleum Co. Other acquisitions included the General Petroleum Corporation of California (1926), which had production properties, refineries, and marketing facilities on the West Coast, and the White Eagle Oil and Refining Company of Kansas City (1930), which had refineries in Wyoming and Kansas. These acquisitions provided considerable new oil reserves and strengthened the company's marketing network throughout the United States.

Socony and Vacuum Oil merged in 1931, forming Socony-Vacuum, with international capabilities to produce, refine, and market petroleum products. Thus, Socony-Vacuum (later to become Mobil) emerged as the youngest and the smallest of the American "sisters." In 1933, Socony-Vacuum pooled its properties and business operations in the Far East with properties owned by Standard Oil Company of New Jersey. Each company owned 50% of the stock of the newly formed company called Standard-Vacuum Oil Company, which handled Far Eastern operations.

In 1939, Socony-Vacuum and Texaco, Inc. each acquired a 50% interest in South American Gulf Oil Co., and a 49.94% interest in Columbian Petroleum Company. Mobil sold its interest in these companies in 1972. In 1955, the company changed its name to Socony Mobil Oil Corporation. (The company later dropped "Socony" from its name and was known as Mobil Oil Corporation until 1976, after which time it was known simply as Mobil Corporation.) By this time, Mobil was already heavily dependent on the Middle East, which supplied 50% of the company's total crude oil. In 1961, Mobil acquired the oil and gas properties and other assets of Republic Natural Gas Co. In the following year the company transferred its business and assets in the Far East, representing its 50% ownership of Standard Vacuum Oil Co., into a new company called Mobil Petroleum Company, Inc. The new firm's affiliates and branches were later brought under the single management of Mobil International Oil Co. (1965).

Other acquisitions in the 1960s and 1970s included Kordite Corp. (1962); Goliad Corp., a gas processor in Louisiana and Texas (1962); Forum Insurance Company (1963); the worldwide paint and chemical coatings interests of Martin Mariett Corp. (1962); Virginia-Carolina Chemical Corp. (1962); Northern Natural Gas

---

**EXHIBIT 4**   Mobil Corporation Distribution of Earnings and Assets-Segments

| (Millions) | 1983 | 1982[a] | 1981 | 1980 | 1979 |
|---|---|---|---|---|---|
| **Total Revenues** | | | | | |
| Petroleum—United States  . . . . . . . . . . | $14,291 | $14,759 | $15,701 | $14,560 | $10,820 |
| —Foreign . . . . . . . . . . . . . . . . | 35,745 | 42,073 | 44,827 | 43,226 | 31,814 |
| Chemical  . . . . . . . . . . . . . . . . . . . . . . . . | 2,424 | 2,246 | 2,437 | 2,027 | 1,718 |
| Paperboard packaging  . . . . . . . . . . . . . . . | 1,779 | 1,953 | 2,068 | 1,946 | 1,647 |
| Retail merchandising. . . . . . . . . . . . . . . . . | 6,646 | 6,143 | 6,122 | 5,916 | 5,652 |
| Other . . . . . . . . . . . . . . . . . . . . . . . . . . . . . | 22 | 46 | 24 | 33 | 13 |
| Adjustments and eliminations  . . . . . . . . . | (1,909) | (3,112) | (2,592) | (3,982) | (3,372) |
| Total  . . . . . . . . . . . . . . . . . . . . . . . . | $58,998 | $64,108 | $68,587 | $63,726 | $48,292 |
| | | | | | |
| **Segment Earnings** | | | | | |
| Petroleum—United States  . . . . . . . . . . | $ 774 | $ 877 | $ 1,174 | $ 953 | $ 689 |
| —Foreign . . . . . . . . . . . . . . . . | 979 | 677 | 1,512 | 2,012 | 1,345 |

*continued*

**EXHIBIT 4**  (*Continued*)

| (Millions) | 1983 | 1982[a] | 1981 | 1980 | 1979 |
|---|---|---|---|---|---|
| Chemical | 8 | 24 | 93 | 119 | 113 |
| Paperboard packaging | 1 | 24 | 57 | 71 | 40 |
| Retail merchandising | 40 | (93) | (160) | (162) | 54 |
| Other | (133) | (136) | (99) | (42) | (83) |
| Corporate expenses | (166) | (160) | (144) | (138) | (151) |
| Income before extraordinary item | $ 1,503 | $ 1,213 | $ 2,433 | $ 2,813 | $ 2,007 |
| | | | | | |
| **Capital Expenditures** | | | | | |
| Petroleum—United States | $ 1,458 | $ 1,617 | $ 1,485 | $ 1,215 | $ 1,160 |
| —Foreign | 1,074 | 1,389 | 1,236 | 1,424 | 825 |
| Chemical | 210 | 328 | 274 | 248 | 146 |
| Paperboard Packaging | 129 | 273 | 255 | 180 | 182 |
| Retail merchandising | 121 | 69 | 144 | 322 | 250 |
| Alternative energy | 16 | 68 | 107 | 48 | 27 |
| Corporate and other | 65 | 77 | 70 | 88 | 52 |
| Total | $ 3,073 | $ 3,821 | $ 3,571 | $ 3,525 | $ 2,642 |
| | | | | | |
| **Depreciation, Depletion, and Amortization** | | | | | |
| Petroleum—United States | $ 1,045 | $ 1,033 | $ 856 | $ 751 | $ 540 |
| —Foreign | 495 | 394 | 445 | 396 | 334 |
| Chemical | 95 | 82 | 76 | 67 | 58 |
| Paperboard packaging | 107 | 93 | 88 | 79 | 71 |
| Retail merchandising | 106 | 105 | 101 | 88 | 74 |
| Corporate and other | 44 | 29 | 20 | 18 | 9 |
| Total | $ 1,892 | $ 1,736 | $ 1,586 | $ 1,399 | $ 1,086 |
| | | | | | |
| **Total Segment Assets at Year-End** | | | | | |
| Petroleum—United States | $10,878 | $10,560 | $ 9,686 | $ 9,107 | $ 7,651 |
| —Foreign | 15,457 | 16,519 | 17,137 | 16,692 | 13,681 |
| Chemical | 2,266 | 2,044 | 1,797 | 1,547 | 1,160 |
| Paperboard packaging | 1,866 | 1,942 | 1,820 | 1,649 | 1,519 |
| Retail merchandising | 4,183 | 4,076 | 4,154 | 3,942 | 3,746 |
| Other | 410 | 391 | 337 | 275 | 271 |
| Corporate assets | 483 | 483 | 443 | 221 | 115 |
| Adjustments and eliminations | (471) | (799) | (598) | (728) | (637) |
| Total | $35,072 | $35,216 | $34,776 | $32,705 | $27,506 |

[a] Restated

*Source:* Mobil Corporation Financial and Operating Statistics 1983.

Producing Co. (1962); Industrias Atlas S.A., a manufacturer of industrial and consumer paints in Mexico (1965); Goodling Electric Co., Inc. (1968); Aral Italiana, an Italian subsidiary of Aral AG, West Germany (1971); Pastucol Cos., three Italian firms which manufactured and marketed polyethylene film products (1971); Marcor Corporation, which operated through two subsidiaries, Montgomery Ward & Co., Inc.

and Container Corp. of America (1974); W. F. Hall Printing Co. (1979); the oil and gas operations of General Crude Oil Co. (1979); and TransOcean Oil Inc. (1980).

In terms of the petroleum business proper, Mobil spent the three decades following its formation in 1931 consolidating its diverse holdings and subsidiaries. Throughout its corporate evolution, Mobil continued to be well known as

**EXHIBIT 5**    Mobil Corporation Distribution of Earnings and Assets—Geographic

| (Millions) | 1983 | 1982[a] | 1981 | 1980 | 1979 |
|---|---|---|---|---|---|
| Total Revenues | | | | | |
| United States | $23,934 | $23,844 | $24,936 | $23,318 | $18,908 |
| Foreign | | | | | |
| Canada | 1,203 | 1,072 | 835 | 850 | 723 |
| Other | 35,399 | 41,898 | 44,901 | 43,189 | 31,806 |
| Total foreign | 36,602 | 42,970 | 45,736 | 44,039 | 32,529 |
| Adjustments and eliminations | (1,538) | (2,706) | (2,085) | (3,631) | (3,145) |
| Total Revenues | $58,998 | $64,108 | $68,587 | $63,726 | $48,292 |
| Geographic Earnings | | | | | |
| United States | $ 659 | $ 660 | $ 1,041 | $ 826 | $ 739 |
| Foreign | | | | | |
| Canada | 104 | 80 | 33 | 97 | 100 |
| Other | 906 | 633 | 1,503 | 2,028 | 1,319 |
| Total foreign | 1,010 | 713 | 1,536 | 2,125 | 1,419 |
| Corporate expenses, net of income taxes | (166) | (160) | (144) | (138) | (151) |
| Income before extraordinary Item | $ 1,503 | $ 1,213 | $ 2,433 | $ 2,813 | $ 2,007 |
| Geographic Assets at Year-End | | | | | |
| United States | $18,706 | $18,123 | $16,898 | $15,644 | $13,696 |
| Foreign | | | | | |
| Canada | 1,329 | 1,314 | 1,138 | 969 | 788 |
| Other | 15,200 | 16,265 | 17,040 | 16,765 | 13,716 |
| Total foreign | 16,529 | 17,579 | 18,187 | 17,734 | 14,504 |
| Corporate assets | 483 | 483 | 443 | 221 | 115 |
| Adjustments and eliminations | (646) | (969) | (752) | (894) | (809) |
| Total Assets | $35,072 | $35,216 | $34,776 | $32,705 | $27,506 |

[a]Restated.
*Source:* Mobil Corporation Financial and Operating Statistics 1983.

a manufacturer of high-grade industrial lubricants. In 1969, Albert Nickerson, Chief Executive Officer at Mobil, noted:

> In most of the world after World War II, the company had really been just a lubricant marketer. Then we started to expand into one European market after another; we constructed refineries; we improved our crude oil sufficiency.[2]

Even so, Mobil continued to be short of crude oil reserves relative to the other majors, and its reputation in lubricants had followed the company into more recent times. An article from the August 1978 issue of *Industrial Marketing* highlighted Mobil's current emphasis on industrial lubricants:

> Mobil Oil Corp. announced a new print ad campaign . . . that will emphasize the company's service and technological expertise in the industrial lubrication market. . . . the new ads are part . . . of an evolutionary communications effort which for the past ten years has been positioning Mobil as the leader in supplying total lubrication programs to industry.[3]

Thus, Mobil Corporation, now the second largest oil company in the United States, still retained part of its heritage, which could be traced to Vacuum Oil, a small producer of petroleum lubricants which had been capitalized in 1866 for $10,000.

## CORPORATE STRUCTURE

Many of the smaller subsidiaries which had been acquired by Socony and Vacuum had not been fully integrated into Mobil's corporate structure. These companies often retained their original staffs, operating procedures, and corporate identities. In 1959, Albert L. Nickerson, chief executive officer of Mobil, initiated an extensive companywide program of reorganization which included the full integration of some of the more independent of Mobil's subsidiaries. Concerted efforts were made to cut fixed costs in the form of redundant staff services, to improve efficiency in exploration and production through better coordination among subsidiaries, and to redefine corporate strategy.

From 1969 until the present, Mobil had been led by two men: Rawleigh Warner, Jr., chairman, and William P. Tavoulareas, president and (later) chief operating officer. Both men rose through the ranks of the company on the financial side. This was somewhat unique, as the engineering ladder was, for most oil companies, the more traditional route. Warner had received a liberal arts degree from Princeton. Tavoulareas started with Mobil in 1947 in the accounting department, and later received a law degree.[4] Tavoulareas was named the first manager of the newly formed planning department in 1959, part of Nickerson's program of reorganization. One oil analyst who worked in planning and finance at Mobil for ten years said, "Mobil is a lawyer-businessman company rather than an oilman-geologist company. Planning is the real essence of this company."[5]

As head of planning, Tavoulareas set out to shake up a company said to be extremely slothful and badly in need of reorientation. Though incurring the ire of some of Mobil's more traditional executives, Tavoulareas and his planning department set in motion a procedure of carefully scrutinizing all projects and killing those which failed to measure up financially.[6]

---

[2]"How to Rob Peter . . . ," *Forbes,* June 15, 1969, pp. 30–31.

[3]"New Mobil Pro Ad Campaign Stresses Expertise in Industrial Lubricants," *Industrial Marketing,* August 1978, p. 22.

[4]"What Makes Mobil Run," *Business Week,* June 13, 1977, pp. 80–85.

[5]*Ibid.*

[6]"Mobil's Maverick: Tavoulareas Puts Firm on a Separate Course From Most of Big Oil," *The Wall Street Journal,* February 14, 1980, p. 18.

Both Warner and Tavoulareas continued the earlier trend toward leaner staffing and greater consolidation. In 1973, Mobil's United States marketing force, which had previously been operating through seven divisions, was consolidated into four regional offices, whose greater efficiency was expected to save the company about $10 million a year.[7]

Prior to 1974, Mobil was organized into four operating divisions. The North American Division was Mobil's operating petroleum division for the United States and Canada. The International Division coordinated the petroleum operations of Mobil affiliates outside the United States and Canada. Mobil Chemical Company was an operating division formed in 1960 which coordinated the chemical operations of Mobil affiliates in the United States and several other countries. This division was involved in the manufacture of agricultural and industrial chemicals, plastics, paints, chemical coatings, and petrochemicals. The fourth division, Transportation, was comprised of domestic trucking, pipelines, and deep sea carriers.

In 1974, the North American Division was reorganized to exclude Canada; the resulting divisions were U.S. Operations and Foreign Operations. Two years later, on July 1, 1976, a holding company was formed called Mobil Corporation, encompassing the Mobil Oil Corporation (which included domestic and foreign energy operations), the Mobil Chemical Company, Montgomery Ward, and Container Corporation. So there were still four operating segments, but they were now distinguished as follows: Energy Operations, including the subdivisions of United States Energy Operations and Foreign Energy Operations; Chemical Operations; Retail Merchandising; and Paperboard Packaging.

Further belt-tightening moves were put into effect in the early 1980s, paralleling efforts made by other industry members. As part of an overall attempt to trim fixed costs, Mobil closed various plants, refineries, and gasoline terminals. The company also scrapped surplus tankers, cut back on travel, and shrank an administrative unit in Europe.

Another reorganization took place in late 1982. This most recent restructuring was said to be setting the stage for the retirement of Warner and Tavoulareas. Warner was scheduled to retire in 1986 and Tavoulareas in 1983. (However, during 1983, the board extended Tavoulareas' tenure until November of 1984.)

Two major operating units were established under Mobil Corporation, which remained responsible for overall policy and strategy decisions. All oil and gas related activities became the responsibility of Mobil Oil. Allen E. Murray was named president of this unit. All other activities, such as chemicals, paperboard packaging, retailing, and alternative energy interests, became the responsibility of Mobil Diversified Business. The creation of this new division lumped the company's most severely troubled businesses into a single group. Richard F. Tucker was named president of this unit. Warner and Tavoulareas were, in turn, named chairman and vice chairman of Mobil's Executive Committee.

Murray and Tucker were often compared to Tavoulareas and Warner and were considerd to be heirs apparent. "Murray is a numbers man, and he came in from the bottom, like Tavoulareas. Tucker is extremely effective in public and came to Mobil at a later stage—and at a fairly high level—as Warner did."[8] Shortly after the reorganization, Warner was quoted as saying, "We will rate these individuals on their capacity to meet established plans."[9]

---

[7]"Mobil Reshuffle Aims at Cost-Cutting," *National Petroleum News,* September 1973, p. 145.

[8]"Mobil's Costly Saudi Strategy," *Business Week,* October 17, 1983, p. 76.
[9]*Ibid.*

## EXPLORATION AND PRODUCTION

Mobil's commitment to a strong exploration program can be traced back to the Suez crisis in 1956, when Mobil's Middle East oil supplies were seriously disrupted and the company paid dearly to acquire crude. A tangible sign of an increased emphasis on exploration was Mobil's increased acreage position, which doubled to nearly 100 million acres throughout the 1960s.

Despite this apparent strategy, the period of the 1960s and early 1970s was a frustrating one for the explorationists at Mobil. The company still concentrated a great deal on downstream (refining and marketing) activities. A number of instances could be cited in which Mobil sold or passed up the opportunity to buy into certain prospects, Alaska being the most costly. Mobil's staff was one of the first to perform seismic work on Alaska's North Slope and vigorously encouraged Mobil's participation. However, the company did not bid aggressively on what later became the Prudhoe Bay field. "The financial people in this company did a disservice to the exploration people," Warner was quoted as saying. "The poor people in exploration were adversely impacted by people (in the company) who knew nothing about oil and gas."[10]

Oil prices substantially increased during the 1970s and Mobil, like the other majors, stepped up its exploration activities. By the late 1970s, Mobil's strategy was finally paying off. The company held an interest in nine giant oil and gas fields which were discovered during 1979 and the first half of 1980, each of which could net Mobil the equivalent of at least 100 million barrels of new reserves. "We've hit on some kind of formula in exploration," said Tavoulareas. "We hope we are in a cycle where each year we can find a big field, and if we do, I'm not worried about our future."[11]

### Saudi Arabia

During the late 1940s, Texaco and Standard Oil Co. of California (Socal), who were then co-owners of Arabian American Oil Company (Aramco), offered 40% of Aramco to Jersey Standard and Mobil. Being a bit nervous about its ability to absorb its share of crude oil, Mobil opted for 10% rather than the 20% it could have bought.

Commented Warner in 1971:

> That (decision) cost us a tremendous amount of money. . . . The oil companies that year in and year out make the most money make it because they are balanced. They move their own crude, they refine their own crude, and they sell their own crude.[12]

By the mid-1950s, the Middle East was supplying approximately 50% of Mobil's crude oil. The company's dependence on Mideast oil was particularly evident during the Arab-Israeli war in 1956. Mobil's earnings suffered much more than its competitors' with the closing of the Suez Canal during that conflict.

William Tavoulareas first went to the Middle East on Mobil business in late 1950. He possessed a no-nonsense manner and a determination to build a strong relationship with the Saudis. As his stature in Mobil grew, Tavoulareas' conviction that the company's best prospects lay in enhancing its access to Saudi oil became engrained in Mobil's strategy. For years this strategy handsomely benefitted the traditionally crude-poor oil company. During the mid-1970s, he skillfully negotiated a five-year contract to acquire another 5% of Aramco.

Originally, the Aramco partners (Exxon, Mobil, Texaco, and Socal) owned the production and the Saudi government was paid a royalty. During the mid-1970s, however, the Saudis began negotiations to buy out the Aramco part-

---

[10]"Mobil's Successful Exploration," *Business Week*, October 13, 1980, p. 112.

[11]*Ibid.*

[12]"The Lively Tortoise," *Forbes,* August 1, 1971, pp. 18–19.

**EXHIBIT 6**    Mobil Corporation Capital, Exploration, and Other Outlays

| (Millions) | 1983 | 1982[a] | 1981 | 1980 | 1979 |
|---|---|---|---|---|---|
| Segment Distribution | | | | | |
| United States | | | | | |
|   Petroleum— ............... | $ 1,742 | $ 2,061 | $ 1,804 | $ 1,429 | $ 1,301 |
|     —Acquisitions[b] ..... | — | 500 | — | 712 | 700 |
|   Chemical ................. | 195 | 311 | 258 | 200 | 130 |
|   Paperboard packaging ....... | 101 | 224 | 208 | 131 | 144 |
|   Retail merchandising ........ | 121 | 69 | 144 | 322 | 250 |
|   Alternative energy .......... | 12 | 82 | 123 | 61 | 40 |
|   Corporate and other ........ | 145 | 162 | 165 | 139 | 72 |
|     Total ................. | $ 2,316 | $ 3,409 | $ 2,702 | $ 2,994 | $ 2,637 |
| Foreign | | | | | |
|   Petroleum— ................. | $ 1,400 | $ 1,774 | $ 1,697 | $ 1,715 | $ 1,026 |
|     —Acquisitions[b] ....... | — | — | — | 3 | 92 |
|   Chemical ................. | 15 | 17 | 16 | 48 | 16 |
|   Paperboard packaging ........ | 28 | 49 | 47 | 49 | 38 |
|   Alternative energy ............ | 12 | 4 | 7 | 6 | 3 |
|     Total .................... | $ 1,455 | $ 1,844 | $ 1,767 | $ 1,821 | $ 1,175 |
| Worldwide | | | | | |
|   Petroleum— ................. | $ 3,142 | $ 3,835 | $ 3,501 | $ 3,144 | $ 2,327 |
|     —Acquisitions[b] ....... | — | 500 | — | 715 | 792 |
|   Chemical ................. | 210 | 328 | 274 | 248 | 146 |
|   Paperboard packaging ......... | 129 | 273 | 255 | 180 | 182 |
|   Retail merchandising .......... | 121 | 69 | 144 | 322 | 250 |
|   Alternative energy ............ | 24 | 86 | 130 | 67 | 43 |
|   Corporate and other .......... | 145 | 162 | 165 | 139 | 72 |
|     Total .................... | $ 3,771 | $ 5,253 | $ 4,469 | $ 4,815 | $ 3,812 |
| Geographic Distribution | | | | | |
|   United States ............... | $ 2,316 | $ 3,409 | $ 2,702 | $ 2,994 | $ 2,637 |
|   Canada .................... | 153 | 138 | 148 | 222 | 206 |
|   Other foreign ................. | 1,302 | 1,706 | 1,619 | 1,599 | 969 |
|   Worldwide ................. | $ 3,771 | $ 5,253 | $ 4,469 | $ 4,815 | $ 3,812 |
| Research Expense ............. | $ 209 | $ 196 | $ 179 | $ 143 | $ 115 |

[a]Restated.
[b]Includes acquisition of a working interest in certain holdings of The Anschutz Corp., 1982, and acquisition of the operations of TransOcean Oil, Inc., 1980, and General Crude Oil Co., 1979.
*Source:* Mobil Corporation Financial and Operating Statistics 1983.

ners. This process was completed in 1980. The partners were granted priority access to significant volumes of Saudi Arabian oil. The price of this oil put the partners at both an advantage and at a disadvantage compared with their competitors during the four years which followed the buyout.

Saudi Arabia, with its small population and vast reserves, had traditionally possessed sufficient foresight to cut back production in times of surplus. Special access to Saudi crude, therefore, was likely to pay off only in an expanding market.

Access to Saudi oil was especially beneficial from 1979 to 1981, when the Saudis were flooding the market with relatively cheap oil to retain world prices. The so-called "Aramco advantage" added some $200 million to Mobil's 1980 earnings.[13]

In 1981, the Aramco advantage became a burden. When world oil prices started declining, Saudi oil became among the world's most expensive, because the country adhered rigidly to OPEC's price structure. As other members of Aramco slashed their purchases, Mobil increased its take, buying as much as 35% of Aramco's contracted volumes. Tavoulareas explained, "We made a commitment to believing continued reliance on Saudi crude would be a benefit to our company. Every time we set out to lift more than our share, other guys (in Aramco) cut back more . . . so we lifted a bit more than we wanted to."[14] Mobil's European refining and marketing arm, once a principal profit center because it used competitively priced Saudi crude, lost $280 million in 1982, a drop of more than $1 billion from 1980.

To further cement its ties to the Saudis, Mobil, in 1980, agreed to build two vast export facilities for the Saudis: an oil refinery and a petrochemical complex in Yanbu, a new industrial city on the Red Sea. In return, Mobil won the right to buy an extra 1.4 billion barrels of extra crude over 19 years. Tavoulareas defended the deal by pointing to the favorable financing and low-cost materials that the Saudis have promised. However, he stated, "These projects must be judged as part of the Saudi 'insurance policy' rather than by their own economics."[15]

Mobil's bold moves in Saudi Arabia were not without criticism from skeptical industry members. Warned one highly placed industry source:

> Mobil's serious risk is that the market won't grow. They made their big, expensive moves in Saudi Arabia in an expansive environment. The expenses they made there have drawn resources that could have been used elsewhere.[16]

Nonetheless, Mobil's Saudi commitment has never waivered. By year-end 1983, $600 million had been spent at Yanbu. In addition, many hours of manpower had been employed to train Saudis to run the complexes. In February 1984, Mobil directors held their board meeting in Saudi Arabia—a first for any U.S. corporation.

In early 1984, Mobil was receiving less than 30% of its total crude supply from Saudi Arabia. Though Mobil was lifting the full amount of oil to which it was contractually obligated, the Saudi portion of Mobil's total crude supply was down from some 50% in 1982.

## Offshore Activities

During the early 1970s, Mobil decided to confine most of its domestic exploration to a search for big fields in offshore waters. The Gulf of Mexico was the area in which Mobil spent the most and received the greatest rewards. Between 1970 and 1983, the company spent over $2.5 billion to acquire federal lease bonuses, second in the industry. For the most part, Mobil

---

[13]"What Makes Mobil Run," *op. cit.*
[14]"Mobil's Costly Saudi Strategy," *op. cit.*

[15]*Ibid.*
[16]*Ibid.*

**EXHIBIT 7**    Mobil Corporation Supplementary Oil and Gas Producing Disclosures
**Table 1**    Estimated Quantities of Net Proved Crude Oil and Natural Gas Liquids Reserves (unaudited)

| | United States | | Foreign | | | | | | |
| | | | Canada | | Europe | | Other | | |
| (Millions of barrels) | Crude | NGL | Crude | NGL | Crude | NGL | Crude | NGL | Total |
|---|---|---|---|---|---|---|---|---|---|
| Year Ended December 31, 1983 | | | | | | | | | |
| Net proved reserves | | | | | | | | | |
|  —beginning of year | 746 | 180 | 180 | 62 | 506 | 11 | 390 | 200 | 2,255 |
|  —revisions of previous estimates | 2 | 3 | 4 | (3) | (6) | — | — | 12 | 12 |
|  —improved recovery | 26 | — | 3 | 1 | 8 | — | — | — | 38 |
|  —extensions, discoveries, and other additions | 18 | 2 | 4 | — | 7 | — | 3 | — | 34 |
|  —production | (86) | (16) | (17) | (2) | (36) | — | (21) | (13) | (191) |
| Net proved reserves | | | | | | | | | |
|  —end of year | 706 | 149 | 174 | 58 | 479 | 11 | 372 | 199 | 2,148 |
| Net proved developed reserves | | | | | | | | | |
|  —beginning of year | 670 | 156 | 180 | 62 | 152 | — | 238 | 200 | 1,658 |
|  —end of year | 638 | 146 | 174 | 58 | 188 | 1 | 231 | 199 | 1,635 |
| Mobil's share of net proved reserves of investees accounted for on the equity method | — | — | — | — | 6 | — | 431 | — | 437 |
| Quantities under special arrangements in which the company acts as producer | | | | | | | | | |
|  —quantities received during the year | — | — | — | — | — | — | 34 | — | 34 |
|  —estimated future quantities | — | — | — | — | — | — | 14 | — | 14 |
| Year Ended December 31, 1982 | | | | | | | | | |
| Net proved reserves | | | | | | | | | |
|  —beginning of year | 766 | 132 | 189 | 55 | 536 | 8 | 520 | 219 | 2,425 |
|  —revisions of previous estimates | 34 | 10 | 4 | 9 | (6) | 3 | (124) | (7) | (77) |
|  —improved recovery | 25 | 1 | — | — | 4 | — | — | — | 30 |

*(continued)*

EXHIBIT 7   (*Continued*)     Table 1 (*Continued*)

| (Millions of barrels) | United States | | Foreign | | | | | | |
| | | | Canada | | Europe | | Other | | |
| | Crude | NGL | Crude | NGL | Crude | NGL | Crude | NGL | Total |
|---|---|---|---|---|---|---|---|---|---|
| —purchases (sales) of minerals in place | — | 33 | — | — | — | — | (1) | — | 32 |
| —extensions, discoveries, and other additions | 7 | 1 | 2 | — | 1 | — | 18 | — | 29 |
| —production | (86) | (17) | (15) | (2) | (29) | — | (23) | (12) | (184) |
| Net proved reserves | | | | | | | | | |
| —end of year | 746 | 160 | 180 | 62 | 506 | 11 | 390 | 200 | 2,255 |
| Net proved developed reserves | | | | | | | | | |
| —beginning of year | 677 | 127 | 189 | 55 | 167 | 1 | 289 | 158 | 1,663 |
| —end of year | 670 | 156 | 180 | 62 | 152 | — | 238 | 200 | 1,658 |
| Mobil's share of net proved reserves of investees accounted for on the equity method | — | — | — | — | 6 | — | 451 | 2 | 459 |
| Quantities under special arrangements in which the company acts as producer | | | | | | | | | |
| —quantities received during the year | — | — | — | — | — | — | 31 | — | 31 |
| —estimated future quantities | — | — | — | — | — | — | 43 | — | 43 |

has been successful in maintaining U.S. reserves through a combination of exploration efforts in the Gulf of Mexico and a series of acquisitions of producing companies.

Mobil acquired 20,000 acres in the Mobile Bay, offshore Alabama, in a state lease sale in 1969 for a low price. The company completed a discovery well in 1979 which flowed 12.2 million cubic feet per day of natural gas. The company then acquired drilling permits for four additional wells, and, in 1981, bought two more leases near the discovery. Mobil estimated reserves on the acreage to be between 200 and 600 billion cubic feet. However, industry analysts believed that the potential of the area was much higher—nearly one trillion cubic feet.[17]

Mobil's long record of success in the Gulf

[17] "Research Brief, Mobil Corporation," Goldman Sachs, April 1, 1981.

**EXHIBIT 7 (*Continued*)** Mobil Corporation Supplementary Oil and Gas Producing Disclosures
**Table 1** Estimated Quantities of Net Proved Crude Oil and Natural Gas Liquids Reserves (unaudited) (continued)

| (Millions of barrels) | United States | | Foreign | | | | | | |
| | | | Canada | | Europe | | Other | | |
| | Crude | NGL | Crude | NGL | Crude | NGL | Crude | NGL | Total |
|---|---|---|---|---|---|---|---|---|---|
| Year Ended December 31, 1981 | | | | | | | | | |
| Net proved reserves | | | | | | | | | |
| —beginning of year | 742 | 148 | 199 | 53 | 574 | 10 | 355 | 170 | 2,251 |
| —revisions of previous estimates | 37 | 2 | 5 | 2 | (12) | (3) | 13 | 61 | 105 |
| —improved recovery | 55 | — | 1 | — | 1 | 1 | — | — | 58 |
| —extensions, discoveries, and other additions | 19 | — | — | 1 | — | — | 177 | — | 197 |
| —production | (87) | (18) | (16) | (1) | (27) | — | (25) | (12) | (186) |
| Net proved reserves | | | | | | | | | |
| —end of year | 766 | 132 | 189 | 55 | 536 | 8 | 520 | 219 | 2,425 |
| Net proved developed reserves | | | | | | | | | |
| —beginning of year | 624 | 135 | 199 | 53 | 164 | 10 | 280 | 169 | 1,634 |
| —end of year | 677 | 127 | 189 | 55 | 167 | 1 | 289 | 158 | 1,663 |
| Mobil's share of net proved reserves of investees accounted for on the equity method | — | — | — | — | 7 | — | 453 | 2 | 462 |
| Quantities under special arrangements in which the company acts as producer | | | | | | | | | |
| —quantities received during the year | — | — | — | — | — | — | 31 | — | 31 |
| —estimated future quantities | — | — | — | — | — | — | 78 | — | 78 |

**Table 2** Estimated Quantities of Net Proved Natural Gas Reserves (unaudited)

| (Billions of cubic feet) | United States | Foreign | | | Total |
| | | Canada | Europe | Other | |
|---|---|---|---|---|---|
| Year Ended December 31, 1983 | | | | | |
| Net proved reserves | | | | | |
| —beginning of year | 6,334 | 1,977 | 2,053 | 6,893 | 17,257 |
| —revisions of previous estimates | (13) | (29) | 48 | 1,353 | 1,359 |

*continued*

**EXHIBIT 7** *(Continued)* **Table 2** *(Continued)*

| (Millions of barrels) | United States Crude | NGL | Foreign Canada Crude | NGL | Europe Crude | NGL | Other Crude | NGL | Total |
|---|---|---|---|---|---|---|---|---|---|
| —improved recovery | | | | 3 | 3 | | 2 | — | 8 |
| —purchases (sales) of minerals in place | | | | (1) | — | | — | — | (1) |
| —extensions, discoveries, and other additions | | | | 400 | 12 | | 152 | — | 564 |
| —production | | | | (448) | (67) | | (96) | (247) | (860) |
| Net proved reserves | | | | | | | | | |
| —end of year | | | | 6,275 | 1,896 | | 2,157 | 7,999 | 18,327 |
| Net proved developed reserves | | | | | | | | | |
| —beginning of year | | | | 5,938 | 1,976 | | 1,192 | 6,893 | 15,999 |
| —end of year | | | | 5,941 | 1,895 | | 1,276 | 7,999 | 17,111 |
| Mobil's share of net proved reserves of investees accounted for on the equity method | | | | — | — | | 61 | 93 | 154 |

*Source: Mobil Corporation Annual Report 1983.*

of Mexico continued with a significant discovery in the Green Canyon areas of the central Gulf. In a 1983 central Gulf lease sale, Mobil added considerably to its holdings in the area, spending more than $400 million for interests in 38 leases. Some of these tracts were located in the vicinity of the Green Canyon discovery.

The company's exploration efforts in other domestic offshore areas have not been as prosperous. Following the launching of a sophisticated $14 million geophysical vessel in 1978, Mobil bid aggressively in a 1979 federal drilling lease sale for tracts located off Massachusetts. Mobil spent $222 million, more than one quarter of the money the government took in.[18] People in the industry questioned whether Mobil had simply overbid or had seen more valuable structures in the area because it had better data. Unfortunately for Mobil, the former turned out to be closer to the truth. The company spudded its first well in the area in 1981. As of 1984, no hydrocarbons had been discovered.

Other offshore U.S. areas have also proved to be disappointing. Expenditures in the Bal-

timore Canyon, where Mobil began drilling in 1978, have been largely written off.

Mobil's partnership with Sohio in a promising offshore Alaska exploration effort ended in further disappointment. Mobil had paid $288 million for 14 federal tracts in the Mukluk area. Failure to discover commercial quantities of oil and gas in the well drilled there caused Mobil to write off its share of the costs to drill the well, as well as part of its investment in tracts in the Mukluk area. This amounted to a $98 million after-tax write-off against 1983 income.

Mobil's efforts to find hydrocarbons in offshore areas in other parts of the world have proved more fruitful, however. In 1971, Mobil discovered Arun, a 13 trillion cubic feet gas field in Indonesia which ranked as the second largest gas field of the decade. To exploit the field, a liquefied natural gas plant was built by Pertamina, the Indonesian state oil company. Arun has been Mobil's most profitable single property, annually contributing more than $300 million to net income.

Mobil was the holder of the largest private interest in the Statfjord Field. This field had been discovered by Mobil and was located off

[18]"Mobil's Successful Exploration," *op. cit.*

**EXHIBIT 7** (*Continued*)   Mobil Corporation Supplementary Oil and Gas Producing Disclosures
**Table 2**   Estimated Quantities of Net Proved Natural Gas Reserves (unaudited)

| (Billions of cubic feet) | United States | Foreign | | | Total |
| --- | --- | --- | --- | --- | --- |
| | | Canada | Europe | Other | |
| **Year Ended December 31, 1982** | | | | | |
| Net proved reserves | | | | | |
| —beginning of year | 6,310 | 2,147 | 2,160 | 6,761 | 17,378 |
| —revisions of previous estimates | 251 | (110) | (162) | 348 | 327 |
| —improved recovery | 26 | — | — | — | 26 |
| —purchases (sales) of minerals in place | 133 | — | — | (1) | 132 |
| —extensions, discoveries, and other additions | 220 | 7 | 151 | — | 378 |
| —production | (606) | (67) | (96) | (215) | (984) |
| Net proved reserves | | | | | |
| —end of year | 6,334 | 1,977 | 2,053 | 6,893 | 17,257 |
| Net proved developed reserves | | | | | |
| —beginning of year | 5,872 | 2,146 | 1,415 | 3,514 | 12,947 |
| —end of year | 5,938 | 1,976 | 1,192 | 6,893 | 15,999 |
| Mobil's share of net proved reserves of investees accounted for on the equity method | — | — | 58 | 206 | 266 |
| **Year Ended December 31, 1981** | | | | | |
| Net proved reserves | | | | | |
| —beginning of year | 6,205 | 2,082 | 2,275 | 3,712 | 14,274 |
| —revisions of previous estimates | 508 | 94 | (59) | 3,248 | 3,791 |
| —improved recovery | 88 | 2 | — | — | 90 |
| —extensions, discoveries, and other additions | 170 | 33 | 62 | — | 265 |
| —production | (661) | (64) | (118) | (199) | (1,042) |
| Net proved reserves | | | | | |
| —end of year | 6,310 | 2,147 | 2,160 | 6,761 | 17,378 |
| Net proved developed reserves | | | | | |
| —beginning of year | 5,754 | 2,080 | 1,514 | 3,712 | 13,060 |
| —end of year | 5,872 | 2,146 | 1,415 | 3,514 | 12,947 |
| Mobil's share of net proved reserves of investees accounted for on the equity method | — | — | 60 | 206 | 266 |

*Source: Mobil Corporation Annual Report 1983.*

the coast of Norway in the North Sea. The company's interest in this project was almost 13%, the largest of any of the twelve company partners except Statoil, the Norwegian State Oil Company. Production from the Statfjord Field, which had reserves of more than 3 billion barrels of oil and 2.5 trillion cubic feet of natural gas, began in November 1979 and reached a total of 391,000 barrels daily in 1983.

The largest single North Sea addition, however, was the Beryl oil and gas field in the British sector. Mobil held a 50% interest in Beryl,

**EXHIBIT 7 (***Continued***)** Mobil Corporation Supplementary Oil and Gas Producing Disclosures
**Table 3** Capitalized Costs Related to Oil and Gas Property Acquisition, Exploration, and Development Activities (unaudited)

| (In millions) At December 31, | 1983 | 1982 |
|---|---|---|
| Capitalized costs | | |
| Unproved properties | $ 2,032 | $ 1,928 |
| Proved properties, wells, plants, and other equipment | 14,259 | 12,848 |
| Total capitalized costs | $16,291 | $14,776 |
| Accumulated depreciation, depletion, and amortization | $ 6,224 | $ 5,360 |
| Mobil's share of net capitalized costs of investees accounted for on the equity method | $ 120 | $ 124 |

**Table 4** Costs Incurred in Oil and Gas Property Acquisition, Exploration, and Development Activities (unaudited)

| (In millions) | United States | Foreign | | | Total |
|---|---|---|---|---|---|
| | | Canada | Europe | Other | |
| Year Ended December 31, 1983 | | | | | |
| Property acquisition costs | $ 473 | $ 2 | $ — | $ — | $ 475 |
| Exploration costs | 508 | 110 | 158 | 148 | 924 |
| Development costs | 493 | 37 | 463 | 161 | 1,154 |
| Total expenditures | $1,474 | $149 | $621 | $309 | $2,553 |
| Mobil's share of investees' costs of property acquisition, exploration, and development | — | — | $ 12 | $ 37 | $ 49 |
| Year Ended December 31, 1982 | | | | | |
| Property acquisition costs | $ 947 | $ 2 | $ — | $ 15 | $ 964 |
| Exploration costs | 712 | 88 | 168 | 290 | 1,258 |
| Development costs | 608 | 44 | 514 | 218 | 1,384 |
| Total expenditures | $2,267 | $134 | $682 | $523 | $3,606 |
| Mobil's share of investees' costs of property acquisition, exploration, and development | — | — | $ 17 | $ 59 | $ 76 |
| Year Ended December 31, 1981 | | | | | |
| Property acquisition costs | $ 383 | $ 1 | $ — | $ 6 | $ 390 |
| Exploration costs | 633 | 115 | 96 | 396 | 1,240 |
| Development costs | 516 | 19 | 385 | 130 | 1,050 |
| Total expenditures | $1,532 | $135 | $481 | $532 | $2,680 |
| Mobil's share of investees' costs of property acquisition, exploration, and development | — | — | $ 14 | $ 37 | $ 51 |

*Source: Mobil Corporation Annual Report 1983.*

**EXHIBIT 7** (*Continued*)     Mobil Corporation Supplementary Oil and Gas Producing Disclosures
**Table 5**   Results of Operations for Oil and Gas Producing Activities (unaudited)

| (In millions) | United States | Foreign Canada | Foreign Europe | Foreign Other | Total |
|---|---|---|---|---|---|
| **Year Ended December 31, 1983** | | | | | |
| Revenues—Trade sales | $ 935 | $150 | $776 | $ 931 | $2,792 |
| —Intercompany sales | 3,059 | 493 | 894 | 1,183 | 5,629 |
| Production (lifting) costs | (1,606) | (213) | (608) | (397) | (2,824) |
| Exploration expenses | (296) | (34) | (119) | (181) | (630) |
| Depreciation, depletion, and amortization | (845) | (39) | (108) | (79) | (1,071) |
| Other operating revenues and (expenses) | (39) | 13 | 45 | (9) | 10 |
| Finance (charges) credits | (75) | (8) | (11) | (1) | (95) |
| Income tax expense | (522) | (258) | (635) | (1,132) | (2,547) |
| Results of operations for producing activities | $ 611 | $104 | $234 | $ 315 | $1,264 |
| Mobil's share of results of operations for producing activities of investees accounted for on the equity method | — | — | $ 20 | $ 29 | $ 49 |
| **Year Ended December 31, 1982** | | | | | |
| Revenues—Trade sales | $1,132 | $135 | $552 | $ 947 | $2,766 |
| —Intercompany sales | 3,134 | 386 | 954 | 1,197 | 5,671 |
| Production (lifting) costs | (1,600) | (195) | (565) | (554) | (2,914) |
| Exploration expenses | (457) | (45) | (104) | (247) | (853) |
| Depreciation, depletion, and amortization | (802) | (27) | (76) | (49) | (954) |
| Other operating revenues and (expenses) | (21) | 25 | 44 | (5) | 43 |
| Finance (charges) credits | (49) | 30 | (94) | 7 | (106) |
| Income tax expense | (599) | (211) | (509) | (1,054) | (2,373) |
| Results of operations for producing activities | $ 738 | $ 98 | $202 | $ 242 | $1,280 |
| Mobil's share of results of operations for producing activities of investees accounted for on the equity method | — | — | $ 15 | $ 37 | $ 52 |
| **Year Ended December 31, 1981** | | | | | |
| Revenues—Trade sales | $1,098 | $127 | $541 | $ 973 | $2,739 |
| —Intercompany sales | 3,422 | 280 | 987 | 1,414 | 6,103 |
| Production (lifting) costs | (1,788) | (152) | (541) | (518) | (2,999) |
| Exploration expenses | (326) | (72) | (61) | (330) | (789) |
| Depreciation, depletion, and amortization | (636) | (31) | (72) | (83) | (822) |
| Other operating revenues and (expenses) | (13) | 25 | 37 | (7) | 42 |
| Finance (charges) credits | (44) | 16 | (15) | 27 | (16) |
| Income tax expense | (803) | (146) | (439) | (1,281) | (2,669) |
| Results of operations for producing activities | $ 910 | $ 47 | $437 | $ 195 | $1,589 |
| Mobil's share of results of operations for producing activities of investees accounted for on the equity method | — | — | $ 14 | $ 42 | $ 56 |

*Source: Mobil Corporation Annual Report 1983.*

**EXHIBIT 7 (***Continued***)**    Mobil Corporation Supplementary Oil and Gas Producing Disclosures
**Table 6**    Standardized Measure of Discounted Future Net Cash Flows Relating to Proved Oil and Gas Reserves (unaudited)

| (In millions) | United States | Foreign | | | Total |
| --- | --- | --- | --- | --- | --- |
| | | Canada | Europe | Other | |
| **At December 31, 1983** | | | | | |
| Future cash inflows | $34,939 | $9,019 | $23,481 | $54,091 | $121,530 |
| Future production costs | (13,963) | (3,115) | (6,888) | (3,817) | (27,783) |
| Future development costs | (890) | (7) | (1,124) | (766) | (2,787) |
| Future income tax expenses | (7,593) | (3,663) | (10,926) | (30,359) | (52,541) |
| Future net cash flows | 12,493 | 2,234 | 4,543 | 19,149 | 38,419 |
| 10% annual discount for estimated timing of cash flows | (5,254) | (1,186) | (1,908) | (10,255) | (18,603) |
| Standardized measure of discounted future net cash flows | $ 7,239 | $1,048 | $ 2,635 | $ 8,894 | $ 19,816 |
| Mobil's share of standardized measure of discounted future net cash flows of investees accounted for on the equity method | — | — | $    83 | $    128 | $    211 |
| **At December 31, 1982** | | | | | |
| Future cash inflows | $37,315 | $8,634 | $26,727 | $59,262 | $131,938 |
| Future production costs | (16,400) | (3,341) | (6,703) | (4,230) | (30,674) |
| Future development costs | (709) | (17) | (1,830) | (963) | (3,519) |
| Future income tax expenses | (7,956) | (3,298) | (12,139) | (33,771) | (57,164) |
| Future net cash flows | 12,250 | 1,978 | 6,055 | 20,298 | 40,581 |
| 10% annual discount for estimated timing of cash flows | (4,875) | (1,051) | (2,319) | (11,111) | (19,356) |
| Standardized measure of discounted future net cash flows | | $   927 | $ 3,736 | $ 9,187 | $ 21,225 |
| Mobil's share of standardized measure of discounted future net cash flows of investees accounted for on the equity method | — | — | $    85 | $    163 | $    248 |
| **At December 31, 1981** | | | | | |
| Future cash inflows | $39,082 | $7,755 | $30,946 | $58,542 | $136,325 |
| Future production costs | (14,956) | (2,765) | (5,507) | (4,813) | (28,041) |
| Future development costs | (796) | (13) | (1,862) | (1,294) | (3,965) |
| Future income tax expenses | (9,744) | (3,451) | (16,348) | (33,683) | (63,226) |
| Future net cash flows | 13,586 | 1,526 | 7,229 | 18,752 | 41,093 |

*Continued*

**EXHIBIT 7 (***Continued***)** Mobil Corporation Supplementary Oil and Gas Producing Disclosures
**Table 6** (*Continued*) Standardized Measure of Discounted Future Net Cash Flows Relating to
Proved Oil and Gas Reserves (unaudited)

| (In millions) | United States | Foreign | | | Total |
| --- | --- | --- | --- | --- | --- |
| | | Canada | Europe | Other | |
| 10% annual discount for estimated timing of cash flows | (6,077) | (758) | (3,343) | (10,404) | (20,582) |
| Standardized measure of discounted future net cash flows | $ 7,509 | $ 768 | $ 3,886 | $ 8,348 | $ 20,511 |
| Mobil's share of standardized measure of discounted future net cash flows of investees accounted for on the equity method | — | — | $ 86 | $ 169 | $ 255 |

**Table 7** Changes in Standardized Measure of Discounted Future Net Cash Flows (unaudited)

| (In millions) At December 31, | 1983 | 1982 | 1981 |
| --- | --- | --- | --- |
| Beginning of year | $21,473 | $20,766 | $19,014 |
| Changes resulting from: | | | |
| Sales and transfers of production, net of production costs | (5,597) | (5,523) | (5,843) |
| Net changes in prices, and development and production costs | (6,980) | (3,308) | (5,674) |
| Extensions, discoveries, additions, and purchases less related costs | 919 | 1,363 | 3,118 |
| Development costs incurred during the period | 1,154 | 1,384 | 1,050 |
| Revisions of previous quantity estimates | 3,250 | (833) | 8,658 |
| Accretion of discount | 5,077 | 4,836 | 4,293 |
| Net change in income taxes | 768 | 2,795 | (3,868) |
| Other | (37) | (7) | 18 |
| End of year | $20,027 | $21,473 | $ 20,766 |

*Source: Mobil Corporation Annual Report 1983.*

and production was expected to begin during the summer of 1984.

Mobil was also active in the offshore areas of Nigeria, where the company produced some 65,000 barrels per day in 1983.

The company paid $37,000 for the rights to 13 million acres off Newfoundland in 1965. It performed seismic activity in the area, which was enough to satisfy the minimal work requirements of the 12-year leases. (Other companies had previously drilled nearly 50 unsuccessful wildcats in the vicinity.) Presumably in an attempt to hold onto their leases, yet unwilling to commit the money needed to drill, Mobil offered farm-outs which eventually reduced its share to 28.1%. Then, in 1980, the massive Hibernia field was discoverd in the area by a Chevron-operated rig. It was estimated that the field would eventually yield 3–4 billion barrels of oil.

Another promising find was the Venture gas field near Sable Island off the coast of Nova Scotia. Mobil held a 42% share in an estimated 4 trillion cubic feet of natural gas at that location.

Mobil officials announced in early 1984 that the company's 1984 capital budget would total $3.4 billion, about the same as the previous year, and would be funded entirely from cash flow. Some 70% of the budget was to be devoted to exploration and development, while some 70% of that was earmarked for North American activities. Mobil's attention in the near future was to be focused on four plays—the central Gulf of Mexico, state and federal waters off Alabama, the Canadian Atlantic, and Offshore Alaska.[19]

### Domestic Onshore Activities

With the exception of the large field that Mobil discovered in Mobile Bay, the company's record at finding domestic reserves had been considered to be only average. While it was "hunting for elephants" offshore, Mobil missed much of the early action in such promising plays as the Rocky Mountain Overthrust, the Williston Basin of the Dakotas, and the Anadarko Basin of Oklahoma.

The company paid dearly during the early 1980s in an attempt to catch up to competitors such as Amoco, Shell, and Chevron. Since 1978, Mobil had devoted 67% of its $5 billion exploration budget to the United States. Without acquisitions, however, Mobil would not have managed to replace the reserves it produced. Since 1979, Mobil had made more attempts to purchase other oil companies than any other major.

By and large, Mobil's U.S. hydrocarbon reserves were primarily in the form of natural gas. Price regulation on some of that gas, along with a growing natural gas surplus, had made much of Mobil's domestic reserves uneconomic. In 1983, the company's domestic gas production fell 20% (to 1,506 million gross cubic feet per day) as a result of flagging demand. Production in the Hugoton field in Kansas proved to be particularly susceptible.

### REFINING

With the merger of Socony and Vacuum Oil in 1931, the company emerged as one of the strongest refiners in the industry. In terms of refining capacity, Socony-Vacuum was the second largest refiner in the United States. By 1960, however, Mobil had dropped back to third place, and its U.S. refining capacity relative to the other major oil companies continued to decline in the following years. By 1978, Mobil was in seventh place behind Exxon, Standard of California, Standard of Indiana, Shell, Texaco, and Gulf. In 1960, Mobil's U.S. refining capacity was 716,700 barrels per day, or 7.4% of the U.S. total. By 1983, however, the company's domestic refining capacity had been restored to 750,000 barrels per day.

---

[19]"Mobil's Spending to Concentrate on Regions in North America," *Oil & Gas Journal,* February 20, 1984, p. 33.

**TABLE 1**　*Refining Statistics*
(thousands barrels daily)

|  | 1983 | 1982 | 1981 | 1980 | 1979 |
|---|---|---|---|---|---|
| Domestic Runs | 618 | 644 | 639 | 734 | 797 |
| Domestic Capacity | 750 | 860 | 860 | 910 | 901 |
| Domestic Runs/Capacity | 82% | 75% | 74% | 81% | 88% |
| Foreign Runs | 976 | 1067 | 1134 | 1225 | 1266 |
| Foreign Capacity | 1436 | 1534 | 1647 | 1709 | 1770 |
| Foreign Runs/Capacity | 68% | 70% | 69% | 72% | 72% |

*Source:* Mobil Corporation Financial and Operating Statistics 1983.

As of December 31, 1983, Mobil owned or had operating interests in 29 refineries in 17 countries. Mobil's total crude oil refinery capacity was 2,186,000 barrels per day, 34% of which was located in the United States. The company's domestic refineries ran at 82% of capacity during 1983, while foreign refineries ran at 68% capacity. (See Table 1.)

Mobil's petroleum product operations were fairly evenly divided among the United States, Europe, and the Far East. Foreign downstream earnings had suffered during 1982, owing to the relatively high cost of Saudi Arabian crude. Foreign margins recovered somewhat in 1983, following a $5/barrel price reduction by the Saudis.

At home, Mobil was still seriously short of crude. Just 45% of the oil used in its domestic refineries came from Mobil's own wells in the United States.[20] Gasoline markets in 1983 were particularly competitive in the United States. Without inventory profits, Mobil would have lost money on its domestic refining and marketing operations in that year.[21]

Speaking before a group of New York security analysts in early 1984, Tavoulareas said

that downstream strategic plans called for Mobil to be "the lowest cost operator wherever we do business or get out."[22] Evidence of this strategy in action was Mobil's announcement in May of 1983 that it would close its refinery in Augusta, Kansas, within a year. Accordingly, Mobil would gradually withdraw from marketing gasoline and distillates in Kansas, Nebraska, South Dakota, and parts of Iowa, Missouri, and North Dakota.

## MARKETING

Between 1950 and 1970, the major oil companies had been competing fiercely to penetrate as many regional markets as possible. Market share, rather than profitability, had been the primary marketing objective. Mobil, on the other hand, had followed a different strategy. Albert L. Nickerson, who was then chairman of Mobil, made the decision to limit domestic marketing expenditures in the effort to develop European markets. In 1969, Nickerson commented on this period of the company's growth:

> From 1948 to 1964 we really starved our marketing people in this country. We just said, "Look,

[20]"Mobil's Costly Saudi Strategy," *op. cit.*

[21]"Company Analysis: Mobil Corporation," Donaldson, Lufkin & Jenrette, March 20, 1984.

[22]"Mobil's Spending to Concentrate on Regions in North America," *op. cit.*

there are many jobs this company has to do. . . . Give us a chance to strengthen some other elements of the company, and the day will come when we can come back to you. . . . " We had a program that almost required us to lose position.[23]

Mobil's domestic market share dropped from 9.9% in 1948 to 6.7% in 1967. By 1965, when foreign sales were approaching domestic sales, Mobil finally began to increase its domestic marketing expenditures. By 1969, Mobil's European market share was about 5%. Since earnings had improved every year since 1958, Nickerson's strategy was viewed as an overall success.

Since the early 1970s, however, there had been a steady decline in the number of marketing outlets for all companies. Even as late as 1977, Texaco was marketing to every state in the union. At the same time, Mobil was in 48 states, Exxon in 44, Shell in 40, and Socal and Gulf in 39.

By the late 1970s, Mobil had decided to get out of the Rocky Mountain States because the firm had no refineries in that area. The decision called for pulling out of five states by 1981, and included closing 276 retail outlets which were supplied directly or indirectly by Mobil. As previously mentioned, Mobil later announced its intention to withdraw from several Midwestern states. From 1969 to 1983, Mobil decreased the number of its retail outlets nationwide from 25,513 to 15,403.

Both at home and abroad, Mobil's strategy was to close down marginal service stations and to consolidate areas of marketing strength. Part of Mobil's domestic marketing retrenchment included the introduction of secondary brands, beginning with the "Sello" brand in the Southwest in 1972, and later with "Big-Bi" stations in the Midwest, and "Reelo" in North Carolina. Most of these secondary outlets were marginal Mobil stations which were converted to self-serve operations designed to compete with lower-priced private brands. The introduction of these secondary brands caused some confusion among competitors and jobbers, since Mobil was not supplying these outlets with its own product, nor was it closing all of its branded outlets in the areas where secondary brands had been introduced. Amid considerable speculation, Mobil consistently maintained that it did not intend to withdraw the Mobil brand from those areas where secondary outlets had been introduced. The company claimed that it was looking at each of its branded outlets on an individual basis to see if they met various investment criteria.

As of December 31, 1983, Mobil's petroleum products were marketed in more than 100 countries. Worldwide the company had approximately 33,000 retail dealer outlets, 47% of which were located in the United States. Thirty four percent of Mobil's petroleum product sales were in the United States. Mobil ranked the fifth-largest gasoline retailer.

During October of 1983, Mobil announced plans to install point-of-sale terminals in 2,400 of its outlets around the country.[24] Station attendants would swipe debit or credit cards through a reader on the terminal, allowing the company to benefit from automated credit checks, inventory controls and electronic funds transfer. Mobil's announcement followed a $2\frac{1}{2}$-year study and $10 million in testing debit card systems. The move was expected to put Mobil in the lead among the majors in a race toward a national electronic fund transfer system.

In February of 1984, Mobil made known its intention to turn as many as possible of its full-service stations into self-service gas islands in combination with convenience stores.[25] The company called them "snack shops." Although

---

[23]"How to Rob Peter . . . ," *op. cit.*

[24]"Mobil's One-Ups Others with Debit Card System," *National Petroleum News,* December 1983, p. 29.

[25]"Mobil Wants to be Your Milkman," *Forbes,* February 13, 1984, p. 44.

**EXHIBIT 8** Mobil Corporation Top 11 Domestic Retail Gasoline Marketers

|          | 1983 | | 1982 | | 1981 | | 1980 | | 1979 | | 1978 | | 1977 | |
|          | Rank | % Share | Rank | % Share | Rank | % Share | Rank | % Share | Rank | % Share | Rank | % Share | Rank | % Share |
|----------|------|---------|------|---------|------|---------|------|---------|------|---------|------|---------|------|---------|
| Amoco    | 1    | 7.23    | 1    | 7.32    | 1    | 7.28    | 3    | 7.40    | 2    | 7.48    | 2    | 7.70    | 2    | 7.30    |
| Shell    | 2    | 6.97    | 2    | 6.77    | 2    | 6.89    | 2    | 7.44    | 3    | 7.30    | 1    | 7.71    | 1    | 7.53    |
| Exxon    | 3    | 6.90    | 3    | 6.75    | 3    | 6.81    | 1    | 7.54    | 1    | 7.65    | 3    | 7.28    | 3    | 7.14    |
| Texaco   | 4    | 5.80    | 6    | 5.62    | 4    | 5.77    | 5    | 5.95    | 5    | 6.01    | 4    | 6.75    | 4    | 7.11    |
| Mobil    | 5    | 5.69    | 5    | 5.68    | 6    | 5.38    | 4    | 6.01    | 6    | 5.78    | 6    | 5.55    | 6    | 5.59    |
| Gulf     | 6    | 5.30    | 4    | 5.78    | 5    | 5.69    | 7    | 5.39    | 4    | 6.36    | 5    | 5.83    | 5    | 5.91    |
| Chevron  | 7    | 5.06    | 8    | 4.84    | 7    | 5.21    | 6    | 5.77    | 7    | 5.30    | 7    | 4.76    | 7    | 4.75    |
| Arco     | 8    | 4.82    | 7    | 4.64    | 8    | 3.80    | 8    | 3.87    | 8    | 3.89    | 8    | 3.79    | 8    | 3.85    |
| Union    | 9    | 3.52    | 9    | 3.31    | 9    | 3.31    | 9    | 3.50    | 9    | 3.49    | 9    | 3.28    | 11   | 3.08    |
| Phillips | 10   | 2.61    | 10   | 2.77    | 10   | 2.88    | 10   | 2.83    | 11   | 2.85    | 11   | 3.02    | 10   | 3.15    |
| Sun      | 11   | 2.54    | 11   | 2.64    | 11   | 2.55    | 11   | 2.74    | 10   | 3.01    | 10   | 3.20    | 9    | 3.39    |

*Source: 1984 National Petroleum News Factbook, p. 117.*

many of the majors, including Arco, Texaco, Amoco, and Tenneco, had already introduced combination gas stations and convenience stores, none were on the scale reportedly envisioned at Mobil.

## TRANSPORTATION

At year-end 1983, Mobil owned 38 ocean-going tankers and had another 20 vessels under charter. The company also made use of voyage charters. Mobil had traditionally been extremely adept at handling its tanker commitments, thus benefitting from consistently low transportation costs.

Mobil's U.S. pipeline system, including partly owned facilities, consisted in December 1983 of 18,855 miles of crude oil, natural gas liquids, natural gas, and carbon dioxide trunk and gathering lines, and 9,158 miles of product lines. The company's pipeline system outside of the United States, including partly owned facilities, consisted of 7,969 miles of trunk and gathering lines, and 1,893 miles of product lines.

Mobil held a 4% interest in the Trans Alaska Pipeline System (TAPS), a 48-inch pipeline system which moved crude oil some 800 miles from the Prudhoe Bay field on Alaska's North Slope to the port of Valdez on the southern coast of Alaska.

## OTHER ENERGY SOURCES

Anticipating the future importance of alternative energy sources, Mobil, in the mid-1970s, began investing more in research and development for new sources of energy. The objectives of Mobil's energy research efforts were to improve technology for finding and extracting current energy resources and to find viable alternatives to petroleum-based energy.

Mobil held proved and probable coal reserves of 4.3 billion tons located in Wyoming, Montana, North Dakota, Colorado, and Illinois. The company first commenced shipments from a mine near Gillette, Wyoming, in late 1982.

Production from the mine was soon expected to reach 2.5 million tons annually.

Initially, coal was thought to be a very attractive alternative if it could be economically liquified or gasified for transportation through the oil industry's huge pipeline system. The major oil companies had, accordingly, increased their ownership of coal reserves since 1970. By the early 1980s, however, serious doubts remained about whether coal liquification and gasification would ever become economical.

Mobil was a majority shareholder in a venture that began exploration for coal in Indonesia in 1983. In Australia, the company was involved in coal exploration, as well, and held reserves of 60 million tons through a joint venture. The company had had a significant position in oil shale lands for many years and was active in shale research. No commercial oil shale operations had yet begun, however.

In New Zealand, a Mobil synthetic fuel plant, which would manufacture gasoline from locally produced natural gas, was expected to come on stream in late 1985.

Mobil had, as well, devoted considerable effort to researching solar technology. Mobil Solar Energy Corporation, a wholly owned subsidiary, planned to build a solar-powered desalination plant in Abu Dhabi. Mobil Tyco Solar Energy Corporation, another subsidiary, was meanwhile involved in the production of solar panels for use in the residential consumer market.

Mobil held proved and probable uranium reserves of 33.5 million pounds, and sold 207,000 pounds of uranium domestically during 1983.

## NON-ENERGY DIVERSIFICATION

Mobil's diversification into areas outside of petroleum included operations involving chemicals, real estate, paperboard packaging, and retail merchandising. Like some of the other major oil companies, Mobil found it difficult to achieve profit margins in these businesses which ap-

**TABLE 2** Non-Petroleum Earnings, 1979–1983

| (millions) | 1979 | 1980 | 1981 | 1982 | 1983 |
|---|---|---|---|---|---|
| Chemicals | $113 | $119 | $ 93 | $ 24 | $ 8 |
| Paperboard packaging | 40 | 71 | 57 | 24 | 1 |
| Retail merchandising | 54 | (162) | (160) | (93) | 40 |
| Total | $207 | $ 28 | $(10) | $(45) | $49 |

*Source:* "Company Analysis: Mobil Corporation," Donaldson, Lufkin & Jenrette, March 20, 1984.

proached those of its core business. In 1983, for instance, Mobil netted just $49 million in net income out of $10 billion in revenues from chemicals, paperboard packaging, and retail merchandising. (See Table 2.)

## Chemicals

The Mobil Chemical Company was formed in 1960 to bring the company's worldwide chemical business into one integrated operating division. This division was equipped with its own research and development, manufacturing, and marketing facilities. The primary domestic facilities produced basic petrochemicals such as ethylene, propylene, and butadiene, and aromatics such as benzene and toluene.

Mobil's strategy in chemicals was said to be one of concentrating on selected areas of business with good growth opportunities, primarily in those fields where the company already had a strong competitive position and could profit from its structural integration and traditional expertise. In addition, Mobil Chemical used much of its output of basic petrochemicals in other manufacturing operations. This large degree of internal utilization made the company somewhat less sensitive to the fluctuations of the petrochemical market.

The company owned or had interest in 63 facilities located in ten countries. Mobil's principal chemical products included: plastics used in the home and in packaging by industry; basic petrochemicals sold to producers of plastics, synthetic fibers, and other chemical products; phosphate rock and di-ammonium phosphate products sold to fertilizer producers; coatings used in packaging, furniture, shipping, and maintenance applications; and specialty industrial chemicals. Brand names identifying Mobil's chemical products included "Hefty," "Kordite," and "Baggies."

Mobil Chemical was, in fact, the largest manufacturer of plastic packaging in the United States, producing such products as garbage bags, food bags, bread wrapping, and industrial packaging. Another highly successful product of the plastics division was polystyrene foam, which was used in the manufacture of egg cartons, fast-food containers, and disposable tableware. There had also been considerable growth in sales of a product called Mobilrap, which was a heavy-duty polyethylene stretch film used to wrap pallet loads for industrial distribution.

Mobil also produced "oriented polypropylene" (OPP) under the brand name BICOR, which was a packaging film replacement for cellophane. This product was receiving rapid acceptance because of its lower cost and higher quality as a cellophane substitute. Mobil was the world's largest producer of this fabricated plastic, and had OPP manufacturing plants in the U.S., Canada, and Europe.

Mobil had attained leadership in the field of high-performance chemical coatings, and was the third largest U.S. producer of phosphate rock, as well.

The company's chemical earnings were barely break-even in 1983, partly because of $23 million of preoperating expenses related to the Saudi petrochemical facility.

## Real Estate

Mobil made its first significant real estate investment in 1966 when it moved its Hong Kong terminal, thereby vacating a choice 40-acre site. Mobil decided to build a huge middle-class apartment complex rather than sell the land for an estimated $15 million. This complex was completed in 1979, and housed more than 70,000 people.

In 1970, a management team was formed to explore further opportunities in real estate. The company's first U.S. purchase was a residential community comprised of 3,300 bayfront acres near San Francisco.

Early in 1977, Mobil began bidding for southern California's Irvine Co., which was the owner of America's largest real estate development. Beginning with an offer of $24 per share (or $202 million), Mobil finally bid more than $336 million for the property before losing out to a private group which included Henry Ford II, John Irvin Smith, Max M. Fisher (a Detroit industrialist), and others. In July of 1978, Mobil purchased the undeveloped half of Reston, Virginia, from Gulf Oil for over $30 million. Gulf previously had sizable interests in real estate, but later divested itself completely of these projects. Gulf maintained that they were not closely enough related to the company's basic business, and that they had not made a meaningful contribution to corporate profits.

The majority of Mobil's real estate was owned by Mobil Land Development Company, a nonconsolidated subsidiary located in San Francisco. Mobil's holdings were generally large tracts of land strategically located in high-growth areas, and were well suited to large-scale communities of at least 1,000 homes.

Despite these investments, real estate remained a relatively minor part of Mobil's overall operations.

## Marcor

In 1968, Mobil made a decision to diversify outside of the energy business in a significant way. A diversification study team was formed to analyze various industries and select individual companies as possible candidates for acquisition. Mobil's objective was not to become a large conglomerate, but to acquire one major diversification subsidiary. Mobil's Rawleigh Warner, Jr., commented on Mobil's motivation:

> We had become aware that governments would interfere with our business. We thought they would be oil-producing countries, not consuming nations. But after the oil embargo we realized that the consuming nations would also play a greater role. That impelled us forward with the diversification program.[26]

Senior management established certain criteria for any potential acquisitions. These criteria required that any company being considered have a strong management team, considerable experience in its own field, good earnings growth and rate of return possibilities, different business cycles and business risks from the oil industry, and a strong competitive position within its own markets.

After reviewing over a hundred companies in a five-year period, Mobil began looking very closely at Marcor, Inc., a holding company formed in 1968 which consisted of two main subsidiaries, Montgomery Ward and Container Corp. Montgomery Ward was a retailer in the U.S., and Container Corp. was the largest U.S. producer of paperboard packaging.

In 1973, Mobil bought 4.5% of Marcor's stock for an average cost of $23 per share. When the Arab oil embargo hit, the stock market fell sharply and oil prices skyrocketed. By 1974, Mobil had a lot of extra cash on hand, and Marcor's stock looked like more of a bargain than ever. In August of 1974, Mobil made a tender

---

[26]"Big Oil's Move into Retailing," *Chain Store Executive*, September 1976, pp. 29–32.

offer for shares that would give it a majority interest in the smaller company. The price at that time was still below $25 per share. Marcor's price per share rose sharply that same year. Later in 1974, three Marcor executives were elected to Mobil's Board of Directors, and four officers of Mobil, including Warner and Tavoulareas, were elected Directors of Marcor.

In July of 1976, Mobil bought Marcor. The 1976 Annual Report contained the following message to the stockholders:

> By merging with Ward and Container, Mobil effectively realized its major diversification objective. Both firms are extremely well managed and have the growth potential to contribute materially to Mobil's U.S. based earnings. They helped Mobil to increase significantly the percentage of total earnings produced in the U.S. Moreover, they operate in business areas with different cycles and risks from oil's and are not subject to the vagaries of oil industry regulation.[27]

During the period of acquisition, Mobil drew considerable criticism from members of Congress and the Federal Energy Administration. John C. Sawhill, chief of the F.E.A., who had previously defended higher oil profits as necessary for capital investment in domestic exploration and production, said the Mobil offer to acquire controlling interest in Marcor was "like having a wet dishrag thrown in your face." Walter F. Mondale (D-Minn.) said in July 1974 that the proposed acquisition:

> . . . is the best sign yet that the oil industry is engaged in a desperate search for ways in which to get rid of embarrassingly high profits. [It] lends substantial weight to the wisdom of repealing the oil depletion allowance immediately.[28]

Sen. Thomas J. McIntyre (D-N.H.) called the acquisition plan "irresponsibility at its worst."[29]

Warner's reply to the criticism that the Marcor acquisition siphoned off cash which should have been used in exploration and production was that Mobil was already exploiting as many E & P opportunities as it could find.

While Mobil never revealed the total price for Marcor, it was estimated that it must have paid about $1.8 billion, spending around $800 million for the first 54% in 1973 and 1974. Mobil put $200 million of cash directly into Marcor's treasury in exchange for new preferred stock, but maintained that it had no plans to pump additional capital into the retailing chain. Ward was definitely expected to pull its own weight, and Mobil emphasized that its new subsidiary would be granted operational autonomy in the conduct of its business.

Although the Marcor acquisition was seen by some analysts as one of the boldest diversification efforts by a major oil company into a nonenergy field, some oilmen viewed the acquisition as overly conservative. One oil executive said:

> They were far ahead with the idea, but maybe they were too timid. Why not diversify into drugs, instruments, office equipment, electronics, or computers—all of which have higher rates of return?[30]

By 1980, Mobil's management was admitting that the scenario surrounding Marcor had not panned out as they had predicted. "We probably wouldn't buy Marcor this year, right now," conceded Tavoulareas.[31]

In order to maintain Montgomery Ward's bond rating in 1980, Mobil was forced to pump

---

[27]Mobil Annual Report, 1976.

[28]"Congressional Barbs Hit Mobil-Marcor Deal," *Oil and Gas Journal*, July 1, 1974, p. 32.

[29]*Ibid.*

[30]"The New Diversifications Oil Game," *Business Week*, April 24, 1978, pp. 76–88.

[31]"Mobil's Successful Exploration," *Business Week*, October 13, 1980, p. 112.

$200 million into the company. Mobil took great care to label the transaction an interest-free loan. At year-end 1980, Montgomery Ward showed a loss of $162 million. Early in 1981, Mobil granted the retailer an additional $155 million in interest-free loans. Earnings, however, continued to deteriorate.

**TABLE 3**   Montgomery Ward Earnings, 1979–1983 (millions)

| 1979 | 1980 | 1981 | 1982 | 1983 |
|------|------|------|------|------|
| $54 | $(162) | $(160) | $(93) | $40 |

Source: Mobil Corp. Annual Reports, 1981–1983.

A 1983 turnaround at Montgomery Ward was attributed to rising retail sales, lower interest rates, more sophisticated merchandising techniques, and cost savings related primarily to a reduction in the number of employees. Credit was also widely given to the guidance of Stephen Pistner, who became chief executive of Ward in 1981.

Results at Marcor's Container Corporation of America, meanwhile, were less than encouraging. Though the paperboard packaging firm showed a $1 million profit in 1983, had gains on sales of properties been excluded, Container Corp. would actually have shown a loss. Moreover, the company had proved to be a drain on capital to Mobil for several years. (See Table 4.)

Mobil's 1983 annual report stressed that man-agement reorganization, major cost-cutting programs, and the introduction of more efficient labor practices were expected to lay the groundwork for better margins at Container Corp. in the years ahead.

## PUBLIC RELATIONS

Beginning in the early 1970s, Mobil developed a public relations strategy which was outspoken, controversial, and decidedly atypical compared with other members of the conservative and usually silent oil industry.[32] This strategy did not appear to have resulted from any single decision by senior management. Rather, "Mobil's 'high profile' operation developed gradually," according to *Fortune* magazine, "in response to an increasingly perceived need for the company to become more visible and articulate."[33]

By the late 1970s, Mobil was also well known for its efforts to sponsor and promote cultural events on both public and commercial television networks. Its first grant was made in 1970 to launch the very successful "Masterpiece Theatre."

Another facet of Mobil's public relations strategy was revealed in the company's willingness to address "issue-oriented" or "advo-

[32]See the case "What Ever Happened to Fair Play? Public Relations at Mobil," by Clark and Barrett, for a thorough description of Mobil's PR efforts.

[33]Ross, Irwin, "Public Relations Isn't Kid-Glove Stuff at Mobil," *Fortune,* September 19, 1976, pp. 106–202.

**TABLE 4**   Container Corporation Funds Flow

| (millions) | 1979 | 1980 | 1981 | 1982 | 1983 |
|------------|------|------|------|------|------|
| Funds from operations | $128 | $141 | $147 | $ 117 | $100E |
| Capital expenditures | 116 | 141 | 206 | 229 | 132 |
| Surplus/(deficiency) | $12 | $0 | $(59) | $(112) | $(32) |

Source: "Company Analysis: Mobil Corporation," Donaldson, Lufkin & Jenrette, March 20, 1984.

cacy" questions in the media. While much of its advocacy advertising was aimed at problems within the oil industry, Mobil also editorialized on other controversial issues which the company thought were of national interest. Mobil was quick to attack any treatment of the oil industry (by the media or the government) which it perceived as unfair. At the same time, many of its views were somewhat surprising when first aired. For example, the endorsement of an effective mass transit policy for the nation's large metropolitan areas initially surprised many observers. At one time or another, Mobil's readiness to defend its interests had led it into extended public conflicts with such powerful media forces as the CBS and ABC television networks, the *Washington Post,* and the *Wall Street Journal.* Mobil had also not hesitated to break ranks with the other members of the oil industry on particularly sensitive issues, such as the question of oil price controls.

## MOBIL ON THE PROWL

Throughout the late 1970s and early 1980s, Mobil redirected its exploration and production efforts toward properties in North America. At the same time, Mobil made repeated attempts to bolster its paltry domestic reserves through acquisition—attempts which met with mixed success.

### General Crude Oil Co.
Mobil entered the high-stakes bidding war for General Crude Oil Co. (a subsidiary of International Paper) in the spring of 1979. Gulf had originally reached a tentative agreement to buy General Crude's oil and gas operations, but was later outbid by a joint offer from Tenneco and Southland Royalty Co. Mobil offered in March of 1979 to buy the operations for $765 million, thus topping the previous offer. General Crude's reserves, located primarily in the United States, were said to approach 160 million barrels. Mobil eventually raised its offer, and a sale for $792 million was completed in July of 1979.

### Belridge Oil Co.
In May of 1979, Belridge Oil Co. let it be known that it was actively seeking a merger with a large oil company. Mobil, the largest single shareholder with 18%, was thought to have an inside track. Belridge attracted a good deal of interest. This was due in part to Belridge's substantial proven reserves, mostly heavy crude located in California. Some speculated, however, that the interest in Belridge was better explained by the company's vast and largely unexplored reserves of light, high-quality oil located in deep geologic formations. A group of big oil companies (which included Mobil) lost out on the bid for the closely held target to Shell Oil, which ultimately purchased Belridge for $3.6 billion. Mobil, in turn, sold its interest in Belridge in January of 1980.

### Texas Pacific Oil Co.
Some months later, Sun Oil bid $2.3 billion for the U.S. oil and gas properties of Texas Pacific Oil, a subsidiary of Joseph E. Seagram & Sons, Inc. Texas Pacific was one of the nation's five largest nonintegrated petroleum producers, with proven U.S. reserves of 120 million barrels of oil and 300 billion cubic feet of natural gas. Sun's bid was a record for proven reserves, and amounted to $12 per barrel. Despite a last-minute secret effort by Mobil to bid for the properties, Sun and Seagram signed a definitive agreement. Mobil was said to have offered to match Sun's price, but with different terms.

### TransOcean Oil
TransOcean Oil was the exploration unit of Vickers Energy Group, which in turn was a subsidiary of Esmark, Inc. In the summer of 1980, Mobil successfully bid $715 million for TransOcean, which owned considerable property in the Overthrust Belt in the Rockies. The deal was structured so that Esmark would be free of capital gains tax. To accomplish this, Mobil bought Esmark common stock, then swapped those shares with Esmark for TransOcean shares—a tax-free transaction. This

arrangement was said to have saved Esmark some $100 million in capital gains taxes.

## Conoco

In July of 1981, Mobil made a $7.7 billion tender offer for slightly more than 50% of the stock of Conoco, Inc. Mobil thus became Conoco's third major suitor, along with DuPont Co. and Seagram. Mobil's offer was immediately rebuffed. Conoco filed an antitrust suit against Mobil, while continuing to press for a DuPont merger.

Mobil continued to press its attack, however, quickly raising its offer to $8.2 billion, and later $8.82 billion. Conoco was an attractive target to crude-short Mobil. Conoco offered stable and abundant acreage, half of which was located in the United States and the remainder in Europe and Canada. Moreover, a Mobil-Conoco merger would more than double Mobil's interest in the North Sea's Statfjord field.

In response to continued reference to possible antitrust violations, Mobil offered to dispose of certain U.S. marketing operations in order to speed the purchase.

Ultimately, Mobil lost out to DuPont when a federal appeals court refused to issue a temporary restraining order to delay a DuPont deal. Mobil had been spurned again, despite a final offer which was $1.28 billion more than DuPont's.

## Marathon

In the fall of the same year, still smarting from the failed Conoco takeover attempt, Mobil made a $5.1 billion ($85 a share) bid for Marathon Oil. Like Conoco, Marathon held reserves in politically secure areas. Marathon, the nation's 17th largest oil company, actually offered greater reserves in the U.S. and Canada than did Conoco. A merger with Marathon at Mobil's bid price would have yielded oil and gas reserves at an equivalent of less than $3 a barrel. Moreover, such a merger would boost Mobil's U.S. oil reserves by some 80%.

Though Mobil had structured its offer so as to entice Marathon stockholders to tender their shares quickly, Mobil's bid was immediately stalled by a court restraining order. That gave Marathon time to search for a white knight (or, friendly suitor). Marathon managed to secure a $100 a share offer from U.S. Steel (subsequently raised to $106 a share).

In a last-ditch effort to salvage the merger attempt, Mobil announced plans to purchase as much as 25% of the outstanding stock of U.S. Steel, its rival bidder. Industry observers questioned the sincerity of Mobil's threat. Though many labeled the announcement "scare tactics," others speculated that a future attempt to buy all of U.S. Steel was not out of the question. Were that to happen, Mobil would pick up massive mineral reserves and could conceivably write down the target company's steel mills, using the loss to shield oil profits.

In order to counter antitrust concerns in the Marathon takeover bid, Mobil offered to bid jointly for Marathon with Amerada Hess. Mobil would then sell Amerada Hess all of Marathon's existing marketing, refining, and transportation properties. A lower court rejected this plan, however.

Though Mobil eventually raised its offer for Marathon to slightly above the U.S. Steel bid, it finally lost out to the steel company when the U.S. Supreme Court rejected a Mobil appeal. Mobil officials would not rule out a run at U.S. Steel in the future, however.

## Anschutz

In 1982, Mobil acquired a working interest in certain domestic oil and gas reserves and exploration acreage from the Anschutz Corporation. Industry sources estimated the purchase price exceeded $500 million. The acquisition was said to net Mobil some 100 million barrels of oil from a giant field located in Utah, and straddling the southwestern corner of Wyoming. Mobil was also said to have received 250,000 acres of undeveloped exploration leases elsewhere. A report from one investment broker called the Anschutz field "potentially one of the most significant finds in North America since the Prudhoe Bay discovery" on the North Slope of Alaska.[34] It was expected that the Anschutz field would be expensive to develop, however.

It had earlier been reported that Anschutz had been seeking a buyer for part of its interest in the field because it was in need of more money to develop the property.

While adding significantly to Mobil's reserves, the acquisition reflected a desire on Mobil's part to bolster its domestic reserves through private, friendly transactions. Mobil thus avoided many of the antitrust complications which hindered earlier takeover attempts.

## Superior

Having twice failed to acquire an integrated oil firm, in March of 1984 Mobil turned its attentions to Superior Oil Company, the nation's largest independent. Industry experts viewed Mobil's interest in Superior as a calculated effort to avoid the antitrust accusations of Mobil's previous attempts. Superior owned neither gasoline stations nor refineries. It did possess, however, vast reserves in the United States and Canada.

A Mobil-Superior merger would increase Mobil's U.S. and Canadian oil reserves by 15% and 48%, respectively. Growth in natural gas reserves would be even more dramatic, with U.S. reserves increasing by 29% and Canadian reserves by 92%. In fact, Superior's 1983 reserve increases would more than offset Mobil's 1983 reserve declines.

[34]"Mobil Buys Part of Utah Oil Field from Anschutz," *The Wall Street Journal,* August 12, 1982, p. 2.

In sharp contrast to its maverick reputation, Mobil's strategy in attempting takeover of Superior was uncharacteristically couched in secrecy and aimed at achieving a friendly deal. Mobil officials first met with members of the founding Keck family, who owned 22% of Superior. Mobil's management knew that the Keck family members, who had recently been fighting among themselves, were willing to sell. Mobil offered them $45 a share and received their agreement to make the purchase for the Kecks' 22% share.

While negotiating with the Kecks, Mobil was simultaneously attempting to strike a deal with Superior's top executives.

On March 11, Mobil made public its agreement with Kecks and announced its intention to purchase the remaining shares at the same $45 price. The total bid of $5.7 billion would make this deal the fifth-largest oil merger in history. Mobil would gain reserves of about one billion barrels of oil and oil equivalent at a price of less than $6 a barrel.

## CONCLUSION

Counting up this list of recent Mobil acquisition attempts, Collier continued to feel somewhat frustrated by his company's apparent strategy. He had to admit, however, that over the past 15 years Mobil had become more than just an oil and gas firm. "Maybe it's not so bad after all," he thought to himself, shutting his briefcase and reaching for his coat. "Could be that all these merger attempts *really* signal a move back toward an emphasis on E & P."

# 10 THE NORTON COMPANY

## Theodore V. Purcell, S.J.
## James Weber, S.J.

*Georgetown University*

## ETHICS AT NORTON: CODIFICATION

The Norton Company is a distinctive concern in that it has both a company code of ethics and a board ethics committee. It is unusual in other respects also but overall it falls within the mainstream of modern industry. Some background is in order:

Norton was founded in Worcester in 1885 as a privately held manufacturer of grinding wheels. It began selling its products abroad at the turn of the century, and in 1909 began building in Germany the first of its overseas plants. Although its sales exceeded $200 million by 1962, it remained privately held and owner-operated until its stock was listed on the New York Stock Exchange in 1963.

Still headquartered in Worcester, the Norton Company now consists of more than 80 separate firms employing some 24,000 workers at 120 plant sites in 28 nations. Norton claims a strong effort in the area of equal employment opportunity and has 7.7 percent minority employment in its 55 domestic plants.

The company manufactures a variety of products, including sandpaper, high temperature durable materials, ceramics, medical plastic tubing, foam sealants, plastics, safety products, products for the oil and gas service industries, and—still going strong—grinding wheels. Sales totaled approximately $960 million in 1978; the abrasives division accounted for 63 percent of total sales, and the largest customer purchased considerably less than 5 percent of the company's output.

It is important to note that Norton has never had absentee ownership. The major stockholders and managers apparently had, from the beginning, a sense of public responsibility and community involvement, with support for civic and charitable activities and sensitivity to social problems. This background may be one reason for Norton's early move toward an ethics code and toward establishing an ethics committee of the board of directors.

Norton makes comparatively few domestic or foreign sales to governments or the military and is therefore less a target for bribe demands or opportunities than, say, a Lockheed or a Boeing. Apart from this, it faces many of the same ethical problems that confront any large, multiplant, multinational corporation.

### A Code Develops

In the early 1960s, ethics and business made headlines. Vice-presidents of major electrical manufacturers were sent to jail for conspiring to fix prices in violation of the Sherman Act. The president of Chrysler Corporation resigned when it was discovered that he had used his position for personal gain. Charles Van Doren and others were found to be involved in fixing television quiz programs. Billy Sol Estes ran afoul of the law for financial manipulations in Texas.

Amid this turmoil, the Norton Company emerged as one firm concerned with institutionalizing ethics. The company adopted a brief code of ethics, stating in general terms that its business must be conducted on a high ethical plane, in strict observance of the law. In formulating this code, Norton created a mechanism for management to introduce ethics into the decision-making structure.

Reflecting the late sixties' mounting concern about civil rights, Norton's board amended the 1961 ethics code in 1967, with a paragraph on nondiscrimination in employment. The focus was entirely on operations in the United States, and no one in Norton management thought it either appropriate or advisable to extend the code to cover overseas operations.

By 1973, following disclosure of ITT's involvement in the downfall of Allende in Chile and the initial reports of multinationals' widespread bribery abroad, Norton undertook to create an ethics code that would have worldwide application. In September of that year, a revised code was drafted that broadened the previous code to encompass all of Norton's operations.

Most of the major questions concerned with this draft centered on its international scope: Should the code apply to all subsidiaries and affiliates or only to some? Should it apply to a Japanese company in which Norton had a 40 percent ownership (with no American on the payroll), or to those firms where there was a 50–50 equity interest, or only to those in which Norton had a controlling interest?

After writing the first draft and submitting it to a number of top executives, Norton's general counsel, Fairman Cowan, decided that he needed more input—from all levels of the company and from all areas of its global network—to develop a comprehensive, worldwide policy statement of acceptable business ethics.

The action that ensued was summed up by then Vice-President Thomas Green, during our discussions with him: "We did not in any way develop a code here in the sequestered walls of corporate headquarters and impose it on our locations. We took this code to various locations, to selected foreign and domestic managers, and said, 'How does it look to you? Is this workable?' "

After responses from Norton's foreign af-

filiates were received, the subject was placed on the agenda of a world conference of Norton's top management, held in Worcester in fall 1976. The 200 managers in attendance further studied the draft that had been submitted to them earlier and revised it to an acceptable state.

The general philosophy of the newly adopted code—termed a *Policy on Business Ethics*—is stated by Norton's chief executive officer, Robert Cushman: "Ours is a highly principled company. Wherever we operate, Norton aims for a standard of conduct well above what the law demands—not just to keep us above reproach, but to nourish our self-respect and sharpen our sense of purpose." Fairman Cowan, who recently retired as Norton's general counsel, continues that theme: "The code of business ethics . . . has given specific notice to the company's employees, suppliers, customers, stockholders, and plant communities, and to the general public that Norton considers ethics to be an essential subject of corporate concern and is endeavoring to conduct its business in conformity with the code."

Concurring, Thomas Green asserts:

A commitment to a socially responsible posture and related programs is the underlying theme of the code of business ethics, along with the emphasis on the observance of individual moral standards. It is also set forth as one of the seven major corporate objectives that are being presented repeatedly to the financial community throughout the country and abroad. . . . Norton's social responsibility activities support a major corporate objective—to maintain and build Norton's reputation as a responsible corporate citizen, which at times means accepting a lower profit.

### The United States versus *Schmiergeld*
Norton judges that the American business firm is held to a higher standard of moral conduct than its foreign counterpart. "Nowhere else in the world," says Fairman Cowan, "is the businessman charged with a higher standard of conduct." This claim is supported by an article

from *The New York Times* on March 5, 1978, entitled, "European Businessmen Don't Take Their Morality So Seriously":

> The more the Senate vaunts its concern about corporate morality, the more European and other foreign businessmen think they are securing a competitive edge over their American rivals. . . . The prevailing philosophy among European companies and European governments is that everything that brings in orders, including bribery, helps in a time of worldwide recession. The United States is now the only industrial country that actually forbids its businessmen by law [the Foreign Corrupt Practices Act of 1977] from bribing a foreign official in order to secure an order.

The German magazine *Der Spiegel* is frank and unashamed in acknowledging standard procedures: "German industrial firms spend hundreds of millions of dollars a year on bribes and gifts to foreign clients that may include yachts, luxury sedans, and the services of call girls . . . such payoffs are generally regarded here as a necessary evil . . . the government in some cases may even advise businessmen about handling this *'schmiergeld'*—literally, grease money." In Germany, payments of this kind—which would draw heavy penalties if made by a U.S.-related company—are not only permitted but are accorded a proper tax deduction status.

Norton realizes that its emphasis on worldwide compliance to a high standard of ethics must be tempered by differences in laws and cultures, and its attempt to achieve this balance by distinguishing between morals and ethics. According to Norton's *Policy on Business Ethics:*

> While moral standards are absolute, ethical behavior is a matter of spirit and intent as well as a matter of law.
> . . . [Thus] honesty and integrity are characterized by truthfulness and freedom from deception and fraud. These qualities are unchanging, not relative, and should vary neither by country nor by culture. They dictate one standard of conduct worldwide. If we are steadfast in this belief, ethical behavioral questions are easily answered in most situations.
> . . . [But] ethics is by definition a philosophy of human conduct, and it is axiomatic that all things human change. This means that our view of ethical behavior must be dynamic—sensitive to changes in values and customs that are certain to take place over time and between cultures.

Amplifying this, former General Counsel Cowan adds:

> The word "morals" is used in the sense of standards which are absolute throughout the world: "Thou shalt not commit murder, bear false witness," etc. "Ethics," on the other hand, reflects philosophies of human conduct, established customs, and mores which may vary thoughout the world and which are subject to change from time to time. It is in this nonabsolute area of ethics where difficulties are encountered in writing a worldwide code of business conduct that cannot possibly answer all the questions which will inevitably arise concerning its application to a particular set of circumstances in a particular country at a particular point in time. It is for this reason that the Norton board of directors, when it approved the code, at the same time appointed a Corporate Ethics Committee.

### The Company, the Law, and the Public

Two major sections of Norton's *Policy on Business Ethics* merit detailed study at this point— "Norton and the Law" and "Norton and Its Publics."

The "Norton and the Law" section deals with entertainment, gifts, favors and gratuities, political contributions, financial integrity, antitrust laws, conflict of interest, and use of confidential information. One of the most important aspects of this section is the requirement that every company transaction be correctly recorded, so that *no* scrutiny of records could prove embarrassing. In Fairman Cowan's words, "Observance of this policy [of recording] will go a long way to minimize the likelihood of company funds being used for an improper purpose."

In setting policy, Norton decided against strict compliance with all laws because it operates in parts of the world where petty officials not only expect but are openly permitted to receive small gratuities for performing their regular duties, despite local laws and regulations to the contrary. Accordingly, Norton specifies that gifts or gratuities may be given "to minor public employees for the performance of their public duty, where it is customary to do so, and where a normal and legitimate transaction might otherwise be impeded, *provided that the gifts or tips are recorded on the financial records of the company.*" (Emphasis is ours.)

Such a situation occurred in Mexico. Norton has a manufacturing operation in the city of Puebla, 85 miles southeast of Mexico City, with its major market in Mexico City itself. Midway between the two cities, there is a truck weight checkpoint at which all commercial vehicles must stop. To clear this point, one must pay a nominal tip to the inspector, whether the vehicle is within the load limits or not. Failing such payment, the shipment is certain to be delayed; in fact, the inspector might even require the driver to unload the truck for further inspection. Norton, which ships daily on this route, makes the requested payment.

Citing this as an instance where an official must be paid to have him perform his required duties, Norton notes that this is part of the practice and culture of the country. Norton honors this particular practice because it does not involve bribing an individual to do what he should not be doing. The driver is asked to enter payment to the inspector on his expense report and so identify it.

Another kind of situation with a different ending occurred in Canada. Norton's policy on ethics prohibits company contributions, direct or indirect, to any political candidate or party or to any other organization that might use the contribution for a political candidate or party. One of Norton's Canadian managers thought political contributions (legal in Canada) should be allowed in order to counterbalance labor union contributions to parties favoring nationalization of industry. Norton decided against making such contributions. Former General Counsel Cowan explained why:

> We were persuaded by arguments to the contrary, such as: There could be a strong resentment by the nationals of a country against political contributions by a U.S.-owned subsidiary. They might be viewed as unwarranted foreign interference with domestic issues—witness the outcry against ITT's interference in Chilean elections. And, if there are many local political parties, how is the recipient party to be selected, or should contributions be made to both major political parties, as some companies have done in Canada? And, under some circumstances, might not a political contribution appear to fall into the category of a bribe?

In the "Norton and the Law" section, the company—which is the world's largest producer of abrasives and so might be accused of limiting competition—has adopted a policy of strict observance of antitrust laws. The policy describes in general terms the types of restrictive or noncompetitive actions that may be illegal, and the Norton legal department has written and widely distributed a separate book on antitrust compliance. Norton has decided that price fixing should not be permitted even in places where it is acceptable, such as Italy, where it is quite permissible when Common Market trade is not involved.

The "Norton and Its Publics" section of the policy on ethics focuses on the company's constituents: employees, customers, suppliers, shareholders, host communities, and the public in general. This section voices support of numerous social responsibility programs such as equal employment opportunity, commitment to a safe and healthy working environment, provision for fair employee compensation, and furtherance of employee self-improvement. "It is our practice," Norton states, "to deal fairly and equitably with employees, and, where unions exist, to negotiate openly with them through their elected or appointed representatives."

Norton pledges product quality and safety to its customers, open and frank business dealings with its suppliers, and a fair return on the invested dollar to its shareholders. Norton also states its recognition of responsibilities in the many countries where it manufactures and markets. These responsibilities include knowing local laws and customs and abiding by them, recognizing that the company is part of each host community, behaving as citizens rather than foreigners, and remembering that the company will be welcome only so long as it makes a responsible contribution to the societies in which it operates.

Reflecting on its concern for the general public, Norton states:

> We recognize that a corporation has more than an economic existence these days . . . and it is important that the company behave as a good citizen wherever it lives. Where Norton operations have an adverse impact on our physical environment, we will continually strive to minimize any harmful effects so as to improve the quality of the environment and conserve energy and natural resources. We live in a political world, one that today tends to look with suspicion upon big business, its motives, and its behavior. In this regard, it is important that Norton conduct itself so as to reflect well upon the business community as a whole.

## ETHICS AT NORTON: ADMINISTRATION

Norton's extensive social responsibility program gives tangible form to company sentiments in a variety of instances: a job placement program for ex-employees, separated because of reorganization, reduction in force, or personal reasons; hiring pre-release inmates from a local correctional institution; 25 separate charitable contribution budgets allocated to local plants; sensitivity and role-playing seminars to dispel psychological roadblocks in upgrading female personnel; reorganization of a local private and public welfare operation; formation of a Loaned Executive Council, which assists municipal officials in improving management practices; and a consultation program for over 100 black-owned, small businesses in South Africa.

In addition, Norton has taken measures to ensure general adherence to its stance on ethics. The first is a simple mechanism to help personnel handle difficult decisions—those "gray areas" where it is difficult to distinguish right from wrong. Norton's directive is succinct—"ask the person to whom you report."

The second move consists of several programs that incorporate the policy on ethics as an integral part of business management. Probably the most important is the establishment of a Corporate Ethics Committee (including both top executives and outside directors), which serves as final authority on the ethics code and monitors its overall enforcement. Other mechanisms include the following directives:

- That managers conduct an annual review with their supervisors and field representatives, to insure that the ethics policy is fully understood.
- That managers investigate any possibility of unethical or illegal activity, enlisting the assistance of the chief auditor if necessary.
- That all corporate officers, divisional general managers, managing directors, and corporate department heads sign a letter affirming their understanding of the ethics policy and testifying that they have, in the year past: (a) reviewed the policy with subordinates, (b) investigated all cases of suspect action, and (c) reported significant violations to the Corporate Ethics Committee.
- That the company's chief auditor inform the Corporate Ethics Committee of any ethical

violations or suspected violations that appear during normal company audits.

Furthermore, Norton asks the cooperation of all employees in enforcing the ethics policy and instructs them to use both good judgment and moral courage "in matters of investigation and reporting covered in this policy." However, as Fairman Cowan puts it, "This does not mean the code calls for an internal spy system, which could create distrust or dissension. On the other hand, reporting improper conduct is in the interests of employee and company alike."

To communicate the *Policy on Business Ethics* to its constituents, Norton printed 20,000 copies in eight languages, distributed the policy to every employee in the United States, and provided copies to all foreign operations. Copies have also been made available to Norton's suppliers, customers, prospective employees, shareholders, and interested individuals.

Attesting to the policy's effectiveness, Fairman Cowan states: "There is no doubt in my mind that, although no major breaches of the policy have surfaced since the adoption of the code, a number of practices which were followed in earlier times have been discontinued."

## Embodiment of Policy: The Corporate Ethics Committee

In 1976, at the time the *Policy on Business Ethics* was adopted internationally, Norton also founded its Corporate Ethics Committee. As Thomas Green told us: "There was a general agreement that if we have a code, we want to arrange for follow-up, ask for enforcement, and set up a procedure for reviewing possible violations, which should ultimately be at the directors' level." Thus, the committee was formed at the board level, so that Norton might also institutionalize ethics in top management decisions.

There are three good reasons justifying establishment of the committee: First, the committee gives emphasis and visibility to the institutionalization of ethics on a worldwide basis; second, the committee guarantees that the *Pol-*

*icy on Business Ethics* will be a long-lived document, to be observed and revised over a period of time; third, an ethics policy inevitably has "gray areas," whose meaning and enforcement require the judgment of a body of top managers and directors.

That said, was there any opposition voiced, from anyone in the company, about formation of an ethics committee? "We didn't have any," recalls Fairman Cowan. "No one argued against it. Nobody. I don't think it was even suggested." And Thomas Green adds, "I think our position was that [an ethics committee] was essential. It would have been one-shot, and meaningless thereafter, if we didn't have a committee. It never occurred to us not to have a committee."

Thus established, the committee was staffed by Robert Cushman, Norton chairman and chief executive officer; Fairman Cowan, general counsel; Richard Flynn, vice-president, finance; Thomas Green, vice-president, administration; Richard Chapin, consultant and president emeritus of Emerson College; and George Harvey, president, Business Systems, Pitney-Bowes, Inc. All committee members, except Green, were also Norton directors.

Norton invited Chapin and Harvey to join because it did not want an exclusively "inside" committee. Richard Chapin, who is also a past assistant dean of the Harvard Business School, was seen as someone very much interested in the whole area of social responsibility; he had served as a consultant to Thomas Green on equal employment opportunity, with special reference to women. Norton also wanted to have a line officer from another company, and because of his association with Pitney-Bowes—a company that has expressed special concern about ethical questions—George Harvey appeared particularly well suited for committee membership.

## The Committee in Action

What specific operations has Norton's Corporate Ethics Committee engaged in? We find four: (1) to answer questions about "gray areas" of the policy and to serve as final authority on the policy's meaning; (2) to issue bulletins on its decisions (as appropriate) in a form that can be added to copies of the basic code; (3) to monitor and investigate policy compliance and report, at least annually, to the board of directors on its actions and findings; and (4) to recommend to the board any changes in the ethics policy it feels should be made.

Committee action on two issues—compensation and discrimination—gives some flavor of the committee's work.

The compensation issue involved possible statutory violations in foreign dealings. As Fairman Cowan explains:

> Sometimes we employ lawyers abroad; we have distributors abroad, and so on. It is not infrequent that when they submit an invoice, they say, "Please deposit your check to my account in the First National Bank, Boston," or maybe they'll say, ". . . in my account in Switzerland," or whatever. That troubled us in the case where we know that the local law has currency restrictions, and where we might suspect there is an avoidance of the local income tax. So we debated: Are we to be our brother's keeper? Are we to put a foreigner in a position where he can violate his own law?
>
> And there was not much written on this at the time we debated it. We finally decided that we will not send a check to an area where the person doesn't appear to have a legitimate business interest. And what we now do is to say, "We are sending the check to you, and you are perfectly free to deposit it or do whatever you want with it." But we will not—where we suspect that there could be a breach of the local law—participate in a potential violation of law.

The discrimination issue involved Norton's payment of dues to clubs that select membership on the basis of race, religion, or sex. It had been company practice to reimburse a limited number of managers for club dues, if the club were used mainly for business purposes, but the committee asked: Should we continue this if it supports a discriminatory policy? The bulk of the cases involved luncheon clubs that declined to accept women as members, and the committee decided that dues would not be reimbursed if discrimination continued. The committee expressed hope that if other companies adopted a similar policy, there might be sufficient pressure to induce these clubs to open their doors on a nondiscriminatory basis.

### Ensuring Worldwide Acceptance

Will doctrines promulgated in Worcester, Massachusetts, hold force halfway round the world? Setting standards of conduct in a way that would not be viewed as an encroachment on the customs or prerogatives of foreign managers has been a challenge, as Fairman Cowan indicates:

> In some countries, the letter that comes from the president of the Norton Company in the [*Policy on Business Ethics*] edition is now signed by the managing director of the local company. It is made clear that this is a worldwide policy, but the directive to the employees in that company comes from the head of their company and not from the United States. The question may be a legal one. The French company has its own board of directors which selects its own president. The latter feels, therefore, that anything that goes out to his people should be over his signature as the president of the company, rather than over the corporate president's signature. He even goes so far as to say that it is not proper for a document of this type to be signed by [Norton Chief Executive] Bob Cushman. They have applied this principle in Italy, too.

# SUPERSCOPE, INC.*

## S. Benjamin Prasad

*Ohio University*

Superscope, Inc., has been prominent in the high-fidelity, consumer-electronics industry. Its main product lines are Marantz audio equipment and a less expensive audio line marketed as Superscope.

In September 1979, the company began shipping its Pianocorder, a device that records on magnetic-tape cassettes for playback on any upright piano, thereby converting a piano into a player-piano. Investment analysts wondered whether the Pianocorder would bring the company success and profit.

In his opening remarks to stockholders, Joseph S. Tushinsky, chairman of Superscope, had described 1977 as a year of extreme contrasts. Earnings had declined through the year, culminating in a first-quarter loss (see Exhibit 1). At the same time, and at considerable expense, the company was strengthening its Marantz line through new-product development. Three years later, in reflecting on 1979, he stated[1]: "For the balance of 1980, management will continue to reduce operating expenses wherever possible and to dispose of any nonessential assets. We believe operations in Europe and Canada will be profitable in 1980."

The mid- and especially the late 1970s posed an ever increasing challenge to the manufacturers of consumer audio electronics. Many new firms entered the industry, offering products of many prices and qualities. Companies incorporated production and technological refinements that permitted automated assembly, with the consequence of better quality at reasonable prices being offered to consumers. These refinements have forced the well-established, brand-name manufacturers to come up with imaginative strategies to cope with the stiff competition. They must also cope with rising manufacturing costs and shorter product life cycles.

Superscope, Inc., along with other companies in the audio industry, had been trying hard to come up with significant innovations, particularly in view of its financial problems. (Stock market reaction can be gauged from Exhibit 2.) Among its innovations were the Marantz higher-priced and higher-quality product line; improved auto- and hand-carried audio products; the Imperial line of compact music systems (which only had a short life); and "Story Teller" prerecorded cassettes featuring fairy tales, Bible stories, Tarzan adventures, and the *Star Wars* soundtrack.

## BEGINNINGS

It was during a visit to Tokyo in 1957 to promote their Superscope anamorphic lens process that Joseph Tushinsky and his brother, Irving, made a discovery which would alter their lives and the direction of the then fledgling audio home-entertainment industry.

The discovery was Sony, whose main facility at the time was a Quonset hut and whose total export business worldwide was no more than $25,000 a year. However, Sony had just developed the first stereo tape recorder with

**EXHIBIT 1**   Consolidated Statements of Operations Superscope, Inc., and Subsidiaries

| Five years ended December 31, 1978 ($000 omitted except per share amounts) | 1974 | 1975 | 1976 | 1977 | 1978 |
|---|---|---|---|---|---|
| *Net sales* | $157,234 | $157,266 | $180,988 | $178,649 | $205,138 |
| Cost and expenses: | | | | | |
| Cost of sales | 104,594 | 107,026 | 121,267 | 127,534 | 157,286 |
| Selling, general, and administrative | 32,570 | 36,410 | 44,273 | 47,052 | 53,923 |
| Interest | 4,706 | 4,952 | 4,067 | 5,562 | 9,283 |
| Discontinuance of Imperial product line | | | | | 5,342 |
| Total cost and expenses | 141,870 | 148,388 | 169,607 | 180,148 | 225,834 |
| Operating income (loss) | 15,364 | 8,878 | 11,381 | (1,499) | (20,696) |
| Minority interests in net income of consolidated subsidiaries | | (189) | (70) | (139) | (32) |
| Share of net income (loss) of Marantz Japan, Inc. | 1,506 | 1,001 | 1,453 | 179 | (287) |
| Income (loss) before income tax provision (benefit) | 16,870 | 9,690 | 12,764 | (1,459) | (21,015) |
| Income tax provision (benefit): | | | | | |
| Current | 6,918 | 3,938 | 4,296 | (2,932) | (3,618) |
| Deferred (reduction) | 415 | (250) | 552 | 1,090 | (1,910) |
| Total | 7,333 | 3,688 | 4,848 | (1,842) | (5,528) |
| Net income (loss) | 9,537 | 6,002 | 7,916 | 383 | (15,487) |
| Net income (loss) per common share | $4.13 | $2.60 | $3.43 | $ .17 | $(6.71) |
| Average common shares outstanding | 2,307 | 2,307 | 2,308 | 2,308 | 2,308 |

**EXHIBIT 2**   Superscope's Stock Prices, 1976–1980

| | | Closing Price |
|---|---|---|
| 1976 | March 15 | 28³/₄ |
| | September 15 | 24¹/₄ |
| 1977 | March 15 | 18¹/₂ |
| | September 14 | 15³/₄ |
| 1978 | March 15 | 10¹/₈ |
| | September 15 | 10³/₄ |
| 1979 | March 15 | 6 |
| | September 13 | 4³/₄ |
| 1980 | March 14 | 4⁷/₈ |
| | September 15 | 3¹/₈ |

Source: *Wall Street Journal,* respective dates.

built-in power amplifiers. The Tushinskys readily saw the enormous market potential at home for this product and, after some negotiations, bought six of the seven units that Sony had produced. Thus Sony, which is now a household word in the United States, made its debut in the United States market. The agreement between Superscope, Inc., and Sony Corporation resulted in a contract that made Superscope the exclusive distributor for all of Sony's tape products.

Superscope, Inc., was also drawn into an industry well suited to the energy and imagination of its founders. In 1964 came Superscope's acquisition of the Marantz Company and

**EXHIBIT 3**   Superscope, Inc.

| | December 31 | | |
|---|---|---|---|
| | **1977** | **1978** | **1979** |
| *Sources of Working Capital: ($000 omitted)* | | | |
| Increase in additional paid-in capital | | | $ 2,061 |
| Issuance of long-term debt | | $ 3,090 | |
| Sales of property and equipment | $ 1,015 | 1,345 | 14,857 |
| Decrease in deferred charges and other | 36 | | |
| Deferred credit on sale of Pianocorder rights | | 2,150 | |
| Dividend from Marantz Japan, Inc. | 153 | 207 | 220 |
| Total Sources | $ 1,204 | $ 6,792 | $17,138 |
| *Decrease (Increase) in Working Capital Items:* | | | |
| Cash | 1,625 | (266) | (1,871) |
| Accounts receivable | (6,004) | (17,417) | 21,151 |
| Refundable income taxes | (4,762) | 510 | 4,252 |
| Inventories | (861) | (19,746) | 19,700 |
| Prepaid expenses | (244) | 784 | (42) |
| Notes payable | 16,918 | 18,742 | 8,516 |
| Accounts payable | (2,718) | 16,593 | (8,465) |
| Accrued expenses | 774 | 5,528 | (2,529) |
| Deferred revenue | | 2,850 | (2,850) |
| Dividends payable | 577 | (577) | |
| Income taxes payable | 90 | (348) | 1,320 |
| Current maturities on long-term debt | 385 | 10,592 | (9,421) |
| Total Decrease | $ 5,753 | $17,245 | $29,716 |

its manufacturing and distribution of high-fidelity stereo components. Superscope's line of audio home-entertainment products reached the market in 1973, following the company's acquisition of the Standard Radio Corporation (now named Marantz Japan, Inc.) in 1971 and the establishment of another Superscope manufacturing facility in Taiwan.

For all its initiative and entrepreneurship, the company has fallen on hard times. Data in Exhibit 3 amplify this point. Superscope's management believed that the external environment was largely responsible for the company's misfortunes. In his letter to stockholders, Joseph S. Tushinsky sketched the 1977 environment as follows[2]:

> The most significant problems Superscope encountered in 1977 were the sharp weakening of the U.S. dollar and intensified levels of competition. Our products originate substantially in Japan, as do those of our competitors. The basic difference is that most of our competitors have substantial domestic sales in their home country

[2]*Annual Report 1977*, Superscope, Inc., p. 2. Note that the yen (¥), was valued in 1976 at ¥295 per $1, and, in 1977, at ¥ 270.

**EXHIBIT 4**  Superscope, Inc., Assets and Liabilities ($000 omitted)

| | 1977 | 1978 | 1979 |
|---|---|---|---|
| *Current Assets* | | | |
| Cash | $ 4,934 | $ 5,200 | $ 7,071 |
| Accounts receivable less allowance for possible losses | 50,784 | 68,201 | 47,050 |
| Refundable income taxes | 4,762 | 4,252 | none |
| Inventories | 60,567 | 80,313 | 60,613 |
| Prepaid expenses | 3,219 | 2,435 | 2,477 |
| Total | $124,266 | $160,401 | $117,211 |
| Property and equipment | 27,838 | 28,025 | 11,916 |
| Investment in Marantz Japan, Inc. | 7,816 | 7,322 | 8,917 |
| Deferred charges and other | 2,861 | 3,525 | 4,704 |
| Total Assets | $162,781 | $199,273 | $142,748 |
| *Liabilities and Stockholders' Equity* | | | |
| Current liabilities | | | |
| Notes payable to banks | $ 38,680 | $ 57,422 | $ 65,938 |
| Accounts payable | 9,046 | 25,639 | 17,174 |
| Accrued expenses | 10,555 | 16,083 | 13,554 |
| Deferred revenue | none | 2,850 | none |
| Current maturities of long-term debt | 415 | 11,007 | 1,586 |
| Other | 1,213 | 288 | 1,608 |
| Total | $ 59,909 | $113,289 | $ 99,860 |
| Long-term debt | 34,692 | 32,809 | 2,530 |
| Deferred credit | none | 2,150 | 2,110 |
| Other | 3,522 | 1,844 | 1,630 |
| *Stockholders' Equity* | | | |
| Common stock, $1 par | 2,308 | 2,308 | 2,308 |
| Additional paid-in capital | 8,895 | 8,895 | 10,956 |
| Retained earnings | 53,455 | 37,968 | 23,354 |
| Total Liabilities and Equity | $162,781 | $199,273 | $142,748 |

currency, the yen, while Superscope has a small base in Japan. This means that the adverse impact of a rising yen is felt less by our competitors. Market share is a key ingredient for current and future success, and price increases to our customers to offset their higher product costs were viewed during 1977 as a threat to our own competitive position and our market share. For the most part, then, higher product costs resulting from a stronger yen were not passed on, but were absorbed, ultimately reducing our pretax income.

Joseph Tushinsky also expressed his belief that the consumer electronics industry in general, and audio in particular, were far from saturated. The main reason why Superscope, Inc., introduced its Imperial brand products was to better use the company's manufacturing capacity.

## BUSINESS OF SUPERSCOPE, INC.

Superscope, Inc., is engaged principally in the manufacture and distribution of consumer audio electronic products designed primarily for home entertainment. In 1979, the company purchased approximately 39 percent of its products from Marantz Japan, Inc., a Japanese corporation in which the company owns 43 percent of the issued and outstanding common stock.

Since 1957, when the company entered the industry as the exclusive United States distributor for Sony consumer-type tape recorders, it has developed and expanded its Marantz, Superscope, and Pianocorder product lines.

The company's products include consumer-type stereophonic and monaural cassette tape recorders, stereophonic hi-fidelity components, compact stereo music systems, loudspeakers, automobile stereos, microphones, accessories, prerecorded audio tape, pianos, electronically controlled player-pianos, and piano systems. Products are marketed in the United States principally under the Marantz, Superscope by Marantz, Superscope, and Pianocorder brand

**EXHIBIT 5**   Principal Company Operations and Location

| Location | Interest | Use | Approximate Square Footage |
|---|---|---|---|
| Chatsworth, California | lease expires 1981 through 1985 | corporate headquarters, plant and warehouse | 276,000 |
| West Carrolton, Ohio | lease expires 1982 | office and warehouse | 77,000 |
| Morganton, North Carolina | owned | office, plant, and warehouse | 124,000 |
| Tsoying, Taiwan | owned | plant and office, excluding leased land | 182,000 |
| Mississauga, Canada | lease expires 1982 | office and warehouse | 46,000 |
| Brussels, Belgium | leases expire 1981 through 1984 | office and warehouse | 25,000 |
| Peronnes-lez-Binche, Belgium | owned | plant, service center, and warehouse | 93,000 |
| Brookvale, Australia | lease expires 1982 | office and warehouse | 12,000 |

The company owns or leases additional smaller facilities for offices, service, and warehousing (ranging from 1,000 to 10,0000 square feet) in the United States, Canada, Australia, Belgium, France, United Kingdom, Norway, Sweden, and West Germany.

names and worldwide under the Marantz, Superscope by Marantz, Superscope, and Pianocorder brands. The company also manufactures certain private-label products for customers desirous of reselling such products under the customer's brand name. Marantz, Superscope by Marantz, and Superscope products are manufactured principally by the company in the United States and Taiwan and, in Japan, by Marantz Japan, Inc.

## DIRECTORS AND EXECUTIVE OFFICERS OF SUPERSCOPE, INC.

JOSEPH S. TUSHINSKY, 69, chairman of the board of directors, chief executive officer, and treasurer. Joined the company in 1954.

DAVID A. CLIMAN, 53, director, president and chief operating officer. Joined the company in February 1979 as senior vice president for finance and administration and chief financial officer. Elected as president and chief operating officer May 10, 1979. Appointed to the board of directors in June 1979. Prior to joining the company, he served as vice president for finance of Phelps Dodge International Corporation for two years and as vice president and treasurer of Northern Telecom, Ltd. (previously called Northern Electric Company, Ltd.), for three years.

FRED C. TUSHINSKY, 52, director, executive vice president and president, Marantz Company, Inc. Joined the Company in 1954. Has been director since 1966 and was elected executive vice president in January 1978. Prior to that time, he held the office of senior

---

**EXHIBIT 6**   Principal Subsidiaries of the Company

| Name | Jurisdiction of Incorporation | Percentage of Voting Securities Owned |
|---|---|---|
| Marantz Company, Inc. | New York | 100 |
| Marantz Piano Co. Inc. | Virginia | 100 |
| Superscope Canada, Ltd. | California | 100 |
| Superscope Tape Duplicating Products, Inc. | California | 100 |
| Superscope (Australasia) Pty. Ltd. | Australia | 100 |
| Superscope Taiwan, Ltd. | Taiwan | 80[1] |
| Marantz Europe, S.A. | Belgium | 100[2] |
| Superscope GmbH | West Germany | 100[3] |
| Marantz Audio (U.K.) Ltd. | United Kingdom | 100[3] |
| Marantz France, S.A. | France | 100[3] |
| Marantz Swenska, A.B. | Sweden | 100[3] |
| Marantz Norske, A.S. | Norway | 100[3] |

[1]20% owned by Marantz Japan, Inc. The company owns 43% of the outstanding voting securities of Marantz Japan, Inc.
[2]Subsidiary of Marantz Company, Inc.
[3]Subsidiaries of Marantz Europe, S.A. (formerly Superscope Europe, S.A.).

vice president for Marketing and sales for five years.

RICHARD D. ROSENBLATT, 54, director of the company since November 1978. He is a private investor and an underwriting member of Lloyds of London.

MARC STERLING, 61, director of the company since 1979. Since 1960 he has served as president of Sterling and Company, a consulting firm in corporate finance, specializing in mergers and acquisitions.

MICHAEL L. TENZER, 49, director of the company since 1979 and director of Leisure Technology Corp., a national developer of retirement communities. He has been the president and chief executive officer of Tenzer & Company, a housing and real estate investment firm, since February 1980, a position which he also held prior to 1976. Prior to assuming his present position and commencing in 1976, he was president and chief executive officer of Leisure Technology Corp.

LAURENCE M. WEINBERG, 70, director, an attorney in private practice in Los Angeles since 1933. He was appointed as a director in November 1978. Mr. Weinberg previously served as a director of Superscope, Inc., from 1967 to 1976 and has provided legal services to the company in the past.

ANTHONY M. BLAZINA, 30, vice president. Joined the company in 1972. Prior to assuming his present position, he served as manager and general manager of Pianocorder Division and in various management positions with Superscope Tape Duplicating Products, Inc., a wholly owned subsidiary.

RICHARD L. CLARK, 35, assistant treasurer, joined the company in present capacity in August 1979. Prior to joining the company, he was, for over five years, manager of financial planning and analysis for United States Borax and Chemical Company, a manufacturer of various chemical products.

RONALD COSTA, 48, senior vice president, Operations. Joined the company in 1971. Has held present position since February 1979, and prior to that he served as vice president and senior vice president of Manufacturing from 1973. Appointed executive vice president, Marantz Company, Inc., in December 1979.

GARY G. COWAN, 43, senior vice president for finance and administration and chief financial officer. Joined the company in June 1979 in his present capacity. Prior to that time, he served as senior vice president and chief financial officer of Leisure Technology Corporation for two years and as executive vice president, chief operating officer of Coastland Corporation for four years. Mr. Cowan previously held financial and executive positions with Dart Industries.

JACK GOLDMAN, 39, vice president, Administration, general counsel, and secretary. Joined the company in 1975. Elected to office of vice president, administration, in March 1977 and to the office of secretary in March 1978. Served as treasurer through May 1977. Prior to that time, he was engaged in the private practice of law in Los Angeles, California, for nine years.

DENNIS E. HUTCHINGS, 38, corporate controller. Joined the company in 1977 as director of internal audit. For over five years prior to joining the company, he was employed by Arthur Andersen & Co., accountants and auditors.

MARTIN W. KATZ, 34, vice president of sales and marketing. Joined the company in June 1978. Prior to joining the company, he was assistant vice president, sales and marketing, for Morse Electro Products Corporation from 1974.

DENNIS K. KINCAID, 45, president of Marantz Piano Company, Inc. He was president of the Grand Piano Company, Inc., for over five years prior to its acquisition by the company in 1978.

## PRODUCT LINES

The company engages in a single line of business, the manufacture, distribution, and sale of audio home-entertainment products. Brand-name contributions to total sales revenues for the last five fiscal years are as shown in Exhibit 7.

The Marantz brand is by far the most significant line marketed by the company, both within the United States and in foreign countries. The Marantz line consists of high-fidelity stereo components and systems for the home and car. In 1979, stereo receivers represented over 28 percent of sales of Marantz products,

followed by high-fidelity loudspeakers, which represented 17 percent of such sales.

## MARKETS AND DISTRIBUTION

The company's Marantz and Superscope products are marketed in the United States through independent sales representatives primarily to retail dealers and to a certain extent by unaffiliated wholesale distributors. Domestic sales through company sales personnel were largely phased out in 1978 and the first quarter of 1979. Imperial products were distributed in the United States through independent sales representatives and independent subdistributors. Distribution in markets other than the United States is effected primarily through foreign-based sales subsidiaries and independent subdistributors or by the company's export sales personnel to independent foreign-based distributors.

Foreign market areas and methods of distribution are

EUROPE, MIDDLE EAST, AND AFRICA—distribution is conducted by

**EXHIBIT 7**

| | 1975 | | 1976 | | 1977 | | 1978 | | 1979 | |
|---|---|---|---|---|---|---|---|---|---|---|
| | ($ Millions) | | | | | | | | | |
| | Sales | % of Total | Sales | % of Total | Sales | % of Total | Sales | % of Total | Sales | % of Total |
| Marantz | $ 84.9 | 54% | $110.3 | 61% | $120.3 | 67% | $135.4 | 66% | $141.0 | 72% |
| Superscope | 35.2 | 22% | 39.5 | 22% | 34.9 | 20% | 34.5 | 17% | 30.7 | 15% |
| Sony[1] | 32.7 | 21% | 24.2 | 13% | 18.9 | 11% | 6.3 | 3% | 1.3 | 1% |
| | — | — | — | — | — | — | 17.5 | 9% | 11.0 | 5% |
| Other[3] | 4.5 | 3% | 7.0 | 4% | 4.5 | 2% | 11.4 | 5% | 12.9 | 7% |
| Total | $157.3 | 100% | $181.0 | 100% | $178.6 | 100% | $205.1 | 100% | $196.9 | 100% |

[1]Pursuant to an agreement with Sony Corporation, distribution of Sony products terminated on March 31, 1979.
[2]This line was phased out during 1979.
[3]Other products consist primarily of the Pianocorder Reproducing System, the Marantz Reproducing Piano, standard pianos, and prerecorded tape products.

Marantz Europe, S.A. (formerly Superscope Europe, S.A. and subsidiaries) directly to dealers and through independent subdistributors;

CANADA—distribution is conducted by Superscope Canada, Ltd., directly to dealers;

JAPAN AND THE FAR EAST—distribution is conducted by Marantz Shoji, KK (formerly Marantz Far East, Inc.), a Japanese corporation wholly owned by Marantz Japan, Inc., directly to local dealers and through independent subdistributors;

AUSTRALIA—distribution is conducted by Superscope (Australasia) Pty. Ltd. directly to dealers;

LATIN AMERICA AND THE CARIBBEAN—distribution is conducted by the Company's export personnel through local independent distributors.

## FOREIGN AND DOMESTIC OPERATIONS

Exhibit 8 sets forth certain information for fiscal years ended December 31, 1978 and 1979, regarding domestic and foreign operations of the Company by geographic areas where sales originated.

The company is largely dependent on foreign production of the products it markets. Approximately 15 percent of the products marketed by the company are produced in Taiwan, and 38 percent are produced in Japan by Superscope Taiwan and Marantz Japan, Inc., respectively. The remaining products are produced by the company in the United States or Europe or purchased from independent foreign or domestic suppliers.

The company purchases raw materials, parts, and finished products from a number of suppliers in the Far East, including Marantz Japan, Inc. Most of these orders are denominated in the local foreign currency, and it is common for several months to elapse between the time orders are placed and products are received. As a result, while orders for products denominated in local foreign currency are outstanding, such local foreign currencies may rise or fall versus the U.S. dollar, exposing the company to the risk that costs of product measured in U.S. dollars may increase or decrease. The company has chosen not to trade extensively in currency futures in connection with its foreign purchase orders; however, in some cases, the company and its suppliers have agreed to share the risk of changes in product costs measured in U.S. dollars resulting from such currency fluctuations. Because of the rapid decrease of the U.S. dollar versus the yen, particularly during 1978, notwithstanding such arrangements, this relative change was reflected in higher costs for products purchased or manufactured in the Far East and carried in inventory and sold through the third quarter of 1979.

With respect to products purchased in 1978 and the first quarter of 1979, the company was largely unable to pass such increased costs to its customers in the form of higher prices because of the intense competition in the United States market. (See "Competition and Competitive Environment.") During 1979, the U.S. dollar strengthened considerably against the Japanese yen, which contributed to higher gross profits during the second half of 1979.

The contribution of domestic and foreign operations to consolidated net sales and consolidated pretax income or losses for the five fiscal years ended December 31, 1979, are summarized in Exhibit 9.

In February 1980, the company announced it had begun discussions with a prospective purchaser for the sale of substantially all of the company's foreign assets and for an agreement whereby the purchaser would supply the company with products in the future. In the event these discussions result in the sale of such assets, the company intends to utilize the proceeds for the payment of bank debt as well as for working capital.

**EXHIBIT 8**

|  | 1978 | 1979 |
|---|---|---|
|  | ($000 omitted) | |
| *Sales to Unaffiliated Customers* | | |
| United States | $119,209 | $ 88,141 |
| Europe[1] | 71,622 | 90,258 |
| Canada | 8,693 | 8,363 |
| Taiwan | 1,126 | 2,947 |
| Australia | 4,488 | 7,155 |
| *Sales or Transfers Between Geographic Areas[2]* | | |
| Taiwan | $ 13,584 | $ 17,406 |
| *Operating Profit (Loss)[3]* | | |
| United States | $(19,980) | $(11,977) |
| Europe[1] | 1,995 | 166 |
| Canada | (1,168) | 61 |
| Taiwan | (368) | (186) |
| Australia | (545) | (661) |
| *Identifiable Assets[4]* | | |
| United States | $103,919 | $ 52,907 |
| Europe | 62,640 | 59,074 |
| Canada | 6,347 | 5,831 |
| Taiwan | 8,956 | 6,027 |
| Australia | 4,267 | 5,456 |
| *Export Sales* | | |
| United States | $ 4,300 | $ 3,500 |

[1]Includes sales to customers in Africa and the Middle East as well as continental Europe.
[2]Transfers between geographic areas are accounted for at prices designed to allocate reasonable gross profits.
[3]Operating profit or loss of each geographic area excludes income taxes, minority interests, and share of income (loss) in Marantz Japan, Inc., and includes foreign exchange gains or losses and interest on all borrowings including loans and advances to the company.
[4]All assets are identified with their related geographic area except for minority interests, investment in Marantz Japan, Inc., and certain corporate assets consisting primarily of cash, tooling, new model costs, and patents.

**EXHIBIT 9**

|  | 1975 | 1976 | 1977 | 1978 | 1979 |
|---|---|---|---|---|---|
| *Net Sales by Point of Origin:* | | | | | |
| Domestic | 72.4% | 64.1% | 64.2% | 58.1% | 44.7% |
| Foreign | 27.6% | 35.9% | 35.8% | 41.9% | 55.3% |
| Total | 100.0% | 100.0% | 100.0% | 100.0% | 100.0% |
| *Pretax Income (Loss)* | | | | | |
| Domestic | 51.9% | 56.6% | (170.6%) | ( 99.6%) | ( 95.7%) |
| Foreign | 48.1% | 43.4% | 70.6% | ( 0.4%) | ( 4.3%) |
| Total | 100.0% | 100.0% | 100.0% | 100.0% | 100.0% |

## COMPETITION AND COMPETITIVE ENVIRONMENT

The company faces intense competition throughout the world in the marketing and sale of its products. The company is a significant factor in the audio home entertainment industry, and it principally competes with approximately twenty full-line major manufacturers and distributors, a number of which are substantially larger than the company. Its larger competitors are based in Japan and enjoy a substantial share of the Japanese audio market. They operate throughout the rest of the world as exporters of similar products, primarily to wholly owned distribution companies based in key foreign market areas. In addition, the company competes with a large number of other manufacturers and/or distributors who offer more limited product lines or specialize in particular markets.

The company's competitive position in its largest market, the United States, has been adversely affected since the repeal of the fair trade laws in 1976. Prior thereto, with few exceptions, audio retailers operated in a predominantly fair-traded market, which enabled them to compete effectively with one another irrespective of size. With the abandonment of fair trade, discount merchandisers and retailers who adopted mass merchandising practices have been able to expand rapidly, based in part upon their ability to obtain lower wholesale prices by placing substantially larger orders and as a result of interbrand competition for such orders. The resulting price competition caused a significant reduction in the number of retail dealers and forced other retailers to withdraw their support from major brands and to specialize in lesser-known brands, which offered a degree of exclusivity and the potential for higher profit margins.

These competitive pressures on order size, wholesale prices, and retail selling patterns severely limited the company's ability to pass on the increased product costs described in the section on "Foreign and Domestic Operations." In mid-1979, the company adopted a marketing strategy in the United States market designed to reposition Marantz and Superscope by Marantz products to restore a high degree of image to these products and to improve profitability. This strategy coincided with the introduction of a new Marantz model lineup. As part of the strategy, the company severely curtailed its prior practice of granting high promotional allowances and discounts which had accompanied the marketing of the prior Marantz model lineup. Also, in connection with the company's overall attempt to move Marantz and Superscope by Marantz products to more stable distribution channels from highly priced sensitive distribution, the company adopted and maintained firm policies regarding terms of sale and prices through the balance of 1979.

The Imperial brand was introduced in 1978 as a response to the needs of the large retail and discount merchandisers for economy-priced audio equipment, which is not sensitive to state-of-the-art demands. The company subsequently discontinued the line in 1979 because of the anticipated lack of profitability in the future.

Additionally, because of increased inter-brand competition and rapid technological development, the average product model life for all product lines has decreased from approximately three years in the early 1970s to approximately eighteen months at the present time. Such rapid reduction in model life has affected not only product manufacture and inventory practices but also pricing decisions and product distribution. This results from the need to continually phase out product models in inventory at reduced prices in order to make way for their replacements.

In the European market, the company is also engaged in intense competition. The company believes its success in Europe to date has resulted from its ability to maintain a high-brand image for its products at the dealer and consumer level, supported by a much more limited and exclusive method of distribution. The company also believes the European consumers' purchasing decision is less influenced by discount-oriented merchandising and more influenced by traditional considerations of quality, reliability, and reputation.

In other foreign markets, conditions are similar to those in the United States.

It has been the practice of the company and others in the audio home entertainment industry to maintain high inventories of a balanced mix of products. This has resulted from the need to stockpile products because of their foreign manufacture and the need to respond promptly to customer orders in a competitive environment where such customers can obtain similar products from their sources of supply. It has

been a normal industry practice for customers to maintain low inventories and to depend on manufacturers to stock adequate levels of finished goods inventories to meet the customers' requirements. Throughout 1978, the company's inventories increased over the levels maintained in 1977 because of product buildup involved in the introduction of the Imperial and Pianocorder product lines.

In 1979, the company undertook a concerted effort to reduce inventories in order to accelerate the sale of products to be replaced by new models, to phase out inventories of Imperial products as quickly as possible, and to generate cash required to fund current operations and reduce bank debt. Consolidated inventories of finished products decreased $20 million during 1979 to $60 million at year end.

The company's outstanding accounts receivable decreased from the levels maintained in 1978 primarily due to lower sales volume in the United States and additions to reserves for doubtful accounts which were made during 1979. In order to accelerate the collection of accounts receivable, the company changed its standard payment terms in the United States to thirty days. In 1979, the average age of the company's accounts receivable decreased from 124 days as of December 31, 1978, to ninety-seven days as of December 31, 1979.

As a result of the policies adopted by the company during 1979 with respect to its inventories and accounts receivable, the company was able to reduce its total borrowings to $101 million from $470 million and to provide cash for operations in spite of continued operating losses. Proceeds from the sale of the company's corporate headquarters building in Chatsworth, California, contributed $13 million to this reduction.

Under an agreement dated May 2, 1977, as amended, between Teledyne Industries, Inc., and the company, the company acquired a worldwide exclusive license, including sublicensing rights, under Teledyne patents to manufacture, market, and sell an electronically controlled automatic piano-playing apparatus (the "Pianocorder Reproducing System"). In consideration for this license, the company agreed to pay Teledyne a royalty based on the worldwide net sales of Pianocorder products to an aggregate royalty of $1,859,000 by December 31, 1987, or sooner. Upon payment of the total royalty, Teledyne shall convey to the company all of its rights, title, and interest in and to such patents and in other Pianocorder technology.

According to Joseph S. Tushinsky:

Pianocorder reproducing system is a computer-type product that easily installs in any piano and plays that piano "live" exactly as an artist would. It also records performances on magnetic tape cassettes that play back a "live" performance by commanding which keys to play and how fast and hard they should be struck.

He went on to say that this new product presents Superscope, Inc., with the opportunity to expand into the worldwide keyboard industry. There are already 30 million pianos in homes and commercial establishments throughout the world. It is estimated that the vast majority of pianos are either never played or only occasionally used for educational purposes. Each of the owners of these pianos could be a potential customer of the Pianocorder system.

The company had made a decision, in light of financial problems emanating from manufacturing operations abroad, in Japan in particular, to manufacture the Pianocorder system in the United States. Also the company hoped that if a substantial demand for Pianocorder software were to materialize, it could then satisfy such demand through its own tape-duplicating production facilities and through licensing other software producers.

The player-piano is not a new idea, but the Pianocorder does contain new technology. Although the initial price of Pianocorder was about $1,800, the company expected to get on the "learning curve" quickly and derive economies of scale. Early sales were brisk and encouraging.

Superscope purchased the Grand Piano Company in July 1978, renamed it the Marantz Piano Company, and began manufacturing pianos with Pianocorders built in. Buoyed by the prospects he saw, Tushinsky commented: "In a few years, I can't visualize anybody investing in a piano without a Pianocorder." The company also negotiated to acquire the Aeolin Corporation, a privately held Memphis (Tennessee) piano manufacturer and the world's largest manufacturer of player-pianos, but talks were discontinued for unknown reasons. At this point, others had remarked that, even if the Pianocorder proves successful, it can't offset the losses in other divisions of Superscope, Inc.

## MONEY MATTERS

On April 2, 1979, Superscope and its domestic banks entered into an agreement in principle, restructuring its aggregate indebtedness ($57.3 million as of April 2, 1979), pursuant to which the domestic banks would make loans to Superscope's domestic operations. The credit facilities included: $34 million revolving line of credit at an interest at the domestic prime rate plus 3 percent; $25 million term loan, at the same rate, and expiring January 31, 1980; and $6 million real estate loan, secured by a second security interest on Superscope's headquarters building, maturing on June 30, 1980. This agreement contained some restrictive covenants on, among other things, creation of additional debt, payment of dividends, creation of new liens, investments or acquisitions, additions to property and equipment, and advances or loans to subsidiaries.

In the midst of its financial woes, at its May 1979 annual meeting, Superscope, Inc., designated David Climan as the new heir-apparent to company founder Joseph S. Tushinsky. After the meeting, Mr. Tushinsky, 68, said he is considering stepping down as chief executive in a year and as chairman in two years. "But I don't plan to leave until this company returns to profitability," he added.

A *Wall Street Journal* staff reporter wrote[3]:

Mr. Climan is faced with a formidable task. Increasing competition in Superscope's product lines and high interest expenses have saddled the

[3]*Wall Street Journal,* May 14, 1979.

company with a continuing string of losses and serious liquidity problems.

The formidable task was probably too formidable for Mr. Climan. In June 1980, he announced his resignation. Joseph Tushinsky resumed the office of the president he had relinquished just a year before and expressed no anxiety to seek an immediate successor to Mr. Climan, but continued to be optimistic.

# 12 THE SWISS CALL IT "THE FIRESTONE AFFAIR"

**Harold Oaklander**

*Pace University*

*Note: about the nature of "cases" used in studies of business administration.* Case studies are used increasingly for education and training in management and business administration. They highlight important decisions, episodes, problems, and issues affecting enterprises. The Harvard Graduate School of Business is well known for its extensive use of cases.

Cases differ from most articles in journals and magazines devoted to administrative affairs. While based on research, a case study does not include the rigorous treatment characteristic of most scholarly reports, or the explanations, discussion, and answers that readers generally expect to find. For these reasons, case studies are seldom published in raw form for use outside the classroom.

The graduate student or manager is supposed to improve his decision-making skills through *his own* analysis of the case. He is encouraged to come up with workable solutions to traditionally mishandled administrative predicaments. Successful analysis often reveals that problems have not been defined adequately in the rush for an answer.

The Firestone Case is the narrative study of a plant closing, an administrative decision whose importance and complexity is overlooked by business, government, and professional education. Although thousands of case studies have been published in the 1970s covering a wide variety of situations, only a handful examine plant closings. Drawing attention to the critical consequences of plant closings can only result in moderating this very costly practice.

Harold Oaklander
New York, Jan. 1979

---

This case was abstracted from a larger work prepared by Professor Harold Oaklander of the Graduate School of Business, Pace University (New York City). It is based almost exclusively on published sources, including newspapers, reports, and studies from German- and French-speaking Switzerland, Germany, France, and the United States. Information is also included from interviews in Switzerland, France, and New York City with government officials of the European countries and informally with the Swiss and American management of Firestone's Swiss subsidiary. Several highly informed Europeans also were interviewed, including members of the Swiss Radio and Television System, the OECD, the ILO, and IMEDE at Lausanne. I am indebted to Mr. Manfred Simon, former Presiding Judge of the French Court of Appeals in Paris, for the translations from the German and to Ms. Anne Louise and Christine Oaklander for translations from the French. The case is intended as a vehicle for class discussion rather than an illustration of either effective or ineffective handling of an administrative situation.
Copyright 1978 by Harold Oaklander.

The Firestone Company, rated as the second-largest manufacturer of tires and rubber products and one of the largest American corporations, celebrated its 70th birthday in 1970. Its net sales of $3.9 billion in 1976 and $4.4 billion in 1977 reflect a diversification that extends beyond the tire business.[1] Its headquarters are in Akron, Ohio.

Production of tires remains its primary business.[2] Its 2,000 tire stores both in the United States and elsewhere and thousands of dealers, distributors, and other retailers sell its tires in 135 countries.

[1]Firestone Annual Report 1977, p. 34.
[2]Ibid., p. 1.

Like other firms with multinational ties Firestone has been buffeted by worldwide inflation and has incurred losses when it invested the fluctuating United States dollar in foreign countries with stronger currencies. Traditionally the decline in the sale of tires for new automobiles is balanced by increased sales of replacement tires for older cars but this was less the case in 1974 and 1975. Reduced speed limits in Europe and the United States meant that tire life was extended. Tires were not replaced as often as formerly. Moreover, weight restrictions imposed on auto manufacturers reduce the size of passenger vehicles and the size of the tires.

Perhaps the most important challenge facing tire makers is the popularity of the radial tire, a European development associated with the French firm of Michelin. There is much to suggest that the popularity of the radial tire exceeded the preparations of the American tire producers. Firestone anticipates that by 1982 some 60% of all passenger tires shipped will be radials.[3] In Europe, where radial tires have been popular for a long time, Firestone predicts that by 1982 approximately 95% of all tires sold will be radials.[4]

At Firestone, the transition from nonradial tire production and marketing to radials has not been smooth. For example, a problem of quality continues to demand the attention of management.[5] Some analysts blame the company's problems with quality for the depressed value of Firestone stock. Firestone's share of the tire market dropped throughout the 1970s and its tire business represents a reduced share of its 1977 sales of $4.4 billion.[6]

The beginning of 1978 saw other problems materialize. Plant closings would occur again in this country, and what was more unusual, they might also be ordered abroad. Said the 1978 First Quarter report:

"As (a) part of management's efforts to reduce the erosion of earnings and improve profitability, a review of tire production capacity ... indicates ... a need ... to reduce or eliminate production at facilities that produce bias ply passenger tires or that are ... uneconomical ... in at least one and possibly two locations in the United States, and to discontinue tire manufacturing operations at two foreign locations."[7]

The Firestone Company's first quarter report for 1978 sketched another problem: a currency exchange loss of $11.9 million was reported in comparison with a $1.5 million gain the year before.[8]

A changing image of Firestone as a firm with deep-seated problems had an effect in Europe where the management of the company reported its tire market as "sluggish."[9] These problems continued to plague the company in 1978, but in a new setting, Switzerland.

At the American Embassy in Bern there are some who say that Firestone's Swiss problems began in 1973 with the purchase of a tire-making plant from its Swiss owners who had run it as a Firestone licensee. Public awareness of the extent of the problems awaited the headlines of March 23, 1978, when newspapers across Switzerland carried the news that Firestone was closing its Pratteln plant outside Basel, second-largest city of Switzerland.[10]

Firestone employees, 40% of whom were foreign workers, would have had no reason for alarm just a few months earlier if they had read the company's 1977 annual report.

[3]Firestone Annual Report 1977, p. 3.
[4]Ibid., p. 13.
[5]Firestone Second Quarter Report, May 23, 1978, p. 4.
[6]Ibid., p. 7.

[7]Firestone First Quarter Report, Feb. 21, 1978, p. 4.
[8]Ibid., p. 3.
[9]Firestone Annual Report, 1977, p. 3.
[10]Swiss Bank Corporation, Switzerland: The Country and Its Economy, 1978, p. 2.

**EXHIBIT 1**    Five-Year Summary: Financial Position of the Firestone Tire and Rubber Company
(Dollars in millions, except per share amounts. Shares in thousands.)

|  | 1977 | 1976 | 1975 | 1974 | 1973 |
|---|---|---|---|---|---|
| SUMMARY OF OPERATIONS |  |  |  |  |  |
| Net sales | $4,427 | 3,939 | 3,724 | 3,675 | 3,155 |
| Gross profit | $ 892 | 797 | 815 | 841 | 782 |
| Interest and debt expense | $ 89 | 78 | 77 | 64 | 46 |
| Income taxes | $ 103 | 90 | 95 | 118 | 121 |
| Net income | $ 110 | 96 | 134 | 154* | 165 |
| Net income as a % of sales | 2.5% | 2.4% | 3.6% | 4.2% | 5.2% |
| Cash dividends on common stock | $ 63 | 63 | 63 | 58 | 51 |
| Average number of shares outstanding | 57,509 | 57,250 | 57,020 | 56,891 | 57,023 |
| Per share of common stock |  |  |  |  |  |
| Net income** | $ 1.92 | 1.68 | 2.36 | 2.71* | 2.89 |
| Cash dividends | $ 1.10 | 1.10 | 1.10 | 1.025 | .898 |
| FINANCIAL POSITION AT YEAR END |  |  |  |  |  |
| Working capital | $ 955 | 926 | 921 | 797 | 797 |
| Current ratio | 2.0:1 | 2.1:1 | 2.2:1 | 2.0:1 | 2.2:1 |
| Stockholders' equity to long-term debt ratio | 2.3:1 | 2.3:1 | 2.1:1 | 2.3:1 | 2.6:1 |
| Total assets | $3,396 | 3,261 | 3,181 | 2,998 | 2,669 |
| Net value of properties, plants, and equipment | $1,423 | 1,387 | 1,393 | 1,347 | 1,158 |
| Long-term debt | $ 690 | 678 | 720 | 633 | 522 |
| Stockholders' equity | $1,618 | 1,568 | 1,529 | 1,453 | 1,357 |
| Book value per share of common stock | $28.12 | 27.33 | 26.79 | 25.54 | 23.85 |
| OTHER DATA |  |  |  |  |  |
| Wages, salaries, and employee benefits | $1,451 | 1,198 | 1,172 | 1,137 | 1,010 |
| Research and development expenses | $ 60 | 53 | 52 | 51 | 45 |
| Taxes deducted from income | $ 300 | 263 | 275 | 293 | 267 |
| Properties, plants, and equipment |  |  |  |  |  |
| Expenditures | $ 205 | 170 | 200 | 330 | 278 |
| Depreciation | $ 167 | 165 | 152 | 136 | 120 |
| Shares outstanding at year end | 57,542 | 57,373 | 57,062 | 56,907 | 56,887 |
| Number of stockholders | 48,754 | 47,910 | 49,778 | 50,337 | 45,984 |
| Return on average stockholders' equity | 6.9% | 6.2% | 9.0% | 11.0% | 12.6% |
| Number of employees | 115,000 | 113,000 | 111,000 | 120,000 | 117,000 |

*Change to LIFO method of inventory valuation reduced net income by $42.2 ($.74 per share).
**Based on average number of shares outstanding during the year.

Despite some expected short-term variations, we believe the basic tire business is good and will continue to grow.... We also believe there are opportunities for growth in our other areas of business, both in the U.S. and internationally.... We extend our appreciation to our employees and dealers everywhere for their achievements in the challenging year of 1977.[11]

The international section of the report appeared less optimistic regarding European operations but still gave little cause to Pratteln workers to worry. For one thing they were aware of their reputation for producing the highest-quality tire of all those made by the company on the Continent. Also, Swiss workers in general enjoy the reputation of being among the most peaceful and cooperative workers.

On March 21, two press releases provided the first news of the location of future plant closings. Frank LePage, Executive Vice President for North American Tire Operations, announced that a bias tire production facility in Akron employing a thousand hourly and salaried workers, approximately one-half the Firestone workers in Akron, would be shut down completely "between now and July."

On that same day Akron announced that Firestone Canada, Ltd. was terminating production at one of its tire plants, and that "a European subsidiary was ending tire production completely." After stating that the specific plants to be closed would be disclosed in locally made announcements, the release detailed the pretax charges that would be made against revenues as a result of all the plant closings. The charges totaled $110 million, including

- $50 million for various payments to affected employees
- $43 million for disposition of fixed assets
- $17 million for other costs including operating losses during the phase-out period

The news release concluded with the declaration of the regular dividend of $0.275 per share for the second quarter.[12]

The following day the managing director of the Swiss subsidiary, John R. Thompson, identified his operation as the European unit marked by Akron for closing. Firestone would continue to provide a full line of tires to the Swiss market. He explained that tires could be imported at a lower cost than they could be made in Switzerland and that the rising Swiss franc had caused tires produced in that country to be noncompetitive for export. "We regret very much that it is necessary to close this plant, since we found the Swiss employees to be very dedicated and cooperative."[13]

The *Wall Street Journal* carried the news of the Pratteln closing on March 23. Subsequent articles in this and other American publications and Firestone news releases could only intimate that the Swiss episode was not like American plant closings.

Five weeks later, a final reference was made to the closing in the Firestone second quarter report. "The tire capacity realignment plan provides for terminating ... production at plants in Calgary, Canada, and Pratteln, Switzerland."[14] What appeared in America as the end of a minor business episode would be viewed in Switzerland as a social crisis of national importance.

## SOME BACKGROUND NOTES ON THE PRATTELN SETTING

What was meant by the statement that Firestone's problems started the day they purchased the plant from its Swiss owners? It was

---

[11]Firestone 77th Annual Report, 1977, p. 3.

[12]Firestone News Service, Akron, March 21, 1978, PR78–100.
[13]Firestone Schweiz A.G., news release dated March 22, 1978, PR78–102.
[14]Ibid., p. 2.

not just the problems of transition from bias tires to radials, nor the rise in labor costs in Switzerland, nor even the fall of the dollar.

When the Swiss owned the tire plant, operated under license from Akron, they used Firestone molds and formulas. Swiss technicians and engineers were so successful with quality and service that their tires were used as original equipment on some models of such cars as Mercedes and BMW. Many of the employees had been with the plant since it opened in the 1930s. They and management had enjoyed labor peace.

In the late 1960s, the Pratteln tire workers approached management with their desire to unionize. The plant is located just across the border from Germany where, under the provisions of new legislation, workers were sharing more and more in the major decisions by means of codetermination.

The Swiss owners of the tire plant, Daetwyler Holding Company, reacted strongly: they discharged several of the leaders of the workers and precipitated the plant's first strike. Now management swung in the other direction. Pratteln became *the* codetermination plant in Switzerland, one of the very few at that time. Their brand of codetermination was mild compared with the German version: it was based on local initiative rather than federal legislation. It did, however, increase labor costs.[15] But the company continued to prosper. It had captured some 35% of the Swiss tire market by 1970. This might have influenced Firestone to purchase the company in 1973. The purchase price was estimated to have been between SFr

120 and 150 million, at that time equivalent to some 35 to 45 million dollars.[16]

Firestone appointed first one managing director, then another, John Thompson, whose previous post had been in the Philippines. Most of the Swiss middle management remained, but an American marketing manager and a manufacturing director were brought into the new subsidiary. Visits from Akron became routine, but few stayed long enough to learn the characteristics of the plant and its people. A memorandum describing local characteristics was produced for the information of the Akron advisers to the Swiss subsidiary, but it apparently met with indifference.

Several important changes were made to improve productivity. Increased standardization reduced the making of minor changes in tire design to accommodate the requirements of automobile designers.

Changing economic conditions, the lower reputation of Firestone tires, and perhaps in part the company's lack of interest in small specialized markets caused demand for Swiss-made Firestone tires to decline. German manufacturers stopped using Pratteln-made tires for their new cars. Production fell from the 10,000 record daily output (1970) to 4,300 units in 1977. Firestone's share of the Swiss market fell from the 1970 high of 35% to 15% in 1977, while Michelin's increased from 20% to 30%.

Effects on local human resources were predictable. Man hours worked were reduced. Later, financial inducements were offered to workers who would resign. Over a period, hundreds of foreign workers elected to return home with severance and pension settlements.[17] Employees numbered 1,500 in 1974, 1,000 in 1976, and 850 by the beginning of 1978. John Thompson reported that his operation had lost $18 million over the four-year period of Firestone ownership.

[15]Codetermination in Switzerland was one element in the evolution of the Swiss labor peace rather than as legislated social change. In the case of the Daetwyler Company that preceded Firestone, codetermination was described by the Swiss labor expert, Dr. Lukas Burckhardt, as "nothing in the way extravagant, but a normal, good result of sound collective bargaining." (from personal correspondence)

[16]*Tribune de Lausanne,* March 29, 1973.
[17]See footnote 46.

## REPERCUSSIONS IN AKRON AND IN PRATTELN

The announcement from Pratteln that the Swiss plant would close was carried in Akron newspapers, where the closing of a local plant had been announced earlier, and in *The New York Times,* the *Wall Street Journal,* and, of course, the Swiss press. The Akron workers knew that they would be receiving unemployment compensation and supplementary compensation, adding up to almost full salary, for a long time, if necessary. They would gain top seniority for job openings in other Firestone plants. The company notified the union, as it had done in the past, that it would welcome discussions so that the remaining plants, also hard-pressed, could continue to operate. There were no demonstrations by the Akron workers nor threats against the company. This was in strong contrast to the reaction of the Swiss.

Word of the Pratteln closing scheduled for July 31, 1978, spread like wildfire. It was carried within 24 hours in every major newspaper in the country. The *Basler Zeitung* reported on Firestone's business conditions in articles covering a whole page.[18] Emphasis was placed on the number of workers to be laid off, the workers' poor expectations in the job market, and the apparent finality of the decision.

In Baselland, consternation was voiced by the head of the canton and similar expressions followed from the head of one of the two unions representing the workers of Firestone. The union felt the action was unwarranted because the workers had been accommodating for several years. They had cooperated by accepting a paring down of the work force, by foregoing wage increases, and by accepting reduced benefits, all with the tacit understanding that production would be maintained.[19] The union also announced that the workers were preparing to demonstrate against this decision. John Thompson responded by assuring the workers that they would not be locked out. The demonstration was peaceful, and in a matter of hours the workers returned to their jobs.[20]

The Federal Council of Switzerland (somewhat similar to but more powerful than the U.S. Cabinet) created a national precedent soon after the announcement. For the first time in its history, it held a plant closing to be grave enough to warrant its intervention. Fritz Honegger, head of the Department of Commerce and a member of the Council, joined with canton officials in appealing to Firestone to reconsider its decision, offering to organize a committee of government officials to meet with the company and explore ways to keep the plant open.[21]

The outcry was loud in the first days following the announcement and Firestone continued to be a topic of national conversation for months. For many Swiss and other Europeans "Firestone" was to become associated with such terms as "brutal," "shocking," and "arrogant." Its actions were described as "unwarranted," "in violation of the labor-management agreement," and "the act of an inept management."

Shortly, a wave of public discussion of the "Firestone Affair" appeared in the media. Now the discussion became analytical. One commentator offered two hypotheses to explain why the enterprise was marked for termination: administrative error on the part of the American management, and a profit-protecting response by a multinational trying to solve a problem caused by the defective quality of its product. According to this account Pratteln-made tires were dumped on the European market, upsetting the price structure for all European producers of Firestone tires and reducing the profitability of European sales. Firestone was also blamed for giving priority to volume of sales at

[18]*Basler Zeitung,* March 23, 1978, p. 15.
[19]*24 Heures,* March 23, 1978.

[20]*Basler Zeitung,* March 23, 1978.
[21]*Journal de Genève,* March 23, 1978.

the cost of quality, thus jeopardizing Switzerland's reputation for high-quality products.

Impetus for the job-saving action attained broad sponsorship. Fritz Honegger emerged as both the spokesman for the Swiss government in the Firestone Affair and the organizing force behind the initiative to save the Pratteln tire manufacturing operation. The Central Committee of Swiss unions sent a telegram to a protest meeting of 3,000 persons, denouncing the cynicism and the errors of judgment that they felt characterized the shutdown decision. The voice of the business and industrial community of Baselland was added, expressing sympathy with the tire workers.[22]

The participation of the private as well as the public sector is one of the most interesting aspects of the Firestone Affair. Mr. Honegger stated that, "It is possible to continue making tires at Pratteln." Honegger reported that a group was developing a "plan of rescue" to be submitted to Firestone management.[23]

Mr. Honegger outlined some specific elements of such a plan. Various enterprises and the Swiss government would agree to buy 25% of the plant's capacity. The plant would be expected to continue under private ownership. A delegation was to travel to Akron and discuss plans for reorganization. It included two members of the Executive Council of Baselland, the former secretary of the Federation of Swiss Unions, and the Swiss ambassador to the U.S.[24]

Press coverage was almost like the attention given to a bizarre murder trial, with the media amplifying each new development and everyone waiting anxiously for the final verdict. Swiss television began to prepare a documentary, with camera crews dispatched to both sides of the Atlantic.

The Swiss ambassador to the United States visited Akron and delivered a formal protest against the announced closing of the Firestone subsidiary. The correspondent of a German newspaper opined: "Akron management won't be impressed by the ambassador, for Firestone has always been critical of the high Swiss wages."[25] The solution to the problem of how to continue making tires in Switzerland was for the Swiss to reapply tariffs on tires. He predicted that the tire workers would have no difficulty in finding new jobs. What the German analyst deemed important was that the Firestone Affair might influence other multinationals to close down their Swiss subsidiaries.

Jacques-Simon Eggly, an opposition member of the Liberal Party, questioned whether Honegger's "spectacular" intervention and his organizing of the mission to Akron represented a "turnaround" in Swiss economic policy.[26] He summarized the traditional Swiss conservatism in economic affairs: "a regime of economic liberty is not a regime of economic assistance." He expressed the opinion that while the central government could not extend its influence each time a foreign enterprise closed its doors, it should be concerned with the welfare of Swiss workers.

Felix Auer, a member of the federal legislature, was critical of the Akron management for not taking the human problem into consideration.[27] He outlined some broader implications of the Firestone layoff. Of some 95,000 workers capable of earning wages in the canton only 70,000 had jobs. Even in the boom of 1973–1974, some 8,000 jobs were lost, "each one changing the destiny of a worker." Auer felt that the Firestone case was typical of this.

Auer also discussed mistakes made by Firestone's top management. Akron didn't react quickly enough to improvements in the Michelin tires. The company produced tires of inferior quality and suffered when consumer ac-

[22]*Tribune de Genève,* March 30, 1978.
[23]*Tribune de Genève,* March 30, 1978, p. 27
[24]*Tribune de Lausanne,* March 30, 1978.

[25]*Frankfurter Allgemeine Zeitung,* April 1, 1978.
[26]*Journal de Genève,* April 3, 1978.
[27]*Basler Zeitung,* April 4, 1978.

ceptance slipped, and while Pratteln labor costs were 20% higher than those in other Swiss industries, the local plant also had to bear high overhead costs from Akron. Finally, to some degree, the lower cost of raw materials imported into Switzerland, owing to the relatively high value of the Swiss franc, would offset high overhead and labor costs.

What might the Swiss do by themselves to continue making tires and maintain jobs? The Swiss lawmaker's opinion was that they lacked the technical knowledge to build tires completely on their own. Neither would they raise tariff barriers to protect jobs since this would draw retaliation. He concludes with the hope that, in its final decision, Akron will take the Swiss population into consideration.

The Executive Council of the canton government voted unanimously to engage a financial specialist to represent the state in matters regarding the financial health of enterprises. This indicated that in future affairs of this sort the canton's government may be willing to provide financial assistance to ailing enterprises.[28]

April 11 witnessed the arrival of the Swiss delegation in Akron and the beginning of daily reports back to Switzerland. At home, Mr Honegger, responding to reporters, mentioned that the unions were willing to accept a 15% reduction in wages which would help decrease the losses from 40 million Swiss francs to 4 million. But Firestone would be asked to take another year's losses.

The "other" Swiss tire company now entered public discussion. Maloja, located in the same canton as Firestone and employing some 400 workers, had also suffered during recent years. Even though its workers had accepted considerable reductions in salary, their jobs were still threatened. Since a variety of measures were being proposed to support Firestone, Maloja claimed equal treatment.[29] Honegger, in

the Zurich weeky *Weltwoche,* felt that it was out of the question for the Confederation to intervene each time an enterprise closes its doors.[30]

Under what conditions should the federal government intervene? Victor Lasserre, editor of a Geneva management weekly, pointed out that the numbers laid off appeared important as well as the military usefulness of the enterprise. While the federal government lent its official support when 600 workers were threatened at Pratteln, it did not appear disposed to support Maloja. It refused in the past to intervene when the failure of a large refinery idled several hundred workers in the canton of Valais, despite pressure exerted by the Valais government. Laserre pointed to the anger expressed by heads of small enterprises when the cantonal government of Geneva attempted in 1977 to save Tarex, a local enterprise with 350 workers. "A shop closes, a small businessman ruined, his workers in the street, this doesn't count, statistically or politically."[31]

The Swiss delegation to Akron returned home on April 14. Were they successful? The consensus appeared to be, "Neither yes nor no." Firestone had agreed to organize a committee to reconsider the closing. It would send two experts in finance and management to examine points raised by the delegation. The committee would make recommendations upon which Akron would base its final decision.[32]

The delegation considered its mission a success. Firestone had been willing to study their proposals. A few additional details were supplied: Firestone would not consider selling the installation, except perhaps the site; they would not accept a Swiss majority partnership but might consider a Swiss minority partnership with American management.

Shortly after the delegation's return, the news came from Paris that the Trade Union

[28]*La Liberté,* April 5, 1978.
[29]*Tribune de Lausanne,* April 12, 1978.

[30]Ibid., p. 3.
[31]*Tribune de Genève,* April 13, 1978.
[32]*Tribune de Genève,* April 14, 1978.

Advisory Committee (TUAC), associated with the 24-nation Organization for Economic Cooperation and Development (OECD), had denounced the Firestone decision to close Pratteln in the name of the Federation of Swiss Unions (USS). Firestone was charged with violating the code of conduct for multinational firms.[33]

Journalists used every bit of available information to predict Akron's final decision. Analyst Rudolf Bachtold feared that union complaints to the prestigious OECD might be disruptive. Looking at the business climate in America, he reminded readers that there was an anti-Nestle campaign taking place in Minnesota. He was dismayed by the return of "Buy American" slogans and concluded that with changes in international economics, plant closings would be unavoidable.[34]

The *Neue Zürcher Zeitung* was also pessimistic about the outcome of the negotiations, calling Firestone's response, "delaying tactics." It brought out that the company had cooperated with the Swiss delegation by showing confidential data and that the delegation had asked Firestone to take a long-term view, recognizing the value of Swiss labor and the advantages of the labor peace that has prevailed in the country since World War II.[35] It expressed its belief that the plant could be made profitable.[36] One correspondent described the approach in the following way: "they put the emphasis on the necessity to adjust American methods to the Swiss turn of mind."[37]

The Zurich newspaper also reported on difficulties which made it unlikely that Firestone would change is decision: The Pratteln closing was part of the general reorganization of the company. Firestone's strategy was to reduce production. The massive layoffs could not be reversed. The correspondent stressed American

astonishment at the Swiss reaction to the closing.[38] He suggested that it would have been better to send private representatives to Akron rather than government officials. He speculated that Akron saw the Swiss approach as an accusation of mismanagement and was irritated by the Swiss plan to reorganize the Pratteln plan to make it more efficient.[39]

What were the expectations of the workers at the Pratteln plant? According to one professional employee, they had reason for optimism based on the quality of the tires they turned out and on the efficiency achieved in the plant. The Swiss middle management, more accustomed to dealing with the American management, were described as more pessimistic.

On May Day, thousands of Swiss workers demonstrated in support of their Pratteln brothers. The President of Switzerland, Mr. Willy Ritschard, gave an address that included a defense of capitalism. He added, however, that the Firestone Affair had exposed some of the harmful consequences of capitalism but had also brought out some unanticipated forces to support the workers in their struggle. In Basel, Lilian Uchenhagen, a member of the National Assembly, addressed a marching crowd which extended nearly a mile to demonstrate solidarity with the Firestone workers. She pointed to the Firestone Affair as an example of the ways of multinationals. In Bern's Federal Square some 2,000 supporters of labor carried banners pledging support for the tire workers.[40]

The Firestone Affair was hardly mentioned in the news media during the week. Was everyone holding his breath for Akron to render its verdict? Their decision on Monday, May 8th: the plant would close on July 31 as announced earlier. This news was released the following day by the government of Baselland and carried in every major Swiss newspaper.

Commentators expressed anger, shock, and

---

[33]*Tribune de Genève,* April 17, 1978.
[34]*Weltwoche,* April 19, 1978.
[35]See Appendix A.
[36]*Neue Zürcher Zeitung,* April 14, 1978.
[37]Ibid.

[38]*Neue Zürcher Zeitung,* April 14, 1978.
[39]Ibid.
[40]*Gazette de Lausanne,* May 2, 1978.

resignation. There was anger because the sacrifices of the workers to keep the plant operational appeared to have been forgotten. The Swiss public was reminded that Pratteln workers had accepted reductions in wages and had cooperated to reduce labor costs. They had complied when asked to give up certain holidays and to speed up production.[41] Firestone had apparently turned a deaf ear. All that had been done to present the Swiss case in Akron seemed to have failed to influence the giant's decision. A few voices asked whether the multinational had any realistic choice but to close the plant. Was it really in the long-term interest of the Swiss to save the factory?[42,43]

Despite the failure of the negotiations, Mr. Honegger, the Federal councilor, responded, "If necessary, I will do it again to save the jobs of workers."[44] He denied that the federal government had offered guarantees to Firestone. He then lifted the curtain on some little-known twists of the negotiations. When Firestone specialists came to Pratteln to start their investigation, a plan evolved to bring the plant out of the red and continue production by reducing personnel by one hundred, cutting salaries by more than 10%, and increasing production. The Firestone experts thought that under these conditions the company could increase its share of the Swiss market. In Akron, they were instructed to add other provisions. Financial guarantees would have to be provided by the canton and Swiss government. Mr. Honegger added that such guarantees were out of the question. He reminded his interviewer of Firestone's current operating debt of 35 million Swiss francs, also that there was no legal basis for such a guarantee.[45] As for future government actions, the federal councilor reminded his interviewer that a grievance had already been brought to the attention of the OECD.[46] He raised the possibility of strengthening national regulations pertaining to multinationals. The modification of Swiss laws applying to corporations was also mentioned as a possibility.[47]

While most journalists supported attempts to save the Pratteln plant, the analysis of Joel Redalie of the *Journal de Genève* was an exception. If there really was 15 to 20% over-capacity in European tire production, perfect management appeared to offer the only chance of survival for the facility, according to Mr. Redalie. But paradoxically, continuation of the plant would imply the presence of the same Firestone management. Looking at the financial side, Redalie asked his readers not only to view the operating losses but also to consider the debt incurred in purchasing the plant in 1973. The company had assumed a debt of 150 million Swiss francs scheduled to be paid back between 1982 and 1986.[48] When the plant was purchased, the dollar exchange was 3 Sfr to the dollar. In 1978 the dollar bought fewer than 2 francs. It was anyone's guess what the dollar exchange would be in the 1980s when the debt was due. Redalie continued, "certainly responsible financial officers of Firestone could not be criticized for wanting to close the operation."[49] He also emphasized the impact of economic changes on many Swiss-owned firms. Some of them were approaching bankruptcy. Why should an American company be rescued when these Swiss firms could not be supported?

---

[46]The Pratteln closing was seen by the unions as an integral part of Firestone's business strategy in Europe. The International Association of Chemical and Energy Workers predicted a movement of facilities to Eastern Europe, where unions had little power and wages were cheaper. The union was aware of the shifting of tire plants by all the major manufacturers that had taken place in the United States with a succession of plant closings in heavily unionized Akron and the opening of new plants in such states as North Carolina, Alabama, and Georgia.

[47]*La Suisse,* May 11, 1978.
[48]*Journal de Genève,* May 10, 1978.
[49]Ibid.

[41]*SMUV Zeitung,* May 10, 1978.
[42]*La Suisse,* May 10, 1978.
[43]*Journal de Genève,* May 10, 1978.
[44]*La Suisse,* May 11, 1978.
[45]*24 Heures,* May 11, 1978.

On May 17 the workers rejected the "Social Plan" offered by Firestone as a termination settlement. The climate became akin to that preceding a strike. The parties became tense; there was talk of a boycott of Firestone products, and the union promised a fight unless competent negotiators were sent from Akron with the power to negotiate to the satisfaction of both parties.[50] The focus had shifted from ways to keep the plant open to ways to indemnify redundant workers.

What was the first proposal made by Firestone to compensate the workers for the loss of their jobs? It was based on the number of years of service and the age of the worker. The range was from 0.3 times the monthly salary to a maximum of 4.5 times monthly salary. The proposal also included settlements to help transfer pension arrangements to other employers and to enable early retirement for older workers. The response of the unions was swift and indignant. The settlement would have to be "several times" such an amount. Charles Levinson, General Secretary of the International Labor Union of Chemical Workers, explained the union's tough position by drawing attention to the benefits received by Akron workers who were laid off. Those with 25 years of service would receive a compensation equal to four years' salary. After 15 years of service the American rubber workers were entitled to 80% of their last salary for a period of 3 $1/2$ years, according to Levinson's account. Why should the Swiss tire workers settle for less, much less?[51,52]

A period of peaceful production marked the month before the workers were to be laid off, in spite of the threats. But "hard bargaining" continued at Pratteln. The first offer from Akron had amounted to some 2.5 million Swiss francs. The unions responded by making specific demands that totaled 13 million. Bargaining produced a plan that amounted to 6.5 million Sfr. On June 14 the workers voted 261 to 81 in favor of this plan. The unions emphasized again that the workers had surrendered an equivalent of 7.2 million Sfr in their earlier efforts to help keep the enterprise open. The settlement didn't even cover this amount. The unions followed by filing a complaint with the Swiss Bureau of Conciliation charging Firestone with violation of the labor agreement.

At that time, in mid-June, only some 25% of those soon to be laid off had found other jobs. Even though the publicity had stimulated scores of job offers from all over the country and beyond, it was reported that new jobs went to skilled workers, with older workers encountering the most problems.[53]

June drew to a close with no clear indication of how the affair would be concluded. With the union charges pending and the indemnities yet to be paid, a power struggle seemed to be shaping up between the two unions and the company.

In Pratteln the company announced on August 7 that 55% of the Swiss workers termi-

[50]*La Liberté,* May 18, 1978.
[51]Ibid.
[52]In Switzerland, compulsory unemployment insurance was instituted nationwide only as recently as 1976. Prior to that time, voluntary plans were used by some employers in some cantons while in others the insurance was obligatory. The determination of an indemnity for the tire workers was thus more a matter of ad hoc collective bargaining than tapping a well-established social security system.
The presence of foreign workers in large numbers may have retarded the need to enact comprehensive un-

employment insurance in Switzerland. With a population of 6.3 million, it had an unemployment rate of 0.8% for 1976. In the United States, with a population of 215.1 million, 7.7% were unemployed during the same year. In 1976, 15.3% of the population was composed of foreign workers and their families. (See *Union de Banques Suisse, Le Suisse en Chiffres,* Edition 1977.) Many were encouraged to return to their Mediterranean home countries with considerable financial settlements which they could spend in familiar surroundings with much cheaper living costs. More than 200,000 foreign workers left Switzerland in the recession years.
[53]*24 Heures,* June 16, 1978.

nated according to plan had found new employment.[54] The severance compensation appeared to have been paid on schedule in spite of forebodings that payments might be held off until the complaint made against Firestone was

[54]*Gazette de Lausanne,* August 7, 1978.

settled. On the last day of the month a hearing was scheduled by the conciliation bureau at which time the union was to deliver a bill of particulars supporting their suit. The document was delivered in mid-September. And so a tangled affair of international misunderstandings appears to be winding down.

# APPENDIX A*

### Industry-Labor Relations:
### Industrial Peace

#### By Dr. Lukas F. Burckhardt,
#### Former Chief of Cultural Section, Swiss
#### Political Dept.

Switzerland's industry-labor relations are famous for their peacefulness. *Arbeitsfrieden* (industrial peace) therefore has become a catchword in any Swiss discussion on labor matters. Is this labor peace a social achievement which should be maintained by all means, or is it an impediment to the fight of the unions for better labor conditions? But are the workers not better off if their demands are peacefully negotiated with employers who are not in a state of war with the unions, but in an unbroken, honest business relationship based on mutual esteem? This discussion is continuously going on, openly and surreptitiously, and its results are not easily foreseeable.

For an American, who is used to big strikes and takes them as an apparently inevitable fact of life in a free society, the emotional aspects of this very Swiss type of discussion may be rather difficult to understand. Why should it not be possible, even after a bitter strike, to establish quite correct and even friendly relations between the former enemies who, after

*Condensed from: J. M. Luck, *Modern Switzerland, The Society for the Promotion of Science and Scholarship.*

the purifying thunderstorm of an open labor conflict, will be free as partners to make another start to the new horizons of the future?

This very supposition, which will seem quite natural to an average American, would certainly hurt many Swiss, presumably even a large majority. But why? To give a true answer one would have to scrutinize the Swiss mind, which is so full of thoughts and afterthoughts that only an investigator with superhuman insight could fully understand it. The following attempt at an explanation is based on the author's experience of 20 years in labor mediation in his home town of Basel. What strikes him most in retrospect, as the main result of those years, is a deep change of mind in the very hearts of the responsible leaders at all levels in management and in the unions. This change might never have come about without the outward threat to the very existence of our country that occurred shortly before and during World War II, but it is nevertheless a reality. Former opponents of the trade unions suddenly realized their qualities, and with the enthusiasm of the newly converted they outdid each other in developing new forms of cooperation within the framework of the renewed and enlarged collective agreements.

This is a very Swiss attitude. But are we ready to continue that tradition? This is an open question. We would like to answer in the affirmative, and the following considerations are our arguments in favor of this optimistic thesis.

It is based on the belief that the idea of a stable industrial peace is already so deeply rooted in the Swiss in that it will be able to adapt itself to new situations because a return to the previous period of bitter, open labor conflicts would seem unthinkable. The future, however, can never be a simple repetition of the past, and it is therefore necessary to instill new life into the notion of industrial peace, instead of using it as a mere cliché to justify the social status quo.

In Switzerland with its federal structure and its highly developed local, cantonal, and regional autonomy, the many agreements between management and labor do not follow any single pattern. Each economic branch has developed its own style of industrial relations. To describe all of them would exceed the limits of this article. We therefore concentrate our main attention upon one outstanding example, the so-called Peace Agreement in the Swiss metal industry, which has attracted more public attention than any similar result of collective bargaining in other Swiss industries or crafts.

The *Friedensabkommen*—the Peace Agreement of July 19, 1937, in the Swiss Engineering and Metalworking Industry—has been and still is the main pillar of Swiss industrial peace. Concluded first for a period of two years, it has been extended several times, most recently from July 19, 1974, to July 19, 1978. Its main partners are: on the management side, the Employers' Association of the Swiss Engineering and Metalworking Industries and, on the union side, the Swiss Metalworkers' and Watchmakers' Union together with four smaller unions of which the largest is the Christian Metalworkers' Union of Switzerland.

The most important minority group in the Swiss trade union movement is the National Christian Trade Union Federation with more than 106,000 members, of whom 30,000 are organized in the metal industry. The group is principally based in the Catholic parts of Switzerland, whereas the Swiss Trade Union Federation has grown in the midstream of the labor movement, together with the Swiss Social-Democratic Party. In the eyes of the employers the Swiss Trade Union Federation is of prime importance. In the context of the Peace Agreement, the Swiss Metalworkers' and Watchmakers' Union, quite obviously the most important partner, has to bear the full responsibility for everything that happens in labor–management relations. Its Christian counterpart, on the other hand, sometimes acts as a ferment for new ideas which still have to be digested by the employers and by the average Swiss. This is quite apparent in recent times and applies particularly to the metal industry and to French-speaking Switzerland under the impact of modern Catholic social doctrines. This attitude differs from the pragmatic approach of the Swiss Metalworkers' and Watchmakers' Union with its concentration on practical issues and its extraordinary capacity to win the confidence of the employers by sharing their concern for the prosperity of the enterprises—a method which has transformed them from opponents into partners. This method can still work if new generations of employers and union leaders will keep it up, not as an excuse for leaving things as they are, but as a stimulus to bold new solutions applicable to their mutual relationship.

The Peace Agreement in the Swiss metal industry, which today covers more than 500 firms and 150,000 workers, begins in its original version of 1937, revised up to 1964, with the following general statement:

In an endeavor to preserve the state of industrial peace desirable to all those engaged in the maintenance and development of the Swiss Engineering and Metalworking Industries, [the parties to this Peace Agreement] undertake to clarify in mutual good faith any major differences of opinion or disputes and to settle them within the terms of this agreement, so as to maintain absolute peace for its entire duration. In compliance with this, such militant measures as labor boycotts, strikes, and lockouts are ruled inadmissible; this shall also extend to disputes concerning working conditions not specified in this agreement.

After this introduction, the Peace Agreement specifies in 11 Articles how these principles are to be implemented by the parties. According to Article 1, "differences of opinion and other disputes shall be first dealt with, and if possible settled, within the enterprise itself." In order to facilitate this, "workers' committees shall be appointed in all enterprises sufficiently large to warrant such committees." In the most recent edition of the Peace Agreement (July 19, 1974), the appointment of such committees is compulsory for all the firms bound by the agreement, and the rights of these committees, barely mentioned in the original text, are now defined. Very clearly the committees are "the legitimate agents for defending the interests of all the employees under the agreement against the employer and for taking care of the problems connected with the application of the agreement in the enterprise."

In apparent contradiction to this long catalogue of important issues to be treated jointly by management and labor, there is one striking exception in Article 2 of the original Peace Agreement: Wages "shall continue to be regulated through individual service agreements., i.e., without the application of minimum, average, or standard wages." The reason for this exception is to be found in the statement that this has to be so "according to custom in the engineering and metal industries." At first glance, this seems to be a severe setback for the union side because collective wage agreements, immediately binding upon each employer, are usually regarded as the very cornerstone of any solid collective bargaining scheme. At second glance, the picture looks somewhat different because of the fact that, otherwise, all kinds of general wage modifications would be subject to discussion between the parties to the Peace Agreement, indirectly also leaving the way open to complaints about individual wages, if they have a general repercussion on the whole enterprise. The very vagueness of the original text has the advantage of including also wage issues which were not foreseeable when the original Peace Agreement was concluded. That a narrowly legalistic approach to the interpretation of a collective labor agreement also has its limitations is visible for instance in the case of an employer who, during a period of crisis, lowers the individual wages down to the minimum permitted under the text of a collective labor agreement, and who points out that this procedure is not in open contradiction to the written contract. Under the Peace Agreement, on the other hand, there would probably never have been any doubt that such behavior could have been brought before the parties, based on the concept of "general wage modifications" in Article 2.

Article 5 states that "should the executives be able to reach a settlement, disputed questions on general wage modifications and on the implementation of special agreements [concerning paid vacations, etc.], shall be submitted to a conciliation board, the function of which shall be to give prompt consideration to collective disputes and, where possible, to settle them. Disputes concerning the interpretation of this agreement shall also be submitted to the conciliation board."

# PART FOUR

# CASES ON MANUFACTURING ORGANIZATIONS

# 13 APPLE COMPUTER, INC.

## William H. Davidson

*University of Virginia*

Chairman Steven Jobs began Apple Computer's annual meeting in January 1983 by introducing President and CEO, Mike Markkula, who summarized the past year's financial results. Sales had grown 74% to $583 million, and earnings had risen 55% to $61 million. Jobs then returned to introduce two new products. The first, the Apple IIe, was an enhanced version of the highly successful 5-year-old Apple II. Before lifting the cloth that shrouded the much-awaited Lisa personal office system, he said:

> The personal computer was created by a hardware revolution of the 1970s. The next dramatic change will come from a software revolution which Apple is introducing here today.

The two product introductions occurred at a time of rising chaos in the merging personal computer industry. New competitors appeared weekly; a profusion of software vendors offered an exploding number of software products, and distribution channels were in a state of flux. Apple's position of leadership in the industry was being challenged from a dozen different directions. The IIe and Lisa provided an immediate response to these challenges, but many observers at the annual meeting were secretly concerned about the company's ability to maintain its unprecedented record of success.

Apple management was not resting on its laurels, however. There was a good deal of effort and pressure within the company to improve the company's competitive position. Among the managers present at the annual meeting no one felt that pressure more than Alan Oppenheimer. Alan had left a consumer products marketing position at General Mills to become Apple's director of market research in 1981. He had recently been selected to head a project to develop Apple's first home computer. Alan's task was to finalize the design for the new home computer and build an organization to manufacture, market, and service the product.

Leaving the community college auditorium where Apple held its annual meeting, Alan thought again about the IIe and Lisa systems. Should the home computer be built around Apple II technology and software, or should it incorporate the new Lisa technology? Questions of price and distribution troubled Alan. He also knew that his work in market research was one of the main reasons he had been selected to head this project, yet he was uncertain about the precise segment he should target. If all these issues could be resolved, Alan then had to push the project through the dynamic chaos that characterized organizational life at Apple.

## HISTORY OF APPLE COMPUTER, INC.

1976 was a transition year for Steve Jobs and Steve Wozniak. Both dropped out of college to work in Silicon Valley, Jobs at Atari and Wozniak at Hewlett-Packard. Their spare time was spent in a Los Altos garage experimenting with video games and electronic circuits. Wozniak was particularly intrigued by the potential power of the microprocessor, a programmable computer-on-a-chip invented by Intel in 1971. He began to build a homemade computer system around a microprocessor.

The machine that emerged was crude but effective. Several friends expressed interest in the new computer, and Jobs began to see commercial potential in the product. Jobs' first effort to sell the computer was at the Byte Shop in Palo Alto, the only known store of its time that sold kits for microprocessor-based computers. He showed them Wozniak's machine, which was only a stuffed and wired circuit board. When Jobs asked if they were interested in buying, they replied they would take a hundred, and asked how much they were. Jobs, not quite believing, but without batting an eye, quoted the price of $666.66 each, COD, to be delivered in 30 days. They agreed, and the deal was done.

Jobs rushed back and asked Wozniak what to do next. They had almost no cash, no components, and no one to assemble the boards. Wozniak sold his H-P calculator and Jobs his VW van to raise $1,300. Jobs' next step was to call component suppliers to ask for credit on parts purchases. One supplier offered him net 30 terms. Jobs agreed, not knowing what net 30 meant but sensing it gave them some time.

They had their components within a week, and Jobs, Wozniak, and Jobs' sister furiously stuffed circuit boards for the next three weeks. They delivered 100 completed boards to the Byte Shop in 30 days, collected and deposited a check for $66,666, and paid their creditors within terms. Jobs and Wozniak were profitable from the time of their first sale.

Jobs sensed the market potential of what he and Wozniak had created. He also acknowledged "we didn't know what the hell we were doing," and sought advice. Wozniak mentioned it to people at Hewlett-Packard, but they turned the design down. Jobs was similarly unsuccessful in interesting Atari in the new product. Jobs then approached Nolan Bushnell, founder of Atari and then a leading Silicon Valley venture capitalist. Bushnell declined any direct involvement, but referred Jobs to a local public

relations firm, Regis McKenna, for help. After turning Jobs down twice, the company finally agreed to accept the venture as a client on a pay-later basis.

While doing the rounds of Bay area venture capitalists, they soon met A.C. "Mike" Markkula, a successful marketing executive who had recently left Intel. He put up $91,000 of his own funds, helped create a business plan, and secured a line of credit with the Bank of America. In return, Markkula received 20% of the equity in the fledgling company. He later raised $600,000 in venture capital from Venrock Associates and Henry Singleton of Teledyne. Markkula also negotiated terms so that Apple received payment from its dealers in 15 days, yet paid its suppliers after 60 days.

Jobs, Wozniak, and Markkula incorporated their new venture in January of 1977. As the deadline for filing the incorporation papers approached, they still had no name for the company. Finally, Jobs, looking at the apple he was eating, said that if no one could think of anything better, he would call it Apple. No one had a better name and the deadline passed, so Apple Computer, Inc. was born.

Jobs and Markkula used the $600,000 in venture capital equity funds not for product development, but for promotion. Regis McKenna created the colorful Apple logo and the 4-color glossy ads that began appearing in magazines. They gave Apple the image of a $100-million company at a time when it had 12 employees. Markkula described this effort as critical because:

We had to gain recognition in the market fast. We could not start small. We had to dominate the business or go bankrupt trying.

Apple's distribution and promotion policies contributed greatly to its rapid growth. Markkula's marketing plan depended on independent distribution rather than Apple's own salespeople. Apple encouraged electronics retailers to carry its computers by offering high markings, dealer training, cooperative advertising, and point-of-sale displays. Apple's suggested retail prices incorporated a 45% profit margin for its dealers. The distribution channel, consisting of specialized retail stores, developed simultaneously with Apple. Apple relied on third-party wholesalers until 1981, when the company took over its own distribution and service operations.

## THE APPLE II

In the meantime, Wozniak continued to improve upon the first computer. Jobs continually pushed him to include additional features. He simplified some of the operating system commands, and incorporated a keyboard and an attachment for a video monitor into his design. They used Markkula's $91,000 for tooling of the high-quality, attractive looking outer case Jobs insisted on using. In May of 1977, Apple introduced the Apple II, the first personal computer with a built-in operating system. The operating system manages the computer's internal operations and executes software programs. An Apple II user therefore did not have to program the computer himself. Instead, he could buy software and run programs that had already been written for the Apple.

The early customers for the Apple were hobbyists already familiar with computers and willing to spend money to have their own. What blocked wider sales was the lack of software to run on the Apple. Jobs and Markkula both realized there were lots of hobbyists and enthusiasts, known in the industry as "hackers," who had bought Apples and wanted to write their own programs. Further, they realized that the Apple II would be useful to large numbers of people only if they could choose from a selection of high-quality software. Only with this wide selection would a microcomputer become a truly personal computer.

Because they recognized Apple didn't have a monopoly on either smart people or good ideas, they revealed the secrets of the Apple II by publishing its technical specifications. This step was unprecedented in the computer industry. The inner workings of computers had heretofore been cloaked in secrecy; now here was the Apple II for the world to see. A programmer would therefore know exactly how this Apple worked, and he could easily write applications for it.

The results of this action were astounding. New programs and application for the Apple poured in from every imaginable source. Apple assisted the authors of the more promising software with documentation and publication of their products. Apple's role became one of identifying and communicating these new ideas and uses to potential Apple purchasers.

In 1978 Daniel Bricklin, a Harvard Business School student, and Robert Frankston wrote a program that used a computer to perform lengthy and tedious calculations involved in creating and altering financial spreadsheets. They wrote their programs, called Visicalc, for the Apple II. For 11 months, Apple was the only computer that supported Visicalc, and that lead time provided a great competitive advantage over other entrants in the personal computer market. Suddenly, the Apple II offered a broadly based, tangibly valuable application, and sales of Apple and Visicalc soared.

In 1978, Apple became the first personal computer manufacturer to offer a floppy disk drive. This magnetic storage medium was compact, reliable, easy to use, and held the equivalent of 35 pages of typed text per disk. An Apple user could simply plug the disk drive into his Apple, and use floppy disks to store his own programs or data, and more significantly, use prewritten programs packaged and sold on floppy disks.

The Apple II was positioned as a personal computer that was easy to use and friendly to the user, whoever the user happened to be. It was small, compact, and neat in appearance. The logo was bright and attractive, and the name connoted a friendly product. Nowhere in the ad copy and promotional material was there

**EXHIBIT 1**   Apple Computer Company
Financial and Operating Statistics
($000)

|  | 1978 | 1979 | 1980 | 1981 | 1982 |
|---|---|---|---|---|---|
| Sales | $7,883 | $47,867 | $117,126 | $334,783 | $583,061 |
| Cost of Sales | 3,960 | 27,450 | 66,490 | 170,124 | 288,001 |
| Gross Margin | 3,923 | 20,417 | 50,636 | 164,659 | 295,060 |
| Marketing and Distribution | 1,170 | 8,802 | 12,619 | 55,369 | 119,945 |
| Research and Development | 597 | 3,601 | 7,282 | 20,956 | 37,979 |
| General and Administrative | 609 | 2,080 | 7,150 | 22,191 | 34,927 |
| Operating Income | 1,547 | 5,933 | 23,585 | 66,143 | 102,209 |
| Interest Income | 0 | 0 | 567 | 10,400 | 14,563 |
| Net Income | 793 | 3,023 | 11,698 | 39,420 | 61,306 |
| Cash and Investments | 775 | 562 | 2,500 | 72,834 | 153,056 |
| Accounts Receivable | 1,379 | 5,006 | 17,400 | 42,330 | 71,470 |
| Inventories | 1,063 | 6,348 | 34,200 | 103,873 | 81,229 |
| Net Plant and Equipment | 268 | 900 | 4,000 | 8,453 | 22,811 |
| Total Assets | 4,341 | 17,070 | 65,400 | 254,838 | 357,787 |
| Accounts Payable | 996 | 5,411 | 18,400 | 26,613 | 25,125 |
| Notes Payable | 0 | 0 | 0 | 10,745 | 4,185 |
| Long-Term Debt | 0 | 200 | 700 | 0 | 0 |
| Shareholders' Equity | 1,916 | 8,155 | 25,900 | 177,387 | 259,402 |
| Apple II Unit Sales | 7,600 | 35,090 | 78,100 | 192,000 | 350,000 |
| Installed Base | 8,170 | 43,260 | 121,360 | 313,360 | 663,360 |

the high-technology image and jargon that frightened most people when the word "computer" came to mind.

The written documentation, or instructions and references, that accompanied the Apple II and its software represented a major innovation in the computer industry. The graphics were attractive, the type large and well laid out, the text friendly and humorous, and most importantly, comparatively easy to understand. Heretofore, computer documentation was written in the arcane language of computer professionals—which can be an incomprehensible mystery to the uninitiated. For the first time, a computer manufacturer provided documentation that invited and encouraged the novice.

In January 1983, the Apple II had the largest installed base of any personal computer priced over $1,000. Through the end of calendar year 1982 over 650,000 Apple II units had been sold. The Apple II continued its phenomenal sales growth despite obvious shortcomings. The hardware had not been upgraded in 6 years, while one advance followed another in semiconductor technology. The keyboard was limited to upper case letters, did not contain the full set of characters used in computer programs, and had no up and down arrow key to move the cursor. The Apple II could display only 40 columns on the video monitor, while 80 columns was the standard display. Yet sales continued to rise right up to introduction of the IIe in January of 1983. In fact capacity constraints had limited sales of Apple II systems throughout the company's history.

Apple's manufacturing operations were based in a modern 250,000 square foot plant in Dallas. Operations were oriented towards minimizing cost and maintaining strict quality control. Significant emphasis was also placed on just-in-time inventory management. Since the Dallas plant was primarily an assembly operation, Apple relied heavily on external suppliers. Printed circuit boards were assembled by subcontractors in Singapore. Apple sourced microprocessors from Synertek, other chips from Hitachi, Texas Instrument, and Motorola, video monitors from Hitachi, power supplies from Astec in Hong Kong, and printers from Tokyo Electric and Qume. Reliance on outsiders is an Apple trademark. Michael Scott, Chief Financial Officer, stated:

> Fast-growing companies should rely on outside help for the manufacture of nonproprietory components and systems. As long as cost-efficient outside alternatives exist, we won't worry about being innovative in such areas as productive procedures. As long as we are protected in terms of quality assurance, there are better things to do with our time here. Our scarcest commodity at Apple isn't cash, it's time.

The Apple II, which retailed for about $2000, contained about $350 in purchased components. Industry observers estimated that the Apple II cost less than $500 to build.

Apple attempted to follow the amazing success of the Apple II with a new personal computer targeted more directly at the business market. This computer was the Apple III, introduced in late 1980. While based on the same relatively slow microprocessor (MOS Technology 6502) as the Apple II, the Apple III featured greater memory and a more sophisticated and simpler operating system. The keyboard offered both upper and lower case type, four directional arrow keys, a separate keypad for entering numerical data, and other improvements over the Apple II.

## COMPETITORS AND NEW ENTRY

From its beginning in 1977, Apple had very little competition. Not only had Apple invented a new product, it had almost singlehandedly created a new industry. Tandy, which distributed through its vast Radio Shack retail network of over 2,000 stores, represented Apple's only rival in its early years. Apple's challenge during that period was to convince people to use personal computers, not to fight the competition for market share.

Stimulating primary demand was the early challenge; in 1983 there was a different threat. More than one hundred manufacturers produced 150 models of personal computers ranging in price from $99 to $37,500. Apple faced the challenge of maintaining leadership in the exploding industry it had helped create.

The players in the personal computer industry in late 1982 comprised a broad representation of businesses from all over the world. Competitors ranged in size from giant computer makers to Silicon Valley start-ups. They included manufacturers of mainframe and minicomputers, such as IBM, DEC, and Data General; semiconductor and electronics firms including Texas instruments, and Hewlett-Packard, Japanese computer and electronic producers such as Sharp, NEC, and Sony; well-known office product companies such as Xerox, Wang Laboratories, and Olivetti; consumer electronic firms, including Zenith and Atari; and a host of start-ups and young concerns who were strictly in the personal computer business, such as Fortune, Corvus, and Altos Computer.

New competitors found it relatively easy

**EXHIBIT 2**   Apple Computer Company
U.S. Personal Computer Market Size and Shares

| | 1980 | 1981 | 1982 | 1983(E) | 1984(E) | 1985(E) |
|---|---|---|---|---|---|---|
| | | | **Market Size ($ billion)** | | | |
| Hardware | 1.5 | 2.9 | 5.6 | 8.8 | 12.8 | 17.3 |
| Software | 0.2 | 0.5 | 1.1 | 2.3 | 4.3 | 6.0 |

**Market Share (1982)**
**Price Range**

| $100–$1,000 | | Over $1,000 | |
|---|---|---|---|
| Commodore | 30% | Apple | 33% |
| Atari | 24% | TANDY | 22% |
| Texas Instruments | 20% | IBM | 17% |
| TANDY | 8% | Osborne | 9% |
| Others | 18% | Texas Instruments | 3% |
| TOTAL Units | 2,550,000 | Hewlett Packard | 3% |
| | | Xerox | 3% |
| | | Others | 10% |
| | | TOTAL | 1,150,000 |

to enter the personal computer market. The technology was not especially difficult, particularly for anyone who wanted to emulate an existing product. Capital was required to fund product development and marketing activities, but access to capital seemed to be a surmountable problem. Venture capital money was readily available. For example, Fortune Systems was capitalized in 1980 with close to $24 million in venture funds. The largest barrier to entry appeared to be access to distribution channels, especially scarce retail shelf space.

## DISTRIBUTION CHANNELS

Distribution channels had evolved together with the personal computer industry. Many retail outlets were owned by independent entrepre-

**EXHIBIT 3**   Apple Computer Company
New Entrants in the Personal Computer Industry

| | 1977 | 1981 |
|---|---|---|
| A. Number of Venture Capital Fundings of Firms in Graphics, Computers, and Software | 6 | 99 |
| B. Number of Personal Computer Firms Started | 17 | 62 |
| C. Number of AEA Member Software Firms* | 10 | 140 |
| D. Number of Personal Computer Manufacturers | 19 | 110 |
| E. Number of Personal Computer Models | — | 160 |

*AEA is the American Electronics Association.
Sources: A, B, C: Venture, Nov. 1982; D, E: IDC Report in Fortune, Oct. 18, 1982.

neurs, but computer retail chains had expanded rapidly. The largest of these, Computerland, had over 250 outlets in the U.S. Some nationwide department store chains, such as Macys, opened personal computer centers in many of their outlets. Sears had built 65 free-standing Sears Business Centers. Computer manufacturers competed vigorously for shelf space in these stores. A few manufacturers, including IBM, Xerox, and DEC, had their own stores, although their personal computers were also sold elsewhere. The IBM product centers sold only IBM products, while the Xerox Stores carried several brands. Most stores carried no more than four or five brands.

Retailers selected the manufacturers they would carry based on several criteria. The profit margin they could earn was an important factor. Retail margins ranged from 25% to over 50%. They relied heavily on the manufacturer for training materials, point-of-sale displays, brochures, co-op advertising, and repair service. Some manufacturers, including Apple, devoted a great deal of time and effort to educating dealers about their products. Both Apple and IBM required prospective dealers to complete product training sessions before they became an authorized dealer. Availability of software and accessories was considered important to dealers, because often a prospective customer would approach a retailer with several applications in mind, and rely on the salesman's recommendation in his purchase decision. If several software packages and hardware accessories were available for a certain computer, the dealer could offer more solutions. Also, margins on software products tended to be higher than for hardware, and dealers would tend to prefer systems wih extensive software over a machine with more limited software.

Personal computers were distributed through channels other than computer stores. Some firms used a direct sales force for large-volume accounts, while others such as Atari, TI, and Commodore sold through mass merchandise outlets. Mail order also accounted for a share of the business. Apple, IBM, and Tandy did not authorize sales of their products through the mail. Apple prohibited the sale of its products by mail in mid-1981. This ban had been generally effective, although several mail order houses were challenging Apple's decision in court. A large amount of software and peripheral equipment was sold through the mail.

## ROLE OF TECHNOLOGY

While technical barriers to entry are relatively low, the personal computer business was nonetheless driven by developments in technology. Advances in microelectronics were the primary driving force behind the growth of the industry. Further advances would play a major role in the evolution of personal computers in the next decade. Advances in software also exerted a great influence on the direction of the industry.

Hardware advances were likely to occur in two areas: memory chips and microprocessors. Most microcomputers in 1982 used 16K RAM (random access memory) chips. However, high-quality 64K RAM chips were available at low cost from several American and Japanese suppliers. The Apple II+ required 32 16K RAM chips to achieve 64K of addressable memory, while the IIe used only 8 64K chips to achieve the same capacity.

The pending availability of low-cost 256K RAM chips promised greater capabilities and price-performance for microcomputers. Fewer chips meant lower cost and higher reliability. Greater available memory permitted more sophisticated and powerful software, faster execution time, and high-resolution graphics. For a microcomputer developer, a key challenge was how quickly he could incorporate more memory into his system design.

Advances in technology were not incorporated into personal computers immediately. The lead time from introduction of a new microprocessor until it was designed into a microcomputer was three or more years. For example, the Motorola's 16-bit microprocessor, the

MC68000, introduced in 1978 and used in the Lisa, first appeared in personal computers in mid-1982. Most personal computers on the market in 1982 used 8-bit micro-processors. The 8-bits refers to the number of bits, or binary digits, that are processed at one time. The successors to 8-bit systems are based on 16-bit processors, which process 16 bits of data simultaneously. These chips execute instructions faster and can utilize much more memory than 8-bit chips. In 1982, Intel introduced its 32-bit microprocessor with the equivalent computing power of an IBM SYSTEM/370.

Acceptance of the latest technology in the marketplace was constrained by the lead time required to develop software. Machines based on the newest memory or microprocessor technology lacked a broad base of software support. Several years were required to develop peripheral hardware, accessories, and applications software to complement the hardware. The purchase of this equipment and software represented significant investments to their buyers, and therefore made them reluctant to replace that investment quickly. Users purchased systems they felt would be useful for several years. This inertia tended to inhibit quantum leaps in microcomputer applications of the latest electronics technology.

Such constraints on the application of new technology were due largely to one element of software, the operating system. Operating systems, the control programs for the computer, are structured around specific microprocessors, as CP/M was for the Zilog Z80. CP/M (control program for microcomputer) is used in more models of personal computers than any other operating system. Introduced in 1975 by Digital Research, CP/M established an accessible industry standard, and thousands of applications have been written for it. As a result, the Zilog Z80 is the most widely used 8-bit microprocessor. Apple DOS (disk operating system), Tandy's TRS-DOS, and Microsoft's MS-DOS for the IBM PC were other widely used operating systems. Their broad acceptance inhibited development of new operating systems, and encouraged new entrants to build their systems around one of the accepted systems. As of late 1982, software could be written to be used on only one operating system. Translating programs to another operating system was expensive and time consuming, although developers such as Microsoft were using languages easily transported to many operating systems.

Software strategy was a key issue for all personal computer makers and users. Established companies and users had the large, sunk investment of proven software written around existing operating systems. At the same time more powerful and sophisticated operating systems were being developed. It was conceivable that a new operating system with the ability to run programs of the other systems might emerge. A microcomputer with this capability would contain several microprocessors and could support virtually any application program. All makers and users also had to consider the possibility that a specific operating system would dominate the personal computer market.

The potential for an operating system to gain such broad acceptance depended in part on who owned the rights on it. Apple's DOS was proprietary to Apple, and not available for license. CP/M and MS-DOS were written by software firms who had financial incentives to promote the use of their systems by hardware and software developers.

## TECHNOLOGY AND COMPETITIVE STRATEGIES

Personal computer manufacturers could use several strategies to break into the personal computer market. One was to develop a machine with superior performance, using the latest technology. For example, the Fortune 32 : 16 used the advanced Motorola MC68000 microprocessor, a highly sophisticated operating system (Bell Labs' UNIX), 1 megabyte of RAM, high-resolution graphics, and supported up to nine users. By contrast, Apple III and IBM PC had slower processing, half the RAM, and lower disk storage. Superior performance could offset a manufacturer's lack of reputation, limited distribution, or small software base.

A company that excelled in hardware engineering, but lacked the resources to distribute its product widely, could sell on an OEM (original equipment manufacturer) basis to systems developers. Convergent Technologies marketed its high-performance workstations this way through Burroughs and Honeywell among others. OEM agreements are not limited to large mainframe makers. Hundreds of small specialized system houses operate on this basis. By integrating and packaging available hardware, systems houses create and install customized turnkey products to user specifications. Sales to such agents, especially in the field of office automation, offered alternative approaches to direct marketing.

Another approach to the market was based on low-price limitation or "knockoff" of a successful computer. Franklin's Ace 100 was a knockoff of Apple II; it looked like the Apple II and was compatible with most Apple II software and hardware accessories. Franklin's ads show a closeup of the Ace 100 keyboard with a shiny red Apple perched on top. Its sales grew despite limited distribution and ongoing lawsuits with Apple. Apple had many other imitators. Ads for the Pineapple appeared in the U.S., and Apple has fought the Lemon in Italy, the Orange in Asia and Australia, and the Apolo in Hong Kong. A host of knockoffs were offered for the IBM PC as well. This strategy required minimal R&D capabilities and no software development. Success depended on low price, permitted by low engineering costs, and an established base of software developed by someone else. Often unable to support a dealer network, knockoffs were commonly distributed through the mail.

For most new entrants, compatibility with a major operating system and software bases was a key element in their strategy. Such firms took this strategy one step further by engineering two microprocessors into the system. These computers were known as dual processor systems. Typically, one of them was the Z80, which ran under CP/M, and therefore guaranteed immediate software availability. However, the Z80 was slower and could address less memory than newer 16-bit processors. The second processor was a faster chip such as Intel's 8086 or Motorola's MC68000. DEC's Rainbow contained the Z80 and the 8088, a scaled-down version of the 8086. IBM's PC has a slot for a second microprocessor of the user's choice. While little software had been developed for these more advanced processors, dual processors allowed the user to upgrade his computing capabilities as new software was published. In the meantime, he could use the full line of software for CP/M. This strategy could become popular, as it hedged against CP/M becoming an industry standard, on the one hand, and against obsolescence of 8-bit systems on the other. The incremental cost of dual processors was relatively small—so it was seen as a powerful means of satisfying both short- and longer-term needs.

## MARKET TRENDS 1983

While the Apple II and III continued to receive excellent response in the market, competition became stiffer by the week. IBM, which introduced its Personal Computer in the summer of 1981, had approached Apple in dollar sales. With its massive financial resources, national sales force, service organization, its brand name, and depth of management, IBM was powerful in nearly every aspect of the business. As monthly unit sales passed the 20,000 mark in 1982, IBM was rumored to plan production of one million units in 1983.

Atari, Commodore, and Texas Instruments all surpassed Apple in unit sales in 1982. Although the bulk of these sales were in low-priced home computers, each had introduced higher-capacity machines. The Commodore 64, a dual-processor machine priced at $595, ran Apple software and offered greater memory and fea-

**EXHIBIT 4**  Leading US Company's Key Financial and Operating Ratios

| | Gross Margin/ Sales % | R & D/ Sales % | S,G&A/ Sales % | P,P&E/ Sales % | Debt/ Equity % | Inventory/ Sales % | Sales/ Employee $ | Cash/ Total Assets % | Pretax Profit/ Sales % | Profit/ Total Assets % | Dividends/ Profit % | AR-AP/ Sales % |
|---|---|---|---|---|---|---|---|---|---|---|---|---|
| Apple | 50.6 | 6.5 | 26.5 | 5.9 | 7.8 | 13.9 | 171,944 | 42.8 | 20.0 | 32.7 | 0 | 7.95 |
| Burroughs | 34.8 | 5.4 | 25.6 | 20.0 | 37.8 | 13.5 | 66,053 | 1.3 | 1.8 | 1.8 | 146.0 | 14.9 |
| Commodore | 47.8 | 5.8 | 23.2 | 16.2 | 41.8 | 30.3 | 121,800 | 2.9 | 16.7 | 21.6 | 0 | 9.7 |
| Data General | 43.8 | 10.5 | 28.3 | 19.4 | 32.4 | 32.6 | 53,019 | 24.4 | 4.5 | 4.6 | 0 | 15.2 |
| DEC | 43.6 | 9.0 | 19.5 | 29.5 | 2.9 | 29.3 | 57,836 | 19.0 | 17.3 | 16.7 | 0 | 17.2 |
| Hewlett Packard | 52.0 | 10.0 | 26.4 | 27.6 | 1.7 | 15.5 | 62,426 | 19.7 | 15.9 | 19.5 | 4.4 | 14.9 |
| IBM | 60.2 | 9.0 | 27.9 | 25.5 | 13.4 | 10.2 | 94,201 | 10.1 | 23.1 | 24.4 | 25.9 | 12.9 |
| Prime | 57.4 | 8.5 | 33.2 | 27.5 | 7.3 | 13.2 | 82,056 | 7.9 | 15.0 | 17.4 | 0 | 27.7 |

tures than the Apple II. Apple's stock price dropped $2 the day this product was introduced.

Apple's management sensed their customer base was being squeezed from both above and below, in terms of price and technical capability. In addition, the personal computer market had become increasingly segmented. Consumers who once could choose between the Apple II and a few other similar systems could now choose from over 150 models in every range of price and capability. The low-cost home models, led by Atari, offered a cheaper solution for casual users than the Apple II did. Corvus and Altos marketed high-powered 16-bit systems that could outperform the Apple III in the office. The Grid Compass and Osborne I offered portability, a feature both the Apple II and III lacked. Apple faced the prospect of losing share to more specialized systems employing newer technology that were positioned in more focused ways.

## MARKET SEGMENTS

The microcomputer market consisted of five broad segments: the home, education, small business, office, and professional categories. The professional market included a range of scientific, engineering, and industrial applications. Users in this segment were often very sophisticated in their knowledge of hardware and software and very demanding in terms of processing power, speed, and capacity. Such users also often required communications capabilities with other computers, scientific instruments, and equipment. Although such users often wrote their own software, several suppliers had recently introduced systems with dedicated software for applications such as computer-aided design, graphics, and process control. The professional market was expected to account for about 10% of 1983 microcomputer sales in dollars.

Communications capability was also important in the office market, where electronic mail and data transfer were important func-

tions. Word-processing and electronic filing were also important functions in the office market. The customer base in this segment consisted of medium to large organizations. Given a trend toward the proliferation of computers in many office environments, there was growing concern among many organizations for standardization and central purchasing of microcomputers. The office market was expected to account for 25% of microcomputer dollar sales in 1983.

The small business market consisted of many small business customers. These customers generally had little experience with computers and required assistance in understanding their functions and uses. They had high service and support requirements. Key applications in this market were accounting, spreadsheet analysis, record-keeping billing and other standard business uses. This segment was expected to represent 25% of the market in 1983.

The education segment ranged from the most simple applications in elementary schools to fairly sophisticated uses in graduate schools. Purchasing often involved bidding procedures in public schools, but high-unit volume purchases were common and there was a strong tendency towards standardization in this market, which was expected to account for as much as 10% of 1983 dollar sales.

The home computer market was the least well defined of all the major segments. Many professionals, managers, and business people owned or used a computer at home to complement the machine they used at work. These individuals had very different needs than the novice who was interested primarily in games or self-instruction. The home computer market covered a variety of price ranges as well. The bulk of unit sales were in the below-$500 range, but home customers accounted for a significant share of sales for more expensive models. While many customers were highly sensitive to price, others demanded ease-of-use, software availability, or brand credibility. The home market was expected to account for 33% of 1983 microcomputer sales.

## APPLE'S ACTIVITIES IN 1983

Apple's products were used primarily in the business and professional market and to a lesser extent in schools and the home. Although Apple III sales exceeded 50,000 units in 1982, almost all of Apple's sales and profits continued to flow from the Apple II system. The IIe, introduced in early 1983, was the third version of this highly successful product. The IIe offered several advantages over the II+, its predecessor. The IIe offered a base memory capacity of 48k, instead of 32k; it featured upper and lower case letters, cursor keys, and other keyboard improvements; it provided an 80-column screen, instead of 40-columns; and it was priced initially at $1,595, four hundred dollars below the price of the II+. Sales of the Apple II continued to be broadly based. Thirty percent of unit sales were for the home market. Business, professional, and education markets were also important. While the Apple II attracted a wide range of users, it was too expensive for many home computer segments and it could not meet the needs of many professional and office segments. Apple III offered greater power and performance, but it had not met expectations in the office and professional segments. The introduction of Lisa marked a major new initiative in these market segments.

## LISA AND MACINTOSH

Apple had two entrants in the office systems market. Lisa, announced at the 1982 annual meeting, was the first entrant. A second project, labeled Macintosh, was headed by Steven Jobs. The Lisa personal office workstation represented a new concept in computers, primarily in the user interface. Lisa incorporated several existing technologies that had never been implemented in the same system. Every element of Lisa's hardware and software design was oriented to facilitating the way a naive user would communicate with the system. The premise behind Lisa's design was to remove the barriers that prevented people from using the computer. Resistance to adoption of computers stemmed from the fact that people were afraid of them; that computers took a long time to learn; that they were difficult to use; and that their software was incompatible. Lisa's features addressed each of these issues. Learning was reduced because Lisa was self-teaching. Each of the six applications programs incorporated in Lisa included an interactive tutorial. Apple claimed the average learning time for one application was close to 20 minutes, as opposed to several hours on other computers.

The screen layout was analogous to a desk top, and the user could arrange it anyway he wanted. By using a language called Smalltalk, developed at Xerox Palo Alto Research Center, Lisa enabled the user to create windows to enter or access information from any of the integrated applications programs. Lisa's six integrated applications programs were word-processing (Lisaword), spreadsheet (Lisacalc), list management (Lisalist), business graphics (Lisagraph), free-form graphics (Lisadraw), and critical path and project management (Lisaplan). Parts of one could be included in another. For example, Lisacalc data can be read by Lisagraph to produce a graph, which can be reformatted in Lisadraw, and cut and pasted into a Lisaword document. Additionally, all six programs used the same commands; the user gave instructions to each application in the same way.

Demonstration units of Lisa were being shipped to selected dealers in March, and quantity shipments were expected to begin late in the spring. Lisa was packaged as an entire system, and was priced at $9,995. The package included the CPU, one megabyte of RAM, the operating system, and six applications software programs, keyboard, mouse, monitor, and 5-megabyte Winchester hard disk storage.

While little was known about Macintosh outside the Mac division, it was said to be based on Lisa technology. Public sources speculated that Macintosh would be a lower-priced version of Lisa. The Macintosh project supposedly was scheduled for completion by early 1984. Lisa and Macintosh represented a two-pronged effort to become a significant factor in the office systems market.

## THE HOME COMPUTER PROJECT

Apple's thrust in the home market had yet to be defined, but Alan Oppenheimer's project had been formed within the Personal Computer Systems Division (PCSD). Many issues had to be resolved before the home computer thrust could be launched, however. Should the home system be based on Apple II technology, with its huge base of software, or should a Lisa-like product be developed? Should the home system be distributed through Apple's 1,400 computer dealers, or should it be carried in chain stores and mass merchandizers? Promotion, pricing, service support, and training policies had to be defined.

With a new product introduction, Apple's management faced the insidious problem of trying to position several new products without cannibalizing others or missing large opportunities. Until 1983, Apple had just two products. Lisa was the third, Macintosh would make four, and the home system, five. The target segments of each overlapped and the problem became more complex as each new system was introduced.

Apple had created a Marketing Council to deal with those and other similar issues. All marketing activities and plans were reviewed by the Council. Alan Oppenheimer commented on the Council and its function:

> We would go the Market Council, which is made up of about ten marketing people, the top marketing person in each division, and get their feedback and recommendations. The Marketing Council exists for interdivisional types of issues, where our division does something that affects others. The Council meets twice a month for about half a day.

Apple's organization and systems were constantly evolving to adapt to the demands of its extraordinary growth. Since its beginning in 1977, Apple had been highly decentralized, reflecting the entrepreneurial nature of its people and industry. As the company grew, it became organized on a product basis. As of January 1, 1983, Apple was organized into five product divisions. Three of the divisions developed and marketed computer systems to end users. The Personal Computer System Division was responsible for the IIe, III, and the forthcoming home system; the Personal Office Systems Division developed and marketed Lisa; the Macintosh Division, headed by Steve Jobs, was engaged in developing a low-priced system based on Lisa technology. The two remaining divisions served primarily as suppliers to the systems divisions.

The Peripheral Division designs and manufactures disk drives. The Accessories Division manufactures and sources products such a keyboards, printers, connectors, and game controls. In addition to these product divisions, there were separate functional divisions for corporate-wide sales, advertising, system manufacturing, distribution, legal, finance, and human resources. There was also a strong functional emphasis within the systems division. In the PCSD, for example, managers within each product group were responsible for applications software development, external software vendor relations, hardware engineering, and many other functions. One set of managers performed these functions for the Apple II, and another set of managers handled these responsibilities for the Apple III. In late 1982, the PCSD reorganized formally along functional lines. For example, applications software activities were centralized and personnel from this group worked on programs for both the Apple II and Apple III, and would also work on the home system. One of Alan's primary efforts involved maintaining a high level of interest and cooperation with the home computer system effort among these functional specialists.

## THE MANAGEMENT ENVIRONMENT

Apple's internal management environment had always been distinctive. Suits and ties were never seen inside an Apple facility. A high level of informality was apparent, as well as a high level of energy and activity. There had always been a high level of commitment to the company's "mission" among its employees. Recently, however, several Apple managers have left the company to start ventures of their own, a consequence of the transition from an entrepreneurial organization to a professional orientation. Peter Levy, a young PCSD manager, commented on how the change has been managed:

> I'm impressed with the way it's been handled. There are many people here who are managers, and we're starting to put together a system that lends itself to the process of getting something accomplished; in other words, I don't have to spend my time thinking about *how* to get something done. I have an established system and organization for that. My time is spent thinking what should get done. And for that, I have a manager who listens and provides feedback.

These changes were a response to increasing demands created by Apple's extraordinary growth. As the company grew, management struggled to provide an organizational structure and system to keep pace. Lines of responsibility were not clear, and communications among divisions were poor. Management spent much of their time figuring out who was supposed to be doing what, instead of putting operating plans together. The reorganization was a major step forward, but information systems lagged behind. Much remained to be done to develop the necessary infrastructure to support Apple's expanding activities in a burgeoning market. As Mike Markkula observed,

> I have a top ten list of priorities for the PCSD, and there's 19 items on it. That should tell you something. That's a real good example of what Apple is.

# 14 CLOVERLEAF DAIRIES, INC.

## Lawrence R. Jauch

*Southern Illinois University-Carbondale*

Cloverleaf Dairies, Inc., is the largest processor of dairy products in the Des Moines, Iowa area. With over $10 million in sales in 1982, the company claimed about 40 percent of the area market in milk, ice cream, and related products. Its main products are given in Table 1.

## A HISTORY OF QUALITY

When asked why Cloverleaf has been able to maintain such a large share of the market, Mr. J. K. Nesbitt, firm president, replied, "Our success can be summed up in one word: 'quality.' People buy our products because they are superior tasting compared to any others in the area. We've been able to keep national brands out of Des Moines because they know they can't top our quality."

Cloverleaf's tradition in quality began with the founding of the company in 1939 by Donald Cochran. The former plant manager for a national dairy company, Mr. Cochran emphasized efficiency and quality, and was able to keep the company on its feet during the Depression years. In 1947, he decided to get into the more profitable ice cream business, and purchased an existing combination milk and ice cream plant. At the same time, he hired Andrew Snider, presently executive vice president, as marketing manager. The company grew rapidly in the

following years. Mr. Snider initiated an aggressive marketing program, using methods never employed before in Des Moines. Delivery trucks were painted bright colors, route salesmen were put in uniform, and a vigorous advertising campaign was inaugurated. The sales of milk expanded so rapidly that the space needed for the processing of milk crowded out the ice cream facilities. In 1952, Mr. Cochran began seeking a new combination milk–ice cream plant. He decided to build a complete new plant, using all the latest features in plant design. Mr. Nesbitt, who had been employed by a national dairy for many years and was thoroughly familiar with the ice cream business, was hired to supervise construction and manage the new plant. After the new plant began operations, sales spiraled upward. The company rapidly passed its competitors in sales. Mr. Cochran died suddenly in 1956, leaving Mr. Nesbitt as the new president. Mr. Nesbitt has continued the emphasis on quality and sales growth.

Much of Cloverleaf's success can be attributed to the lifelong devotion of its executives. Top management includes the following people:

*President:* John K. Nesbitt. Fifty-eight years old, Mr. Nesbitt has worked in dairy operations since graduating from a dairy institution 37 years ago. He has been described by fellow workers as "aggressive" and "hard driving." He has a fierce competitive instinct. He once remarked, "There are no rule books in this game. You kick them [competitors] while they are down, and keep kicking." Mr. Nesbitt is very active in

This is a disguised case. That is, the facts in it are based on a real company. But the names of the persons involved, the location, and the quantitative data have been changed because the company requested it. It serves no useful purpose to try to determine which company is the "real" company. Based on an original case by William F. Glueck.

**TABLE 1**  Percent of Sales of Cloverleaf's Main Products

| Product | Percent of Sales |
|---|---|
| Cloverleaf milk (homogenized, whole milk) | 36.2 |
| Vita-cal milk (fortified, low-fat milk) | 21.8 |
| Cloverleaf ice cream | 14.0 |
| Delite frozen dessert | 8.0 |
| Other assorted products | 19.6 |
| Total | 100.0 |

community affairs and recently held a top position in the local Chamber of Commerce.

*Executive Vice President:* Andrew H. Snider. Mr. Snider has also spent most of his working life in the dairy business. A capable person, he moves more slowly than Mr. Nesbitt, but seldom makes mistakes. He is regarded as Mr. Nesbitt's closest adviser and confidant. Mr. Snider is well liked by Cloverleaf employees and spends much of his time in employee relations.

*Vice President of Sales and Promotion:* Jay Cochran. The son of the founder, Donald Cochran, Mr. Cochran has been with the company since graduating from high school in 1962. Mr. Cochran is in charge of all promotions, but since the company has a contract with an advertising agency, he does little of the actual planning himself. Most of his time is spent in working as a liaison between Cloverleaf and the advertising agency.

*General Manager:* Bruce Bitner. Mr. Bitner is office manager and head of accounting, finance, and purchasing functions. He has worked for Cloverleaf for 15 years. Before that, he was superintendent for a large dairy in Knoxville, Tennessee.

*Marketing Manager:* Robert Anderson. Mr. Anderson's main job is to maintain relations with the various retailers who handle products. With Jay Cochran, he aids in setting up displays, investigates complaints, and in general promotes goodwill between the company and retailers. He has worked for Cloverleaf only two years. Before that, he had a sales position with a national lumber firm.

*Assistant General Manager:* Richard Foley. Mr. Foley is in charge of production and quality control, including storage, maintenance, and fleet operations. He has 14 years of supervisory experience in dairy production and processing.

All of Cloverleaf's top officials are active in community affairs. Mr. Nesbitt thinks that since Cloverleaf is a locally owned and operated business, "We have an obligation to be good citizens and to help Des Moines grow and prosper to become a better place to live."

The company's organization is shown in Figure 1.

## THE DAIRY INDUSTRY

Tables 2 and 3 present recent statistics on sales for the dairy industry in the United States.

Sales of fluid milk and cream (product pound basis) totaled almost 56 billion pounds in 1979, nearly the same as in 1978. This continues the flat sales trend prevalent since 1975 which has resulted in slowly but steadily declining per capita sales.

Sales per person of fluid milk and cream were 256 pounds during 1979, down nearly 3 pounds from 1978 and 16 pounds from 1969. An increase in sales of cream and specialty items only partially offset a decline in milk beverage sales.

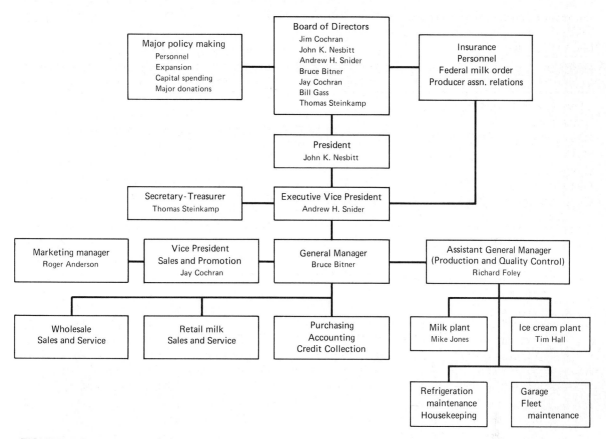

**FIGURE 1** Organization Chart

The long-run tendency toward greater low-fat milk consumption away from whole milk use continued in 1979, as per capita sales of low-fat milk were up 3 pounds while whole milk sales declined by 5 pounds. Per person sales of skim milk, which has exhibited no trend in the last two decades, increased last year from 1978. Meanwhile, per capita sales of flavored drinks declined for the second year in a row while the popularity of buttermilk continued to wane.

Cream sales per person were down slightly in 1979 mainly due to lower sales of half and half and light cream items. Per capita sales of eggnog and heavy cream in 1979 matched 1978 sales.

Among cultured products, per capita sales of yogurt, which experienced tremendous growth through the 1970s, declined slightly in 1979, the first decrease on record. Meanwhile, sales per person of sour cream and dips increased. Since 1970, sales of sour cream have risen by two-thirds.

The dairy industry is important to Iowa as can be seen in Table 4. The milk industry is not equally important to all states, and some must import their milk from neighboring areas. Table 4 presents industry data on production of the dairy industry in selected regions of the United States.

In the Des Moines area, there are four other

**TABLE 2** Milk and Dairy Product Sales (Domestic Disappearance, Commercial Sources) Total and Per Capita, Selected Years, United States, 1970–1979[1]

| Year | Fluid Milk Product Sales | | | | | Butter | Cheese | | Cottage Cheese[6] | Evaporated and Condensed | |
| | Fluid Whole Milk | Cream[2] | Low-Fat Milk[3] | Product Weight | Whole Milk Equivalent[4] | | Whole and Part Skim Milk[5] | | | Whole Milk | Skimmed Milk |
| | | | | | | | American | Other | | | |
| --- | --- | --- | --- | --- | --- | --- | --- | --- | --- | --- | --- |
| | | | | | Million Pounds | | | | | | |
| 1970 | 42,956 | 1,067 | 10,289 | 54,312 | 51,998 | 902 | 1,393 | 892 | 1,060 | 1,349 | 1,016 |
| 1971 | 42,108 | 1,076 | 11,485 | 54,669 | 51,853 | 878 | 1,452 | 971 | 1,108 | 1,303 | 1,039 |
| 1972 | 41,851 | 1,093 | 12,826 | 55,770 | 53,227 | 861 | 1,573 | 1,110 | 1,133 | 1,236 | 980 |
| 1973 | 40,443 | 1,130 | 14,062 | 55,635 | 52,413 | 846 | 1,661 | 1,193 | 1,103 | 1,194 | 894 |
| 1974 | 38,358 | 1,143 | 14,815 | 54,316 | 50,514 | 917 | 1,771 | 1,267 | 992 | 1,154 | 732 |
| 1975 | 38,256 | 1,175 | 16,558 | 55,989 | 51,123 | 948 | 1,692 | 1,317 | 1,006 | 1,097 | 761 |
| 1976 | 37,061 | 1,189 | 17,710 | 55,960 | 51,505 | 932 | 1,912 | 1,446 | 1,025 | 1,046 | 783 |
| 1977 | 35,638 | 1,199 | 18,988 | 55,825 | 51,383 | 860 | 1,912 | 1,493 | 1,032 | 915 | 854 |
| 1978 | 34,937 | 1,214 | 19,813 | 55,965 | 51,223 | 894 | 2,050 | 1,627 | 1,039 | 885 | 772 |
| 1979[7] | 33,995 | 1,231 | 20,689 | 55,915 | 51,421 | 923 | 2,116 | 1,703 | 1,010 | 895 | 748 |
| | | | | | Per Capita[8] | | | | | | |
| | | | | | Pounds | | | | | | |
| 1970 | 214 | 5.3 | 51.3 | 271 | 259 | 4.4 | 6.8 | 4.4 | 5.2 | 6.6 | 5.0 |
| 1971 | 207 | 5.3 | 56.5 | 269 | 255 | 4.3 | 7.0 | 4.7 | 5.4 | 6.3 | 5.0 |
| 1972 | 204 | 5.3 | 62.5 | 272 | 259 | 4.1 | 7.6 | 5.3 | 5.4 | 5.9 | 4.7 |
| 1973 | 195 | 5.5 | 67.9 | 269 | 253 | 4.0 | 7.9 | 5.7 | 5.3 | 5.7 | 4.3 |
| 1974 | 184 | 5.5 | 70.9 | 260 | 242 | 4.3 | 8.4 | 6.0 | 4.7 | 5.5 | 3.5 |
| 1975 | 181 | 5.6 | 78.5 | 266 | 243 | 4.4 | 8.0 | 6.2 | 4.7 | 5.1 | 3.6 |
| 1976 | 174 | 5.6 | 83.3 | 263 | 242 | 4.3 | 8.9 | 6.7 | 4.8 | 4.9 | 3.6 |
| 1977 | 166 | 5.6 | 88.4 | 260 | 240 | 4.0 | 8.8 | 6.9 | 4.8 | 4.2 | 3.9 |
| 1978 | 161 | 5.6 | 91.5 | 259 | 237 | 4.1 | 9.4 | 7.5 | 4.8 | 4.1 | 3.5 |
| 1979[7] | 156 | 5.6 | 94.6 | 256 | 235 | 4.2 | 9.6 | 7.7 | 4.6 | 4.1 | 3.4 |

**TABLE 2** (Continued)

| Year | Frozen Products | | | | | Dry Products | | | |
|---|---|---|---|---|---|---|---|---|---|
| | Ice Cream | Ice Milk | Sherbet | Other | Mellorine | Whole Milk | Nonfat Dry Milk | Buttermilk | Whey[9] |
| | Total | | | | | | | | |
| | Million Pounds | | | | | | | | |
| 1970 | 3,656 | 1,577 | 318 | 40 | 249 | 43 | 960 | 51 | 294 |
| 1971 | 3,676 | 1,582 | 317 | 47 | 232 | 32 | 958 | 55 | 319 |
| 1972 | 3,685 | 1,599 | 325 | 53 | 218 | 24 | 853 | 48 | 377 |
| 1973 | 3,714 | 1,604 | 346 | 70 | 191 | 21 | 1,056 | 39 | 384 |
| 1974 | 3,753 | 1,629 | 325 | 56 | 166 | 15 | 839 | 44 | 453 |
| 1975 | 4,015 | 1,643 | 316 | 66 | 144 | 16 | 668 | 44 | 477 |
| 1976 | 3,928 | 1,574 | 322 | 64 | 112 | 33 | 743 | 38 | 527 |
| 1977 | 3,887 | 1,694 | 324 | 72 | 90 | 34 | 698 | 59 | 530 |
| 1978 | 3,914 | 1,705 | 312 | 77 | 78 | 56 | 640 | 50 | 543 |
| 1979[7] | 3,893 | 1,632 | 293 | 72 | 75 | 66 | 692 | 42 | 597 |
| | Per capita[8] | | | | | | | | |
| | Pounds | | | | | | | | |
| 1970 | 17.9 | 7.7 | 1.6 | 0.2 | 1.2 | 0.2 | 4.7 | 0.3 | 1.5 |
| 1971 | 17.8 | 7.7 | 1.5 | .2 | 1.1 | .2 | 4.6 | .3 | 1.6 |
| 1972 | 17.7 | 7.7 | 1.6 | .3 | 1.0 | .1 | 4.1 | .2 | 1.8 |
| 1973 | 17.7 | 7.6 | 1.6 | .3 | .9 | .1 | 5.0 | .2 | 1.8 |
| 1974 | 17.8 | 7.7 | 1.5 | .3 | .8 | .1 | 4.0 | .2 | 2.1 |
| 1975 | 18.8 | 7.7 | 1.5 | .3 | .7 | .1 | 3.1 | .2 | 2.2 |
| 1976 | 18.3 | 7.3 | 1.5 | .3 | .5 | .2 | 3.5 | .2 | 2.5 |
| 1977 | 18.0 | 7.8 | 1.5 | .3 | .4 | .2 | 3.2 | .3 | 2.5 |
| 1978 | 17.9 | 7.8 | 1.4 | .4 | .4 | .3 | 2.9 | .2 | 2.5 |
| 1979[7] | 17.7 | 7.4 | 1.3 | .3 | .3 | .3 | 3.1 | .2 | 2.7 |

[1]Excludes milk used on farms where produced and distribution from USDA supplies; includes sales to the Armed Services for use in the United States.
[2]Includes milk and cream mixtures.
[3]Includes skim milk, buttermilk, flavored milk drinks, and yogurt.
[4]Fat solids basis.

**TABLE 3**   Sales of Individual Fluid Products as a Proportion of Average Daily Fluid Milk Sales, All Federal Order Markets, 1965, 1970, and 1975–1979

| Fluid Items | 1965[1] | 1970 | 1975 | 1976 | 1977 | 1978 | 1979 |
|---|---|---|---|---|---|---|---|
| Whole milk[2] | 83.7 | 76.1 | 65.6 | 63.4 | 61.1 | 59.8 | 58.4 |
| Flavored whole milk | 2.6 | 2.5 | 2.6 | 2.7 | 2.7 | 2.5 | 2.3 |
| Total whole milk items | 86.3 | 78.6 | 68.2 | 66.21 | 63.8 | 62.3 | 60.7 |
| Low-fat (2%) milk[4] | [4] | 12.1 | 21.4 | 22.8 | 24.4 | 26.0 | 27.5 |
| Plain | [4] | 3.3 | 11.6 | 14.3 | 15.8 | 18.0 | 20.4 |
| Solids added | [4] | 8.8 | 9.8 | 8.5 | 8.6 | 8.0 | 7.1 |
| Skim milk | 8.6 | 4.3 | 4.2 | 4.3 | 4.5 | 4.4 | 4.5 |
| Plain | 2.8 | 1.1 | 1.7 | 1.9 | 2.1 | 2.3 | 2.7 |
| Solids added | 5.9 | 3.2 | 2.5 | 2.4 | 2.4 | 2.1 | 1.8 |
| Buttermilk[5] | 2.0 | 1.9 | 1.8 | 1.8 | 1.8 | 1.7 | 1.6 |
| Yogurt | — | .3 | .7 | .8 | 1.0 | 1.0 | .9 |
| Flavored milk drinks | .7 | .8 | 1.5 | 2.0 | 2.4 | 2.4 | 2.5 |
| Total skim and low-fat milk item[3] | 11.3 | 19.4 | 29.6 | 31.7 | 34.1 | 35.5 | 37.0 |
| Milk and cream mixtures | 1.3 | 1.1 | .9 | .9 | 1.0 | .9 | 1.0 |
| Light cream | .4 | .2 | .2 | .2 | .1 | .2 | .2 |
| Heavy cream | .3 | .2 | .2 | .2 | .2 | .2 | .2 |
| Sour cream | .3 | .4 | .6 | .6 | .7 | .7 | .7 |
| Total cream items[3] | .9 | .8 | 1.0 | 1.0 | 1.0 | 1.1 | 1.1 |
| Eggnog | .1 | .2 | .2 | .2 | .2 | .2 | .2 |
| Total fluid milk and cream[3] | 100.0 | 100.0 | 100.0 | 100.0 | 100.0 | 100.0 | 100.0 |

[1]Excludes New York–New Jersey market.
[2]Includes whole milk equivalent of small quantity of concentrated milk.
[3]Totals may not add due to rounding.
[4]Included with skim milk.
[5]Includes small quantities of yogurt and cultured specialties.

processors besides Cloverleaf. The largest of these, Hillsdale Dairy, accounts for 22 percent of the area market. Over the years, Cloverleaf has steadily increased its market share at the expense of its competitors. In recent years this growth has slowed, and Hillsdale, which markets low- to medium-priced products, has made some gains.

Within the past eight years two companies have been formed to compete directly with Cloverleaf. Soon after the first opened, a mysterious fire destroyed the entire plant. The second plant was closed by a prolonged and extremely violent truck drivers' strike. Neither plant has attempted to reopen. Some store owners, probably not friendly to Cloverleaf, implied that Cloverleaf had engineered these "misfortunes" by ties with unsavory elements on the fringes of the union movement or even the underworld. Recently, Sealtest, a large national dairy, announced that it would soon begin selling in the Des Moines area. At this writing, over one-third of the retail foodstores in the area have made preliminary agreements with Sealtest to handle their products.

**TABLE 4**   Milk: Production by Selected Production Regions, 1974–1981 (Millions of Pounds)

| State and Region | 1974 | 1975 | 1976 | 1977 | 1978 | 1979 | 1980 | 1981 |
|---|---|---|---|---|---|---|---|---|
| Michigan | 4,350 | 4,411 | 4,620 | 4,761 | 4,793 | 4,830 | 4,970 | 5,103 |
| Wisconsin | 18,713 | 18,900 | 20,296 | 21,041 | 21,252 | 21,850 | 22,298 | 22,705 |
| Minnesota | 9,382 | 8,946 | 9,239 | 9,483 | 9,089 | 9,145 | 9,535 | 10,061 |
| LAKE STATES | 32,445 | 32,257 | 34,155 | 35,285 | 35,134 | 35,825 | 36,803 | 37,869 |
| Ohio | 4,221 | 4,259 | 4,435 | 4,455 | 4,275 | 4,265 | 4,310 | 4,385 |
| Indiana | 2,260 | 2,210 | 2,240 | 2,248 | 2,178 | 2,175 | 2,210 | 2,292 |
| Illinois | 2,522 | 2,446 | 2,485 | 2,515 | 2,399 | 2,391 | 2,540 | 2,604 |
| Iowa | 4,025 | 3,893 | 3,954 | 4,030 | 3,960 | 3,920 | 4,108 | 4,298 |
| Missouri | 2,989 | 2,840 | 2,919 | 2,918 | 2,719 | 2,714 | 2,876 | 2,877 |
| CORN BELT | 16,017 | 15,648 | 16,033 | 16,166 | 15,531 | 15,465 | 16,044 | 16,446 |
| North Dakota | 980 | 917 | 948 | 954 | 903 | 874 | 907 | 968 |
| South Dakota | 1,642 | 1,556 | 1,650 | 1,652 | 1,540 | 1,549 | 1,669 | 1,757 |
| Nebraska | 1,477 | 1,431 | 1,409 | 1,344 | 1,269 | 1,260 | 1,315 | 1,400 |
| Kansas | 1,403 | 1,392 | 1,447 | 1,442 | 1,372 | 1,330 | 1,355 | 1,397 |
| NORTHERN PLAINS | 5,502 | 5,296 | 5,454 | 5,392 | 5,084 | 5,013 | 5,246 | 5,517 |
|  | 115,586 | 115,398 | 120,180 | 122,654 | 121,461 | 123,411 | 128,425 | 132,634 |

## THE HUMAN PROBLEMS AT CLOVERLEAF

Most of Cloverleaf's 300 employees are engaged in unskilled or semiskilled tasks. Most of the labor hired has had no prior dairy experience, and it is the responsibility of the individual departments to train them through on-the-job training. The more skilled workers and supervisors get some training from nearby colleges and through Cloverleaf's own training programs. Employees are sometimes sent to participate in educational programs presented by associations such as the Milk Industry Foundation or the International Association of Ice Cream Manufacturers.

Pay received by Cloverleaf employees is consistent with pay scales in the Des Moines area. Although not high by national standards, it is deemed "adequate" for this locality. A number of benefits are offered to employees. After 10 years of service, employees are entitled to retire with a pension. Insurance policies are offered to employees on a "half-and-half" basis, meaning that the employees pay half of the insurance premium and Cloverleaf pays the remainder. Such policies cover medical and hospitalization expenses for the entire family. The pension plan is funded entirely by Cloverleaf.

Cloverleaf plant employees do not belong to a union. One attempt has been made to unionize these employees. In this instance, a union, without identifying itself as such, sent out cards to the employees asking them questions such as "Would you like to make more money?" and "Do you want shorter hours, longer vacations?" Later, the union notified the management that it had the signatures of the employees and that they wished to unionize. Mr. Snider reported that they paid little attention to the union effort, and the employees, upon learning of the union involvement, did not pursue the matter further.

But the drivers are unionized. They shifted back and forth between the Teamsters Union and a smaller Milk Drivers Union. One individual close to the company told the case writer that at times the management found "ways" to keep labor trouble (slowdowns, strikes, etc.) low by being very friendly with union leaders. One member of management supposedly met the union leader regularly in private to "talk things over." Cloverleaf had so little labor trouble that some union members suspected that the manager exchanged more than talk with the labor leader. Of course, Cloverleaf had to walk a tightrope when the two unions were battling over representation rights and there had been minor violence, mostly roughing up of drivers at times like that.

It is known that the union would like to get the plant employees to join and may be putting pressure on Cloverleaf to "encourage" them to join. When asked if union problems were a major concern of Cloverleaf, Mr. Snider said, "I think union problems are the major problem Cloverleaf has."

## PROCESSING CLOVERLEAF PRODUCTS

Milk is produced at a rate of about 26,000 gallons per day by Cloverleaf. Cloverleaf purchases all fresh milk from a dairy co-op (116 producers) at prices set by the Federal Milk Marketing Order. Quality control begins with the purchase of milk. Mr. Bitner said that the best check for quality products is to make sure that only Grade A milk is purchased from the farmers in the first place. All drivers of the tank trucks are licensed milk testers and have the responsibility of checking the milk for quality, smell, and taste.

After the milk is delivered by the company-owned tank trucks, samples are taken for laboratory tests. Then the milk is approved for quality and it goes into giant stainless steel refrigerated storage tanks, where it is held at a temperature of 35°. From there, it is first preheated, and then run through stainless steel pipes to the homogenizer. In the homogenizer, the milk is subjected to high pressures which force the cream to be distributed evenly throughout the milk. After homogenization, the milk is piped to the pasteurizer, where it is heated to a temperature of 163° for 15 seconds. It is then put in bottles or cartons and sent to the cold storage room to await delivery. Mr. Foley tries to keep a 1-day inventory of milk.

The equipment used to make ice cream is of the latest in design. Fully automatic, it features an electronic quality control device which constantly monitors quality, assuring that all output meets standards for taste, content, and texture. A 3-day inventory of ice cream is carried in the frozen storage vault. Mr. Foley emphasized that ice cream does not age appreciably and can be kept for up to three years if the proper temperatures are maintained.

In addition to milk and ice cream, the company produces a variety of other dairy products, including whipping cream, half and half, cottage cheese, sour cream, and sour-cream party dips. Cloverleaf finds it more practical to buy some products from outside than to produce them. Cottage cheese, for example, is imported from Missouri. Milk is used to produce all Cloverleaf products. One quart of milk weighs 2.15 pounds.

The quantity of milk actually used to produce one pound of each product depends chiefly upon the butterfat test of the milk, and this varies in different sections of the country and, to some extent, with the season.

Milk is presently being produced on an 8-hour shift at about 50 percent of capacity; ice cream production is running nearly 100 percent of capacity on a 14-hour shift. The production volume of each product varies according to the season, with ice cream output reaching a peak in April, May, June, July, and August, and mild output rising in October, November, December, January, and February.

"Our ice cream capacity is actually rather flexible," said Mr. Bitner. "Right now, we could increase our capacity by as much as 35 percent by not changing flavors as often. To change flavors requires 20 minutes of downtime on the freezer so that it may be cleaned. Still, I can see the time, probably within 1.5 years, when we won't be able to produce enough to meet our needs. One way of alleviating this problem would be to add more frozen storage space so that we could stockpile in the winter months." Presently, about 50 percent of total ice cream production is vanilla-flavored, 11 percent German chocolate, 10 percent chocolate, 9 percent strawberry, and 20 percent in about eight other flavors.

Cloverleaf is proud of its quality products. All products exceed the minimum standards set by the government. For example, Cloverleaf ice cream contains 12 percent butterfat by weight, whereas the specified minimum is 10 percent. "We could sacrifice just a little quality and obtain great savings in our production costs," said Mr. Nesbitt, "but in the end, we'd just be cutting our own throats. Our quality is our best promotion."

Management is convinced that "the *package* sells the product." Recently, Cloverleaf introduced double-coated (inside and out) ice cream cartons. Although more costly than normal cartons, they prevent moisture leakage which gives cartons that "bulging at the sides" look. "All the advertising in the world will do no good if a housewife picks up a carton which is slimy to the touch or unattractive," remarked Mr. Snider. Ice cream bearing the Cloverleaf trademark Princess label is sold in round cartons, which are supposed to add to the quality image.

## THE DES MOINES MARKET

Cloverleaf's main sales effort is aimed at the retail grocery market, since this is where management feels that the most profit is. Virtually every major food store in Des Moines handles Cloverleaf products. "There's simply no one else around here selling Cloverleaf quality," said one retailer. Another retailer, when asked why he thought no one was competing with Cloverleaf, said, "Everyone knows that someone's looking out for J. K. Nesbitt. He's got this town 'sewed up.' People seem to have more than their share of problems if they try to compete with him."

Yet, few retailers are complaining about the situation. They feel that the prices they pay for Cloverleaf products are reasonable, and that the products are good. Many retailers said that they would be willing to handle Sealtest products in addition to Cloverleaf products, but only because they wanted to give the customers a broader range of selection, not because they were dissatisfied with Cloverleaf products. There is only one national chain food store in the city; the rest are locally owned.

In addition to the food stores, Cloverleaf sells to hospitals, schools, lunch counters, and various other institutions. Cloverleaf bids for the milk contract at the public schools, although there is little profit in this business. The purpose of school sales is to "keep the Cloverleaf name in front of the kids." Such sales amount to about $200,000 per year. School accounts are payable 60 to 90 days after delivery. It would be possible for Cloverleaf to bid for the milk contract at a nearby military installation, but since profit margins would be slim, and since the inhabitants would not be long-run potential buyers of Cloverleaf products, this has not been done.

"Bid business is a ruthless one. You gain or lose a bid on fractions of a cent per carton. At times, we wonder if this business is worth all the effort, time, and grief it involves," said Mr. Cochran. "When it's all said and done, we probably lose money on this business. But what with our production situation on milk, we hang on; but we're not sure how long we should."

Another part of the milk business is the home delivery business. This is more competitive than retail store business. Maintenance of the trucks, labor problems with the drivers, and the detailed records involved are factors Cloverleaf considers. Again the management feels that it keeps the name before the public and of course it builds volume. About 25 percent of their milk sales are through home delivery, but tend to be much less profitable than retail store business.

Frequently other dairies whose volume is low will try to take some of Cloverleaf's home delivery business away from them. They usually do this by offering discounts for an introductory period to the homemakers. Cloverleaf drivers usually match these, and so a small milk war can develop. One device Mr. Anderson has found effective in stopping a milk war was explained by him. "In an area where there is a war, I'll go into a large grocery store where I'm not known. I'll fill my basket and take some of the competitor's milk. When I get to the checkout and the clerk starts to ring up the price, I'll say, 'Hey, what's the matter with you? You're charging $X$ cents for a quart of milk. My sister can get that brand delivered at home for 3 cents a quart lower [the price the war has brought it down to].' At this point, I say, 'Well, if that's what you charge for things here, I don't want any' and I stalk out of the store. This usually makes quite a scene for I always pick a busy time. The retailer then puts pressure on the competing dairy, wanting to know why they are underselling him with home delivery business. Since the retail business is more profitable, frequently the competition then reduces the fervor of its home delivery expansion plans."

Cloverleaf does not have a formal policy for new product development. "We use the old time-honored method of trial and error," said Mr. Nesbitt. "There are four factors that determine whether or not a product will succeed: (1) there must be a demand for that product, (2) it must be conveniently available, (3) the product must be the best, and (4) the public must be made aware of it through advertising." Mr. Nesbitt said that they depended on flavor and ingredient suppliers for new ideas, and that some suggestions came from employees. The company is presently considering the addition of novelty treats, such as ice cream bars and ice cream sandwiches, to its product line. Similar items sold in Des Moines are now supplied by an Illinois firm.

A local advertising agency, Miller-Brown Advertising Company, has handled Cloverleaf's advertising for many years. Once a week, usually on Wednesday, a member of the Miller-Brown staff meets with Mr. Cochran and Mr. Anderson to plan promotional activities. Most advertising is done inside the retail stores and includes displays and "flavor-of-the-month" sales. Each month, one flavor of Princess ice cream is selected to be sold at special prices. A "theme" is selected for the flavor of the month, such as "Hawaiian Holiday," for Royal Pineapple flavor. This theme is carried through on colorful posters and displays on the frozen foods section of the stores. This sale is popular with the retail store owners, who report increased sales as a result. Their profit margin remains the same on sale products, as Cloverleaf gives them discounts to make up for the lower selling price.

Although the flavor-of-the-month sale is a continuous campaign, more intense "saturation" campaigns are conducted about twice yearly. These include extensive radio and television advertising which is designed to convey Cloverleaf's "quality message."

One such campaign served to inform the public about the company's new electronic quality control system for ice cream production. Public suspense was first built up by repeated reference to the letters "EQC," without explaining what the letters represented. Radios blared the letters against an echo background, "E . . . Q . . . C . . . ," and newspapers and television emphasized the EQC theme. At the peak of the campaign, EQC was explained to the public in detail. Mr. Cochran said that they were not certain whether or not this campaign was successful, since the results were difficult to measure. He did not feel that such advertising had much value.

One of the company's recent advertising successes was a "kiddy auction," in which young children saved Cloverleaf bottle caps and labels in order to bid for toys and games. Sales were noticeably increased during this campaign.

Cloverleaf has an aggressive promotion campaign for store openings. They usually feature their Princess ice cream and Cloverleaf milk. The customer may be offered 1/2 gallon of ice cream free when purchasing one at the regular price. Or Cloverleaf can give the retailer a similar "one free with one" offer on milk, but not both at the same opening. These store opening deals are made to all stores likely to carry the Cloverleaf line. For some time, stores in the vicinity of the new store have complained to Cloverleaf, asking for a special deal at the time of the opening. They don't necessarily want the same deal (for it is quite costly and they had their turn), but feel special arrangements should be made to keep them fairly competitive.

Customers have come to expect specials like this at store openings and stock up the limit of the sale (usually two gallons to a customer). Cloverleaf wonders what it should offer competing stores at the time of a nearby opening. Mr. Anderson and Mr. Cochran worry about this because they want to keep the retailers on their side, especially with Sealtest entering the market.

The case writer asked the marketing executives what their strategy was for the other products (after all, it is 20 percent of their business) and home delivery. Mr. Cochran replied, "You have us there, I guess. These parts of the business have not been aggressively merchandised. Most of the 'other products' are very profitable and volume has been growing but we've been so busy with milk and ice cream we haven't given them much push. Have you got any ideas on what we should do to merchandise them?"

"Well," the case writer said, "that's an interesting problem and perhaps we can discuss it, but what about the home delivery business?"

"You sure raise questions about things we don't think much about," said Mr. Anderson. "I guess we just haven't made exact cost studies on that business. If we did, I suspect profit wouldn't look good on that end of the business, but we'll look into it and think about it."

"Recent concern over the company's new competitor, Sealtest, is forcing management to reevaluate its promotional policies. Sealtest is presently conducting an intensive television and newspaper campaign to acquaint the Des Moines residents with its products. Mr. Nesbitt thinks that Cloverleaf should step up its own advertising efforts to counter the possible effects of the new competition. The matter was discussed at the meeting between Mr. Nesbitt, Mr. Cochran, and Mr. Miller, of the Miller-Brown advertising agency, in which the following conversation took place:

Mr. Nesbitt: "It appears as though they [Sealtest] will be hitting us straight on, up and down the product line. As far as quality is concerned, I think our products are slightly better, but most customers probably won't be able to tell the difference. What we need to do is emphasize the quality difference in our advertising."

Mr. Miller: "That's right. What we can do is emphasize the greater freshness of the locally processed Cloverleaf products as compared to those transported from other areas, as Sealtest will be. This is something that the customer can readily understand and relate to quality."

Mr. Cochran: "I think we're being slightly paranoid about the situation. Sure, people will try the new brand at first, just to see how they will like it. But after the newness wears off, they'll go back to buying Cloverleaf. Why? Because we still have the best products. Oh, we might step up advertising a bit at first, but I think an extended campaign would cost more than it would be worth."

Mr. Nesbitt: "Sure, we can count on a lot of customer loyalty. Our prices are reasonable, and I don't think we'll be undercut. But still, we can't ignore competition. For every sale Sealtest makes, we'll lose a sale. It won't be our present competitors who are hurt—they're not selling in the same market."

Mr. Miller: "What I feel we need to do is to begin an intensive campaign very soon that will firmly implant the Cloverleaf quality image in the minds of our customers. This will make them more resistant to the Sealtest sales pitch."

Mr. Nesbitt: "One thing is for certain. We haven't got where we are today just by sitting around and letting it happen. If we're going to maintain our position, we've got to act, and act now."

By the time the case writer had concluded his study, Sealtest had already begun to sell in the Des Moines area. Predictably, Cloverleaf orders fell off moderately. Management was still uncertain what strategy they would employ to handle the new competition.

## PROFIT PLANNING AND RESULTS

The Dairy Processing Industry reports how the average processor allocates his funds (see Figure 2).

Separate accounting procedures are used for retail and wholesale accounts. Wholesale accounts are processed by a small computer, which automatically shows sales, accounts receivable, and accounts payable. A weekly printout breaks sales down by product and geographical sales area. This information is then forwarded to Mr. Anderson.

The retail (home delivery) system must be processed by hand since the accounts are too small and too frequently changed to be placed on the computer feasibly. Retail routemen play an important role in the accounting process. Each day, they bill customers (billing is done at the time of delivery) and calculate sales per customer and total sales for the day. Records prepared by the retail men are given to the accounting department for further processing.

Most wholesale sales are on credit, payable in 30 days; home retail accounts are paid at the end of the month. Bad debts stem mainly from the home retail sales. This is also the least profitable area of operation. Although home retail operations account for 22 percent of total sales, they account for only 14 percent of profits. Mr. Snider attributes the lower profit margin to the cost of salesmen's commissions and the maintenance and upkeep on the company's 150 trucks. Overall, about 75 percent of costs are direct

**FIGURE 2** How the average dairy processor allocates income.

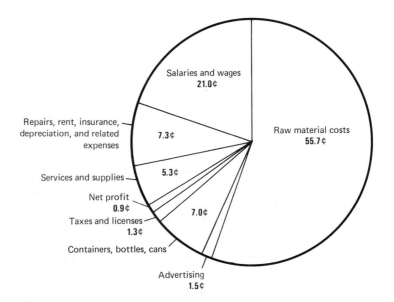

Salaries and wages
21.0¢

Repairs, rent, insurance, depreciation, and related expenses   7.3¢

Services and supplies   5.3¢

Net profit 0.9¢

Taxes and licenses 1.3¢

Containers, bottles, cans

7.0¢

Raw material costs 55.7¢

Advertising 1.5¢

**TABLE 5** Cloverleaf Dairies, Inc.
Comparative Income Statements for the Years Ended December 31

| | 1980 | 1981 | 1982 |
|---|---|---|---|
| Sales | $8,779,320 | $9,563,530 | $10,173,967 |
| Cost of sales | 5,844,366 | 6,380,313 | 6,809,299 |
| Gross Profit | 2,934,954 | 3,183,217 | 3,364,668 |
| General & administrative expenses | 2,287,066 | 2,485,943 | 2,639,005 |
| Income from operations | 647,888 | 697,274 | 725,663 |
| Other income | 114,505 | 117,058 | 124,665 |
| Total | 762,393 | 814,332 | 850,328 |
| Other income changes | 7,121 | 9,023 | 7,993 |
| | 755,272 | 805,309 | 842,335 |
| Contributions to pension trust | 209,860 | 212,789 | 215,983 |
| Income before taxes | 545,412 | 592,520 | 626,352 |
| Income tax expense | 257,450 | 254,784 | 270,134 |
| Net income | $287,962 | $337,736 | $356,218 |

costs, with 50 percent for raw products and 25 percent for wages. Recent financial statements for Cloverleaf are given in Tables 5 and 6.

Annual operating budgets are prepared by Mr. Bitner, who was proud to point out that last year's budget proved to be extremely accurate. Predicted sales were within $70,000 of actual sales, with actual selling expenses 3.5 percent under the budget, and general and administrative costs 1 percent under. Manufacturing expenses were 2.5 percent under the budget, and material costs 0.75 percent over.

The company keeps a $5000 standing balance in every bank in each community in the selling area. Presently this is 60 banks. Mr. Bitner did not approve of the practice, but Mr. Snider defended it, saying that it helps build their public image and stimulated the economy of the community. He added that if the funds were put in CDs or notes, they would not bring in enough profit after taxes to make it worthwhile.

Mr. Nesbitt, Mr. Anderson, and Mr. Bitner jointly prepare the capital budget. No plant ex-

**TABLE 6** Cloverleaf Dairies, Inc.
Comparative Statement of Changes in Retained Earnings for the Years Ended December 31

| | 1980 | 1981 | 1982 |
|---|---|---|---|
| Retained earnings, January 1 | $921,549 | $1,079,928 | $1,242,042 |
| Add: Net income for the year | 287,962 | 337,736 | 356,218 |
| | 1,209,511 | 1,417,664 | 1,598,260 |
| Deduct: Dividends paid during year | 129,583 | 175,622 | 201,210 |
| Retained Earnings December 31 | $1,079,928 | $1,242,042 | $1,397,050 |

**TABLE 7**   Cloverleaf Dairies, Inc.
Comparative Balance Sheets at Years Ended December 31

|  | 1980 | 1981 | 1982 |
|---|---|---|---|
| **Current Assets** | | | |
| Cash | $529,373 | $748,458 | $737,593 |
| Accounts receivable (less allowance for bad debts) | 816,476 | 937,653 | 1,074,215 |
| Inventories | 140,469 | 162,580 | 188,693 |
| Prepaid expenses | 21,091 | 25,153 | 26,844 |
| Total current assets | 1,507,409 | 1,873,844 | 2,027,345 |
| Land, buildings, & equipment | | | |
| Land | 253,850 | 253,850 | 253,850 |
| Buildings & equipment (less depreciation) | 1,501,451 | 1,626,580 | 1,747,283 |
| Other assets | 17,130 | 13,759 | 3,844 |
| Total assets | $3,279,840 | $3,768,033 | $4,032,322 |
| **Current Liabilities** | | | |
| Accounts payable | $282,341 | $427,693 | $466,133 |
| Income taxes payable | 80,960 | 102,508 | 110,386 |
| Withholding and Social Security payable | 26,696 | 37,025 | 45,756 |
| Total current liabilities | 389,997 | 567,226 | 622,275 |
| Stockholders' equity | | | |
| Outstanding capital stock | 1,898,788 | 2,050,409 | 2,104,641 |
| Less treasury stock | 88,873 | 91,644 | 91,644 |
| Retained earnings | 1,079,928 | 1,242,042 | 1,397,050 |
| Total stockholders' equity | 2,889,843 | 3,200,807 | 3,410,047 |
| Total liabilities & stockholders' equity | $3,279,840 | $3,768,033 | $4,032,322 |

pansion is planned for the near future. In the past, small dairies have been purchased in outlying areas to provide new markets, but the plants proved too costly to operate and were shut down. It is not anticipated that anymore such purchases will be made.

Eighty percent of the Cloverleaf stock, which is sold over the counter, is owned by four families. These include the Cochran, Nesbitt, and Snider families, and one other family not connected with management. Each family owns between 15 and 20 percent of the stock and 20 percent is held by the general public in smaller amounts.

## FINAL COMMENTS

"All in all, I think we're a profitable and progressive company and will have no problems in the future," Mr. Nesbitt told the case writer as he was ready to leave. "After all, Des Moines is our home base and we know how to run a business here," he said. The case writer wondered if Mr. Nesbitt was right about that.

# 15 MAJESTIC MACHINING COMPANY

**Charles Schwenk**

*University of Illinois*

Roy and Elaine Hart said little to each other during their drive back to Majestic Machining after their meeting with the loan officer at National Bank. They were both preoccupied with the same question, "Why is it with all the business we are doing now that we are still showing such low profits and getting into financial jams like this that require short-term loans to pull us out?" The loan officer at the bank had agreed to loan Majestic Machining enough money in order to meet its payroll and machinery payments for the month of June but only after the company had completely exhausted its line of credit on its accounts receivables.*

Roy Hart summed up the Harts' confusion in the following way, "I wonder what we are doing wrong. We have the best machinists in the area. We pay one of the highest wage rates in the area. We have some of the best equipment. Our sales have been growing by leaps and bounds these last few years and maybe that has something to do with it. As soon as we stop growing and stabilize, things might get better for us in terms of these short-run cash shortages. Also, the local economy plays a big role in all of this. Our volume of business fluctuates so much that we just have to expect to have times when money is tight."

*Majestic Machining can borrow up to 70% of the value of their accounts receivables to meet short-run expenses. However, the interest rate on these funds is rather high and they would prefer not to use this form of financing.

## HISTORY OF MAJESTIC MACHINING AND ROY HART

Like many small businesses, until recently, Majestic Machining could have been described as the lengthened shadow of a man; in this case, Roy Hart.

Roy Hart was born in a small town on the Washington–Canadian border and showed early interest in machinery and metalworking. After graduating from a vocational high school in Portland, where he concentrated on preparing for a job as a machinist, he served four years in the Air Force in India during World War II as an airplane machinist. At the end of this time, he went to work in Portland as a tool and die maker and, within a few years, started his own tool and die shop, Hart Tool and Die. For nearly eight years, he operated his small shop, employing from two to three people at all times. In 1963, he decided to expand his operation. He moved to a different location, with more floor space, and began to purchase more machinery on credit and hire more tool and die makers, expanding the number to 12 at the peak of Hart Tool and Die's operation.

During the period from mid-1969 to early 1971, the Oregon economy suffered a slight downturn which had disastrous consequences for Hart Tool and Die. The company had been heavily dependent on a few large companies as their principle customers and with the recession, these companies cancelled purchase orders to Hart Tool and Die. The company found itself in a position of being unable to meet its fixed expenses and for a time, bankruptcy seemed to be the only solution. However, the company was able to sell much of its machinery (often at a loss) and avoid this alternative.

1972 found Hart Tool and Die in much the same position financially as it had been in 1968. In late 1972, as the Oregon economy was beginning to recover, Roy Hart went into partnership with Ned White, who put up $10,000, matched by $10,000 from Roy to start a new business which would have a broader product-market focus than Hart Tool and Die. The new business would focus on general machining, rather than the specific area of tool and die making. A corporation was formed and the name of the company was changed to Majestic Machining.

To avoid the problems with overextension which Roy Hart had experienced with Hart Tool and Die, the two men agreed on a policy of slow growth, financed partly by retained earnings and partly by debt. However, they avoided heavy debt financing. The business was moved to a new location outside Portland and they began the slow growth process.

As in the past, the company continued to remain tied to a few large customers since a substantial part of their work came from these customers. For this reason, the company continued to experience problems with fluctuations and large swings in business during parts of the year. However, the company continued to grow and even during the worst of times was able to meet its salaries and fixed expenses.

## ECONOMIC ENVIRONMENT

The overall level of business activity in Oregon has shown a good deal of fluctuation since 1967 but has shown an upward trend overall. Manufacturing employment, one indicator of the level of activity in the manufacturing sector, has shown wide fluctuations. Wage and salaries have shown a general increase.

Expectation of a recession to begin early in 1979 has Roy Hart and others at the company worried. The prime interest rate has been rising and recent articles in the *Wall Street Journal* have been predicting a mild recession soon. Since past recessions have been so dangerous for the company, Roy is looking for ways to minimize the possible damage of a recession in the near future.

Majestic's own volume of sales typically has undergone much wider fluctuations than the manufacturing industry as a whole. One cause of this is the fact that the company has previously been tied to several large customers. When economic conditions worsen, these customers have less work for Majestic and are slower to pay for work they have had done. Majestic has been reluctant to press large customers for payment at these times for fear of losing business.

## MAJESTIC'S MAJOR DEPARTMENTS

Since 1972, Majestic has expanded from a simple machine shop to a more complex operation. Within the past year, Majestic has added a fabricating department and plans are being laid out now for the creation of a new department to deal with repair and rework on equipment for pulp and paper mills.

The machine shop, Majestic's oldest operation, deals with the building and repair of various types of production machinery and the design and construction of various types of tooling.

The fabricating department deals with the construction of such items as tractor canopies and metal frames through the welding of their individual components.

## COMPETITIVE CONDITIONS

There are approximately 140 machine shops in the Portland area which perform some or all of the activities discussed above, including maintenance work on various types of industrial machinery, milling machine work, welding, fabricating, and machine design. Majestic Machining is larger than most of the machine shops in the Portland area and offers a wider range of services than most. Roy Hart feels that this is the key to a large volume of sales. The companies which supply work to machine shops often require a number of types of work on any given job. A typical job might require welding and fabricating work in addition to milling, etc. Such a job, sent to a small machine shop which did not have the capabilities to do all these things, would have to be subcontracted out to another machine shop for part of the work. Typically a shop which subcontracts work must add a percentage to the amount charged by the subcontracting shop when they pass the costs on to the customer. This has the effect of making work done by smaller shops more expensive than the same work done by a larger shop which can do it all in-house.

Many large manufacturing companies have their own small machine shops in which they can do simpler machining jobs. However, larger jobs must be done outside. Some of these are submitted to a number of shops for competitive bidding. However, in many cases the selection of a shop to do a given job is not determined by a competitive process. Companies have certain shops with which they are familiar and which they feel will offer them work of acceptance quality, with rapid delivery, at a reasonable price. In the case of rush jobs, where speed is more important than price or even quality, these companies will not ask the shop to quote or estimate prices beforehand but will require a firm commitment on an early delivery date. Because of the number of rush jobs (which tend to be the smaller jobs) some shops in the area offer 24-hour-a-day, 7-day-a-week service. These shops tend to be the larger shops and Majestic Machining is not yet of sufficient size to offer such service, preferring to concentrate on larger orders with less urgent delivery schedules. However, in the case of jobs which are determined through competitive bidding, Roy Hart feels Majestic should have an advantage over many smaller shops in the area for the reasons mentioned earlier.

The competitive conditions have remained relatively stable since 1973, with the number of machine shops growing slowly as the population in the Portland area increased.

## FINANCE

Roy sees no real difficulties for Majestic in the area of financial health. His main concern, as stated previously, is the short-term shortages of cash which the company faces periodically. Exhibits 1 and 2 contain financial data on the company from 1976 through 1978. Since gross profits and sales have risen since 1976, Roy is, in general, pleased. The company is considering institution of some form of financial controls or budgets in view of the increases in cost of goods sold and selling and administrative expense.

## MARKETING

Recent expansions were undertaken with little thought given to an increased marketing effort which would be necessary to generate work to keep these expanded facilities busy. However, Roy and Elaine Hart soon realized that such an expanded effort would be necessary. John West, who had originally been hired to head up the welding and fabricating department, was given the job of contacting potential customers for this operation. Though he had had little selling experience prior to this, he felt he could handle this assignment and has brought in some new business. No effort has been made at this point in time to assess the effectiveness of his sales efforts or to determine whether the new business he is bringing in justifies his salary.

Majestic also recently hired Ray Luck who does some selling in addition to various managerial duties. The sales effort is still not well coordinated and has no targets for volume of sales. Work still needs to be done in this area. Recently, a single very large customer stopped doing business with Majestic because of a dispute on the quality of some work Majestic had done for them and this severely reduced the company's volume of business temporarily. This experience lead Roy and Elaine Hart to the conclusion that they had been essentially a captive

## EXHIBIT 1

| | 1976 | 1977 | 1978 |
|---|---|---|---|
| **Current Assets** | | | |
| Cash in banks | $ 575.95 | $ 1,492.85 | $ 1,257.66 |
| Accounts receivable | 42,533.16 | 48,681.85 | 108,424.41 |
| Work in progress | 24,314.25 | 7,680.92 | 17,903.60 |
| | 67,423.36 | 57,855.62 | 127,585.67 |
| **Property, Furniture and Equipment** | | | |
| Furniture and fixtures | 4,023.30 | 4,215.42 | 7,363.16 |
| Trucks | 11,900.00 | 13,153.00 | 13,800.00 |
| Equipment | 131,648.36 | 139,384.95 | 317,048.79 |
| Tools | 13,614.00 | 14,270.55 | 15,244.63 |
| Leasehold Improvements | 11,487.01 | 11,811.77 | 31,250.07 |
| | 172,672.67 | 182,835.69 | 384,706.65 |
| Less accumulated depreciation | (70,323.80) | (93,355.80) | (141,269.02) |
| | 102,348.87 | 89,479.89 | 243,437.63 |
| **Other Assets** | | | |
| Prepaid deposits | 1,287.50 | 1,287.50 | |
| Prepaid expenses | 10,184.26 | 9,110.30 | |
| Goodwill | 9,664.00 | 9,664.00 | 1,095.50 |
| Organization expenses | 35.45 | — | 9,664.00 |
| | 21,171.21 | 20,061.80 | 10,759.50 |
| | $190,943.44 | $167,397.31 | 381,782.80 |
| **Current Liabilities** | | | |
| Accounts payable | $ 24,396.49 | $ 4,594.14 | $ 45,237.49 |
| Payroll taxes payable | 6,646.97 | 2,912.32 | 11,330.15 |
| State income taxes payable | — | 194.00 | — |
| Accounts receivable notes payable | 25,355.94 | 22,945.26 | 60,901.88 |
| Contracts payable—pickup | 1,874.65 | — | 3,500.00 |
| Current portion of long-term debt | 16,019.76 | 10,399.68 | 35,854.31 |
| | 74,293.81 | 41,045.40 | 156,823.83 |
| **Long-Term Debt** | | | |
| Contracts payable—lathe | 19,521.00 | 16,481.44 | 20,236.67 |
| Contracts payable—boring mill | 35,951.16 | 25,679.40 | — |
| Contracts payable—truck | — | 3,579.75 | 1,897.59 |
| Contracts payable—Westinghouse | — | — | 96,971.14 |
| Contracts payable—forklift | — | — | 2,062.50 |
| Contracts payable—jeep | — | — | 5,579.02 |
| Contracts payable—building | — | — | 9,049.50 |
| Notes payable | — | — | 93,751.62 |
| Loans payable—officer's | 14,900.00 | 6,735.27 | 43,109.71 |
| Less current portion above | (16,019.76) | (10,399.68) | (35,854.31) |
| | 54,352.40 | 42,076.18 | 236,803.44 |

**EXHIBIT 1**   *(Continued)*

| | 1976 | 1977 | 1978 |
|---|---|---|---|
| Stockholders' Equity | | | |
| Capital stock | 44,000.00 | 46,275.00 | 46,275.00 |
| Retained earnings | 18,297.23 | 38,000.00 | 41,880.53 |
| Treasury stock | — | — | (100,000.00) |
| | 62,297.23 | 84,275.73 | 11,844.47 |
| | $190,943.44 | $167,397.31 | $381,782.80 |

vendor for these large customers and that they needed a shift in their marketing focus toward more aggressive selling. However, Roy has never felt he had strength in this area and there is some question about how effective this new thrust will be.

With the creation of the welding and fabricating department, and with the hiring of Ray Luck, a potential market has opened up for the company in repair and maintenance in the Oregon pulp and papermill industry. Roy Hart feels that Majestic will soon have the capabilities for doing all the repair work which would be required on papermill equipment. Ray Luck, who has had some experience in this area, feels that repair orders from sawmills would typically be very large orders and rush jobs and, therefore, be very lucrative. One aspect of this market which is particularly attractive is that it moves counter to the rest of the economy and would, therefore, provide needed work in the event of an economic downturn. When an economic downturn occurs, papermills are more likely to have equipment repaired rather than purchase new equipment. Therefore, the repair and maintenance work from papermills are making them aware of Majestic's capabilities in the area of repair and maintenance.

With the newly expanded marketing effort came a need for the company to more clearly define its target market. No attempt had been made to do this in the past because the marketing function was not as important to Majestic as it is now. Roy Hart, on first considering

this issue, defined Empire's target market as the Northwest (Oregon, Washington, Idaho, and northern California) and indeed, orders have come from Washington and northern California. However, for companies which are a great distance from Majestic, transportatation costs eliminate any cost advantages which Majestic might have over local shops. Further, there is reason to believe that large manufacturing concerns may prefer to do business with local shops with whom they are familiar. In the past, the greatest share of the company's business came from companies within the Portland area.

## ORGANIZATION AND PERSONNEL

In April of 1978, an expansion in the volume of work to be done for Majestic resulted in a need for the hiring of a number of qualified machinists.

Because of the fluctuations in workload in the shop, the number of machinists employed typically fluctuates widely, at times dipping below ten and at other times approaching twenty. Majestic is a nonunion shop but pays wages higher than most union shops. Roy Hart feels that the benefits of being a nonunion shop outweigh the drawbacks of the higher wages. He feels that he is able to arrange things in his shop so that the men are much more productive than they would be if he had to operate within the constraints established by a union.

Unable to attract qualified machinists when he needed them, he decided to raise wages even

**EXHIBIT 2**

|  | 1976 | 1977 | 1978 |
|---|---|---|---|
| **Income** | | | |
| Sales | $ 384,108.37 | $ 455,538.68 | $ 684,568.12 |
| Less discount allowed | (6,486.71) | (734.35) | — |
| Miscellaneous income | 3,215.27 | 6,438.93 | 14,489.98 |
|  | 380,836.93 | 461,243.26 | 699,058.10 |
| **Cost of Sales** | | | |
| Beginning inventory | 13,100.28 | 24,314.25 | 7,680.92 |
| Materials | 68,740.07 | 37,382.58 | 106,960.40 |
| Shop supplies, tools | 20,506.87 | 22,259.83 | 47,257.17 |
| Subcontracts | 10,037.90 | 32,584.63 | 34,972.51 |
| Labor | 136,657.29 | 146,068.26 | 245,020.99 |
| Payroll taxes and benefits | 28,268.54 | 33,255.23 | 58,129.40 |
|  | 277,310.95 | 295,864.78 | 500,021.39 |
| Less ending inventory | (24,314.25) | (7,680.92) | (17,903.60) |
|  | 252,996.70 | 288,183.86 | 482,117.79 |
| Gross Profit | 127,840.23 | 173,059.40 | 216,940.31 |
| Operating Expenses–Schedule I | 134,556.82 | 152,331.97 | 214,496.66 |
| Operating income (loss) | (6,716.59) | 20,727.43 | 2,443.65 |
| **Other Income and (Expenses)** | | | |
| Officers' life insurance | (1,040.40) | (898.20) | (170.21) |
| Penalties | — | (125.73) | (1,379.64) |
| Federal tax refund | 3,418.25 | — | 2,986.00 |
|  | 2,377.85 | (1,023.93) | 1,436.15 |
| Net Income (Loss) | $ (4,338.74) | $ 19,703.50 | $ 3,879.80 |
| Officers' salaries | $ 46,350.00 | $ 62,400.00 | $ 56,683.00 |
| Advertising | 852.31 | 1,317.62 | 1,103.28 |
| Auto | 4,807.36 | 5,500.33 | 8,449.12 |
| Insurance | 4,261.50 | 4,439.00 | 5,295.87 |
| Interest | 3,974.19 | 11,450.97 | 23,016.44 |
| Professional services | 1,625.92 | 1,903.59 | 2,525.91 |
| Taxes and licenses | 1,767.57 | 2,413.42 | 3,068.97 |
| Maintenance | 4,834.05 | 7,265.82 | 11,898.08 |
| Office salaries | 15,620.00 | 2,722.50 | 15,951.50 |
| Office | 854.16 | 1,035.71 | — |
| Rent | 12,555.00 | 15,810.00 | 2,201.04 |
| Equipment rental | 3,148.20 | 524.70 | 9,568.77 |
| Travel and subsistence | 715.10 | 492.59 | 50,677.22 |
| Travel and entertainment | 1,492.01 | 1,083.26 | — |
| Utilities | 5,803.75 | 7,071.23 | — |
| Depreciation | 25,824.70 | 26,552.00 | — |
| Other | 71.00 | 349.23 | 445.00 |
|  | $ 134,556.82 | $ 152,331.97 | $ 214,496.66 |

further, by an average of $1.00 per man per hour, to an average of $10.25 per hour for qualified employees. At this rate, he felt he would be able to attract the most qualified and productive men and their productivity would more than cover their increased wages. At this wage rate, he was able to attract the qualified people he needed but it significantly increased his variable costs and there is some reason to believe it created resentment on the part of other machine shop owners because of the pressure it put on their wage rates.

Because the responsibilities of the individuals in supervisory positions in the company are not clearly defined, because of the recent expansion which has lead to several shifts in job responsibilities, and because more than one individual often shares responsibility for certain duties, it would be very difficult to develop an organization chart for the company and indeed this has never been attempted in the past. Day-to-day operating decisions are made by the individual in charge of whichever department the decision concerns. More important matters are decided by Roy Hart, who is also consulted if problems arise in decisions made by department heads. Decisions on major purchases or major shifts in the focus of company actions are made by a vote of the board of directors consisting of Roy and Elaine Hart.

## FUTURE DIRECTIONS FOR MAJESTIC MACHINING

Early in 1978, negotiations began for the purchase of Ned White's half-interest in Majestic. The company agreed to pay Ned for his interest in monthly payments for the next 15 years. As long as the company does not default on the agreement or any of the monthly payments, it would enjoy all the rights of ownership of the stock.

One clause of the agreement which is of particular interest deals with provisions for a merger or sale of the company. The agreement reads:

If there is a merger or consolidation of the corporation with any other corporation or the sale of substantially all of its assets except in the regular course of business, the interest rate applicable to the unpaid balance of the purchase price for Seller's (Ned White) shares shall change from six percent to nine percent per annum, said change being effective as of the date of sales or merger and payable with the first installment due after that date.

A second clause of interest reads:

As security for payment of the balance of the purchase price of Seller's shares, the corporation grants to seller a security interest in machinery and equipment owned by the corporation which, to the extent permitted by Oregon law, shall be prior interest to all other security interests.

The purchase of Ned's interest gives Roy Hart more latitude in terms of managerial decisions affecting future directions for the company. However, Roy is seriously considering reducing his own managerial responsibilities and turning over control of the company (partially) to someone else. There are two basic reasons for this. First, he recognizes his own limitations in terms of managerial background and feels that as the company expands it will be increasingly necessary for it to be managed by someone with more extensive business background and education. Second, at age 60, he is ready to retire within a few years and will need someone to take over soon so that he or she may begin learning the business. He is considering a number of long-range alternatives, each of which seems to meet his personal objectives only partly:

A. Find a suitable buyer for the company.
B. Merge with another machine shop or manufacturing company who can supply the needed management talent.
C. Retain control of the company but locate an individual from outside the company to take over Roy Hart's job in a few years and begin training him.

**D.** Retain control but locate an individual within the company and begin grooming him to take over Roy Hart's job.

**E.** Put the decision off.

Finally, in addition to the long-range considerations, there is the immediate concern of the actions the company should take to minimize the ill effects of a possible recession in the near future.

Ray Luck has his own ideas about the future of Majestic, which are summarized below:

## FINANCE

Majestic is a job shop. A job shop does not have a product that can be manipulated saleswise. Moderate improvements can be executed in growth rate through the sales portion of marketing; however, this is practically limited. As such, financial health depends largely on operations as they affect the current financial position of the organization.

Growth must be financed almost entirely from revenues. This business is not highly leveraged—capital budgeting is more difficult, requiring a conservative approach to expansion.

## MARKETING

A jobbing machine shop is simply a service company. One must evaluate carefully which segment of the overall market is best suited to be served efficiently and profitably at the time. This segment is then high-graded to produce service activity.

Beyond this, the growth will depend on specific *goals* of the company. Thereafter, accelerated growth depends on the company's ability to create and market additional services. This requires careful planning—people and equipment must be timed and brought on stream as the market is developed. Growth in this field is conservative because the market tends to be geographically controlled.

The company can target for sales that result from new or added industrial growth within the region plus converting a portion of the existing business over to our operations. This new level, if properly handled, will expand approximately at the average rate of the geographic area serviced.

The better method for Majestic Machining Company to meet current needs is to stabilize the market to the existing capabilities. Once consistency has been achieved on this level, future plans can be followed. The major control mechanism is the ability to finance additional service capabilities from revenues.

Majestic currently is out of phase with the financial requirements for this structure. The immediate aim is to manage existing operations profitably until debt can be reduced and cash for future growth accumulated.

Optimizing existing service abilities will meet the desire for diversification and concurrently provide quality growth for the next two or three years.

## ORGANIZATION AND PERSONNEL

Historically there have been marked fluctuations in service activities for Majestic. This has occurred while most shops in the area have remained stable. There has also been a general shortage of qualified machinists.

Because machinists are not readily available and it takes a considerable amount of time and money to train them to be profitable, one must also be stable. This requires the company to control the growth and level of activity such that time is available to superintend these factors.

Any time an organization depends on a skilled and technically oriented work force, in short supply, it must do everything possible to provide relative stability. To do otherwise is an open contradiction. Therefore, Majestic must utilize management energy towards winning and keeping men that fill our needs.

Retaining qualified people does not necessarily mean we pay the most per hour, directly. Sensitivity to overall needs of individuals requires our attention. It becomes part of the management function to include this in our marketing structure.

Majestic has reached a size and stage of development that is precarious. To go forward will require decentralized control of specific functions and an overall definition of responsibilities.

## FUTURE DIRECTIONS FOR MAJESTIC MACHINING

As I see it, there are two possibilities. Reduce the growth or size of the company such that it can stay below the critical stage, or structure the company and manage it to obtain the level beyond this status. Retaining the status quo is not a possibility.

# 16

# PENTRON INC.

## Lawrence R. Jauch

*Southern Illinois University-Carbondale*

In the early months of 1984, Pentron Inc. was acquired by Painter Enterprises, Incorporated, a small Seattle-based conglomerate. Pentron is a Seattle firm engaged in the manufacture of pens and mechanical pencils used by businesses as advertising specialties.

In late 1984, Mr. Janson Painter, president of Painter Enterprises, Inc., asked the casewriter to analyze his new acquisition in detail. In a conversation with the casewriter he said, "Find out what makes Pentron tick. I want to learn as much as I can about the company—what its strong and weak points are, and where changes or improvements might be necessary. Be my eyes and ears for a while. I'll see that you get full cooperation from everyone involved."

Although the casewriter did not learn all about the parent company in the beginning of his visits, he was able to piece together the following information about Painter Enterprises.

Painter Enterprises, Inc., began as an outgrowth of the Painter Paper Company, a Los Angeles paper products company. The firm specializes in napkins and disposable dinnerware. PPC, as the firm was known, was founded in 1951 by Mr. Sherman Painter, Janson Painter's father. The younger Painter took over as owner and president when his father died in 1976.

Since that time, Mr. Painter has sought to diversify his operations. With a strong capital and earnings base provided by the paper prod-

ucts company, Mr. Painter acquired the Rollok Containers Corporation in 1979 and Ross Accessories, Ltd. in 1981. Rollok is a liquids packaging firm with assets of $63 million and sales of $3.2 million. Ross Accessories makes automobile floor mats, grossing $1.6 million in sales with assets of $750,000.

It was Mr. Painter's strategy to acquire small companies which, although operationally strong, were experiencing financial difficulties and needed additional capital. He felt that he could acquire such companies at a low price and make them into profitable operations. Rollok and Ross Accessories both fit Mr. Painter's requirements. They both showed a history of strong sales growth but operating inefficiencies, and in the case of Rollok the need for new capital equipment forced the need for more funds and reorganization.

Mr. Painter used much of the experience and knowledge he had acquired in the manufacturing business in solving some of the major difficulties at both companies. He reshuffled the organizations, introduced new production techniques, and modernized plants and equipment. Rollok showed a profit for the first time in three years in 1980; Ross Accessories reached the break-even point in 1982 and showed small profits in 1983 and 1984.

The move to acquire Pentron began in mid-1983. As Mr. Painter sees it, this acquisition did not fit into his "buy-cheap-and-rebuild" strategy. He said,

I viewed the purchase of Rollok and Ross Accessories as medium-risk acquisitions, and in fact, still regard them as such. Along about 1981, I wanted to balance this risk with the acquisition of a solid and profitable firm. I guess you could

Adapted from a case study prepared by William F. Glueck and John Abendshien. This is a disguised case. Names and locations and some data have been altered because the firm requested it. No useful purpose is served by attempting to discover the "real" company.

almost call it a 'hedge.' I heard through various channels that Mr. Hopkins was thinking of selling Pentron and contacted him about this. The rest of the story you know.

Unlike his other purchases, which were largely cash transactions, Mr. Painter borrowed heavily to buy Pentron. Almost 80 percent of the purchase was financed by issuing twenty-year convertible debenture bonds. In addition, the Painter corporation assumed the balance of two long-term loans already on Pentron's books.

Then, in 1984, two of Painter's firms began to falter. Rollok lost two of its major contracts to other firms. At the same time, intense competitive pressures in the paper products industry brought certain weaknesses in Painter's sales organization to light. Rollok showed a net loss in 1984; Painter Paper Company posted the smallest earnings amount in over eight years.

Sales and income data for 1984 are given for the four Painter firms as follows:

|  | Sales | Earnings |
| --- | --- | --- |
| Painter Paper Co. | $ 7,658,902 | $ 51,163 |
| Ross Accessories, Ltd. | 1,676,266 | 71,618 |
| Rollok Container Corp. | 3,176,044 | (132,548) |
| Pentron | 8,525,716 | 306,344 |
| Total | $21,036,928 | $296,570 |

Mr. Painter is optimistic about the prospects of what he calls his "corporate family." He said:

Problems at PPC and Rollok have absorbed almost all of my time and energy over the past few months. For that reason, I have been able to devote little attention to Pentron. Fortunately, Pentron had enough basic strength and momentum that it did not need our assistance. We were extremely fortunate to have the previous owners stay on the job. Indeed, I made this a part of the contract and would perhaps not have made the purchase in the first place if I didn't have that kind of assurance.

But now we're getting some of the wrinkles in our operations ironed out. I see much promise for Painter Enterprises in the years ahead. Pentron, which has emerged as the largest and strongest company, will serve as the cornerstone for future growth. That's why I'm interested in probing further into Pentron and determining what future changes will have to be made now. The company will play an important role in our future.

## THE SUCCESS STORY

The casewriter next attempted to learn as much as he could about the history of Pentron. He arranged an interview with Mr. Robert Hopkins to discuss the company's past history and present conditions.

When the casewriter arrived at Pentron, he was shown to Mr. Hopkins' office. Mr. Hopkins, a well-groomed gentleman apparently in his mid-forties, met him at the door: "So Painter's checking up on us," Mr. Hopkins said cheerfully. "Well, I'm sure that you'll find things well run around here. Here, let me show you something." Mr. Hopkins pointed to sales and profits charts on one wall of his office. "This is where we started thirteen years ago," he said, indicating 1971 figures on the charts, "and this is where we are now. Sales have risen over 500 percent and are still going up. Profits have been following the same trend, you can see that from our Statements." Mr. Hopkins handed Exhibits 1 and 2 to the casewriter.

"So, I guess what I'm trying to tell you is that although there may be problems here and there in our operations, you can't argue with our overall results. We're a pretty darn successful company, anyway you look at it. Still, if you happen to find any worms in our apple, I'll be happy to listen," he chuckled. "We're always looking for ways to improve."

Mr. Hopkins then began to give the casewriter a thumbnail sketch of his company's history. He stated that the company started in the business in 1959 as the Olson Pencil Company. At that time, it was engaged in the manufac-

**EXHIBIT 1**   PENTRON
Balance Sheet
December 31, 1984

Assets

Current assets:

| | |
|---|---|
| Cash | $ 2,541,258 |
| Accounts receivable | 777,549 |
| Inventory | 2,971,921 |
| Total current assets | 6,290,728 |
| Stock investments | 37,957 |
| Net plant and equipment | 4,157,948 |
| Total assets | $10,486,633 |

Liabilities and Net Worth

Current liabilities:

| | |
|---|---|
| Accounts payable | $ 370,304 |
| Notes payable | 1,957,730 |
| Reserve for income taxes | 965,614 |
| Total current liabilities | 3,293,648 |
| Notes payable | 3,537,456 |
| Total liabilities | 6,831,104 |

Stockholders' equity:

| | |
|---|---|
| Common stock outstanding | 2,581,171 |
| Earned surplus | 1,074,358 |
| Total stockholders' equity | 3,655,529 |
| Total net worth | $10,486,633 |

ture of mechanical lead pencils. The demand for such pencils peaked in the mid-1960s and then began to decline. The company sought to revive sales by introducing a line of ball-point pens, but competition in this field was so intense that the pens never became profitable. Finally, liquidity problems forced the company to close it doors in 1970.

Mr. Hopkins, who at that time was in the wholesale grocery business, heard that the Olson business was for sale and became interested in it. "Through my own business, I knew about the widespread usage of pens for advertising purposes," Mr. Hopkins said. "I thought that the old Olson plant could be used to turn out these pens. Besides, I was growing weary of the wholesale grocery business. There's just too much hassle involved in trying to stay on top."

And so, Mr. Hopkins negotiated to buy the Olson facilities. He needed additional capital for the purchase, so he invited two long-time friends, Paul Hoffman and Dwight Thomas, to join him in the venture. Initially, Mr. Hopkins owned 40 percent of the shares outstanding, Mr. Hoffman and Mr. Thomas each owned 20 percent, and the remainder was held by several of Mr. Hopkins' friends. The name of the firm was changed from Olson Pencil Company to PENTRON.

Mr. Hopkins explained what he termed his firm's "phenomenal" growth:

I think it's unusual for a company to start up and set the kind of growth record that we have. It's even more amazing when you consider that neither the product nor the market was new when we started. No, to survive and grow in this business, you have to offer a product that is imaginative for a price that is competitive. Fortunately, we've been able to do both. One of the big reasons why we've done so well is that by doing our own manufacturing, we're able to undercut most of the outfits that buy ready-made pens and perform advertising alterations for their customers. Besides the cost savings, this enables us to tailor our product to more nearly suit the needs of the customer.

After several years of selling ball-point pens successfully, the company decided to begin making mechanical pencils again. Most of the equipment used by the old Olson company to make the pencils still remained, so tooling costs were minimal. PENTRON found a ready market for mechanical pencils as an advertising specialty, and overall the firm's sales increased by 10 percent the first year the pencil was offered.

Then, in late 1983, the three PENTRON owners were approached by Mr. Painter. Mr. Painter offered to buy PENTRON for a dollar sum, which, according to Mr. Hopkins, "was too much to turn down." Mr. Hopkins went on, "None

**EXHIBIT 2**  PENTRON
Selected Income Statements
1972–1984

| | 1972 | 1974 | 1976 | 1978 | 1980 | 1982 | 1984 |
|---|---|---|---|---|---|---|---|
| Net sales | $2,448,427 | $3,393,521 | $4,357,280 | $5,285,381 | $6,575,014 | $7,850,567 | $8,525,716 |
| Operating expenses | 2,218,267 | 2,959,150 | 3,751,619 | 4,450,290 | 5,628,211 | 6,767,189 | 7,383,270 |
| Gross operating income | 230,151 | 434,371 | 605,661 | 835,091 | 946,803 | 1,083,378 | 1,142,446 |
| Other expenses | | | | | | | |
| Depreciation expense | 172,130 | 178,357 | 247,562 | 315,373 | 331,767 | 365,065 | 372,530 |
| Advertising | 31,570 | 33,962 | 60,011 | 112,369 | 130,015 | 176,050 | 184,399 |
| Miscellaneous deductions | 9,884 | 17,083 | 23,149 | 34,639 | 19,511 | 13,135 | 26,224 |
| Total other expenses | 213,584 | 229,402 | 330,722 | 462,381 | 481,293 | 554,250 | 583,153 |
| Income before taxes | 16,567 | 204,969 | 274,939 | 372,710 | 465,510 | 529,128 | 559,293 |
| Taxes | 3,738 | 90,186 | 118,775 | 169,210 | 202,031 | 228,583 | 252,949 |
| Net income | $ 12,829 | $ 114,783 | $ 156,167 | $ 203,500 | $ 263,479 | $ 300,545 | $ 306,344 |

of us figured to stay in this business forever. There was sort of a mutual understanding among us that once we had the company to the point where we could sell it at a large profit, we would get out. We didn't anticipate selling so soon, but Mr. Painter's price was right, so we took it."

Thus, PENTRON became a subsidiary of Painter Enterprises, with the shift in ownership taking place on January 2, 1984. The three former owners, Mr. Hopkins, Mr. Hoffman, and Mr. Thomas, received a three-year contract to continue managing the business. Mr. Hopkins said that he wasn't sure whether he or the other two ex-owners would stay with PENTRON after the three-year period is up. He added that he has no alternative plans at the present time.

## PENTRON'S EXECUTIVE TEAM

Many management experts believe that you can learn a lot about a company's future by looking closely at its top executives. This is especially true of smaller companies. PENTRON has an interesting group of executives.

Mr. Hopkins was described by his associates with such words as shrewd and careful. In his conversation with the casewriter, Mr. Hopkins offered some insights into his own personality and managerial philosophy.

> I guess my approach to management lies somewhere between being either completely authoritarian or democratic. People may find me to be rather autocratic at times, but after all, someone has to make the big decisions. On the other hand, I feel that within the scope of authority assigned to him, a person should be able to make his own decisions and plan his own activities. I realize the value of having others contribute to decision making, and appreciate hearing differing points of view on matters. That is why many years ago I instituted our management committee.

Mr. Hopkins explained that the management committee consists of himself; Mr. Hoffman; Mr. Thomas; Mr. Davis, the production manager; Mr. Branson, the sales manager; and Mr. Adams, controller. Each committee member represents his particular department or area of operation at the meetings, but is invited to participate in overall policy and decision making for the entire firm, as well. The working relationships and responsibilities among the committee members are not strictly defined, and neither an organization chart nor job descriptions have ever been printed.

"A more rigid, bureaucratic organization would not work well here," Mr. Hopkins contended, "because you can't run a small company that way. We don't get too hung up about overlapping functions and responsibilities. Each man can do a better job if he has some idea of the activities and problems involved in operating areas other than his own."

Mr. Hopkins said, "When it comes to major decisions, I have the final responsibility. Sometimes it may appear that I'm dragging my feet on some matters, but then, no one else around here has the kind of responsibility attached to decision making that I do. I feel that my appropriate role is to set the pace for the future and to put on the brakes whenever necessary."

In talking about his managerial philosophy Mr. Hopkins said that the one thing he demands of all employees is their complete loyalty. "I don't believe that a person can be an effective manager or employee unless he has a personal interest in the company and believes in what he is doing," he stated.

Nearly one-half of Mr. Hopkins' time is spent with contacts outside the firm. This activity is related to finding new sales opportunities and maintaining old customer relationships. He estimates that he spends about two-thirds of the remaining time in his office, handling on-the-spot problems, receiving calls, and going over reports. The rest of the time he spends walking around the plant talking to supervisors and employees. He personally supervises budgeting and capital expenditures for each operating area.

Mr. Hopkins receives several monthly reports. These include sales summary data and

**EXHIBIT 3**  PENTRON
Description of Management Personnel

Name: Robert L. Hopkins
Title: President
Age: 58
Education: B.S. Business Administration, University of Washington, 1950.
Background: Worked in his father's wholesale grocery business for several
            years; commissioned as Army officer in 1954, advancing to grade
            of full colonel; retired from Army, 1965; took over father's grocery
            business, sold grocery firm, and purchased PENTRON, 1971.
Duties: Development of overall company policy.


Name: Paul R. Hoffman
Title: Vice-President in charge of Sales
Age: 46
Education: Completed high school, two years of college.
Background: Commissioned in U.S. Army, 1962, served in Mr. Hopkins' unit;
            began work as salesman for Mr. Hopkins' grocery business in
            1976, advancing to account executive in 1976; became part-
            owner and vice-president of PENTRON, 1980.
Duties: Sales promotion, customer relations.


Name: Dwight W. Thomas
Title: Secretary-Treasurer, General Manager
Age: 42
Education: B.S., Business Administration, University of California.
Background: Worked as executive trainee in family's clothing business for three
            years starting in 1974, became assistant to president in 1967; left
            to become part owner and general manager, PENTRON, 1971.
Duties: Financial management; in charge of office, bookkeeping, and
        accounting staffs.


Name: Carl M. Davis
Title: Production Manager
Age: 36
Education: B.S., Industrial Arts Education, University of Wyoming.
Background: Taught high school 1969–1971; worked as production supervisor
            for plastics firm six years; came to PENTRON as molding
            supervisor in 1978; promoted to production manager in 1980.
Duties: Supervises mold design, production and assembly, purchasing.


Name: Brian L. Branson
Title: Sales Manager
Age: 39

*continued*

**EXHIBIT 3**　PENTRON (*Continued*)
Description of Management Personnel

Education: Completed one year of college.
Background: Worked as insurance salesman 1964–1966, became salesman,
　　　　　and later, jobber-distributor of miscellaneous hardware items; took
　　　　　over as sales manager at PENTRON in 1976.
Duties: Sales promotion, customer service, orders receipt and products
　　　　shipment.

Name: Roger A. Adams
Title: Controller
Age: 34
Education: B.S. Accounting, Pacific Lutheran College.
Background: Began working for national CPA firm, 1974, became chief
　　　　　accountant at PENTRON in 1977; named as controller in 1980.
Duties: Financial management and control, preparation of internal and external
　　　　financial reports.

Name: Mary Gordon
Title: Personnel Manager
Age: 54
Education: High school and one year secretarial school.
Background: Began as a clerk in the Hopkins' grocery store; hired as office
　　　　　manager when PENTRON began in 1971; became personnel
　　　　　manager in 1980.
Duties: Hiring, training, benefits, and personnel record keeping.

records of orders-on-hand, shipments, backlogs, and inventory. Balance sheets and income statements, with cumulative totals compared with last year to-date are received monthly. Mr. Hoffman and Mr. Thomas both receive these same reports.

A summary of the backgrounds and duties of the other officials of PENTRON as gathered by the casewriter is given in Exhibit 3.

## HUMAN RESOURCES AT PENTRON

PENTRON employs approximately 425 employees, most of whom are engaged in production activities. Nearly 90 percent of the work force is female. About 40 percent of the production employees have a high school diploma. The work at PENTRON involves mainly unskilled tasks, with the exception of some craftwork in the tool rooms and in the molding process.

Mrs. Mary Gordon has the title of personnel manager. Mrs. Gordon has worked for Mr. Hopkins for many years. She is in charge of hiring and training workers, administering benefits, and other record-keeping and administrative tasks associated with personnel management. Most personnel policies are set by members of the management committee. Grievances are normally handled by the line supervisors, but in some instances are brought to the attention of top management.

Mr. Gordon considers personnel relations to be quite good, pointing out that the company is genuinely interested in the personal and work problems of the employees and that it attempts to solve or accommodate these problems whenever possible. She cited as an example the lenience which PENTRON displays toward absenteeism. ("Many of the girls have young chilflen. We accept the fact that they need to be absent more than usual.")

One employee recalled that several years ago there was a general feeling that there was too much favoritism involved in selecting employees for promotion. Formerly, the three owners of the business had been known to suggest to the line supervisors that a certain employee be advanced or given a particular job. The worker added that now that the plant has become unionized, this is no longer a problem, since promotions are determined by seniority. In 1980, all production employees were organized under Machinist's Local 1208.

Most of the persons the casewriter talked to seemed to think that employee turnover is the greatest personnel problem. For the past several years, the turnover figure has remained at approximately 25 percent. Mrs. Gordon says that the main reason for such a high turnover is the fact that many of the employees leave to have children, or as their husbands transfer or change jobs. Others, she says, regard their jobs as temporary from the beginning. Mrs. Gordon does not believe that very many resignations result from grievances or complaints about working conditions, since the union has reported very few such complaints. Mr. Davis said that turnover is not a serious problem as far as he is concerned, since most production jobs do not involve extensive training.

The pay schedule for nonskilled work starts at $4.19 per hour, with a 30 cent raise after the initial six weeks. Leadmen can earn up to $5.65 per hour. There is no piece-rate incentive. Wage and salaries for many personnel are given in Exhibit 4.

**EXHIBIT 4**  California Pen and Pencil Company Wage and Salary Scale

| Position | Annual Salary/Wage |
| --- | --- |
| President | $90,000 |
| Vice-President, Sales | 55,500 |
| Secretary-Treasurer, General Manager | 55,500 |
| Controller | 28,000 |
| Production Manager | 21,200 |
| Sales Manager | 22,000 |
| Personnel Manager | 17,500 |
| Production Supervisors | 14,100–15,500 |
| Sales Representatives | 14,000–17,000 (straight salary) |
| Mold Designer | 14,600 |
| Molding Supervisor | 13,500 |
| Production Employees | 4.19–5.65/hr. |
| Secretarial-Clerical Personnel | 4.00–4.29/hr. |

## MANUFACTURING PENS AND PENCILS

The casewriter next wanted to examine the production facilities and manufacturing team at PENTRON. He first interviewed a frustrated production manager and supervisors. First he talked to Mr. Davis.

### Life in the Pen Factory

In a frank interview, Mr. Davis described his personal dilemma at PENTRON:

In many respects, the story of my last five years here at PENTRON is a story of disappointment and frustration. I was initially attracted to PENTRON in 1978 because it was a fairly small company—seemingly the environment that would enable a person such as myself to grow and acquire responsibility. For the first two years everything went well and I was optimistic about my future here at PENTRON. Then in 1980 Mr.

Jackson, our production manager, resigned suddenly and I took over the job. It was my dream come true, or at least, so I thought. I was unaware that Mr. Jackson had been having a number of difficulties with the owners, as indeed, did his predecessor; but I thought that I had the temperament and ability to stay out of that kind of trouble.

So what happened? Well, very soon I found that although I have considerable authority and flexibility, so does everyone else. I issue directives and someone else—I'm speaking mainly of the three ex-owners—comes along and countermands them and issues his own. The result is that neither I nor anyone in my department knows just where we stand. Furthermore, nothing is ever in writing. The orders that bypass me are verbal, so I don't get a memo, and oftentimes, cannot verify them.

In many respects, my authority is very strictly circumscribed. For instance, I cannot approve new mold designs. This has to be done by the management committee. The same thing holds true for major equipment acquisitions, or even major repairs. The result is that I spend a great deal of time running around trying to get approval for these things. This can be difficult, since no one is even around here any more. Mr. Thomas is the only person you can depend on to show up regularly. Mr. Hopkins and Mr. Hoffman are only here a few hours a week anymore, it seems. A lot of important matters, such as new product development, are being largely ignored. I certainly can't do anything about it. Even if I had the authority, my hands are completely tied by day-to-day considerations.

Of course, the fact that Hopkins and Hoffman are seldom here anymore has its side benefits. For one thing, they're not in my hair as much. Things go more smoothly when they're gone. None of the former owners has much of a feel for production. The management process here is not one of consulting and supplying technical expertise, but one of meddling and being preoccupied with everyone else's job.

Mr. Davis philosophized about the company's current state of affairs. He stated that, in his opinion, the underlying cause of many of the problems he mentioned is that PENTRON has outgrown its organizational structure. He feels that whereas informal relationships and overlapping responsibilities may have been desirable when the firm was smaller, this type of organization is now causing the company to become bogged down. He would like to see more standing rules and procedures, a better-defined line of authority, and clear job descriptions. He said that he is still in favor of the management committee arrangement, but not as it presently exists. He remarked that it very seldom meets (about once every two weeks), and that when it does, he is not made to feel like a full member.

Further, Mr. Davis feels that the decision-making process is hampered by conservative and indecisive decision making on the part of the three ex-owners. He stated flatly that most new ideas come from him and other members of middle management, and that the committee is therefore reluctant to accept them. He sees very little evidence that long-range planning is being done.

"I'm telling you these things not in order to sabotage anyone," Mr. Davis ended by saying, "but in the hopes that something can be done about the situation. If the people at Painter really knew what was going on around here, some changes would be made. I just hope I'm around to see these changes. I don't think I can live with the situation as it exists much longer."

The casewriter next examined the facilities and factory available to produce PENTRON products. He was escorted through the plant by Mr. Thomas. But the casewriter returned to talk to Mr. Davis and others after the tour.

## Pen Manufacturing

The company's products are manufactured in a two-story building of 110,000 square feet. The first floor contains office space, employees' rest area, space for storing material and finished goods, and docking areas. All manufacturing facilities are on the second floor. Major plant and equipment additions were made in 1975

($504,000), 1978 ($1,092,000), and 1980 ($914,400).

According to Mr. Davis, the production process is fairly simple. The pens and pencils are made of plastic, which is formed in high-pressure injection molds. The advertising names and slogans are then imprinted on the products through a heat-printing process. The metal parts are machined in another area of the plant and are assembled along with the plastic components on the final assembly benches.

There are four final assembly lines, which means that three different styles of pens and one style of pencil may be produced at any one time. The ink ball and cartridge, or refill mechanism for the ball-point pens, is purchased from another manufacturer under contract. PENTRON makes all of its own parts for mechanical pencils.

Presently, PENTRON produces from between 90,000 to 102,000 units per day. Mr. Davis estimates that total production capacity is approximately 110,000 units. "At our present rate of growth, I estimate that we will need additional capacity within eighteen months," he said. He stated that any further extension of capacity will require building expansion.

Mr. Davis claims that most of the production processes and machinery used represent the current state of the art in the business and are highly efficient. But he is quick to admit that production operations do not flow as smoothly as he would like. He blames part of the problem on production scheduling:

> Production scheduling is really complicated because of the wide variety of styles and designs we produce. Ideally, we can run together several orders back-to-back which call for essentially the same style of pen or pencil. This cuts down on unnecessary changes in molds, equipment, and procedures. But we're limited by our production schedule, since we usually have deadlines to meet on our shipments. An order averages 10–14 days in process, which gives us very little flexibility on rush jobs.

In the early days of the company's history, production scheduling became such a problem that customer relations deteriorated because of late shipments. According to Mr. Davis, the sales department had almost complete control over scheduling and rushed some orders through to curry the favor of certain customers. Other orders were set aside, deadlines were not met, and production efficiency suffered. "Mr. Hoffman knew about these goings-on," Mr. Davis told the casewriter, "but he just turned his head and looked the other way. The salesmen kept running things because they knew they could get by with it."

Then, in 1981, the company programmed its newly acquired computer to keep track of production. The computer is used to facilitate scheduling by keeping the department up-to-date on the orders in process, printing out daily reports on the status of each order. The computer also reports on any order which has been delayed in the production process or which is late in shipment.

Mr. Davis feels that some important advantages have accrued from the computer reports. He said, " . . . For the first time we are able to determine the actual status of orders in process. But we still could improve. The next step is to have the computer actually perform the scheduling operations."

As the casewriter probed further into the production area, we talked to others who had more to say about problems in production scheduling.

One of the most vocal was Mr. Walton, a production supervisor. Mr. Walton complained that the schedules are always changing, and that many times change notices are received after the molds have already been set and other tooling modifications made. Mr. Walton is convinced that production schedules are still being unduly influenced by the sales department, and cited one instance where Mr. Hoffman personally initiated a change order without either Mr. Branson's or Mr. Davis's knowledge.

Mr. Bass, a molding supervisor, told the casewriter that his men are repeatedly having to readjust the settings on the molding machines, a practice which causes frequent broken molds and damaged production due to overheating. He claims that mold changes can be cut in half if production schedules are properly arranged.

Mr. Bass and Mr. Walton both agree that the lack of formal procedures in the area of production control is partly responsible for some of the problems that occur. They believe that there is some confusion about who can make changes in the production schedule and when such changes can or should be made.

Prior to visiting with the marketing department, the casewriter consulted the literature, visited some specialty jobbers, and in general tried to find out what he could about the business. Some of what he learned is discussed next.

## THE SPECIALTY BUSINESS

The advertising specialty industry is large and fast-growing. In 1982, the dollar sales in this field exceeded an estimated $2 billion. The industry's growth can be seen when one realizes that sales in 1972 were $800 million and in 1961 were $435 million.

Advertising specialties are used by practically all types of business concerns to promote the firm's name and build goodwill among its customers. The articles used as advertising specialties include calendars, ash trays, paperweights, cigarette lighters, yardsticks, matchbooks, and many others. Advertising specialties are chosen by their customers because they can be used very flexibly: specific items can be sent to particular customers in a very personalized way. Specialty advertising also has the advantage that it serves as a lasting reminder to the customer. For a few cents, a seller can give an item that will be used and seen repeatedly for months or perhaps years. Some items, such as a clock in a retail store, may receive constant

exposure to large numbers of people. This form of advertising may be particularly useful to the small business which cannot afford mass advertising.

PENTRON has found that its sales are greater whenever the specialty has a "tie in"—a relationship between the product given and the giver. For example, a pen might be given to dealers by a wholesaler bearing the inscription, "You'll write up more sales with XYZ products!"

Experts contend that specialties serve the following marketing functions:

Cultivate known prospects
Regain old friends
Promote frequent contacts
    A fire brick manufacturer used three ideas—first a neat pocket lighter; second, playing cards; and third, heavy ashtrays, sending them to contractors who specify materials.
Attract consumers
Repeat the company's sales message
    A Chicago neighborhood florist started with the use of a monthly calendar some fifteen months ago. Today he is using seven times as many as at first in addition to leaving two decks of playing cards on each table in the home of customers who have ordered their party floral decorations from him. Wedding decorations and floral orders have come from his circle of buyers.
Gain children's support of a trademarked product
Introduce new brands and new products
Make a trademark a household word
Repeat and impress sales messages
Open doors for salesmen
Offer appreciation for past order
Reward trade loyalty
Attract new sales
    A manufacturer of castings started using 100 billfolds of excellent leather which carried a catchy advertisement. In the

second year he used a far larger number of billfolds, and added seasonable greetings cards, leather memo pads, and key cases. In some of his customers' plants he supplied the drinking cups. He uses 5,000 and they go to every logical prospect.

Aid in checking mail advertising

A chemical manufacturer places a novel name and phone index on the desks of purchasing agents in all prospect plants within a radius of 150 miles.

Repeat and obtain more consideration for the salesman's message

Keep the company's name before logical prospects

Promote a product

Provide constant reminder—the intimate personal touch—throughout the year

A wire and rubber goods manufacturer has obtained wide attention with a miniature automobile-license keytag. More than 100,000 motorists have been supplied with these tags and chains. Each applicant gets a tag bearing his own license number with the state name and the state's own colors.

Impress a trade name

Advertise a trademark

Paint manufacturers have never found a substitute for the cotton cap for painters. Some caps are provided with visors—some merely skullcaps—with the name of the company boldly printed from the back.

Advertising specialties are dealer and agent goodwill builders.

Behr-Manning Corporation finds mechanical pencils valuable for use among dealers and jobbers who handle their products. One year its salesmen distributed 40,000 of them, as well as 34,000 small knife-sharpening stones by way of promoting the name Norton Abrasives. Pillsbury Flour salesmen through many years have given out pencils, one by one, to grocers and their employees.

Provide trademark reminders

Obtain remembrance

Build goodwill

Political convention and exposition goodwill is built through the use of metals, badges, name buttons, and a whole list of items which appear and are expected as part of the show.

PENTRON, with annual sales of approximately $8.5 million, accounts for only a small part of the total industry sales. The industry is composed primarily of small firms. PENTRON is the fifth-largest maker of specialty pens and pencils. Nearly two-thirds of the firm's sales are concentrated in the western half of the U.S., primarily in California, Oregon, Washington, and Texas. PENTRON products have been shipped to places throughout the continental United States and also to countries in South America, Europe, and Africa.

## PENTRON'S PRODUCT-MARKET SCOPE

PENTRON manufactures ball-point pens and mechanical pencils on a job-order basis for customers who wish to have their business name or advertising slogan placed on the writing instruments. Unlike some makers of specialty pens who purchase the basic product from another manufacturer and then make the inscription or perform other modifications, PENTRON does all of its own manufacturing.

Ideas for designing PENTRON pens and pencils come from several sources. Often, a customer will suggest a particular style pen that he would like to have made. It is then up to the company's designer, Mr. Rose, to make the idea work. After determining materials and molding specifications, Mr. Rose sends the design sheets to Mr. Davis, who estimates the cost of producing it and gives tentative approval. Or the customer will choose a line of pens or pencils which previously have been manufactured by PENTRON. Since the molds from past production runs are kept, this substantially lowers producing costs and reduces the price to the customer.

Mr. Branson said that the company's three primary requirements for design are that a pen must be useful, durable, and attractive.

"We don't go in for overly elaborate or highly unusual styles," Mr. Branson said.

> We want to develop products that will be useful and in good taste. Just to give you an example, we had a request the other day from a large tire distributor to make a pen with a model of their product—a tire—fastened to the top. It took a good deal of convincing and more than a little diplomacy to convince them that such a pen would not be desirable. But the fact is, it would have been looked at, put in a drawer, and never used. Why? Because it would have been too bulky; and further, it would look a little ridiculous for a store manager or executive to carry a pen like that in his pocket. So, we risked losing a sale, but feel that it was worth it. After all, our reputation and the success of our products is all that counts.

Mr. Branson credits much of the company's sales success to the designer, Mr. Rose. He said that Mr. Rose, who had been with PENTRON since the company began, has consistently come up with ideas that are original and appealing, and that he has a "good feel" for the technical considerations and costs involved in producing a given style.

## SALES MANAGEMENT AND MARKETING STRATEGY

Mr. Hoffman described how PENTRON'S marketing strategy developed.

> In the beginning we had two primary objectives: first, to gain as wide a market coverage as possible; and second, accomplish this at reasonable cost. We believed that the use of jobber-distributors would best fulfill these requirements. We

were not too concerned about launching a hard-sell, door-do-door campaign, simply because the idea of using advertising specialties already had wide acceptance among our potential customers. We felt that it was a matter of pricing under our competition and delivering a product of high quality. As the record shows, our strategy worked out pretty well.

Mr. Hoffman stated that PENTRON now uses over 400 jobbers located throughout the country. Many of these jobbers also carry other lines of advertising specialties, including competitors' pens and pencils.

PENTRON also began running advertisements in various retailing and trade magazines. It was the response to these ads that convinced management that jobbers alone were not adequate to handle a large market segment: the small business. So in 1975, the company started its own sales representative organization. The sales representatives, who now number fourteen, are to meet the service requirements of customers who respond to the company's advertisements. They sit down with the customer and help make decisions regarding style, quality, and quantity; then they relay this information to the production department. The percentage of sales accounted for by sales representatives has been steadily rising and now exceeds 40 percent of total sales.

Both Mr. Hopkins and Mr. Hoffman make it a point to maintain personal contact with some of the very large accounts. This includes, for example, a large insurance company which places a sizable order each year with PENTRON.

### Pricing at PENTRON

The prices of pens and pencils offered by PENTRON range from $.22 to $1.49. Prices depend upon materials used, the style of the pen, and order quantities. Pens having unusual features such as elaborate retracting mechanisms, oil-filled or clear tops for displaying clients' products, etc., are generally more costly. On very large orders, companies often solicit bids from several pen manufacturers. Generally, prices are lower when bids are used.

PENTRON has a discount system of pricing, with discounts ranging from 35–50% depending on the size and type of order. The jobbers and their salesmen split the discounted amount according to their own prearrangements. Terms for payment are 2%, ten days; net, sixty days.

Mr. Hoffman stated that the use of jobbers throws the company into direct competition with other makers of advertising specialties. "That's why," he said, "I feel that price, design, and quality factors are so important."

> And, I might add, we've been extremely competitive in this regard. One reason we've done so well has to do with our size. We're small enough that we can easily tailor our services to meet the desires of our customers. We're more flexible than the larger pen companies who do some advertising imprinting only as a sideline. But we're large enough to produce efficiently and undercut some of the smaller firms on price. If we ever lose our price advantage, we could be in trouble.

Mr. Hoffman claims that much of PENTRON's competition comes not from other pen and pencil makers, but from other types of specialty advertising products. He said that in many instances a jobber or salesman handles a full line of specialty items made by various manufacturers. Thus, PENTRON's products must compete with the others for the customer's time and attention. The salesman is apt to push hardest the product carrying the greatest discount or commission. "This is undoubtedly the weak link in our marketing setup," Mr. Hoffman conceded, "but it doesn't appear that this has had much of an effect on sales."

Mr. Hoffman believes that the rising GNP over the years has contributed to PENTRON's sales growth, but emphasized that sales are not directly related to the state of the economy. He recalled instances where sales actually rose during economic slumps. He feels that this might be explained by the possibility that companies cut down on their advertising expenditures during lean years, putting more dollars into the less expensive media such as advertising specialties.

"And," he concluded, "our strategy has worked where it counts the most: the order books. Look at the figures." He handed the casewriter sales figures since 1971.

| Year | Sales($) |
|------|----------|
| 1971 | 1,454,249 |
| 1972 | 2,448,427 |
| 1973 | 3,008,760 |
| 1974 | 3,393,521 |
| 1975 | 3,889,088 |
| 1976 | 4,357,280 |
| 1977 | 4,783,876 |
| 1978 | 5,285,381 |
| 1979 | 5,875,693 |
| 1980 | 6,575,014 |
| 1981 | 7,251,738 |
| 1982 | 7,850,567 |
| 1983 | 8,195,974 |
| 1984 | 8,525,716 |

## A DISSENTING VIEW

Not everyone in marketing agreed with Mr. Hoffman's enthusiastic report as an interview with Mr. Branson revealed.

"There's just no room for creativity in this company," Mr. Branson complained to the casewriter one day. "New ideas are not invited, but are seen as a threat. First, let me dispel any ideas that you may have received that participative management exists here at PENTRON." He continued,

> Oh, yes, we have our committee meetings, and supposedly everyone is to contribute their ideas and participate in making decisions. On the surface, this is the way it appears. But in reality, there is very little about these committee meetings that could be considered democratic. In the first place, in order to have an idea accepted you

must somehow convince the three men at the top that the idea is theirs, not your own. In other words, you have to dangle the light in front of their eyes so that they can see it, but you can't say that you saw it first. Some people around here haven't gotten around to learning this, and have absorbed all their time and energy trying to go through this barrier rather than around it. Davis is an example of what I am talking about. His ideas are good, but he tries to force them on Hopkins and the others all at once instead of spoon-feeding them a bit at a time. Now he's gun-shy. He seldom makes suggestions for fear of being shot down. Several others have developed more or less of a pipeline which works much of the time. Basically, it works like this: First, suggestions are fed to me, and then I relay them to Dwight Thomas. Dwight, who is generally fairly receptive, then brings up these matters with the others. A specific proposal is then initiated at the next committee meeting, and we rubber-stamp it. It's a long, time-consuming process, but it often works.

Mr. Branson talked about what he termed the "stagnation" of the company's product and promotion policies. He said that he felt that the company's reaction to the market has been sluggish at times. He cited as an example PEN-TRON's delay in introducing a fiber-tip pen. Mr. Branson foresaw the trend to this type of pen as early as 1976, but was not able to convince management of its potential until late 1979. By this time, important sales had been lost, he felt. PENTRON began tooling up for a fiber-tip pen, and was producing limited quantities in early 1982 with full output capabilities in 1983.

Mr. Hickson is now concerned that PEN-TRON is not moving fast enough to keep pace with the future. He stated;

> Management may be disillusioning itself into thinking that we are doing better than we really are. Oh, yes, sales are still rising and profitability is good. But where are we in relation to the rest of the market? Are we getting more or less of the market share? It is a fact that sales

are a little harder to come by than they once were. For instance, we're relying more and more on our sales representative and less on jobbers. But is this due to a tightening market situation or is it because of a change in customer buying patterns? This we don't know.

Mr. Branson went on to say that he thinks PENTRON should consider broadening its product line to include other advertising specialties. He pointed out that the molding machines used in making pens could be easily converted to make plastic articles such as icescrapers, flyswatters, and other items. He feels that it would benefit the company to have a complete line of specialty items marketed through company-paid salesmen.

He concluded:

> We've been very successful so far. I have to credit much of this success to Hopkins, who smelled a very hot opportunity in this business and followed through with action. But now that we're well established and doing well, the prevailing attitude seems to be, "don't anyone move because it worked before and it is working now." I don't think we can afford this kind of complacency. We need to step back and examine our position, and come up with some concrete objectives.

## A FINAL VISIT WITH MR. HOPKINS

As the casewriter finished his last interview and was wrapping up his study, he stopped by Mr. Hopkins' office for a final chat:

"Well, I hope you got some feel for how we operate around here," Mr. Hopkins said. "The flexibility of our management structure has been the secret of our success. I very much hope that Mr. Painter will retain the best features of our organization."

The casewriter asked Mr. Hopkins about his personal plans. He replied,

> I guess you might call me a builder. I like to start an organization from the ground up—to nurture it and watch it grow. Now that PEN-

TRON has become firmly established as a success, I'm interested in starting over again. Just what it will be I don't know. Right now I'm waiting for the same kind of opportunity that will give me the potential I had with the company. But meanwhile, I'm conmitted to PENTRON. Perhaps I'm a little like a proud father who, after raising and protecting his child, is watching it make its way into the world on its own. I'm doing everything I can to make that transition an easy one.

The casewriter is now wondering what he should report to Mr. Painter.

# 17

# THE TURCO STORY

**Lawrence R. Jauch**

*Southern Illinois University-Carbondale*

## EARLY DEVELOPMENT (1945–1969)

Turco Manufacturing Company was formed in 1945 as a manufacturer of outdoor gym sets. The company was originally owned by Sam Turken and his four sons, and was located in St. Louis, Missouri. Robert E. Feigenbaum, David Turken's son-in-law, came to the firm in its early years and was to become its president in the years to come.

In September 1959, Turco moved its operation to DuQuoin, Illinois, due to a desire to reduce labor costs resulting from escalating contracts with the machinists union in St. Louis, and to acquire a larger facility with room for future expansion. Interestingly, Turco encouraged the formation of another union in Du-Quoin (then called the Laborers International Union of North America) which was less antagonistic than the machinists.

Turco began selling a large portion of its playground equipment to Sears in 1956. This was to become a large and important relationship for the company. Its first year in DuQuoin, sales were about $2 million, and over the next ten years, sales expanded to $10 million.

Turco had an expensive strategic learning experience when it made a move to acquire the American Toy Company, a Massachusetts company, in early 1962. Top management and operations were moved to Sesser, Illinois, and Kinder Toy Products, a subsidiary of Turco, was formed. The intent was to expand the children's toy products line. American Toy Products produced wood toys, as well as table and chair sets for young children. It seemed at the time to be a natural extension of the product line. However, consumer demand for wood products of this nature was declining. Further, Turco did not possess woodworking skills or experience. In November of 1964, after almost 3 years of operations, the decision was made to close Kinder Toys due to low volume and lack of profitability. By this time Mr. Feigenbaum had become Vice President and General Manager of Turco.

In late 1964, the decision was made to produce steel ladders and slides for swimming pools. In this case, there was greater synergy in the manufacturing process than in the case of wood products. The fabrication of steel tubing used in the production of playground equipment was similar to the kinds of equipment, processes, and labor skills used in the production of slides and ladders.

There was yet another strategic decision made in 1964 regarding the possible opening of a new plant in California. At the time, 35 percent of Turco's sales of playground equipment to Sears went to the west coast. In the years before, Sears had four suppliers of swing sets: Turco in the Midwest, Hedstrom in Alabama, Southern California Pipe and Supply in the West, and a supplier on the east coast. The west coast supplier had a falling out with Sears and decided to close. Sears had approached Turco in need of increased suppliers of the equipment, and Turco was able to supply more and more of the necessary goods. Now Sears wanted Turco to open a plant in California to facilitate ever-increasing sales in that area. A careful study

Editor's note: Bruce Stocco assisted in gathering information and transcribing tape recordings with key executives, and preparing the first draft of the case.

was made including the hiring of a factory location search firm, since the transportation of bulk items like steel tubing was a significant cost factor. The prohibitively high cost of transporting the raw materials needed (steel tubing) from the East and Midwest where it is produced, as well as high overhead and startup costs, were believed to outweigh the benefits of opening the new plant, so the plans were scrapped. Turco would continue to produce the swing sets in DuQuoin and then ship them to the west coast distribution centers that Sears operated.

By 1965, Turco had become a favored source of supply for Sears. From 50 to 60 percent of Turco's output was distributed to Sears at the time. Sears was rapidly expanding in hard goods in the 1960s and this favored relationship led to expansion at Turco.

In addition to swing sets and pool equipment, Sears urged Turco to supply bar stools and steel tube folding outdoor clothes dryers. The DuQuoin plant was expanded about 55 percent and the payroll was doubled to accommodate producing these new products. Partial financing for this expansion was the rollover of a nine-year note from local residents and businessmen. A total of $160,000 in 10-year notes at 6 1/4 percent interest were subscribed by the community. About this time, Dave Turken, one of the founder's sons, became Chairman of the Board, Mr. Feigenbaum became President, Charles Bookstaver was hired as Executive Vice President and Operations Manager, Irv Korte was named Vice President of Sales, and Duane Olson was named Secretary and Controller. Mr. Korte was hired specifically to expand sales of the non-Sears products.

In June 1969, a tornado knocked down a wall at the DuQuoin plant; luckily no one was hurt and production and distribution was minimally affected. The following month, Turco received an award from Sears for excellence in product quality and operations management. The award was prestigious in that only 300 of Sears' 20,000 suppliers received such recognition on the basis of quality of products, on-time delivery, cost control, and superior operations and employee management. Of greater importance, the award signified the increasing warmth and appreciation Sears had for Turco. This relationship with Sears would prove to be even more profitable, because increased demand for bar stools dictated further expansion. In late July 1969, Christopher Industries opened in Christopher, Illinois, in order to sell bar stool seats to Turco. The sole stockholder in Christopher Industries was Turco. By December 1969, sales of Turco had reached about $10 million, with profits of about $256,000, on a firm whose net worth was around $600,000. Turco employed about 600 people, and they had just finished negotiating their third 3-year contract with what had become the Laborers International Union Local 799.

## THE MATTEL DEBACLE (1969–1973)

In the late 1960s, with a booming economy, a wave of conglomerate mergers had become the corporate fad. Mattel was caught up in the feverish expansion. In June of 1969, they had bought Metaframe Company for $27 million in Mattel stock, and had built a new plant in Canada. Sales at Mattel had grown to $210 million and profits were $7.4 million in the fiscal year ending in February 1969. The company's earnings were growing at a brisk 40 percent, and their stock price was up 10 times the 1966 level. They were the darlings of Wall Street, and expanding quickly. One of the firms Mattel was interested in was Turco. After 8 or 9 months of negotiations Turco agreed to an exchange of stock with Mattel. In early 1970, Mattel traded approximately 53,000 shares of their stock worth $3.5 million in exchange for all of Turco's stock. Before this time Turco stock was divided as follows: Mr. and Mrs. Feigenbaum owned one-sixth, one-third was owned by David Turken, and one-sixth of the shares were owned by each of his three brothers. Mr. Feigenbaum indicated that the family believed the financial gains possible in this agreement would outweigh their loss of control of the business. Besides, the Turkens had indicated that they were ready to retire. While Mr. Feigenbaum personally opposed the move, the stock exchange was made. The president of Mattel, Ruth Handler, had personally assured Mr. Feigenbaum that the present top management would still continue to operate the company, but would now report to Mattel. Mrs. Handler also confided to Mr. Feigenbaum that without his personal approval, Mattel would not go through with the transaction. Mr. Feigenbaum agreed to the transaction because the company's founder, his father-in-law, wanted to make the sale.

Turco retained essentially the same management team after the takeover with Mr. Feigenbaum remaining as President. But a new Vice President of Operations was appointed from Mattel. The new executive was given control of all manufacturing and purchasing operations. In addition, Mr. Charles W. Bookstaver, who had been Vice President for Operations, was appointed as Director of Marketing.

In 1970, Mr. Feigenbaum issued a press release indicating that sales were terrible, but he expected improvement with the economy. In spite of poor sales during the winter, Turco still managed to make a small profit that year. Early 1971 saw a series of mishaps in the plant. In late January and early February, fires broke out in the paint booth operation. The labor force was also becoming a problem as dissatisfied employees demanded more of their union during labor contract negotiations. The negotiations broke down in July and 230 union workers went on strike. Twenty days later the union narrowly passed a new 3-year contract which called for the termination of the current piecework incentive system in exchange for higher hourly wages. Even though Sears had given Turco its third consecutive excellence award, a new record for Sears suppliers, sales and productivity began to plummet, and profits were down again.

In June 1972, Turco experienced another fire in the paint booth. By November, Mr.

Bookstaver had resigned. Meanwhile, with reduction in sales, employment had dropped to about 250. In mid-1973, Sam Easterly, Director of Industrial Relations, issued a press release that production levels should be back to normal in the near future.

But Mr. Feigenbaum was of the opinion that the Mattel purchase and management influence seriously jeopardized the future of Turco. For example, Mattel established a profit goal of $550,000 for Turco in 1970. When Mr. Feigenbaum indicated that actual profits were only in the $350,000 to $375,000 range, Mattel management refused to accept this figure. Meanwhile, Mattel itself was beginning to suffer from its acquisition binge.

In the early 1970s, Mattel suffered huge losses as well as a scandal that later led to the indictment of one of its founders for fraud and false financial reporting. Mattel was forced to sell its Ringling Brothers Barnum and Bailey Combined Shows, Inc., along with several other of its subsidiaries, including Turco manufacturing, in order to raise cash to meet a $32 million payment on a $100 million long-term bank debt. Four years to the day of the Mattel takeover, Mr. Feigenbaum negotiated a buyback agreement with Mattel. The Mattel marriage had gone on the rocks, and Mr. and Mrs. Feigenbaum became substantial owners of the restructured Turco. At the time of the transaction, sales had dropped to $12 million, and the company had suffered a $1.5 million loss.

## THE SEARCH FOR A NEW STRATEGY (1974–1979)

After the buy-back from Mattel, Mr. Feigenbaum's main objective was to regain control of the company and to make a profit. In 1974, the productivity of the company was low, but they still managed to make a profit. They had begun to search for new products, and in May 1975, Turco purchased the tools, dies, machinery, and equipment to manufacture gas and electric barbecue grills from Armco Recreational Products

Company of Denver, Colorado. Mr. Feigenbaum would later say, "it was the perfect product for us—it was an established growing market; it was a bulk, high-ticket item, the kind of thing we were accustomed to doing; and it was a non-Sears item, which also made it desirable."

In addition to the barbecue grills, Turco also decided to produce juvenile furniture. The furniture was made of rugged steel tubing, with baked enamel finish. It had padded chairs with vinyl tops, which were supplied by Christopher Industries, which by now had become a wholly owned subsidiary of Turco. The furniture was marketed through such stores as J.C. Penney, Montgomery Ward, and K-Mart. By the end of 1975, Turco had two new products in production, but profits were down from the previous year, possibly due to the recession.

From the onset of 1976, it looked like it was going to be a spectacular year for Turco. However, in February and March there were fires in the paint booths and production was at the seasonal peak in anticipation of increased sales of the new product lines. In June the labor union approved a new 3-year contract after long negotiations. It was also at that time that the first of the new gas grill line was being purchased by customers from the retail outlets, and sales were brisk. By year end, it was clear that the gas grill line was a great success. Turco had projected $4.7 million in sales for the grills, but had realized $7.5 million. Profits in 1976 were the highest in the history of the company.

By 1977, sales of folding outdoor clothes dryers had dropped off at Sears, so Turco decided to discontinue that product. Sales for the new grill would more than make up for the lost volume. But there was growing concern over the increasing cost of steel tubing used to produce the other products. Inflation was rising, and the company had no control over the cost of the steel tubing, and thus minimal control over the cost of their products. In mid-1977, Turco responded to these influences by purchasing two mills to produce their own tubular

steel. Sales for 1977 were up once again, but profits didn't keep pace with this growth.

1978 was another year of expansion into new products. Sears had contacted Turco and asked them to produce weight-lifting benches. Sears was experiencing trouble with their supplier, and Turco was approached because of the past history of reliability as well as the synergy of the benches with other Turco/Sears products. Also, during this time, three models of Speed Scooters were introduced. A major reason given for adding scooters was to use excess plant capacity and to cover some of the fixed overhead. Turco ran a test marketing survey for the scooters, and only 115 units of an initial inventory of over 500 were sold. But management believed that with proper promotion and a price reduction, the line would sell well, even though profit margins would be low. In addition, the Champion batting line was introduced. It consisted of a plastic baseball on a cord connected to a stake placed in the ground. With all the additions of new products, sales volume went up again. But profit was once again decreasing.

1979 was to be one of the most painful years in the history of Turco. There were fires in the paint booth in February and March once again. Another tragedy occurred when a man fell to his death in the plant warehouse. Overall labor relations were strained, but a contract was approved without a strike. Further, it was becoming increasingly clear that the seasonal nature of the entire product line was causing great difficulty. Production peaked in Fall through February, followed by level production through May. But May to September production was very low, and as a result layoffs were the norm. The company's plant was also a real problem. Productivity had fallen to the point where costs were rising uncontrollably. Mr. Feigenbaum stated, "It got to the point where the plant was running us, we weren't running the plant." Another major problem was the profit margin on the product lines. Turco was unaware of which products were making money, but it was clear that some products had very low or no profit margin. The company was growing very quickly, as sales rose from $12 million the first year after Mattel to $34 million 5 years later. But as the sales volume went up, the profit results were getting worse. The company also had cash flow problems due to low profitability. This led to problems with the banks who gave them credit and the confidence in Turco was diminishing quickly. The year-end results for 1979 were terrible; Turco had a substantial loss.

## THE TURNAROUND (1980–1982)

Mr. Feigenbaum began to worry about the future for Turco. Volume was up, but profits kept dropping and cash flow and bank relationships were strained. He called in Jerry Goldress, a turnaround specialist based in Encino, California. The two of them began to look at the company's strengths and weaknesses. Rather than examine the business as a whole, they broke it down into its component parts and analyzed them individually. In so doing, Feigenbaum and Goldress discovered that quite a few of the products that Turco was manufacturing were profitable. However, they learned that quite a few others were costing them money to make. Some of Turco's customers were valuable; again, others were costing them money.

In 1979, Turco had six product lines, two of which—the backyard playground equipment and the gas barbecue grills—were responsible for 95 percent of sales. The playground equipment had been Turco's bread and butter for years, but the industry as a whole had declined by nearly 50 percent during the 1970s. Turco felt they would have to become an industry leader to remain in the business, so they cut prices. Volume grew, but profit margins shrank. In 1979, this line comprised 35 percent of Turco's business, but was a loser as a whole.

However, when the playground line was analyzed, Turco discovered that it wasn't a total loss. Sears and K-Mart, their two biggest customers, were buying over 80 percent of Turco's

playground equipment; the other customers were creating more headaches than profits.

In addition to their two main lines, Turco had four minor products that were accounting for 5 percent of their business. Of these, only the weight benches, which they manufactured on an ongoing contract basis for Sears, were profitable. The others—the baseball batting practice game, bar-type counterstools, and scooters—comprised only 2 percent of Turco's sales and were losers. In some instances, Turco had failed to recognize the nature of competition. Mr. Feigenbaum indicated they were up against "garage shop operations"—competitors who had small operations and low overhead who could produce these types of products much more cheaply than Turco.

More importantly, they recognized the folly of the "volume game." "When there's an oversupply in the industry and you're scratching for volume, you sometimes take on things that you shouldn't," says Feigenbaum. "A customer would say, 'Make an item special for me.' We would make it for him, and he would say, 'I'm going to use 2,000 pieces.' He'd end up using 1,000 and wouldn't take the other 1,000. What can you do? You can't go out and sue everybody you do business with."

So Turco had a huge inventory of playground equipment which they couldn't sell to their bulk buyers because each lot was a little different from the next. Turco decided to get out of the playground equipment business, except for Sears and K-Mart, and determined to concentrate on their gas grill line, which they had first marketed in 1975 and which seemed to have the best future.

At that time, gas grills represented 65 percent of the company's business, and the line had become very broad. Turco was manufacturing several different sizes of these grills and was making several different models in each size. When this product line was segmented, Turco again found that some models had to go.

"One of the major problems a manufacturing company has is the proliferation of their product lines, and Turco's gas grill line was a good example of that," says Goldress. "They had too many different models within each basic size. That's expensive, and that makes you the high-cost producer. The reason they were doing it," he continued, "is that everybody wanted a grill that was a little bit different from their competition's. Turco found, through experience, that they really couldn't afford to do that, so they eliminated a lot of special models. They went more to basic, standard models."

Turco cut back on the losers. Their sales volume dropped in 1980, yet they made a profit that was large enough to offset the previous year's loss. In 1981, their volume started to grow once again, but this time, profits rose as volume did. New operations and finance managers were hired to regain control of the factory and the financial position of the firm.

Turco began to control inventories and lower its costs considerably as a result. Control over purchasing, manufacturing, and sales was restored. A new union labor contract, partially federally mediated, was accepted. Turco offered few concessions and the union accepted less than the usual 8 to 10 percent wage increase. While these were obviously important to the turnaround, Mr. Goldress offered another viewpoint—"If you were to ask me what the real key to the turnaround was, the key was that they went from being a manufacturing company in philosophy to a method-of-distribution-type company." Turco found that although they billed themselves as manufacturers, their true strength lay in their ability to sell. They had a sound marketing program; they had a good knowledge of their market and very good sales representatives. Turco turned their approach around. Rather than sell only products that they could manufacture, they began to look for new products that they could sell successfully, whether they manufactured them or not. "We said, 'You know something? This was a mistake from the beginning,'" Feigenbaum recalls.

"We're like a fish out of water. We're in a business we're not really in. We got out of that. We took our licking and walked away from it. They were taking our attention away from someplace it should have been."

By 1981, Turco had stabilized and was making a good profit. They then put the new strategy to work. Turco managers went to Japan and worked with Toshiba to help them create the first portable kerosene heaters to be Underwriters Laboratories approved, and then began to import them. Turco paid $550,000 for a DuQuoin building for warehouse space, hired 40 new people to assemble and package the product, and became exclusive U.S. distributors for the Toshiba heaters with the Turco label. The kerosene heaters caught on quickly in the United States and just as quickly became Turco's biggest product, accounting for about 60 percent of total sales volume in 1981–1982. Turco expected to sell 40,000 units in 1981–1982. Instead, they sold 170,000 units, and profits tripled.

## ONGOING ACTIVITIES (1983–?)

Even though sales of kerosene heaters were expected to be down in 1983, Mr. Feigenbaum was looking at a possible sales volume of $70 million overall in 1983, if things continued as they were. But his five-year goals were to double sales volume and maintain the profit margin. This called for new products which fit the concept of a "method-of-distribution" company. In order to assess the firm's capabilities to pursue such a strategy, it is useful to examine the current environment and activities of the functional areas at Turco.

## MARKETING AT TURCO

Mr. Stanley R. Sudman, Vice President of Marketing, came to Turco in 1975 from Kenner Products, a toy manufacturer in Ohio where he was V.P. of Product Planning. After receiving a B.S. from Boston University, he spent many years at a trading stamp company prior to his work with Kenner. Mr. Sudman sees his primary responsibility at Turco now to be in new product development, but he controls all marketing activities.

## Products

Turco's share of the gym set market was about 30 percent. Prices to consumers ranged from $50 to $150. There was about a 30 percent markup from the retailer's cost to consumer list price, and the gym sets were sold to retailers with a 16 percent markup over manufacturing cost. No consumer ads for this line are run by Turco. Sears is the only account being served presently. They buy direct from Turco. Turco had no intention of increasing the present share of the gym set line due to unit volume declines with a declining birth rate, even though dollar volume had increased slightly.

Gas barbecue grills was the other major line prior to kerosene heaters. Turco, known as an innovator here, had about a 20 percent market share with a goal of 25 percent. Prices to consumers ranged from $99 to $249, with a typical markup to the retailer of 40 percent. Turco took approximately a 25 percent markup from production costs. K-Mart accounted for about 20 percent of the business.

In commenting on the nature of newer products at Turco, Mr. Sudman concluded that "Probably today we are more an energy-saving company than anything else. More than 50 percent of our volume this year and next will be taken up with these products." This includes the kerosene heaters and unvented wall-mounted natural gas reflection heaters which were new to Turco in 1983.

The idea for a gas heater, a natural extension from the kerosene heater business, came from a major customer of kerosene heaters—a farmer's supply store in Toledo, Ohio—who indicated that they were doing a fairly large business in unvented gas heaters. After a study of feasibility and legal issues, an outside design firm (since there was little need for internal designers for gym sets) was consulted, as was a gas engineering consultant who designed the working mechanism to pass American Gas Association (AGA) approval. Finally, an oxygen depletion valve (to cut off the unvented heater when $O^2$ levels fell below a certain tolerance) was developed by a firm in England, with Turco underwriting 60–70 percent of the cost.

**EXHIBIT 1**    1983 Turco Unvented Gas Heater Specifications*

|  | 5100 Horizon II | 5150 Horizon II | 5200 Horizon II | 5250 Horizon III |
|---|---|---|---|---|
| Type of Gas Heater | Natural | LP | Natural | LP |
| Heat Output (BTU) | 6000/12000 | 6000/12000 | 6/12/18(000) | 6/12/18(000) |
| Infrared Tiles | 2 | 2 | 3 | 3 |
| Controls | 4 position | 4 position | 5 position | 5 position |
| Individual Heater | | | | |
| Dimensions | W: 21" | W: 21" | W: 25" | W: 25" |
|  | H: 17" | H: 17" | H: 17" | H: 17" |
|  | D: 11" | D: 11" | D: 11" | D: 11" |
| Shipping Weight | 24# | 24# | 27# | 27# |
| Shipping Cube | 2.8 | 2.8 | 3.3 | 3.3 |

*All heaters include automatic ignition, oxygen depletion sensor system, and pilot light.

The final gas heater design was presented to sales representatives at one of the twice-annual presales meetings who "went to feel out the market for potential sales." Based on responses, a catalog with four various models was developed for presentation at a trade show in Dallas. (See Exhibit 1.) While unvented gas space heaters have been around for years in Europe, only 12 firms were showing models in Dallas. Turco was the only U.S. manufacturer, and they left the show believing they could sell every unit they could produce. Plans were to import tiles from Ontario, Canada, valves from England, and to manufacture cases and assemble

100,000 units in DuQuoin for an expected 20 percent of the 1983 industry shipments. Mr. Sudman expected that 10 percent of the kerosene heater customers would pick up gas heaters the first year, maybe 50 percent the year after, and 80 percent by the third year.

## Distribution and New Product Development

With the exception of Sears, who buys direct from Turco, a commissioned sales representative force of about 60–65 travels out of seven regional distributor operations (see Exhibit 2). These reps are bulk sales people who primarily

---

**EXHIBIT 2**   Sales Representatives for Turco

Colman & Hirschmann, Inc.
200 Fifth Avenue, Room 1453
New York, NY 10010
(212)691–8500
States of AL, CT, DC, DE, FL, GA,
MD, ME, MS, NC, NH, NJ, NY,
PA, RI, SC, TN, VA, VT, WV

John Tanner, Inc.
26902 La Sierra
Mission Viejo, CA 92691
(714)831–0806
States of CA, HA

Marshall Associates, Inc.
Suite 1214–22
666 North Lake Shore Drive
Chicago, IL 60611
(312)266–8500
States of IA, IL, IN, KY, KS, MI,
MN, MO, ND, NE, OH, SD, WI

Bell, Beyer & Assoc.
1406 130th Ave., N.E.
Bellevue, WA 98005
(206)454–4992
States of WA, OR, AK

Marshall Associates, Inc., S.W.
P. O. Box 581129
8224 World Trade Center
Dallas, TX 75258
(214)742–5930
States of OK, TX, AR, LA

Canada
Irwin Leisure Products
Division of Irwin Toy Ltd.
165 North Queen Street
Etobicoke, Ontario, Canada M9C1A7
(416)626–6600

Mel Pearson and Co.
1860 South Acoma Street
Denver, CO 80223
(303)744–2323
States of ID, WY, CO, UT, MT,
AZ, NM, El Paso, Las Vegas

carry high-bulk, high-ticket ($100–$150) items to be mass mechandised through 5,000 or so independent retail stores or chains. They usually receive 3–5 percent of net sales to retailer as a commission.

Mr. Sudman commented that distribution was an important criterion in new product development. "Every time we've gone away from this, we've gotten killed. We're really a bulk mover—a truckload mover." The trucking operation is all by contract carrier F.O.B. Du-Quoin, with goods shipped directly to retailer warehouses. The sales reps never touch the product.

In-house trucking operations had been considered, but the investment in equipment plus the past seasonal nature of the business with its attendant downtime precluded this vertical integration. Also, a large percentage of sales in the past were to K-Mart or Sears (who still commands 15 percent of Turco business), who had their own trucks or specified a carrier. A concern about shipping shutdowns and a change in smoother production may lead to a reconsideration of this strategy. But Mr. Sudman indicated that "In the long run it might make economic sense, but we probably won't become that involved in it."

As indicated above, then, certain criteria influence Turco's new product development ideas. Mr. Sudman's comments on these criteria are instructive:

We are looking at the energy-saving area and a lot of other areas. We are looking at a super-expensive coffee-making system. The item we can't seem to find is one that would (1) fit our manufacturing—because we are really a pipe bender and a painter; (2) fit our sales force—who are bulk salesmen; and (3) fit our bulk shipping department. This is what we're really looking for today. If you came along with the greatest needle that could sew, we couldn't handle it. This isn't Turco. It used to be where we might have done it, but not any more. We need a line of a product. You can't sell a single item—you get killed with a single product.

## Environmental Influences

Mr. Sudman noted that several environmental factors had an influence on the sales of Turco products. For example, in 1981 and 1982, the recession diminished disposable income. As a consequence, he believed the usually stable sales of gas grills had been adversely affected from the typical industry volume of about 1,200,000 per year. The weather was another uncontrollable. In this instance, warm winter weather in 1982–1983 reduced demand for kerosene heaters. But he was semioptimistic about kerosene industry sales for the near future, anticipating 4.2–4.3 million units of sales, or more if the weather turns bad. However, the Japanese had shipped excess units in 1982, and with inventories at over 3 million units in warehouses, revenues of kerosene producers were expected to be down sharply, even with a pickup in sales. Margins have eroded about 10 percent. Turco's response was to offer a $20 rebate for the next selling season to reduce their inventories on their Heritage Convection Heater. This rebate was expected to help move over 100,000 of this unit at the rebate price of $139 retail. Said Sudman, "It's going to cost us money, but it helps us maintain our relationship in Japan, which is not too good right now."

Of even more significance for heaters, perhaps, were legislative and consumer groups concerned with health and safety. Kerosene heaters came under attack for potentially unsafe oxygen depletion, heat burn, and fires in 1982. Mr. Sudman states his position as follows:

We participate in the National Kerosene Heater Association. I serve on the executive board as Treasurer. We at Turco, with 10 percent of the kerosene heater business, do not have resources to fight this on our own. The Association is out doing the P.R., the fighting, for us. A P.R. firm in Washington used most of the money preparing for the Consumer Product Safety Commission (CPSC) hearings in June. The Association spent about $300,000 on in-home testing to check emission levels. The problem is that the E.P.A. has not established a standard for in-home emission levels. We've pulled out all the money in the state-by-state fight—New Jersey legislation, Michigan legislation, California, Indiana, Massachusetts—to go in and say that if we lose the CPSC we don't have to worry about all those states. We honestly believe they'll only require an additional warning label. For kerosene heaters, the unit is fire safe, the hot surface burn incidences are low considering the high quantity of units sold, and there really isn't an emission standard to measure against.

Indeed, staff scientists of the CPSC indicated in July of 1983 that problems resulted from inadequate ventilation in the home, improper operation of the heater and the use of gasoline-contaminated fuel. Since the heaters could be of concern to people with respiratory illnesses, the CPSC recommended several design changes to improve safety and promote safer use. Manufacturers basically agreed with the recommendations.

Mr. Sudman did not believe these kinds of problems were as likely with the unvented gas heaters. There is no emission, they burn clean, there is no smell problem, and there is little or no chance of carbon monoxide due to the cutoff valve built in. But he admitted there was a volatile, flammable, and potentially explosive product in the home; and due to past experience, Turco plans to put numerous warnings on the label.

Of course, another factor of importance to the "energy-saving product concept" is the managerial expectations about the energy future. Mr. Sudman's statements on this matter indicate his thinking.

The price of oil has dropped drastically, but I believe it will go back up. The price of electricity has been constant or up slightly. The investment in nuclear plants will keep electricity costs up. Natural gas is going up like crazy. 60 percent of the living environment of people in the U.S. is heated by natural gas, and as long as these prices keep going up people will continue to look for a means to reduce that consumption.

## Market Research and Advertising

Marketing research at Turco was characterized as "nonscientific" by Mr. Sudman. One of the early product lines (scooters) was test-marketed at one store location. Results were poor, but the product was introduced anyway. As for kerosene heaters, Mr. Sudman indicated that "Kero-Sun did it for us. We figured they sold a unit for $299 in a 2-step distribution, and we could turn out as good a unit, maybe better, go to our one-step people, and sell it for $199." As far as gas heaters were concerned, "We haven't done a darn thing and we probably should. But really it's nothing new. What we're doing is taking the niche between the two-step distribution which sold at a higher price, and put ourselves at a one-step distribution and under price them." As a result, margins were expected to be about 35 percent, out of which 8 percent was to be spent on advertising in full-color ads in national magazines like *House Beautiful, Better Homes and Gardens, Changing Times, Popular Mechanics, Country Living, New Shelter,* and others. Customer service was provided by Turco with a toll-free number for assistance with operation and replacement parts.

## PRODUCTION OPERATIONS AT TURCO

Mr. Robert J. Kotarba is V.P. for Operations at Turco. After attending two years of college in industrial engineering, he was trained for quality control at Alcoa Aluminum. After three years he went to Ford Motor Company's Business Management School. During the next seven years he was trained in areas such as production, finance, scheduling, quality control, and inventory planning. He spent another seven years with Parker-Hanafin, working his way up to plant manager. Another 7-year stint was put in as Scheduling Manager, Manufacturing Manager, and V.P. and General Manager at Curtis-Toledo, a division of Wyle Laboratories, Inc., until the firm was sold. He began his own consulting firm and was called in by Jerry Goldress as part of the turnaround work in 1979–1980. Mr. Feigenbaum offered the current position, and Mr. Kotarba joined the firm.

A major task for Mr. Kotarba was to regain control of the plant in the turnaround. He believed the top management team was out of balance. Marketing and sales was very strong but manufacturing was weak. According to Kotarba, "they didn't stand up and say 'hey, we've got too many models to have an efficient operation'." Product pricing was based on manufacturing costs of 10,000 unit production runs, but runs were often made of only 1,000 units, so costs were very high. With marketing willing to sell at any volume, this contributed to inefficient plant operations. Mr. Kotarba indicated that he successfully pushed for runs of 2,000 units. The first year this came into play a lot of items were dropped. Efficiency went up and inventory went down. With this better balance, manufacturing can better react to marketing.

## Production Scheduling

One of the main areas of Mr. Kotarba's work is scheduling production. The process begins with a planning session in March for the following year's production. Spring and summer seasonal products (barbecue grills and swing sets) are produced during the winter and fall months. Marketing initially provides an estimate of sales for each model of a specific product line. One problem frequently encountered is the estimation of sales volume because product line designs often change drastically. Since scheduling of production is dependent on accurate forecasts of demand, production scheduling must be frequently changed. Changing product lines can also create problems because major changes in a line or a new line such as gas heaters involves acquiring new tooling, labor changes, and setup changes. Of course, the contraseasonality of heaters may help smooth production in the long run. For instance, beginning August 8, 1983, Turco expected to pack 1,000 gas heaters a day and do 15,000 for the month. Plans

were to run 30,000 units in September and again in October, with an additional 100 employees added to the work force.

Still, the production system is geared to a seasonal schedule. Mr. Kotarba commented as follows:

It is difficult to go into a year like we had last year where we had a whole new product line change. Tooling was late and sales and orders were fairly heavy. We're still trying to catch up. We're trying to do in 4 months what we did last year in 6 1/2 months. Since almost everything is brand new it causes a lot of headaches.

In mid-January we start to ship products, and catalog showrooms start selling, and all of a sudden we find we ran 10,000 of a grill that marketing said would sell and it's a dud. They need something else, so we have to scramble to get it. After February, if the units are still in, we have to have specials, reduce prices, use closeouts, etc.

Next year we will have a carry-over of identical grill models with only 15 to 20 percent changes; it is basically the same line. So our requirements will be much easier to predict. We run in cycles like that. Every other year we have an aesthetic change (about a 20 percent change for us), then into a massive change where almost everything changes.

Of course, the process could be confounded or helped with the kerosene and gas heater business.

While marketing may have trouble forecasting sales volume of a brand new line due to uncertain public reaction, production has no history either. An overabundance of material can easily result, or the lack of a nail or a screw can put production in limbo.

To help integrate marketing and operations, a marketing manager sits in on daily production meetings who can carry back to sales a realistic idea of production problems and when a job will get done. A new computer program was installed to help all activities at Turco. The impact of this on production is described below.

For 20 years, Turco had operated as more

or less a job shop operation. But a computerized scheduling system known as MAPICS was installed. The master schedule was to go into the computer, and the program would indicate when to buy parts, when materials should be received, when to do manufacturing runs, and how long it would take to go through the system. For instance, one part may go on six grills. The computer is told what grills are produced when, and it indicates how many parts to order when needed. Mr. Kotarba commented as follows:

It worked 99 percent up to January 1. But after that we started to lose a handle on things because we circumvented the lead times, we expedited, we pushed back what we thought we would need because of changes. A customer says a product isn't selling and they cancel their orders, or vendors fail to fill orders on time. This goes back into the computer and the whole schedule changes again.

If we can fill orders that change (like a vendor who orders 2,000 and suddenly asks for 6,000 extra), it's a plus for marketing when they go in next year to negotiate new prices or try to sell new products.

The computer told us in January that we couldn't possibly make a production run goal in two days. The computer said three weeks. But we said 'No. We can make the run in two days.' At this time of year the exception becomes the rule? Everything goes through the shop in two days. This is not the most efficient way of doing it. At the end of the year, we will be able to see how much we could have saved by flattening out the production. I'm sure the savings would be substantial. But the bottom line is we're keeping a lot of customers happy by jumping through the ring of fire daily.

As noted above, effectiveness and customer demands appear to take priority over production efficiency at Turco. The MAPICS system can theoretically indicate when orders should be filled, and even prioritize among customer orders in terms of maximizing operating efficiency. But the actual Turco operating system

has circumvented the program to satisfy customer demands. Hence, "the figures you get out of the computer as to inventory on hand or work in process are almost meaningless," says Kotarba.

Nonetheless, management is committed to making the system work.

We can't operate in the same chaotic manner as before. The system will work and has to work if we intend to get into other models or different product lines. Our production control people have gained a lot of education, but they're not as proficient as they will be next year.

MAPICS is doing a lot for us, but we have to understand it collectively—production, finance, and marketing. It almost puts marketing up against a wall and forces them to make a forecast that will be 90 percent accurate. They have a better chance this year because we are going in with a product line that will run for a year. Last year we had a new grill product line, new tooling, and new forecasts almost daily, *and* we were trying to live with the new MAPICS system.

Another major responsibility of Mr. Kotarba is dealing with the labor force. Labor difficulties have occurred in the past as a result of seasonal production, even though highly skilled workers or supervisors are not needed. The products do not require close tolerance for manufacturing of parts, and much of the work is assembling and preparing inventory for shipping. For example, Turco hired an extra 145 workers and three supervisors in January of 1982 for 2 to 3 weeks to assemble grills, swing sets, and weight benches. By early March of that year, it was determined that the extra workers were still needed for gas grill production. The warm winter had hurt kerosene heaters, but grill sales were expected to be up. Mr. Kotarba indicated that the impact of such seasonal hiring was a reduction in efficiency due to inexperienced supervisors. Mr. Kotarba was surprised that no major problems had resulted, such as putting the wrong part in a box.

We had one last year. We had cooking grills that were wrong and we ended up flying a cooking grill back and flying a replacement out. K-Mart has over 1,000 stores so we ended up taking parts from 1,000 stores and shipping to 1,000 locations. That is extremely costly. We know that if we hire 3 supervisors and 150 workers (packing 2 shifts with overtime when we normally stay on one shift and stay as lean as possible), we lose quality control with inexperienced people.

Turco must also deal with their labor union. In southern Illinois, the coal mining union is very strong, and it "rubs off" on other unions. The union impact was an important factor when Mr. Kotarba came in as part of the turnaround.

We had a radical union leader—very radical. I came in here and in 90 days had fired him. The arbitrator ruled in our favor and labor relations after that changed from night to day.

The last union contract was very favorable for the company, but the one prior to it was extremely favorable to the union. In 1979 scrap was high, efficiency was low, the company was in bad financial shape, and it was hard to get a point across to the union. Weak managers failed to use the union contract language to discipline employees. Kotarba's efforts apparently changed these conditions.

First we started to discipline some people and we could see an immediate efficiency increase. Then we fired the union leader and we saw efficiency go up again. We had somewhat of a give-away incentive plan. The direct people had a standard to work with, but the indirect people floated along on the same percent of a plantwide basis. Once we got over 100 percent, we started paying shipping people, maintenance people, materials handlers, fork lift servicers—if the plant was at 105 percent, they all got a 5 percent pay increase. That slowly crept up until all of a sudden they were getting a 27 percent increase, but they weren't doing any more work. So we changed that in the last contract. Direct labor is still on an incentive plan, but indirect labor is on an hourly wage. We also save on the fringe-benefits

part of it. Right now, efficiency is at 145 percent (measured against a standard pieces-per-hour).

## Plant and Equipment

As mentioned earlier, two major buildings totaling 470,000 square feet are used for production of parts, assembly, painting, and warehousing operations, as well as office space. In addition, two tubing mills are owned by Turco, but only operate part time. Mr. Kotarba commented as to their use.

If we had to run everything we have right now we would only need one mill. But we work with a product that is volatile. This year we won't make anything for Sears that is painted; they are all galvanized gym sets. But two years ago we had to run three months of production on both mills to satisfy Sears' gym sets. And next year we may have all Sears' painted sets which Hedstrom has this year. We also use it for chrome tubing in weight benches and for a small part we use for gas grills on the cart model. Sales of these carts are expected to go up so it becomes a necessary piece of equipment. I can't sell one mill and buy it back when I need it. And we don't want to buy pieces; you pay someone else's profit and are at their mercy for delivery. We have been looking for a buyer for one mill; but those who want to buy it want us to pay them to take it.

Very limited use is made of mechanized or "robotic" type of equipment. The multitude of parts, sizes, and model changes is thought to limit the ability to program a robot. But Turco plans to purchase a new computerized "palletizer" to stack finished "boxed" goods. This should eliminate the problem of the worker who fell to his death from stacked boxes, and will allow greater space utilization, and should reduce insurance costs.

## Staffing and Management Philosophy

The production operations staff, other than the normal work force of 350 or so, consists of the following individuals who report to Mr. Kotarba.

- Purchasing—director, purchasers, secretary, and temporary purchaser during peak times to expedite
- Production control—7 or 8 people who plan and control certain product lines; Mr. Kotarba believes they are overstaffed because they are on a learning curve for some new products
- Plant manager with 23 supervisors regularly (3 extra supervisors for the additional 150 workers on a short-term basis at this time)
- Materials control manager—in charge of inventory, receiving, raw material warehouse, and the production planners
- Personnel—a manager and a secretary

It might be noted that shipping and warehousing of finished goods is the responsibility of marketing.

Mr. Kotarba was asked whether he believed the pressure facing the operations at Turco could be diminished. Aside from his earlier comments regarding the use of MAPICS, he noted the following:

> As an officer of the company I like to see manufacturing under pressure at all times. When the economy is going up we will sell everything we can produce. It keeps people working at 120 percent efficiency. It's hell trying to satisfy everyone though. We couldn't operate at this pace all year. Our people are giving 150 percent today. It's a good thing we're seasonal, because you would burn out at that pace. But they know it will come to an end by June, and they will be able to sit back and breathe for 2 weeks before we start planning for next year.

## FINANCE AT TURCO

Mr. James D. Leven, C.P.A., became Vice President of Finance at Turco in 1979 as part of the turnaround. After earning his M.B.A. at Northwestern University he spent four years in public accounting until he was offered a job by one of his clients. He spent several years with Hunt Foods on the west coast and later moved to Angelica Corporation in St. Louis, where he stayed

for 10 years. He spent three years with the garment industry before joining Turco. In many of those firms he received valuable turnaround experience in financial functions.

When Mr. Leven arrived he found that the firm had no idea what it was costing to make the merchandise. He indicated that Turco installed "good hard-nosed cost accounting." He went on: "Bob Kotarba is an extremely hard-nosed operations man. His thinking and mine run very much alike, and neither of us could have accomplished the job without the other." Gaining production control was an important element in the turnaround. Mr. Leven indicated one of the prime ways Turco now uses to gain production control.

> We say the fixed cost is fixed each month but the variable cost isn't. The indirect labor is the key to the ballgame. The indirect labor per shift stays the same whether you are producing 50 percent or 100 percent. A forklift driver will drive slower when the work slows down. So if we can compact the production cycle into as small a period as possible, we control those variable costs—that's the key to making money in this type of seasonal production operation.

### The Finance Function

Mr. Leven views the finance function at Turco as twofold. First, in a service function—the primary job is to provide information. "You can put the proper people in an operational situation, but if they aren't provided information, nothing will happen." Second, he sees finance as a watchdog.

> Our job is to keep people honest. You can highlight anything in the world with information, but if you don't have cooperation to take advantage of a situation, it won't happen.

A basic tool Mr. Leven uses to monitor production operations is the MAPICS system described earlier. He argues that the system helps control and bring down inventory levels, which in turn reduces interest costs. Plus, it gives factory management firm information on job costing. However, when it was first installed in March, he found a massive control hole. "You could make work in process disappear and steal the place blind." IBM was asked to reprogram the software. Meanwhile, Turco is developing a separate forecasting system which, in conjunction with MAPICS, will provide "added frosting on the cake" according to Mr. Leven.

Of course, financial inputs in marketing operations are also critical. A good example of financial thinking here deals with the decision to offer the $20 rebate on kerosene heaters. At first, Mr. Leven was skeptical, because it appeared that the rebate would cost the firm 20–30 percent of $6 to $8 a unit. However, a more careful examination led to the following line of reasoning by Mr. Leven.

> From a sunk-cost standpoint, I've got inventory of one stockkeeping item taking up floor space. That's about 35 percent of our heater inventory. I don't feel I've got any fixed cost to warehouse it other than insurance and interest. I don't put a value on floor space unless I'm running out. (You can't get rid of it because there isn't a very good market for a 450,000 square foot building here.)
>
> Second, we have a unique situation because I bought that inventory when the Japanese yen was 270 to the dollar. That item now is roughly 225 yen to the dollar, so it costs about $6 more than we actually paid for that inventory. All I've given away is the profit on the hedge, which I wasn't entitled to anyway.[1]
>
> So what have we given away (by a rebate)? Nothing. It will move existing inventory; we'll sell 30,000 units we otherwise keep in inventory, on a product where there are no unknowns except selling it or not selling it.

Another financial policy affecting marketing was the use of a plan to try to move kerosene heaters in June and July (off-season). In this case, goods were sold F.O.B. Japan to customers on a letter of credit arranged through a finance company. This allowed Turco to give abnor-

mally low prices because the customer was not paying Turco's profit on the freight cost of goods (about 15 percent out of the Far East) or on miscellaneous items representing 20 percent of the cost of the goods in total. As for the impact on Turco, when they sell goods "F.O.B. letter of credit," they don't give terms. They are paid in Japan immediately on loading goods on the ship. Turco saves 1 percent per month in interest. On the usual 5-month terms otherwise given, that's a 5 percent margin for Turco.

## Sources of Working Capital

At the time of the turnaround, Turco had a credibility problem with its financial institutions. They didn't know their costs of manufacturing, so the firm showed a profit for eleven months; but all of a sudden in the twelfth month a huge loss would appear after taking inventory. As the turnaround progressed and cost controls were introduced, bankers were no longer faced with an "unpleasant surprise." As profitability and credibility increased so did banker flexibility. It became easier to borrow larger amounts of money. The firm had two financial institutions at the time. One was as unhappy with Turco as they were with the banker and they came to a "polite parting of the ways." This institution was subsequently replaced with a second bank with a $5 million line of credit. A third institution, a finance company, is also used for partial financing. Mr. Leven commented about this relationship:

> There is nothing wrong with a finance company for a firm like Turco. We are really halfway between a prime banking situation and a true finance company situation. We can negotiate some rather unusual terms with them. When you look at the spread on your money—1 percent a year costs us $80,000 or $90,000—it's minimal in relation to the total interest we pay. The key is flexibility and that's where leverage and a finance company offers tremendous advantages. While banks are lending at a lower rate, they want more protection than a finance company does.

[1]Hedging operations are described later in the case.

Turco also smooths its cash flows through terms with vendors. And by being a collateralized borrower, borrowing against a percent of inventory, Turco really ends up just factoring their receivables. Such a maneuver doesn't bother Leven at all. "I don't think of us as a collateralized borrower, because any bank that thinks it can get 70 cents on the dollar in liquidation of raw materials is insane."

One would expect that Turco might also achieve some financing through special terms with its suppliers. The same operational seasonality at Turco would influence suppliers who might want to level their production. So if Turco were to buy parts on, say, 120-day terms, they could "live" off supplier money. Plus, a price reduction might occur because the supplier wants to keep the factory in operation. But as mentioned earlier, Turco looks at the seasonal production spread a little differently in terms of compacting the production cycle to control indirect labor costs.

Of course, working capital also came from internal profits as the firm worked through its turnaround. And a line of credit with Sears helped finance their product lines.

## Financial Position

Turco had roughly doubled sales in a 2 1/2 year period with 1982 sales at about $70 million. The sales increase had been financed without new equity, and at the same time the interest cost increases have been minimal in terms of total dollars. The balance sheet has improved through interest rate reductions and offshore financing. Total borrowing was down 1 or 2 million dollars to a total of $16 million by 1983. However, this represented about a 2.5 to 1 ratio of debt to common stock equity. Returns on common stock equity were around 50 percent. These profits were mostly plowed back into the company. "Our dividend payout will never exceed 10 percent, because we are a closely held company."

There was discussion of increasing equity to help finance the growth goal of doubling sales

again in 5 years and reducing the degree of leverage. Mr. Leven commented on this issue:

> Mr. Feigenbaum and I disagree on the subject. From his standpoint, a large infusion of equity would dilute him terribly. But realistically, what do we have to offer? We have nothing that makes us an attractive equity situation that's going to allow us to sell stock at 20 times earnings. Maybe in today's market, if we're lucky, we could get 10 times earnings.

The breakeven point for Turco is about $33–$36 million in sales currently, depending on changes in margins. A 20 percent increase in a low-margin product can be minimal while a 5 percent negative swing in a high margin line can have a drastic effect. The turnaround was centered on elimination of no-margin lines, but Turco was left with some low-margin lines. The margins on new gas heaters were expected to be high initially since it was a unique product. But this would decrease as new competitors were attracted. This happened with kerosene heaters for the first time two years where Turco did little more than broker the product. But then market forces led to the situation described earlier (see Environmental Influences).

## Leverage and Risk Reduction

As noted above, the leverage (calculated by Mr. Leven as total long- and short-term debt to equity) was about 250 percent. This was the lowest it had been since the company was bought back from Mattel. It was as high as 650 percent in March of 1980. Mr. Feigenbaum was concerned about this, but Mr. Leven was more sanguine.

> I don't consider our leverage very excessive, truthfully. The key to leverage is very simple: How do you make money and pay a lot of interest? If you plan properly and you know what your cost of leverage is going to be, you build it into product cost one way or another. In 1981 and 1982 when the prime rate got as high as 21 percent, our profits increased because we factored

cost of money into our product costs. I would love to see the leverage at 1 to 1, but this is basically an undercapitalized company.

The leverage would still be higher if it hadn't been for kerosene heaters whose profits contributed substantially to the bottom line. And the interest rate savings and leverage reduction came from several other methods Mr. Leven used. First, he used short-term money to finance fixed assets because he could arbitrage the interest rates more cheaply.

Why spend the extra percent on long-term as long as I can get the line of credit on short-term and we plow back 90 percent of our returns as cash? The only people involved in our financial statements are our stockholders, who are all internal, and our banks. Moving dollars between short-term and long-term debt is just financial manipulation that you can play with banks. Our banks know where the money's coming from, so what's the point in playing a game?

The second maneuver to reduce leverage was the use of letters of credit through the finance company described earlier. However, Mr. Leven believed that if leverage could be reduced below 200 percent in a year, he would be able to get the banks to take over the finance company's position at more favorable terms. This would save about $200,000 per year.

His third approach was to try to reduce exchange rate risk through hedging on money markets, as briefly mentioned earlier. As of March 1983, Turco owed $16 million worth of yen with August to December expirations. In dealing with the Japanese, kerosene heater contracts negotiated in dollars will cost 3 to 5 percent higher than the same merchandise contracted in yen. Thus, Turco negotiates in yen and hedges the contract. So the purpose is not to gamble on the market.

We cost our product based on X yen to the dollar. The hedge is how much cheaper I can buy yen than X yen to the dollar on which we've based our margin. The issue is the spread I can get from the standard cost on which those goods were costed, up to the actual value we're paying for those yen in the future.

Yet the exchange rates are subject to substantial fluctuations and are hard to predict. OPEC's price reductions led to a 2 percent rise in the yen's value after a short-term devaluation. Bankers in November of 1981 expected the yen to be down to about 195 a year later, but in November of 1982 it was up to 270. Mr. Leven believes the yen is undervalued in relation to the dollar because of market hysteria about U.S. interest rates. He expects the yen to stabilize later in 1983 at about 220. He also commented as to why he did not hedge against the British pound for the gas heater valve produced there.

When the price of North Sea oil dropped 50 cents a barrel, the pound went up because people have more confidence in the currency's stability. The gas valve was costed at $1.55 to the pound. Today I could cover that with a 4 percent profit on a hedge, because the profit margin is figured as if the pound will be $1.55. But it's less, and I think the pound will weaken further against the dollar.

Hedging other currencies where imported goods were involved was not necessary since contracts were for purchases F.O.B. country of origin and involved pure dollar trading.

All in all, then, Mr. Leven was not overly concerned about the risks in the financial position at Turco. Pure interest cost savings were not the prime consideration. As the working capital position built, leverage was dropping, loans were being reduced, interest costs were going down, and the bottom line was going up.

## TOP MANAGEMENT AND TURCO'S FUTURE

Bonuses for top executives were based exclusively on Turco profit as a whole. They could earn up to double their salary—bonuses and salary could range from $70,000 to $160,000 depending on the bonus. If external factors over which management had no control reduced profits, no bonuses would be received. Response to this approach from the three vice presidents was unanimously favorable.

It appears that the top management group is in sympathy with Mr. Feigenbaum's goal of doubling volume in five years. But each member of the team had different views of the impact of such a move on their areas. Mr. Sudman commented as follows:

> We wouldn't have to increase our sales reps if we stay in the lines they can handle. If we came up with a product which had to be sold directly to the retail level, we would have to go out and get a new or additional sales organization.

Perhaps the Sears relationship could again become more important in the future of Turco. Mr. Kotarba also reacted to the future expansion goals.

> If we get a new product line that is contraseasonal we can smooth and extend the production cycle so the 4- to 5-month layoff in production can be reduced to 30 days. But if we end up with some new line which runs concurrent with grills and gym sets, that would just make the production period more unbearable. We would have to run 2 or 3 shifts which can be done, but every-

thing would have to be done at once. With large inventories of parts, everything has to flow.

Mr. Leven believed that internal financing and external bank lines of credit would support the growth goal. As indicated earlier, he did not believe further equity financing to be feasible. But he also reacted to the casewriter's suggestion of a replay of the Mattel merger which would not result in existing equity dilution.

> The company is not as naive today as when they got involved with Mattel. When you sell out, the main reason is you want the money. The buyer will dictate the level of capital flow into the firm in the future, and he is going to do it based on R.O.I. Now we have a 50 percent return on common equity. But the buyer looks at the infusion of money, whether it's borrowed or not, as capital. On that basis we have a horrible return. Most major American corporations have a very simple standard—they measure the EPS this quarter a year ago, and want to know what the EPS will be this quarter. Most of them don't think too long-term.

The casewriter wondered whether Turco could achieve its goals and how that would be accomplished. But Mr. Feigenbaum expected a good kerosene heater year in 1984, and a great year for the gas heater business.

# 18 WHEELING-PITTSBURGH STEEL COMPANY

## Neil Snyder

*University of Virginia*

Wheeling-Pittsburgh Steel Company (W-P), the 8th largest domestic steelmaker, produced 3,895,000 tons of raw steel (2.9 percent of the industry total) and shipped 2,889,000 tons of finished products in 1978. The remainder of their output was sold in raw form to other producers of finished products.

W-P is a vertically integrated firm with annual raw steel capacity of about 4,400,000 net tons. Their production operations are geared primarily toward producing flat-rolled steel— steel which is made by rolling up long, thin bands of steel like a roll of paper towels. Rolled steel, which is adaptable to most processes, is used extensively for products in the auto, farm construction, container, and pipe markets. Due to the combined influence of economic and business cycle trends, W-P has experienced especially sharp cyclical swings in earnings for the past several years.

## HISTORY OF THE FIRM

In 1968, two small companies (Wheeling Steel and Pittsburgh Steel) agreed to merge to improve their position in an industry which is dominated by big producers. When the two companies merged to become Wheeling-Pittsburgh

Steel Company, Pittsburgh was an old-line, low-profit, limited-product-mix producer. Similarly, Wheeling was an unprofitable company because they possessed more steel making capacity than their finishing operations could handle. For Wheeling Steel (the 11th largest domestic producer), a merger with Pittsburgh Steel (the 14th largest domestic steel producer) offered the opportunity to reverse a dangerous trend. Between 1964 and 1967, Wheeling lost $29 million. Both companies produced flat-rolled steel, and each had equipment that would dovetail.

Wheeling's excess capacity had been a central issue during the company's hard times. Thus in the merger arrangement, Pittsburgh agreed to give Wheeling technical assistance on production and sales and to relieve Wheeling's financial pressures so that money could be raised for much needed facilities. Outside observers, however, were not enthusiastic about the marriage. One industry analyst stated that "the only thing synergistic about this merger will be its problems."

For the next several years, W-P's performance supported this skepticism. Saddled with debt, top heavy with management, and scarred by a reputation as an unreliable supplier, W-P did little more than survive. But in 1974, everything came together. Net income increased eightfold to $73.7 million and sales jumped to $1 billion (up 36 percent over 1973). The company's profit surge in 1974 reflected the worldwide increase in demand for steel which began late in 1973. But the surge was also due to the corporate revamping engineered by Robert E. Lauterbock (who, in 1976, became Chairman and Chief Executive Officer). Lauterbock made the following changes:

- He reduced the number of top executives from 16 to 6—all of whom had more than 25 years of experience in the steel industry.
- He reduced the company's debt.
- He reduced the number of production lines.
- Bucking an industry trend toward increased diversification, he concentrated on shrinking the company down to its essential core—the making of flat-rolled steel products.

Lauterbock's reason for focusing on the essential core was quite simple. He said, "We're not going to remain in any business where our competitors can beat us to death with small plants, low labor costs, and low capital costs." Instead, he looked for markets with growth potential. According to Lauterbock, in the strong markets "we'll compete head on with the big guys."

But the 1974–1975 recession dealt W-P a stunning blow in 1975. Due to continuing cost pressures without adequate price increases in major product lines and weak demand for products such as automobiles, appliances, and containers, W-P's earnings were depressed in 1975. In 1976 this trend continued, and in 1977 W-P sustained a $25.6 million loss.

In 1978, Dennis J. Carney became Chairman of the Board of W-P. He had served as President and Chief Operating Officer since 1976. Immediately after assuming the Chairman position, Carney began to make changes. He renegotiated debt contracts, restaffed executive positions, and eliminated unprofitable finished steel items from W-P's product line. Additionally, Carney launched an offensive against W-P's big competitors by accusing them of perpetrating a "coldly calculated campaign" of underpricing flat-rolled steel products at W-P's expense.

On March 15, 1979, W-P won approval for a loan package in excess of $150 million substantially guaranteed by state and federal agencies. These funds were earmarked for two major projects—building a railroad rail plant and purchasing pollution control equipment to comply with Environmental Protection Agency (E.P.A.) pollution standards. The rail plant portion of the loan package produced substantial controversy in the United States steel industry.

Currently, domestic competition in railroad rails is virtually nonexistent; Japanese producers supply most of the high-quality rails to purchasers in the United States. But due to the energy situation in the United States and the resulting increase in demand for mass transportation of people and freight, railroad usage has increased significantly. While the increase in demand for railroad transportation represented a significant opportunity for the depressed railroad industry, firms in the industry had allowed their roadbeds to deteriorate. Furthermore, railroad trains today are much faster and heavier than they once were. Thus, the opportunity afforded by increased demand resulted in the need for railroad firms to improve their roadbeds.

Faster and heavier trains require straighter and stronger rails. Because of the loan guarantees, W-P was prepared to become the domestic industry leader in railroad rail production at a time when demand was increasing rapidly. Major steel producers such as U.S. Steel objected to government interference in a potentially lucrative market segment. Thus, steel producers became embroiled in another controversy which pitted domestic producers against one another and the government.

## THE STEEL INDUSTRY: OVERVIEW

In June of 1979, prospects for the steel industry looked good. The industry was producing at 90 percent of capacity, and products such as flat-rolled steel were experiencing generally strong demand despite the softness of the domestic auto industry. Demand for steel in capital goods industries was quite strong since important users of steel such as farm equipment manufacturers, machinery manufacturers, and the heavy construction industry were experiencing brisk demand. Thus, the demand for steel did not decline dramatically.

By the second half of 1979, however, a weakening of demand for steel could be detected. The softening of the consumer goods market finally materialized in a very pronounced way, and orders from the users of flat-rolled steel products declined across every market. Many steelmen feared that declines in orders might spread to the industrial markets. Thus, companies such as Wheeling-Pittsburgh and Jones and Laughlin, whose major product is flat-rolled steel, began to schedule maintenance on their heavy equipment. (Maintenance on heavy equipment used in steel production is delayed frequently until demand slackens to avoid costly delays in production.)

In the first half of 1980, the bottom fell out of the steel industry as the nation settled into a recession. High interest rates finally crushed the demand for steel products in industrial markets, and by June of 1980, the steel industry was mired in its worst slump in ten years. The industry as a whole was producing at only 60 percent of capacity. Cost-cutting measures, such as layoffs, shorter work weeks, and plant closings were scheduled as the industry braced itself for an onslaught of red ink. To make matters worse, steel imports continued to increase at an alarming rate. Continued strong import competition and the 1980 recession serves to emphasize that the steel industry faced several long-term problems which threaten its current health and future competitiveness.

## STEEL INDUSTRY PROBLEMS

### Imports

Steel imports have accentuated the downside of the domestic steel industry's business cycle and deprived it of shipments and sales revenue needed to purchase new plant and equipment and modernize existing facilities. According to

William A. Delancey, Chairman of Republic Steel Corporation and President of the American Iron and Steel Institute, "I don't imply that imports alone are the root of the steel industry's problems, but imports have taken all of the growth in the domestic market in the past 10 years and have substantially depressed the domestic industry's profitability."

The steel import problem is exacerbated because many foreign governments own or subsidize their steel industries. Thus, foreign steel producers can sell their products in the U.S. market at prices below their costs of production. In a 1981 report prepared by the American Iron and Steel Institute entitled *Steel at the Crossroads: One Year Later,* news releases were presented as evidence of this fact. Several of the news releases follow:

> IN CANADA—"A report calling for a $350-million infusion to nudge Sydney Steel Corp. (Sysco) along a 10-year road to recovery has been released by Nova Scotia Premier John Buchanan, who said federal-provincial negotiations for the money are just starting.
>
> With the release of the business plan, Buchanan said Ottawa would release the initial $7.5-million rehabilitation grant. The previous federal government of Joe Clark had promised the grant, but the present liberal government had held back until it saw the plan.
>
> The business plan says the ailing, turn-of-the-century steel mill needs $350-million over 10 years for modernization, and then a further $175-million if a decision is made to introduce an oxygen steelmaking process.
>
> A spokesman in Ottawa said it is expected that most of the money would come through normal federal-provincial financing agreements, such as those worked out with the department of regional economic expansion."
>
> *American Metal Market*
> November 20, 1980

**EXHIBIT 1**   Imports and Apparent Steel Supply (Million Net Tons)

| Year | Total Imports | Apparent Steel Supply* | Imports As % of Apparent Steel Supply |
|------|------|------|------|
| 1970 | 13.4 | 97.1 | 13.8 |
| 1971 | 18.3 | 102.5 | 17.9 |
| 1972 | 17.7 | 106.6 | 16.6 |
| 1973 | 15.1 | 122.5 | 12.4 |
| 1974 | 16.0 | 119.6 | 13.4 |
| 1975 | 12.0 | 89.0 | 13.5 |
| 1976 | 14.3 | 101.1 | 14.1 |
| 1977 | 19.3 | 108.5 | 17.8 |
| 1978 | 21.1 | 116.6 | 18.1 |
| 1979 | 17.5 | 115.0 | 15.2 |
| 1980 | 15.5 | 95.2 | 16.3 |

*Shipments from domestic mills plus imports minus exports.
*Source:* American Iron and Steel Institute.

IN MEXICO—"When the first slab of steel rolled out at Mexico's huge new mill here (Las Truchas) four years ago, President Luis Echeverria and other government dignitaries at the ribbon-cutting ceremonies were ecstatic. The government's decades-old dream of building a "pacific Pittsburgh" here in a west coast jungle was finally coming true. President Echeverria saw an era of self-sufficiency in steel.

Today, as the government prepared to sink billions more into Las Truchas and other steel-expansion projects, a basic question is being raised: Can Mexico really achieve its planned threefold increase in steel output over the next decade? Plagued by poor planning, low productivity, labor strife, management corruption, and myriad other problems, the struggling state-dominated steel industry clearly faces an enormous challenge."

So the government moves ahead with plans to invest more than $17.2 billion over the next decade to raise state steel production to 20.3 million metric tons an-nually, up from 4.5 million now. The Las Truchas plant alone is scheduled to produce 10 million tons a year in 1990, up from less than one million to-day, making it the largest steel mill in Latin America."

*Wall Street Journal*
January 27, 1981

IN WEST GERMANY—"Even though the West German steel industry could compete with the world's most cost-effective producers, it 'cannot compete with the combined forces of Europe's tax-payers who subsidize their steelmakers to the tune of up to $60 a ton,' Willy Korf, president of the newly-formed European Independent Steelworkers Association, said here last week.

'Roughly 70 percent of all European steel enterprises, particularly those in Great Britain, France, Belgium, Luxem-bourg, and Italy are either national-ized or financially dependent on the state,' he said."

*American Metal Market*
March 25, 1981

"West German government officials will take up the matter of public steel subsidies with other European heads of state at a summit meeting in Maastricht, the Netherlands, on March 23–24.

A document published by the West German Iron and Steel Federation showed that steelmakers in other countries had been granted or promised aid totalling 60 billion German marks ($28.3 billion) in the 1975–1983 period, or an average of about $47 for each metric ton of crude steel production. The average financial assistance worked down to 55 marks ($26) a ton for the French government, 64 marks ($30) for the Italian, 102 marks ($41) for the Belgian, and 185 marks ($87) for the British."

*American Metal Market*
March 18, 1981

"The generous state aid promised to Hoesch to build a new steel plant in Dortmund has irritated its hard-pressed competitors. Hoesch is to invest some DM550m ($314m) in the project in the next four years and it is getting more than $137m of this in cheap loans—half each from the West German government and the government of North Rhine-Westphalia.

The terms are indeed favourable. The interest rate on the loans is a mere 4%, instead of the customary 8%. And after three years without having to make repayments Hoesch has been given 15 years in which to pay the money back—at its own pace."

*The Economist*
March 1, 1980

IN FRANCE—"Agreement has been reached on one of the two stages of the French government's plan for restructuring the special steel industry and an accord on the second stage is likely before the presidential elections in late April, officials at the Industry Ministry said.

In all, the restructuring program is expected to cost the equivalent of $325 million. The French taxpayer will pick up half the tab in the form of state aid to help four steel companies trim excess production capacity and improve productivity."

*Wall Street Journal*
March 18, 1981

## Dumping

Dumping is a term used to describe the selling of steel products in the United States by foreign competitors at prices below production costs. This practice is viewed as unfair competition by the Commerce Department and the United States steel industry because many foreign governments own or subsidize their steel industries.

The trigger price mechanism (TPM) was set up by the Commerce Department in 1978 to protect the U.S. steel industry from unfairly priced imports. Trigger prices are indexed according to the prices paid for Japanese steel products because Japan is considered the world's most efficient producer of steel. In effect, the trigger price is the minimum price at which foreign producers may sell their products in this country. Any attempt by foreign producers to sell their products below the floor price automatically results in dumping investigations.

According to the American Iron and Steel Institute report entitled *Steel At The Crossroads: One Year Later* (June 1981),

The American Steel industry supports an open world trade system. Foreign steel should have an opportunity to compete in the American steel market so long as it is fairly traded. The industry has been a supporter of the Tokyo Round Trade Agreement involving more than 100 countries, which reduced tariffs and promoted efforts to remove nontariff barriers.

Domestic steelmakers believe they are the principal low-cost producer for the American market. But the U.S., the only major open steel market in the world, cannot ignore the penetration of unfairly traded imports. Heavy flows of such imports cripple the domestic industry and undermine its capability to continue as the principal supplier of steel for this market.

There are no import restrictions on steel traded in the U.S. market in accordance with U.S. trade statutes and with internationally agreed upon trade rules. The TPM is not a restriction, but rather an administrative procedure for identifying potential violations of U.S. trade law.

U.S. trade law is consistent with international rules established in the Tokyo Round Agreements. These rules have become the international legal basis for expansion of world trade.

The need for the TPM is accentuated by the currently depressed state of the world steel industry, in which more than one-half of the steel produced comes from government-controlled or government-subsidized steel companies. In a depressed world steel market, these producers sell their products at prices below average costs, in order to maintain home employment and obtain foreign exchange.

Unfair steel imports transfer to American steel producers and workers the unemployment adjustment problems that foreign producers and their governments are seeking to avoid.

Enforcement of U.S. trade law through the TPM is the most effective answer to the problem and is essential to the industry's revitalization program.

Accurate, up-to-date calculations of Japanese costs of steel production—the basis for the TPM—are integral to the success of the entire program. Expeditious use of the import surge provision is also a vital component of the TPM program. Removing products from coverage, failure to audit related party transactions which result in evasion of the system, and granting unjustified preclearances which weaken the TPM should be avoided. If imports take a significant share of the U.S. market by means of dumping or subsidization, American steel producers will not be able to accomplish their modernization goal.

**EXHIBIT 2** Production and Shipments (Million Net Tons) Raw Steel

| Year | Production | Percent of Capability* | Steel Shipments |
|------|-----------|------------------------|-----------------|
| 1970 | 131.5 | N.A. | 90.8 |
| 1971 | 120.4 | N.A. | 87.0 |
| 1972 | 133.2 | N.A. | 91.8 |
| 1973 | 150.8 | N.A. | 111.4 |
| 1974 | 145.7 | N.A. | 109.5 |
| 1975 | 116.6 | 76.2 | 80.0 |
| 1976 | 128.0 | 80.9 | 89.4 |
| 1977 | 125.3 | 78.4 | 91.1 |
| 1978 | 137.0 | 86.8 | 97.9 |
| 1979 | 136.3 | 87.8 | 100.3 |
| 1980 | 111.8 | 72.8 | 83.9 |

*Raw steel output as a percent of tonnage capability to produce raw steel for a sustained full order book. Not published prior to 1975.
*Source:* American Iron and Steel Institute.

## Poor Financial Performance

Many domestic steel companies are experiencing a vicious cycle of inadequate returns on investment, which results in an inability to raise capital for modernizing existing facilities or building new facilities, which results in inefficiency, which results in poor profit performance, which further reduces return on investment. Furthermore, industry depreciation expenses understate inflation-impacted replacement costs of plant and equipment which results in overstated earnings and high taxes. Additionally, steel industry cash flow trails industry in general, and government demands for antipollution devices to protect the environment have greatly increased operating costs and intensified the problem of low returns on investment because such expenditures do not produce any dollar return.

Thus, many producers in the domestic steel industry are liquidating permanently millions of tons of steel capacity. Rather than investing in new facilities or modernizing existing facilities, many domestic steel producers are investing in nonsteel related products in an attempt to protect themselves through diversification. Ironically, liquidation could result in a shortage of domestic capacity by 1985.

Exhibits 2, 3, 4, and 5 present data pertaining to production and shipments, cash flow,

## EXHIBIT 3
CASH FLOW DATA
(Millions of Dollars)

| Year | Profits After Taxes | Depreciation, Depletion, etc. | Gross Cash Flow | Cash Dividends | Net Internal Sources | Capital Expenditures |
|------|------|------|------|------|------|------|
| 1964 | $ 992 | $1,046 | $2,038 | $462 | $1,576 | $1,600 |
| 1965 | 1,069 | 1,117 | 2,186 | 468 | 1,718 | 1,823 |
| 1966 | 1,075 | 1,199 | 2,274 | 483 | 1,791 | 1,953 |
| 1967 | 830 | 1,444 | 2,274 | 481 | 1,793 | 2,146 |
| 1968 | 992 | 1,316 | 2,308 | 452 | 1,856 | 2,307 |
| 1969 | 879 | 1,173 | 2,052 | 489 | 1,563 | 2,047 |
| 1970 | 532 | 1,128 | 1,660 | 488 | 1,172 | 1,736 |
| 1971 | 563 | 1,123 | 1,686 | 390 | 1,296 | 1,425 |
| 1972 | 775 | 1,216 | 1,991 | 402 | 1,589 | 1,174 |
| 1973 | 1,272 | 1,329 | 2,601 | 443 | 2,158 | 1,400 |
| 1974 | 2,475 | 1,553 | 4,028 | 674 | 3,354 | 2,115 |
| 1975 | 1,595 | 1,591 | 3,186 | 658 | 2,528 | 3,179 |
| 1976 | 1,337 | 1,614 | 2,951 | 637 | 2,314 | 3,253 |
| 1977 | 22 | 1,888 | 1,910 | 555 | 1,355 | 2,850 |
| 1978 | 1,277 | 1,968 | 3,245 | 536 | 2,709 | 2,595 |
| 1979 | 1,154 | 2,453 | 3,607 | 593 | 3,014 | 3,312 |
| 1980 | 1,632 | 2,235 | 3,867 | 602 | 3,265 | 3,319 |

*Includes changes in reserves.
*Source:* American Iron and Steel Institute (for those companies reporting financial information).

**EXHIBIT 3** (*Continued*)    Cash Flow Data
(Millions of Dollars)

| Year | Excess (+) or Deficit (−) Net Internal Sources over Capital Expend. | Change in Long-term Debt | Capital Expenditures As a Percent of Net Internal Sources |
|------|------|------|------|
| 1964 | − $    24 | + $    179 | 101.5 |
| 1965 | −    105 | +    245 | 106.1 |
| 1966 | −    162 | +    659 | 109.0 |
| 1967 | −    353 | +    423 | 119.7 |
| 1968 | −    451 | +    396 | 124.3 |
| 1969 | −    484 | +    7 | 131.0 |
| 1970 | −    564 | +    526 | 148.1 |
| 1971 | −    129 | +    10 | 110.0 |
| 1972 | +    415 | +    85 | 73.9 |
| 1973 | +    758 | −    85 | 64.9 |
| 1974 | + 1,239 | −    312 | 63.1 |
| 1975 | −    651 | − 1,054 | 125.8 |
| 1976 | −    939 | + 1,262 | 140.6 |
| 1977 | − 1,495 | +    992 | 210.3 |
| 1978 | +    114 | +    804 | 95.8 |
| 1979 | −    298 | −    46 | 109.9 |
| 1980 | −    54 | +    659 | 101.7 |

corporate profit rates, and estimated capital expenditures for environmental control facilities, respectively.

### Labor and Productivity Issues
Labor costs in the steel industry are higher than labor costs in any other manufacturing industry. This fact exacerbates steel's poor return on investment. Companies in the steel industry must take a large share of the credit for this situation: in order to protect themselves from the disrupting effects of strikes, the ten largest steel producers signed an experimental negotiating agreement which prohibits steel unions from striking in case of bargaining deadlocks and substitutes binding arbitration as the remedy for resolving such deadlocks.

Steel's collective bargaining agreement has produced an unparalleled record of peaceful negotiations—20 years without a nationwide strike. But the cost of peace in terms of wages has been high. Even though profitability and productivity have been declining for years, the 1980 labor negotiations did not reverse the steel industry trend of paying extremely high wages. Adjusted for inflation, the labor agreement of June 1980 called for a 2.3 percent increase in hourly earnings and a 3.0 percent increase in hourly earnings, benefits, and Social Security combined. As wages have increased, however, industry employment has declined. In 1970, there were 531,000 employees in the steel industry, but by 1980 there were only 399,000.

Exhibit 6 presents data on hourly employment costs and average hourly earnings for the steel industry. Additionally, it shows increases

**EXHIBIT 4**    Corporate Profit Rates: Steel Versus All Manufacturing Average

| Year | Steel Company Profits after Taxes (millions of $) | Steel Company Profits after Taxes As a Percent of Revenues | Profits after Taxes As a Percent of Stockholders' Equity* | |
|---|---|---|---|---|
| | | | Steel Companies | All Manufacturing |
| 1964 | 992 | 6.1 | 9.0% | 12.6% |
| 1965 | 1,069 | 5.9 | 9.4 | 13.9 |
| 1966 | 1,075 | 5.9 | 8.9 | 14.2 |
| 1967 | 830 | 4.9 | 6.9 | 12.6 |
| 1968 | 992 | 5.3 | 8.2 | 13.3 |
| 1969 | 879 | 4.6 | 7.0 | 12.4 |
| 1970 | 532 | 2.8 | 4.1 | 10.1 |
| 1971 | 563 | 2.8 | 4.3 | 10.8 |
| 1972 | 775 | 3.4 | 5.8 | 12.1 |
| 1973 | 1,272 | 4.4 | 9.3 | 14.9 |
| 1974 | 2,475 | 6.5 | 17.1 | 15.2 |
| 1975 | 1,595 | 4.7 | 9.8 | 12.6 |
| 1976 | 1,337 | 3.7 | 7.8 | 15.0 |
| 1977 | 22 | 0.1 | 0.1 | 14.9 |
| 1978 | 1,277 | 2.6 | 7.3 | 15.9 |
| 1979 | 1,154 | 2.1 | 6.7 | 18.4 |
| 1980 | 1,632 | 3.0 | 9.0 | 16.6 |

*Based on Equity at beginning of year.
*Sources:* American Iron and Steel Institute, Citibank N.A.

in both statistics in relation to the Bureau of Labor Statistics' Consumer Price Index (Base Year 1961). Exhibit 7 presents statistical highlights for the United States Iron and Steel Industry from 1970 to 1980.

## THE UNITED STATES GOVERNMENT

The government, until recently, has been unsympathetic about steel industry complaints of excessive pollution regulation and unfair imports. However, the government has had to change its position because the industry's plight has become so acute. William J. DeLancey of Republic Steel characterized the change in the following way:

We can now be confident of moving into the eighties with the assurance of receiving a congressional audience which will give sympathetic attention to proposals aimed at strengthening the steel industry and making it healthy for the years ahead . . . It would be unrealistic to fail to recognize that in the area which has been the ultimate source of most of our problems, namely the federal establishment, there has been a positive change from apathy at best toward better understanding and, in some areas, support.

**EXHIBIT 5**   Estimated Capital Expenditures for Environmental Control Facilities*
(Millions of Dollars)

| Year Facilities Began Operations | For Water Improvement | For Air Improvement | Total |
|---|---|---|---|
| 1951–1965 | $ 209.6 | $ 238.8 | $ 448.4 |
| 1966 | 18.8 | 37.7 | 56.5 |
| 1967 | 54.7 | 39.4 | 94.1 |
| 1968 | 61.5 | 40.2 | 101.7 |
| 1969 | 71.0 | 67.1 | 138.1 |
| 1970 | 110.0 | 72.6 | 182.6 |
| 1971 | 73.4 | 88.2 | 161.6 |
| 1972 | 57.0 | 144.8 | 201.8 |
| 1973 | 34.7 | 65.4 | 100.1 |
| 1974 | 79.4 | 119.4 | 198.8 |
| 1975 | 131.8 | 321.3 | 453.1 |
| 1976 | 158.7 | 330.5 | 489.2 |
| 1977 | 205.7 | 329.1 | 534.8 |
| 1978 | 180.8 | 277.2 | 458.0 |
| 1979 | 201.2 | 449.6 | 650.8 |
| 1980 | 168.2 | 342.3 | 510.5 |
| Total 1951–1980** | 1,879.6 | 3,015.0 | 4,894.6 |
| Authorized for 1981 and Later | 219.7 | 641.1 | 860.8 |

*Between 1951 and 1974 capital expenditures were for facilities placed in operation. Effective with 1975, the data represent actual capital expenditures made during the year.
**Includes capital expenditures in years prior to 1975 for facilities not placed in operation as of January 1, 1975: $63.1 million for water, $51.4 million for air, $114.5 million in total.
*Source:* American Iron and Steel Institute.

The two best examples of the improved relationship with the government are the Carter Administration's express desire to establish a policy which addresses the problems of the industry and the establishment of a Steel Tripartite Committee with labor, steel, and government representatives, dedicated to the formulation of a National Steel Policy.

According to the American Iron and Steel Institute report entitled *Steel At The Cross-Roads: One Year Later,*

Numerous studies have since supported the steel industry's position and have made policy rec-ommendations virtually identical with those of the industry. For example, the study of the OTA concluded, "A well-defined and vigorously implemented government policy has nurtured the Japanese steel industry's expansion and adoption of new technology. The U.S. steel industry, on the other hand, has been hurt by a long series of federal government policies that have frequently been uncoordinated, contradictory, and inattentive to critical issues.

Similarly, the GAO report said, "On the whole, both general and specific Government policy has not been consistently responsive to requirements for modernization. At times, it worked directly against modernization, as through

**EXHIBIT 6**    Hourly Employment Costs and Average Hourly Earnings in the Iron and Steel Industry

| Year | Consumer Price Index on 1961 | | Average Hourly Earnings per Hour Paid for Index 1961 | | Employment Costs per Hour Worked Wage Employees Index 1961 | |
|------|------|------|------|------|------|------|
| | 100 | | Actual | 100 | Actual | 100 |
| 1961 | 100.0 | | 3.20 | 100.0 | 3.989 | 100.0 |
| 1962 | 101.1 | | 3.29 | 102.8 | 4.155 | 104.2 |
| 1963 | 102.3 | | 3.36 | 105.0 | 4.247 | 106.5 |
| 1964 | 103.7 | | 3.41 | 106.6 | 4.355 | 109.2 |
| 1965 | 105.5 | | 3.46 | 108.1 | 4.475 | 112.2 |
| 1966 | 108.5 | | 3.58 | 111.9 | 4.633 | 116.1 |
| 1967 | 111.6 | | 3.62 | 113.1 | 4.758 | 119.3 |
| 1968 | 116.3 | | 3.82 | 119.4 | 5.032 | 126.1 |
| 1969 | 122.5 | | 4.09 | 127.8 | 5.375 | 134.7 |
| 1970 | 129.8 | | 4.22 | 131.9 | 5.677 | 142.3 |
| 1971 | 135.4 | | 4.57 | 142.8 | 6.261 | 157.0 |
| 1972 | 139.8 | | 5.15 | 160.9 | 7.075 | 177.4 |
| 1973 | 148.5 | | 5.56 | 173.8 | 7.681 | 192.6 |
| 1974 | 164.8 | | 6.38 | 199.4 | 9.078 | 227.6 |
| 1975 | 179.9 | | 7.11 | 222.2 | 10.590 | 265.5 |
| 1976 | 190.3 | | 7.86 | 245.6 | 11.744 | 294.4 |
| 1977 | 202.6 | | 8.67 | 270.9 | 13.036 | 326.8 |
| 1978 | 218.0 | | 9.70 | 303.1 | 14.303 | 358.6 |
| 1979 | 243.0 | | 10.77 | 336.6 | 15.921 | 399.1 |
| 1980 | 275.7 | | 11.84 | 370.0 | 18.451 | 462.5 |

the application of environmental regulations making it needlessly difficult for the industry to replace polluting old plant with cleaner, new plant. Each of the Federal policy decisions affecting the industry was framed with its own purpose in mind; no effort was made to assess their total impact on the industry's health."

Further, the Steel Tripartite Committee prepared a detailed examination of policy combinations which could cover the industry's capital shortfall (faster capital recovery and refundability, faster capital recovery and reduced capital expenditures, etc.) and then argued, "A piecemeal approach to the steel industry will accomplish little. The problems of the industry cover a number of areas including capital formation, trade, environmental regulation, technology, and

the adjustment of workers and communities to changes in industry conditions. Programs in any one of these areas depend upon progress in others. With or without Government assistance, measures directed only at one of these areas cannot set the industry on a new path. A coordinated and integrated set of initiatives, maintained for a three- to five-year period, or longer, is required to remedy the industry's situation."

Finally, the GAO report, summing up OTA's, the Tripartite Committee's, and its own views, said, "Our overall conclusions parallel those of both the Office of Technology Assessment (Technology and Steel Industry Competitiveness: 1980) and the Steel Tripartite Committee, which served as the basis for the Administration's latest program proposals. We also agree on priority policy action areas for industry revitalization. These include assistance with capital formation to promote modernization investment; an effective trade policy to insure reasonable control of steel imports; and, increased flexibility in administering environmental laws."

## KEY EXECUTIVES AT WHEELING-PITTSBURGH

*Dennis J. Carney—Chairman and Chief Officer*

Carney, 59, was elected Chairman of the Board on January 25, 1978. He had served as President and Chief Operating Officer of Wheeling-Pittsburgh since March 1, 1976.

Following his retirement from U.S. Steel after 32 years, where he was elected Vice-President Long-Range Planning in 1965, and Vice-President Research in 1972, he joined Wheeling-Pittsburgh as Vice-President Operations.

Educated at the University of Pennsylvania, Harvard, and MIT, Carney became widely known for his many technical papers on metallurgy, and iron and steel manufacturing.

In March 1978, Carney was awarded the Benjamin F. Fairless Award for distinguished achievement in iron and steel production and ferrous metallurgy by the American Institute of Mining, Metallurgical and Petroleum Engineers. In 1979, Carney was awarded a Distinguished Life Membership by the American Society for Metals for outstanding contributions to the advancement of the metal industry.

*John E. Wright, III—Vice President, Purchases, Traffic, and Raw Materials*

Wright, 44, joined Wheeling Steel in 1961, and he has served in his current position since 1977. At Wheeling, he advanced in the areas of plant industrial engineering and production control to become Manager, Production Planning, at Wheeling Steel's General Offices. He became Director of Production Control in 1971, and Vice President, Purchases and Traffic in 1976.

*Cornel Bolog—Vice President, Commercial*

Bolog has been with the Corporation for 14 years. Prior to his election to his present position, he served as Manager, Coated Products Sales from 1970 to 1975, as General Manager of Sales for the Eastern Sales Districts from 1975 to 1976, and as Vice President, Sales for Wheeling Corrigating Division from 1976 to 1979.

*Roger McLean—Vice President, Operations*

McLean has held operations responsibilities with Wheeling-Pittsburgh since joining the Company in 1969 as Director of Manufacturing of Wheeling Corrigating Company.

McLean became Vice President, Operations on May 28, 1980. Since 1976, he had served as Vice President and General Manager of Wheeling Corrigating Company, a division of Wheeling-Pittsburgh Steel. In addition to assuming operating responsibilities for the parent company operations, he will also remain in charge of Wheeling Corrigating Company.

## INTERNAL OPERATIONS AT WHEELING-PITTSBURGH

### Raw Materials

W-P owns or has a significant ownership interest in six large iron ore producing operations. These operations, located in Minnesota, Michigan, and Canada, supplied 93 percent of Wheeling-Pittsburgh's iron ore needs of 3,796,000 tons in 1979.

The corporation also owns or has a signif-

**EXHIBIT 7**  Statistical Highlights, U.S. Iron and Steel Industry

| | | 1980 | 1979 | 1978 | 1977 | 1976 | 1975 | 1974 | 1973 | 1972 | 1971 | 1970 |
|---|---|---|---|---|---|---|---|---|---|---|---|---|
| Production (millions of net tons) | TOTAL U.S. Pig Iron | 68.7 | 87.0 | 87.7 | 81.3 | 86.9 | 79.9 | 95.9 | 100.8 | 88.9 | 81.3 | 91.4 |
| | Total U.S. Raw Steel | 111.8 | 136.3 | 137.0 | 125.3 | 128.0 | 116.6 | 145.7 | 150.8 | 133.2 | 120.4 | 131.5 |
| | Open Hearth | 13.0 | 19.2 | 21.3 | 20.0 | 23.5 | 22.1 | 35.5 | 39.8 | 34.9 | 35.6 | 48.0 |
| | Basic Oxygen | 67.6 | 83.2 | 83.5 | 77.4 | 79.9 | 71.8 | 81.6 | 83.3 | 74.6 | 63.9 | 63.3 |
| | Electric | 31.2 | 33.9 | 32.2 | 27.9 | 24.6 | 22.7 | 28.7 | 27.7 | 23.7 | 20.9 | 20.2 |
| | Total Canadian Raw Steel | 17.5 | 17.7 | 16.4 | 15.0 | 14.6 | 14.4 | 15.0 | 14.8 | 13.1 | 12.0 | 12.3 |
| | Total World Raw Steel | 792.1 | 824.5 | 790.6 | 741.8 | 745.6 | 712.0 | 782.8 | 768.6 | 694.6 | 639.9 | 654.2 |
| Shipments (millions of net tons) | Total Steel Mill Products | 83.9 | 100.3 | 97.9 | 91.1 | 89.4 | 80.0 | 109.5 | 111.4 | 91.8 | 87.0 | 90.8 |
| | Carbon | 73.4 | 87.9 | 86.2 | 81.2 | 80.3 | 70.8 | 98.0 | 100.9 | 83.2 | 79.3 | 83.2 |
| | Alloy | 9.4 | 11.0 | 10.5 | 8.8 | 8.1 | 8.4 | 10.2 | 9.4 | 7.8 | 7.0 | 6.9 |
| | Stainless | 1.1 | 1.4 | 1.2 | 1.1 | 1.0 | .8 | 1.3 | 1.1 | .8 | .7 | .7 |
| Shipments, Major Products, All Grades (millions of net tons) | Shapes, Plates and Piling | 13.3 | 14.6 | 13.6 | 11.9 | 11.3 | 13.9 | 18.1 | 16.8 | 13.2 | 13.6 | 14.1 |
| | Bars and Tool Steel | 13.3 | 17.6 | 16.9 | 15.4 | 14.2 | 13.4 | 18.5 | 18.2 | 15.5 | 14.2 | 14.6 |
| | Pipe and Tubing | 9.1 | 8.2 | 8.4 | 7.5 | 6.3 | 8.2 | 9.8 | 9.1 | 7.6 | 7.6 | 7.8 |
| | Wire and Wire Products | 1.8 | 2.4 | 2.5 | 2.4 | 2.5 | 2.2 | 3.2 | 3.2 | 3.0 | 2.8 | 3.0 |
| | Tin Mill Products | 5.7 | 6.3 | 6.1 | 6.4 | 6.4 | 5.7 | 7.5 | 7.3 | 6.1 | 6.8 | 7.2 |
| | Sheets and Strip | 33.6 | 43.5 | 43.6 | 41.7 | 42.3 | 30.8 | 45.0 | 49.4 | 39.9 | 35.6 | 35.1 |
| Shipments, Major Markets (million of net tons) | Automotive | 12.1 | 18.6 | 21.3 | 21.5 | 21.4 | 15.2 | 18.9 | 23.2 | 18.2 | 17.5 | 14.5 |
| | Steel Service Centers | 16.2 | 18.2 | 17.3 | 15.3 | 14.6 | 12.7 | 20.4 | 20.4 | 16.8 | 14.4 | 16.0 |
| | Construction & Contractor's Products | 11.9 | 13.7 | 13.1 | 12.1 | 12.0 | 12.0 | 17.6 | 17.2 | 13.6 | 13.6 | 13.4 |
| | Containers & Packaging | 5.6 | 6.8 | 6.6 | 6.7 | 6.9 | 6.1 | 8.2 | 7.8 | 6.6 | 7.2 | 7.8 |
| | Industrial & Electrical Machinery & Equipment | 7.0 | 8.8 | 8.8 | 8.2 | 7.9 | 7.3 | 9.7 | 9.7 | 8.2 | 7.5 | 7.9 |
| Employment | Average Number of Employees (thousands) | 399 | 453 | 449 | 452 | 454 | 457 | 512 | 509 | 478 | 487 | 531 |

| | | | | | | | | | | | |
|---|---|---|---|---|---|---|---|---|---|---|---|
| Annual Wages and Salaries (billions) | $10.9 | $11.5 | $10.3 | $9.2 | $8.3 | $7.4 | $7.9 | $6.8 | $5.8 | $5.2 | $5.2 |
| Financial — Total Employment Cost/Hr. Worked (hrly. employees) | $18.45 | $15.92 | $14.30 | $13.04 | $11.74 | $10.59 | $9.08 | $7.68 | $7.08 | $6.26 | $5.68 |
| Net Assets (billions) | $33.0 | $31.0* | $30.1 | $28.7 | $27.4 | $25.1 | $22.8 | $21.2 | $20.5 | $20.0 | $19.7 |
| Total Revenue (billions) | $55.0 | $55.7* | $49.5 | $39.7 | $36.5 | $33.7 | $38.2 | $28.9 | $22.6 | $20.4 | $19.3 |
| Net Income (millions) | $1,632 | $1,154* | $1,277 | $22** | $1,337 | $1,595 | $2,475 | $1,272 | $775 | $562 | $531 |
| Long Term Debt (billions) | $9.4 | $8.7* | $8.8 | $8.0 | $7.0 | $5.7 | $4.7 | $5.0 | $5.2 | $5.1 | $5.1 |
| Capital Expenditures (billions) | $3.3 | $3.3* | $2.6 | $2.9 | $3.3 | $3.2 | $2.1 | $1.4 | $1.2 | $1.4 | $1.7 |
| Total Dividends Paid (millions) | $602 | $593* | $536 | $555 | $637 | $658 | $674 | $443 | $402 | $390 | $487 |
| Profit Per Dollar of Sales | 3.0¢ | 2.1¢ | 2.6¢ | 0.06¢** | 3.7¢ | 4.8¢ | 6.6¢ | 4.5¢ | 3.5¢ | 2.8¢ | 2.8¢ |
| Percent Return on Stockholders' Equity† | 9.0% | 6.7% | 7.3% | 0.1%** | 7.8% | 9.8% | 17.1% | 9.3% | 5.8% | 4.3% | 4.1% |
| Debt/Equity Ratio | 49.0 | 48.3* | 49.5 | 45.5 | 38.9 | 33.1 | 29.0 | 34.5 | 38.0 | 38.3 | 39.2 |
| Expenditures for Air and Water Quality Control — Capital Expenditures (millions) | $510.5 | $650.8 | $458.0 | $534.8 | $489.2 | $453.1 | $267.2 | $100.1 | $201.8 | $161.6 | $182.6 |
| Water (millions) | $168.2 | $201.2 | $180.8 | $205.7 | $158.7 | $131.8 | $106.9 | $34.7 | $57.0 | $73.4 | $110.0 |
| Air (millions) | $342.3 | $449.6 | $277.2 | $329.1 | $330.5 | $321.3 | $160.3 | $65.4 | $144.8 | $88.2 | $72.6 |
| Foreign Trade (millions of net tons) — Imports, All Steel Mill Products | 15.5 | 17.5 | 21.1 | 19.3 | 14.3 | 12.0 | 16.0 | 15.1 | 17.7 | 18.3 | 13.4 |
| Carbon | 14.8 | 16.6 | 20.2 | 18.5 | 13.6 | 11.4 | 15.4 | 14.6 | 17.1 | 17.7 | 12.9 |
| Alloy | .559 | .728 | .753 | .580 | .483 | .448 | .413 | .434 | .448 | .415 | .349 |
| Stainless | .153 | .169 | .200 | .178 | .175 | .167 | .176 | .128 | .149 | .192 | .177 |
| Dollar Value (billions) | $6.9 | $7.0 | $6.9 | $5.5 | $4.0 | $4.1 | $5.1 | $2.8 | $2.8 | $2.6 | $2.0 |
| Market Penetration (percentage) | 16.3 | 15.2 | 18.1 | 17.8 | 14.1 | 13.5 | 13.4 | 12.4 | 16.6 | 17.9 | 13.8 |
| Exports, All Steel Mill Products | 4.1 | 2.8 | 2.4 | 2.0 | 2.7 | 3.0 | 5.8 | 4.1 | 2.9 | 2.8 | 7.1 |
| Dollar Value (millions) | $2,557 | $1,878 | $1,329 | $1,037 | $1,255 | $1,862 | $2,118 | $1,004 | $604 | $576 | $1,010 |

*Revised figure.
**Reflects substantial impact of permanent plant closings.
†As of January 1 of each year.
*Source: American Iron and Steel Institute.*

icant ownership interest in four coal mining operations in Pennsylvania, West Virginia, and Kentucky. Approximately 75 percent of Wheeling-Pittsburgh's coal requirements in 1979 were supplied by companies in which it has a significant ownership interest.

Coal and iron ore needs not met by company interests are fulfilled by open market purchases. The corporation's requirements of zinc, manganese, pig tin, limestone, and other raw materials needed to produce steel are purchased from other companies.

W-P does not have a parent. The subsidiaries of the Corporation, all included in the consolidated financial statements, and the percentage of their voting securities owned by the Corporation are listed in Exhibit 8.

## PRODUCTS AND MARKETS

W-P has two major steel producing plants: the Steubenville plant headquartered in Steubenville, Ohio, and the Monessen plant headquartered in Monessen, Pennsylvania. Both plants produce raw steel ingots which are processed into "hot rolled" steel bands. The steel bands are either processed into rolled sheet steel for sale to steel users, or they are processed into finished steel products by W-P.

Exhibit 9 presents the contributions to sales revenues of W-P's classes of similar products; Exhibit 10 shows W-P's shipments (net tons) by product class; Exhibit 11 shows W-P's shipments (net tons) by major market classification; and Exhibit 12 shows W-P's principal markets

---

**EXHIBIT 8**     Wheeling-Pittsburgh's Subsidiaries

| | | |
|---|---|---|
| Consumers Mining Company[2] | Pennsylvania | 100% |
| Ft. Duquesne Coal Company | Kentucky | 100 |
| W-P Coal Company[2] | West Virginia | 100 |
| Daly Gas Company[1] | Pennsylvania | 100 |
| Harmar Coal Company | Pennsylvania | 75 |
| Mingo Oxygen Company | Ohio | 100 |
| Monessen Southwestern Railway Company | Pennsylvania | 100 |
| National Steel Fabric Company[1] | Pennsylvania | 100 |
| Pittsburgh-Canfield Corporation | Pennsylvania | 100 |
| Pittsburgh Steel Sales Company[1] | Pennsylvania | 100 |
| Standard Land and Improvement Company[1] | Pennsylvania | 100 |
| Three Rivers Coal Company[2] | West Virginia | 100 |
| Wheeling-Pittsburgh Trading Company | Delaware | 100 |
| Wheeling-Itasca Co. | Delaware | 100 |

The Corporation also owns a substantial percentage, but in each case no more than 40%, of voting stock of each of eight other corporations or partnerships engaged in the mining or beneficiation of iron ore or the holding of iron ore reserve properties, and owns various percentages, but in each case not more than 40% of the voting stocks of certain other corporations. These corporations have been omitted since, considered in the aggregate as a single subsidiary, they have not been considered to constitute a significant subsidiary.

---

[1]Inactive.
[2]Consumers Mining Company owns 100% of the outstanding stock of W-P Coal Company and Three Rivers Coal Company.

**EXHIBIT 9** Contributions to Sales Revenues

| Products | 1979 | 1978 | 1977 | 1976 | 1975 |
|---|---|---|---|---|---|
| Hot & Cold Rolled Sheet & Strip | 43.3% | 42.8% | 45.0% | 44.1% | 35.6% |
| Tin Mill | 13.2 | 13.4 | 12.2 | 13.4 | 13.2 |
| Coated Sheet | 12.4 | 10.8 | 11.1 | 11.2 | 9.9 |
| Fabricated | 13.3 | 12.2 | 13.1 | 11.8 | 12.2 |
| Seamless Tubular | 8.1 | 10.8 | 9.6 | 8.6 | 15.1 |
| Welded Tubular | 5.8 | 7.0 | 6.5 | 5.5 | 7.8 |
| Other | 3.9 | 3.0 | 2.5 | 5.4 | 6.2 |
| | 100.0% | 100.0% | 100.0% | 100.0% | 100.0% |

**EXHIBIT 10** Shipments (Net Tons) by Product Class

| Products | 1979 | 1978 | 1977 | 1976 | 1975 |
|---|---|---|---|---|---|
| Hot & Cold Rolled Sheet & Strip | 56.4% | 56.1% | 59.0% | 58.6% | 51.7% |
| Tin Mill | 11.5 | 12.0 | 10.8 | 11.6 | 12.2 |
| Coated Sheet | 11.5 | 9.8 | 9.9 | 10.3 | 9.6 |
| Fabricated | 9.2 | 8.5 | 8.9 | 7.9 | 8.3 |
| Seamless Tubular | 4.2 | 5.6 | 5.1 | 4.4 | 7.8 |
| Welded Tubular | 4.9 | 5.5 | 5.1 | 4.2 | 6.2 |
| Other | 2.3 | 2.5 | 1.2 | 3.0 | 4.2 |
| | 100.0% | 100.0% | 100.0% | 100.0% | 100.0% |

**EXHIBIT 11** Shipments (Net Tons) by Major Market Classification

| Market Classification | 1979 | 1978 | 1977 | 1976 | 1975 |
|---|---|---|---|---|---|
| Automotive | 16% | 19% | 23% | 24% | 20% |
| Service Center | 19 | 19 | 21 | 21 | 19 |
| Construction | 16 | 15 | 15 | 12 | 12 |
| Converting & Processing | 12 | 14 | 12 | 13 | 16 |
| Containers | 12 | 11 | 9 | 11 | 11 |
| Appliances | 8 | 8 | 8 | 9 | 8 |
| Oil & Gas | 4 | 6 | 5 | 3 | 5 |
| Misc. | 13 | 8 | 7 | 7 | 9 |
| | 100% | 100% | 100% | 100% | 100% |

**EXHIBIT 12**  Principal Markets and Major Market Classifications to Which Respective Classes of Products Were Sold, Based upon Shipments (Net Tons)

| Products | Automotive | | Construction | | Containers | | Appliances | | Oil & Gas | | Misc. | |
|---|---|---|---|---|---|---|---|---|---|---|---|---|
| | 1979 | 1978 | 1979 | 1978 | 1979 | 978 | 1979 | 1978 | 1979 | 1978 | 1979 | 1978 |
| Hot & Cold Rolled Sheet & | | | | | | | | | | | | |
| Strip | 23% | 26% | 7% | 6% | 7% | 5% | 12% | 10% | —% | —% | 10% | 8% |
| Tin Mill | 7 | 7 | 3 | 5 | 64 | 62 | 7 | 6 | — | — | 5 | 2 |
| Coated Sheet | 20 | 15 | 23 | 16 | 1 | — | 7 | 4 | — | — | 11 | 7 |
| Fabricated | — | — | 93 | 93 | — | — | 3 | 3 | — | — | — | — |
| Seamless Tubular | 3 | 7 | 3 | 4 | — | — | — | — | 70 | 77 | 11 | 3 |
| Welded Tubular | — | — | 22 | 15 | — | — | 2 | 1 | 6 | 6 | 25 | 26 |
| Other | 7 | 3 | — | — | — | — | — | — | — | — | 80 | 79 |
| Total Products | 16 | 19 | 16 | 15 | 12 | 11 | 8 | 8 | 4 | 6 | 13 | 8 |

**EXHIBIT 13**   Per Share Data (in Dollars)

| Yr. End Dec. 31 | 1980 | 1979 | 1978 | 1977 | 1976 | 1975 | 1974 | 1973 | 1972 | 1971 |
|---|---|---|---|---|---|---|---|---|---|---|
| Book Value | 90.75 | 88.80 | 79.00 | 75.12 | 83.56 | 84.06 | 85.68 | 79.38 | 74.96 | 71.46 |
| Earnings[1] | 2.85 | 12.16 | 4.23 | d7.70 | 0.05 | d0.68 | 19.23 | 4.10 | 2.78 | 0.42 |
| Dividends | Nil | 1.00 | Nil | Nil | Nil | 1.05 | 0.35 | Nil | Nil | Nil |
| Payout Ratio | Nil | 8% | Nil | Nil | Nil | NM | 4% | Nil | Nil | Nil |
| Prices—High | 24 | $24^3/_4$ | $14^1/_4$ | 20 | $23^7/_8$ | $31^7/_8$ | $23^1/_4$ | $21^5/_8$ | $24^1/_4$ | $20^1/_2$ |
| —Low | 15 | $10^5/_8$ | 8 | $8^1/_2$ | 16 | $14^1/_4$ | $13^1/_4$ | $10^1/_4$ | $15^5/_8$ | $11^1/_2$ |
| P/E Ratio | 8–5 | 2–1 | 3–2 | NM | NM | NM | 1–1 | 5–3 | 9–6 | 49–27 |

Data as orig. reptd. 1. Bef. spec. item(s) of + 0.35 in 1973, + 0.55 in 1972, + 0.20 in 1971. NM-Not Meaningful. d-Deficit.

and the major market classifications to which respective classes of products were sold, based upon shipments (net tons).

## FINANCIAL MATTERS AT WHEELING-PITTSBURGH

Exhibit 13, 14, and 15 show W-P's per share data, income data, and balance sheet data, respectively.

**New Product Development**

Wheeling-Pittsburgh is currently constructing the world's most modern railroad rail mill at their Monessen location. It is scheduled for completion in 1981 and will cost Wheeling-Pittsburgh an estimated $105,000000. Rail production will diversify the Wheeling-Pittsburgh product mix. The company predicts that 12 percent of their total yearly shipments will come from rail production once the new plant is fully

**EXHIBIT 14**   Income Data (in Millions of Dollars)

| Year Ended Dec. 31 | Revs. | Oper. Inc. | % Oper. Inc. of Revs. | Cap. Exp. | Depr. | Int. Exp. | Net Bef. Taxes | Eff. Tax Rate | [3]Net Inc. | % Net Inc. of Revs. |
|---|---|---|---|---|---|---|---|---|---|---|
| 1980 | 1,054 | 14 | 1.4% | 147 | 39.1 | 22.9 | [2] 9 | NM | 14.7 | 1.4% |
| 1979 | 1,242 | 100 | 8.0% | 54 | 35.7 | [1]18.4 | [2] 60 | 16.7% | 49.7 | 4.0% |
| 1978 | 1,155 | 67 | 5.8% | 32 | 34.5 | 15.5 | [2] 23 | 18.8% | 19.0 | 1.6% |
| 1977 | 966 | 9 | 0.9% | 45 | 34.7 | 14.5 | [2]d33 | NM | d25.6 | NM |
| 1976 | 931 | 41 | 4.4% | 51 | 31.8 | 12.3 | [2] 1 | NM | 3.2 | 0.3% |
| 1975 | 827 | 34 | 4.1% | 61 | 30.3 | 12.8 | [2]Nil | NM | 0.6 | 0.1% |
| 1974 | 1,037 | 138 | 13.3% | 54 | 28.5 | 10.4 | [2]105 | 30.4% | 73.4 | 7.1% |
| 1973 | 761 | 64 | 8.4% | 28 | 30.1 | 10.2 | [2] 26 | 30.8% | 18.1 | 2.4% |
| 1972 | 608 | 58 | 9.5% | 22 | 29.9 | 9.7 | [2] 20 | 35.0% | 13.2 | 2.2% |
| 1971 | 528 | 41 | 7.7% | 18 | 29.4 | 9.7 | [2] 6 | 19.2% | 4.6 | 0.9% |

**EXHIBIT 15**   Balance Sheet Data (in Millions of Dollars)

| Dec. 31 | Cash | —Current— Assets | Liab. | Ratio | Total Assets | Ref. on Assets | Long Term Debt | Com- mon Equity | Total Cap. | % LT Debt of Cap. | Ref. on Equity |
|---------|------|--------|-------|-------|--------|--------|------|--------|------|---------|--------|
| 1980 | 101 | 395 | 238 | 1.7 | 983 | 1.6% | 280 | 353 | 717 | 39.0% | 3.2% |
| 1979 | 74 | 374 | 235 | 1.6 | 847 | 6.0% | 170 | 341 | 593 | 28.6% | 14.3% |
| 1978 | 51 | 345 | 211 | 1.6 | 793 | 2.4% | 189 | 298 | 561 | 33.7% | 5.5% |
| 1977 | 39 | 309 | 184 | 1.7 | 766 | NM | 209 | 282 | 562 | 37.2% | NM |
| 1976 | 37 | 277 | 146 | 1.9 | 728 | 0.5% | 183 | 310 | 561 | 32.6% | 0.1% |
| 1975 | 49 | 258 | 116 | 2.2 | 676 | 0.1% | 160 | 309 | 536 | 29.8% | NM |
| 1974 | 81 | 347 | 199 | 1.7 | 722 | 10.6% | 113 | 314 | 495 | 22.8% | 23.3% |
| 1973 | 31 | 313 | 134 | 2.3 | 661 | 2.7% | 140 | 290 | 498 | 28.2% | 5.3% |
| 1972 | 23 | 315 | 139 | 2.3 | 666 | 2.1% | 155 | 274 | 495 | 31.2% | 3.8% |
| 1971 | 23 | 258 | 113 | 2.3 | 611 | 0.7% | 138 | 260 | 465 | 29.7% | 0.6% |

Data as orig. reptd. 1. Reflects acctg. change. 2. Incl. equity in earns. of nonconsol. subs. 3. Bef. spec. item(s) in 1973, 1972, 1971. NM-Not Meaningful. d-Deficit.
Standard NYSE Stock Reports. Vol. 48/No. 78/Sec. 24. April 24, 1981. Standard Poor's Corp., 25 Broadway, New York, N.Y. 10004. Copyright © 1981. Standard & Poor's Corp.

on line. Company officials also state that the completion of the rail mill will relieve the critical shortage of quality railroad tracks in the U.S. today.

Currently C.F.&I. Steel's rail facility in Pueblo, Colorado, is the most modern rail mill in the United States. But aside from that plant, which supplies western rail needs, the eastern rail-making operations of Bethlehem and U.S. Steel were built in the early 1900s. Rail products of the older mills were suitable when trains carried lighter loads and traveled at slower speeds, but they cannot stand up under the constant pressure they get from faster and heavier trains. Domestic railroad companies have for years been demanding longer and stronger rails which stand up better, but they have been forced to rely on foreign rail makers to obtain quality rails.

Prior to entering the rail market, W-P conducted in-depth studies and held discussions with major domestic railroads. Based on their research, it was concluded that domestic de-

mand was sufficient to justify building a new rail mill. The new mill will be an ultramodern design using the latest in French and Japanese technology.

In December of 1978, one year after President Carter announced his Inter-Agency Task Force on Steel, W-P took advantage of one of the task force's recommendations. They announced that they had obtained tentative federal loan guarantees from two U.S. agencies, contingent on a third state loan guarantee and an Environmental Protection Agency (EPA) consent decree. In March of 1979, the Pennsylvania Industrial Development Authority approved a $10 million loan to Wheeling-Pittsburgh. The company also signed an EPA consent decree setting up a timetable for instituting environmental controls. The state loan and the consent decree cleared the way for loan guarantees by the Economic Development Administration (EDA) and the Farmers Home Administration of $100 million and $40 million, respectively. In the same month, Wheeling-

Pittsburgh signed agreements for the purchase of up-to-date technology and equipment from Japanese and French producers for the rail mill.

W-P's government-guaranteed loans have caused much controversy and anger within the U.S. steel industry. Bethlehem Steel, U.S. Steel, and C.F.& I. Steel Corporation have argued that the use of guarantees in this way was improper. The three companies claimed that the program is not intended for and should not be used to finance new product development and plant expansion.

In August of 1979, the loan agreement with the federal agencies was signed. C.F.&I. Steel Corporation immediately filed suit in Federal Court to stop the loan agreement. C.F.&I., which had just started an expansion of rail capacity using private funds, argued that the government should not finance a large company's move into a new product line.

T. J. Slater, President of C.F.&I. stated,

> . . . the decision to support Wheeling-Pittsburgh's entry into the rail business is "totally illogical" and is apt to create excess capacity in a presently healthy segment of the steel industry. Such decisions only serve to dry up sources of private risk capital available.

While C.F.&I. is concerned about the impact this action will have on future financing alternatives available to steel producers, they and other steel companies perceive it as the first step toward nationalization of the steel industry. Bethlehem Steel's Chairman, Lewis W. Fry, had this to say:

> We are distressed by the government's decision to use tax dollars to permit Wheeling-Pittsburgh

to diversify its product lines. We believe the decision by two federal agencies to help a private company finance a new steel facility in the Greater Pittsburgh area violates the basic principles of our free enterprise system.

Wheeling-Pittsburgh does not agree with their competitors. They have said that the loan guarantees are just that—guarantees. W-P's management believes there is no question that they can and will be able to repay the loans when they are due. Additionally, they believe the controversy represents an attempt by the companies who currently produce railroad tracks to protect their market position. Wheeling-Pittsburgh's Chairman, Dennis J. Carney, has stated,

> Three major producers have had a corner of the market for rails in this country for over 50 years. No new rail mills have been built in this country since the early 1900's . . . the real fact is that they don't want competition in rails, either domestic or foreign.

In May of 1980, with legal proceedings still pending in Federal Court, Wheeling-Pittsburgh reached agreement with nine institutional lenders on a loan structure with the above-mentioned federal guarantees. The package furnished $160 million in funds. These loans along with $38 million raised privately were slated to (1) cover $86.5 million worth of pollution control equipment under the EPA consent decree, and (2) to finance the nation's newest rail mill, worth $105 million.

Recently, the C.F.&I. Corporation dropped its appeal case after losing the first decision, but top managers at W-P are convinced the battle is not over yet.

# PART FIVE

# CASES ON SERVICE AND NOT-FOR-PROFIT ORGANIZATIONS

# 19 HUMANA, INC.

### George S. Vozikis

*University of Oklahoma*

### Timothy S. Mescon

*University of Miami (Florida)*

Michael M. Le Coney, security analyst for Merrill, Lynch, Pierce, Fenner and Smith, has said, "With Humana, investors are dealing with what I believe may be the most aggressive and smartest major company in the U.S. That's a lot to say about any company, but Humana's success, and the absolutely, uncanny accuracy of its corporate strategy, make it a supportable statement" (*Wall Street Transcript,* June 9, 1980).

## HISTORY

Humana, Inc. was begun in 1961, when David A. Jones and Wendell Cherry, two young lawyers, built their first nursing home. Humana, Inc. was incorporated in Delaware, on July 28, 1964, as Extendicare Inc. It became the successor to Heritage House of America Inc., which commenced operations in 1961.

By 1967, government health programs such as Medicaid and Medicare had been implemented by Congress, and Humana, Inc. was running eight nursing homes. In 1968, a flu epidemic struck New Haven, Connecticut, and a hospital placed its overflow in their local nursing home.

The "Gold Dust Twins," as business associates sometimes call Jones and Cherry, discovered that hospitals earned six times as much from Medicare and Medicaid than nursing homes.

In 1968, a boom year for nursing home stocks, they took their company public. Humana began to buy up existing private hospitals at a rate of one per month, and by selling their nursing homes and mobile home parks (and by borrowing heavily), in 1972 and 1973 embarked on a $300 million dollar hospital construction program, completing some 39 hospitals in the South and Southwest by 1976.

The National Health Planning and Resources Development Act was passed in 1974, which prohibited the renovation, construction, or purchase of equipment costing more than $100,000.00, unless state and local health planning agencies approved it as necessary. Humana, Inc. was convinced that this law would practically halt new construction, and they began to supplement hospital purchases by buying out competitors such as American Medicorp, number two in the industry and in 1978 when it was purchased by Humana.

Little cash was used. The acquisitions were accomplished by exchanging stock with doctor-owners. Success in acquisition efforts precipitated an internal growth strategy of construction of additional hospitals, coupled with a divestment of the nursing homes. By 1977, this strategy increased revenues to $316 million from $85 million in 1971, and long-term debt to $224.3 million from $87.8 million.

In 1980, Humana's revenues increased to $1.1 billion from 1977's $316 million, and profits from $11.8 million to $64.6 million. Significantly, Humana's ten-year compounded growth rate of 32 percent exceeded all but eight companies in *Financial World* magazine's annual ranking of 10-year performance by companies with revenues above $500 million.

Humana, known as an industry leader with a strong financial background, presently owns and operates ninety-three facilities with a total of 17,138 beds, in short-term, acute-care community hospitals in twenty-three states, and in two European countries.

Humana's stated goal is "to provide hospital services of measurable, unexcelled quality, without waste, in response to the needs and values of patients and their physicians" (*Humana 1980 Annual Report*, p. 7). Emphasis is not placed upon research or extensive medical-educational programs.

## COMPETITIVE AND INDUSTRY ISSUES

Widely diverse forms of ownership and control are found in the hospital industry. There are networks of hospitals operated by the U.S. government to serve segments of the poplulation for which it assumes a special obligation. There are also many publicly owned hospitals operated under the control of state and local governments. For the most part, however, the ownership of hospitals serving the general community is in the private sector. The great majority of community general hospitals are voluntary not-for-profit institutions, and many are operated under religious sponsorship. The private sector includes also a significant number, but relatively small proportion, of proprietary, investor-owned institutions.

There are approximately 7,700 hospitals of all types in the United States. Nearly one-half of this number are operated by charitable organizations other than the government. The number of the facilities owned by investors-private sector is approximately 1,300, which covers 11% of America's hospital beds. Among the top six of the for-profit hospital companies, which control one-third of the for-profit hospitals, Humana has inspired entrepreneurs with phenomenal growth.

The for-profit hospital sector is made up of many small doctor-owned facilities. The six largest companies have intensely competed for beds to achieve market share and economies of scale and they now control over 50 percent of the for-profit hospital industry's beds. At the end of 1979, the 15 largest investor-owned multihospital firms were as shown in Table 1.

At present, most hospitals need not be price competitive, since 95 percent of all Americans are covered by some form of third-party reimbursement.

**TABLE 1**    The 15 Largest Investor-Owned Multihospital Firms

| Company | Number of Beds | Number of Facilities |
|---|---|---|
| Hospital Corp. of America | 20,240 | 130 |
| Hospital Affiliated Int'l.* | 16,620 | 126 |
| Humana | 16,289 | 89 |
| Hyatt Medical Enterprises† | 6,467 | 35 |
| American Medical Int'l. | 6,176 | 48 |
| Nat'l. Medical Enterprises | 4,909 | 41 |
| Lifemark | 4,305 | 36 |
| Charter Medical | 1,474 | 10 |
| Brookwood Health Services | 1,404 | 14 |
| General Care‡ | 1,294 | 8 |
| General Health Services | 1,287 | 7 |
| Southern Health Services | 1,178 | 11 |
| A. E. Brim & Associates | 1,097 | 25 |
| American Health Care Management | 757 | 5 |
| Universal Health Services | 706 | 5 |

*Acquired by Hospital Corporation of America in 1981.
†Acquired by American Medical International in 1980.
‡Acquired by Hospital Corporation of America in 1980.
*Source:* Standard & Poor's Industry Surveys. *Health Care.* March 19, 1981. Volume 149, No. 12, Sec. 1.

The for-profit hospitals aim more at serving the privately insured, short-term patient to achieve a higher profit margin. This leaves the non-profit organizations more responsibility to serve the uninsured patients who cannot pay for services. This is indicated by the loss of bad debt ratio for non-profit organizations of 4.5% of revenues compared to 2.5% for the leading company.

## Legislative Issues

The cost, quality, and accessibility of health and medical services have always been an issue of government and society's concern. Public confidence in the efficiency of medical services is expressed in a national policy affirming a universal right of access to health care according to need. Governmental programs to implement this policy are directed largely to lowering financial barriers to medical and hospital services.

But currently, governmental programs are being developed for a limit to government involvement and for increased encouragement of efficient private companies through deregulation. Various bills pending in Congress would deregulate the hospital industry and encourage competition and consumer choice. The National Health Care Reform Act of 1980 calls for replacing government regulations with market and tax incentives, allowing health care providers to compete in terms of the price and quality of their product, lowering cost-based reimbursements, decreasing government-mandated health planning, and revising the Medicare and Medicaid programs.

From 1965 to 1978, the percentage of total health care expenditures that was government-financed rose to 41%, from 25%. In 1985, some 42% of total health spending is expected to be financed from public funds, of which 72% will be paid by the federal government. This trend of increasing government should moderate, however, under a conservative administration. No large increases in the number of new recipients or major new benefits are expected to be added during the next few years.

Expected changes in the hospital industry might include:

- Cutbacks in Medicare/Medicaid
- Changes in the reimbursement system (the present cost-based system forces neither the consumer nor the provider of health care to be concerned about price)
- Legislation to increase competition in the health care industry (this would be aimed at improving the quality of health care while limiting the increases in its costs)
- Changes in health care delivery [a sharp rise in the number of health care maintenance organizations is anticipated over the next few years]

*Health Care Maintenance Organizations (HMOs)* A 3-year extension of the Health Planning and Resources Development Act of 1974 was signed into law in October 1979. This law exempts from certificate-of-need coverage federally certified health maintenance organizations (HMOs) with more than 50,000 enrollees and acquisitions of health care facilities unless there is a change in bed capacity. This will make changes in health care delivery.

Private health insurers are promoting a number of efforts for HMOs. For example, the Blue Cross-Blue Shield Association, the nation's largest insurer, has invested some $30 million in the development of HMO programs. According to a recent study, HMOs can save their members as much as an estimated 40% over traditional plans, due primarily to a reduction in the number of hospital days because of fewer admissions.

Some competitors have sponsored or established HMOs which emphasize illness prevention and health promotion, and encourage the use of less expensive outpatient services instead of more expensive hospitalization. Because of this trend, HMOs might be encouraged to expand and take patients away from hospitals.

## Labor

One problem affecting profit margins that the industry must tackle is the current severe shortage of nurses. An American Hospital Association's survey reported that nearly 100,000 nursing positions in its 6,100 member hospitals are unfilled. Hospital profit margins are affected by higher overtime fees, costly hourly compensation for temporary replacements, and lost revenue through closed beds. Hospitals now spend millions of dollars on help-wanted advertising and recruitment enticements. The National Association of Registered Nurses estimates that the current turnover rate for nurses is 32% annually with an average $1,010 spent by hospitals to hire each nurse.

According to the nurse organizations, the major reasons for shortages include low pay, poor working conditions, and lack of respect from physicians. In addition, career opportunities in fields not traditionally open to women have increased and have diverted potential nurses.

## Science and Technology

Hospital organizations use an intensive technology that draws on a variety of methods and techniques to achieve improvement in the condition and health of the patient. Because advances in technology can provide great advantages to patients and physicians, hospitals intend to keep their facilities in the forefront of medical developments. The advanced technology helps the hospitals to achieve productivity and high-quality services.

Since the 1970's, there have been very rapid developments in the medical equipment industry parallel with the growth of the computer industry. These developments made possible the usage of some very sophisticated equipment by hospitals. These are far more cost-effective than traditional procedures. For example, without computerized axoid tomographic (CAT) scanners, a typical case using conventional processes and generally requiring several days of hospitalization would cost more than $2,400; but with a CAT scanner, it would cost $223.

The advanced computer technology helps the hospital industry in some other areas as well as medical areas. For example, aided by computers, hospitals are keeping tight controls over inventories. Another example, a central processing unit handles patient billing for several facilities at a location away from the hospitals. This arrangement provides a productive business environment for processing patient accounts.

## Financing

Financial relationships between the hospitals and its clients are mediated commonly by third parties: private health insurance organizations and governmental programs of health services financing. As government has enlarged its role in the financing of health services in the private sector, it has also adopted measures to implement an explicit policy of cost containment. At the same time, since borrowing has come to be the principal means whereby the hospital meets its growing capital requirements, capital costs account for an even larger share of hospital expenses.

The federal government has a vested interest in keeping a lid on hospital costs, the most heavily funded health care expenditure; an estimated 54.5% of such costs were reimbursed by the government in 1980.

In an effort to limit health care spending, the government has instituted various programs. Among these is the Certificate of Need (CON) program. The goal is to avoid duplication of hospital services. Expansion of capacity is an important source of revenue growth for the hospital management industry. But the CON requirement discourages the addition of new hospital beds through construction, encouraging, instead, expansion through acquisitions. This adds to the industry's trend toward consolidation and increases the value of each existing hospital. The cost of acquiring hospitals is now often more than $100,000 a bed. This high price limits the return on investment that a hospital management chain can achieve from each new acquisition. And there are other heavy costs. For example, chains spend much time and money becoming conversant with the planning criteria in the various states in which they operate. On the other hand, the cost of borrowing money is getting prohibitive.

Increased project costs cut into profit margins of the hospital chains and must eventually be passed on to the consumer in the form of higher hospital charges. Construction limits would reduce the ability of hospitals to raise funds through relatively inexpensive tax-exempt financing. The resulting higher debt burden of hospitals would be passed on to the government through higher Medicare reimbursements.

Most of the future expansion of health care will come from technological advances that lead

to the replacement of outdated equipment, or from the replacement of existing facilities with better-equipped structures.

## Health Care Costs

Health care expenditures continue to absorb an increasing proportion of gross national product (GNP), due to several persistent national trends over the last decade: expanded public and private health insurance coverage, making medical care available to an increasing number of Americans; the growing number of older Americans; increases in the intensification of services resulting from advances in medical technology; and rising costs per unit of service, partly due to higher energy and medical supply prices.

Between 1965 and 1979, health care expenditures as a proportion of GNP rose to 9.0% from 6.1%, with a further rise to 10.5% projected by 1985. National health care expendi-

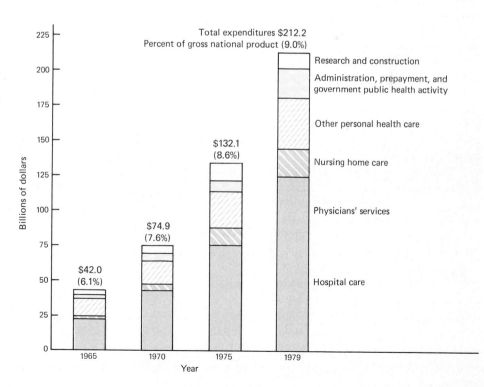

**Figure 1 National health expenditures (in billions of dollars).** *Source: Department of Health and Human Services.*

**Figure 2 Projected national health expenditures as a percentage of the GNP (in billions of dollars).** *Source: Office of Research, Demonstrations and Statistics, Health Care Finance Administration, U.S. Department of Health and Human Services.)*

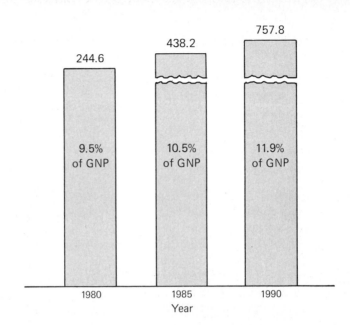

tures rose at an annual rate of 12% from 1965 to 1979, versus a 9% growth rate for GNP (see Figures 1 and 2.)

Hospital bills represent America's largest single health care cost. According to the Health Care Financing Administration (HCFA), of the $244.6 billion Americans will spend on health care in 1980, 40%, or $97.3 billion, will go for hospital care. Hospital costs accounted for about 40% of total health care expenditures in 1979, up sharply from 32% in 1965. By 1985, this figure should reach 42%.

Despite the heavy regulation of their industry, hospitals have been able to pass inflation on in the form of price increases, thus protecting profit margins. Increased "census," or patient-days, provided only a small part of the growth in hospital costs. Much of the rise came from increased usage of facilities. Outpatient services have been growing, spurred not only by more highly sophisticated medical technology, such as the CAT scanner, but also by increased use of emergency rooms and radiological and diagnostic departments and greater use of clinical laboratories.

## GENERAL ORGANIZATION AND MANAGEMENT OF HUMANA

The medical, professional, and ethical policies of each hospital are controlled by a Board of Trustees appointed by Humana, Inc. Each Board of Trustees is composed of staff physicians, local residents, and employees of Humana, Inc. Subject to the control of the Board of Trustees, the medical staff of each hospital supervises and regulates its medical and surgical procedures. The day-to-day fiscal and administrative operation of each of the Purchaser's hospitals is under the supervision and direction of a full time professional administrator. Five regional managers are responsible for operations in their designated areas.

Centralized management services are supplied to the hospitals by the Purchaser's home office. These services include financing, recruiting and personnel development, accounting, data processing, consulting, and purchasing.

Humana, Inc., does not operate any hospitals under management contract with unrelated third parties.

Humana's effective management is increasingly dependent on the expertise of specialists in financial management, information processing, quality control, systems engineering, personnel management, and labor relations. Mr. Jones and Mr. Cherry believe, at the top executive level, decision-making strategy is essentialy judgmental but increasingly requires formal analysis of quantitative data. At staff and operational levels, Humana uses the specialized skills and tools of management technology.

The specialization of medical services, along with the functional differentiation of professional and paraprofessional roles, generates multiple, often competing, demands for hospital-based resources. The problem of balancing these demands is solved by Humana's managers very innovatively. Years ago, Humana pioneered the meaurement of hospital quality by establishing goals for patient care. The management staff, working with hospital representatives, determines what is important in each hospital area and develops operating goals. After being reviewed by a physician council, the goals are field-tested in several hospitals to see if they are important and attainable before they are implemented throughout the company.

Humana remains the only major hospital management company not engaged in the "management of hospitals for others on a fee basis." This allows them to use centralized facilities such as their San Antonio central business office, which serves ten hospitals in three states and is pioneering electronic claims processing.

Through this centralizing process, Humana achieves not only economies of scale, but also a pyramid organizational structure. With the hospitals, being the base, and Humana being the pinnacle, there is a direct, upward communication flow and a reciprocal flow of benefits based on economies of scale.

David A. Jones, Chairman of the Board and Chief Executive Officer, was quoted in the *New York Times* as saying that Humana's managerial depth is "unmatched in the fledgling investor-owned health care industry." This same attitude of confidence is reflected by all levels of corporate management. The mobility of subsidiary and affiliate employees is definitely upward. The corporate ranks are full of former subsidiary and affiliate employees. This policy has proven to be profitable for both the company and its employees. Humana's management is also characterized by its stability. The same top executives have led the company throughout its 19-year history.

David A. Jones, Chairman of the Board and Chief Executive Officer, and Wendell Cherry, President and Chief Operating Officer, are the focal point of strategic planning, formulating long-range goals and policies compatible with the function of the company and the laws of community health services. As operating heads of the organization, both men are responsible for management of the company and are accountable to the governing authority.

Outside organizations also recognize exceptional performance by Humana executives. David A. Jones was selected as the outstanding chief executive officer in the hospital industry by *The Wall Street Transcript*. The newspaper commended Humana's chairman for guiding its rapid expansion, for devotion to excellence, for achieving great operating efficiency through centralized management, and for the rapid assimilation of American Medicorp.

At Humana, executive roles differ with respect to levels of accountability for formulating institutional objectives and policies, monitoring the quality of medical services, acquiring and allocating institutional resources, and shaping external relationships. While the chief executive officer is specifically accountable to the governing authority for the conduct of the hospitals, the challenge is to chart the long-range development of the company in accordance with the principle of accountability to the larger community.

| Name | Age | Position |
| --- | --- | --- |
| David A. Jones | 49 | Chairman of the Board and Chief Executive Officer |
| Wendell Cherry | 45 | President and Chief Operating Officer |
| Carl F. Pollard | 42 | Executive Vice President |
| William C. Ballard, Jr. | 40 | Executive Vice President–Finance and Administration |
| Thomas J. Flynn | 43 | Senior Vice President and General Counsel |
| H. Linden McLellan | 43 | Senior Vice President–Facility Management |
| Harold C. Rimes | 49 | Senior Vice President–Pacific Region |
| P. Duane Walker | 49 | Senior Vice President–Management Systems |
| Jerry L. Bowling | 40 | Vice President–Reimbursement |
| Jack Clark | 48 | Vice President–Mid South Region |
| F. Donald Davis | 46 | Vice President–Administration, Hospital Division |
| Beuregard A. Fournet | 40 | Vice President–Hospital Services |
| Paul A. Gross | 43 | Vice President–Florida Region |
| Rodney E. Jedlicki | 38 | Vice President and Associate General Counsel |
| John V. Kessler | 58 | Vice President–Insurance |
| George M. Lansdell | 42 | Vice President–Western Region |
| John P. Laverty | 52 | Vice President–Education and Documentation |
| William H. Lomicka | 43 | Vice President–Finance and Treasurer |
| Larry P. Lowe | 47 | Vice President–Marketing |
| Daniel Mayeux | 50 | Vice President–Delta Region |
| Kathryn Mershon | 37 | Vice President–Nursing |
| Gary W. Metcalf | 36 | Vice President and Controller, Hospital Division |
| H. Herbert Phillips | 52 | Vice President–Human Resources |
| Fred Pirman, Jr. | 45 | Vice President–Information Systems |
| Paul B. Powell | 53 | Vice President–Purchasing |
| Lyndol J. Rogers | 43 | Vice President–Employee Relations |
| F. David Rollo, M.D., Ph.D. | 41 | Vice President–Advanced Medical Technology and Medical Affairs |
| Joseph E. Shiprek | 47 | Vice President–Internal Audit |
| Wayne T. Smith | 34 | Vice President–Central Region |
| Robert B. Steele | 48 | Vice President–Taxes |
| Charles E. Teeple | 52 | Vice President–Communications |
| James J. Walters | 36 | Vice President–Design and Construction |
| Henry J. Werronen | 37 | Vice President–Planning and Development |
| Alice F. Newton | 42 | Secretary |

The company has 5,700 stockholders. Insiders control 29% of common stock. Doctors are partners in hospital ownership, have vested interests in hospital operations, and swap stock with doctors who own hospitals which are being purchased. They set up limited partnerships with doctors who own real estate where they build.

Set forth in the accompanying table are the present executive officers of the company, their ages and their positions held with the company.

Officers are elected annually by the Board of Directors and serve for a one-year period and until their successors are elected. No officers have employment contracts with the company. Almost all of the above named officers have been employees of the company for more than the last five years.

## MARKETING

Humana followed a policy of selective distribution of its services to achieve its rapid growth strategy while attracting the specific target market which management defined.

*Market segmentation* was a corporate strength utilized effectively by Humana. Young families living in suburbs located primarily in the sunbelt were the primary target. This segment is likely to be privately insured, require routine surgery, and have short stays in the hospital. These factors yield a high profit margin and increase utilization of diagnostic facilities. The babies will provide a second generation of customers.

*Pricing* policies are profit oriented. Humana charges what the market will bear for privately insured patients. Medicare and Medicaid charges are based on the maximum allowable overhead allocations.

Humana justifies expenditures by analyzing the expected returns. Diagnostic equipment and services are readily provided to meet doctors' and community needs when the costs are justifiable. Humana's average costs are higher than the industry averages, but this is a difficult comparison. Non-profit operations control 89% of America's hospital beds and their costs and structure are different from Humana.

*Service* receives strong emphasis from Humana management. Every patient receives initial contact within minutes after admission. Gourmet meals are part of the menu with complimentary wine at certain facilities. Use of computer analysis aids streamlining service procedures to enhance service while controlling costs.

*Promotion* consists of a strategy to "push" the hospital through the channel by hard sell methods aimed at local doctors. Humana constructed offices and clinics adjacent to hospitals and offered doctors one-year-free leases. Doctors were given guaranteed salaries of $60,000 in some cases. Humana then "encouraged" doctors to send patients in the target segment to Humana, and records were maintained of the number of admissions per doctor. Those not cooperating with the system did not have leases renewed.

Insta-Care cards were sent to homes mapped in strategic areas surrounding company hospitals. The cards guaranteed speedy admission and treatment to patients entering the emergency room. These cards play on people's fears of helplessness in a crisis, stressing that since card-carriers are considered financially sound, they will receive faster treatment without the delay of red tape. The Insta-Care cards waive the $180.00 deductible that Medicare patients pay. Humana also began a Cradle Club which offers expectant mothers pre-natal care classes and discounts from local merchants. David Jones admits that these cards don't do much. A patient should get 60-second treatment with or without the Insta-Care card. Because people don't know that, the cards are comforting to them. In 18 months, Humana's marketing blitz increased revenues $2.7 million and occupancy seven percentage points.

Recently, Humana introduced a four-sided brochure placed in rooms of Florida motels near Humana facilities. It is designed to direct travelers to nearby medical services.

# OPERATIONS

The mission of Humana is to achieve and maintain, through a system of hospital management, an unequaled level of measurable quality and productivity in the delivery of hospital services which are responsive to the values and needs of patients and their physicians. This goal applies to every phase of Humana's operations.

Work continues on formulating measurable quality goals for each important process that takes place in company hospitals. At the same time, productivity is vital to the cost-effective delivery of hospital services. Humana ranks first in the industry in the important area of holding down operating expenses as a percentage of gross revenues. Humana's operating expenses in 1980 were reduced to 61.9% of gross revenues from 64.8% the year before. This was substantially better than that achieved by any of the other major hospital companies.

Humana is very successful with the cost-control problem. The company applies sharp cost-cutting treatments to each hospital. Since labor costs represent 50% to 60% of a hospital's budget, industrial engineers used computers to compare each department with those in Humana hospitals.

Humana handles its goals of providing unexcelled care at the lowest possible cost very well. Interviews with doctors in several communities where Humana operates indicate that the quality of care equals or exceeds that of other area hospitals.

Humana measures its efficiency as expenses per case. In fiscal year 1979, its average cost per in-patient case came to $1,453 vs. the community hospitals' average of $1,564.

The company has an excellent purchasing system. Purchasing groups demanding quantity discounts have been formed and hospitals in some areas are sharing certain services in an attempt to limit expenditures. Humana purchases its supply in large quantities and gets higher volume discounts under nationwide contracts.

Because advances in technology can provide great advantages to patients and physicians, Humana intends to keep its hospitals in the forefront of medical developments. Recently, F. David Rollo, M.D., Ph.D., joined the company as Vice President for advanced medical technology and medical affairs. Dr. Rollo monitors research and development by leading manufacturers of medical products and helps define the clinical systems required to introduce emerging technologies to Humana hospitals.

Inventories are valued at the lower of cost (first-in, first-out) or market. Aided by computers, Humana's hospitals are keeping tight control over inventories.

In the hospital industry, capacity is measured by the number of beds. Humana's capacity is the second in the industry. Humana owns and operates 90 hospitals containing 16,765 licensed beds. This gives to the company a great strength within the for-profit hospital industry. (See Table 2.)

As used in Table 2, the term "licensed beds" is the maximum number of beds permitted in the facility under its license regardless of whether the beds are actually available for patient care. The term "weighted licensed beds" is the number of licensed beds after giving effect to the length of time the beds have been licensed during the period. "Patient days" is the total number of days of patient care provided by the company's hospitals. Occupancy rates are calculated by dividing average patient days (total patient days divided by total number of days for the period) by weighted licensed beds.

The occupancy rate of a hospital is affected by a number of factors, including the number of physicians using the hospital, the composition and size of the population, general economic conditions of the area serviced by the hospital, variations in medical and surgical practices in local communities, the degree of outpatient use of hospital services, the length of patient stay, and the number, type and quality of other hospitals in the area. Humana has

**TABLE 2**   Occupancy Rates for Humana Corp. 1976–1980*

| | Fiscal Year Ended August 31 | | | | |
|---|---|---|---|---|---|
| | **1980** | **1979** | **1978** | **1977** | **1976** |
| Number of hospitals in operation at end of period | 90 | 91 | 96 | 60 | 60 |
| Licensed beds in operation at end of period | 16,765 | 16,147 | 16,214 | 8,507 | 8,370 |
| Weighted licensed beds | 16,753 | 16,267 | 13,006 | 8,542 | 8,236 |
| Patient days | 3,611,282 | 3,401,663 | 2,724,327 | 1,693,580 | 1,658,136 |
| Occupancy rate | 59% | 57% | 57% | 54% | 55% |

*The Medicorp Hospitals for the fiscal years ended August 31, 1977 and 1976 had occupancy rates of 56%.

generally experienced lower occupancy rates at its hospitals during the first half of its fiscal year, when major holidays occur, than during the second half. During fiscal 1980, 1979 and 1978 occupancy was favorably affected by the maturation of the company's newer facilities resulting in increased occupancy rates in those facilities and by the decrease in the company's rate of construction of new hospitals in recent years. However, if fiscal 1980 occupancy was adversely affected by the opening of a 356-bed and a 120-bed hospital, the acquisition of a 240-bed hospital and several replacements or expansions totaling 231 beds. Fiscal 1979 occupancy was adversely affected by the openings of a new 400-bed hospital, a 174-bed expansion at one hospital and decreased occupancy in certain of the company's California hospitals and certain older hospitals which have been sold or were replaced. Humana believes that the downward trend in its overall occupancy rate during fiscal 1976 and 1977 was attributable to the opening of new hospitals, which typically initially experience lower occupancy rates than mature facilities, and decreasing occupancy in several of the older hospitals which were being replaced or have been sold. Humana believes that since the beginning of fiscal 1976 the average occupancy rate of its hospitals (exclusive

of the Medicorp Hospitals for 1976 and 1977) has been below the average occupancy rate for investor-owned hospitals in the United States.

**Properties**

Table 3 sets forth the location and number of licensed beds in the 90 hospitals operated by the company at August 31, 1980. The number of licensed beds represents the maximum number of beds permitted to the facility under its state license. The number of beds actually in use in the facility may be less than the number of licensed beds for various reasons, such as beds being placed in service over a period of time as required in newly-opened hospitals or removal of beds from service for renovation.

In selecting locations for new hospitals, Humana considers the local demand for hospital beds, interest expressed by local physicians in having additional or improved facilities, the availability of desirable sites and financing. In some instances, the company is approached by local physicians or the owners of other hospitals with requests to construct a new hospital or to replace an obsolete one. The company conducts its own in-depth feasibility study before undertaking a new hospital project. Although Humana engages independent architects and general contractors in connec-

**TABLE 3** Existing Hospital Locations and Their Capacity, and Hospitals under Construction (1981)

| State | # Locations in State | # Beds in State | Smallest | Largest | Under Construction |
|-------|---------------------|-----------------|----------|---------|--------------------|
| Alabama | 5 | 822 | 100 | 294 | — |
| Arizona | 1 | 314 | — | — | 1 @ $ 4,501,000 |
| California | 12 | 1,716 | 89 | 236 | 1 @ $ 19,051,000 |
| Colorado | 2 | 450 | 200 | 250 | — |
| Florida | 16 | 3,783 | 65 | 458 | 3 @ $ 13,615,000 |
| Georgia | 2 | 494 | 120 | 374 | — |
| Illinois | 2 | 556 | 200 | 356 | 1 @ $ 920,000 |
| Kansas | 2 | 510 | 110 | 400 | — |
| Kentucky | 5 | 1,279 | 90 | 484 | 1 @ $ 22,252,000 |
| Louisiana | 6 | 549 | 55 | 126 | — |
| Mississippi | 2 | 263 | 101 | 162 | — |
| Nevada | 1 | 661 | — | — | 2 @ $ 20,616,000 |
| New Jersey | 2 | 512 | 204 | 308 | — |
| North Carolina | 1 | 100 | — | — | — |
| Oregon | 2 | 275 | 66 | 209 | — |
| Pennsylvania | 2 | 419 | 196 | 223 | — |
| South Carolina | 1 | 52 | — | — | — |
| Tennessee | 5 | 552 | 52 | 137 | — |
| Texas | 11 | 2,451 | 65 | 416 | — |
| Utah | 1 | 100 | — | — | — |
| Virginia | 3 | 585 | 135 | 250 | — |
| Washington | 2 | 278 | 123 | 155 | — |
| West Virginia | 2 | 194 | 72 | 122 | 1 @ $ 8,673,000 |
| *International* | | | | | |
| England | 1 | 105 | — | — | 1 @ $ 37,432,000 |
| Switzerland | 1 | 240 | — | — | — |
| Total | 90 | 17,260 | | | 11 @ $127,060,000 |

tion with the construction, renovation and expansion of its hospitals, the construction department supervises both the design and construction of hospitals. In the United States the construction of new and replacement hospitals and the renovation and expansion of existing hospitals are generally subject to health planning agency and/or certificate of need approvals. Humana also has jumped onto the bandwangon of "minor emergency clinics." This new wave of health-care treatment by what is sometimes called an "emergicenter" aims to siphon off all but the most serious cases from hospital emergency rooms. The clinics usually charge less than conventional emergency rooms, but are open fewer hours and are not so versatile. Humana already has opened seven units in what will be—maybe just for starters, the company says—a $43 million chain with 66 clinics in 15 cities. These clinics, according to the new, Dallas-based National Association of Freestanding Emergency Centers numbered about 500 as of November 1981 compared to 50 in 1978.

### Liability Insurance

A wholly-owned subsidiary of the company licensed by the Colorado Department of Insurance (the "Insurance Subsidiary") insures professional liability risks of Humana's hospitals for initial losses of up to $2,000,000 per occurrence, $2,000,000 per facility and $15,000,000 in the aggregate and insures general liability risks of up to $2,000,000 in the aggregate. Additional insurance purchased from commercial insurers provides total coverage for professional and general liability claims of $47,000,000 per occurrence and $60,000,000 in the aggregate. The aggregate limits of the company's coverage apply to all liability risks, and payments for losses from risks other than malpractice would reduce the coverage available for malpractice claims during the policy period. A professional insurance management organization has been retained to manage the operations of the Insurance Subsidiary. Humana intends to utilize the Insurance Subsidiary's assets solely for the payment of claims and does not intend to withdraw any of the subsidiary's assets for any other purpose. The Insurance Subsidiary insures risks of Humana only, and generally does not provide insurance to physicians except those who are actually employed by the company.

## PERSONNEL

Humana places strong emphasis on quality employees and keeping them happy. As of August 31, 1981, Humana, Inc. had approximately 40,400 employees: 29,500 full-time; 10,900 part-time. 14,400 of these employees were registered or licensed practical nurses, and 14,000 were licensed physicians of which one-half were members of the active staff. Physicians are usu-

ally not members of the hospital staff, but some may provide ancillary services under contract. Application to the medial staff may be made by any licensed physician or dentist with approval coming from the medical staff and either one of the Boards that apply. Humana medical staff personnel may also serve on the staffs of other hospitals.

Humana recruits only doctors to its hospitals who service ailments most common to young, privately insured patients: family doctors and specialists (i.e. general surgeons, gynecologists, neurologists, and doctors who work with sports related injuries). Humana does actively investigate and recruit only for these doctors. It will construct office buildings next door to its hospitals which offer the doctors offices at a discount with up to one year's free rent. The latest in medical technology will be provided for the doctors along with office staff, furniture, and partners. Salaries of up to $60,000 are guaranteed for the first year. Any difference below this salary is made up by Humana.

Humana has incentive compensation plans whereby employees, some of whom are directors and officers, may earn as much as 60% of their base salaries based upon actual performance measured against certain financial objectives. In addition, the stock bonus plan provides that hospital administrators may be granted shares of Humana common stock having a value equivalent to 20% to 50% of incentive compensation if they achieve certain operating objectives. Shares awarded under this plan are deliverable over a five-year period and any shares not delivered are forfeited if the administrator's employment is terminated.

Humana aims to make its hospitals the place where nurses will prefer to work. To achieve this objective of employee satisfaction, Humana appointed Kathryn Mershon as the industry's first vice president for nursing. Mrs. Mershon is developing a recruitment, training, and retention program to attract and hold top nurses. Nurses have also been utilized in the corporate management process and the employee relations department.

The company also conducts training programs to prepare employees for positions as hospital administrators. It has trained 350 persons in ten years.

Humana has a reputation for dismissing the management of companies it takes over. "Humana takes no prisoners" has become a widespread comment among industry competitors and analysts. This reputation dates to its acquisition, in September, 1978, of American Medicorp. Upon completion of the merger, Humana dismissed 250 Medicorp employees, mainly executives. It is this reputation that apparently caused Brookwood Health Services Inc. to actively fight the takeover bid by Humana. Brookwood management actually solicited a bid by American Medical International to take them over.

Close to 144 employees at 3 hospitals are members of labor unions. Humana's hospitals have experienced satisfactory relations with periodical union organizational activity in some of its hospitals. Union activity in future operations has been hard to predict (see Humana 10-K Report, 1981).

## FINANCE AND ACCOUNTING (SEE EXHIBITS 1–4)

### Accounting Policies

Inventories are valued at the lower of cost (first-in, first-out) or market.

Depreciation expense is computed by the straight-line method. Depreciation rates for hospitals are equivalent to useful lives ranging generally from 20 to 25 years. Estimated useful lives of equipment vary from 4 to 10 years.

Substantially all goodwill is amortized over forty years by the straight-line method.

Revenues are based on hospitals' established billing rates. Contractual allowances represent the differences between these rates and amounts reimbursable under Medicare, Medicaid and similar cost-based programs.

Primary earnings per share are based on the weighted average number of common shares outstanding and common stock equivalent for dilutive stock options. Fully diluted earnings per share give effect to dilutive stock options and to the assumed conversion of convertible debt.

Investment credits are treated as reductions of tax expense of the year in which they arise ("flow-through" method).

**EXHIBIT 1**   Consolidated Balance Sheet, August 31 *(Dollars in thousands except per share amounts)*

| | 1981 | 1980 | 1979 |
|---|---|---|---|
| **Assets** | | | |
| Current assets: | | | |
| Cash and cash equivalents | $ 197,411 | $ 116,299 | $ 101,716 |
| Accounts receivable less allowance for losses of $52,904–1980 and $47,612–1979 | 149,664 | 128,429 | 115,508 |
| Inventories | 29,971 | 28,436 | 22,756 |
| Other current assets | 11,441 | 9,794 | 8,226 |
| | 388,487 | 282,958 | 248,206 |

*continued*

**EXHIBIT 1** *(Continued)*

|                                                                                                                   | 1981 | 1980 | 1979 |
|---|---|---|---|
| Property and equipment at cost |  |  |  |
|   Land | 95,891 | 82,717 | 64,259 |
|   Buildings | 702,437 | 675,698 | 559,365 |
|   Equipment | 329,130 | 296,653 | 253,935 |
|   Construction in progress (estimated cost to complete and equip after August 31, 1980–$118,100) | 75,147 | 37,424 | 73,629 |
|  | 1,202,605 | 1,092,492 | 951,186 |
|   Less accumulated depreciation | 223,845 | 173,044 | 129,275 |
|  | 978,760 | 919,448 | 821,913 |
| Other assets | 134,985 | 66,132 | 59,459 |
| Goodwill | — | 58,046 | 60,521 |
|  | $1,502,232 | $1,326,584 | $1,190,099 |

**Liabilities and Stockholders' Equity**

|                                                                                                                   | 1981 | 1980 | 1979 |
|---|---|---|---|
| Current liabitilies: |  |  |  |
|   Trade accounts payable | $ 52,992 | $ 46,137 | $ 33,552 |
|   Salaries, wages and other compensation | 37,859 | 27,878 | 51,571 |
|   Other accrued expenses | 40,543 | 35,140 | — |
|   Income taxes | 100,156 | 60,268 | 52,938 |
|   Long-term debt due within one year | 43,110 | 34,748 | 28,476 |
|  | 274,660 | 204,171 | 166,537 |
| Long-term debt | 733,060 | 722,376 | 699,674 |
| Deferred credits and other liabilities | 133,273 | 117,763 | 88,822 |
| Contingencies |  |  |  |
| Redeemable preferred stock, $1.00 par; authorized 10,000,000 shares; $ 2.50 cumulative; issued 2,848,161 shares; outstanding 2,706,861 shares—1981 and 2,844,461 shares—1980; mandatory redemption price $67,672 | 63,925 | 65,961 | 65,535 |
| Common stock, $16\frac{2}{3}$¢ par; authorized 100,000,000 shares; issued and outstanding 37,125,912 shares—1981 and 36,230,248 shares—1980 | 6,188 | 6,038 | 2,986 |
| Capital in excess of par value | 94,317 | 79,117 | 79,695 |
| Retained earnings | 196,809 | 131,158 | 86,850 |
|  | 297,314 | 216,313 | 169,531 |
|  | $1,502,232 | $1,326,584 | $1,190.099 |

**EXHIBIT 2**  Consolidated Statement of Income for the Years Ended August 31
*(Dollars in thousands except per share results)*

|  | 1981 | 1980 | 1979 |
|---|---|---|---|
| Revenues | $1,703,597 | $1,392,412 | $1,122,003 |
| Provisions for contractual allowances and doubtful accounts | 360,691 | 275,588 | 195,349 |
| Net revenues | 1,342,906 | 1,116,824 | 926,654 |
| Operating expenses | 1,036,878 | 861,901 | 726,505 |
| Depreciation and amortization | 69,216 | 59,237 | 50,899 |
| Interest | 59,880 | 75,831 | 67,964 |
|  | 1,165,974 | 996,969 | 845,368 |
| Income before income taxes | 176,932 | 119,855 | 81,286 |
| Provision for income taxes | 83,755 | 55,253 | 40,399 |
| Net income | $    93,177 | $    64,602 | $    40,887 |
| Earnings per common share |  |  |  |
| Primary | $2.33 | $1.53 | $ .99 |
| Fully diluted | $2.33 | $1.51 | $ .97 |

Approximate maturities of long-term debt (including amounts representing principal on capital leases) in the years 1982 through 1985 are $47,553,000, $54,718,000, $61,997,000 and $65,569,000, respectively.

Substantially all property and equipment is pledged on senior collateral debt. In addition, the capital stock of 29 subsidiaries, representing approximately 31% of licensed beds, has been pledged on senior collateral debt.

The senior term bank loan agreement requires compensating balances (which may be withdrawn on a day-to-day basis without restriction) of 20% of the average outstanding loan or a fee on any compensating balance deficiency at 125% of the interest rate on the loan. After August 31, 1982, the interest rate increases to $1^{1}/_{2}\%$ over prime, not to exceed an average of $12^{1}/_{2}\%$ over the term of the loan agreement.

Agreements relating to long-term debt, among other things, require maintenance of working capital at certain levels, limit long-term and other debt, generally restrict the company from engaging in any new business other than that of furnishing health care and related

services, and restrict payment of cash dividends, prepayment of debt and retirement of capital stock.

The company continuously evaluates contingent liabilities and provides or revises allowances for loss based upon the best available current evidence. In addition, allowances for loss are provided each year for disputed items which have continuing significance, such as certain third-party reimbursements and tax deductions and credits which continue to be claimed in current cost reports and tax returns.

The company has designated 7,500,000 shares of its 10,000,000 authorized preferred shares as $2.50 cumulative preferred stock. The remaining 2,500,000 authorized preferred shares have not been designated.

The preferred stock is subject to mandatory redemption in 15 equal annual installments of approximately $4,747,000 commencing in February 1984 at $25.00 per share (plus accrued but unpaid dividends). Any or all outstanding shares were to be redeemed by the company for $25.83 per share until February 1981 and $25.00 thereafter.

**EXHIBIT 3**  Consolidated Statement of Changes in Financial Position for the Years Ended August 31 *(Dollars in thousands)*

|  | 1981 | 1980 | 1979 |
|---|---|---|---|
| **Funds provided:** | | | |
| From operations: | | | |
| Net income | $ 93,177 | $ 64,602 | $ 40,887 |
| Changes which did not require working capital: | | | |
| Depreciation and amortization | 69,216 | 59,237 | 50,899 |
| Deferred income taxes | 9,330 | 14,599 | 10,907 |
| Other | 5,503 | 6,725 | 7,754 |
|  | 177,226 | 145,163 | 110,447 |
| Additions to long-term debt | 106,681 | 95,603 | 221,849 |
| Issuances of common stock | 15,350 | 2,411 | 42,537 |
| Increase in allowance for professional liability risks | 13,917 | 13,654 | 9,360 |
| Disposition of properties | 40,936 | 18,818 | 11,370 |
| Proceeds from disposal of other investments | — | 14,725 | — |
| Decrease in long-term receivables | — | — | 8,789 |
| Other | 13,567 | 2,712 | 15,472 |
|  | 367,677 | 293,086 | 419,824 |
| **Funds applied:** | | | |
| Additions to property and equipment | 165,617 | 170,444 | 147,959 |
| Reduction of long-term debt | 92,983 | 74,371 | 65,722 |
| Payment of cash dividends | 27,038 | 19,802 | 14,777 |
| Acquisition of minority interest in subsidiary | — | — | 147,531 |
| Insurance subsidiary's investments | 17,053 | 15,335 | 11,550 |
| Other investments | 6,041 | 5,492 | 11,870 |
| Other | 23,905 | 10,524 | 7,806 |
|  | 332,637 | 295,968 | 407,215 |
| Increase (decrease) in working capital | $ 35,040 | $ (2,882) | $ 12,609 |
| Increase (decrease) in working capital consists of: | | | |
| Cash and cash equivalents | $ 81,112 | $ 14,583 | $ 46,452 |
| Accounts receivable | 21,235 | 12,921 | (1,899) |
| Inventories | 1,535 | 5,680 | 4,381 |
| Other current assets | 1,647 | 1,568 | (1,160) |
| Trade accounts payable | (6,855) | (12,585) | (5,411) |
| Salaries, wages and other compensation | (9,981) | (6,196) | (5,535) |
| Other accrued expenses | (5,403) | (5,251) | (2,840) |
| Income taxes | (39,888) | (7,330) | (24,223) |
| Long-term debt due within one year | (8,362) | (6,272) | 2,844 |
|  | $35,040 | $(2,882) | $12,609 |

**EXHIBIT 4**   Consolidated Statement of Common Stockholders Equity for the Years Ended
August 31
*(Dollars in thousands except per share amounts)*

| | Common Stock | | Capital in Excess of Par Value | Retained Earnings | Total |
| --- | --- | --- | --- | --- | --- |
| | Shares | Amount | | | |
| Balances, August 31, 1978, as previously reported | 15,341,580 | $2,557 | $37,362 | $61,233 | $101,152 |
| Adjustment to give retroactive effect to 2-for-1 stock split | 15,341,580 | 2,557 | (2,557) | | — |
| Balances, August 31, 1978, as adjusted | 30,683,160 | 5,114 | 34,805 | 61,233 | 101,152 |
| Net income | | | | 40,887 | 40,887 |
| Cash dividends on common stock ($.23$\frac{1}{4}$ per share) | | | | (7,656) | (7,656) |
| Cash dividends on preferred stock ($2.50 per share), and $493 provision for redemption value | | | | (7,614) | (7,614) |
| Public offering of common stock, net of expenses of $2,070 | 4,000,000 | 667 | 36,451 | | 37,118 |
| Stock options exercised and related tax benefits | 553,216 | 92 | 2,435 | | 2,527 |
| Conversion of convertible debentures | 579,128 | 96 | 2,796 | | 2,892 |
| Other | 12,288 | 2 | 223 | | 225 |
| Balances, August 31, 1979 | 35,827,792 | 5,971 | 76,710 | 86,850 | 169,531 |
| Net income | | | | 64,602 | 64,602 |
| Cash dividends on common stock ($.35$\frac{1}{8}$ per share) | | | | (12,685) | (12,685) |
| Cash dividends on preferred stock ($2.50 per share), and $492 provision for redemption value | | | | (7,609) | (7,609) |
| Stock options exercised and related tax benefits | 136,146 | 23 | 1,119 | | 1,142 |
| Conversion of convertible debentures | 254,150 | 42 | 1,227 | | 1,269 |
| Other | 12,160 | 2 | 61 | | 63 |
| Balances, August 31, 1980 | 36,230,248 | 6,038 | 79,117 | 131,158 | 216,313 |
| Net income | | | | 93,177 | 93,177 |
| Cash dividends on common stock ($.54$\frac{3}{8}$ per share) | | | | (19,956) | (19,956) |
| Cash dividends on preferred stock ($2.50 per share), and $488 provision for redemption value | | | | (7,570) | (7,570) |

**EXHIBIT 4** *(Continued)*

| | Common Stock | | Capital in Excess of Par Value | Retained Earnings | Total |
|---|---|---|---|---|---|
| | Shares | Amount | | | |
| Shares issued in business combinations | 357,564 | 60 | 9,337 | | 9,397 |
| Stock options exercised and related tax benefits, net of 30,503 shares tendered in partial payment therefor | 322,695 | 54 | 4,740 | | 4,794 |
| Conversion of convertible debentures | 199,357 | 33 | 962 | | 995 |
| Other | 16,048 | 3 | 161 | | 164 |
| Balances, August 31, 1981 | 37,125,912 | $6,188 | $94,317 | $196,809 | $297,314 |

## EPILOGUE

The following excerpts from the cover letter of the 1980 Humana Annual Report to the stockholders expresses the optimism about the future of the company:

To our Stockholders: With another outstanding year, Humana continues to be one of America's fastest growing companies and the leader in the hospital industry.

Earnings per common share increased by 55% in the year ended August 31, surpassing the 32% compound annual growth rate of the preceding 10 years.

Despite the recession that plagued many businesses during 1980, Humana's earnings per common share rose to $3.07 from $1.98 the year before (adjusted for the 4-for-3 stock split that took place February 1, 1980).

Dividends, which were effectively increased by 33% with stock split, are at the rate of 75 cents a year. We have increased dividends sevenfold since we started payments in 1976. It is our policy to pay dividends amounting to at least 25% of earnings.

Humana retained its position as the largest company in the hospital business as revenues grew 24% to $1,392,412,000 from $1,122,003,000.

Our position as the industry leader results from more than just being the largest company. It includes having outstanding managers for every corporate and hospital department, responding to challenges with innovative solutions, pursuing opportunities aggressively, and having the foresight to know where we are going and how we will get there.

We have an absolutely clear-cut sense of purpose in this company. Our goal is to provide hospital services of measurable, unexcelled quality, without waste, in response to the needs and values of patients and their physicians. This simple goal applies to every phase of our business.

Work continues on formulating measurable quality goals for each important process that takes place in our hospitals. At the same time, productivity is vital to the cost-effective delivery of hospital services. Humana ranks first in the industry in the important area of holding down operating expenses as a percentage of gross revenues. Our operating expenses in 1980 were reduced to 61.9% of gross revenues from 64.8% the year before. This was substantially better than that achieved by any of the other major hospital companies.

Growth in demand for hospital services provides a steady, predictable course of increasing revenues and net income as our hospitals mature. In 1975 our hospitals had revenues of $216 million. During 1980 revenues from those same hospitals reached $512 million. Hospitals that we built or bought since 1975 added another $880 million to bring us to $1,392 billion for the next year.

We expect further significant growth in volume, accompanied by improved profit margins. For fiscal 1981 we expect revenues to increase between 15% and 20%, and pretax margins to exceed the 8.6% margin achieved in 1980, which was up from 7.2% the year before.

Return on average common stockholders' equity continued to improve, reaching 29.5% in 1980, compared with 26.7% a year ago.

The most important accomplishment of the past year was the completion of the assimilation of American Medicorp. These results demonstrate the great success of this acquisition.

We salute our fellow employees for their past accomplishments and know we can count on them for future successes because of their commitment and their ever-growing skills.

# THE LAFAYETTE CIVIC CENTER

## Jeffrey D. Schaffer

*Virginia Polytechnic Institute and State University*

Lafayette, Louisiana, is a city of approximately ninety thousand people located in the Arcadian section of Louisiana. Arcadiana comprises most of the southwestern section of Louisiana ranging from Baton Rouge on the east to Lake Charles on the west. Most of the area is rural and populated relatively sparsely by people of French-Canadian descent. There are, however, a number of cities and towns ranging from approximately 250,000 people in Baton Rouge to small cities like Thibodaux and New Iberia with populations of 50,000 and 80,000, respectively.

The economy of the area is based on sugarcane, cotton, and rice farming, the fishing and seafood industries, and oil exploration. Some of the finest shrimp, oysters, and crabs come from the waters along the coast of Louisiana. Also many oil companies engage in exploration and production activities along the Louisiana coast and offshore in the Gulf of Mexico.

## HISTORY OF THE LAFAYETTE CIVIC CENTER

### When Conceived

In the late 1950s, Lafayette's only public gathering facility, the Lafayette Municipal Auditorium, caught fire and burned to the ground. At that time, Lafayette was a sleepy town and had been experiencing increasing decay in its downtown area. Some slum areas had developed and the general quality of life in the city suffered from a lack of cultural activity.

The burning of the old auditorium sparked some of the city fathers to begin thinking about what was happening to their downtown area.

### The Reasons for a New Civic Center

Shortly after the fire, discussions began in the Lafayette City Council regarding the future of downtown and of Lafayette. Lafayette was headquarters for many of the oil companies' field operations in Louisiana. As a result, a substantial portion of the population were executives of oil companies and their families. The oil industry had experienced continued substantial growth in Louisiana and new oil leases were being sold by the government on a regular basis. Other cities and towns in Arcadiana had begun to compete for the new field offices that were being developed as a result of the oil industry's growth.

The city fathers recognized that in order to continue to attract the interest of the oil companies to locate their offices in Lafayette, they would have to do something about the decaying environment and lack of cultural and entertainment activities in the city. In addition, there was little in the way of suitable meeting space for civic groups which were made up of the executives, bankers, merchants, and professionals in Lafayette. These groups, such as Kiwanis and Rotary, had been growing in membership.

Discussion also centered around what appeared to be a growing trend in convention and trade show activities throughout the south. The city fathers felt that the central location of Lafayette, between New Orleans and Houston, would provide opportunities for regional and statewide conventions and trade shows. They hoped this would help promote the overall economy of the city and bring economic benefits to the retail businesses, motels, and restaurants. They discussed the need for facilities that could be used for social events such as weddings and banquets, as well as the need for a sports arena for the local high school basketball games, gymnastics events, etc.

## The Development Process

During the next two years much discussion took place regarding the development of a new civic center that could be designed to fulfill the needs of the community and help to reverse the decline of the downtown area. The area adjacent to the site of the old auditorium had become a full-fledged slum.

It was finally decided by the City Council to take action and to design the proposed civic center. In order to keep the project "within the community" a decision was made to call upon all five of the architectural firms in Lafayette.

The five firms created a consortium and undertook to design a new civic center for Lafayette. The site to be used was that of the old auditorium plus the slum area adjacent to it. If feasible, the city intended to condemn the buildings in the slum area and thereby be in a position to purchase and utilize the land.

## Design of the Lafayette Civic Center

Working together under a project director chosen from among the five architectural firms and utilizing specialized consultants—such as acoustical consultants, theater consultants, and food service consultants from New York and

Lafayette Civic Center

other cities—the architects designed a three-segmented structure. It comprised an auditorium, an exhibit hall, and an arena. They presented their designs to the City Council nine months after the initial assignment.

### Cost of the New Facility

Shortly after the design was completed the City Council passed a proposition accepting the design that the architects had prepared and authorizing a cost estimate to be made for both construction of the civic center and the purchase of the additional land necessary for the site.

By late 1963, the costing process was complete and the total amount necessary to develop the facility and purchase the land was $14,800,000.

### Financing the Civic Center

After much debate it was decided that the city would finance the development of the new civic center by issuing general revenue bonds for $7,800,000 at 7 percent interest for 15 years and finance the remainder from the city treasury (a surplus of $10,000,000 existed at that time) to be repaid by increasing the utility tax on its citizens.

The proposal was put to a vote in early 1964 and defeated soundly. At that time only property owners were permitted to vote on matters concerning city financing. In 1965, a new ordinance was passed permitting all citizens of the city to vote on all matters and in 1966 a second proposal to build the Lafayette Civic Center was put up for a vote. This time it was easily passed and preparations for the condemnation and purchase of the necessary land were begun immediately.

### Building the Facility

Construction was begun in 1968 with a great citywide celebration at the ground-breaking ceremony. Finally, after three years of construction, the new civic center was opened in March 1971.

## THE IMAGE OF THE LAFAYETTE CIVIC CENTER

### Early Years

There was considerable excitement and enthusiasm when the new civic center opened in 1971. Great things were expected. However, within two years it became evident that the civic center was in trouble financially. Where operating revenues were expected to cover all operating costs, substantial losses were being incurred. These losses had to be made up from city revenues. The civic center soon became known as the "White Elephant" and with a little help from the local newspaper, public criticism grew.

The initial manager was soon fired and his replacement, a local Chamber of Commerce executive, continued to experience criticism and growing financial losses.

### Current Management

In 1977 George Smith was hired to manage the Lafayette Civic Center. George had been in the amusement management business for the past 15 years. His most recent position was manager of the Baton Rouge Municipal Auditorium, a facility of about 8,000 seats. He was quite familiar with the City of Lafayette. Over the years he had watched the development of the Lafayette Civic Center, had observed the local criticism grow, and was aware of the financial problems of the facilities.

George felt that in order to be successful in his new position he would have to do something about the image of the civic center in the local community. He felt that in order to change local feeling about the civic center he needed to give lots of attention to the local community. He felt that his efforts and that of his staff must be directed toward pleasing the memberships of the local organizations and especially the local press. He proceeded to set up VIP tours for local people and went out of his way to roll out the red carpet whenever a member of the press came to visit. George and his staff spent a major portion of their time entertaining local dignitaries and trying to find ways to please the local press.

George was also well aware of the civic center's history of substantial loss. He had seen from his past experience how the Baton Rouge City Council had zeroed in on the annual operating statements of the Baton Rouge Municipal Auditorium and was highly critical of any increase in operating losses. George knew that he had to find a way to achieve operating results that were better than his predecessors'. Cultural events, conventions, and trade shows were all part of the potential market; unfortunately, they usually paid only minimum fixed rentals. Thus, while they added much in the way of economic and cultural benefit to the city, they were not profitable to the civic center.

The big money was in concerts, especially those which could attract large numbers of people. The usual arrangements for these types of shows (mostly rock, country, and gospel concerts) was one in which the auditorium would share in gross receipts. Usually 12 percent of the gross take went to the auditorium in the form of rent plus an additional 3 percent as a "box office" advance for selling tickets. With 11,000 seats in the coliseum, a healthy amount of revenue could be generated for a good concert.

It cost no more to set up the space for a concert than it did for a convention or trade show. In fact, it was generally easier because you only had to deal with the concert's man-ager, who usually was well organized and knew the ropes, as opposed to a multitude of exhibitors for conventions and trade shows. Table 1 shows a comparison of the fixed-rate structure with the potential rates for various levels of concert ticket prices.

## MANAGEMENT HIERARCHY

### The Commission

The Lafayette Civic Center is owned and operated by the City of Lafayette. It is organized as a department within the city. The primary difference from other city departments is that, by City Council ordinance, a seven-member civic center commission was established. The function of this commission is to act as an independent body and set policy for the civic center in the areas of advertising, promotions, rates, ticket sales, parking, concessions, and catering contracts. The commission is composed of private citizens of the City of Lafayette. The City Council also has seven members.

Each member of the commission is appointed by the entire City Council; candidates can be recommended by one or more of the councilmen or any citizen can petition the council and be considered for membership.

One member of the City Council sits on the commission as a liaison to the council. This person has no voting right on the commission. The commission serves at the pleasure of the council

---

**TABLE 1** Comparison of Civic Center Revenue Potential
(Coliseum Only)

|  | Daily Revenue Potential |
| --- | --- |
| Regular fixed rate (Convention, Trade show, etc.) | $ 1,200.00 |
| Concert revenue potential (11,000 seats—12% of gross) | |
| Ticket Price—$4.00 | $ 5,300.00 |
| Ticket Price—$5.00 | $ 6,600.00 |
| Ticket Price—$8.00 | $10,600.00 |
| Ticket Price—$10.00 | $13,200.00 |

and appointments to the commission are for a one-year period.

## Structure Within the City

The City of Lafayette is operated through the office of the city manager. The city manager is the chief operating officer of the city. He is appointed by and reports directly to the city council. The city council is composed of six councilmen elected at large and the mayor. The mayor is primarily a figurehead position. He serves as a member of the council and has the same voting power as a council person.

The director of administration and public safety reports to the city manager and has, as one of his many duties, responsibility for the Lafayette Civic Center. The manager of the Lafayette Civic Center reports to the director of administration and public safety. He in turn is responsible for the day-to-day operation of the civic center.

## Responsibility of the Civic Center Manager

The manager of the civic center's responsibilities include all activities related to the booking and handling of events, sales, administration of the operation, maintenance of the facility, preparation of all operating and capital budgets, and staffing. However, the civic center manager is not directly responsible for any of the food service or concessions. This aspect of the operation is handled through a private operator under contract with the civic center commission. The contract is negotiated and set by the civic center commission. The civic center manager must coordinate with this contractor for the food service and concession needs of the activities booked into the civic center.

## The Operating Organization for the Lafayette Civic Center

The internal structure of the Lafayette Civic Center is composed of 18 full-time people. The organization consists of the civic center manager, the assistant civic center manager, a box office supervisor, four box office attendants, a parking lot supervisor, two secretaries, a promotions coordinator, an operations superintendent, four lead men, and two laborers.

Many other people are needed when events are set up and taken down. These additional part-time employees are drawn when needed from the City of Lafayette's centralized labor

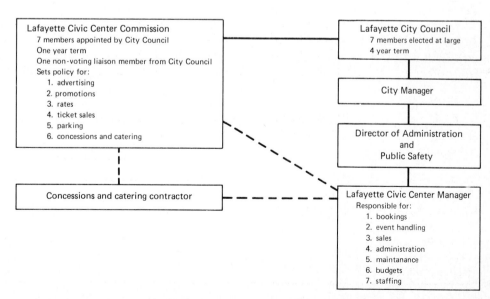

**EXHIBIT 2**

Organization of the City of Lafayette Relative to the Civic Center

Lafayette Civic Center Commission
7 members appointed by City Council
One year term
One non-voting liaison member from City Council
Sets policy for:
1. advertising
2. promotions
3. rates
4. ticket sales
5. parking
6. concessions and catering

Lafayette City Council
7 members elected at large
4 year term

City Manager

Director of Administration and Public Safety

Concessions and catering contractor

Lafayette Civic Center Manager
Responsible for:
1. bookings
2. event handling
3. sales
4. administration
5. maintanance
6. budgets
7. staffing

**EXHIBIT 3**
Lafayette Civic
Center
Management
Organization

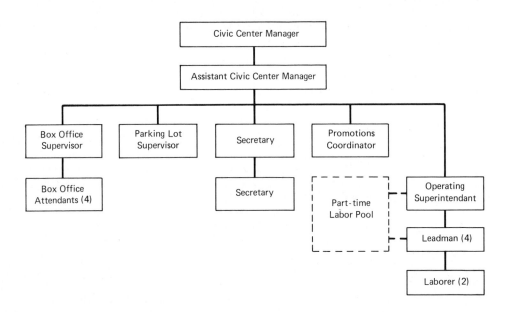

pool. They consist of janitors, electricians, engineers, plumbers, carpenters, and general laborers. The civic center is charged for the time of these additional employees based upon rates established by the city Finance Department. These rates include all city overhead and benefits plus an administrative cost factor. The civic center management has no control over the rates charged by the city for temporary labor. The rates charged are substantially higher than that which would have to be paid for comparable part-time help hired directly. (See Table 4.)

**The Promotions Coordinator**
The position of promotions coordinator was approved as an addition to staff about 18 months ago. The intent of adding this position was to be able to generate more business for the civic center. However, according to George Smith, little has been done yet in the way of actual sales development. Most of the promotions coordinator's time has been spent dealing with local activities and publishing the calendar of events. George Smith said that the primary reason for not engaging in more direct selling is that they don't have the 4 to 5 additional

**TABLE 4**     Lafayette Civic Center City Labor Pool vs. Market Wage Rates

| Jobs | City Labor Pool Rate | Market Rate[1] |
|---|---|---|
| Janitorial/Laborer | $ 8.72/hr. | $3.35/hr. |
| Building maintenance services (elect., plumb., etc.) | $10.84/hr. | $5.50–7.50/hr. |
| Grounds maintenance | $10.85/hr. | $3.35/hr. |

[1] In most instances unskilled minimum wage people are all that would be required. In addition, fringe benefits would be nil due to the part-time nature of the jobs required.

slide presentations that they need as a selling tool. The one slide presentation that they do have, entitled "Booking a Concert," has been shown frequently at local civic club meetings and at a city high school presentations.

### The Operating Superintendent

The operating superintendent and his four leadmen actually handle the setting up and taking down of the booked events. It is the operating superintendent's responsibility to decide on the number of extra employees he needs and to make arrangements for them through the city labor pool. The superintendent knows, based on his "experience," how many and what kinds of people are needed for a particular event.

## MARKETING AND SALES

### Uses of the Lafayette Civic Center

According to George Smith each of the areas of the civic center are used somewhat differently. There is, however, substantial overlap in some of the types of use. The following is a breakdown provided by George Smith as to the use of which the various areas can be put.

*Coliseum*

Ice shows
Circuses
Rodeos
Concerts
Basketball
Hockey
Wrestling
Boxing
Trade shows
  Antiques
  Cars
  Boats
  Homes

Conventions
Political rallies
Association meetings
Religious meetings
Banquets

*Exhibit Hall*

Trade shows—most frequent use
Banquets
Dinners
Dances
State Testing
  Bar Exam
  CPA Exam
  Citywide Tests
Weddings
Proms
Council meetings
Corporate meetings

*Auditorium*
*(primarily an entertainment facility)*

Broadway road shows
Symphonies
Ballets
Opera
Individual artist presentations (concerts)
Beauty pageants
Religious meetings
Corporate meetings

### Key Markets

"The big money is in booking concerts in our coliseum," according to George Smith. "If we want to maintain a bottom line that won't cause the City Council to get into an uproar we've got to make sure we book enough concerts during the year to generate the revenue we need. . . . Conventions bring a lot of people to the city but all we get if the fixed daily rate. With the labor rates we have to pay, it costs us more than we take in. The same is true for operas and symphonies because they get the fixed civic rate."

"Our plan is to try to keep everyone happy. We have to book some conventions and cultural events as well as cater to local civic groups. But we can't let them get in the way of our concert business." Smith conceded, therefore, "we try not to commit our facilities to these activities too far in advance because you never know when a concert promoter will call."

### Sources of Revenue

"It's obvious that our greatest source of revenue is the concert business although I can't say exactly how much it is. We don't keep those kinds of records. . . . We are interested in how many days we have the civic center in use. That's what the city council wants to see . . . that the facility is being used as many days as possible."

Table 5 is a summary of the occupancy and attendance records that are kept on a monthly basis. A listing of the events held during each month and a breakdown of the attendance by the area of the civic center facility is kept. The amount of ticket sales generated by each event is also recorded. However, the ticket sales reflected on these reports do not reflect civic center net revenue; they represent gross ticket sales. (See Table 6 for net revenue information.)

### Advertising

Since the Lafayette Civic Center, according to George Smith, is in the amusement business, most of the advertising is done through magazine ads placed in the "Bibles of the Industry." About $2–3,000 per year goes toward advertising. The budget figure is arrived at by adding the cost of placing ads in the periodicals chosen. They usually are

> Talent and Booking Magazine
> Meetings and Conventions
> Trade Show and Concert Guide
>     (annual issue)
> Bill Board Magazine

Special ads are placed in magazines when there is an editorial comment about the city or region. For example, last year *Successful Meetings Magazine* ran an article about Arcadiana and the Lafayette Civic Center took an ad in that issue.

### Sales Promotions

"Most of our business comes because we are here," said George Smith. "Our sales promotion is on a day-to-day basis. . . . The city doesn't have enough hotel rooms for us to go after the big conventions and our airport is served by only one carrier."

"In addition our meeting rooms are not adequate for most convention groups. We need smaller rooms and more flexibility to be able to satisfy the conventions and meetings that do come."

"What I think we need is a community room for about 400 people or less. This room should be flexible so that it can be broken down into smaller rooms. We also need more exhibit space and parking is at a premium. When we have concerts and conventions that draw heavily we don't have enough room for all of the cars and we have to make arrangements with one of the hotels in the area so that we can use its lot for our overflow. The problem is we've got nowhere to expand. There is no more land available around our site."

Smith added, "To really make the Lafayette Civic Center complete, we want to have an on-site restaurant and a small community theater of about 400 seats. That way, everything will be under one roof. People could have dinner and then see a show without going outside."

### Competition

"We really have to work hard to compete with other civic centers and auditoriums in cities throughout southwestern Louisiana. We're all vying for the same concerts, conventions, and trade shows. People in the area who attend these concerts will gladly drive 100 miles or more to see a show."

"We are careful to treat the concert pro-

**TABLE 5** Lafayette Civic Center
Summary of Occupancy and Attendance

| Month/Yr | Coliseum | | | | Auditorium | | | | Exhibit Hall | | | | Total Complex | | | |
|---|---|---|---|---|---|---|---|---|---|---|---|---|---|---|---|---|
| | Atten-dance No. of People | Tkt Sales $ | Occupancy Days | Occupancy % | Atten-dance No. of People | Tkt Sales $ | Occupancy Days | Occupancy % | Atten-dance No. of People | Tkt Sales $ | Occupancy Days | Occupancy % | Atten-dance No. of People | Tkt Sales $ | Occupancy Days | Occupancy % |
| July '80 | 6,667 | 45,518 | 3 | 10 | 10,142 | 16,122 | 10 | 32 | 3,548 | 2,459 | 8 | 26 | 20,357 | 64,098 | 18 | 58 |
| August '80 | 11,110 | 63,093 | 4 | 13 | 4,867 | 8,415 | 6 | 19 | 6,549 | 4,862 | 15 | 48 | 22,526 | 76,370 | 19 | 61 |
| September '80 | 15,458 | 104,505 | 7 | 23 | 5,550 | 0 | 2 | 7 | 4,971 | 1,898 | 15 | 50 | 25,979 | 106,403 | 18 | 60 |
| October '80 | 38,910 | 166,913 | 17 | 55 | 18,037 | 27,769 | 11 | 35 | 2,328 | 0 | 16 | 52 | 59,275 | 194,682 | 25 | 81 |
| November '80 | 30,648 | 169,472 | 10 | 33 | 9,334 | 30,446 | 14 | 47 | 12,162 | 11,943 | 19 | 63 | 52,144 | 211,861 | 24 | 80 |
| December '80 | 18,528 | 102,180 | 14 | 45 | 10,646 | 28,269 | 8 | 26 | 5,697 | 246 | 15 | 48 | 34,871 | 130,695 | 23 | 74 |
| January '81 | 40,812 | 154,290 | N/A | N/A | 3,434 | 2,320 | N/A | N/A | 3,147 | 5,893 | N/A | N/A | 47,393 | 162,503 | N/A | N/A |
| February '81 | 8,886 | 30,808 | N/A | N/A | 5,525 | 12,424 | N/A | N/A | 4,737 | 0 | N/A | N/A | 19,148 | 43,232 | N/A | N/A |
| March '81 | 44,351 | 246,765 | N/A | N/A | 14,594 | 42,245 | N/A | N/A | 4,588 | 0 | N/A | N/A | 63,533 | 289,010 | N/A | N/A |

moters right so that they will remember us when they have another show."

## BUDGETS AND FINANCIAL REPORTS

### Accounting
All accounting for the civic center is done centrally by the city Finance Department. The civic center is required to follow the budgetary and planning process as prescribed by city management.

### Monthly Operating Statement
Table 6 is the operating statement for the Lafayette Civic Center covering the nine months ending March 1981. A financial statement in this format is prepared monthly, on a cumulative basis, by the city finance department.

### Budget
"When I'm not entertaining someone from the local community or a newspaper representative I'm working on our budgets." That's the way George Smith described the budgetary process

**TABLE 6**  City of Lafayette, Louisiana, Civic Center Fund
Comparative Income Statement for the 9 Months Ended March 13

| Operating Revenue: | 1981 | 1980 |
|---|---|---|
| Rentals | $186,249 | $205,068 |
| Event Expenses | 57,693 | 62,383 |
| Advertising | 2,600 | 2,140 |
| Admissions Tax | 48,840 | 61,657 |
| Commissions | 50,290 | 52,944 |
| Event Profit—City Sponsored | 6,775 | 70 |
| Parking Fee | 48,938 | — |
| Total Operating Revenue | 401,385 | 384,262 |
| Less: Operating Exp. before Depreciation | | |
| Administrative: | | |
|   Personal Services | 249,385 | 218,351 |
|   Utilities and Communications | 190,768 | 194,969 |
|   Administrative Expenses | 340,139 | 565,655 |
| Promotional Expenses: | | |
|   Personal Services | 38,392 | 32,622 |
|   Services and Charges | 1,591 | 5,309 |
| Total Operating Exp. before Depreciation | 820,275 | 1,016,906 |
| Operating (Loss) before Depreciation | (418,890) | (632,644) |
| Less: Depreciation | 243,178 | 238,912 |
| Operating (Loss) | (662,068) | (871,556) |
| Add: Nonoperating Income | | |
| Supplement from General Fund | 240,000 | 375,000 |
| Miscellaneous | 4,649 | 9,133 |
| Interest on Investments | 849 | 3,438 |
| Total Nonoperating Income | 245,498 | 387,571 |
| Net (Loss) | $(416,570) | $(483,985) |

used at the Lafayette Civic Center. The actual information required to complete the budget amounted to over 200 pages. The following is a list of the major summary forms and reports that are included in the budget report:

1. A statement of objectives and activities
2. Personnel recap
3. Budget work sheet A
4. Detail of budget request
   Reason and justification of basic budget request
5. Computerized form #2A
6. Equipment request forms
7. Revenue estimate form
8. Budget request form
9. Revenue estimate income generated
10. Detailed description of each budgetary account
11. Budget recap
12. Supplemental budget request recap
13. Supplemental budget request cover
14. Improvements, maintenance, and capital budget cost request and budget estimates
15. Equipment request recap
16. Reason and justification of supplemental budget requests
17. Justification for additional personnel requests
18. 5 percent decrease budget
19. 5 percent decrease account summary

# 21 THE RUSHFORD TELEPHONE COMPANY

## Lawrence R. Jauch

*Southern Illinois University-Carbondale*

On November 14, 1984, the Rushford Telephone Company of Rushford, California, applied to the California Public Utilities Commission for a 10 percent rate increase. In response to this application, the Public Utilities Commission answered that approval for this rate hike ". . . would require a complete review of the company's operations and an assessment of its ability to discharge its reponsibilities to the public." The Commission further stated that ". . . certain specific customer complaints would be examined to determine if the company is taking all necessary and appropriate measures to resolve these complaints."

Complaints received by the California Public Utilities Commission concerning Rushford telephone service include the following:

Calls are frequently misplaced.
There are undue delays in the installation and repair of telephone equipment.
During certain times of the day, one must often wait for a dial tone.
Customers frequently receive busy signals before they finish dialing.
Direct-distance dialing calls often do not go through.

Adapted by Lawrence R. Jauch from a case study by William F. Glueck and John Abendshien. This is a disguised case. The facts in it are based on a real company, but the names of the persons involved, the location, and the quantitative data have been changed because the company requested it. It serves no useful purpose to try to determine which company is the real company.

Telephone lines in some outlying areas are not well maintained.
Operators sometimes do not answer for long periods.
Operators are occasionally discourteous and generally not helpful.
Customers are improperly billed for telephone service, particularly for long-distance calls.

To help support its claims that it is doing all it can to improve service and to help justify the need for a rate increase, Rushford management hired a university professor from San Francisco as consultant. Dr. McGowan, an economist, has on several previous occasions done consulting work for other telephone companies. In late November, Dr. McGowan arrived at the company and began gathering data. Much of the information which he was able to obtain is contained below.

## COMPANY BACKGROUND

The Rushford Telephone Company is a privately owned telephone company serving residents in Rushford, California, and in several surrounding smaller towns. In 1974, when the long-established Shawnee Telephone Company was sold to a group of investors, Rushford Telephone Company was formed. In 1978, the present system was completed, as another small company serving three adjoining towns was acquired. Presently, the company has over 90,000 telephones serving an estimated population of 190,000. Exhibit 1 shows the company's operating statistics.

**Exhibit 1** Rushford Telephone Company
1984 Operating Statistics

| | |
|---|---|
| Estimated population served | 192,086 |
| Exchanges | 9 |
| Counties served | 4 |
| Total assets | $47,297,591 |
| Total telephones | 90,301 |
| Residence telephones | 64,114 |
| Business telephones | 26,187 |
| Employees | 542 |

The company has been plagued with service problems from the very beginning. Mr. Kimball, company vice-president and general manager, told Dr. McGowan that most of the early problems were inherited from the previous company:

Actually, we knew when we took over operations that the going would be rough for quite a while. The equipment—poles, lines, exchanges, relays, telephones . . . everything—was very old and in a poor state of repair. In fact, that is the main reason why the old Shawnee Company finally went out of business. After a long period of poor management and inefficient operations, they simply didn't have the resources needed to replace this equipment. Although we immediately began a vast program to replace and modernize equipment it wasn't possible to bring the whole system up to date overnight. We had to use old equipment along with the new, an arrangement that does not result in optimal performance. We still have problems caused by some of the older equipment in the system. No matter how new or sophisticated some parts of the system are, failures are still going to result from the older equipment that is still in use.

Dr. McGowan learned that further problems stemmed from the original company's failure to plan and anticipate increases in service demands adequately. For many years, equipment was added piecemeal as the need arose, resulting in overloaded lines and central equipment. This problem was compounded by an unexpected surge in the area's population during the 1970s. As Mr. Kimball put it, "The company was barely able to keep pace with the rise in service demands, let alone update equipment or improve service." Only in recent years has Rushford been able to meet consumer demand and begin solving some of the more persistent service problems, he said.

Mr. West, the company president, emphasized that the planned rate increase is necessary, since the company needs to generate additional capital to be used for the improvement and expansion of plant facilities. He also stated that Rushford needs to build up cash assets. "We're skating on thin ice, financially speaking," he commented.

Financial information for the years 1978 through 1984 is given in Exhibits 2, 3, 4, and 5.

## INDUSTRY NOTES

The telephone industry can basically be divided into two segments: the various components of the old Bell System and the independents. As of January 1, 1984, the industry, which had been deregulated over the past ten years reached a turning point when AT&T divested itself of its seven operating companies, namely, the Bell System. With this breakup, the competition became intense. The cost of services began to change significantly, declining in some areas and rising in others. More competition began to change many companies' capital investment patterns. Technology is changing so rapidly that telecommunications equipment which formerly enjoyed a 30-year life is becoming obsolete at an alarming rate. As quickly as technology changes customers demand increased services. The single greatest impact on communications is being made by digital computers. As these machines multiply throughout business, telecommunications becomes a necessity to all com-

**EXHIBIT 2**   Rushford Telephone Company
Income Statement for Year Ended December 31, 1984

| | |
|---|---:|
| Operating revenues: | |
| Local service | $7,563,101 |
| Toll service | 7,009,684 |
| Miscellaneous | 328,080 |
| Uncollected revenues dr. | 114,446 |
| Total operating revenue | $15,015,311 |
| Operating expenses and taxes: | |
| Plant changes, move equipment | 413,642 |
| Repairs—plant | 1,869,444 |
| Traffic | 1,481,722 |
| Commercial | 948,786 |
| Office salaries and expenses | 1,006,926 |
| Other operating expenses | 861,020 |
| Total above expenses | 6,581,540 |
| Depreciation and amortization | 2,799,707 |
| Total operating expenses | 9,381,247 |
| Federal, state, and local income tax | 2,300,192 |
| Total operating expenses and tax | 11,881,439 |
| Net operating income | 3,133,872 |
| Miscellaneous income—net | 52,996 |
| Income for fixed charges | 3,186,868 |
| Fixed charges* | 1,773,954 |
| Net income | $1,412,914 |

*Fixed charges represent contractual payments on long-term debt.

panies. Instead of just transmitting calls and telex messages, companies are now sending huge volumes of computer data at high speeds, transmitting facsimiles of blueprints, and holding video conferences.

As deregulation opens up markets, selling directly to users is becoming of the utmost importance. Users were expected to buy nearly $19 billion worth of equipment in 1984 ranging from simple telephones and telex machines to sophisticated private branch exchange telephone systems.

Telephone companies around the world are racing to renovate their networks. Yesterday's copper wires and mechanical switching relays were designed to carry only a single type of information: telephone calls, telegrams, or telex messages. Today's high-capacity optical fiber and sophisticated digital computers can transmit everything—voice, data, or image—in the same way by connecting them into a stream of computer on-off pulses. Once the equipment is updated to handle everything in digital form, networks can carry anything from a simple telephone call to computerized airline reservations and television pictures. At the same time, new ways of moving digital information, such as microwave radio, satellites, and optical fiber

**EXHIBIT 3** Rushford Telephone Company
Income Statement
December 31, 1984

| | |
|---|---|
| *Assets* | |
| Current assets: | |
| Cash | $ 477,588 |
| Temporary investments | 175,164 |
| Prepayments | 107,268 |
| Receivables | 2,255,030 |
| Materials and supplies | 475,256 |
| Other deferred charges | 362,153 |
| Total | 3,852,459 |
| Investments | 18,126 |
| Net fixed assets | 43,427,006 |
| Total assets | $47,297,591 |
| *Liabilities and capital* | |
| Current and accrued: | |
| Accounts payable | 1,728,600 |
| Accrued taxes | 975,738 |
| Debt due | 110,081 |
| Accrued interest | 500,632 |
| Deferred income tax | 939,289 |
| Deferred investment credit | 677,016 |
| Total current | 4,931,356 |
| Funded debt | 25,662,040 |
| Earned surplus | 2,772,195 |
| Capital stock | 13,932,000 |
| Total liabilities and capital | $47,297,591 |

cables, are dramatically lowering the cost of sending messages across vast distances.

As a result, Rushford executives contemplated the need for heavy capital investments to keep pace with changes occurring in the industry.

## ORGANIZATION

James West is president of Rushford Telephone Company. The fifty-four-year-old chief executive began his career in 1956 starting as an accountant for a small independent telephone company. He became controller and then vice-president of that firm before he was hired to become president of Rushford. He has served in that capacity since the company was started in 1974.

Reporting directly to Mr. West is Mr. Hank Kimball, vice-president and general manager. Mr. Kimball, age 61, has worked in a variety of capacities since be began working for the Shawnee Telephone Company in 1949. He started as a lineman, and then successively became field superintendent, assistant plant supervisor, plant supervisor, chief engineer, and general manager. In describing his top-ranking subordinate, Mr. West stated that, "He is with-

**EXHIBIT 4**  Rushford Telephone Company
Income Statement for Years Ended December 31
Selected Years 1978–1983

|  | 1978 | 1979 | 1980 | 1981 | 1982 | 1983 |
|---|---|---|---|---|---|---|
| Operating revenues | $ 2,285,466 | 3,655,543 | 6,639,644 | 9,736,207 | 12,607,568 | $13,203,716 |
| Operating expenses | 1,648,686 | 2,344,507 | 4,024,841 | 6,046,184 | 7,514,111 | 8,054,267 |
| Gross operating income | 636,780 | 1,311,036 | 2,638,804 | 3,690,023 | 5,093,458 | 5,149,450 |
| Federal, state, and local tax | 285,410 | 412,282 | 1,075,614 | 1,496,923 | 2,405,636 | 2,399,312 |
| Income for fixed charges | 351,370 | 898,754 | 1,563,190 | 2,193,100 | 2,687,821 | 2,750,137 |
| Fixed charges | 195,959 | 705,172 | 738,696 | 1,306,378 | 1,522,612 | 1,600,988 |
| Net income | 155,411 | 193,583 | 824,494 | 886,722 | 1,165,210 | 1,149,149 |

**EXHIBIT 5**  Rushford Telephone Company
Consolidated Balance Statements
Selected Years: 1978–1983

|  | 1978 | 1979 | 1980 | 1981 | 1982 | 1983 |
|---|---|---|---|---|---|---|
| *Assets* | | | | | | |
| Current assets | $ 1,642,748 | 2,822,647 | 3,075,433 | 3,040,313 | 3,084,874 | 3,496,402 |
| Investments | 3,601 | 48,098 | 67,898 | 70,666 | 14,929 | 25,675 |
| Net fixed assets | 21,525,928 | 29,644,550 | 30,730,093 | 34,423,749 | 37,490,643 | 40,646,690 |
| Total assets | $23,172,277 | 32,515,295 | 33,873,424 | 37,534,728 | 40,590,446 | 44,168,767 |
| *Liabilities and Capital* | | | | | | |
| Current and accrued liability | $ 2,155,021 | 3,219,014 | 3,051,388 | 3,659,636 | 3,985,982 | 4,648,369 |
| Funded debt | 9,600,000 | 14,878,802 | 16,114,689 | 18,730,578 | 20,784,354 | 23,192,880 |
| Retained earnings | 245,256 | 485,478 | 775,348 | 1,212,514 | 1,888,110 | 2,395,518 |
| Common stock | 11,172,000 | 13,932,000 | 13,932,000 | 13,932,000 | 13,932,000 | 13,932,000 |
| Total liabilities and capital | $23,172,277 | 32,515,295 | 33,873,424 | 37,534,728 | 40,590,446 | 44,168,767 |

out a doubt one of the most knowledgeable men in the business," and "practical" in his approach to management. Mr. Kimball was the only top-ranking executive of the Shawnee Telephone Company to be retained by the Rushford Company.

Mr. Stanley Smith is marketing director. Forty-three years old, Mr. Smith has a B.S. degree in Business Administration from the University of Arizona. Before coming to Rushford, he worked in the sales department of the Bell System. In addition to sales activities, Mr. Smith is responsible for handling public relations.

Also, reporting to Mr. West are T. L. Gross, controller; F. R. Wright, secretary-treasurer; and M. E. O'Connor, personnel director. Mr. Gross is the only one of these three individuals who has a college education. Mr. O'Connor has previously worked for Mr. West as assistant commercial director before coming to Rushford. Exhibit 6 is an organization chart of Rushford Telephone Company.

## THE COMMERCIAL DIVISION

The commercial division's responsibility is customer billing and collection functions, including the collection of toll telephone deposits. Customers are charged a flat monthly rate for local calls, with rates dependent upon whether a customer has a single- or multiple-party telephone, the style of the receiver, number of extensions, etc. However, user-sensitive service (USS) was being considered whereby a charge for local calls might vary depending on the number and length of these calls. Further, multiple-party lines were likely to be phased out.

All rates are subject to approval by the California Public Utilities Commission. The base rates reflect costs, competitors' rates, and ceilings on profits imposed by the federal and state regulatory commissions. Under regulations to 1984, telephone companies in California were permitted a maximum return of about 6 percent of net plant assets. The effects of deregulation

**EXHIBIT 6**
Organization
Chart

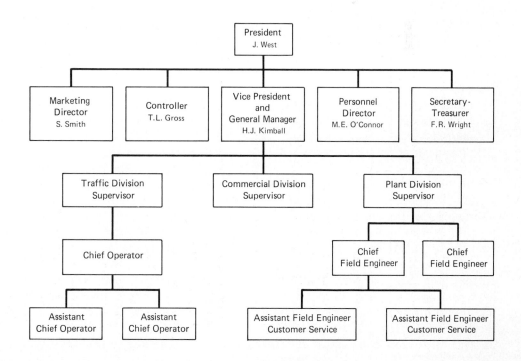

**EXHIBIT 7** Rushford Telephone Company Monthly Residential Telephone Rates 1975–1984

|  | 1975 | 1978 | 1979 | 1982 | 1984 |
|---|---|---|---|---|---|
| Private line | $5.72 | $6.30 | $6.95 | $7.65 | $8.10 |
| Two-party line | 4.72 | 5.30 | 5.95 | 6.65 | 7.10 |
| Three-or-more party line | 4.72 | 5.30 | 5.65 | 6.35 | 6.80 |

*Note:* As of July 1, 1984, each extension telephone is $2.80 additional per month.

were not known. The state commission has placed a valuation of $34,490,000 on Rushford's fixed assets. Currently, average Rushford rates are approximately the same as those charged by nearby independent companies, and are slightly higher than those charged by the Pacific Telesis Group in surrounding areas. Exhibit 7 presents recent Rushford telephone rates.

## THE TRAFFIC DIVISION

The traffic division handles local and long-distance calls, and is responsible for seeing that placed calls reach their proper destination. The division employs 195 operators, 10 assistant operators, and 2 chief operators. Specific functions include:

    directory information assistance
    local and long-distance dialing assistance
    long-distance directory service
    placement of person-to-person calls

In his investigation, Dr. McGowan noted an unusually high number of customer complaints concerning operator service. In particular, it is complained that operators are frequently difficult to reach.

Mrs. Carolyn Watson, one of the chief operators, told Dr. McGowan that during peak load periods the operators could not always handle all incoming calls. She explained that the demand for long-distance service was quite uneven, with most calls occurring during the evening hours. Mrs. Watson pointed out that it is not always possible to staff adequately for the evening periods, since this is an unpopular work shift.

Other problems are caused when unexpected surges in demand occur at other times of the day. This may be caused by local emergencies, or other unanticipated local or national events.

From 25 to 100 operator stations are manned at all times. The company normally tries to keep about 60 stations open during the 7 A.M.–4 P.M. shift, up to 90 on the 4–12 P.M. shift, and 25 on the night shift. Due to difficulties in staffing for the evening shift the number of stations open may be as low as 65 to 70.

Mrs. Watson sees the biggest problem in the traffic division as being employee turnover. "The hours are not always the best, and for some, the work is rather monotonous and confining," she commented. She feels that these factors are largely responsible for the high turnover in the department.

Several developments in recent years have affected the demand for operator services. One significant influence has been the use of direct-distance dialing, a concept which diminishes the role of the operator in placing long-distance calls. Also, Wide Area Telephone Service (WATS) has seen increased usage. With this system, three area bands—statewide, regional, and nationwide—are available at fixed monthly rates.

The key to profitability, according to Mr.

Kimball, is long-distance service. Up to the time of deregulation, over 45 percent of the company's revenues were generated through toll calls. The independent companies were at a disadvantage in long-distance service because all interstate calls had to pass through the Bell System "long line." Toll contracts were negotiated with Bell, with rates being based on average revenues per message. Independent firms received about 50 percent of the total revenues generated on each call. After deregulation, however, the independents faced a more perplexing set of circumstances. AT&T was only one of several companies who could carry long-distance messages, and the rates were likely to be lower. However, AT&T was a leader, particularly in serving smaller communities.

## THE PLANT DIVISION

The plant division is responsible for installing and maintaining all telephones, connections, transmission lines, and central exchange equipment. Presently, the system consists of about 90,000 telephones. There are eight exchange substations and one central exchange station. Two of the three substations have been built within the past five years. The main plant was recently doubled in size.

Unlike the largest telephone companies, who obtain most of their equipment from their manufacturing subsidiaries, independent companies such as Rushford buy from a variety of sources. Rushford usually buys from companies such as North American Phillips, Stromberg Carlson, and Northern Electric. Mr. Jordan, the company's chief engineer, feels that independents are losing some of their competitive edge with respect to buying equipment. In the past, Bell was forced to buy all its equipment from Western Electric, a subsidiary of the AT&T monopoly.[1] Independents were more flexible in

---

[1]Western Electric was dissolved as part of the AT&T restructuring; but its production facilites remained a part of the new AT&T Technologies Group.

buying equipment because they could buy from several manufacturers. These companies don't have the heavy investment in particular items that the large suppliers do, and are therefore able to quickly incorporate changes or make modifications to suit the customer. However, with the breakup of AT&T, this situation will change. The Bell companies will also be able to purchase from any supplier, therefore destroying what was once an advantage for the independent companies.

Still, the company's gross plant investment per telephone is only $400, as compared with over $650 for most companies. This figure reflects the high proportion of older, more fully depreciated equipment owned by the company. In particular, the equipment in two towns acquired as a result of a takeover of another company is quite old and obsolete.

Mr. Jordan admitted to Dr. McGowan that in many instances the company's equipment is not performing satisfactorily and needs to be replaced. Mr. Kimball agreed that it should be replaced, but said that the company has had to expend so much money just keeping up with the rapidly growing population and service demands that it has not had the resources to make needed replacements of equipment. The result is an unusually higher incidence of equipment failures, particularly in the circuit relay equipment. Mr. Kimball said that present construction budgets call for replacement of most of this obsolete equipment within five years. "That is, if we can get the needed funds," he added. He said that equipment replacements alone would cost the company an estimated $12,000,000 over the next four years.

Efforts are also being made to upgrade customer equipment. The company has generally lagged behind most telphone companies in introducing new telephone devices. Rushford has not, for instance, made available built-in panel telephones, or any of the so-called "hands-free" instruments. Mr. Kimball feels that improving the quality and reliability of service is a first priority, and the frills, such as fancier and more elaborate user equipment should come later. The customer service department is one of the most important areas of the plant division. The functions of this department include the installation, maintenance, and repair of lines, cables, relays, and user equipment. Mr. Samms, the service department supervisor, described for Dr. McGowan some of the company's service problems. He explained that most service outages are not caused by faulty equipment, but instead are the result of unexpected occurrences:

> In my opinion we keep up quite well with routine service. It's when a violent storm occurs, or whenever a street repair crew slices through a cable, for instance, that we have problems. But when this happens, people aren't concerned with why their phones won't work; all they know is that they don't. This is understandable, I suppose, but it puts us in a difficult position.

Dr. McGowan asked about long-standing customer complaints concerning long delays in installing telephones. Mr. Samms answered, saying,

> Here again it's not so much a matter of poor service, but rather public expectation of service. People take telephones for granted so much today that they expect them to be available for use at all times. Whenever people move to a new location and have to wait just a short time for installation, or whenever repair becomes necessary, they become impatient.

Mr. Samms conceded, however, that the service organization is not all that he would like it to be. He pointed out that the average wait for telephone installation is about one week, and that the average wait for repair service is over 24 hours. He considers these time periods to be excessive, particularly when compared with figures for the large telephone companies. But he emphasized that the company simply cannot afford to make the heavy investment in service equipment and personnel needed for faster service. This, he claims, would result in the under utilization of equipment and manpower, increasing costs and possibly reducing service in other areas.

Mr. Samms also pointed out to Dr. McGowan that it is becoming more and more difficult to find qualified personnel to install and maintain equipment. He talked about the long and expensive training period necessary for employees in the service department and the need to reduce turnover among these employees. (Employee turnover in this area is about 20 percent annually.) Mr. Samms stressed the fact that communications equipment is becoming extremely complex, and that frequent retraining of employees is necessary to keep up with the latest developments.

Rushford has divided its territory into eight districts for purposes of telephone installation and repair service. A dispatcher in each district makes out the work schedules and assignments for the service crews working in the district. Repair service and telephone installation is performed for customers on a first-come, first-serve basis, although, as Mr. Samms explained, repair work takes precedence over telephone installation if personnel are insufficient to handle all jobs in a given period of time.

## THE EMPLOYEE TURNOVER PROBLEM

Mr. O'Connor, personnel director, agrees with the department heads and supervisors that labor turnover is one of Rushford's most persistent and pressing problems. Currently the turnover for switchboard and information operators is about 70 percent per year, as compared with a 30 percent average for the industry. The turnover in the other divisions averages about 25 percent.

Mr. O'Connor attributes the high turnover in the traffic division to several reasons:

> First of all, the typical traffic division employee is young, female, and married. These character-

istics alone mean that we will have a higher turnover. The girls have children, their husbands get out of school or are transferred, or they decide that they want to be at home with the family during evenings or at night.

And let's face it. The cream of society do not want to work as telephone operators. We get girls who are essentially undertrained and who have had relatively little education. Usually, one of two things happens when such a person is employed. Either they are irresponsible and fail to show up or do the job properly, or they improve their skills and confidence level to an extent that they move on to a better paying job elsewhere.

Mr. O'Connor told Dr. McGowan that the only way to deal with absenteeism and work infractions is by use of strict disciplinary methods. He explained that it is company policy to automatically fire an employee after two unexcused absences. Employees who refuse to work their assigned shifts are also fired.

But Mr. O'Connor admitted that the company can do little to prevent conscientious, well-trained employees from moving on to better jobs. "We simply can't compete on a wage basis with a lot of other employers in this area," he lamented. Exhibit 8 shows the wages of hourly employees.

In recent years, Rushford has been under some community pressure to employ some of the area's unemployed minorities. Mr. O'Connor has resisted this pressure, saying that they cannot afford to worsen their already critical turnover problem by taking a chance on uneducated, unemployed, or itinerant persons. He has publicly stated that Rushford already hires a high percentage of minority employees (minority employees comprise about 25 percent of the total Rushford work force), but that ". . . such people must meet the standards and qualification for employment, the same as everyone else."

Rushford offers incentives and wage differentials for employees to work the less pop-

---

**EXHIBIT 8**  Rushford Telephone Company Wage Classifications for Hourly Employees Effective June 18, 1984

|  | Operators | Clerks, Cashiers, Representatives |
|---|---|---|
| Start | $4.68 | |
| Beginning  7th month | 4.73 | |
| 13th month | 4.78 | $4.79 |
| 19th month | 4.83 | 4.86 |
| 25th month | 4.89 | 4.91 |
| 31st month | 4.95 | 4.97 |
| 37th month | 5.01 | 5.03 |
| 43rd month | 5.07 | 5.09 |
| 49th month | 5.13 | 5.15 |
| 55th month | 5.19 | 5.22 |
| 61st month and thereafter | 5.25 | 5.30 |

Differentials

For any tour ending after 7:00 p.m. and before or at 9:00 p.m. 40¢ per hour
For any tour ending after 9:00 a.m. excluding all night tours 50¢ per hour
All night tours ending at 6:00 a.m. 80¢ per hour

ular shifts. In addition, time and a half is paid for work in excess of 40 hours per week. Employees called in to work overtime receive a minimum of 3 hours pay, and their pay period starts when they are called and continues until they return home. (All operators and service employees are technically "on call" at all times they are off-duty, but are not expected to stay at home or near a phone while on call.) Taxicab service is offered at company expense for employees whose shift begins or ends between the hours of 7:30 P.M. and 6:00 A.M.

Training is given starting employees in each division. Traffic operators, for instance, have a three- to four-week training period. Other employees receive training according to the type and complexity of their work. Some employees attend training schools at centers set up by the manufacturers of the particular equipment which they are to operate or service.

The employees of the company are represented by the Communications Workers of America, a national trade union. Mr. O'Connor says that company–union relations are "good." Two strikes in the past seven years have been promptly settled following wage increases.

## SELLING AN IMAGE

Mr. Smith, marketing director, says that his department sees itself in a public education role rather than in primarily a selling one. In an interview with Dr. McGowan, he contended that company officials are cognizant of the public criticisms which have been directed at Rushford in recent years, and that there is a general consensus that the company's promotional efforts should be aimed at improving its public image.

Recent television ads, for example, have carried the theme, "Service is Our Product," emphasizing the telephone company's vital role in the community. Other advertising has illustrated the efforts being undertaken to expand and improve service. Recently, a newspaper ad showing equipment and staff additions for the previous year were captioned, "We're Doing a Better Job."

Although Rushford has expanded its public relations advertising in recent years, over three-fourths of the total marketing budget is still spent on the promotion of services. Such promotion is primarily aimed at the commercial businesses or large organizations in the area who have need for highly elaborate and specialized communications services. Three comunications consultants, who work directly under Mr. Smith, are responsible for evaluating communication needs and designing communications systems for large organizations and commerical firms.

Most advertising directed at residential users touts the advantages of extras, such as extension phones and optional colors and styles of telephone receivers.

Little effort is made to attract additional subscribers. This is because, as Mr. West put it, "the market is so saturated anyway" (87 percent of all residences in Rushford have telephones), and because "the company is already pressed to keep up with the existing demand for installations and services."

The Rushford Telephone Company regularly advertises on three local television stations, four radio stations, and in two newspapers. A local advertising agency handles most of the radio and television spots. Mr. Smith and an assistant lay out the content and format for all newspaper ads.

## THE BOARD TALKS ABOUT THE FUTURE

At a recent meeting of the board of directors, Mr. West talked about the future of Rushford Telephone Company. He began by saying that he believes the thrust of the company should not be toward rapid growth or expansion, but rather, should be aimed at improving services within the present area. He presented the data in Exhibits 9, 10, and 11 to illustrate Rushford's growth. He suggested that, "The greatest chal-

**EXHIBIT 9** Number of Telephones in Use

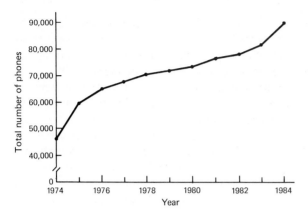

**EXHIBIT 10** Service Population Growth

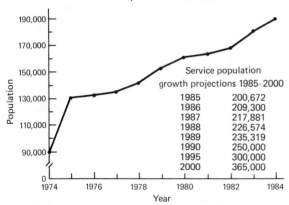

Service population
growth projections 1985-2000

| Year | Population |
|------|-----------|
| 1985 | 200,672 |
| 1986 | 209,300 |
| 1987 | 217,881 |
| 1988 | 226,574 |
| 1989 | 235,319 |
| 1990 | 250,000 |
| 1995 | 300,000 |
| 2000 | 365,000 |

**EXHIBIT 11** Capital Expenditures

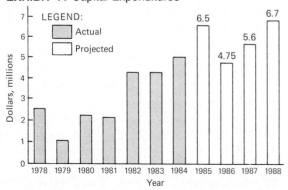

lenge in the years ahead will be in gaining the full confidence and support of the public." He continued:

We've done a lot in the past few years to eliminate some of our weak areas and shortcomings. We can now say that we're offering good service to the public. But "good" isn't good enough. We've got to offer service that is excellent, and which the public recognizes as being excellent. This means that we've got to continually stay abreast of new developments in the field; and in particular, we've got to keep pace with some of our neighboring companies in implementing these developments. I don't need to tell you that the one thing which has really hurt our image in the past is not that we're standing still—because we're not—but the fact that other companies have had the jump on us in updating their systems. For example, when people visit or move from areas where they are able to use touch telephones, they wonder why we don't have them. We can't afford these kinds of lags in the future.

Mr. West told the board about some of the trends in user equipment, such as built-in panel telephones and video telephone. He described an altogether new concept in voice transmission called *pulse code modulation,* which has the potential of improving fidelity, efficiency, and economy over conventional methods of communication.

Of particular importance, thinks Mr. West, is the growing demand for data transmission services for electronic data processing systems. He estimates that soon data transmission will account for up to 50 percent of telephone usage. He stated that if the telephone companies did not take the initiative in this area, that business would develop their own transmission system. He pointed out that several firms in the Rushford area were already developing their own communication systems for both voice and data transmission.

But perhaps more than being able to implement technological developments, Mr. West said that he is worried about the mechanics of installing and servicing increasingly complex equipment. He talked briefly about some new concepts which other companies are trying which might have application for Rushford. One is the "fast-response" program being successfully used by one of the large systems. This concept involves the development of program centers for service, trouble analysis, and program expansion. These centers bring together the personnel of various departments to coordinate and facilitate the handling of new installations, repair, and system changes. Another idea which Mr. West feels would cut down on installation time and service problems is the prewiring of homes and apartment buildings during construction.

Of course, the uncertainties with the breakup of AT&T were also on the minds of senior executives. The impact of potentially lower long-distance revenues and increased competition were uncertainties which plagued the thinking about funding new capital investments.

"These are just some of the things we're going to be dealing with in the future," Mr. West concluded. "But for right now, we're going to have to shape up some of our present problems before we can commit our resources to these ideas."

# SPEED SERVICE LAUNDRY COMPANY

## Lawrence R. Jauch

*Southern Illinois University-Carbondale*

The Speed Service Laundry Company recently surpassed its chief competitor to become the largest laundry and dry-cleaning company in East Lansing, Michigan. Only 4 years ago, the company was merely one of the many neighborhood dry-cleaners in the East Lansing area, and was about seventh or eight in size. The rapid growth began when the company changed hands in 1980.

The company was founded by Michael Burke in 1948. Located in the downtown section of East Lansing, the firm quickly gained a reputation for quality work and friendly service. The business was profitable and provided a comfortable living for Mr. Burke and his family for many years. About a year before the owner's death in 1971, he followed the trend to move to the suburbs and relocated the plant near an older, middle-class neighborhood. His widow ran the business for the next 9 years, until she was forced to sell it because of ill health. Tom Kigin and Karen Kessler purchased the business in the summer of 1980.

Mr. Kigin, a native of Ohio, graduated from Michigan State University with a degree in personnel management in 1976. From 1976 to 1979 he was the manager of a dry-cleaning company in East Lansing. Kigin saw the advertisement to sell the Speed Service Laundry in the newspaper and was immediately inter-

ested. He felt that the potential for a dry-cleaning business in the East Lansing area was a promising one, and also saw this as a chance to be his own boss. Mr. Kigin was able to persuade Ms. Kessler, whom he met at a civic club, to leave her job with a state agency and form a partnership to purchase Speed Service. Ms. Kessler is 32 years old and has a degree in accounting.

The new owners decided to expand operations rapidly by borrowing heavily and reinvesting all profits for the next 5 years. During the first year of operations one dry-cleaning plant and one combination dry-cleaning and laundry plant were purchased. Three dry-cleaning plants were added in 1983 and one more in 1984. Two combination dry-cleaning and laundry plants were added in 1984. In addition, five pickup stations were established. Gross sales increased from $120,000 in 1980 to over $1,000,000 in 1984.

Mr. Kigin is operations manager and director. He supervises purchasing, advertising, production, personnel, and transportation. He spends most of his time troubleshooting, traveling to various plants. Ms. Kessler serves as treasurer, accountant, and finance officer. Since she spends most of her time at the main plant, she also acts as manager of that plant.

## HOW SPEED SERVICE OPERATES

Plant 1 is the original facility and is used for laundry, dry cleaning, and clothes storage. It is located in a deteriorating neighborhood on a heavily traveled street. The area has been the subject of much local criticism due to its high concentration of businesses and generally in-

**TABLE 1**  Speed Service Laundry
Comparative Income Statements
for the Years Ended December 31

| Financial Statement | 1984 | 1983 | 1982 |
|---|---|---|---|
| Net sales | $1,000,300 | $613,909 | $297,362 |
| Cost of sales | 532,000 | 332,739 | 172,470 |
| Gross profit | 468,000 | 281,170 | 124,892 |
| All other expenses net | 438,000 | 259,683 | 113,116 |
| Profit before taxes | 30,300 | 21,487 | 11,776 |
| Income taxes | 7,899 | 4,945 | 2,136 |
| Net profit | 22,401 | 16,542 | 9,640 |

**TABLE 2**  Speed Service Laundry
Comparative Balance Sheets
at the Years Ended December 31

| Financial Statement | 1984 | 1983 | 1982 |
|---|---|---|---|
| ASSETS | | | |
| Cash | $62,898 | $32,954 | $21,247 |
| Receivables, net | 72,771 | 59,058 | 29,635 |
| Inventory, net | 28,796 | 18,492 | 11,380 |
| All other | 15,260 | 12,634 | 9,598 |
| Total current | 179,725 | 123,138 | 71,860 |
| Fixed assets, net | 515,493 | 344,451 | 230,237 |
| All other | 28,179 | 28,135 | 23,742 |
| Total noncurrent | 543,672 | 372,586 | 253,979 |
| Total assets | 723,397 | 495,724 | 325,839 |
| LIABILITIES | | | |
| Due to banks | $78,685 | $54,226 | $37,082 |
| Due to trade | 71,001 | 45,645 | 22,943 |
| Income taxes | 7,899 | 4,945 | 2,136 |
| All other | 19,226 | 12,270 | 8,598 |
| Total current | 176,811 | 117,086 | 70,759 |
| Long-term debt | 515,797 | 348,012 | 226,231 |
| Total debt | 692,608 | 465,098 | 296,990 |
| EQUITY | | | |
| T. Kigin | 13,323 | 13,323 | 13,323 |
| K. Kessler | 13,323 | 13,323 | 13,323 |
| Earned Surplus | 4,143 | 3,980 | 2,203 |
| Total liabilities and equity | 723,397 | 495,724 | 325,839 |

adequate parking space. There is room for three cars in Speed Service's parking area. Curb service is featured.

Plant 2 is a dry-cleaning plant located near Michigan State University and close to a number of apartment buildings. It is a modern building on a main traffic route. Parking is adequate.

Plant 3 was the first plant built by the partnership. It has both dry-cleaning and laundry facilities, and contains the cold-storage vault used by the whole company. It is a physically attractive building located on a commercial street next to a middle-class neighborhood and close to a number of high-income apartments.

The fourth plant is a dry-cleaning establishment located in the same building as a self-service laundry (not owned by the company). The neighborhood contains rather cheap houses and includes a large primary-secondary educational complex. Parking is shared with a grocery store. On the day the case writer visited the outlet, there was a great deal of litter strewn both inside the building and on the parking lot. On this and a subsequent visit, the attendant was very slow in appearing.

Plants 5, 6, and 8 are all dry-cleaning plants located in newer, middle-class suburban areas. In all cases, the buildings are fewer than 5 years old and are well maintained. Plant 7 is a combination dry-cleaning and laundry unit in an old and somewhat aristocratic neighborhood.

The ninth unit is in the process of being built. It is Speed Service's first venture into an area which consists of luxury housing and apartments. The new facility will be a combination of dry cleaning and laundry.

The five pickup stations are located in areas where customers do not have ready access to any of Speed Service's main facilities. Most are located in neighborhood shopping centers. In each instance, these stations share the same building with coin-operated laundries owned by another firm. One attendant takes care of both facilities.

Speed Service Laundry is a full-service company, serving the laundry, dry-cleaning, and clothes storage (both normal storage and cold storage for furs) needs of their customers. These services are available at all stations. If the receiving station does not have the facilities to perform the desired work, the items are transferred to another station and then returned to the original station for pickup. One-hour service is available for all dry cleaning. Laundry is on an "in-by-nine, out-by-five" basis. In most areas of the city, laundry accounts for about 30 percent of the business. Near the university, however, it amounts to nearly 60 percent of the total volume. "Instant" curb service is advertised. A study showed that the average time spent by a customer at a drive-in facility is 2 minutes.

The full cycle for dry-cleaning operations includes the actual dry-cleaning and drying process, steam pressing (pants, coats, and dresses), steam finishing (pants), clothes wrapping, racking, and delivery.

In the laundry, clothes are marked, and then washed and dried. Shirts, pants, and dresses undergo both a preliminary and a final steam pressing. Sheets are pressed only once. After an item has been pressed, it is folded or packaged for delivery.

The equipment for a laundry facility consists of a boiler and compressor to supply steam, washing machines, a dryer (although most clothes are ironed wet), three or four types of ironers, a packaging rack, and a repair area. The dry-cleaning equipment includes a dry-cleaning machine, a dryer, a number of semiautomatic ironers, a packaging rack, and a repair station. With the exception of the original plant, the equipment is fairly new and modern in design. The equipment in the old plant is less efficient and has caused some maintenance problems. Mr. Kigin stated that labor is the major production cost in this industry, and that they are using automated equipment whenever possible. He added that he subscribed to an industry periodical, and that he closely followed any recommendations on how to improve efficiency.

The design of the work areas in most of the plants is generally good from the standpoint of efficiency. Storage areas are inadequate, however. For example, the passageways at some of the plants are cluttered with large drums of detergent. There are no plans to expand existing facilities although they are presently operating at 80 to 90 percent capacity. Management would rather build new plants to meet future needs than expand old ones, as they feel that small plants are more efficient.

## SPEED SERVICE'S MARKET

Mr. Kigin said that as far as he can predict, Speed Service Laundry will limit its marketing area to East Lansing. Lansing, which is the capital and third largest city in Michigan, is located midway between Grand Rapids and Detroit. The city contains a wide variety of medium and light industry, with products such as machinery, metal products, paper products, auto parts, and clothing, and state government offices. The town is also the home of Michigan State University, which has an enrollment of approximately 40,000. It is not a rapidly growing community. In fact, many people seem to be moving from Michigan to other areas in the country, as a result of the economically depressed auto industry of the late 1970s and early 1980s.

Speed Service serves many types of persons in the community, and management has tried to vary its promotions accordingly. For example, an appeal is made to the town's established residents with advertising slogans such as "Serving You with Quality for Over 35 Years," and "We Care—and Have Cared for Over 35 Years." On the other hand, ads are placed in a student newspaper emphasizing the growth and progressiveness of the company. Members of the football team sometimes pose for these ads.

Some advertising is aimed at the town's wealthier residents, giving assurance that expensive clothes will be handled competently, and explaining in detail the elaborate precautions taken in clothes and fur storage. Delivery service is furnished to a small number of customers who live in the town's most exclusive residential area. Delivery service is not provided to other customers.

Speed Service advertises on radio, on television, and in the newspapers. Radio advertising consists of spots on the 7:30 morning and 6:15 evening weather reports of a local station. Sixty-second television commercials are placed on an eleven o'clock news program on Sunday and Monday nights. It is estimated that 85,000 people watch this program. Ads are placed in a major newspaper every few days although management does not feel that this has yielded worthwhile results. Mr. Kigin said that at one time they tried a direct-mail campaign, but did not find it very effective. Mr. Kigin writes all of the company's advertising copy and delivers the television advertisements himself. The total advertising budget is $2,100 a month. An independent organization estimates that 168,000 people are being reached by the advertising campaign. Occasionally, one of Mr. Kigin's children delivers the television commercials.

Speed Service's prices are comparable to those of competitors in the area, with one exception. A fast-growing chain, Stotlar Cleaning and Laundry, is underselling all the others. Mr. Kigin commented, "They're wearing out their equipment, but they're not making any money. I don't think they can keep offering such low prices for very long." He admitted, however, that he was surprised that they had been able to keep prices low for as long as they had. Stotlar dropped prices to a level about 10 to 15 percent below the prevailing rates in late 1983 and has not raised them since. Stotlar is now the second largest of the three major chains in the area.

The Speed Service marketing concept contends that all dry cleaning and laundry are basically the same. "We're selling service, nothing else," said Mr. Kigin.

> There's not much difference in quality from one outfit to the next. Even if there is a difference, people are not apt to notice it. What they do notice, however, are things like how fast they are waited on, whether or not they can get a nearby parking place, how friendly the people behind the counter are, and whether or not the ashtrays have been emptied recently. It's the little things that really make the difference.

Mr. Kigin said that persons employed to work behind the counter are carefully selected on the basis of appearance and personality. Many college students are hired part-time for this job.

## PERSONNEL

Mr. Kigin does all the hiring and firing. In reference to hiring policies, he said, "My first impression of a person usually determines whether or not he gets hired. I look at his personal appearance, personality, interest in the job, and whether or not he's got a wine bottle in his pocket." All references are checked, and no applications are taken over the phone. The company does not discriminate racially, and this is reflected by the fact that nearly one-third of the work force is black.

Labor turnover, a serious problem in most cleaning businesses, is no problem to Speed Service. Management feels that this is largely due to the fact that their pay scales are above the area average for the industry. The major job categories and hourly wages are as follows:

1. Laundry pressers      $3.35 per hour
2. Dry-cleaning pressers      $4.25–4.75 per hour
3. Dry-cleaning operators      $4.85–5.25 per hour
4. Checkers      $3.95 per hour
5. Laundry markers      $3.35 per hour
6. Front personnel      $3.35 per hour
7. Managers of outlets      $250/week, plus 3% of sales

Mr. Kigin said that each worker is guaranteed a minimum weekly wage of $75, regardless of how many hours he or she has worked. Time and a half is given for all time over 40 hours.

Fringe benefits include a "surprise" cake given on an employee's birthday, cokes sold at cost, with free cokes during rush periods, a 50 percent discount on all work, and a 1-week vacation. In addition, a $10 award is given to all employees when no garments are lost in a given month. This is awarded for most months.

Promotion, like hiring, is based on Kigin's personal evaluation of the employee. Mr. Kigin emphasized that qualified employees who have the desire to "better themselves" have the opportunity to work up in the organization. Part of the 135-member work force comes to work at 7 A.M. and works until 4 P.M., whereas the others work from 8 A.M. until 5 P.M. Only the dry-cleaning staff works on Saturday, working from 8 until 11 A.M. There are two coffee breaks per day, one at 10 A.M. and the other at 3 P.M.

Most training is done on the job. Many applicants have had previous experience in the production end of the business, and an effort is made to hire these individuals. If their past experience has been limited or specialized, they are rotated through a number of jobs so that they will be able to work wherever needed. There is no educational requirement for production workers. The front workers, who are often high school or college students, do not normally have prior experience. Mr. Kigin trains them personally, emphasizing the importance of good customer relations.

There are no written personnel policies, but Mr. Kigin has a number of informal policies that reflect several precepts which are especially dear to him. These include:

1. Never ask of a worker what you would not do yourself.
2. The success of the company depends on the worker, and workers produce in a direct re-

lationship to the way management treats them.

3. Employees are people, and they bring their personal troubles to work with them. Help the employees solve their problems, and they work better. (Mr. Kigin has been known to cosign notes, secure legal aid, and perform other services for his employees.)

4. The workers are sensitive to changes in production processes and management. It is better to explain things than to have the employees come to the wrong conclusions.

Mr. Kigin pointed out that the employees have a strong sense of identification with the company, and that this would tend to thwart any attempts at unionization. Many cleaners in the area, including Speed Service's largest competitors, are unionized.

Speed Service has no centralized personnel records. Records for each employee are kept at the plant in which he works for a period of 1 year.

## FINANCING AT SPEED SERVICE

The company has relied upon debt to provide the funds for its rapid expansion. All new locations are 100 percent debt-financed with 10-year notes. It costs the company about $50,000 to set up a dry-cleaning plant, and about $100,000 to build and equip a full-service plant. Everything needed to start a facility is financed with a "package" note at the company's bank. Pickup stations are leased. Mr. Kigin said that the break-even points for pickup stations, dry-cleaning plants, and full-service plants are $550 per month, $5,000 per month, and $11,000 per month, respectively.

Short-term debt is occasionally used to finance inventory. Ms. Kessler said that she never uses a budget, but she prepares trial balances monthly. Balance sheet and income statments are prepared semiannually. Depreciation is figured under the S/L provisions allowed by the accelerated cost recovery method of depreciation on a straight-line basis, which assumes a 5-year life for all machinery and equipment.

Ms. Kessler said that she was worried that the financial structure of the company was becoming debt-heavy. "I'm not certain that we can continue to expand indefinitely using long-term debt as a source of funds," she said. "The way I see it, we're driving ourselves up against a wall as far as future financing is concerned. The more we go into debt, the higher interest rates we must pay to offset the increased risk." She continued:

> This also limits the possibility of future equity financing, since investors would not be willing to pay as much for the stock because of the risk factor. No, I'm becoming more and more convinced that we should start a franchising operation.

She went on to describe the details concerning a franchise plan which she has been "playing around with." Under this plan, the original partnership would act more or less as a holding company, owning two-thirds of the new plants and providing "professional services" for a fee. The franchise holder would put up $15,000 of his own money. Ten thousand of this would pay for the franchise, $3,500 would go into "paid-in-surplus," and $1,500 would go into "paid-in-equity." He would then be entitled to draw $16,000 in salary plus one-third of net profits. The controlling partnership would pay two-thirds of expenses and take two-thirds of the profits. For 5 percent of sales, the parent company would furnish advertising and bookkeeping services. Laundry service would be provided to plants having only dry-cleaning facilities at a 25 percent discount.

"I think that in the long run this arrangement would work out best for us," Ms. Kessler concluded.

> I've talked it over with Tom, but he's not willing to go along with the idea at the present time.

He's concerned that we might lose control over the operation, and that it would be difficult to maintain our quality image. I feel just the opposite about this. It's becoming virtually impossible for two people to personally supervise the entire chain. Why, we're spending almost all of our time traveling from one unit to another as it is. Right now, we're placing an enormous reliance on the individual plant manager. If they owned a piece of the action, they would work even harder to increase sales.

The two partners are still arguing over the possibility of a franchise operation.

# 23 VOLUME BOOKSTORES

## W. Harvey Hegarty

*Indiana University*

## HISTORY

Kenny Lieberman, age 29, is the operator of three bookstores, a houseplant store, and a children's clothing store in the Chicago area. On a day-to-day basis, he spends most of his time working on the bookstores. They are the focus of this case.

Overall, Lieberman seems satisfied with his bookstores. As he himself says,

> I got into the book business ... *not* to get rich; we had no [such] intention. I'm making far more now than I thought I'd ever make in the book business. I went in with my eyes open, but we wanted to have a little mellow bookstore, a nice little business. ... My ideas have not changed. I may be making a little more than I thought I would be making, but my ideas on the situation haven't changed.

### Volume I (OLD)

Lieberman entered the book business in November 1970, with the opening of Volume I Bookstore in Chicago's Piper's Alley, a well-known, youth-oriented shopping mall. In this venture, he formed a partnership with his wife, Barbara Lieberman. Financing was obtained through their families and local banks.

At the time, Piper's Alley was an ideal location: it was in a part of the city popular with young people and intellectuals with money to

spend. Furthermore, the terms of the lease and the opportunity to purchase the store's fixtures were excellent then, considering the high demand in 1970 for this location. Initially, the Liebermans worked all 72 hours a week that the store was open by themselves. Later, they brought in Kenny's sister as a clerk, and added some other part-time help.

Volume I remained open four years, until November 1974. Originally the dollar volume of business was satisfactory, but in the last two years it dropped off considerably. Piper's Alley turned out to have been a fad, and once its newness wore off, it was ignored by the public. Operating expenses began to seem backbreakingly high, largely due to the exorbitant rent the location once deserved and now continued to demand. Lieberman managed to get a break in his lease and move his employees to other bookstores which he had begun in the meantime. This first bookstore was the only one which failed.

### Volume II

Lieberman always has been interested in expanding his book business. Part of his strategy for expansion has been scouting for attractive new locations. Early in 1972, he found a storefront for rent on Sheridan Road, a major North Side arterial. He rented it immediately because of its ideal location: Loyola University and Mundelein College are right across the street; the neighborhood is prosperous and filled with young people just out of college with intellectual interests; the street is busy and lined with other successful businesses; public transportation (train and bus) stop next to the store; and there is a heavy amount of pedestrian traffic in the area. This storefront, which had previously housed a submarine sandwich stand, was divided into two parts. Half became Volume II Bookstore. The other half became Dawn, a houseplant and card store named for Lieberman's young daughter. Two of Lieberman's friends initially managed these new stores.

Lieberman found that it was easier to start this second bookstore because of the line of credit he had established through Volume I. Volume II is operated as a partnership between Lieberman and his wife. Its inventory was financed largely through trade credit and some small bank loans, with these sums being repaid out of the store's sales. Further information on Volume II will follow later in the case.

## Volume III

Volume III opened in November of 1974, shortly after the Volume I store in Piper's Alley closed. Pat McDonald, who had been a clerk at Volume I, was promoted to manager of Volume III. This store was organized as a partnership between Lieberman and a young businesswoman–investor named Anne Riback. It is located in a residential neighborhood in Evanston, a suburb situated immediately north of Chicago along Lake Michigan.

Volume III is on Central Avenue, which is a neighborhood business street but not a major arterial. The only other bookstores in the immediate area are two used book stores which offer Volume III no competition. Evanston is the home of Northwestern University, but this is not a lucrative detail because the store and the university are on opposite sides of town. The Evanston bus stops across the street, giving the store some exposure to the elderly people who ride it. Their purchasing books for their grandchildren helps explain Volume III's high sales of juvenile books. Volume III adjoins Mudpies, a lucrative children's clothing store run by Lieberman and Riback.

At the present time, Volume III is just barely breaking even. Certain aspects of its difficulties will be presented later in this case.

## Volume I (NEW)

Lieberman's latest bookstore, opened on July 1, 1976, is the *new* Volume I, located on Broadway and Belmont on Chicago's Near North Side. This store, aside from its name and owner, has no connection with the original Volume I. It is in the middle of an extremely busy business district in a very heterogeneous neighborhood. To the east lies Chicago's Gold Coast, that strip of expensive high-rise apartment buildings which line Lake Michigan. To the west is a very poor immigrant neighborhood. In addition, many gay people are attracted to the area because of the wide open life-style it offers. The public transportation (train and bus) is good. Another factor which strangely enough makes Volume I's location attractive is the high local crime rate. While there are three other nice bookstores within four blocks of Volume I, many people would rather not go four blocks further into the neighborhood and therefore prefer to shop at Volume I.

Volume I has been characterized by high and steady sales since its opening day. This section of Broadway has always been a good business location. While expenses are higher due to the particularly choice location, the added traffic and sales more than make up for these additional fixed costs. It is organized as a corporation with Lieberman and an unnamed second party as the primary shareholders.

## FINANCE

Lieberman has always attempted to use as much trade credit as possible in running his bookstores. The book business is known for its slow payments (publishers will accept 90–120 days), and thus the Volume Bookstores have been able to adopt a policy of paying in 60 days on shipments which are invariably marked as 2/10, net

30. During the Christmas season, when stock builds up on the shelves before the sales crush begins, many accounts are not paid for 90 days. Immediately after Christmas, with extra cash on hand, the bills are paid up again to the 60-day point.

Lieberman has an interesting method of determining how much of each month's sales should go toward paying for inventory. Since books are usually sold by the publishers at a 40% discount, he simply allocates 60% of gross sales to go for paying publishers. This is all they will get. Of the remaining 40% of gross sales, 15% goes to salaries, approximately 5% is for fixed expenses, and 20% is allocated to Lieberman and his associates, employee bonuses, and improvement of stores and their inventories. This is the goal set for the bookstores; expenses

have in actuality been running at more than 5%. The financial data for Volume II for 1975 are given in Exhibit 1, with comparisons with what the figures would be if they followed Lieberman's plans.

Lieberman simply feels that when his expenses exceed this goal, they are just "blowing it." He thinks that it is just a matter of carelessness and internal and/or external theft that expenses get out of hand. In 1976, sales at Volume II were expected to be $206,000. The actual figure was $186,000.

Since sales are rising at Volume II, there has been some attempt on the part of management to define just where this growth is coming from. It is felt that 10% is inflationary. The cost of books is still rising. This automatically would add to a dollar increase in sales volume without

**EXHIBIT 1**    Volume II Income Statement Est. for Calendar Year 1975

|  |  | Actual | Desired |
|---|---|---|---|
| Gross Sales |  | $164,000.00 | $164,000.00 |
| Less COGS |  | 98,400.00 | 98,400.00 |
| Gross Margin |  | $ 65,600.00 | $ 65,600.00 |
| Less Expenses: |  |  |  |
| Wages and Bonuses Exp. | $25,000.00 |  |  |
| Rent Exp. | 3,600.00 |  |  |
| Payroll Tax | 2,500.00 |  |  |
| Insurance Exp. | 2,500.00 |  |  |
| Electricity Exp. | 1,500.00 |  |  |
| Advertising Exp. | 1,500.00 |  |  |
| Interest Exp. | 5,000.00 |  |  |
| Store Telephone Exp. | 750.00 |  |  |
| Supplies | 1,000.00 |  |  |
| Miscellaneous Exp. | 1,500.00 |  |  |
| Lieberman's Phone | 1,000.00 |  |  |
| Lieberman's Car | 700.00 |  |  |
| Net Expenses |  |  |  |
| Profit for Dist'n to Partners |  | $ 46,050.00 | $ 41,000.00 |
| and Store Improvement |  | $ 19,550.00 | $ 24,600.00 |

Note: Financial Information not available on Vol. I and Vol. III due to financial organization of stores. Income statements for Vol. I and Vol III are very similar to Vol. II, with the notable exceptions of gross sales, rent expense, and wages.

a corresponding increase in actual unit sales. The remainder of the sale increase, however, is thought to be due to other factors, such as,

- more people on the street.
- more people finding the store.
- more people using public transportation and walking.
- more people giving business to dependable neighborhood stores.
- more people growing with the store, staying with it as income goes up and more income goes for books.
- more people wanting to browse and avoid the department store atmosphere of the larger bookstores.

All of the stores' space is rented. Volume I is on a 10-year lease at $1,250 per month, with nominal increases for inflation. Volume II is currently paying $300 per month; its lease will be renegotiated shortly for a 5-year term at an undoubtedly higher, but as yet unfixed, rate. Volume III has two years left on a lease with an option to renew; rent there is currently $300 per month.

Cash flow is at present the stores' biggest problem. In Lieberman's words, it is the problem of, "How to get enough to pay for the books before you sell the books." Because sales at all the stores are so predictable, it is his practice to write checks against the next week's deposits. He uses literally every cent just to pay the bills. When sales are higher than normal, this extra cash goes to pay for additional inventory that the managers have had their eyes on. However, because space is limited, especially at Volume II, there is not a tremendous push to over-fill the shelves. Eventually, higher sales will mean more cash in the checkbook for all the stores.

## INVENTORY

Inventory excesses are the bane of all bookstores, and the Volume Bookstores are no exception. The basic challenge lies in the tradeoff between keeping inventory low enough so that publishers' bills do not eat the stores alive and maintaining a sufficiently broad selection of books so that customers will continue to frequent the stores.

The managers, who also do the buying, must always fight off the publishers' representatives. The problem is that the representatives come and always have nice things to offer. The more nice books the managers see, the more they want to buy. There frequently is no question but that the books would sell. But there still must be limits on orders, for three reasons: (1) there is not room on the shelves for all the good books available; (2) the increased inventory would send the bills through the roof; and (3) while the books might sell, there is no guarantee as to how quickly they would sell, and rapid turnover is essential.

The Volume Bookstores thus have developed a formula for inventory ordering. All managers work on a quota system. If the store sells 1,100–1,200 books per week, that is all that will be ordered weekly. Inventory replacement, then, is tied to sales. The mixture of price ranges on books tends to average out, so there has been no attempt to restrict ordering on the basis of list price.

The point at which things begin to work less smoothly is when a manager will over-order on a week when the publisher's representative is in town, and then fail to cut his orders accordingly in the following weeks. Inventories can easily go from $50,000 to $60,000 through such mistakes.

Lieberman is aiming for an inventory turnover of four times a year. At Volume II, with gross sales of $206,000, this would then indicate that inventory should be about $50,000. This year, they have been successful at holding to this except as Christmas approached, when, due to early shipments by publishers, inventory went to $60,000. $240,00 in gross sales are anticipated for 1977; inventory will remain at $60,000 for that year, maintaining the inventory turnover at 4.

**EXHIBIT 2** Books
Sold by Category

<u>     Vol II     </u>

Week ____ 21st–27th ____  Month ____ Nov. ____  Year ____ 1976 ____

### SUBJECTS and SALES

15 Art  卌 卌 卌

25 Biography  卌 卌 卌 卌 卌

1 Business  /

10 Cooking  卌 卌

9 Crafts  卌 ////

25 Drama  卌 卌 卌 卌 卌

4 Education  ////

246 Fiction  卌 卌 卌 卌 卌 卌 卌 卌 卌 卌 卌 卌 卌 卌 卌 卌 卌 卌
卌 卌 卌 卌 卌 卌 卌 卌 卌 卌 卌 卌 卌 卌 卌 卌 卌 卌
卌 卌 卌 卌 卌 卌 卌 卌 卌 卌 卌 卌 /

14 Film  卌 卌 ////

12 Games and sports  卌 卌 //

26 Hardcovers  卌 卌 卌 卌 卌 /

22 Humor  卌 卌 卌 卌 //

21 Juvenile  卌 卌 卌 卌 /

22 Language  卌 卌 卌 卌 //

41 Medicine  卌 卌 卌 卌 卌 卌 卌 卌 /

17 Music  卌 卌 卌 //

79 Mystery  卌 卌 卌 卌 卌 卌 卌 卌 卌 卌 卌 卌 卌 卌 卌 ////

10 Nature  卌 卌

9 Natural living  卌 ////

50 Occult  卌 卌 卌 卌 卌 卌 卌 卌 卌 卌

29 Philosophy  卌 卌 卌 卌 卌 ////

10 Photography  卌 卌

24 Poetry  卌 卌 卌 卌 ////

11 Political science  卌 卌 /

108 Psychology  卌 卌 卌 卌 卌 卌 卌 卌 卌 卌 卌 卌 卌 卌 卌 卌 卌 卌 卌 卌
卌 卌 卌 卌 ///

11 Reference  卌 卌 /

15 Religion  卌 卌 卌

6 Remainder (sale books)  卌 /

17 Science  卌 卌 卌 //

209 Science fiction  卌 卌 卌 卌 卌 卌 卌 卌 卌 卌 卌 卌 卌 卌 卌 卌 卌 卌
卌 卌 卌 卌 卌 卌 卌 卌 卌 卌 卌 卌 卌 卌 卌 卌 卌 卌 卌 卌 卌
卌 卌 卌 卌 ////

27 Sociology  卌 卌 卌 卌 卌 //

7 Travel  卌 //

20 Calendars  卌 卌 卌 卌

10 Feminism  卌 卌

1162

As the retail price of books continues to rise, however, a predictable phenomenon occurs: sales dollars from old, cheaper books won't buy an equal number of new, more expensive books. This is a factor which is being watched by Lieberman and the managers. Any need for more cash to maintain a balanced inventory in terms of both dollars and units is expected to be fulfilled by:

- sales increases.
- no increase in drawings by partners nor any increase in dividends.
- lower interest payments as loans are paid off, thus decreasing fixed expenses.

A careful eye must also be kept on inventory because of publishers' attitudes toward trade credit. Lieberman has found that the more business the Volume Bookstores do with the publishers, the better credit risk they are seen as being, and thus the more leeway the publishers will give on late payments. Therefore, he now can pay on a late but regular basis. Smaller publishers do tend to ask for payment sooner than the larger companies due to their more precarious cash flows. But, generally speaking, the more debt the Volume Bookstores maintain (within reasonable limits), the more the publishers seem to like them.

The Volume Bookstores all use the same method of day-to-day inventory control. The numbers and categories of books sold are recorded on a tally sheet at the cash register, as shown in Exhibit 2. This method, of course, is only as accurate as the people using it. From the tally sheets at each store, a profile of each store's best-selling book categories, has been worked up and is shown in Exhibit 3.

To reorder particular books, the stores use an inventory card system. When books initially come in, a certain number of them will get these cards, and the date of arrival is marked on the cards. When these books are sold, the sales clerk removes the cards. The cards are then sorted by publisher. When an order is being prepared for a particular publisher, the cards are studied to determine what books are selling, how many copies have been sold, and how quickly they have sold. This system helps the Volume Bookstores maintain a good backstock of books which are not current best sellers, but which are nevertheless quality material. This system can fall into trouble if too many customers mistakenly pocket the cards, thinking them to be unimportant or bookmarks.

A final inventory control the Volume Bookstores use is book distribution companies. Distributors carry a selection of books which are in high demand. If a publisher is slow to send orders out, if the publisher is holding a shipment while demanding payment, if there is a

| **EXHIBIT 3** | Best-Selling Categories of Books* | | |
|---|---|---|---|
| | **Volume I** | **Volume II** | **Volume III** |
| #1 | Fiction | Fiction | Juvenile |
| #2 | Science Fiction | Science Fiction | Fiction |
| #3 | Psychology | Psychology | Psychology |
| #4 | Mystery | Mystery | Science Fiction |
| #5 | Medicine and Health | Occult | — |
| #6 | Occult | — | — |

*The exhibit is simply a ranking by category, i.e., #3 at Volume I does not represent the same number of units at Volume II or Volume III. This exhibit just shows which types of books are most popular at each store.

run on a certain book—in all these situations, a distributor is good for quick shipment. The stores have special equipment for reading the microfiche which the distributors send out, giving the title, author, and call number for each book. Volume II and Volume III use Baker and Taylor Distributors. Volume I uses Ingram, Inc. Baker and Taylor is felt to have better selection of books.

## PERSONNEL

The Volume Bookstores' employees fall into two categories: managers and hourly employees. In this section, the hourly employees' situation will be examined. For a look at the organizational structure of the Volume Bookstores, see Exhibit 4.

Lieberman has experienced no difficulty in hiring hourly employees. Far more people come in to ask about work than he could ever hire. The pay is not what attracts them—everyone, regardless of experience, starts at minimum wage. Most of them are simply looking for a happy work experience. Lieberman seems to know what the job entails and what he wants in his workers, and he has expounded on this at length:

Although we don't pay very decent wages, we pay the going rate for the kind of job it is. And really what it is, it's clerical; it's checking in books, putting books on the shelf, and helping customers. It's not where anyone would have to have any training outside of here to come here. In fact, we prefer no one having worked in a bookstore, outside of having a liking for books. But what we do look for—we look for a certain type of person within that framework. We won't just take a body, because a body makes everyone else have to deal with it. We've had bodies, and it's brought down the whole place. What we're looking for is, we're looking for people who are not trying to climb a corporate ladder, who are trying to get by, who are trying to have a decent job with decent people working around them, and decent people to deal with. They're not feeding anyone's ego, they're not into the clothes busi-

**EXHIBIT 4**
Organization
Structure

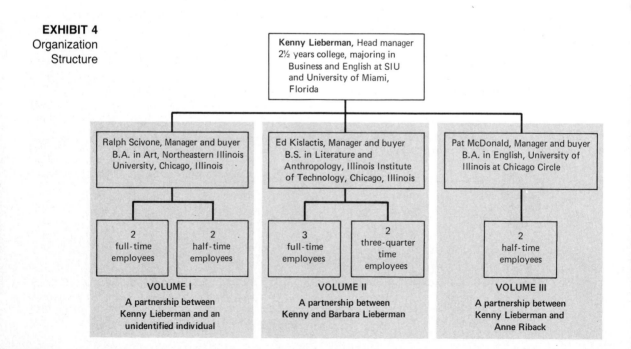

ness. It's a low-key kind of thing. We don't want anyone to pressure anyone. They're not working on commission. They can get by on the salary they make, but they're not going to get ahead on it, to be honest. . . . We get a lot of students that way. . . . We get a lot of people who are doing other things, who are actors, artists, musically inclined, which is fine with us, because they have the right temperament for what we're looking for. We're looking for someone who's somewhat outgoing, somewhat mellow, who can talk to people, and who isn't uptight about that, and who isn't coming here with blindfolds where he thinks he'll make any big deal of money, where he's also not going to steal from us. If you're going to steal, you're going to go for someone where there's lots of money. We've been fortunate that way. There are a lot of people who fit that mold, who come to us. The turnover rate is there, in a job that pays $2.50 an hour. And it's no different if you pay $3.00 an hour. They have other things—they're going to move along. . . . I have mixed emotions about whether that's right or wrong, but that's the way the society is. We try to do little things that mean something here and there . . . a little consideration.

Part of this consideration is paying small bonuses to employees (based on the number of hours worked) whenever sales are over $15,000 for the month. In 1976, it's been paid every month.

Lieberman continues:

I hope that everyone who works in all the stores can at least say that going to work isn't a hassle for them, any more than going anywhere else to work; that they have some fun and they like the people they work with.

Lieberman's supportive attitude toward his employees really does appear to work. His hourly employees have stayed on with him, some moving from store to store, others moving up into manager's positions as the openings came up. All of his current managers were once hourly employees. Furthermore, working hours for each person are flexible. Many of the workers have outside interests in the arts, and they can readily adjust their working hours to permit them to freely participate in outside activities. There is a remarkable amount of give and take in this area.

For the most part, the managers agree with Lieberman's interest in hiring friendly, non-egotistical people. The one thing they sometimes want to change is the low wages. The managers are very interested in the personnel aspects of their work, and thoughtfully expressed themselves on the topic.

Ralph Scivone, 23, manager of Volume I, talked about hiring practices:

I'd rather have somebody with experience [but I can't afford to wait for them to apply for the work]. . . . We put a sign in the window, and people come in and fill out a card, and then just judge on the basis of personality and what appeared to be intelligence. I'd just as soon hire somebody on the basis of personality. If you can think straight, that's all you have to do. And if you're likable, then everybody gets along.

Scivone's ideas on the minimum wage payment with no premium for experience are

I wouldn't do it that way. . . . 15% of gross is for salaries, and [Kenny] doesn't want to go above that. So even if you have somebody with experience, he would just as soon hire somebody without experience. He'd end up doing the same job anyway. But I don't want to do it necessarily that way. I would probably start people off higher, even if they didn't know anything. I think we're having trouble getting people who are serious about the job, because if you can't pay them, they don't care. But it just happened that I ran into a lot of people who are working here now who knew that there wasn't going to be much money. So it's more that the money is secondary [working as pleasure is primary].

If Scivone had his way, the basic thing he'd change about the treatment of hourly employees is their pay. He says that he'd be willing to pay people more, and take less profit.

Ed Kislaitis, 28, manager of Volume II, says bluntly, "We pay too low." He feels that this contributes to some difficulty in holding on to employees, though his three most recent turnovers have occurred due to factors entirely out of the store's realm, and had little or nothing to do with wages. Kislaitis has a pragmatic attitude toward his employees. He doesn't meddle much, and lets them resolve their own problems:

> There's been some pressure. One of the folks hasn't been pulling his weight, and since everybody's doing the same damn job, it becomes obvious to everybody else that they're putting away more books than they had to and everybody gets crabby. But then again, also, everybody knows who's doing it, too.

Pat McDonald, 24, manager of Volume III, is in charge of two part-time employees. His current workers please him, but usually his day-to-day concerns involve juggling his own responsibilities as buyer and the part-time employees' occasional lack of concern over their jobs:

> You can only expect so much from someone who is only working 20 hours a week. Sometimes they're working by themselves, and you can't expect them to have a whole lot of initiative when they're unsupervised. The only thing I could wish is that we were doing a little better here, so I would be more free of waiting on customers, and would be more free to think about the store and analyze what's happening and what we need and what we don't need.

Overall, the Volume Bookstores' employees seem satisfied with their work, largely because of the friendly atmosphere in the stores. Life has not always been so carefree, though. Volume II recently went through a rash of shoplifting and robberies, some of which looked as though they could have been inside jobs. After much anxiety on everyone's part, Lieberman finally settled on lie detector tests for all people connected with the store, in order to defuse the issue. Lieberman had this to say about the problem:

> We just gave all our people polygraph tests. . . . I fired a guy. . . . So many things were going on, and so many shortages. Everyone starts accusing everyone. So what we decided to do was just clear everyone and when we hire them from now on, they're going to be told that they may have to take it sometime. And everybody came out beautifully, which is what we wanted. But at least we know we can count on everyone.

## THE MANAGERS

Lieberman has organized his businesses so that most of the typical day's work can be done by his managers with the help of the hourly employees. These managers are not managers in the typical sense. They do not make major financial decisions for the stores. These managers are buyers/supervisors/direction-givers for the stores. Because of their own interests in literature, this role seems to satisfy them. They do seem to realize that they are not financial managers, and generally seem relieved about this. In the words of Pat McDonald, Volume III manager, this is his job:

> . . . I'm the store manager, not really a bookkeeper type of manager. Mainly, what we're a combination of is, I guess, super store clerk, which amounts to a store clerk who is the buyer . . . which gives us quite a bit of control as to the overall impact of the store, much more than the fellow who actually owns it, in terms of what kinds of stock we're carrying, the overall physical appearance, and the diversity of the store as the public sees it. So far as that's concerned, I find it very interesting, much more interesting doing what I'm doing, than being, say, the working partner who's paying the bills and worrying about that. I'm worrying about things that interest me, like literature and new writing and getting a first peek at all the new books, which, because of my interests, is very sufficient.

Or, as Ralph Scivone, Volume I manager, puts it:

> The managers for the Volume Bookstores aren't managers—they're bookbuyers. And they keep things running. It's financial for Kenny. For the rest of us, it's sales work. It's something fun to do.

The managers are in fact a bit underinformed about the financial condition of the stores. They revealed in their conversations a lack of hard figures, and one was even working without a clear understanding of how his yearly bonus would be paid.

The organization is really not quite as simple as McDonald and Scivone make it sound, however. Each manager is given freedom within guidelines to make his store what he wants. The major guideline is that Lieberman still be able to pay the bills under the manager's format. Therefore, the inventory changes with each manager. They can go off into their own specialties. This is okay in Lieberman's eyes, since the managers are the ones who have to sell the books, and their interest is important to the success of the store. As Lieberman says, "There's nothing easier to sell than something you care about."

Part of the managers' motivation is money. In addition to their base salaries, they receive bonuses, which are 1%–2% of gross sales. This encourages them to keep a good stock of books on hand, treat the customers well, and run the store smoothly. Right now, Kislaitis and Scivone make $14,000 to $17,000 per year with bonuses. McDonald makes less than this due to his store's struggle to do more than just break even. Lieberman feels that "Pat's hands are tied with low volume. There's nothing he can do." The other two managers, though, should be making $18,000 to $20,000 per year in a few years. And Lieberman "looks for good things for them." He is "satisfied with the managers—extremely pleased." He thinks that "they're doing a super job."

## CUSTOMER AND STORE PROFILES

### Volume I

Volume I is located at Broadway and Belmost, in a densely populated neighborhood that runs the gamut from the very rich to the very poor. Lieberman had long considered putting a store in this area, and was delighted when a storefront finally became available. There are three other bookstores within four blocks, but due to the high crime rate in the area, people prefer not to walk far and thus like Volume I's location.

The store is spacious, 1,300 sq. ft., and has plenty of extra room for later expansion. Rent is $1,250 per month. Sales are $300–350 per day on weekdays, and $700–800 on Saturdays and Sundays. In units, this is about 1,000 books per week.

Customers are mostly 23–30, and very transient—employees say that they never seem to see the same faces more than once. They are out of school, working, and like to read. They really tend to read what they know is worth reading. On the other hand, the older, wealthier clientele listen to reviews and buy what they're told to buy in *The New York Times Review of Books*. Most customers buy more than one book at a time.

Magazines are a sideline at this store. Best sellers are the *Paris Review, Africa,* and *Vogue*. Because many gay people live in the area, there is also a brisk trade in gay magazines.

The selection of books at this store has not yet narrowed much because the store has not been in existence long enough to define what type of customer is most attracted to it. Right now, the store is emphasizing science fiction, mass market paperbacks, and older fiction. They are also finding a good market for hardcover books in this neighborhood.

### Volume II

Kislaitis, the manager, is trying to better resolve this store's character, so that he can create a sharper image of quality in the customer's mind:

. . . . [A] reason we've been getting stronger and stronger [is] that we've been cutting our weak points. Instead of trying to compete with Whole Earth (a counterculture bookstore) and trying to compete with Beck's Bookstore (student textbook store) . . . we've said, they're doing a damn good job in their natural living section. We're carrying a really nice poetry section. And when we keep stocking books that don't sell in those places, we're taking money away from those places that we do sell. So we cut natural living. We trimmed a lot of sections that, you know, were moderate, and we've been investing heavier in science fiction, heavier into the literary aspect. I found out if you want literary paperbacks, if you want literary criticism in any form you're up the creek. . . . We're one of the few people around that have complete [works]. . . . It's developing its character. It's in an amiable relationship with the other bookstores in the area. We're not cutting each other's throats. And all of us, I think, are prospering because of that. . . . We're not out to be all things to all people now.

We found a good formula. We found our ecological niche for this area. Now, every area has a different ecology, and if you sit there, and if you can last long enough to figure it out, you're going to survive as a species.

Since science fiction is such a strong seller, Kislaitis is expanding it, and bringing in hard-to-find English titles. This is earning the store mention in science fiction fan magazines. The store has a dependable image in this area, in the manager's opinion:

If it's not on the shelf and it is in print, it's in transit, because we order every science fiction book that's written unless it's really a piece of garbage.

The store has sales of $500–550 on weekdays and $650–800 on Saturdays and Sundays. This is a unit volume of 1,100–1,200 books per week. Volume II has 900 sq. ft.

The store sells magazines as a sideline, but Kislaitis doesn't like them, unless they're unusual:

[They're a] real pain. Discount's pretty crummy. We're not going to expand the space, that's for sure. We're just carrying them as a service. I have no intention of trying to do anything with it. We're always going to try to carry more odd magazines.

At this store, the manager feels he tends to underestimate the intelligence of his customers. He wants to do more with hardbound books, since he finds that they are starting to sell better. He also has his eye on the financial situation at Dawn, the sister store, whose sales have dropped off dramatically. That operation is now just breaking even. Kislaitis thinks about expanding Volume II into Dawn's area, but he knows Lieberman isn't likely to close a store named after his daughter.

## Volume III

This store is having real problems doing more than just breaking even. It is in a residential neighborhood dominated by young families who do not read much. Juvenile books are the biggest sellers, bought by mothers and grandmothers. The street is quiet, so much so that this store closes earlier than the other two Volume Bookstores and is also closed on Sunday. The store is structurally sound and has 1,200 sq. ft. Unit sales per week are approximately 300.

Sales are $130 per day on weekdays and little over $200 on Saturdays. On some weekdays sales do not break $100. There are months when the store falls into the red. Employees see the same few customers all the time. Customer relations are very important, according to manager McDonald:

We break our backs here for the customers, to special order things, which is not necessary if you're doing better.

Volume III does face heavy competition from several larger bookstores located in the main shopping area of downtown Evanston, where public transportation is better. Volume III seems to draw the most attention when it has a sale.

Volume III is located in the least "literate" part of a very literate town. It sells perhaps one book per month in the philosophy, poetry, and oriental religion sections. The depression of the employees over their inability to increase sales is further accentuated by the rousing success of its sister store, Mudpies, a children's clothing store, which opened in July 1976, is growing quickly, and will apparently be quite successful.

Even Lieberman admits the store is doing poorly. He says it's barely worth the trouble to own it—he hasn't taken a cent out of it in the two years it's been open.

## THE FUTURE

Kenny Lieberman feels that there are a number of possible changes that could be carried out in the future. However, he is not overly anxious to make any dramatic changes. Below are some comments pertaining to future directions for the Volume Bookstores.

. . . We might get more into plants and cards. You know the same people who buy books buy plants and cards. They're all very compatible, you know.

. . . The kids clothing business will be faded out. There's a high profit margin on that stuff, but Anne is getting out and I don't get much personal satisfaction from that. You always have to worry about a new season—who needs it?

. . . I'm not looking to get into textbooks. We are located near a number of schools. Markup on those books is less and you have a real problem in determining enrollment. The professors either don't know or they tell you too damned late. Then you get all those students screamin' at you. That's not where I'm at.

. . . We'll try to turn Volume III around in the next couple of years. Right now we're buying back books after the customers have read them. This is not an affluent area—people are very price conscious.

. . . I really don't have any idea where I'll be three years from now. I may not even be here, but my best guess is I will be. I've got a partner that is pushing me in that direction. But if that means not having mellow stores and that kind of life-style, its not for me.

. . . Publishers are increasing their prices of books drastically. That's going to be a big problem for us, especially at a store like Volume III.

# 24 WALL DRUG-STORE, 1983

## James D. Taylor, Robert L. Johnson, and Philip C. Fisher

*University of South Dakota*

The Wall Drug Store is a complex of retail shops located on the main street of Wall, South Dakota, population 770, owned and managed by the Hustead family of Wall. It includes a drugstore, a soda fountain, two jewelry stores, two clothing stores, a restaurant with four dining rooms, a Western art gallery, a bookstore, and shops selling rocks and fossils, camping and backpacking equipment, saddles, and boots as well as several souvenir shops. In 1983, a major expansion was underway which would add five more shops and a chapel. "The decision, as when you first wrote the case in 1974,[1] is, are we going ahead with our building program or not? That hasn't changed," announced Bill Hustead as he talked about his plans for Wall Drug. The tourist season was just beginning on June 1. The spring had been cool and wet, and sales for the year to June 1 were down considerably from the previous year. Bill continued,

> We are still going ahead with the building program. The building program is not necessarily to make more money, but mainly it is to enlarge and enhance the store, so that it makes more of an impression on the traveling public. The church, the art gallery, the apothecary shop—we naturally feel these things will pay their way and make money, but the good part is, when the signs go down, we will have a place that people just won't miss. The place is so crazy, so different— it's the largest drugstore in the world, it may get

in the *Guiness Book of Records* as the only drugstore with a church in it. People and writers will have a lot to talk about. We will continue to seek publicity. We will advertise in crazy places, we will have packets for writers, and we will try to seek national and international publicity.

## WALL DRUG HISTORY

Ted Hustead graduated from the University of Nebraska with a degree in pharmacy in 1929 at the age of 27. In December of 1931, Ted and his wife Dorothy bought the drugstore in Wall, South Dakota, for $2,500. Dorothy and Ted and their four-year-old son Bill moved into living quarters in the back twenty feet of the store. Business was not good (the first month's receipts were $350) and prospects in Wall did not seem bright. Wall, South Dakota, in 1931 is described in the following selection from a book about the Wall Drug Store.

> Wall, then: a huddle of poor wooden buildings, many unpainted, housing some 300 desperate souls; a 19th century depot and wooden water tank; dirt (or mud) streets; few trees; a stop on the railroad, it wasn't even that on the highway. U.S. 16 and 14 went right on by, as did the tourists speeding between the Badlands and the Black Hills. There was nothing in Wall to stop for.[2]

Neither the drugstore nor the town of Wall prospered until Dorothy Hustead conceived the idea of placing a sign promising free ice water to anyone who would stop at their store. The

---

[1]Professors James D. Taylor and Robert L. Johnson are co-authors of "Wall Drug Store," a case written in 1974.

This case was prepared by Professors James D. Taylor, Robert L. Johnson, and Philip C. Fisher of the University of South Dakota as the basis of class discussion.

[2]Jennings, Dana Close, *Free Ice Water: The Story of Wall Drug* (Aberdeen, South Dakota: North Plains Press, 1969), p. 26.

**EXHIBIT 1**

sign read "Get a soda/Get a beer/Turn next corner/Just as near/To Highway 16 and 14/Free ice water/Wall Drug." Ted put the sign up and cars were turning off the highway to go to the drugstore before he got back. This turning point in the history of Wall Drug took place on a blazing hot Sunday afternoon in the summer of 1936.

The value of the signs was apparent and Ted began putting them up all along the highways leading to Wall. One sign read "Slow down the old hack/Wall Drug Corner/Just across the railroad track." The attention-catching signs were a boom to the Wall Drug and the town of Wall prospered too. In an article in Good Housekeeping in 1951, the Hustead's signs were called "the most ingenious and irresistable system of signs ever derived."[3]

Just after World War II, a friend traveling across Europe for the Red Cross got the idea of putting up Wall Drug signs overseas. The idea caught on and soon South Dakota servicemen who were familiar with the signs back home began to carry small Wall Drug signs all over the world. Many wrote the store requesting signs. One sign appeared in Paris, proclaiming "Wall Drug Store 4,278 miles (6,951 kilometers)." Wall Drug signs have appeared in many places including the North and South Pole areas, the 38th parallel in Korea, and on Vietnam jungle trails. The Husteads sent more than 200 signs to servicemen requesting them from Vietnam. These signs led to news stories and publicity which further increased the reputation of the store.

By 1958, there were about 3,000 signs displayed along highways in all 50 states, and two men and a truck were permanently assigned to service signs. Volunteers continue to put up signs. The store gives away 14,000 6-by-8-inch signs and 3,000 8-by-22-inch signs a year to people who request them. On the walls of the dining rooms at Wall Drug are displayed pictures from people who have placed signs in unusual places and photographed them for the Husteads.

The signs attracted attention and shortly after World War II articles about Ted Hustead and Wall Drug began appearing in newspapers and magazines. In August 1950 *Redbook Magazine* carried a story which was later condensed in October's *Readers Digest*. Since then, the number of newspapers and magazines carrying feature stories or referring to Wall Drug has increased greatly. In June of 1983, Wall Drug Store files contained 543 clippings of stories about the store. The number by 10 year periods was as follows[4]:

| | |
|---|---|
| 1941–1950 | 19 articles |
| 1951–1960 | 41 |
| 1961–1970 | 137 |
| 1971–1980 | 260 |
| 1981 through April 1983 | 59 |

The store and its sales have grown steadily since 1936. From 1931 until 1941 the store was in a rented building on the west side of Wall's Main Street. In 1941, the Husteads bought an old lodge hall in Wasta, S.D., (15 miles west of Wall) and moved it to a lot on the east side of the street in Wall. The building which had been used as a gymnasium in Wasta became the core around which the current store is built.

Tourist travel greatly increased after World War II and the signs brought so many people into Wall Drug that the Husteads claim they were embarrassed because the facilities were not large enough to service them. The store did not even have modern restrooms. Sales during this period grew to $200,000 annually.

In 1953, Bill Hustead, now a pharmacy graduate of South Dakota State University at Brookings, joined his parents in the store.

In 1953, Wall Drug was expanded into a former storeroom to the south. This became the Western Clothing Room. In 1954, they built an outside store on the south of the Western Cloth-

---

[3]Ibid., p. 42.

[4]Twenty-seven clippings were undated.

ing Room. This was accompanied by a 30 percent increase in business. In 1956, a self-service cafe was added on the north side of the store. In the early 1950s sales were in the $300,000 per year range and by the early 1960s had climbed to $500,000. (A map of the store with the dates of expansion are shown in Exhibit 2.)

In the early 1960s, Ted and his son Bill began seriously thinking of moving Wall Drug to the highway. The original Highway 16 ran by the north side of Wall, about two blocks from the store. It was later moved to run by the south side of Wall, about two blocks also from the

drugstore. In the late 1950s and early 1960s a new highway was built running by the south side of Wall paralleling the other highway. Ted and Bill Hustead were considering building an all-new Wall Drug along with a gasoline filling station alongside the new highway just where the interchange by Wall was located.

They decided to build the gasoline station first, and did so. It is called Wall Auto Livery. When the station was finished, they decided to hold up on the new store and then decided to continue expanding the old store in downtown Wall. This was a fortunate decision, since soon

**EXHIBIT 2**
Floor Plan

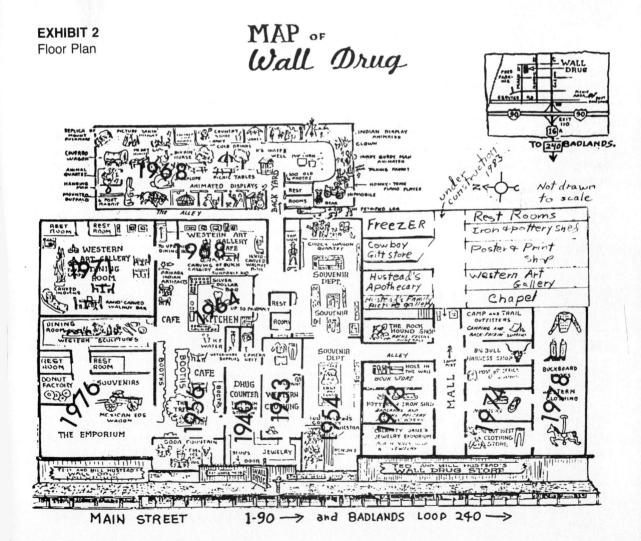

MAP OF
Wall Drug

after that, the new interstate highway replaced the former new highway and the new interchange ran through the site of the proposed new Wall Drug.

In 1963, a new fireproof construction coffee shop was added. In 1964, a new kitchen, again of fireproof construction, was added just in back of the cafe and main store. In 1964 and 1965 offices and the new pharmacy were opened on the second floor over the kitchen.

In 1968, the back dining room and backyard across the alley were added. This was followed in 1971 with the Art Gallery Dining Room.

By the late 1960s and early 1970s, annual sales volume went to $1,000,000.

In 1971 the Husteads bought the theater that bordered their store on the south. They ran it as a theater through 1972. In early 1973 they began construction of a new addition in the old theater location. This is called the "Mall." By the summer of 1973 the north part of the Mall was open for business. The south side was not ready yet. That year the Wall Drug grossed $1,600,000, which was an increase of about 20 percent over 1972. Bill believes the increase was due to their new Mall addition.

The development of the Mall represents a distinct change in the development of Wall Drug. All previous development had been financed out of retained earnings or short-term loans. In effect, each addition was paid for as it was built or added.

## THE MALL

The owners of Wall Drug broke with their previous method of expansion when they built the Mall by borrowing approximately $250,000 for 10 years to finance the Mall and part of 20 large new signs which stand 660 feet from the interstate highway.

During the last half of the 1960s and early 1970s Bill Hustead had thought about and planned the concept of the Mall. The Mall was designed as a town within a large room. The main strolling mall was designed as a main street with each store or shop designed as a two-story frontier Western building. The Mall is thus like a re-created Western town. Inside the stores various woods are used in building and paneling. Such woods as pine from Custer, South Dakota, American black walnut, gumwood, hackberry, cedar, maple, and oak are among the various woods used. The storefronts are recreations of building fronts found in old photos of Western towns in the 1880s. Many photos, paintings, and prints line the walls. These shops stock products that are more expensive than the souvenir merchandise found in most other parts of the store. The shops are more like Western boutiques.

The northern part of the Mall was open for business shortly after July 10, 1973. In the fall of 1973, Bill was uncertain whether or not to open the south side. The Husteads perceived a threat to the tourist business in the 1974 season. They agonized over whether to finish the Mall and order the normal amount of inventory, or to hold up the Mall and order conservatively. Among the conditions that seemed to threaten tourism were rising gasoline prices, periodic gasoline shortages in parts of the country, and trouble with American Indian Movement (AIM) at Wounded Knee and on the Pine Ridge Reservation. The more long-term threat to the businesses that depend on tourists, especially Wall Drug, was the highway beautification laws of the 1960s that threatened the removal of roadside advertising signs.

Bill finally decided in the winter of 1973 to prepare for a full tourist season and therefore had the Mall finished and ordered a full inventory for the 1974 season.

The decisions the Husteads confronted in the fall and winter of 1973 marked the first time they had seriously considered any retrenchment in their 27 years of growth.

In May and June, the opening of the 1974 tourist season, there were nine shops in the Mall. Bill estimated in the winter of 1974 that the year would be a record breaker of $2 million. June, July, and August sales were up 15 to 20 percent. September business was up 20 to 30 percent, October was up 40 percent, and November was a record setter for that month.

Bill gave the following reasons for the 1974 season:

1. Many other businesses bought light, Wall Drug bought heavy. Therefore, while others ran short, Wall Drug had merchandise toward the end of the summer.
2. Expensive items sold well in spite of the recession scare of the late 1974 period. Bill indicated that articles in Eastern merchandising journals indicated luxury items were doing well all over. Wall Drug had to reorder even into the fall on hot items, such as books, jewelry, and Western clothes.
3. Wall Drug had more goods and space than it ever had before, and each person was buying more.
4. There were more hunters than ever before in the fall. Signs on the highway advertising free donuts, and coffee for hunters brought many in and they bought heavy.
5. Although visitations to Mt. Rushmore were down in the summer of 1974, Wall Drug sales were up. Why? Bill speculates that more people from South Dakota and bordering states took shorter trips this year, and thus went to the Black Hills. These people had likely been in the Black Hills before and had seen Mt. Rushmore on their first trip. However, these people like to pay another visit to Wall Drug to eat, see what has been added, and to shop.

In the fall of 1974, Wall Drug invested in more large signs to set 660 feet back from the interstate. By 1976, they had 29 of these signs. These were the only legal-type signs that they could put up along the interstate, but by the spring of 1976, the language of the Highway Beautification Act was changed to put these signs outside the law also. Their signs (smaller ones) in neighboring states have been removed.

In 1975 and 1976, expansion continued with the addition of the Emporium, more dining area, and more rest rooms at the north end of the store. (See map of Wall Drug.)

In 1978, the location of the Wall post office at the south end of the store beyond the Mall, which had previously been purchased, furnished expansion for the Western clothing stores and the boots and harness shop.

Currently, in 1983, there is further expansion under construction east of the Mall to the alley. The new area will feature a chapel modeled after a church built by Trapist Monks in Dubuque, Iowa, in 1850. Also featured will be a replica of the original Wall Drug Store, which will be called Hustead's Apothecary and will serve as the Drug Store Museum. The store will sell Caswell-Massey products from the store of that name in New York which is the oldest drugstore in the U.S. Other shops will be a Western art gallery, a poster shop and Western gift shop, an iron and pottery shop, and Hustead's Family Picture Gallery. The shops will be modeled after famous old Western establishments. There will also be a new set of rest rooms. In effect, the new addition will be an extension of the Mall.

## STORE OPERATION

Wall is a small town of 770 people as of 1980. The economic base of the town is primarily built around the Wall Drug and is dependent on tourist business.

Wall is situated right on the edge of the Badlands and 52 miles east of Rapid City. For miles in either direction, people in autos have been teased and tantalized by Wall Drug signs. Many have heard of the place through stories in the press, or have heard their parents or friends speak of the Wall Drug. In the summer of 1963, in a traffic count made on the highway going by Wall, 46 percent were eastbound and 54 percent were westbound. Of the eastbound traffic, 43 percent turned off at Wall. Of the westbound traffic, 44 percent turned off at Wall.

When people arrive at Wall (those westbound usually after driving 40 miles or more through the Badlands), they are greeted by the large Wall Drug sign on the interchange and an 80-foot-high, 50-ton statue of a dinosaur. The business district of Wall is two blocks long and is about three to five blocks from the interchange. The town has eleven motels and a number of gasoline filling stations.

Cars from many states line the street in front of and several blocks on either side of the drugstore. Tabulation of state licenses from autos and campers parked in front of Wall Drug, June 1, 1983, at 12:00 noon are summarized as follows:

| | |
|---|---|
| South Dakota (not local county) | 20% |
| South Dakota, local county | 22% |
| Balance of states and Canada | 58% |

Wall Drug is more than a store. It is a place of amusement, family entertainment, a gallery of the West, a gallery of South Dakota history, and a place that reflects the heritage of the West. Nostalgia addicts find Wall Drug particularly interesting. Children delight in the animated life-size cowboys singing, tableau of an Indian camp, a stuffed bucking horse, a six-foot rabbit, a stuffed buffalo, old slot machines that pay out a souvenir coin for 25¢, statues of cowboys, dancehall girls and other characters of the old West, a coin-operated quick-draw game, and souvenirs by the roomful which make up part of the attractions.

The food is inexpensive and good, and although as many as 10,000 people might stream through on a typical day, the place is air-conditioned and comfortable. The dining rooms are decorated with beautiful wood paneling, paintings of Western art are displayed, and Western music plays. One can dine on buffalo burgers, roast beef or steak, 5¢ coffee or select wine, and beer from the rustic, but beautiful, American walnut bar.

About one-fourth of the sales in the Wall Drug is food, plus about 5 to 10 percent for beverages and soda fountain. (This varies with the weather.) About 10 to 15 percent is jewelry, 15 percent clothing and hats, 35 to 40 percent for souvenirs, and 5 to 10 percent for drugs, drug sundries, and prescriptions.

The store is manned by a crew of 201 people, 76 of whom are college girls and 25 are college boys who work there in the summer. Student help is housed in homes that have been bought and made into dormitory apartments. There is a modern swimming pool for their use, also. The clerks are trained to be courteous, informed, and pleasant.

Orders for the following summer season begin being placed in the preceding fall. Orders begin arriving in December, but most arrive in January, February, March, and April. Many large souvenir companies postdate their invoices until July and August. Each year brings new offerings from souvenir companies and other suppliers. Much of the purchasing is done by Bill, who admits he relies on trusted salespeople of their suppliers who advise him on purchasing. Many of these companies have supplied Wall Drug for 30 years or so. Wall Drug generally buys directly from the producers or importers including photo supplies and clothing.

Years ago, much of what Wall Drug bought and sold was imported or made in the Eastern part of the country. In recent years, much of the merchandise is being made regionally and locally. Indian reservations now have small production firms and individuals who make much handicraft which is sold through Wall Drug. Examples of such firms are Sioux Pottery, Badlands Pottery, Sioux Moccasin, and Milk Camp Industries.

The Husteads rely a great deal on the department managers for buying assistance. The manager of the jewelry, for instance, will determine on the basis of last year's orders and her experience with customer reaction and demand how much to order for the next season. All ordering is centered through Bill.

## HIGHWAY BEAUTIFICATION AND PROMOTION

In the year 1965, Congress passed the Highway Beautification Act, which was designed to reduce the number of roadside signs. Anticipating the removal of the many Wall Drug advertising signs, Bill Hustead invested in new signs that were allowed under that legislation. These signs were to be placed no closer than 660 feet to the road. To be read, these signs must be larger than the older signs, and cost close to $9,000 each. Now even these large signs are included in the laws for regulation or removal.

There has been slow compliance with this legislation by many states including South Dakota, since many states in less populated areas have many tourist attractions, and find road signs the only practical way to advertise these attractions. Since the administration of President Reagan has been in office, there has been little enforcement of the sign legislation since there has been less money available for federal enforcement. There is new legislation being proposed by the Federal Highway Administra-

tion of the Department of Transportation as of 1983 that could have an impact on Wall Drug and other tourist-dependent establishments.

Bill and Ted also decided that they must gain as much visibility and notoriety as possible, and to help achieve this, they began using advertising in unusual places. In the 1960s, Wall Drug began taking small ads in unlikely media such as the *International Herald Tribune* and *The Village Voice,* in New York City's Greenwich Village, advertising 5¢ coffee and 49¢ breakfast as well as animal health remedies. This brought telephone calls and some letters of inquiry. It also brought an article in the *Voice* and probably attracted the attention of other media. On January 31, 1971 (Sunday), *The New York Times* carried an article about Wall Drug. This article may have led to Bill Hustead's appearance on Garry Moore's television program "To Tell the Truth." In the year 1979, there were 75 articles in newspapers and magazines about Wall Drug. In the August 31, 1981, edition of *Time,* a full-page article in the American Scene featured the store and the Husteads. Also, in 1981, Wall Drug was featured on NBC television's "Today Show" and Atlanta Cable "Winners."

For awhile, the Wall Drug was advertised in the London city buses and subways, in the

**EXHIBIT 3**  Income Statements (in 000's) Wall Drug

|  | 1982 | 1981 | 1980 | 1979 | 1978 | 1977 | 1976 | 1975 | 1974 | 1973 |
|---|---|---|---|---|---|---|---|---|---|---|
| Sales | 4,733 | 4,821 | 3,970 | 3,552 | 4,125 | 3,777 | 3,464 | 2,679 | 1,991 | 1,607 |
| Cost of Sales | 2,644 | 2,676 | 2,230 | 2,072 | 2,228 | 2,098 | 1,879 | 1,484 | 1,100 | 806 |
| Gross Profit | 2,089 | 2,145 | 1,740 | 1,480 | 1,897 | 1,679 | 1,586 | 1,195 | 891 | 801 |
| G. + A. Exp. | 1,802 | 1,857 | 1,473 | 1,433 | 1,578 | 1,453 | 1,312 | 1,000 | 754 | 691 |
| Inc. from oper. | 287 | 288 | 267 | 47 | 319 | 226 | 274 | 195 | 137 | 110 |
| Other inc. exp. | 36 | 81 | 43 | −8 | 35 | 23 | 2 | 3 | −8 | −10 |
| Inc. before tax | 323 | 369 | 310 | 39 | 354 | 249 | 276 | 198 | 129 | 100 |
| Tax | 120 | 144 | 125 | 6 | 148 | 94 | 111 | 80 | 54 | 41 |
| Net income | 203 | 224 | 185 | 33 | 206 | 155 | 165 | 118 | 75 | 59 |

**EXHIBIT 4** Balance Sheets on Dec. 31 (in 000's)

| | 1982 | 1981 | 1980 | 1979 | 1978 | 1977 | 1976 | 1975 | 1974 | 1973 |
|---|---|---|---|---|---|---|---|---|---|---|
| Cash and short-term invest. | $240 | $282 | $449 | $ 11 | $ 82 | $ 65 | $ 51 | $ 93 | $145 | $ 74 |
| Inventories | 631 | 547 | 369 | 403 | 338 | 276 | 249 | 248 | 174 | 144 |
| Other current assets | 60 | 57 | 53 | 99 | 51 | 58 | 50 | 32 | 26 | 26 |
| Total current assets | $931 | $886 | $871 | $513 | $471 | $399 | $350 | $373 | $345 | $244 |
| Property, equipment | 2907 | 2591 | 2380 | 2297 | 2230 | 1960 | 1739 | 1484 | 1234 | 1130 |
| Accumulated depreciation | −1355 | −1254 | −1147 | −1030 | −906 | −790 | −674 | −576 | −496 | −428 |
| Other assets | 24 | 25 | 27 | 53 | 55 | 33 | 29 | 31 | 34 | 34 |
| Total assets | $2507 | $2248 | $2131 | $1833 | $1850 | $1602 | $1444 | $1312 | $1117 | $ 980 |
| Current maturities of LTD | $ 43 | $ 40 | $ 46 | $ 8 | $ 11 | $ 5 | $ 8 | $ 7 | $ 21 | $ 20 |
| Notes payable | 0 | 0 | 0 | 68 | 20 | 0 | 0 | 5 | 70 | 20 |
| Accounts payable | 56 | 58 | 63 | 47 | 43 | 64 | 36 | 42 | 31 | 23 |
| Accruals + other current liab. | 252 | 244 | 310 | 124 | 232 | 167 | 178 | 193 | 136 | 110 |
| Total current liab. | $ 351 | $ 342 | $ 419 | $ 247 | $ 306 | $ 236 | $ 222 | $ 247 | $ 258 | $ 173 |
| Long-term debt | 191 | 149 | 179 | 238 | 133 | 130 | 133 | 136 | 222 | 244 |
| Deferred tax | 7 | 1 | | | | | | | | |
| Stockholders' equity | 1958 | 1756 | 1533 | 1348 | 1411 | 1236 | 1089 | 929 | 637 | 563 |
| Total liab. + equity | $2507 | $2248 | $2131 | $1833 | $1850 | $1602 | $1444 | $1312 | $1117 | $ 980 |

Paris Metro (subway) in the English language, and on the dock in Amsterdam where people board sight-seeing canal boats.

## FINANCES

Exhibits 3 and 4 present summary income statements and balance sheets from 1973 through 1982. The Wall Auto Livery was consolidated into Wall Drug Store, Inc., in May 1975. Had this transition occurred prior to 1973, sales for 1973, 1974, and 1975 would have been about $192,000, $248,000 and $52,000 larger, and net profit would have been about $19,000 larger in 1973, and $21,000 larger in 1974, with a negligible effect in 1975. The value of the acquired net assets was about $180,000.

The company's growth and expansion has been financed primarily by retained earnings, temporarily supplemented at times with short-term borrowings. A major exception was a $250,000, ten-year installment loan in 1973 used to help finance the mall and some large signs located 660 feet from the highway. In 1975, this loan was prepaid through 1980. At the end of 1982, only $34,500 remained to be paid on this loan. Other long-term debt at the end of 1982 includes installment contracts for the purchase of real estate and a stock redemption agreement (occurring in 1979) for the purchase by

the company of some Class B, nonvoting stock. As indicated on the December 31, 1982, balance sheet, current maturities of long-term debt were $43,436. Of this amount, $34,496 is the final payment on the 1973 loan due in 1983.

Both the growth and the volatility of the business should be apparent from the income statements presented in Exhibit 3. Exhibit 5 presents the income statements as a percentage of sales. Exhibit 6 is an analysis of the rate of return on equity broken into the component parts using the format:

$$\frac{sales}{assets} \times \frac{gross\ profit}{sales} \times \frac{operating\ income}{gross\ profit}$$

$$\times \frac{net\ income}{operating\ income} \times \frac{assets}{equity} = \frac{net\ income}{equity}$$

Between 1973 and 1982, prices, as measured by the Consumer Price Index, increased by about 115 percent. Percentage increases in some balance sheet and income accounts for Wall Drug over this period are

| | |
|---|---|
| Sales | 163% |
| Total G. + A. expense | 145 |
| Net income | 159 |
| Total assets | 115 |
| Equity | 169 |

---

**EXHIBIT 5**  Percent of Sales Statements

| | 1982 | 1981 | 1980 | 1979 | 1978 | 1977 | 1976 | 1975 | 1974 | 1973 |
|---|---|---|---|---|---|---|---|---|---|---|
| Sales | 100.0 | 100.0 | 100.0 | 100.0 | 100.0 | 100.0 | 100.0 | 100.0 | 100.0 | 100.0 |
| Cost of sales | 55.9 | 55.5 | 56.2 | 58.3 | 54.0 | 55.6 | 54.2 | 55.4 | 55.2 | 50.2 |
| Gross profit | 44.1 | 44.5 | 43.8 | 41.7 | 46.0 | 44.4 | 45.8 | 44.6 | 44.8 | 49.8 |
| G. + A. exp. | 38.1 | 38.5 | 37.1 | 40.3 | 38.3 | 38.4 | 37.9 | 37.3 | 37.9 | 43.0 |
| Inc. from oper. | 6.0 | 6.0 | 6.7 | 1.3 | 7.7 | 6.0 | 7.9 | 7.3 | 6.9 | 6.8 |
| Other inc. exp. | .8 | 1.7 | 1.1 | −.2 | .9 | .6 | .1 | .1 | −.4 | −.6 |
| Inc. before tax | 6.8 | 7.7 | 7.8 | 1.1 | 8.6 | 6.6 | 8.0 | 7.4 | 6.5 | 6.2 |
| Tax | 2.5 | 3.0 | 3.1 | .2 | 3.6 | 2.5 | 3.2 | 3.0 | 2.7 | 2.5 |
| Net income | 4.3 | 4.7 | 4.7 | .9 | 5.0 | 4.1 | 4.8 | 4.4 | 3.8 | 3.7 |

**EXHIBIT 6**    Components of Rate of Return on Equity

|  | 1982 | 1981 | 1980 | 1979 | 1978 | 1977 | 1976 | 1975 | 1974 | 1973 |
|---|---|---|---|---|---|---|---|---|---|---|
| Gross profit |  |  |  |  |  |  |  |  |  |  |
| Sales | .441 | .445 | .438 | .417 | .460 | .444 | .458 | .446 | .448 | .498 |
| Inc. fr. oper. |  |  |  |  |  |  |  |  |  |  |
| Gross profit | .137 | .134 | .153 | .032 | .168 | .135 | .163 | .163 | .154 | .137 |
| Sales |  |  |  |  |  |  |  |  |  |  |
| Assets | 1.89 | 2.14 | 1.86 | 1.94 | 2.23 | 2.36 | 2.40 | 2.04 | 1.78 | 1.64 |
| Inc. from oper. |  |  |  |  |  |  |  |  |  |  |
| Assets | .114 | .128 | .125 | .026 | .172 | .141 | .190 | .148 | .123 | .112 |
| Net income |  |  |  |  |  |  |  |  |  |  |
| Inc. from oper. | .707 | .778 | .698 | .702 | .646 | .686 | .602 | .605 | .547 | .536 |
| Assets |  |  |  |  |  |  |  |  |  |  |
| Equity | 1.28 | 1.28 | 1.39 | 1.36 | 1.31 | 1.30 | 1.33 | 1.41 | 1.75 | 1.74 |
| Net income |  |  |  |  |  |  |  |  |  |  |
| Equity | .103 | .128 | .121 | .025 | .146 | .126 | .152 | .126 | .118 | .105 |

These percentages are based on combining Wall Auto Livery with Wall Drug in 1973 as if the merger occurring in 1975 has taken place.

Given below are percentage changes in some of the general and administrative expenses from 1976 through 1982:

| | |
|---|---|
| Total G. + A. | 37% |
| Utilities | 137 |
| Officers' salaries | 2 |
| Other salaries | 42 |
| Depreciation | 5 |
| Advertising | 116 |
| Profit-sharing contribution | 49 |

The items mentioned accounted for 77 percent of total general and administrative expenses in 1982 and 76 percent in 1976. These same items as percentages of sales were

| | 1982 | 1976 |
|---|---|---|
| Utilities | 1.7% | 1.0% |
| Officers' salaries | 2.9 | 3.8 |
| Other salaries | 18.5 | 17.7 |
| Depreciation | 2.3 | 2.9 |
| Advertising | 2.1 | 1.3 |
| Profit-sharing contribution | 2.0 | 1.8 |

Depreciation methods on various assets vary from straightline to 200 percent declining balance and over lives of from 15 to 40 years for buildings and improvements to 5 to 10 years for equipment, furnitures, and fixtures. Although not evaluated or recognized on the financial statements, it is likely that some assets, such as the Western art and the silver dollar bar, have appreciated.

## STORE MANAGEMENT

Recruiting and training the seasonal work force is a major task at Wall Drug. College students are recruited through college placement services. Training is of short duration but quite intense. Summer employees are tested on their knowledge of store operations and their ability to give information about the area to tourists.

Bill Hustead commented:

I really think that there isn't anything more difficult than running a business with 20 to 30 employees in the winter and then moving into a business with 180 to 200 employees, and you have to house a hundred of them and you have to supervise them, and train them. This lasts through June, July, and August, then the next year you start all over. It's kind of exciting and fun for the first 25 years but after 30 years you begin to think it's a tough racket.

The store had a permanent nucleus of 20 to 30 employees. While the business could operate with fewer employees during the winter, the Husteads believed that they needed the experienced employees to give stability to the operations in the summer. Permanent employees with seniority could get as many as six weeks paid vacation. Commenting on this policy Bill said,

We probably go through the winter with more employees than we really need, but we give them time off in the winter because a seasonal business is so demanding. When the Fourth of July comes, you're working, when Memorial Day comes, you're working; when all those summer fun times come, you're working six days a week and it's quite a sacrifice. So, we try to be very generous with our paid vacations.

Dependence on seasonal tourists for the major portion of Wall Drug's business has inherent risks, and uncertainty over the future of the roadside signs, which have brought customers to the store for nearly 50 years, is a grave concern to the Husteads.

We will try to have ideas to modify our outdoor advertising program to adapt to changes in the law which we are sure will be forthcoming. If they are drastic changes, they could put us out of business. If they nail it down so there isn't a sign on the interstate, that will do the job.

---

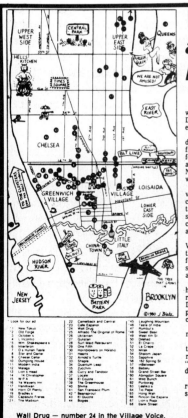

Wall Drug — number 24 in the Village Voice.

# Wall Drug ads mystify New Yorkers

**By RUTH HAMEL**
Argus Leader Staff

SoDak is a long way from SoHo, where west can mean New Jersey and Wall Drug could reasonably be thought to exist near Wall Street.

But, as usual, mere distance has not deterred Wall Drug owner Bill Hustead from advertising his business. Off and on for the past 20 years, Hustead has bought advertising space in the Village Voice, a New York City weekly based in Greenwich Village.

In every recent issue, a Wall Drug advertisement can be spotted between the columns devoted to Manhattan's vegetarian lunchspots and sushi bars. The small box may advertise petrified wood clocks one week, flying jackalopes on another and free ice water on another.

The tiny advertisements do not tell Voice readers where Wall Drug is, nor that it is more than a subway jaunt away for any New Yorker who might want to shop around for a petrified wood clock on a Saturday afternoon.

And the Voice's accompanying Manhattan map that shows where various restaurants are located denotes Wall Drug with a small arrow that simply points west from New York's Hell's Kitchen.

All of which adds to the Wall Drug mystique.

"We do get inquiries from time to time," Katherine Rogers, Village Voice restaurant sales coordinator, said. "'What is that?' We give them the address."

Once told where Wall Drug is, people respond with the same question, she said: "'Why?'"

But the baffling ads work. Over the
**\*WALL DRUG**
Continued on page 2A

# \*Wall Drug

Continued from page 1A

July 4th weekend, Wall Drug served five busloads of New York-area youth, some of whom knew of the drugstore from reading the Village Voice, Hustead said.

"One time, late at night, a guy from Massachusetts called" after spotting one of the Voice ads, Hustead said. "He wanted to know, 'What is a horse hitch?'."

New Yorkers passing through South Dakota will stop at Wall Drug to read the copies of the Village Voice Hustead receives every week and advertises on Interstate-90.

(Wall Drug signs, of course, are legendary. The small-town drugstore with the multi-national advertising campaign has placed signs in Amsterdam, London and along the French Riviera, among other places.)

Hustead's account with the Village Voice began about 20 years ago.

Always a fan of New York City, the drugstore owner was sitting in a Greenwich Village coffeehouse reading the paper when "I thought it might be a good move to advertise in the Voice," he said. "I knew that a lot of writers take that paper."

So Hustead placed an ad that emphasized the reasonable price of Wall Drug food compared to New York food.

Eventually, the Village Voice ads led to a Newsweek article about Wall Drug.

Ms. Rogers said a recent ad for Wall Drug's rattlesnake bite kits prompted many calls to the Village Voice offices.

Another recent ad boasting of free ice water hit a chord when New York was in a drought and its restaurants would only give customers a glass of water if they asked for it, Ms. Rogers said.

Hustead is proud of the Village Voice ads but has reservations about the paper itself.

"I'm a little conservative," he said. "I feel it's not as wholesome a paper as it used to be. The language ... it isn't something you want to lay around and let your 10-year-old girl read."

On a given week, Wall Drug may share Voice advertising space with naughty bakeries and naughtier film houses. And the newspaper that Hustead said used to resemble the paper in Wall now contains articles that might make some South Dakota jaws drop.

But the Voice association has allowed Hustead to meet interesting people between his forays to New York and New Yorkers' forays to Wall.

Wall Drug, Hustead says, "is a stop that those New Yorkers will make" as they pass through the state.

Asked about diversification as a hedge against this risk, Bill replied,

> We will try to diversify within our own community. By that I mean probably on our highway location in and around our Auto Livery. We have several hundred acres there (in sight of the interstate), and a motel and a modified drugstore would be our last straw if we were wiped out in town.

The Husteads hoped to be able to create a fund to provide self-insurance for their dormitory houses. This fund would then also provide some measure of security from business risks as well.

Although over 80, Ted Hustead is still active in the management of the store, involved in everything from physical inspections of the premises to acting jointly with Bill in making policy decisions. Ted can frequently be seen on the grounds picking up litter. Dorothy, Ted's wife, comes to the store every day, summer and winter, helps with the banking, and spends from two to six hours each day on various chores. Bill's son Rick, 33, joined the store in 1980 and now shares in the management. Rick has a Master's Degree in guidance and counseling and spent four years as a guidance counselor and teacher in high school. Rick also spent two years in the real estate business and one year in the fast-food business before returning to Wall. During his school years, Rich spent ten seasons working in Wall Drug. His wife, Kathy, is a pharmacist and also works in the store.

Bill Hustead expressed his continuous concern with the future of Wall Drug in light of future action concerning roadside sign advertising. Can the store expansion continue; should diversification be attempted in the community; should diversification be considered away from being affected by the tourist? Will Wall Drug be able to continue to gain publicity as they have in the past to keep people aware of their "attraction" characteristics? The costs of doing business are rising, such as the increase in utilities which is sizable. How can they plan for a bad year or two given the increasing uncertainty in the tourist industry? With these thoughts in mind, the 1983 tourist season at Wall Drug was underway.